ANTON RUPERT

A BIOGRAPHY

Ebbe Dommisse

with the cooperation of
Willie Esterhuyse

TAFELBERG

Tafelberg Publishers
a division of NB Publishers (Pty) Limited,
40 Heerengracht, Cape Town 8000
© 2005 authors

Cover photograph by Jansje Wissema
Cover and book design by Nazli Jacobs
Translated from the Afrikaans by Linde Dietrich
Index by Mary Lennox
© Photographs Rupert family, Rembrandt Archive or
Peace Parks Foundation, unless otherwise indicated
Set in Palatino

Printed and bound by Paarl Print,
Oosterland Street, Paarl, South Africa
First edition, third impression 2006

ISBN-10: 0-624-04150-6
ISBN-13: 978-0-624-04150-4

Contents

Foreword

T his is the first publication to attempt a comprehensive overview of Dr Anton Rupert's career and life since his early childhood. Although books about aspects of his activities and his view of life had been published, he remained unwilling that a biography should be written. When Hannes van Zyl, then head of Tafelberg Publishers, who had over a long period expressed an interest in Dr Rupert's story, mentioned the idea again at the turn of the century, Dr and Mrs Rupert finally agreed.

In 2001, shortly after my retirement from active journalism, the publisher approached me to undertake this task, one that proved both daunting and demanding, yet thoroughly fascinating. Despite his public profile, Anton Rupert is a very private person who has wide-ranging interests, while his career also partly overlaps with the rise of the Afrikaner in the economy.

Prof. Willie Esterhuyse of the University of Stellenbosch Business School, who had written a short volume on Rupert as an 'advocate of hope', was asked to cooperate. He assisted with both the research and with analysis. Together, we decided that it was best that one author should write the final text.

Research and writing spanned nearly four years and a broad spectrum of people and a variety of sources, both in South Africa and abroad, were consulted.

Although the Rupert family cooperated with the authors, their wish, as well as that of the authors, was that this should not be an authorised biography. Such an approach to biography sometimes creates credibility concerns as well as other problems, and for a biographer it is certainly advisable to maintain some distance from the subject. Also, to the extent that one can strive for complete objectivity, to provide a perspective that will withstand the test of time. In a few cases where details were divulged to the author in confidence, this confidentiality was honoured.

Sincere appreciation goes to all who assisted with the research, especially members of the Rupert family as well as their friends, acquaintances and colleagues whose assistance was invaluable. Throughout the publisher provided strong support. Equally supportive were Willie Esterhuyse and his wife, Annemarie, not only because of his valued contributions, but also because of their insight and support. Three respected adjudicators who read the manuscript,

PA Joubert, Koos Human and Danie van Niekerk, provided valuable advice and suggestions on earlier drafts.

Lastly, a special word of thanks to my wife, Daléne, for her love, patience and increasing understanding that retirement need not mean doing nothing or gardening.

EBBE DOMMISSE

PART I
TURNING POINT

CHAPTER 1

Atom bombs and parks for peace

O nly once in his career did Anton Rupert deliberately stay away from his office for a whole day.

This was when he heard of the world's first war-time nuclear explosion: the morning the devastating news reached South Africa that an atom bomb had been dropped on Hiroshima on 6 August 1945, destroying the Japanese seaport. The brief prelude to Japan's surrender and the end of the Second World War had begun.

The nuclear horror, a direct result of the splitting of the atom through which humankind developed the ability to annihilate itself, irrevocably changed the course of history. It also changed Anton Rupert's view of life irrevocably.

The young Afrikaner industrialist, trained in the natural sciences and destined to become his country's most innovative entrepreneur and the head of one of Africa's two wealthiest families, immediately sensed that this was a defining moment in history: one of those rare events that would forever be remembered as a turning point in human existence.

Rupert was at that stage still in Johannesburg, an inexperienced young entrepreneur with a factory processing pipe tobacco that struggled to keep afloat in the tough wartime conditions. That morning in early August when he heard of the devastation of Hiroshima, he telephoned his office to announce that he would be unavailable for the whole day. Instead, he stayed home to ponder on the destructive force of the atom bomb: 'I realised that the human race had become like scorpions in a bottle, with the power to destroy one another totally.'[1]

Expressing a similar sense of awe after witnessing the giant mushroom cloud forming over the stricken city, Robert Lewis, who had been the co-pilot of the *Enola Gay*, the B-29 bomber of the American Air Force that dropped the bomb on Hiroshima, wrote in his journal: 'My God, what have we done?'

One hundred thousand of the 245 000 inhabitants of Hiroshima perished that day, obliterated by the force of nuclear power, with a further 100 000 dying in the aftermath. Three days later the second and last atom bomb destroyed the picturesque port city of Nagasaki, killing another 80 000 people.[2]

The devastating atom bombs heralded the final episode of Japan's participation in the war. Five days later Emperor Hirohito acknowledged that Japan had been vanquished for the first time in its history. The images of total annihilation by the two atom bombs, Little Boy and Fat Boy, not only broke Japan's spirit but stunned the whole world.

Anton Rupert, with a master's degree in chemistry, understood that something cataclysmic had occurred. At his Johannesburg home, which he was to leave a few months afterwards for Stellenbosch to build a business empire that would eventually stretch across the globe, he reflected on the implications of the atomic era. He sensed that the military use of the nuclear bomb was probably the most portentous event he would experience in his lifetime, and came to the conclusion that the world would see no more great wars for fear of mutual annihilation. The inevitable consequence would be constant smaller wars, making lasting peace in the future highly unlikely.

'Since the unlocking of the power of the atom – since Hiroshima – everything has changed, except our way of thinking. In this atomic era there is no longer any country remote enough to become a place of shelter. The biblical notion that "I am my brother's keeper" has become a cold reality; depressions are now global, as is welfare. In this century where at least two nations possess enough bombs to destroy everything, we live like scorpions in a bottle – and he who wants to retain all, will lose all.'[3]

In future, humanity could only save itself through coexistence. 'People simply have to learn to live together.'

Coexistence, a conviction that had been taking root in Rupert since his student days, now became the core concept that would inspire him all his life, and a vision that he would proclaim persuasively. The well-known Rodin bronze *The Cathedral*, acquired in the 1960s, stands in his office as an enduring reminder. The sculpture of two right hands symbolises for him the coexistence between people, the foundation on which he developed his business philosophy. On this philosophy of coexistence, or partnerships forged from country to country, he built a worldwide international business chain long before globalisation became a fashionable concept.

This vision of partnership is coupled with social responsibility, which he considers one of the three major responsibilities of a successful business enterprise. Not only should there be coexistence between human beings, but also coexistence between human beings and nature. It is with this philosophy that Rupert as conservation-oriented philanthropist was to carry the concept of peace parks, or transfrontier conservation areas, across international borders.

Peace parks – with peace between peoples and nations as a desirable prerequisite for the survival of threatened species in spite of a human population explosion threatening the biological cycle – became a compelling vision that brought the octogenarian Rupert to his head office at Millennia Park in Stellenbosch each day. With the energy of a much younger man, he campaigns for the development of transnational game and nature parks that require multilateral cooperation between governments of various countries.

The peace parks are perhaps the most imaginative project initiated by the philanthropist Rupert in a long business career that he has applied to the benefit of society on many fronts.

The Ruperts appear on the *Forbes* business magazine's list of the world's wealthiest people, the billionaires with estimated assets of more than 1 000 million American dollars. Besides the Ruperts, *Forbes* only lists one other family from Africa: the Oppenheimers, the heirs of the South African mining magnate Sir Ernest Oppenheimer and his son Harry.[4]

The main difference between these two South African families, both of whom have contributed enormously to the development of their country as well as to community welfare, is that Rupert started with next to nothing when he built his international business empire, nor did he depend on the country's abundant mineral riches as a base.

Labelled in the media as the 'king of luxury', the 'secretive marketing giant', the 'shy king of snob smokers' and the 'true gentleman of the business world', he built an international reputation.

The chemistry student – who with a personal investment of a mere £10 started a worldwide group of companies that would make him a world-famous entrepreneur – is linked to some of the best-known international trademarks, the foundation on which his business empire is built. From Cartier, the 'king of jewellers and the jeweller of kings', to the luxury goods of Alfred Dunhill, from Mont Blanc's stylish writing instruments to the oldest Swiss watchmakers, all fall under Richemont, the international arm of the Rupert umbrella. It was preceded by the establishment of a global chain of tobacco interests under the banner of Rembrandt and Rothmans, as well as the production of the most famous South African wines and spirits.

During his long career Anton Rupert developed into a man for all seasons, with active interests outside the business sphere: conserver of his country's historical heritage; patron of the arts; navigator over political minefields; benefactor helping others to help themselves.

Still, in spite of the media attention that accompanies his public appearances, Rupert remains an intensely private person, someone who does not readily grant media interviews and whose private life is as mysterious as some of his weighty business transactions.

The eminent Afrikaans poet Dirk Opperman celebrated Rupert's restless spirit and many-sidedness by describing him as the 'prince of commerce' who could reconcile commerce, science and the arts.[5] His versatility is also the source of his interest in nature and animal life, the foundation on which the idea of peace parks developed.

Rupert was the first chairman of the Peace Parks Foundation (PPF), which has former President Nelson Mandela as emeritus patron. This icon of the 20th century likes to refer to Rupert as his 'older brother'.

Eight heads of state of southern African countries serve as honorary patrons of the PPF, which facilitates the establishment and development of transfrontier parks. Rupert regards the Foundation as a catalyst, a concept from his background as chemist that he has used frequently in his long career – a substance that, without itself undergoing any change, precipitates a change in another substance.

The PPF's funds, mainly derived from private individuals as well as institutions and big multinational companies, are used to develop the transfrontier conservation areas and also to train people in the tourism and service industries as well as game wardens.

To a world with shrinking natural resources, Africa with its vast, still unpopulated spaces can be a last refuge for irreplaceable wildlife and unspoilt natural beauty. This is why Rupert started linking the idea of peace parks to national parks. Besides, wildlife and conservation can provide a foundation for counter-acting the poverty and unemployment of many African countries. These activities prepare the way for tourism, the world's biggest industry, the enormous potential of which has scarcely been exploited on the conflict-ridden continent.

He was able to experience the achievement of six peace parks being connected directly to his fatherland only a few years after the inception of the project. These transnational parks and conservation areas that are joined to South Africa and for which agreements have been signed with the respective governments, have already considerably extended the 'African safari' as a sought-after tourist destination.

Together with two other peace parks in southern Africa, these eight, with their abundance of animals and plant life, will cover about 60 million hectares. A further fourteen transfrontier conservation areas in southern Africa have been identified for development in the next decade. The 22 peace parks will ultimately extend over 100 million hectares, an area the size of France, Germany and Switzerland combined.

The idea of peace parks is gaining ground in other parts of the world as well, such as the demilitarised zone between South and North Korea, the Mont Blanc mountain park, South America and elsewhere.

The most extensive project in which South Africa is directly involved is Greater

Limpopo, the game park that may become the biggest animal kingdom in the world. The renowned Kruger National Park of South Africa will be united with three national parks in Mozambique and Zimbabwe's Gonarezhou National Park. The envisaged peace park, four times the size of the already large Kruger National Park, will be home to an unrivalled collection of Africa's animals, plants and trees. It is envisaged that this transnational park, extending across the borders of three countries, will initially cover 35 000 km², which could eventually be extended to 100 000 km² – bigger than Portugal, Hungary or Austria.[6]

Big game has already been translocated from the Kruger National Park to Mozambique. Among other wildlife, more than 1 000 elephants will eventually be moved to the Mozambican side: to a region where animals were destroyed ruthlessly during Mozambique's civil war, but also the country from which the first elephants for the later Kruger National Park were donated decades ago.

The translocation of the first herd of elephants to the envisaged peace park took place on 4 October 2001, Rupert's 85th birthday. For him this was a birthday present without equal: the realisation of a ten-year-long dream.

Still at Rupert's side in this great experiment is his wife, Huberte. This strong and attractive woman has been a tower of strength and his sounding board throughout his career, his life partner with whom he celebrated their 60th wedding anniversary a week before on 27 September 2001.

Rupert often reiterates his belief that the idea is stronger than the man. His conviction that nothing can stop an idea whose time has arrived echoes an observation by the economist John Maynard Keynes: 'The ideas of economists and political philosophers, both when they are right and when they are wrong, are more powerful than is commonly understood. Indeed, the world is ruled by little else. I am sure that the power of vested interests is vastly exaggerated compared to the gradual encroachment of ideas.'[7]

Now, in his advanced years, Anton Rupert is experiencing the satisfaction of seeing the idea of peace parks becoming increasingly popular – an idea that may still become the biggest and most enduring trademark of the business leader who is regarded by an international trademark expert as the oracle of trademarks. Nothing would give Rupert greater pleasure than seeing such an inspirational, hope-giving idea expanding internationally from South Africa, the fatherland to which he has always returned after his world travels.

He draws inspiration from Albert Schweitzer's thoughts on reverence for life. The German medical missionary, philosopher and philanthropist, winner of the Nobel Peace Prize in 1952, devoted his life to healing Africans in his hospital at Lambaréné in Gabon. Schweitzer regarded ethics as nothing other than reverence for life. 'Reverence for life affords me my fundamental principle of morality, namely that good consists in maintaining, assisting, and enhancing life, and that to destroy, to harm or to hinder life is evil,' he declared.

Reverence for life is also reflected in a poignant bronze statue placed in the entrance hall of Rupert's office building in Stellenbosch. Here visitors walk past the German artist Käthe Kollwitz's *Mutter mit Zwillingen*, depicting a mother cradling her twins in her arms.

Now the once energetic dark-haired entrepreneur walks with a stoop as a result of a curvature of the spine. He also reads with some difficulty, and all correspondence and reading material have to be enlarged by means of a video screen on his desk. A solar eclipse 60 years ago may have caused his eye problem. In October 1940 in Graaff-Reinet he and his youngest brother Koos, who has similar eye problems, watched a total eclipse of the sun through film that possibly did not offer adequate protection. Typically, Rupert regards his weakening sight as an asset – just as more than once in his career he tried to convert a disadvantage into an advantage. Because he is able to read less, he 'has more opportunity to think'.

The remarkable life story of this entrepreneur-philanthropist, a business leader regarded as one of Africa's legends, covered almost a quarter of modern South Africa's history by the turn of the century. It started nearly nine decades earlier with his birth during the First World War in his beloved Karoo, the vast semi-desert in the interior of South Africa where the Rupert family became part of the land and the land became part of them.

PART II

FORMATIVE YEARS

CHAPTER 2

Eastern Cape roots

T he first Rupert arrived in South Africa in 1857.
Johann Peter Ruppert, the founder of the South African Rupert family and Anton Rupert's great-grandfather, was a native of Prussia. According to family lore he came from Gräfrath near Solingen, although his death certificate in the Cape Town archives gives his birthplace as Trier, the oldest city in Germany. He was one of the many German founders of Afrikaner families – 33,7% of Afrikaners of the period from 1657 to 1867 were of German descent, the second-largest group after those of Dutch descent (34,8%).[1]

After the outbreak of the Crimean War (1854-56) Johann Peter Ruppert enlisted in the British army, which was recruiting reinforcements on the European continent. With the rest of what was known as the German Legion, he was stationed at Colchester near London under the command of Major-General Baron Richard von Stutterheim. The war ended before the Legion was sent to the Black Sea, and Ruppert and his comrades were given the option to settle on the eastern frontier of the British colony at the Cape. With the cost of the frontier wars a drain on the treasury, the British government was keen to settle military pensioners on small-holdings so that they could be called up for military duty when the need arose.

The volunteers were told that there was a dearth of women at the Cape and were advised to find wives before they set forth. On 19 October 1856 the eighteen-year-old Ruppert wed seventeen-year-old Emma Susanna Grandfield-Crosby, a Colchester girl. Thus the South African Ruperts – Ruppert soon lost its second p – are descended from British and Prussian stock.

By that time the Cape, strategically situated on the sea route to the East, had burgeoned into a prosperous colony. Trade in wine and wool was flourishing and the government could launch large-scale public projects. But there was a serious shortage of skilled labour and European immigrants could help fill the gap.

Two events had given rise to the shortage of labour. Many craftsmen and workers died in the smallpox epidemic of 1857, while the 'national suicide' of the Xhosa in the same year, the consequence of visions reported by the prophetess Nonqwase, resulted in large-scale loss of life.[2]

By 1858 a contingent of 2 362 officers and privates of the German Legion, accompanied by only 361 women and 195 children, had been settled in the drastically depopulated frontier area later known as the Ciskei. In due course they were joined by a further 2 700 German civilian settlers, friends and relatives of the military settlers.

Johann Peter Ruppert (private number 1678, in the third company of the German Legion's second regiment) disembarked in East London. According to family tradition he was musically talented, and a violinist in the military band. He was initially stationed at Berlin, one of a number of Eastern Cape towns that were given German names, where he was granted land.

The British government's plan with the German settlers in the buffer zone at the frontier did not work out as intended. The frontier problem was becoming less acute and, at the outbreak of the mutiny in India, over 1 000 members of the German Legion volunteered for service on that subcontinent. Only 386 eventually returned. The ones who remained were mostly unable to farm successfully on their five-acre holdings, much of which was not even arable. In 1861 the German Legion was disbanded.

Johann Peter Ruppert and his wife were among the settlers who moved to Graaff-Reinet, where the Ruperts would have a lasting influence. This Karoo town with its colourful history had been established in 1786 as the centre of the fourth district at the Cape, with a *drosdy* (magistrate's residence) as the seat of local government, and a military commandant. The district encompassed a vast area stretching from the Indian Ocean almost to the Gariep River, with an indigenous population ranging from the Xhosa in the east to the Griqua and San in the west. By the time the district was proclaimed there were already 600 farmer families of European descent.[3]

As early as 1795 the people of Graaff-Reinet showed their mettle when they rebelled against the authority of the Dutch East India Company, earning a reputation as the first Boer republic. The town also has a niche in early South African history as the home base of eminent figures like Andries Stockenström (1792-1864) and Andrew Murray (1794-1866), moderator of the synod of the Dutch Reformed Church (DRC). Murray ministered in Graaff-Reinet alongside members of the London Missionary Society like Dr John Philip and Dr JT van der Kemp, whose views differed greatly from his.

In the confrontational climate of the eastern frontier Stockenström, the district's first *landdros* or magistrate, later lieutenant-governor of the Eastern Cape, stood for coexistence with the indigenous population and advocated truth and justice as fundamental principles. The views of this influential and far-sighted leader resemble the philosophy Anton Rupert was to adopt more than a century later.

Stockenström was responsible for laying out the charming town, which, with its water furrows, was known as the 'Jewel of the Karoo'. Set in the horseshoe bend of the Sundays River, it boasted an imposing church and parsonage (later the Reinethuis), as well as Cape Dutch, Georgian and Victorian residences cheek by jowl with flat-roofed Karoo houses. Today it is a picturesque museum town with 220 proclaimed historical sites, the most in any town in South Africa.

The descendants of the rebels of 1795 gradually developed more and more grievances against the British colonial administration, and by 1838 the Great Trek, the migration of Afrikaners to the interior, was in full swing. Several eminent Trekker leaders had close ties with Graaff-Reinet. Gerrit Maritz was a wealthy wagon maker in the town, with an outlying farm called Welgevonden, eventually owned by Anton Rupert's son Anthonij. Andries Pretorius of Blood River fame farmed in the district. Two provincial capitals – Pietermaritzburg and Pretoria – were named after them. The marriages of renowned Trekker leaders Piet Retief and Louis Trichardt were solemnised in the local church, and Andries Hendrik Potgieter was baptised there. Another prominent Trekker leader, Sarel Cilliers, was born at nearby Nieu-Bethesda.

Two presidents of later Boer republics – JN Boshof of the Free State and TF Burgers of the Transvaal – hailed from Graaff-Reinet. Further down the line, Dr DF Malan, later prime minister of South Africa, left his position as minister of the DRC in Graaff-Reinet to become the first editor of *Die Burger*, the oldest Afrikaans daily newspaper. And Robert Mangaliso Sobukwe, founder-leader of the Pan Africanist Congress, the Africanist resistance movement that broke away from the African National Congress in the late 1950s, went to school and now lies buried at Graaff-Reinet.

Many other cultural leaders, business people, educationists, medical doctors and agriculturalists put their stamp on Graaff-Reinet. The town was quite 'cosmopolitan'; the strong Afrikaner presence was complemented by English-speaking and Jewish families as well as initially a smaller group of black people and a considerably larger population of coloured people.

The first Rupert arrived in Graaff-Reinet during a worldwide depression in the aftermath of the Crimean War and the American Civil War. The wool market was flat and mildew was wreaking havoc in the vineyards of Graaff-Reinet. In 1868 the mildew was brought under control through the use of sulphur, and the town became renowned as a source of brandy and a potent home-distilled brew called *withond*, 'white dog'. The discovery of diamonds at Kimberley in 1867 and of gold at Pilgrim's Rest in 1874 restored the fortunes of the town. Fortune hunters from all over the world landed at Port Elizabeth and travelled to the minefields via Graaff-Reinet. There were over 60 camping sites for ox-wagons travelling north. In 1879, amid great festivity, Graaff-Reinet became the terminus of the new railway line from Port Elizabeth. At one stage the town had no fewer than four newspapers.

The pioneer Johann Peter Ruppert started off as a foreman on the farm Bloemhof, but then worked in Graaff-Reinet as a wagon maker until his death in 1882. According to family tradition he was killed in a shooting accident while hunting, which is not implausible, since the plains of the Karoo teemed with game in those days.[4]

He and his wife Emma Susanna belonged to the Anglican parish of St James at Graaff-Reinet. In 1865, a few years after their arrival in the town, the colonial government decreed that instruction at all government schools in the Cape Colony would henceforth be conducted in English. English newspapers at the Cape, convinced that the English were the 'dominant race', propagated a militant form of cultural imperialism; the *Cape Argus* dismissed Afrikaans as a 'bastard jargon', unworthy of the name 'language'. Despite this the Ruperts, like many other immigrant families, gradually adopted Afrikaans as their home language. After the marriage of the pioneer couple's surviving son to an Afrikaans-speaking girl, the family eventually joined the Dutch Reformed Church.

Three of the pioneer couple's four children died in childhood, two of them of diphtheria within ten days of each other in the epidemic of 1869. Only the eldest son, Anton Rupert's grandfather Anthony Edward, survived to adulthood. Like his father, he died at the age of 44 years. Emma Susanna died in 1919.

Grandfather Anthony Edward Rupert was a builder. During his last illness in 1906 he wrote a document – it is still in the family's possession – describing his humble beginnings at the village of Petersburg, plying his trade from one farm to the next. Sometimes he went around on horseback, but when in dire straits he travelled on foot. Before his marriage to Maria Elizabeth Dippenaar in 1885 he rented a house from the coloured congregation of the London Missionary Society for £2 per annum. He had to cover the thatched roof with a canvas wagon tent to keep out wind and rain.

After his marriage his fortunes improved. He built a school at Graaff-Reinet and another on the farm Letskraal, where Andries Pretorius had farmed before the Great Trek. At Petersburg, on the ox-wagon route to Kimberley, he built a church whose cornerstone still bears his name. His reputation spread. In 1899, shortly before the outbreak of the Anglo-Boer War, he and his family settled in Graaff-Reinet itself, where he restored and renovated houses. Although all building materials had to be transported by ox-wagon, he could complete a farmhouse within six weeks – an achievement that required considerable organisational abilities.[5] Ds Rooi Abraham Louw, who had known the builder Rupert at Graaff-Reinet, once told Anton Rupert: 'Your grandfather was the most hard-working man I ever met.'

The eldest of the skilled builder's eight children, John Peter Rupert, born in 1888, practised as an attorney at Graaff-Reinet, where his family would live for nearly a century. In this town, with its eventful history, his son Anton was born 28 years later.

CHAPTER 3

Boyhood years in the Karoo

A nthony Edward Rupert the second was never called by his baptismal names. In his boyhood he was known as Boetie (lit. 'little brother'), and at university he became Anton. The oldest of three brothers, he was born on 4 October 1916. Jan (John Peter) was born in 1922, and Koos (Jacobus Albertus) in 1929. Both Rupert's bothers would follow him to the Rembrandt Group. The three brothers in the tobacco industry have been compared to the three brothers Reemtsma in Germany and the three brothers Reynolds in the USA, who built up the biggest cigarette factories in their respective countries.

Their father, universally known as *Oom* (Uncle) John, was a respected community leader in Graaff-Reinet. In the hard times during the Anglo-Boer War (1899-1902), when the Cape Colony was subject to martial law and many Cape Afrikaners, although British subjects, were as poverty-stricken as their fellow Afrikaners and relatives in the war-torn northern republics, he had to go out to work at a young age. After the war he was able to complete his high-school education at the Graaff-Reinet College in 1909.

After serving articles at the local law firm of CH Maasdorp, John Rupert worked as an attorney in towns such as Kimberley, Mossel Bay and Prince Albert, which was booming in the heyday of the ostrich-feather industry. Here he was offered a partnership in a law firm but he smelled a rat and turned down the offer – wisely, as it turned out, since two of the partners were later prosecuted. It left him with a lasting mistrust of partnerships, in contrast to the philosophy of partnership his eldest son would implement so successfully.

John Rupert, who established his own law practice in Graaff-Reinet, took a keen interest in education and child welfare. The secretary of the local Child Welfare Society during his term of office as chairman was the town's social worker, Tini Malan, who was to marry the later Prime Minister John Vorster. Another future prime minister who crossed his path was JG (Hans) Strijdom, whose uncle brought the young law graduate from nearby Willowmore to Rupert requesting that he employ him as an articled clerk. Rupert was of the view that Graaff-Reinet offered too little scope and advised him to try his luck in the Transvaal. Strijdom evidently heeded the advice and moved to Pretoria and then to Nylstroom, where he became known as the Lion of the North.

Years later, before Strijdom became prime minister, he visited Anton Rupert in Stellenbosch. Strijdom, Transvaal leader of the governing National Party in the 1950s, wanted to break away from the then Prime Minister DF Malan on account of differences about whether South Africa should become a republic. Rupert walked twice around the house with the agitated Strijdom and persuaded him to be patient; he would get his chance as leader. Strijdom did take over from Malan, but became ill and died in office.

John Rupert and his wife both served on the committee of the Dutch Literary and Drama Society in Graaff-Reinet. The deputy chairman was Dr Bennie Keet, eventually a theology lecturer at Stellenbosch who became known for his rejection of apartheid. The names of the Ruperts and Keet appear in a brochure about an exhibition of 'antiques and curiosities' held in Graaff-Reinet in 1918, for which several townspeople had contributed antique furniture and possessions of historical value. Anton Rupert's later interest in antiques was probably stimulated at an early age.

John Rupert became involved in politics as the secretary of the first branch of the National Party established in the town after General JBM Hertzog's sensational speech at De Wildt on 7 December 1912. Hertzog increasingly differed with the conciliation politics of Generals Louis Botha and Jan Smuts as well as their views on the language question, with Hertzog advocating language equality for Afrikaners. He declared himself a 'definite opponent' of imperialism where imperial interests clashed with national interests, and stated that he put South Africa first. As a result of his unshakable views Botha omitted him from the first Union cabinet and the Free State judge and war hero Hertzog formed a new party, the National Party (NP). In 1913 Hertzog, who was to become South Africa's longest-serving prime minister, created a commotion at a Stellenbosch language festival when he read out a telegram from former Free State President MT Steyn, a giant figure in South African history, that contained the following quotation in Dutch: 'In the mouths of the conquered, the language of the conqueror is the language of slaves.'

The NP grew into the strongest party in Graaff-Reinet as scores of supporters of Botha and Smuts's South African Party (SAP) joined its ranks. John Rupert's wife Hester chaired the women's branch of the party, which would come to power in 1924 in coalition with the Labour Party.

John Rupert's hobbies were writing and reading poetry and studying languages; he could read nine languages. At the age of 70 he took up French, and could soon read classic works in that language. But he was unable to avail himself of a bursary to the Netherlands in his student years and never travelled abroad.

In his legal career John Rupert appeared in several much-discussed court cases, some arising from the Rebellion of 1914 during the Second World War. He defended the editors of the *Graaff-Reinet Onze Courant* and the Aberdeen paper *Nuwe Tijd* when they were charged with the capital crime of sedition on account of reports on Gen. Manie Maritz's treasonable act of joining the Germans with his troops during the Rebellion. The charges were withdrawn. On another occasion he defended the editor of *Onze Courant* when the paper was sued for reporting that the British airforce had bombed cities in a neutral country. The report turned out to be true, and again the charge was withdrawn.

At that time quite a number of coloured people, who then still had the vote in the Cape Province, lived in the town of Graaff-Reinet. In Cradock Street alone there were 25 houses belonging to coloured families. John Rupert did not hesitate to appear for coloured people, sometimes pro bono, at a time when such actions were viewed with scepticism by conservative white communities like Graaff-Reinet's. Coloured townspeople referred to him as *Groot Seur* (Big Sir); later his son Anton was called *Klein Seur* (Little Sir). Anton Rupert was to consider the later removal of coloured people from the centres of towns such as Graaff-Reinet and Stellenbosch under the Group Areas Act of 1950 one of the great follies of the NP's policies of rigorist racial separation.

John Rupert counted among his good friends and clients the local DR minister Ds Jozua Francois Naudé, and his wife, Mrs Ada Naudé. Ds JF Naudé was a co-founder and the first president of the *Afrikaner Broederbond* (AB), the secret organisation established to promote Afrikaner interests as a counterweight to the Freemasons and Sons of England. The couple were the parents of the later anti-apartheid activist Dr CFB (Beyers) Naudé, named after Christiaan Frederick Beyers, the Boer general under whom his father had fought in the Anglo-Boer War and who drowned in the Vaal River in the Rebellion of 1914.

Ds Naudé was also chairman of the governing body of the *Hoër Volkskool* in Graaff-Reinet, the first Afrikaans-medium secondary school in the Cape Province, where Anton Rupert was to matriculate. John Rupert was a co-founder and for 21 years honorary secretary of the governing body. At one stage he successfully waged a one-man campaign against the abolition of Latin, which he considered an essential basis for language instruction, as a subject at the school.

In 1922, a year before Boetie Rupert started school, the Hoër Volkskool – with its motto *Ons Sal Handhaaf* expressing a commitment to uphold the linguistic and cultural aspirations of Afrikaners – moved into the stately premises of the erstwhile Midlands Seminary. The principal Dr G von W Eybers, who had obtained his doctorate in London, was a firm believer in mother-tongue education. Already in 1919, six years before Afrikaans was recognised as an official language, he started teaching in Afrikaans instead of Dutch. This unleashed an educational language dispute in the town that resulted in the establishment of the Union High School, an English-medium boarding school.[1]

The language question also led to division in the DRC. In 1921 Ds Naudé, one of the six *Bittereinders* (bitter-enders) who at the end of the Anglo-Boer War had refused to sign the terms of surrender at Vereeniging, gave his inaugural sermon in Afrikaans. Aggrieved members of the congregation, many of whom considered Dutch the appropriate language for church services, protested vehemently against the use of 'kitchen Dutch' in the 'Great Church' of the Murrays. One Sunday the organist, Amy Asher (born Murray), even played 'God Save the King' after the service. It ended in schism when the 'New Church' seceded.

Anton Rupert's wife Huberte recounted in an interview that her father-in-law had lost clients during a court case in which he acted for the wife of a friend. It offended some people that John Rupert had defended her – a portent of the loyalty principle that would count for so much in his son's career.

When Anton's father died in 1961, he thought he would ask Beyers to bury his father, Huberte said. Dr Beyers Naudé, then minister of the DR congregation of Aasvoëlkop in Johannesburg, related during the funeral service that as a child, he often had to take messages from his father to the deceased. He had been struck by John Rupert's 'sincere modesty, genuine love for his people, broadness of vision and sense of justice'.

John Rupert met his future wife Hester Adriana van Eeden, sister of a friend, on a train from Port Elizabeth to Klipplaat, a small railway siding near her father's farm in the Jansenville district. They were married in December 1915 and a year later Anton was born in their stone house at 110 Cradock Street, Graaff-Reinet. The family later moved to 84 Cradock Street.

Anton Rupert was born two years after the outbreak of the First World War on 4 August 1914. In South Africa, Botha and Smuts's decision to invade German South-West Africa (today Namibia) in support of the hated British Empire once again divided the country. A rebellion broke out after Gen. Manie Maritz had joined the German forces. Although the Rebellion of 1914 was quelled, resistance grew against the conciliation politics of Botha and Smuts aimed at national unity between Afrikaans- and English-speaking South Africans and cooperation within the Commonwealth, especially after Hertzog had proclaimed his policy of 'South Africa First'. Smuts's execution of the rebel leader Jopie Fourie also earned him bitter reproaches that would dog him for the rest of his life.

An important consequence of the Rebellion was the establishment of the *Help-mekaarvereniging*, a mutual-aid society to assist rebels with the payment of fines and compensation claims, at a time when the Poor White problem was worsening in the aftermath of the Anglo-Boer War. Following from the Helpmekaar movement's first fundraising drive that yielded £250 000, a national congress was held at Graaff-Reinet's neighbouring town of Cradock in 1916, the year of Anton's birth, to investigate the problem of poverty. It turned out that there were 105 518 indigent whites, 39 021 of them in dire straits, and that a quarter of the country's 280 000 white children were not attending any school.

Although the congress was unable to do much to stem the impoverishment, the Helpmekaar movement provided one of the most important launching pads for the economic independence of Afrikaners. The mustering of Afrikaner capital during the First World War led to the establishment of a number of big Afrikaner enterprises that became success stories, notably the media company Nasionale Pers (later Naspers) in 1915 and the insurance giants Sanlam and Santam as well as the *Koöperatiewe Wijnbouwersvereniging van Zuid-Afrika Beperkt* (Cooperative Wine Farmers Society of South Africa Ltd, the KWV) in 1918. Some of these enterprises were to play a role in Anton Rupert's life, while he would also later become involved in the Helpmekaar educational fund.

A major driving force behind the Helpmekaar movement was Ds JD Kestell, who would later be a decisive influence in the young's Rupert's life. Kestell conducted the funeral service of former Pres. Steyn, who was buried at the foot of the Women's Monument in Bloemfontein after having said in his last speech on the day of his death in 1916: 'The Helpmekaar has been born from God.'

Anton Rupert's mother Hester, one of ten children, was a caring, loving woman who 'kept the family together' and had a great influence on her eldest son. He often quoted moral guidelines she had given him, such as: 'Of what use is it to conquer the world and lose one's soul?' And: 'Cast thy bread upon the waters: for thou shall find it after many days.' At her funeral in 1944 a coloured woman told her daughter-in-law Huberte Rupert that 'she had given much to our people'.

After Dr DF Malan's departure from Graaff-Reinet Mrs Hester Rupert became the secretary of the *Jong Zuid-Afrika* (Young South Africa) association. It had originally been called *Zonen van Zuid-Afrika* (Sons of South Africa) as a counterweight to the Sons of England, with the aim of promoting a common South African patriotism, supporting the Dutch language and advancing the material and spiritual interests of the Afrikaner people. In 1912 it was decided to admit women as well and the name was changed. In due course Jong Zuid-Afrika sided with Hertzog's NP against Prime Minster Louis Botha.

Mrs Rupert's father, Mr Jacobus Albertus (Oom Kootjie) van Eeden, a Cape Patriot and co-founder of JH Hofmeyr's *Afrikanerbond*, South Africa's first political party, also had a significant influence on his grandson Anton. Up to Oom Kootjie's death at the age of 84, this successful farmer who had 500 morgen agricultural land under irrigation on his farm Gannavlakte often discussed national affairs with his grandson. Oom Kootjie was a descendant of one of the oldest Dutch families in South Africa – the first Van Eeden arrived at the Cape in 1662. On his mother's side Anton Rupert is a ninth-generation South African.

Oom Kootjie had a chequered history. His father died when he was nine and he was indentured to a wealthy farmer, for whom he had to perform hard manual labour. After his mother's remarriage she reclaimed him, but he was again put to menial work, this time as a goatherd on his stepfather's farm. He ran away to fight in the frontier war. Wounded, he turned to transport riding and married Anna Gertruida Lötter, also an orphan, who bore him ten children. After some daring land speculation he bought Gannavlakte, which he developed into a prosperous farm. It boasted an orchard, vineyards, a smithy, a brandy distillery, a mill, flocks of sheep and ostriches, whose plumage was worth a fortune in those days.

Even though he had little formal education, Oom Kootjie was a prominent member of his community and district chairman of the Afrikanerbond for over 22 years. He often addressed the annual sports meetings on Union Day (31 May) on a farm in the Jansenville district, and wise words from this grandfather Anton Rupert learnt to respect were quoted in a newspaper report: '. . . the common fault on the sportsground, as well as in life, is to look at the man who is behind you. If we could keep the man in view who is ahead of us and make it our object to catch up with him the number of poor people would certainly decrease.'[2]

He was interned at Port Alfred for his pro-Boer sympathies in the latter days of the Anglo-Boer War, when Boer commandos were invading the Cape Colony and recruiting young Afrikaner rebels. Two of these were Oom Kootjie's eldest sons, Frederick (Frik) and Francois (Soois), who joined up in 1901. After enduring hardship on commando they surrendered to British forces. As a Cape rebel and British subject Soois, aged seventeen, was found guilty of the capital offence of high treason by a military court in Graaff-Reinet. He was granted clemency by Lord Kitchener and received a prison sentence of one year, but benefited from the Peace of Vereeniging on 31 May 1902 and only served six months.

Oom Kootjie's youngest son, born in 1901 while his older brothers were on commando, was christened Smartryk – grief-stricken, sorrowful. In the aftermath of this war that would be regarded as the beginning of the end of British imperialism, the name expressed the emotions of thousands of Afrikaners, also in the Cape Colony, who had suffered and been pauperised as a result of the conflict. Many were on the brink of famine and the British government's meagre compensation for war damage caused further bitterness. General Louis Botha, first prime minister after the formation of the Union of South Africa in 1910, was offered £900 in settlement of his claim for £20 000. He returned the cheque.

A war story that made a profound impression on the young Boetie Rupert was that of the legendary scout and Scarlet Pimpernel of the Boer forces, Gideon Scheepers, executed at the age of 23 by the British after being convicted of 30 alleged war crimes. In Anton Rupert's own view, the story of Scheepers as told to him by his father, who as a thirteen-year-old boy had been present at the verdict of the military court on Church Square in Graaff-Reinet, changed his life.

The prosecution of Scheepers was a show trial intended as a lesson to Cape republicans – while in Rudyard's Kipling words, the war had been 'no end of a lesson' to Britain itself. On Major-General John French's orders the execution was carried out in public. Blindfolded, sitting on a chair, the ill Scheepers faced the firing squad of the Coldstream Guards on his mother's birthday, 17 January 1902. His body was put in a grave on the scene and covered with quicklime, but was probably removed that same night. His remains were never found.

Like the concentration camps where 28 000 women and children died and the 'scorched earth' policy of the British Commander-in-Chief Lord Kitchener in terms of which hundreds of farmhouses were burned down and herds of livestock destroyed, the show trials and executions of Cape rebels and Boer prisoners of war elicited bitter resentment. Scheepers, for instance, was not a Cape rebel but hailed from the Transvaal and was a commander of the Free State state artillery, therefore rather a prisoner of war than a disloyal British subject. Some 40 rebels were executed in the Cape Colony, with eight executions taking place in Graaff-Reinet. As elsewhere, the executions hardened the attitudes of republicans in the divided town.

The long search of Scheepers's mother for his remains was never rewarded. On her hundredth birthday in 1956, she said she had not forgotten, but forgiven: 'Let us rather live together in love and peace as an undivided people.'[3] Scheepers became a legend in South Africa that also inspired Afrikaans poets. In his moving poem 'Gebed om die gebeente' (Prayer for the bones), Dirk Opperman reflects the plea of the grieving mother of Scheepers, an expert heliographer:

> Bless, Lord, all the bleached bones of our struggle –
> that we as one great nation in the tough terrain
> with every scrap of roofing iron and every wheel
> and, like tin foil behind clean glass, the white, the black, the brown,
> may catch your sunlight, Lord, and signal each to all.[4]

Opperman, a close friend of the Ruperts, captures with his imagery the idea of partnership and coexistence that would run as a leitmotif throughout Anton Rupert's career, after he had been inspired at a young age by the legend of Scheepers.

At the Anglo-Boer War centenary in 1999 Rupert bought a priceless file on Gideon Scheepers, previously in the possession of British Intelligence, from a Cape Town bookseller. It contains Scheepers's last letters and diary entries, as well as unique photographs of Scheepers and other Boer prisoners of war.

A monument to Scheepers and the others executed at Graaff-Reinet, unveiled in 1908, was erected on land donated by Jurie Laubscher, owner of the factory that manufactured the famous Graaff-Reinet Doll. The later fate of this doll-making factory with its seventy workers was something that made a lasting impression on the future industrialist Rupert. When the Pact Government of the National and Labour parties came to power in 1924 after the mineworkers' strikes in Johannesburg, they introduced progressive labour laws with strict requirements for the physical layout of factories. 'Oom Jurie Losper, as he was known, couldn't meet those requirements – and Graaff-Reinet's biggest factory had to close down,' Rupert remembers.

In Boetie Rupert's childhood days Graaff-Reinet, like most country towns, had no electricity, running water or tarred streets. Drinking water was collected from the runoff of rainwater from rooftops. Gardens were irrigated from furrows fed by Maggie's Well, a perennial spring that produced two million gallons of fresh water daily on the site where the town reservoir is today. This water, boiled, was used for ablutions. Piped water did not come till the late 1920s. Lighting was provided by candles and paraffin lamps. When electricity finally arrived, it was expensive at a shilling a unit. In the early 1920s John Rupert drove a Model-T Ford, which was replaced with a Chevrolet in the mid-twenties. Later the vintage Chev was displayed in the Transport Museum at Heidelberg, Gauteng.

One of Boetie Rupert's earliest memories was a visit to his great-grandmother Emma Susanna at an old-age home in Cape Road, Port Elizabeth, shortly before she died in 1919. His mother also showed him a letter to her from this Colchester-born ancestor, which ended with five crosses and a message in her native English: 'And remember to give my love to Anthony.'

Port Elizabeth was where the Ruperts spent their holidays. Grandmother Rupert lived there from 1923 till her death in 1930. So did her daughter Florence, Aunt Florrie, a teacher who introduced Boetie to experiences that stimulated his early interest in industry and museums. He was taken to the snake park and the museum and, when he was old enough in the early 1920s, to various factories around Algoa Bay. Places they visited included the first assembly plants of Ford and General Motors, the Wool Exchange, the Pyotts biscuit factory and the Mobs shoe factory. Years later Anton Rupert told visitors at a Port Elizabeth show: 'Coming from Graaff-Reinet where there were no industries, it was a dream and a magical world to me to see how "something" was manufactured.'[5]

South Africa's transition from agriculture and mining to an industrial country left such a lasting impression that it influenced his choice of career. 'Production has always fascinated me. Later at university I realised how important industry was as a source of employment opportunities,' he said in a radio interview.[6]

In Port Elizabeth he also saw his first talkie, 'The singing fool', starring Al Jolson. Before that he had seen only silent films, like the cowboy films of Tom Mix. But he never became a film enthusiast and showed no particular interest in the cinema in later years.

In Anton Rupert's boyhood years the most important people in South African country towns and villages were authority figures like the school principal, the magistrate and the minister of the local congregation. Sundays were strictly Calvinist in Graaff-Reinet, a town very much under the influence of the Murrays, who like other austere Scottish church fathers had become ministers of the South African DRC. Children had to attend church and Sunday school, sport on Sunday was considered sinful and even sewing was forbidden on the sabbath lest the needle pierce God's watchful eye. John Rupert never went to church, but his wife Hester took the children while he went mountaineering. Although she did not flaunt her religion, she was devout. And whatever his religious convictions, her husband's values were staunchly Calvinist: an ethos of hard work, integrity and sobriety governed Anton's upbringing and indelibly stamped his character. So rigorous was John Rupert's moral code that he never defended an accused who had confessed his or her guilt to him. Yet the absence of rigid orthodoxy on the part of his parents left the eldest son with a lasting distaste for niggling rules and regulations that curb innovativeness and individuality.

Boetie Rupert started school in 1923 at the age of six. Although there was no school uniform, the children had to wear shoes. On his first day at school Boetie was pushing his baby brother's pram and ended up in a water furrow. His brand-new shoes and outfit were drenched and he had to go home to change into old clothes and shoes before venturing out on his school career. Boetie completed substandards A and B in one year. He was left-handed but, counter to the common practice in those days, he was not forced to write with his right hand. For that he could thank Dr Karl Bremer, their family doctor, who had recently qualified abroad and brought home some enlightened ideas. He lived across the road from the Ruperts and his daughter Elizabeth (Van der Merwe, a writer of children's books) was a classmate and close friend of Boetie.

Initially his scholastic performance was mediocre: in Sub B he came ninth in his class. Then a rebuke by his teacher in front of the whole class shamed him into excelling. Soon he was top of his class, to the chagrin of Elizabeth Bremer, his inveterate rival. She remained at the Volkskool till they were in Standard 7; then her father became a member of parliament – later Minister of Health – and the Bremers moved to Cape Town.

Hester Rupert was much loved by the young, who shared many childhood joys and sorrows with her. She read books with Boetie, a voracious reader in his own right. Apart from the family's collection of children's books, he scoured the well-equipped town library for newspapers and magazines like *Scientific American* and *Illustrated London News*, besides any book that captured his lively curiosity. At night his mother sat up with him while he read and studied and brought him a hot drink at bedtime.

With his father he went for long walks across the veld, sometimes to the Valley of Desolation (the Ruperts called it the 'mountain cathedral'). He loved this wide, arid landscape, so ancient a dinosaur footprint would cause no surprise, and considers it 'an absolute privilege' to have grown up in the Karoo. According to Anton Rupert's brother Koos, their father preferred mountain climbing to going to church – in a poem he had written about the Valley of Desolation, he described it as 'the church where I want to pray'. Years later Anton Rupert pointed out in a newspaper interview that many of the great faiths came from the desert – Moses, Jesus and Mohammed had all been desert dwellers. 'That is where you get seven-year droughts, where the starry night skies make you aware of your puniness, and where you are forced to think.' By contrast, he quipped, Karl Marx found the inspiration for the communists' bible, *Das Kapital*, in the vaults of the British Museum.[7]

The young Anton spent time at his father's office, learning about the legal profession. John Rupert impressed on him the importance of meticulous attention to detail, a virtue that Anton was to inculcate in his own children and employees in later life. He also taught him to be wary of praise: 'Today they shout hosanna, tomorrow they crucify you.' A compliment, he added, entailed responsibility: you had to live up to it. Among the values John Rupert imparted to his son was the importance of honesty and being true to one's word.

Boetie Rupert's introduction to radio was a crystal set broadcasting the 1929 election results. What impressed the twelve-year-old Boetie no less than the second victory of his hero Hertzog was the novelty of radio waves. He and a friend decided to build their own crystal radio. For an aerial they chose a length of galvanised wire, which they wanted to fasten to the roof of the house. While they were on the roof the aerial dropped onto the power lines, causing a short circuit that left the neighbourhood without power for hours. His father was furious.

It was at about the same time that Boetie and his friend Elizabeth stood watching a municipal vehicle procession one day when they saw a billboard advertising cigarettes. In what could have been a prophetic moment, the young Rupert told

Elizabeth South Africa should not be importing such cigarettes: 'We should be making them ourselves.' He was expressing a sentiment that had been gaining ground among Afrikaners for quite some time. Already in 1880 *Di Afrikaanse Patriot* had referred to 'foreign fortune seekers who are completely in control of commerce in our country'.[8]

In the late 1920s Japie Heese founded the Voortrekker movement for youths at the Hoër Volkskool. Boetie joined and wore the little green badge in his buttonhole. In 1931 it became a countrywide movement, an Afrikaans counterweight to Baden-Powell's Boy Scouts. Boetie did not excel at sports, although he enjoyed a friendly game of tennis or rugby. Later in life when a journalist from the American magazine *Fortune* asked Rupert what his favourite forms of exercise were, he remarked: 'I do mental gymnastics and I jump to conclusions!'

As a child he often played 'Cowboys and Indians' with the other boys. On one occasion one of the town's pranksters, Robey Leibbrandt, was involved. Leibbrandt, the Olympic boxer and Nazi sympathiser who would receive a death sentence for treason during the Second World War, had been born in 1913 and as a teenager went to school in Graaff-Reinet. His father, a Boer combatant described by Smuts as one of his bravest men when clemency was granted to Robey in 1948, was stationed at Graaff-Reinet as an officer in the permanent force from 1914 to 1924. One day during a game Robey and his brothers hanged the son of the school principal with a rope from a tree. Fortunately, his toes were touching the ground and some older men cut the rope to release him. The much younger Boetie, who had just started school, witnessed the incident.

In 1928 the school magazine included an essay by the twelve-year-old Boetie that gave an indication of his later interest in wildlife. Describing a visit to the Pretoria Zoo, he wrote: 'The first thing which attracted my attention was the gorgeously coloured speaking-parrots. Then I came to the cage of the gorilla – a mighty big and strong animal. After a few minutes walking I came to the monkey cage from where I walked to the hippopotamus, a very large animal with the largest mouth I have ever seen.' He concluded: 'I thoroughly enjoyed this well-spent and interesting afternoon.'

When Boetie was in Standard 6 he went on what was meant to be a one-day visit to his uncle Fred Knoetze, a printer at Somerset East who published the local newspaper. The driver who had given him a lift there forgot to pick him up and he spent a whole week with his uncle, who showed him everything at the printing works. 'The whole printing process, the type faces, the colour samples absolutely fascinated me,' he related later. This early interest in printing, colour and form would culminate in the scrupulous attention that Rupert as a master of marketing would give to each new product in the tobacco and liquor trade.

In Standard 8 he obtained four distinctions and was among the ten top students in the Cape Junior Certificate examination. In 1933, his final year at school, he was one of a class of 35, some of whom had started school in 1922, the year the Volkskool was founded, and had completed their entire school career there. At a reunion of eighteen of the surviving members of that class 50 years later Anton Rupert – by then an honorary citizen of Graaff-Reinet – on behalf of the three Rupert brothers presented the school with a Bill Davis sculpture entitled *His Hands*, inspired by a poem by the Afrikaans poet WEG Louw.

Anton matriculated in 1933 with three distinctions, for English (lower grade), Chemistry and Physics, and a remarkable 92% for Mathematics. His marks for Afrikaans (higher grade), Latin and History were slightly lower, but he averaged 78,9% and won a £10 prize for the best matriculant at Graaff-Reinet. By then he was finding schoolwork boring and was glad to put it behind him. He had just turned seventeen and was planning to study medicine.

That was not to be. By 1933 the Great Depression had hit South Africa. The Wall Street crash happened in 1929, when the Dow Jones index dropped from 312,76 to 230 points in five days. The slump continued for three years to a low of 40,56 points and American industrial shares fell by as much as 90%. The ripples spread around the globe, as far as South Africa. Here, meanwhile, rural poverty in the wake of the Anglo-Boer War had led to rapid urbanisation: between 1900 and 1926 the rate of urbanised Afrikaners rose from 10 to 41%. By 1933 the Carnegie Commission of Inquiry on the Poor White Question found that the number of desperately poor whites had grown from an estimated 106 000 in 1921 to 300 000, hence 30% of Afrikaners and seventeen percent of the white population as a whole. The Great Drought of 1933-1934 did not improve matters and many more farmers were forced to migrate to the cities, where they were largely dependent on welfare organisations and many women eked out a living for their families by running boarding houses.

The Hertzog government's stubborn insistence on sticking to the gold standard exacerbated the situation. In 1931 England devalued its pound but South Africa, a gold-producing country, did not follow suit. Exports became uncompetitively expensive: South African wool cost 40% more than that of Australia. Currency speculation caused an outflow of capital and South African mining houses, which sold gold for sterling, hoarded their profits abroad.

The Ruperts did not escape the general hardship. John Rupert's annual income dropped from £3 000 to £120. The family car stood idle in the garage for several years. At the age of sixteen young Anton had sufficient prescience to realise that South Africa would be compelled to leave the gold standard. His father, trusting Finance Minister Klasie Havenga to stick to his word, refused to believe him. This led to what was to be Anton's first business deal. He had been begging his father to exchange his paper currency for gold. On 28 December 1932 Havenga announced that South Africa was abandoning the gold standard. John Rupert manfully admitted that his son had been right. He opened his safe, which contained seven gold pounds. 'Take them, you deserve them,' he said. Each pound was worth 27 shillings instead of 20 – a lucky windfall for a young man who had to make his way through university.

Nonetheless he had to review his plans for the future. The only two medical faculties at the time, at the universities of Cape Town and the Witwatersrand, were way beyond his means. For £100 a year he could do a BSc at the University of Pretoria. At the beginning of the 1934 academic year he enrolled.

Commenting on this life-changing decision in later life, he said: 'I have often thanked Providence for things I didn't get when I wanted them.'

CHAPTER 4

Student during the depression

E arly in 1934, in the midst of the Great Depression, Anton Rupert left the Karoo for Pretoria, the administrative capital of the Union with a burgeoning Afrikaans university. On 26 February he registered for a first-year BSc course at what was popularly known as TUCs[1] – the University of Pretoria (UP), his alma mater, of which he would later become chancellor and Alumnus of the Century. The course was designed to serve as an admission qualification to a medical degree at one of the other universities.

His decision to attend the UP instead of the older universities of Stellenbosch or Cape Town was directly related to his love for Afrikaans. When he read in a newspaper report in 1933 that the city council of Pretoria had withdrawn its annual contribution to the UP on account of the university becoming an Afrikaans-language institution, he decided that this was where he wanted to study, as one of the first generation of Cape school children who had been educated fully in Afrikaans.

In Rupert's first year he was in Sonop men's residence. The first ten days the newcomers were subjected to a gruelling initiation programme. Most of it happened at night, so they got precious little sleep. They were tossed out of their beds, had to crawl through a stream, which they were told contained hidden barbed wire, and sent on long-distance jogs across the city on senseless errands like counting the steps of the Union Buildings. The young entrepreneur sized up the situation and, on his way to purchase a box of matches for a senior student at the railway station several kilometres away, he stopped off at the house of his former headmaster Dr Eybers, who had moved to Pretoria in the meantime. From him he borrowed enough money to buy a dozen boxes, which he hid on the sports grounds in case he was sent on the same silly errand again. At the end of the ten days two first-year students were in hospital and a third in a psychiatric institution. On 7 March 1934 the rector, Prof. AE du Toit, put a summary end to all initiation in the residences and instituted a committee to investigate the matter. On its recommendation, initiation rituals entailing physical exhaustion and nocturnal activities were declared taboo.

In the midst of this ordeal Rupert for the first time in his life wrote an intelligence test. The result was sufficiently impressive to secure him a bursary of £40 per annum for three years. On his slender budget it was a substantial amount. By then the Depression was affecting student numbers at the UP. In 1930 there had been 1 074 students. By 1934 enrolment was down to 829, including extramural students, plus 25 in Johannesburg. Those on the Pretoria campus knew each other well and Rupert was soon actively involved in student life, where he emerged as a natural leader.

At the end of his first year he was one of two students out of a class of seventeen to qualify for admission to study medicine at the universities of Cape Town or the Witwatersrand. Still unable to afford it, he changed to a straight BSc with chemistry as his major subject. His academic performance suffered a setback in his second year when he incurred inflammation of the middle ear and missed several months' lectures. There were no antibiotics in those days, and the somewhat primitive treatment left a permanent scar behind his ear.

In his final year Rupert met Huberte Goote, a first-year BA student. He had first heard about her when his close friend Colijn van Bergen sang her praises while they were sitting in a car outside the house of Fritz (FS) Steyn, the university's propaganda secretary and later a member of parliament, diplomat and judge, where Rupert was staying at the time. Student friends told Huberte about the *Afrikaans-Nasionale Studentebond* (ANS, Afrikaans National Students' Association), where she met Rupert. She represented the first-year students on the students' representative council (SRC), of which he was chairman. Huberte would spend the coming decades at the side of the tall, dark-haired student of whom she said in an interview: 'Anton was shy, but he had charisma. I was already fascinated by him at the first mass meeting.'

Huberte came from a Western Transvaal family, one that had also experienced hardship. She was the daughter of a Dutch immigrant teacher, Hubertus Johannes Goote, who had died five months before her birth during the 1918 Spanish influenza epidemic, and Johanna Adina Goote, née Bergh. When her grandfather in the Netherlands received a cablegram announcing her birth, he got the impression that he had a grandson and proposed that the baby be given the family name of Hubertus Gerardus, which was duly done. Understandably, the name gave rise to a lot of teasing, also from a good family friend, Prince Bernhard of the Netherlands. Hubert, as she spelled her name initially, objected to Prince Bernhard calling her 'Hubertus Gerardus'. He suggested she should be Huberta but she refused – Huberta was a hippopotamus, she said. In the end they agreed on Huberte, the French feminine form, which she prefers.

Like her daughter, Huberte's mother had also been born after the death of her father. Mrs Johanna Adina Goote was orphaned at the age of six when her mother Mrs Bergh (née Riekert) died. Huberte's grandfather Bergh was a descendant of the Swedish adventurer Olof Bergh, a member of the Political Council at the Cape, who gained fame through exploits such as leading the journey of exploration to Namaqualand in 1682-'83. He had been married to Anna de Koning. After the loss of her mother, Huberte's mother was raised by her grandparents, Comdt PJ and Mrs Lenie Riekert, on the farm Derdepoort. It was in the same district, near Pilanesberg, that Huberte's mother met her Dutch father, who was then head of a farm school with three teachers.

One of Huberte's clearest memories, one that she has carried with her since childhood is the story of the infamous murders on Derdepoort on 25 November 1899, a few weeks after the outbreak of the Anglo-Boer War. Her great-grandfather Comdt Riekert owned the large farm Derdepoort along the Marico River on the border between Marico-Bushveld and the then Bechuanaland. An attack on a Boer settlement of about thirteen families on the farm was the first in which the British forces used black people and in which Boer women and children were victims.[2]

In later years when Huberte told her grandchildren about the wartime suffering, she also cautioned them to remember the kindness and humanity of those who had helped her ancestors: 'You should always keep a balanced view, because wars are not caused by people; the cause is greed. Wars are always about greed.'

Huberte was born in 1919 in Pres. Paul Kruger's official residence in Church Street, Pretoria, at a time when the house was rented by the Moedersbond maternity hospital before it became the Kruger House museum. Until the age of seven, she lived with her mother and older sister Bets at Rustenburg. The widow supported her daughters by sewing dresses for friends. She had inherited the family farm but derived no income from it: 'just firewood and beetroot,' Huberte recalls. As her husband had died so soon after starting to teach in South Africa, Mrs Goote only qualified for a tiny pension. 'That is why I have respect for people who can make the most of their talents and can survive. I detest handouts; you have to retain your independence and honour,' Huberte relates.

In 1927 Huberte's mother remarried. Her new husband, Piet Wessels, was also a teacher and eventually became headmaster of Krugersdorp's Monument High School, which Huberte attended. A clever child, she did her first three standards in one year and matriculated at a young age. Her interest in all forms of the arts dates from the time she first went to school. She acted in plays, sang leading roles in operettas and was a member of the choir, while also playing basketball and hockey. After matriculating she worked as children's librarian at Krugersdorp for a year. Then, with the aid of three interest-bearing loans, she proceeded to university in Pretoria.

Huberte registered for a BA with Afrikaans-Nederlands and Afrikaans cultural history as major subjects. When her cultural history lecturer Kotie Roodt-Coetzee, who had become a good friend, learned about her library experience, she organised a post for Huberte in the university library and her tuition fees were waived. This lucky break enabled her to register for a diploma course in librarianship concurrently with the BA, which was permitted on condition she worked in the library two nights a week. With all that on her plate, she still found time for the SRC as well as her many other interests, mainly the arts. She was a member of the Castalides art committee and on the editorial board of its journal, *Castalia*. She belonged to a small group that met regularly to discuss art exhibitions. Intensely musical like the father she had never known, she was part of a group of music lovers that met on Sunday nights to listen to records. On top of that she chaired the ANS drama group and acted in productions at the *Volksteater* along with well-known actresses like the passionate Anna Neethling-Pohl. (In later years, whenever Huberte became somewhat agitated, Rupert would admonish her: 'Don't be like Anna Neethling-Pohl!') Even with all her extramural interests, however, Huberte completed both her BA and the librarianship diploma successfully.

Rupert, who has often acknowledged his gratitude to Huberte for her support throughout his career, paid tribute to his wife in his chairman's address at the 1996 AGM of Rembrandt Beherende Beleggings (Rembrandt Controlling Investments): 'She has been my most loyal and faithful supporter and also my greatest critic. I think that is how it ought to be.' On the same occasion he called to mind their student years, stressing that they were both children of the Depression, when about a third of Afrikaans-speaking whites were unemployed. 'I think it leaves a mark on one and maybe makes one look at capital in a different way. Those who had cars – three out of UP's total of 820 students – did not do well.' Both of them had to borrow to pay for their studies. They knew money could do a lot of good but it could also be the cause of great evil. 'It is like a rope: it can be used as a lifeline to save a drowning person, or as a noose to hang someone. That is money. It talks.'

At the end of 1936 Rupert obtained his BSc, majoring in chemistry with second-year courses in physics and mathematics. The next year he registered for an MSc in chemistry. He would be studying part-time, for he had to start earning a living. Jobs were scarce, but he was fortunate to get a post at the Pretoria Technical College lecturing to part-time pharmaceutical students. Their average age was 28. He was twenty.

It dawned on him even then that he was training Afrikaners to work for 'the English' – the language divide, reinforced by economic inequality, ran deep. Over the next few years he became increasingly convinced that Afrikaners would have to fight for their own niche in the business world and in public life, a view he shared with other Afrikaner intellectuals. Ever since Lord Milner's 'Kindergarten' – the British team imported from Oxford after the Anglo-Boer War to run the administration – the civil service had been predominantly English speaking. In 1925 nearly a third of all public servants were unilingual; the lingua franca at the office was English. In the business world, too, Afrikaners had to relinquish their ethnic ties and communicate in English if they wanted to become part of the business elite. Many Afrikaners sensed that English speakers condescendingly looked down on them and considered their language and culture inferior. A considerable number of English-speakers still harboured feelings that had been rife during the Anglo-Boer War, when the English press in South Africa was predominantly imperialist and anti-Boer. Some of the worst jingoism was displayed in the area around Graaff-Reinet.[3]

In the anti-Afrikaans atmosphere, which would increase as a result of divisions after South Africa's entry into the Second World War in 1939, Dr HJ van Eck, a brilliant chemical engineer and father of the South African industrial revolution, was refused membership of the prestigious Rand Club. (In 1945 Rupert cited this as his reason for declining nomination for membership, which, given his English name, might well have been granted by the club, considered the canteen of the mining fraternity.)

In 1937, the year Rupert started lecturing, a new Afrikaans morning paper, *Die Transvaler*, was launched in Johannesburg. He applied for a position at the paper and was interviewed by the editor, Dr HF Verwoerd, who offered him a job on the editorial staff. Since it would have meant furthering his study by correspondence, however, Rupert turned down the offer: he recalls his decision to return to the university and concentrate on his postgraduate studies as one of the most important in his early life. Besides, he had not been favourably impressed by Verwoerd, who came across as 'restless, rather autocratic and opinionated' during the interview – impressions that were confirmed in later life, when he and Verwoerd crossed swords on various occasions.

The centenary of the Great Trek took place in 1938. There was a huge upsurge of Afrikaner nationalism throughout the country, also on the UP campus. The *Afrikaanse Taal- en Kultuurvereniging* (ATKV, Afrikaans Language and Culture Society) organised a symbolic ox-wagon trek to remind the trekkers' descendants of the arduous journey and many tribulations their forebears had endured on their way into the interior. The symbol was apposite and stirred up great emotion among the vast majority of Afrikaners.

Rupert, in 1938 already a lecturer in chemistry, chaired both the extramural SRC and the extramural students' branch of the ANS, precursor of the later *Afri-*

kaanse Studentebond (ASB). He was also on the national executive of the ANS, at that time chaired by Dr Nic Diederichs, a future minister of finance. By that time Rupert was a supporter of Dr DF Malan's Purified National Party, the opposition to the ruling United Party of Hertzog and Smuts that had been formed through the fusion of the NP and the SAP in 1934.

Rupert and Huberte were among the ringleaders of the centenary celebrations on the UP campus, where Afrikaner ardour was opposed by members of the National Union of South African Students (Nusas), the dominant organisation on English-language campuses. Huberte was incensed by their snide comments on the Voortrekker costume that was widely worn by Afrikaners in that centenary year. She organised a special day when she and her friends would attend classes en masse wearing long Voortrekker dresses and traditional bonnets. They borrowed costumes from the Volksteater with the aid of Huberte's actress friend Anna Neethling-Pohl. The appointed day happened to be 14 September, which, someone pointed out, was the anniversary of the day when Afrikaans became the official teaching medium at the university. They decided to celebrate this event and it became the first 'Spring Day', as the annual commemoration of the day at the UP came to be called.

Some weeks later on 4 October 1938, Rupert's birthday, he and Wouter le Roux went to Bloemfontein as SRC delegates to attend a tribute to Ds JD Kestell, a revered Afrikaner church leader known as Father Kestell. Rupert was deeply moved by the venerable old man's message: 'A nation saves itself.' Kestell's message, reinforced by later experiences that turned him away from a career in politics, played a crucial role in Rupert's decision to enter the business world. It strengthened his conviction that Afrikaners should be self-sufficient and pull themselves up by their own bootstraps – in his own case, that he should venture into small business. Kestell, who had accompanied the Boer commandos on horseback as field chaplain throughout the Anglo-Boer War, had been a driving force in the Helpmekaar movement and provided the inspiration for the *Reddingsdaadbond*, an association formed to promote the economic advancement of the Afrikaner people. On the train journey back to Pretoria, Le Roux proposed that they celebrate. Only then, on such a decisive day in his life, Rupert remembered it was his birthday, and they toasted the occasion with a glass of white wine.

Rupert participated actively in the Ox-wagon Trek of 1938. As part of the celebrations a lighted torch had been carried all the way from Jan van Riebeeck's statue in Cape Town to the uncompleted foundations of the Voortrekker Monument in Pretoria, and it was also kept burning on the university campus. Rupert's younger brother Jan, a member of the Voortrekker youth movement, was on a visit from Graaff-Reinet at the time. Rupert recalled that Jan had to hold the torch while he drove his open car carefully so the flame would not go out.

On 10 October Rupert and Fritz Steyn, as representatives of the UP community, had travelled to Bulhoek to commemorate Pres. Paul Kruger's birthday in
the company of the Trek party. On this occasion they had requested the leader of
the Ox-wagon Trek to donate a wagon that could serve as a lasting inspiration to
students at their university. On 14 December – two days before the centenary
reached its climax on the Day of the Covenant, the commemoration of the Voortrekker victory over the Zulu at Blood River – it was announced at a mass rally
on Monument Hill that the wagon of Louis Trichardt was to be entrusted to the
students of the University of Pretoria for safekeeping. On 17 December students
pulled it to the university campus.[4] It became traditional for every outgoing chairman of the SRC to formally hand over custody of the wagon to his successor, as
Rupert duly did to Hans Nel in 1938.

At the peak of the Ox-wagon Trek celebrations Rupert edited and published a
newspaper, *De Oude Emigrant*, with the historian Gustav Preller as honorary
editor-in-chief. He consulted the news editor of *Die Transvaler*, Piet Meiring, also
from Graaff-Reinet and later head of the South African Information Service.
Rupert worked night and day on the four editions of the jubilee paper that appeared on 13, 14, 15 and 16 December, writing the editorial, collating copy – articles
and news about the Ox-wagon Trek and the centenary celebrations of the Great
Trek – and getting each edition printed by morning. But he failed to get a distribution network going and after the celebrations thousands of unsold copies
had to be burnt. 'I learnt a valuable lesson there,' Rupert was to say later. 'Your
product could be good, and still be a failure if your sales organisation and distribution aren't good.'

Afrikaner nationalism swept the Pretoria campus after the centenary, so much
so that the UP was unofficially called the Voortrekker University for a while.
Emotions ran high and UP students pelted the screen with eggs filled with ink
when 'God Save the King' was played in cinemas, as was customary in those
years. At a mass rally on 10 April 1939 Rupert proposed that 14 September (the
day when, seven years earlier, the university became an Afrikaans-medium institution) be celebrated annually at a student function, its nature to be determined
by the SRC. The proposal was adopted unanimously. In fact, the date was one
day out: 13 September in due course became Commemoration Day, or Spring
Day. Initially it took the form of a morning gathering on the campus, at which the
Louis Trichardt wagon, Voortrekker apparel and national flags featured prominently. In the afternoon there were sporting events and in the evening a ball. This
continued until 1944 when, on the proposal of the then SRC chairman, it was
declared an annual university holiday.

As invited speaker on Spring Day in 1961, Rupert recalled how in 1938, without official permission, they had taken the principal prisoner, carried him to the old club hall in a huge chair and started celebrating. Compared to the world's great universities – from Salerno, the oldest of all, dating back to the ninth century, to relative latecomers like Leiden and Harvard – South African universities were young, he said. 'But we have our own tradition, a tradition we should maintain with pride. We have a tradition of youthful vitality and resilience; a tradition of life instead of bricks and concrete. It is a tradition which should govern our actions, thought and attitudes, because in our country and with our challenges we need to be able to think clearly.'

On the 40th Spring Day in 1978 Rupert presented his alma mater with the hand-embroidered sash of office of Pres. Paul Kruger, taken to England as booty by a British soldier after the Anglo-Boer War, that he had traced and bought back. In an impassioned speech he reminded the students of the importance of symbols like the ox-wagon and the flaming torch to keep them aware of their origins and destiny. 'The ox-wagon was [for the Voortrekkers] the church, the childbed and the cradle of a new generation. And that is why this small wagon stands here as a symbol and a guard in order that we should never forget how small our beginnings were and how humble and grateful we should remain,' he said.

Yet even in the emotionally charged atmosphere of the late 1930s Rupert's patriotic fervour did not overrule his sense of justice. This is evident in his attitude towards an incident involving an English-speaking lecturer, John Agar-Hamilton. It was the upshot of the protracted language struggle that persisted even after Afrikaans was declared the official medium at the university in 1932. That move had been triggered by the tarring and feathering of a French lecturer at the UP, HP Lamont, who was suspected of pseudonymously writing a book entitled *War, Wine and Women* that contained denigratory comments about Afrikaners. At his assailants' trial Lamont admitted to writing the controversial book and was dismissed by the university.[5]

Despite the 1932 decision on the language medium, the UP senate decided that English-speaking lecturers merely had to improve their proficiency in Afrikaans to a level where they could understand the language but not necessarily be able to lecture in it. So John Agar-Hamilton, senior lecturer in history, continued to deliver his lectures in English amid mounting student objections that culminated in a boycott of his classes in April 1939. At the instigation of the chairman of the SRC, Albert Geyser, a protest meeting was held on campus, at which the *Vierkleur*, flag of the old Transvaal Republic, was hoisted.

Rupert was deeply perturbed by Geyser's action. Officially Agar-Hamilton was still permitted to lecture in English until the end of the year. At a mass meeting of students he proposed that Agar-Hamilton should receive an apology: as a guest on their campus he ought to be treated hospitably. He also suggested that English-speaking students abstain from voting, since it was the Afrikaners' honour that was at issue. Although Rupert's proposal was accepted by an overwhelming majority, Geyser refused to apologise to Agar-Hamilton. At the outbreak of the Second World War the lecturer joined the air force and left the campus for good.

This episode illustrates Rupert's early awareness of the need for coexistence, but also reveals a conviction that would become a philosophy of life: that Afrikaners should conduct themselves civilly and courteously towards people from other cultures. Geyser was not prepared to accept that. A *Hervormde Kerk* theology student, he did not have full student support during his chairmanship of the SRC. One of the council members, Ria Hugo (the later history lecturer Dr Maria Hugo), accused him of undermining Rupert, then chairman of the ANS, and proposed a motion of no confidence, which was passed. Geyser and his henchmen then proceeded to assault Rupert supporters, and one night they lay in wait for Rupert himself. He drove a battered red MG convertible, bought second-hand when he became a lecturer. They forced him out of it and led him to a nearby hall. Colijn van Bergen, who was with him in the car, managed to escape and ran to the library where Huberte was on duty. He shouted to her to summon the police, who arrived soon afterwards and came to Rupert's rescue. He was already being stripped by his assailants, who intended to tar and feather him.

Rupert refused to lay charges against the Geyser group, either with the police or the university authorities. He dismissed their conduct as plain jealousy. One by one his assailants came to him to apologise. Geyser was the very last to do so. That was in 1977, when he represented the University of the Witwatersrand at Anton's inauguration as chancellor of the University of Port Elizabeth.

After the Ox-wagon Trek Rupert and his good friend Colijn van Bergen, then in charge of the ANS Film Bureau, went on tour with a film show that included a film made of the Trek, together with films on the sculptor Anton van Wouw and the Afrikaans literary figures Jan FE Celliers, DF Malherbe and Totius. The only music they had was a recording of the national anthem, 'Die Stem van Suid-Afrika' (The Call of South Africa). In Rupert's second car, a DKW convertible, they set out for Graaff-Reinet from Pretoria around six in the evening, loaded with equipment. On a dirt road near Trompsburg in the Free State the car overturned. Since they were travelling at low speed, neither suffered more than slight injuries, but the record with the national anthem broke in half. Undeterred, they went ahead with the tour and drew big audiences wherever they went, even though at half a crown per ticket admission was not cheap. The film, which had considerable historical value, disappeared during the war years.

Van Bergen often stayed with the Ruperts at Graaff-Reinet. He remembers

Anton's mother as a 'wonderful woman' who was very hospitable and made people feel at home. And the first of the local attractions that the young Rupert pointed out to his friends was the statue of Gideon Scheepers.

Towards the end of his student career Rupert was given a lecturership in the Department of Chemistry at the UP. At the end of 1939 he obtained an MSc in applied chemistry. In 1939 and 1940 he also completed courses in law and commerce at the University of South Africa, and embarked on a doctorate in spectroscopy at the UP.

In 1939, while war clouds were gathering in Europe, Rupert chaired the on-campus committee of the ANS, of which Huberte was a member. He was also a member of the executive committee of the ANS and on the editorial board of the movement's official publication, *Wapenskou*, which published its freedom manifesto that reflected the strong feelings prevalent among Afrikaans students in the tension-filled late 1930s. In this document the ANS demanded that the Union of South Africa, a member of the British Commonwealth under the British crown, should be converted into a republic with an authoritative government. White population growth should be encouraged, including a considered immigration policy with assimilability as a requirement. 'Indigenous non-whites' should be under state tutelage. 'By means of a differentiation policy parallel development according to their own traditional cultural beliefs and equality through apartheid should be made possible for them.' Natural and production resources should be used equitably for the benefit of the entire community, in which regard the state should not hesitate to infringe on vested interests. As for language, it was proposed that Afrikaans should be the official language, with English enjoying full rights as a second language.

Several of the ideas in the manifesto were not to survive the overheated atmosphere of the war years; the proposed ideas also included some with which Rupert would differ increasingly explicitly in key respects in years to come.

In 1939 the ANS took a militant stand in favour of neutrality with regard to the war, but its protest meetings were to no avail. In parliament Gen. Hertzog's neutrality motion was defeated by 80 votes to 67 and when Governor-General Patrick Duncan turned down his request for a general election, he resigned as head of government. Gen. Jan Smuts became prime minister and on 6 September 1939 South Africa entered the Second World War. The war was to last till 1945, and once again divided the country.[6]

Shortly after the outbreak of war Rupert was invited for sundowners at the house of physics professor JS van der Lingen, who had worked under Albert Einstein in Europe. To Rupert's amazement he declared categorically that Germany would lose the war. He argued that for all its technological expertise, Germany did not understand mass production. When the USA entered the war Germany would be flattened by bombardment from the air. Besides, said Van Lingen, the Germans always wanted to improve a product instead of mass-producing the armaments required in a war situation. This far-sighted view was confirmed many years later by Dr Joachim Zahn, chairman of Daimler-Benz in the 1970s, who was astounded by the South African's insight when Rupert told him about Van Lingen's prediction. Zahn himself had worked on an intercontinental ballistic missile during the war, a sophisticated version of the V1 and V2 rockets that rained death and destruction on British cities during the blitz. The war was over and lost before the new missile was ready.

Shortly after the conversation with Van Lingen two incidents occurred that were to change Rupert's political views profoundly. Both occurred in the company of his student friend Dirk Hertzog, who would become a co-founder of the Rembrandt group. Hertzog was a nephew of General JBM Hertzog, who was living in retirement on his farm Waterval near Witbank.[7] He had initially planned to major in political science, but Stephen Leacock's warning that reconciling electioneering with statecraft was the cardinal problem of the parliamentary system made him turn to law. According to Hertzog, he and Rupert first met as a result of student anti-war activities. At a meeting to protest against the internment of a member of the SRC, first Rupert and then Hertzog spoke: 'Everybody else kept mum, as there were too many detectives in the audience,' he related.[8] It was Hertzog's interest in politics that triggered the two incidents in question.

The first was an interview with Gen. Hertzog that his nephew organised shortly after the outbreak of war. Their party comprised six members of the ANS executive, including himself, Rupert and Demps van der Merwe. They wanted the veteran leader to advise them as to where their duty lay in these turbulent times. At first the septuagenarian Boer general was sceptical. Why come to him for counsel after vilifying him all these years, he asked. He pointed out that until recently many students had questioned his Afrikaner identity and loyalty. In the end he wanted an assurance that they would follow whatever advice he gave them. The young men asked leave to deliberate. When they returned Rupert, acting as spokesman, agreed that they would accept his advice unconditionally: for his part, he had requested it because he needed it. They recall Hertzog's words to them as follows:

'If you ever want to exercise control, you must first learn to obey. And the true test of obedience is not when you are in agreement but especially when you disagree. Jan Smuts has declared a war that you do not agree with. As you know, I do not agree either. But it was done legally under a constitution that I helped to write, so as law-abiding citizens we are bound by it. Smuts assured me that he would not conscript South Africans for duty beyond our borders. I told him if he introduced conscription or martial law I would personally lead you to the hills [i.e. head a rebellion]. I think he learned a lesson in 1914, he won't repeat that mistake.

'Now I am telling you: go back and prepare yourselves to take over. The wheel will turn and the day will come when you have to take the reins, and then you must be ready. Go back to your studies, do your duty and obey the law. And remember, whatever you do unto others will be done unto you.'

The former prime minister then insisted on personally pouring the coffee and slicing the bread.

Rupert was profoundly impressed. He had expected Hertzog to instigate them to rebel against the Smuts government. He decided then and there that he would desist from protest in future and rather engage in positive, practical action. To his mind this was an even more life-changing resolve than his decision to turn down Verwoerd's offer to join *Die Transvaler*. Hertzog died two years later in November 1942. His former private secretary, Wennie du Plessis, described him as 'Boer, Soldier, Statesman, Prince among humans'. Du Plessis eventually became an MP when he defeated Smuts in his stronghold, the Highveld constituency of Standerton, in the watershed election of 1948, which brought to an end the era of the Boer generals who had ruled the Union of South Africa since 1910.

The group of student friends all followed Hertzog's advice and completed their academic training, except Demps van der Merwe, who was interned during the war. He was a theology student, newly returned from the Netherlands, who eventually headed the *Gereformeerde Kerk*'s Transvaal training centre for black theology students at Hammanskraal. In Huberte's opinion it was Hertzog's 'wonderful' advice that inspired Anton to join the Reddingsdaadbond when he was asked to do so.

The other crucial incident that influenced Rupert during the war years took place in 1940, when Dirk Hertzog persuaded Rupert to accompany him to Swart-ruggens to attend a political meeting at which Oswald Pirow was to speak. In 1939 Pirow, minister of defence in Hertzog's government, had started a right-wing totalitarian movement, the New Order. Back in Pretoria after the meeting, Rupert was invited to tea by Pirow's sister Sylva Moerdyk, wife of the well-known architect Gerard Moerdyk and member of a political triumvirate in the Transvaal, together with Adv. JG (Hans) Strijdom, later prime minister, and Prof. LJ (Wicus) du Plessis of Potchefstroom University for Christian Higher Education.

When he arrived she did not mince words. 'Anton, why are you throwing away your future like this?'

Surprised, he asked what she meant.

'Why do you mix with the likes of Oswald Pirow?'

Bewildered, he told her he didn't understand. She replied: 'We're grooming you as leader in our party.'

He was shocked to hear a sister speak about her brother in such terms. That evening he told Huberte: 'If that's what politics is like, I want nothing to do with it. I'm through with politics.'

Rupert's decision to steer clear of politics differed from that taken by Harry Oppenheimer, heir to an earlier South African family fortune, at about the same time. In 1947 he was elected a United Party MP. After the death of his father, Sir Ernest, in 1958 he became chairman of Anglo American and left politics, no doubt because he sensed a conflict of interests which the dual role as politician and head of a mighty gold, diamond and mineral empire would have entailed.

Dirk Hertzog in his turn received advice that turned him away from politics from his uncle Gen. Hertzog, whom he often visited at Waterval, although he did stand for election once. In his memoirs he records that when he questioned Hertzog about Stephen Leacock's view of politics, the old man replied: 'Yes, my boy, Leacock's right. Smuts and I entered politics with the prestige we had gained over three years during the Anglo-Boer War. We could still achieve something on occasion. But if you have to start from the bottom, you have to kiss so many hands to get to the top that by the time you do, you are powerless. Besides, it's always difficult to decide whether you should do the popular thing – and it's never hard to tell what that is – or rather do what your own knowledge and experience tell you is in the public's long-term interest. If you choose to do what you believe to be right, you must accept that you may become unpopular. And if you want to be popular, you must accept that you will have to act against your own judgment, if not your conscience.'

Rupert retained great respect for Gen. Hertzog, whose stature grew after his death. And he considers the international statesman Gen. Jan Smuts, prime minister from 1939 to 1948, and the poet and naturalist Eugène Marais to have been the two real geniuses that South Africa produced.[9]

His decision to shun politics was indeed life-changing. Most of his university friends believed he was destined for a political career. Dr Colijn van Bergen expressed a firm view in this regard: 'If Anton had become prime minister instead of Hendrik Verwoerd, South Africa would have been a totally different world.'

During the war years the relationship between Rupert and Huberte was formalised. Rupert duly approached Huberte's stepfather, Piet Wessels, to ask for her hand in marriage. His future father-in-law responded: 'I know you can't support her, but I'm sure you will manage in the end.'

Although far from the war arena, South Africa felt the reverberations. Strict rationing and other wartime measures were introduced and towards the end of the war 200 000 South Africans in uniform took part in the war effort. In the midst of this comparative austerity the young couple were blissfully in love. They went to buy an engagement ring at the Amsterdam Diamond Cutting Works in Johannesburg. The counter staff made such a fuss of them that they quite forgot to pay for the ring. They were nearing Pretoria when Huberte realised the oversight. Horrified, she remembered that they had even been told that when they came for the wedding ring, it would be a present. When they hastened back the next day to settle the bill the staff were unfazed. 'They said they knew we would come back to pay them, can you believe it?' Huberte related in 2001.

They announced their engagement on Kruger Day, 10 October 1940. Their photograph appeared prominently on the social page of *Die Transvaler*, with the caption stating that the engagement was bound to 'arouse general interest in republican circles'. The same issue contained an article on the heroines of the Anglo-Boer War, with a long quotation from a letter Gen. Smuts wrote to Pres. MT Steyn in 1901, describing the devastation of the country and the abuse of women and children. The article made a lasting impression on Huberte because the quoted letter included a reference praising her great-grandmother Lenie Riekert.[10]

A year later, on Saturday, 27 September 1941, the couple were married in the *Gereformeerde* church in Krugersdorp. (Rupert was Dutch Reformed, but Huberte belonged to the smaller sister church popularly known as the *Dopperkerk*.) The wedding, a major social event in the close-knit Afrikaner community, was covered in great detail in *Die Transvaler*.

After the reception the couple drove off in Rupert's battered little DKW, registration number TK 714. The canvas roof leaked so that when it rained Huberte had to open an umbrella to keep dry. They were embarking on a life in which she was to be a constant support at Rupert's side, having taken to heart the advice given to her before the wedding by Sen. Martin Vermeulen, father of her student friend and bridesmaid Theresa Vermeulen: 'You are going to marry a leader of people, a man of whom we expect much. Decide early on that you want to be his helpmate. Someone must keep the home fires burning.'

PART III

BUSINESSMAN

CHAPTER 5

Small beginnings in business

upert's change of direction, his entry into the business world, was small and modest, but it was to be like the mustard seed from which a giant tree would grow.

His business career started on a modest scale while he was still lecturing at the UP. Rupert, his student friend Dirk Hertzog, then an articled clerk at a Pretoria law firm, and Dr Nic Diederichs, later minister of finance and state president, decided to open a dry-cleaning business. This was consonant with a conviction that Afrikaners had to fight their way out of national obscurity, if not inferiority, by non-political means. Hertzog shared the view that too few Afrikaners were involved in commerce – for many years they had restricted themselves to agriculture and the professions. The choice of dry cleaning was based on sound reasoning: wartime austerity meant that new clothes were hard to come by and dear, so people had to wear what they had – and have it cleaned regularly. Besides, with his training in chemistry Rupert felt he was cut out for the business.

The dry-cleaning business, *Chemiese Reinigers Edms Beperk* (Chemical Cleansers Pty Ltd), was situated at 535 Voortrekker Road, Pretoria. Four partners each contributed £100 to the starting capital of £400: Rupert borrowed his £100, repayable with interest, from the fourth director, Hertzog's half-brother Dawid de Waal Meyer, then South African trade commissioner in Canada.

The name itself tells a story. Their advertisement in *Ons Reddingsdaad* (Our Act of Rescue), a brochure published by the head office of the Reddingsdaadbond (RDB) in 1941, appealed directly to Afrikaner nationalist sentiment and shows how these new entrants into the commercial world initially saw their market:

Always support the True Afrikaans CHEMIESE REINIGERS (like you, we prefer this name to the erroneous, anglicised word: Dry-cleaners).

We undertake chemical cleansing (dry-cleaning) of every kind of garment, carpets, etc., as well as refurbishing of hats.

Our equipment is the latest and the best. Our workers are specialists.

A BETTER, FASTER AND EXCLUSIVELY AFRIKAANS BUSINESS. Ask your Dealers to send your clothes to us.

Directors: Dirk Hertzog, BA, LLB; Anton Rupert, MSc. [Our translation.]

Their advertising provided an early lesson to an entrepreneur who would later gain international renown for his sophisticated marketing techniques. In retrospect Rupert himself admitted that the word 'chemical' was an unfortunate choice – after all, dry-cleaning was meant to obviate the use of chemicals. And the focus on an exclusively Afrikaans clientele narrowed their market considerably. An appeal to sentiment was not a winning recipe, as some of his tobacco products would also later prove. Rupert noticed that the competitors to whom they later sold the business focused on serving a wider market comprising both language groups.

The new business also faced other problems. It was wartime and the benzine for the cleaning process had to be used and reused. Their German manager did not replace the filters of the machines regularly and white tennis shorts were returned to the customer a pale shade of grey. Customers complained because deliveries were not punctual. A valuable lesson from these first experiences was that quality and service delivery, in short, value for money, was crucial to the success of a business enterprise. It is not surprising that 'the customer is king' would become one of the chief maxims in the Rembrandt Group. They were contemplating getting Huberte to run Chemiese Reinigers, but before that could happen Rupert had launched out in a very different direction.

Yet the business was not a total failure. 'But people were reluctant to put their money in dirty laundry – you could not get capital for it,' Hertzog wrote in his memoirs. 'We then thought they may put their money in liquor. We bought a bottle store and behold, the first thousand pounds we received came from a dominee; all his life he fought against the devil and then he put his money in it.'

When the partners eventually sold the dry-cleaning business, the money came in handy at an opportune time. For Rupert, the venture represented a beginning that was inspired by a dream as well as an unyielding resolve to be successful. In years to come he would often quote the Flemish adage: 'Where there's a will, there's a way – the will itself becomes the way.'

This will to succeed was reinforced by the nationalist and republican ideals prevalent among Afrikaners at the time. The Reddingsdaad movement, inspired by Ds Kestell, was actively promoting the very kind of venture in which Rupert and his partners were engaged. The aim was to mobilise Afrikaners to go into commerce – and, ultimately, industry as well – rather than stay within the safe confines of the professions. At that time teaching, the church and the law were the limits of their ambition. Afrikaners had started off as farmers, the first courageous immigrant entrepreneurs on the continent with which they had come to identify, but the cumulative effects of the Anglo-Boer War, the Great Drought and the Depression had reduced many of them to penury. Poverty had eroded their cultural, religious and educational life and in the urban slums, many Afrikaner families lapsed into social disintegration and moral depravity. In an article on the Reddingsdaad movement, Diederichs expressed the need for the economic advancement of Afrikaners as follows: 'It is the poverty that tears families apart, forcing thousands to the slums in the cities, where crime and social evils abound. It is the economically backward position of our people that makes us a nation of employees, dependent on others for their daily bread. And thus it lies at the root of a sense of dependency and a sense of inferiority that eat into the soul of our people.'

Among many English-speaking compatriots there was little empathy for the distress of poor Afrikaners. Sir Robert Beattie, vice-chancellor of the University of Cape Town, was quoted by the writer MER (ME Rothman) as casually telling a public meeting that 'poor whites' were 'intellectually backward' and that 'something inherent in the Afrikaners' was the reason why the phenomenon of poverty was taking on such alarming dimensions in their case.[1] While the Carnegie Commission of Inquiry on the Poor White Question had refuted the allegation about intellectual inferiority, Afrikaners were manifestly not holding their own in the urban, capitalist structure that came in the wake of the mineral discoveries. The commission's statistics on the poor white problem were, as noted already, horrifying, with 300 000 out of a total white population of 1 800 000 classified as poor whites. The Stellenbosch economist Prof. CGW Schumann calculated that the per capita income of Afrikaners in 1936 averaged £86, as opposed to the £142 of other South African whites.

This was the situation that Kestell and other concerned Afrikaner leaders sought to address with an 'act of rescue'. Rupert had been deeply moved by Kestell's appeal when he visited Bloemfontein for the arrival of the Ox-wagon Trek on his birthday in 1938. In later life he often pointed out that a man of the cloth, Kestell, had motivated him to embark on a business career, starting out with virtually nothing. In certain respects the Reddingsdaad campaign and the spirit it embodied foreshadowed the Black Economic Empowerment movement of post-1994 South Africa, though the earlier movement was not based on the transfer of capital with favourable financing schemes or share options.

A year after the Great Trek centenary, in October 1939, the *Eerste Ekonomiese Volkskongres* (First National Economic Congress) was held at the initiative of the Economic Institute of the *Federasie van Afrikaanse Kultuurverenigings* (Federation of Afrikaans Cultural Associations, FAK, the cultural front of the *Afrikaner Broederbond*, AB). The overriding goal was to rouse the impoverished, demoralised people to take on the challenges of entrepreneurship. But, like both Rupert and Hertzog with their first venture, they would need capital.

Capital and capitalism had been a bone of contention among Afrikaner intellectuals for some time. Early in the century Gen. Smuts, in *A century of wrong*, had thrown down the gauntlet to tyrannical international capital, which British imperialism in South Africa represented at the time. By the 1930s pent-up resistance to British imperialism was still rife among Afrikaners, alongside an aversion to hated excrescences of capitalism, as expressed through DC Boonzaier's cartoon character, the arch-exploiter Hoggenheimer, who featured regularly in the Afrikaans daily *Die Burger*. But by 1939 Hitler's national socialism and Stalin's communism – both epitomising the totalitarian state – were looming as a counter threat. The Afrikaner intellectuals who were spearheading the economic struggle did not reject capitalism outright, but instead advocated a variant that became known as *volkskapitalisme* (national capitalism). Prof. Wicus du Plessis stated at the congress that the new economic movement had as its aim 'no longer to tolerate the Afrikaner nation being devastated in an effort to adapt itself to a foreign capitalist system, but to mobilise the nation to conquer this foreign system in order to transform it and adapt it to our national character.'

One after another prominent Afrikaans intellectuals made a case for the mobilisation of capital to launch Afrikaner businesses that were capable of achieving that aim. One outcome of the congress was the founding of *Federale Volksbeleggings* (Federal National Investments, FVB), which would do just that. The other – the answer to Ds Kestell's appeals over the years for the economic upliftment of Afrikaners – was the establishment on 8 December 1939 of the Reddingsdaadbond (RDB). Its task would be to dispense funds to suitable applicants who wanted to venture into business.

This was the organisation that finally lured Rupert away from academia. Various people had been prodding him to join it and in the end he was invited by his partner Dr Nic Diederichs himself, by then at the helm of the RDB. At the end of 1940 Rupert resigned from his post at the University of Pretoria. He abandoned his studies – the doctorate in chemistry and his legal and commercial courses – and stepped out into the world outside the ivory tower. At the age of 24 he found himself heading the small-business section of the RDB at its headquarters next to the railway station in Johannesburg on the bustling Highveld, the centre of South Africa's industrial heartland.

In this decisive period of his life Rupert acquired an intimate knowledge of the needs of small-business entrepreneurs. His mentor was Dr AJ Stals, another remarkable man who would have a lasting influence on his life. Rupert had a deep respect for Stals, the kind of Afrikaner he would probably typify as a member of the Afrikaner aristocracy. He relates that Stals, the son of a tenant farmer at Tulbagh in the Western Cape who obtained doctorates in medicine and law at the universities of Berlin and Dublin, did not hesitate to scrub floors for his widowed mother during holidays at home. After 1948 he became a member of Malan's cabinet, but died within three years. Stals's political views were moderate – according to his wife he walked out of a National Party congress where unfavourable decisions were being taken about the rights of coloured people. In this respect, too, he influenced Rupert, who said in later life that if Stals had lived long enough after 1948, coloureds would never have been removed from the common voters' roll. When a close friend of Stals once commented that he was not a good politician because he was too fair to indulge in nepotism, Rupert's response was, 'If fairness makes you a bad politician, I don't belong in politics. My father was therefore right to turn down political positions.' In fact, he came to believe that Afrikaners managed to build their economic muscle for the very reason that in times of crisis, like during the Second World War, they channelled their energies into non-political fields.[2]

In the early 1940s Stals was a director of Volkskas Bank and Voortrekker Press, two of the rather few sizeable Afrikaner businesses at the time. Twice a week he travelled from Pretoria as financial adviser to help Rupert vet loan applications from prospective entrepreneurs, who could be granted loans up to £500. A top economist, Stals trained Rupert in his new job of helping beginners find their feet. One of the success stories was DW Pienaar, who for many years ran a barber's shop in the Groote Kerk building in Cape Town, where several parliamentarians came for their haircuts. But many fledgling Afrikaans enterprises folded – in Johannesburg alone at least 50 of them.[3]

Nonetheless, at the RDB's second official congress in Bloemfontein on 14 July 1943, Dr Eben Dönges could maintain with some justice that the organisation – acting as the 'fieldworker' of the FAK's Economic Institute – was breaking down Afrikaner prejudice against capital investment in business enterprises, especially Afrikaans ones. In due course the Afrikaans universities (Stellenbosch, Pretoria, Orange Free State and Potchefstroom) would also play a role in cultivating business leaders by producing growing numbers of commerce graduates. In 1945, five years after its inception, the RDB had close on 400 branches countrywide and some 70 000 members. Numerous Afrikaans enterprises had been assisted with loans. Thousands of job opportunities had been created and hundreds of people had received counselling or been helped with the financing of their studies by the RDB, which later linked up with the Helpmekaar study fund.

By the time the RDB was dissolved in 1957, Rupert had left the organisation. But his involvement with small business had made him aware of tantalising possibilities. Besides, he was itching to try his hand at manufacture, for, as he saw it, 'chemistry and industry are first cousins'. His choice of a branch of industry stemmed from his experience as a child of the Depression: he came to the conclusion that an entrepreneur keen on entering the business world should concentrate on products that would sell even during a depression. And if any two products were depression proof, they were liquor and tobacco.

As early as 1941, while Rupert was still involved with the RDB, he heard about an insolvent tobacco company that was for sale. He himself could raise only £10, but as in the case of Chemiese Reinigers he found willing partners: Dr Nic Diederichs and his mentor Dr Stals. The new venture received loans of £2 500 each from FVB and *Kopersbond*, a big wholesale concern, and the new company was launched with a starting capital of £5 000. A week before Rupert's wedding, on 21 September, *Voorbrand Tabakmaatskappy*[4] was formally established and was registered the next day, 22 September 1941 – the official founding date of the Rembrandt Group. On the 23rd the directors held their first meeting.

Voorbrand was established at a time when the South African business world was dominated by English speakers. In trade, industry, finance and mining the turnover of Afrikaner enterprises comprised only five percent of the total in 1938-1939; in industry, only three percent. The few established Afrikaans companies included the insurance companies Sanlam and Santam, the media companies Nasionale Pers (later Naspers) in the south and Voortrekkerpers in the north, the undertaker Avbob and Volkskas, the first Afrikaans commercial bank, founded in 1934.

Two other pioneer entrepreneurs who were creating empowerment and job opportunities for Afrikaners in parastatal institutions were the chemical engineer Dr Hendrix van Eck and the equally brilliant electrotechnical engineer Dr Hendrik van der Bijl. Van der Bijl, chairman of Escom and thereafter of Iscor, realised his ideal of supplying inexpensive electricity and steel as the basis for industrial development. The industrial town of Vanderbijlpark was named after him. His successor as chairman at Iscor was Dr Frikkie Meyer, who as chairman of the council of the UP established the first business school in the world after that of Harvard University. Under Van Eck's chairmanship of the Industrial Development Corporation (IDC) important parastatal institutions such as Sasol, Foskor, Safmarine and Alusaf were established and financed. Michael O'Dowd, a director of Anglo American, wrote about these institutions: 'The primary credit (for the policy) belongs to the Afrikaners, and it was in effect opposed by many, if not all, English-speaking South Africans.'

As a result of the calls for economic mobilisation in the 1940s many new enterprises in the private sector sprung up among Afrikaners, most of which failed. Ultimately, out of the initiatives of those years two private-sector enterprises in particular were to grow and flourish. The one was Rupert's Rembrandt, which developed out of Voorbrand. The other was Veka, subsequently known as Veka/ Bertish, a clothing manufacturing company established by Albert Wessels. Wessels would later make his greatest strides after acquiring the South African trading rights of the Japanese vehicle manufacturer Toyota.

After the establishment of Voorbrand, Rupert continued at the RDB in a supervisory capacity for the time being. In fact, his honeymoon was spent touring the country to publicise and promote the organisation. Well-meaning friends thought it quixotic to take on a formidable industry – 90%-dominated by the giant United Tobacco Company (UTC) – with just £10 to his name. Some travelled from far afield to persuade him to abandon the plan. People like the journalist Willie Muller from Port Elizabeth, a fellow student in Pretoria, wanted to know 'what on earth he thought he was doing'.[5]

Rupert himself could only contribute £10 in cash, but ultimately this £10 was to become an investment from which a multibillion rand global business empire would grow.

He had been approached by Stals to undertake the new task at the insistence of Jan de Kock, general manager of the Magaliesberg Tobacco Growers' Society (MTKV), which he had built up into a model cooperative. De Kock had been a key figure in the establishment of the Tobacco Control Board, which sought to regulate the market in the best interests of tobacco producers and consumers, and headed an umbrella body of ten tobacco cooperatives. This dynamic leader thought so highly of Rupert that he wanted to do business with no one but the young UP lecturer at Voorbrand. He knew it would take brains and stamina to make even a dent in UTC's virtual monopoly and he thought Rupert had the character and perseverance required for the task – if he failed to get a grip on the tobacco industry, other Afrikaners would not follow. De Kock and Rupert became close friends after the latter had taken over the management responsibilities at Voorbrand. De Kock also made a grader from the MTKV available to help Voorbrand with the manufacturing of pipe tobacco.

De Kock's prescience was shared by others. Not long after the establishment of Voorbrand one of its directors tried to entice Rupert to join Kopersbond, at a higher salary. He turned down the offer.

The new company embarked on their task with a number of directors who would make their mark in South African business life. The calibre of the people involved also indicated a tendency that would characterise later, also foreign boards of directors of the Rembrandt Group: Rupert could draw together able associates around him.

The first chairman of Voorbrand's board was Dr Stals, who served as minister of education, health and social welfare in the Malan government from 1948 to his death in 1951. One of the first directors of Voorbrand was Dr Diederichs, later minister of finance and eventually state president, who would succeed Stals as chairman of Rembrandt after the latter's appointment to the cabinet. Kopersbond was represented by two directors, BJ Pienaar, at one time South African consul in Milan, and JJ Fouché. Other directors were the Afrikaans cultural figure Ivan Makepeace Lombard, who thought up the name Voorbrand; WB Coetzer, the chartered accountant who was later chairman of *Federale Mynbou* (Federal Mining) and Gencor as well as a director of up to 60 companies; Dr Etienne Rousseau, later chairman of Sasol, which became a world leader in the large-scale manufacture of oil from coal; and CC (Oupa) Kriel of *Wol Groeiers Afslaers* (WGA, Woolgrowers' Auctioneers).

Rupert's salary at Voorbrand was £500 per annum, £41.13 per month. He was also allocated two shares in the company. The factory occupied rented premises at 200 Commissioner Street, close to His Majesty's Theatre and the radio corporation in those days, hence not far from the present Carlton Centre in the city centre. At this early stage Voorbrand was joined by an associate with whom Rupert was to travel a long road: the accountant Daan Hoogenhout. Hoogenhout, a B.Com. graduate from UP and a 'child of the depression' like Rupert and Huberte, was a grandson of CP Hoogenhout, a campaigner for Afrikaans in the late 19th century.[6] Rupert and Hoogenhout shared a room at the entrance to the building. They partitioned it into two tiny offices, each barely big enough for a desk with a chair on either side. The ceiling rained dust on everything. One day when Hoogenhout climbed up there to clean the mess, he fell straight through the ceiling onto his desk.

The hallway was big enough to accommodate another desk. Within a few months it was occupied by Huberte, who became the unpaid clerk, typist, telephonist, secretary and messenger. Her typing was rudimentary – she used only four fingers – but she made up for it in other ways. Rupert soon also charged Huberte, according to her own description the 'only female being' at Voorbrand, with managerial duties. Among other things, she studied the Companies Act so she could draft notices of board meetings, letters to interested parties and other documents for the expanding company. She attributes their good working relationship to the good understanding between them. 'While the speed of my typing wasn't up to scratch, the accuracy of the data was good,' she remembers. In effect, she was the Rembrandt Group's first company secretary.

Adjoining the front offices was a room where six women, the first employees, sat around a block moulding containers for Voorbrand's sole product – pipe tobacco – by hand. At the back was a workshop with a few machines taken over from their insolvent predecessor. Of these they used only the tobacco-cutting machine. Carl Langenstrass was the foreman in charge of this small domain.

For quite a while the new enterprise struggled to keep going, sometimes finding it difficult to pay the employees' weekly wages on Friday afternoons. Once when a bank clerk from Volkskas refused to give Hoogenhout the amount of £25 needed for the wages because there was not enough money in Voorbrand's account, Hoogenhout had to telephone Dr Stals, then a director of Volkskas. Stals deposited a personal cheque in Voorbrand's account and requested the bank manager to pay out the amount. On another occasion Voorbrand was unable to pay its auditors, Meyernel, for their services. The auditors were obliged to write off the £5 they were owed. Rupert never forgot this, and after his move to Stellenbosch Meyernel, a precursor of PricewaterhouseCoopers, remained the auditors of the Rembrandt Group despite the difficulties caused by distance.

Without money or equipment they were unable to produce the big money-spinner, cigarettes. Besides, the wartime currency and import restrictions prohibited importation of the necessary machinery and packaging material.

At the early stage of Rupert's entry into the tobacco industry there were already four other cigarette companies in the South African tobacco market, which yielded an annual profit of £2 million, but in which some 60 cigarette brands were vying for a market share. Tobacco farmers complained that they were being crippled by price fixing, while the net profit UTC transferred to its overseas parent company, British-American Tobacco, exceeded the gross annual income of everybody engaged in the local industry, including the – mainly Afrikaner – farmers. It was a situation calling for stronger competition, and Anton Rupert saw this as an opportunity.

He started studying companies that were depression-proof and found that, worldwide, tobacco companies were among the most successful. These included the major companies in the USA, such as RJ Reynolds, Lorillard, American Tobacco and Liggett & Myers. He also studied companies in Spain, Italy, Japan and China. In France, the state monopoly Seita owned famous brands such as Gauloises and Gitanes. Tobacco companies in the United Kingdom included Player, British-American Tobacco and Imperial Tobacco, whose chairman, Lord Winterstoke, head of the Wills family, was the richest man in Britain in 1901 after Cecil John Rhodes, who had made his fortune in South Africa.

As a new entrant to the industry Voorbrand was given a maximum allocation of only one percent by the Tobacco Control Board, and that was for snuff, pipe and cigarette tobacco. The latter had to be stored for seven years, until 1948 when Rembrandt was at last able to enter the South African cigarette market. Meanwhile the 'Afrikaans impostor' in the tobacco industry faced fierce competition, some of it conducted in underhand ways such as whispering campaigns and rumour mongering.

As early as 1941 Voorbrand received a substantial offer from ME Risien, chief executive of UTC: he was willing to pay £50 000 if Voorbrand undertook not to manufacture cigarettes, thus entrenching UTC's near monopoly of the market. Stals's response was swift and categorical: 'We're not selling our birthright.'

Rupert, while always courteous and considerate, early on showed the steel that would inspire his employees as well as his competitors with awe. On an occasion when he encountered Risien at a gathering of tobacco manufacturers, the man from UTC inquired somewhat snidely, 'So how is little Voorbrand doing?' Rupert immediately retorted: 'Mr Risien, by all laws of probability we have a good chance of outliving you.' Risien never condescended to him again, but many years later his son applied to Rembrandt for a job. At that time there was no suitable vacancy.

Times were hard and for the first few years the young company showed a mounting loss. By 1948 it had risen to £30 000 – 'Not much, if you think back on it today,' Rupert comments in retrospect, 'but a loss just the same.' Its competitors had the benefit of existing quota allocations not granted to newcomers. The inability to manufacture cigarettes did not help either. It inhibited expansion to such an extent that some directors were considering selling their shares. A major lesson he learned from the difficult times during and after the war, according to Rupert, is that Voorbrand was mainly selling products he would typify as C products. He distinguishes three classes of products: A products, better than those of his competitors; B products, which are equal to the products of competitors, and C products, inferior to those of competitors. The lesson he would later impress upon his employees was to launch only A products or at least B+ products. The only other way was imitation or discount prices, which he rejected as not normally options for quality entrepreneurs. Rupert's exceptional emphasis on quality was to become a supreme feature of the Rembrandt Group.

Another major problem was to find a market for snuff tobacco. This they were able to solve with the help of two Indian businessmen, Yusuf Ahmed Cachalia, who had a textile shop, and Donath Desai. These two individuals assisted Rupert to find outlets for the snuff tobacco with the help of other Indian merchants. Huberte is of the view that the snuff tobacco success is probably what ensured Voorbrand's survival.

The Ruperts became close friends of the Cachalias and the Desais, visiting each other at home. Both Cachalia, a brother of the activist Mauldi Cachalia, a leading figure in the Transvaal Indian Congress, and Desai were fiercely opposed to British imperialism and later played a prominent role in the political struggle against apartheid. Desai's daughter Zureena, a medical practitioner, made news headlines as a result of her relationship with Prof. John Blacking, professor in social anthropology at the University of the Witwatersrand. The security police got wind of the relationship and started harassing the family. Desai asked Rupert to intervene, but there was nothing he could do: Section 16 of the then Immorality Act, which prohibited amorous relationships across the colour line, was in full force and spared nobody. The couple had to emigrate in order to marry.[7]

Pipe tobacco, too, was not without problems. Wartime restrictions on imports of packaging material hit new enterprises hard; they were unable to obtain permits at all. 'Our packaging was simply not good enough,' Rupert recalls. 'Our competitors were established manufacturers, they could make beautiful plastic packets with a lead lining and foam rubber on the inside.' His eventual obsession with packaging and marketing stems from that early experience.

Voorbrand registered several brand names with Afrikaans and patriotic connotations, such as Oom Bart, Drosdy, Patriot, Landdros ('the good things from the past improved to the very best in the present – medium strength)', Voorbrand, Spoor (spur, track) and Vonk (spark). English-speaking customers could buy Stop Press ('extra special edition'), Bandmaster, Carefree and Sunkist Golden Mixture.

Drosdy, a pipe tobacco, was advertised as 'a unique discovery: tobacco matured in old wine casks – medium strength'. One of Rupert's good friends in Johannesburg, the poet WEG (Gladstone) Louw, approved the advertising slogan 'matured in old wine casks' for the pipe tobacco. Louw, who was awarded the prestigious Hertzog prize for poetry at the age of 21, also worked at the RDB at the time, in the arts and culture section. Like other friends of the Ruperts, this younger brother of the leading Afrikaans poet and writer NP van Wyk Louw contributed ideas to the new company Voorbrand, which initially stored Drosdy tobacco in old wine casks. The Ruperts also got to know Van Wyk Louw through Anna Neethling-Pohl, sister of his second wife, Truida Pohl. The Rupert and Pohl children had all grown up in Graaff-Reinet.

During the war years while he was still in Johannesburg, Rupert was, without his knowledge, proposed by friends for membership of the AB. Other members of the AB at the time were the prominent literary figures Dirk Opperman and Van Wyk Louw. Rupert's name was put forward in a circular, as was then customary in the secret organisation. He became member number 3088.

Dirk Hertzog, also a member, points out in his memoirs that the membership of the AB was a little more than 2 000 during the war years, when Smuts had proclaimed emergency regulations forbidding public servants and teachers to be part of the movement. Afrikaners like Hertzog were incensed that Smuts had forced highly esteemed fellow Afrikaners to resign from the public service on account of their AB membership.

On 24 August 1942 Rupert was one of 75 delegates and businessmen at the founding congress of the *Afrikaanse Handelsinstituut* (AHI, Afrikaans Institute of Commerce) in Bloemfontein, another product of the Ekonomiese Volkskongres and an RDB initiative to promote the interests of existing and emerging Afrikaans business people and entrepreneurs. The chairman of the first executive was JG (Kaalkop) van der Merwe, businessman and lawyer from Heilbron in the Free State, and MS (Tienie) Louw of Sanlam was the first deputy chairman.[8] In 1949 Rupert became a member of the executive of the AHI and in 1950 chairman of the industry committee, but he eventually resigned because of the growing demands of his international business concerns.

According to a highly secret and confidential circular of 14 January 1944 in the Rembrandt archives at Stellenbosch the production of Voorbrand increased by 300% in 1943 after the company had entered the pipe-tobacco industry in 1942. At that time the company had 40 registered brand names, eleven kinds of packed tobacco and eight kinds of loose tobacco. In a circular in Afrikaans addressed to 'You as a connoisseur of pipe tobacco', dated 15 February 1943, Rupert emphasised to clients that Voorbrand makes provision for a variety of tastes and maintains the quality of the various kinds of tobacco. 'Our factory is totally under the control of Afrikaners and Afrikaans capital. Our tobacco is processed and packed in elegantly designed packets by Afrikaner hands,' he continued, and invited clients to order directly from the factory at retail prices.

In board minutes, however, it was noted that the appeals to sentiment did not have the desired effect on Afrikaans consumers. 'Partly as a result of early disappointments of failed businesses and largely because of a sense of inferiority, the Afrikaans public do not regard their own as good enough.' It was also noted that Afrikaans businesses were generally perceived as 'expensive'. These seemed to be the reasons why they started manufacturing products with English names, while attempts were also made from early on to enter the markets for black and Indian consumers.

At the beginning of 1943 Rupert presented Voorbrand's directors with a comprehensive report on the tobacco industry. It included a careful, scientific analysis of the various types of tobacco, drying procedures and additives. There were statistics on the number of tobacco growers, tobacco corporations, their products and the Tobacco Control Board's quota system, which was heavily biased against new entrants. In addition, wartime shortages and austerity measures curbed progress. From all this he concluded that any new factory could only expand slowly and by degrees.

Voorbrand was hampered in that it was not allowed to manufacture cigarettes, but already at that stage Rupert recommended that the cigarette tobacco should be kept and preserved in view of 'the size and scope of the cigarette industry'.

Nonetheless, the wartime restrictions on the manufacture of cigarettes posed such a severe obstacle to expansion that certain directors were keen to sell their shares.

Among further problems listed in the report was the shortage of fuel for Voorbrand's travelling salesmen, since the chief fuel controller refused to allocate any fuel to new travellers during the war years. It was also difficult to obtain supplies of materials, as the company had to face other controllers – the controllers of paper, of vehicles, of rubber, of bags and of industrial chemicals. Moreover, owing to the shortage of matches, Voorbrand was 'the further victim as we cannot supply matches with the tobacco'.

Rupert pointed out the dominant position of UTC and the control this company could exert over wholesale and retail traders as well as publicity and advertising space. He came to the conclusion that the answer was advertising. More and more advertising at every level, by every means, was an essential expenditure and one of the cornerstones of success.[9] This conviction stayed with him, culminating in the sophisticated advertising and marketing approach with which he would build an international reputation.

Voorbrand's third AGM was held in December 1944, the year in which it became a public company. Its capital was increased from £25 000 to £50 000 by means of a share issue of £36 980. But the immediate outlook was bleak. Government regarded smoking as a luxury and continued to impose heavy excise duty and import restrictions. The quota system still benefited established manufacturers and stifled new enterprises. Somewhat dispirited, Rupert and his friends asked at the AGM: 'What hope is there for young industrial enterprises to establish themselves under such circumstances?' But with unfailing idealism they themselves provided the answer: '. . . we believe in our future, and we shall be victorious.'

Twenty-five years later, at Rembrandt's 21st anniversary celebrations on 4 June 1969 in Paarl, Rupert recalled the early beginnings of Voorbrand and the spirit that had sustained them. 'It is very simple and I try to teach it to my children: when you walk on the beach at Hermanus and you see the sand that stretches for miles, you realise that the human being is nothing more than a grain of sand . . . But always remember, the other person is also nothing more than a grain of sand. Then you can never be conceited. You are humble, but you will never lack confidence. This is to me the basic concept that has sustained our small group of people who started and those who are sitting here today, to the point where we are one of the biggest groups in the world at present. You yourself are nothing, but the other people are no more than you.'

Tobacco was indeed a product that would sustain the later Rembrandt Group through thick and thin. It helped to make it possible that setbacks could be converted into opportunities – a perennial philosophy of Rupert's, who has often pointed out that the Chinese word for 'crisis' comprises two pictographs meaning 'calamity' and 'opportunity' respectively.

'If we want to avoid the calamity, we must seize the opportunity with all our might,' he said on opening the agriculture and industry show in Port Elizabeth in 1967.

An early example of how he seized a setback as an opportunity occurred in late 1942 when FVB became dubious about Voorbrand's prospects and threatened to sell its 2 000 shares. This plunged the fledgling company into crisis. The ironic consequence was a further far-reaching initiative, an inventive solution conceptualised by Rupert: to launch a new investment company, *Tegniese en Industriële Beleggings Beperk* (TIB, Technical and Industrial Investments Limited), that could strengthen its capital base through the sale of shares. The start of TIB was financed by the sale of the dry-cleaning business Chemiese Reinigers. That was when Dirk Hertzog, Rupert's old friend and first business partner, joined the board of Voorbrand.

Rupert threw himself into the campaign to sell shares in the new company, thus raising the necessary capital to buy back not only the 2 000 FVB shares, but those of Kopersbond as well. When FVB was dissolved years later, those 2 000 shares were worth more than all its assets. With the blessing of Voorbrand's board, Rupert was allowed to place shares in TIB.

The establishment of TIB gave the first indications that Rupert was starting to move. The investment company was to lay the foundations for one of the most spectacular expansions in South African industry, the House of Rembrandt.

CHAPTER 6

Call of the grape

T he beginnings of the new investment company that would become Rupert's vehicle for gaining access to the liquor industry were modest, as was the case with tobacco. The starting capital of TIB was a mere £5 000, but within three years it grew into the parent company of the Rembrandt Group, by then worth £1 million. By the time TIB reached the £100 000 mark Rupert became its managing director. Before that he had repaid Voorbrand all the money he had earned there and also returned to the RDB, in the form of Voorbrand shares, an amount of £700 he had been paid as salary.

On the establishment of TIB in 1943, Dirk Hertzog said to Rupert: 'Anton, our first little venture [Chemiese Reinigers] wasn't exactly a failure, and I trust you and can after all lend you my name.' These words were quoted in the first edition of *Tegniek* (Technology), the Afrikaans business magazine started by Rembrandt that would later become *Finansies & Tegniek* (with an English counterpart, *Finance Week*) in the Naspers stable. *Tegniek* was in its own right an important attempt to provide Afrikaners with insight and information about business life, as Afrikaans newspapers published almost no business news in those years, not even stock exchange prices. Business news aimed specifically at the Afrikaans business community came mainly from *Volkshandel*, the magazine started by JG (Kaalkop) van der Merwe from Heilbron in the early 1940s.

For the first three months of the Ruperts' marriage they lived with Huberte's mother and stepfather in Krugersdorp before moving to Johannesburg where they rented a furnished flat in Joubert Park at fifteen guineas per month, half Rupert's salary. Later they moved to 59 Auckland Avenue, a suburban house in Auckland Park, where they stayed until their move to Stellenbosch in 1946.

At one stage the couple shared the flat with Rupert's younger brother Jan, then a clerk with a law firm in the city. The commercial artist Kobus Esterhuysen, from whom TIB rented an office, also moved in for a while – he had to sleep on the balcony. Esterhuysen, the brother of Joubero Malherbe, *grande dame* of the South African music world, was the designer of the country's bank notes and also did freelance work for Voorbrand.

The office Rupert rented from Esterhuysen had only the most basic furniture and no telephone. When AGMs were held, chairs had to be borrowed to seat everybody. During the first year there was no money for directors' fees or salaries.

Huberte was for a long time the unpaid secretary, typist, clerk and messenger. Rupert's principle was: 'As long as we don't have our own capital, we have to avoid costs.' Huberte was a thrifty housekeeper and for many years made her own clothes – later their children's as well until Hanneli was five years old. But as children of the Depression, they did not mind living frugally. 'We knew that where one lives has nothing to do with the quality of one's life,' she said about those early days.[1] 'What did worry us, however, was that Anton should make something that produced no profit.'

Huberte saw her role as that of Anton's helpmeet, companion and sounding board. 'When he had a problem, he'd tell me about it. I'd listen and then he'd go out and solve it. The main thing was, I was in it with him. I learned the business from the inside.'

In the stimulating atmosphere of Johannesburg her life was a buzz of friends from different walks of life, entertaining Rupert's business associates and – in between spells of unpaid office work – a job as secretary at a girls' high school, *Hoër Meisieskool Helpmekaar*, and freelance work for the South African Broadcasting Corporation (SABC).

Huberte was to maintain her close involvement in Rupert's business enterprises over decades. At an early stage in Johannesburg she was offered a position at Voortrekkerpers at a salary higher than that of her husband's. She declined the offer, however, 'because I had to work for Anton for free, and I knew their set-up. But everything one accomplished was an adventure.'

TIB was registered on 16 March 1943 and would eventually develop into a company with diversified interests in tobacco, liquor, coal mines, wool brokers, tea and coffee. Contrary to what is sometimes told in business circles, Rupert already started to diversify at a very early stage in his career.

The entry of Rupert and his partners into the liquor market – the second depression-proof product – was prompted by the rather poor performance of Voorbrand as a result of wartime constraints and, perhaps, over-reliance on Afrikaner sentiment. Rupert realised that the highly competitive tobacco industry would not give them enough of a foothold in industry. They had to look wider, also southwards.

In September 1943 he and one of his co-directors, Coenie (Oupa) Kriel, started making inquiries. In October they travelled to Paarl in the Western Cape where they met Canzius Pretorius, accountant of the Koöperatiewe Wynbouersvereniging (KWV). He advised them that the only way to enter the liquor industry would be to buy a Cape company, Forrer Brothers. With the aid of the company auditor, Roux van der Poel, they negotiated the purchase of a 50% interest for £17 500.

In the north of the country money for capital expansion was scarce on account of the failure of institutions such as Kopersbond and Spoorbondkas. Rupert therefore started selling five-shilling shares to the more established, wealthier community in the Western Cape, notably the wine and export grape farmers, who would become the mainstay of his business empire. His investors were all Afrikaners; nobody else was interested.

De Wet Theron of the farm Montpellier near Tulbagh, who had previously been a wine expert at the KWV where his father, Hennie, was chairman, assisted Rupert in his recruitment drive. Among the earliest investors who put their trust in Rupert were Frank le Roux and Paul Roux of Paarl, founders of the KWV.

Rupert had to divide his time between business interests in Johannesburg and Cape Town, a thousand miles to the south. For three years he commuted, mainly by rail. In one year he spent 63 nights – more than two months – on bunks in train compartments. He had sold his little DKW after a shop owner in Linden, Johannesburg, studying the battered jalopy, observed: 'Rupert, I won't be able to do business with you.' Eventually he replaced it with a second-hand Studebaker. But by then he had crisscrossed the winelands in the DKW in the company of De Wet Theron, selling shares to leading farmers in those fertile valleys.

In early 1944 the outstanding debt on the purchase price of the Forrer Brothers' company still stood at £9 000, money Rupert did not have. This was not an unusual situation for an entrepreneur; contrary to popular belief, entrepreneurs are often not people who start off with ample supplies of money or have access to big capital. They are rather enterprising individuals who spot opportunities and strive passionately to exploit them. Nevertheless, times were hard at a stage that Huberte has described as a 'dark period' in their lives.

On 29 January 1944 the Ruperts were in Cape Town when they learned that Anton's mother had died the previous night at a hospital in Port Elizabeth, where she was due to have a heart operation. She was only 50. They left for Graaff-Reinet immediately. Fuel was rationed and they had no coupons left. At Oudtshoorn Jurgens Schoeman, a businessman and farmer who was one of Rupert's directors, filled their tank and they managed to reach Graaff-Reinet in time for the funeral. On the way they stopped for a while so Huberte could, as she put it, 'finish crying': she had loved her mother-in-law dearly, describing her as 'a lovely woman'. They also discussed what to do about Rupert's youngest brother Koos, then only fourteen. The moment they arrived in Graaff-Reinet, Koos hugged Huberte and asked: 'You're taking me with you, aren't you?' Huberte reassured him. He would come to live with them. After the funeral Rupert returned to Cape Town to attend to unfinished business. Huberte stayed behind to make the necessary arrangements for her and Koos's departure for Johannesburg.

A few days after his mother's funeral Rupert was booking into a hotel in Paarl when a report in the afternoon newspaper caught his eye: his good friend and staunch supporter Jan de Kock of MTKV had died tragically. He and the chairman of MTKV were crossing a flooded low-level bridge when their car was swept away by the torrent and they had both drowned. De Kock was the one who had shown such confidence in Rupert's unproven ability when Voorbrand was founded. To Rupert this was a double blow, losing both his mother and one of his best friends in the space of week.

Less tragic but nonetheless distressing was the news soon afterwards that his accountant and friend Daan Hoogenhout was resigning from Voorbrand to go farming in Botswana. That venture folded after a year and Daan returned to the fold, this time as accountant of the latest venture, Distillers Corporation. In 1948 he was to return to the tobacco group.

But 1944 started badly for Rupert. And he still had to find the £9 000 to pay the Forrer Brothers. The day in March when the money was due Rupert addressed a group of wine farmers at De Doorns in the Hex River valley, known for its export grapes. 'I showed them a few labels for wine bottles and sold them my ideas. I sold them a dream,' he said afterwards.[2] His dream earned £11 000 in TIB shares within a couple of hours. It was one of the closest shaves of his career up to then. He drove back to Cape Town via Wellington and Bainskloof – the Du Toits Kloof Pass had not yet been built – and before closing time the money was in the bank. That evening he made his first long-distance call ever to Huberte to share the glad news. She treasured the memory, a memento of comradeship.

Rupert, who has prized loyalty so highly throughout his career, would never forget the support he received in the 1940s from the wine farmers in particular. This loyalty and continued involvement in an industry that yields relatively small returns compared to the management attention devoted to it would again be strongly manifested during the restructuring of the South African liquor industry in 1979.

In due course, the farmers' investment in TIB shares would prove to be an investment of a lifetime. Several Rembrandt shareholders from the early years became millionaires, some multimillionaires. The wealth of quite a number of other affluent Western Cape families, thus to a large extent also the prosperity of the region itself, rests on the foundation of Rembrandt shares. One farmer at Paarl bought £2 000's worth of shares for each of his four children. Shortly after the turn of the century each child's shares were worth R132 million. At the De Doorns gathering, which had saved Rupert's skin that autumn morning in 1944, a woman bought shares for £500. In 2001 her son told Rupert that his mother's investment had secured him and his sister a comfortable retirement.

Someone who later regretted not having bought shares was Piet Meiring, the South African head of information Rupert had consulted in Johannesburg about the festival newspaper he published during the Great Trek centenary. Meiring was especially regretful as he and Dr Hendrik Verwoerd were plunged into debt in the war years as a result of two business ventures in which they had been involved as co-directors, a garage and a market agency delivering market produce to housewives. 'Extravagance and mismanagement led to the failure of the two enterprises, with Dr Verwoerd and I as sureties at the bank, ' Meiring wrote in his memoirs. They owed R50 000 each to Volkskas and Sasbank. The banks were lenient and wrote off part of the amount, but Meiring had to sell his car and some of his paintings to redeem the debt.[3]

The affair also left a mark on Verwoerd, who was accommodated by the banks through the mediation of Fritz Steyn. Rupert is convinced that this financial failure led to Verwoerd's hostility towards capitalism. 'He was prejudiced against the business sector because of his own negative business experience.' One of the consequences was that the policy of separate development Verwoerd later wanted to extend as prime minister, failed, among other reasons, because he did not want to allow white capital in the black homelands.

In its first years TIB was spreading its wings, selling shares and acquiring new enterprises. Soon its capital was fully subscribed, paving the way for further share issues and expansion. But the big breakthrough came in March 1945, when TIB – acting as trustee of Union Distillers SA (Pty) Ltd on behalf of a company still to be floated – bought the land, machinery and equipment of an insolvent Stellenbosch company, South African Farm Products Protective Association Limited, for £25 000. The price at that time was quite steep, but it secured seven hectares of prime land on the outskirts of the picturesque university town. On 11 June 1945 Distillers Corporation was registered, the first Afrikaans company to be listed on the Johannesburg stock exchange.

The first board of directors of Distillers was constituted as follows: SA (Sidney) Schonegevel (the company's first chairman, for twenty years), Anton Rupert (managing director), Dirk Hertzog, CC (Oupa) Kriel, JJ (Jurgens) Schoeman, JF (Freddie) Kirsten, PC du Toit and FS (Fritz) Steyn. In a memorandum in which he reacted to criticism that the board was controlled by the National Party, Dirk Hertzog wrote: 'There was no NP connection and, what's more, there were SAP members on the board.'[4]

Distillers started with a substantial capital of £1 300 000, divided into 2 200 000 ordinary shares of ten shillings each and 200 000 preferential shares of £1 each. The share issue was soon oversubscribed – further evidence of the wine farmers' confidence in Rupert. From within the industry, however, criticism of the new player with its eight liquor stores ranged from vehement to venomous. The editor of the KWV's journal *Wine and Spirit* observed somewhat viciously that he found even the criticism strange, 'as we know that businesses without prospects of a future are usually left severely alone; left to their own fate.' He also criticised the leadership of the new company's use of Afrikaans: 'Why they should continually refer to the Afrikaans origin of the company, they alone know.'

For Rupert there was a good reason to use Afrikaans in addition to English. True to his roots and imbued with the desire to prove that Afrikaners could succeed in industry, he has never been ashamed or hesitant to fly the flag for Afrikaans. He also had another motive: to champion the predominantly Afrikaans wine farmers' right to proper recognition. And he wanted to promote estate wines, a dream that would occupy him for most of his life and that would also lead to the Ruperts' involvement in estates that produce quality wines.

In the initial years there was not much he could offer the wine farmers, who were naturally aggrieved by their marginalised position in the industry. As one of them put it, the wine trade was in the hands of 'whisky drinkers who stood wine bottles upright on liquor store shelves'.

Rupert's conviction that such people had no respect for wine was a major reason why he started promoting estate wines, and why he wanted the wine farmers to receive the honour due to them. His first estate wines were from the farms Montpellier, Theuniskraal and Alto. He also introduced the French and German custom of *appellation contrôlée* in South Africa, that is, labelling wines as products of a specific estate and its vineyards.

'It was an interesting marketing strategy,' he says. 'It drew the farmers into the industry and put their names on the map.' By 1946 about twenty wine farmers had joined the umbrella organisation for estate wines that became known as the *Bergkelder* (Mountain Cellar). Among the best known of these pioneers were Andries Jordaan of Theuniskraal, Tulbagh; De Wet Theron of Montpellier, Tulbagh; Manie Malan of Alto, Stellenbosch; Baron von Carlowitz of Uitkyk, Muldersvlei; Danie Roux of Provence, Franschhoek; P Bruwer of Mont Blois, Robertson; and P Beyers of Riversmeet, Groot Drakenstein. It was not until 1972, however, that estate wines gained general recognition and legal protection in South Africa.

Another astute move of Rupert's was to push up the shelf prices of good estate wines. When Paul Sauer, later a cabinet minister and owner of a top Stellenbosch wine farm, Kanonkop, chided Rupert for this, his response was: 'Look at the wines people order when they entertain. They buy foreign wines because they're more expensive. They don't want to appear mean by offering their guests cheaper wine.'

Distillers started under very difficult circumstances. The immediate post-war period was a time of scarcity, with both money and goods hard to come by. Building materials were sold under a government-imposed quota system.

Rupert's new company had to make do with old buildings left by the bankrupt company. The only proper structure comprised a large room and four small partitioned offices. Three of these were occupied by Rupert, his secretary J van R Maartens and Daan Hoogenhout; the fourth accommodated a few clerks, including Fanie Botha, later minister of labour. Rupert managed to secure a permit to purchase building materials to the value of £5 000, which had to be used to build essential facilities like tanks and a laboratory. Undercover working accommodation was a secondary consideration and a luxury cellar unthinkable. Open-sided sheds were constructed to provide some shelter. They were walled in gradually as bricks became available.

An early setback was the rationing of rebate brandy by the KWV, which had instituted quotas for proof spirit for the liquor industry based on past purchases. So although Distillers had initially envisaged 40 000 gallons a year, on account of rationing it was allocated only 9 000 gallons based on its takeover of the much smaller Forrer Brothers. For all its healthy capital investment and processing facilities Distillers was 'all dressed up and nowhere to go', as Dirk Hertzog put it in an internal memorandum. 'It took sweat and toil to do business successfully despite these constraints imposed by the state.'[5]

Distillers had to relinquish some 80% of its allocated quota of proof spirit to the older, more established companies like Castle Wine and Brandy. The wheel came full circle in 1969, however, when the Oude Meester Group, an offshoot of Distillers, took over this giant company.

Rupert's obsession with quality made up for constraints with regard to supplies and infrastructure. From the outset Distillers concentrated on producing quality brandies, of which Oude Meester was but one. In 1949 Distillers outranked all other South African companies at the Empire Wine Exhibition in London. This feat was repeated in 1950, the year in which Oude Meester was named the best brandy produced in the British Commonwealth. Rupert had personally designed the famous Oude Meester trademark for Distillers. Later he also proposed the name Amarula for the cream liqueur that became a worldwide favourite.

Huberte Rupert often visited the cellar and showed visitors around. At that stage there was no glass factory in the Cape that produced bottles, so they had to avail themselves of used ones. Bottle cleaning was a major operation, conducted just outside the laboratory. It was not a prepossessing spectacle for visitors. So

Milton, the gatekeeper, would give a few shrill blasts on a whistle whenever Huberte and her visitors arrived. This was the sign for the bottle-washers to vanish into the cellar, leaving access to the laboratory unobstructed.

Within the company Distillers' personnel relations attested to Rupert's personal values. Despite the growing number of employees, he kept his ear close to the ground and shared their well and woe, in a sense honouring the ethos of earlier, more intimate family businesses. Huberte was very much involved in this aspect of her husband's career.

Soon after he became Distillers' wine technologist in 1946 Alfred Baumgartner, a German who hailed from Swakopmund in present-day Namibia, was under threat of deportation to Germany as a hostile alien. Awaiting the dreaded deportation order, he and his wife had already sold most of their possessions and kept only their beds and five suitcases. Huberte, deeply moved by their plight, offered to look after their three children and return them to their parents once they had found their feet in war-ravaged Germany. But eventually Baumgartner, father of the Stellenbosch artist Regine Kröger, was not deported and in 1948, when the Malan government took over, the family was granted permanent residence. But the Ruperts' generous offer earned their lasting gratitude and Baumgartner's lifelong loyalty to Rembrandt.[6]

There are many such stories of assistance to employees, such as the case of Annies Breytenbach's wife Loretta who needed eye treatment that was not available in South Africa at the time; she was sent abroad at the company's expense. On one occasion a female employee told Huberte that married women were not members of the pension fund. Huberte wasted no time in having the anomaly set right. She and other company wives arranged Christmas parties with presents for staff and their children, and she personally congratulated employees who excelled at sport in any way. Her view was that as empathetic wife of the chief executive she could mean much more to the staff than she would have been able to accomplish as a career woman with an occupation of her own.

In Huberte's view, Rupert had the ability to inspire people to achieve beyond themselves, based on qualities like integrity, purposefulness and honesty. 'The people who worked with him all ended up as inspired, better people, intensely loyal. This is what makes a leader; someone who can achieve this. It is not enough to be entrepreneurs with capital in the bank. Without the human material Anton had around him, people he could inspire, he wouldn't have been able to accomplish anything.'[7]

Loyalty would become one of the core concepts of the Rembrandt Group. On the occasion of Rupert's 80th birthday in 1996, the business journalist David Meades wrote that Rupert gave 'new meaning' to the word: 'It is probably the single strongest building block of his business empire. His people are willing to sacrifice everything for the group.'[8]

Rupert expressed his own views on character as the most important ingredient of leadership in a lecture given in 1965 that was published in 1967 in his book *Leiers oor leierskap* (Leaders on leadership). A good manager lives by 'a code of values that emanates from his ethical and spiritual life'. He singles out loyalty as the quality of character he prizes above all others – 'the one quality that cannot be bought with money and has to be earned.'

Indeed, Rupert demanded undivided loyalty. For him it began in the family circle. He believed that an unfaithful husband or wife who became disloyal to a marriage partner could also become disloyal towards the group, and how could someone like that be trusted in his or her work? For him, office relationships between married and unmarried staff were a cardinal sin. Everyone in the Rembrandt Group knew that, and a few individuals who transgressed were transferred or went to work elsewhere in the days before the community norms became more accommodating.

Rupert regards loyalty as one of the supreme virtues to such an extent that he relishes an anecdote about himself. Once when he had to handle a difficult situation concerning a colleague, his friend Prof. James Yeats of Stellenbosch told him: 'Anton, you are too loyal.' Rupert stood up, walked round his desk and shook Yeats's hand: 'Thank you, Jamie, thank you; it is the biggest compliment you could have given me.'

When married staff of Rembrandt had to go overseas on business their spouses often accompanied them. This was at Huberte's insistence. She felt strongly that neither partner's personal development should lag behind: they should share mind-broadening experiences and build their marriages on a basis of equality, with successful marriages also being an asset to the group. When Johann Rupert took over the reins of Rembrandt he continued the policy.

The Ruperts' humane empathy ensured a committed workforce. In 1997 their son Johann, testifying before the Truth and Reconciliation Commission, could claim a staff turnover of only two percent over more than 50 years.[9]

Loyalty was one of the factors that helped Distillers as well as the later Rembrandt to go from strength to strength. Another contributing factor to his business success was Rupert's ability to be ahead of his competitors as far as scientific innovation was concerned. A trained scientist himself, he constantly exploited new technologies as they became available.

Distillers' first technical manager, the Berlin-trained perfectionist Gerhard Schröder, quickly established a laboratory despite the rather primitive conditions. Schröder left most of the laboratory work to Alfred Baumgartner, who had obtained his doctorate in plant physiology summa cum laude at the University of Freiburg. In Baumgartner's opinion Rupert could not have had anyone better than Schröder: 'Gerd Schröder was married to Distillers. He never rested until a task had been completed to perfection and he was always prepared to be on duty at any hour, night or day.'[10]

As early as 1947 Schröder ordered from France the equipment needed to launch the only modern, fully automated sparkling-wine cellar in the country. Four kinds of sparkling wine were produced under the brand name La Residence.

In 1951, when Rupert first heard about cold or 'controlled' fermentation, a process devised by the German Wilhelm Geiss in California, Distillers immediately ordered four high-pressure tanks from Germany. With state-of-the-art equipment and stringent quality control they were able to produce wines of standardised, predictable quality for the mass market. Popular brands like Grünberger Stein with its distinctive flagon (modelled on the *Bocksbeutel* used by the Franks in Germany) and Kupferberger Auslese are still top sellers today.

As in the case of tobacco, Rupert initially marketed a wide range of brands to suit all tastes. Some were competing with each other, a technique he often followed since it kept everyone in the group on their toes. In the end, however, they reduced the number of brands, concentrating on the top sellers – household names like Oude Meester and Richelieu brandy, Old Master medium sherry, Theuniskraal Riesling and Stellenheimer Rooderust, La Residence sparkling wine and liqueurs like Van der Hum and Amarula.[11]

While a success story was unfolding in the liquor industry, the dramatic expansion of Rupert's tobacco empire as well as a controversial beer war lay ahead.

CHAPTER 7

Rembrandt: birth of a masterpiece

R upert's study of world markets as well as his own observations during the Depression had convinced him that 'tobacco and liquor had the best growth potential because I noticed during the depression of the Thirties that people didn't smoke less and, if anything, they probably drank more'.[1] Undaunted by the unsuccessful attempts of Voorbrand to produce cigarettes for this lucrative market, he persisted in pursuing his dream of manufacturing cigarettes. The *Rembrandt Tabakvervaardigingskorporasie van Suid-Afrika Beperk* (Rembrandt Tobacco Manufacturing Corporation of South Africa Limited), in which Voorbrand was taken up, was founded in 1946. As a whole the group concentrated on tobacco and liquor because of the growth potential Rupert saw in these markets, but also because the first shareholders were mainly wine and tobacco farmers.

In the initial years Rupert devoted himself more to the tobacco interests while Hertzog mostly attended to the liquor interests. Hertzog tended to keep a lower profile – it was better that way, he often told friends and relatives, as a team could only have one captain: 'Anton is the masthead.'

The shift in emphasis represented by the name Rembrandt was an important innovation in its own right. Rupert gave much thought to a new name: 'As much labour (thinking) goes into a good name as into the whole product.' He knew that Voorbrand was not suitable for the cigarette with which he wanted to conquer the world market; especially not the choosy Afrikaner market that tended to mistrust its own. He was contemplating Cigarette Cézanne when one night he dreamt about Rembrandt's paintings. When he woke up, he knew instantly what the name of his company would be, and roused Huberte to share his brainwave. 'We were so excited, we never thought about sleep again,' she recollects. 'We made tea and talked till daylight. Both of us knew the name was spot on.'

Rembrandt was a name with universal appeal and a symbol of quality, with the emotional force of the works of Rembrandt Harmenszoon van Rijn (1606-1669), the greatest painter of his time and creator of the world-famous *Nightwatch* that hangs in the Rijksmuseum in Amsterdam. As a name, Rembrandt was immediately recognisable and easily pronounceable in both Afrikaans and English and other world languages. And it had no sectional overtones.

Rembrandt was to benefit greatly from a brilliant move Rupert had made even before the formation of the group. Towards the end of 1945 he went on his first overseas business trip, in search of the necessary machines and to make arrangements to obtain essential technical services. In England he met Sydney Rothman, head of the celebrated tobacco house Rothmans of Pall Mall, and concluded a strategic agreement that would have far-reaching consequences.

The 29-year-old Rupert, who was then still based in Johannesburg, had become friendly with Gordon Douglas, head of Rothmans' South African agency. Douglas was of great help to Rupert in the early years. With a view to the young Afrikaner's overseas trip, he briefed him on the finer details of travelling an international businessman had to master, such as tips for chambermaids and at which hotels to stay. Douglas also wanted to propose Rupert as a member of the exclusive Rand Club, regarded as the canteen of the Chamber of Mines and with a membership of wealthy English businessmen and mine-owners. Although Rupert, with names like Anthony Edward, would probably have been accepted without any difficulty, he declined the offer politely, explaining to Douglas that he could not become a member of a club where someone like the respected Afrikaner industrialist Dr Hendrik van Eck was not welcome.

In October 1945 Rupert boarded a BOAC airship for the trip to London that lasted six days and six nights. Flying low over the vast African continent, he was awed by its grandeur and unspoilt natural beauty. It was just two months after the nuclear explosions in Japan, which weighed heavily on his mind. Large cities in Europe and Britain had been flattened. With such powers of destruction at its disposal, humankind had to see reason or it faced extinction. Imperialism and colonialism, he concluded, were dead. Africa was moving towards a new, independent future. His view of Africa from the air, coupled with the realisation that humanity had acquired the power to destroy itself, strengthened his conviction that coexistence had become imperative – between humans, but also between humans and nature.

'The era of paternalism, where everything had to be done for others, had failed. In future, success could only be achieved if one planned and acted together with others. The time of doling out fish to the hungry was past. It had to make way for an approach of teaching them to fish. Hence the concept of *coexistence* through *partnership*,' he said in a magazine article.

On his arrival in war-ravaged London, Rupert phoned Rothman's office to confirm the appointment he had made from Johannesburg. He was told that Rothman could only see him in ten days' time. Rupert replied that he had a four-day booking at Grosvenor House, the Mayfair hotel where he was to occupy the same suite on all his visits to London over the years (just as he would remain a client of the same bank, Volkskas, and the same insurer, Sanlam, for many years). If he could not see Rothman within those four days, he would have to go home. Rothman checked his diary again and arranged to meet Rupert that same afternoon at four o'clock.

The meeting with Sydney Rothman was in many respects a watershed event. That afternoon, Rupert entered into an agreement with Rothmans of Pall Mall to manufacture Rothmans' brand in South Africa in exchange for technical expertise. They clinched the deal with a handshake – a formal contract was not signed until 1948, when the first cigarettes had been produced in the factory in Paarl.

Rothmans became the company that provided Rupert with technical advice. In the typical fashion of a true entrepreneur, he would go to immense lengths to obtain the right advice. He appointed people who could complement his own entrepreneurial abilities and established networks at an early stage.

Rothmans' technical advice proved invaluable to Rupert, as Sydney Rothman had grown up in the tobacco industry. His father Louis, a Russian Jew who had been born in the Ukrainian capital Kiev, had learnt the trade as a young boy in a cigarette factory owned by his father and uncle. Louis Rothman immigrated to London in 1887 and by 1890 was making cigarettes in his spare time. His outlet was a small Fleet Street tobacconist. In 1900 the innovative retailer moved to Pall Mall, which became a world-famous brand name he had registered. The inventor of mentholated cigarettes, Louis Rothman was given the royal imprimatur – 'By appointment to His Majesty the King' – in 1905. Sydney became an apprentice in his father's business in 1919 and, in 1923, a partner. Rothmans was listed on the London stock exchange in 1929. Among its regular clients were the media mogul Lord Northcliffe, the British premiers Lloyd George and Winston Churchill, and King Alfonso of Spain.

Rupert's journey home was ill-starred. The airship came to grief on the Nile and the passengers were stranded in Khartoum for six days before they could return to Cairo. In Cairo he was told there was no room on a flight to South Africa for the following week, also not for the two weeks after that, perhaps in two months' time. Only VIPs like generals could get preference. As an insignificant young Afrikaner, he was well and truly stuck. In desperation he decided some gallantry might do the trick. Recalling that the woman behind the counter at the airline office was past her prime, he bought a magnificent bunch of roses in a street in Cairo, and had it delivered to her. 'I was on the next flight back to South Africa,' he later told a group of amused Pretoria commerce students.

It was by no means all plain sailing in the founding years of the Rembrandt Group. Before Rupert's departure for London TIB had a bank balance of £120 000, proceeds of an issue of ten-shilling shares sold at 12s 6d. It was agreed that any financial transactions after the listing had to be approved by two of the three TIB directors – he, Dirk Hertzog and Fritz Steyn, then a lawyer in Johannesburg. On Rupert's return to Johannesburg he was notified by Jan Hurter, accountant and later managing director of Volkskas, that shares had been bought back and their account was heavily overdrawn – would they please do something about it? Rupert was astonished. Dirk Hertzog was equally in the dark. It turned out that Fritz Steyn had bought back shares, issued shortly before at 12s 6d, at 16s 3d on the advice of a broker to support the price – allegedly to maintain Afrikaner prestige! Rupert could only describe this as 'sheer nonsense'. In his view, 'the prestige lies in establishing the company and then in doing good business.'

Although the company was not insolvent, it had suffered a significant setback. It took a long time to pay back the overdraft. Rupert said afterwards that the episode had taught him a big lesson: 'Always make sure you get the right advice.'

One important consequence of this misfortune was that in 1946 they formed a second investment company, *Tweede Tegniese en Industriële Beleggings* (Second Technical and Industrial Investments), later to be renamed *Tegniese Beleggingskorporasie* (Technical Investment Corporation) or *Tegkor* for short. This was again Rupert's inventive plan to raise cash and to help TIB meet its obligations regarding the take-up of further shares in Distillers. Investments were spread over a range of industries: tobacco (Voorbrand and Rembrandt), wool (Wolgroeiers Afslaers Beperk), coffee and tea (Theal Stewart and *Biesheuvel Eiendoms Beperk*), and coal (the Klipfontein group of companies). The upshot was a pyramidal structure with the Ruperts and Hertzogs in overall control. *Rembrandt Beherende Beleggings* (Rembrandt Controlling Holdings), in which Tegkor had a 40,6% interest, retained 51,1% in Rembrandt Group Ltd. At the top of the pyramid was Rembrandt Trust (Pty) Ltd, in which the Hertzogs had a fairly small 5,6% interest compared to Rupert's lion's share of 80 to 90%. The Rembrandt Trust became the basis of his wealth, but also the reason why in later years he bought or sold virtually no shares on the open market – his view was that whatever he did could influence the market.

In 1946 TIB vacated its Johannesburg headquarters – by then they had moved to the Volkskas building, where they had two vermin-infested offices with few amenities – and the entire staff moved to Distillers' premises in Stellenbosch. These were still under construction, the windows unglazed. Most of the staff members were later transferred to Ou Rosenhof across the road in Dorp Street, with Rupert retaining his office at Distillers, until the new Rembrandt building was ready.

Rupert preferred the peaceful, rustic environment of the university town of Stellenbosch to the hustle and bustle of city life. In the late 1940s the town had only some 12 000 residents, 2 400 of them students. Yet it was conveniently close to Cape Town's airport, where he could catch international flights.

The Ruperts would eventually become one of Stellenbosch's most famous assets, in certain respects even more widely known than the university. With Rupert and Rembrandt becoming synonymous with Stellenbosch, he also turned the name of this tranquil Western Cape town into a world-famous trademark.

Their first home was in Thibault Street in the suburb of Mostertsdrift, where their eldest son – Johann Peter, after the family's Prussian progenitor – was born in 1950. Soon afterwards they moved to no. 13, diagonally across the tree-lined street, where they would live for the rest of their marriage. Here the younger children, Anthonij Eduard and Hanneli, were born in 1952 and 1955 respectively.

The dusty pink, double-storeyed house on the bank of the Eerste River cost them £6 100 (R12 200) at a time when Rupert decided to invest in a home rather than further shares; he held that a managing director should not surround himself with debt. At the turn of the century he pointed out humorously that if he had bought shares for the same amount instead, they would have been worth R300 million by then – so the family home was perhaps the most expensive in the South Africa!

The house is situated on a large stand with a swimming pool, but it is in no way ostentatious like some of the sumptuous palaces of the mega-rich. The two silver-grey Mercedes cars are parked in a lean-to carport. Indoors there are cosy armchairs, a bookshelf reflecting the occupants' catholic tastes, antique furniture, Persian rugs and paintings by well-known artists collected over many years. The atmosphere radiates relaxed comfort and the Ruperts' sober lifestyle.

To have lived in the same house for such a long time is something they have in common with some of the world's top entrepreneurs. The American billionaire Warren Buffet, ranked second on the 2004 Forbes list of 500 richest people in the world below Bill Gates of Microsoft, has spent decades in the same grey stucco house in Omaha, Nebraska. Known as the 'Oracle of Omaha', Buffet is also the only American businessman Rupert met who had studied Rembrandt's business in depth. Another renowned entrepreneur, Henry Ford of Model-T fame, lived in the house he had built for him in Dearborn, close to his automobile factory in Detroit, Michigan, from 1915 until his death in 1947.

In Thibault Street, the Ruperts maintained their simple, sober lifestyle. 'What do you do with a larger and larger and larger house?' he said 50 years later. 'What do you do with these things? It's boring. It doesn't actually make me happy. I need to help create.'[2]

Huberte made their home a peaceful haven from the stressful world of business. She kept a close eye on the family's diet, establishing a vegetable garden and serving fresh fruit and vegetables. Lunch was the main meal of the day. During their school days the children often came home to salads – grated carrots and apples soaked in orange juice, also tomatoes and pineapple. Annie Booysen, the family cook for over 40 years, conjured up plain, tasty dishes. Thick vegetable broths were often served for supper. Huberte believed it kept Rupert healthy and made him sleep well. He never had stomach ulcers. They rarely dined out and steered clear of formal functions whenever they could. Huberte kept up her interest in music and the theatre and attended performances with friends.

When the Ruperts first settled in Stellenbosch, the town was still mostly dominated by academics. In the somewhat cliquish community the newcomers were initially treated like outsiders and late arrivals, except by a few shareholders who became good friends. One of their first friends was Prof. James Yeats of the university's law faculty, a former Rhodes scholar who had co-authored some of the most important Afrikaans law books with Prof. JC de Wet at Stellenbosch. Yeats, who also became a director of the Rembrandt Group, took them under his wing. He introduced the Ruperts to academics and other residents and they were gradually drawn into the community.

A number of academics with whom the Ruperts enjoyed intellectual conversations provided stimulating company. Among those who lived close by in Mostertsdrift were CGW Schumann, the economist who would later describe Rupert as 'a practical dreamer and a realistic idealist'; Len Verwoerd, agriculturist brother of HF Verwoerd (ideologically poles apart from his brother); the literary scholar FEJ (Fransie) Malherbe, whose brother Prof. F du T Malherbe had been Rupert's chemistry lecturer in Pretoria; and the composer Arnold van Wyk. Dirk Hertzog and his wife lived nearby at Rus Roes in Tuin Street, across the road from the poet Dirk Opperman and his wife Marié, friends of both the Ruperts and the Hertzogs, whose house was at no. 3 Thibault Street. Although Rupert's brothers Koos and Jan spent much time overseas, they also made Stellenbosch their base and lived in the same area. In later years Mostertsdrift and specifically Thibault Street became less affordable to academics, and by the turn of the century the residents of the suburb were mostly business people and medical doctors.

As a location for the new cigarette factory Rupert chose an old mill in Paarl, a town in the Berg River valley. He thought the climate ideal for maturing tobacco and manufacturing cigarettes. It was to this valley that Jan van Riebeeck, governor of the Dutch East India Company, had sent an expedition in October 1657. Two hundred and ninety years later Rupert came to Paarl as a new pioneer. Like

Van Riebeeck he had a dream, but with it the determination and initiative to turn it into reality.

Rembrandt's starting capital was a modest £125 000. There were also other problems. Hennie van Zyl, who had succeeded Hoogenhout as manager of Voorbrand, left in 1946 to join the leather-suitcase company SAPRO in Port Elizabeth. Like Hoogenhout, he returned to Rembrandt two years later when his business at SAPRO failed. There were no recriminations in either case. In the interim, however, the only suitable person Rupert could find to take over at Voorbrand was his own brother Jan, newly qualified as a lawyer and working for their father John Rupert. Jan agreed to join Rembrandt and organised the move of the cigarette factory in Johannesburg to Paarl. He crossed over to the new company at the time of the merger, when Voorbrand's production assets and brand names were transferred to Rembrandt for a sum of £70 000. Voorbrand shareholders obtained a share in Rembrandt, which still continued to process pipe tobacco. Rupert himself was authorised to apply for shares of £70 000 in Rembrandt.

The other co-founder of the group, Dirk Hertzog, was in the early stages still a partner at the law firm Couzyn, Hertzog & Horak in Pretoria. He joined the group in Stellenbosch, where his astute legal brain was an asset, but after a year he wanted to return to Pretoria. An asthmatic with a heart defect, he believed he needed a lot of exercise and the Cape weather interfered with his tennis. His wife Lorraine (née De la Harpe) also found it hard to settle into the new surroundings and missed her friends in the north. After a few years in Pretoria, however, the couple returned to Stellenbosch and Hertzog devoted the rest of his career to Rembrandt. Rupert observed in his founder's notes that Hertzog, who had taken up golf in the meantime, was rarely available outside of office hours. Hertzog's own view was that after devoting a full day's energy and concentration to business, he did not want to be disturbed at home or on the golf course. As a result of a car accident in 1968 Hertzog's wife became an invalid, which also made it practically difficult for him to travel overseas.

Hertzog had tried to interest Rupert in golf, but after a few attempts Rupert declared frankly that he was only making a fool of himself on the golf course. Years later his older son Johann would become an enthusiastic golfer. Johann Rupert counts golf heroes such as Ernie Els and Trevor Immelman among his friends, serves as chairman of the PGA in South Africa and encourages the development of young golfers.

Two other well-known associates of Rupert's, JF (Freddie) Kirsten and Fritz Steyn, also left the group at an early stage. Kirsten, a farmer from Paarl, left the board of TIB after acquiring an interest in a liquor store. Steyn resigned as a director of

TIB in 1948 after he had laid personal claim to a liquor licence financed by TIB and obtained on behalf of the company, and Rupert pointed this out to him. They parted ways for good and Steyn went on to become a member of parliament, ambassador and judge.

In his chairman's address of Rembrandt Beherende Beleggings in 1996 Rupert referred to those who came and went in the first ten years, and those who returned and stayed to the end. 'There are few of us left who had the faith. I think only Dr Stals and I truly believed. We kept on believing that these things were possible; that he who does not believe in miracles, is not a realist.' Stals, chairman of Voorbrand, became Rembrandt's first chairman, with Rupert the first managing director. When Stals was appointed to the cabinet in 1948, he was succeeded as chairman by Dr Nic Diederichs. In addition to Stals and Rupert, other members of Rembrandt's first board were CC (Oupa) Kriel, DWR (Dirk) Hertzog, IM (Ivan Makepeace) Lombard, JH (Jan) Steyn and RL (Roulou) Barry.

Rupert confirmed his high regard for Stals in an article published in *Tegniek* in September 1950, on the occasion of his mentor's 70th birthday, shortly before his death in 1951. Stals's 'refinement of spirit' – one of the highest compliments Rupert could pay a person – had left an indelible impression: 'I have never in all my life encountered someone who, to my mind, is a more perfect, honest, sincere Christian.'[3]

With the move to Stellenbosch Rupert also linked up with a division of the Afrikaner-Broederbond (AB) in the new environment. Between September 1945 and January 1947 discussions on economic affairs were conducted in the AB in which he participated as one of some 40 members who were representative of the biggest Afrikaans businesses. During this period the earlier debate between a socialist and a free-market approach was concluded with a commitment of loyalty to free-market principles.[4]

In these discussions, where Rupert argued for the free-market system, he also pleaded for a better understanding between North and South (a division in Afrikaner politics marked by suspicion and distrust that dragged on for many years) and for the bigger institutions to help create circumstances more favourable to the development and growth of the smaller enterprises. As Rupert himself put it, 'I stated my views' within the AB where there were great differences on a variety of issues. Among other things, he advocated coexistence.

At a *bondsraad* meeting of 4-5 October 1956 where the Afrikaner's economic aspirations were high on the agenda, some speakers proposed a quota system as a 'powerful instrument' to ensure a foothold in trade and industry for young and emerging Afrikaans businesses. The executive council of the AB was requested to lobby members of the cabinet to find a basis 'on which Afrikaner enterprises can be favoured to a greater extent by means of the allocation of quotas.' Rupert, who delivered one of three papers at the bondsraad, pointed out, however, that an own business style, realism, enthusiasm and loyalty were the most important requirements for success. A second speaker, Dr AD Wassenaar of Sanlam, emphasised that, over and above outside forces obstructing the advancement of Afrikaners, the major obstacles lay in Afrikaners' own view of and approach to their problems.

The executive council responded 'rather unenthusiastically' to resolutions about matters like a quota system, an idea also propagated earlier by Dr Hendrik Verwoerd. Quota systems, which would again figure in the new government's transformation plans and affirmative action after the ANC came to power in 1994, were scrapped from the executive council's agenda within a few months after the bondsraad decisions of 1956.[5]

Rupert gradually saw less need for an organisation such as the AB after 1948, 'when our own people had come to power'. His father had been opposed to secret societies and never joined the AB, even though his friend Ds Jozua Naudé had been a founder and the first president. John Rupert believed that a secret society always gave rise to machinations and intrigue. His father's view made Rupert increasingly uncomfortable with participation in the AB; as he put it, it had become 'an absurdity' and 'counterproductive' over time. In the 1960s an AB circular noted that he had only attended two of the year's monthly meetings of the Helderberg division.[6] Eventually his membership lapsed. But he never violated the confidentiality of the organisation, as did Beyers Naudé (a member for 22 years and the chairman of an AB division in Emmarentia) and Albert Geyser (who was never considered for AB membership).

In response to an allegation in Dan O'Meara's book *Volkskapitalisme* that 'the Bond-connection was vitally important to the early development of Rembrandt', Hertzog wrote in an internal memorandum: 'The members of the Broederbond, the Reddingsdaadbond and also many other people supported Rembrandt, but it is nonsense to say it was founded by the Broederbond.' He concluded: 'Rembrandt met a need at the time to bring the Afrikaner into business life on a sound basis and thereafter became widely known on account of its pioneering work in 50/50 partnership with all the benefits this entailed in terms of international and inter-group cooperation. For this and for the consistently high quality of its products and services Rembrandt will remain known, regardless of the mud flung from time to time by those who have their own axes to grind.'[7]

Rupert is adamant that membership of the AB was never used as a criterion for appointments. 'AB membership was to me no reason for preferential treatment.' It was also his policy not to force anyone in his group to speak Afrikaans. One such English-speaker with whom he would have a long association visited Stellenbosch in 1946 – the London marketing expert Patrick O'Neill-Dunne of Rothmans, for whom a draft contract was drawn up to assist with the marketing of Rothmans' products in South Africa. Dirk Hertzog recalls how O'Neill-Dunne once commented on their struggle against the mighty UTC: 'You two boys trying to bash British American Tobacco make me think of two fleas crawling up the back of an elephant with rape in their mind!'[8]

O'Neill-Dunne was entitled to 2,5% of Rembrandt's net profit, which also applied to Rupert as the managing director. This led to a far-reaching decision in 1949 that would provide an early foundation for his philosophy as businessman-benefactor. Rupert requested the board to use this 2,5 percent of the net profit to which he was entitled for good deeds and worthy causes, a decision that would eventually lead to numerous philanthropic actions and foundations, as well as important strategic partnerships in the area of social responsibility.

An old flourmill next to the Berg River in Paarl was adapted to serve as the group's first cigarette factory. In 1947 the first two cigarette machines arrived from Canada, bought with the help of Dawid de Waal Meyer, South Africa's trade commissioner in Montreal, from a small Dunhill factory that had folded after the war. At the beginning of 1948, as Rupert put it, 'with two old primitive machines we at last took the plunge to start making cigarettes, with overseas expertise and South African capital.'

The small band of pioneers took the risk of venturing into an industry with a long history. Tobacco smoking dates back to ancient North and South American civilisations. In the 16th century Sir Walter Raleigh popularised pipe smoking at the English court, and in Spain tobacco plants were used medicinally. By the 17th century the use of tobacco had been prohibited in Austria, China, Persia (where a tobacco dealer was burnt at the stake) and tsarist Russia (first offenders were flogged, a second offence meant the death penalty). Still the smoking habit spread. In 1880 two Americans, James A Bonsack and James Buchanan Duke, designed and patented machines to manufacture cigarettes. Especially in wartime tobacco consumption rocketed. During World War I Gen. John Pershing said: 'You ask me what we need to win the war? I answer tobacco as much as bullets.' Pres. FD Roosevelt regarded it as essential war material during World War II and exempted tobacco growers from military duty. The non-smoker Adolf Hitler, by contrast, launched the first anti-smoking campaign of modern times in the 1930s and the tobacco rations of Nazi soldiers were restricted to six cigarettes a day.

The cigarette industry was also boosted by the film industry. Ordinary people could not afford the yachts, fur coats and luxury goods displayed by Hollywood stars in films, but they could smoke the cigarettes their screen idols were enjoying so freely. Cigarette consumption rose after World War II and peaked in the 1950s.[9] Opposition to smoking started gradually after a 1952 *Readers Digest* article, 'Cancer by the Carton', described the health hazards of tobacco. The American surgeon-general's first report on smoking was issued in 1964. But it was not till the latter part of the century that measures against smoking and tobacco advertising were introduced internationally – in South Africa only in the 1990s.

The first Rembrandt cigarette was made by AP (Pappa) Thierack, who had met Rupert in 1945 and two years later installed the first steam kettle and standard packaging machines in the old mill. Among those who helped assemble the first cigarette machines were Moos du Preez and James Martin, two coloured workers who would remain with the group for decades. According to Thierack the initial output was 100 000 cigarettes a day. Mrs HJ Muller relates how she sealed the cellophane around the first packet with a flatiron and affixed the first excise duty sticker by hand; 'after much pondering and measuring, Bakoor Smit then built a machine that consisted of a sewing-machine wheel and a bicycle chain'.[10]

The first cigarette was taken off the conveyor belt in the factory in Paarl by Dr MS (Tienie) Louw, president of the Afrikaanse Handelsinstituut (AHI), on 4 June 1948. It was still the old format of 70mm, 15mm shorter than the eventual king size. 'The first Afrikaans cigarette is on the market', *Tegniek* reported joyously. The new cigarettes were released on the market a week after Dr DF Malan's National Party, which had entered into an election pact with Klaas Havenga's Afrikaner Party, ousted Gen. Smuts's SAP in the May 1948 elections. Nationalistic feelings were rampant among Afrikaners. Some political analysts contend that the NP's policy of 'apartheid' had been the decisive factor in the new Afrikaner government's victory at the polls. Others hold the view, however, that far more important factors had been Smuts's decision about participation in the war that had not been subjected to a referendum, the hardship in the war years after the Depression, discrimination against Afrikaners in the public service and elsewhere, as well as the grievances of ex-combatants who felt Smuts's promises to them had not been kept. Malan expressed the emotions of many Afrikaners when he said: 'We feel at home again in our own country.'

At first Rembrandt concentrated on the Western Cape. Wary of overextending themselves, they literally fought their way northwards area by area, creating a demand for the new group's products. From the Western Cape the outposts shifted to the Southwestern Districts, the Karoo, Namaqualand, the Eastern Cape,

Kimberley, the Free State. A year later they crossed the Vaal River to reach Johannesburg, the City of Gold.

Manufacture of Rothmans' cigarettes under licence, with all the benefits of the overseas company's technical know-how, forged ahead from 1949 onwards, giving Rembrandt a significant competitive edge. Initially, Rembrandt paid royalties to Rothmans for its expertise. In the end it would take control of Rothmans of Pall Mall in England.

In the early stages there was not much cash, but the employees were fired by the conviction: *'n Boer maak 'n plan* (An Afrikaner makes a plan). A poster on the Rembrandt factory wall bore a likeness of the great artist, with his name and the slogan: 'Every cigarette *must* be a masterpiece.' Quality, not protectionism, was Rupert's recipe for success. The caption of a drawing in the group's offices depicting the race between the hare and the tortoise read: 'It's the last ten paces that count'. The message was intended to make employees aware that 'one shouldn't rest on one's laurels and lie down to take a nap.'[11] This was typical of Rupert himself, who never became complacent. Always impatient with the status quo, he challenged it in his constant search for new possibilities and opportunities.

Another characteristic for which Rupert became known was his capacity for hard work. His unflagging energy and powers of concentration were legendary. A twelve-hour working day was nothing unusual, his brain racing all the while – notably in the late afternoon. His work rate put pressure on his senior staff, but also inspired them to put in long hours themselves. Did this put his marriage under stress? Not at all, says Huberte. 'Other men also get home late, but maybe via the golf club or the pub. It's ridiculous to complain if you know your husband is hard at work.'[12]

The staff in the Paarl factory was small because money was tight. The little band worked day and night. The mill was far too small for what they had in mind, but construction work was not allowed to interfere with production. Walls for extensions were erected around the existing building while work continued. Then, over a weekend, the inside walls were demolished and the debris removed. The cornerstone of the Paarl building was laid by Mrs Annie Stals, widow of Dr AJ Stals, first chairman of Rembrandt, on 22 September 1951, but expansion continued and eventually all that remained of the original building of 1948 was a solitary wall and two palm trees.

One of the most serious problems Rembrandt faced at the outset was the quota system that continued to exercise a stranglehold on industrial development. After the wartime rationing of goods, the new government reimposed this system that was based on the status quo – established manufacturers benefited, but new entrants were hamstrung by the restrictions. In 1948 Rupert joined forces with other Afrikaans enterprises in establishing a new business journal, *Tegniek* – the second Afrikaans publication of its kind. He used it to launch an attack on the quota system.

The first issue contained an outline of his vision of the Afrikaner's role in industry, plus an article under the heading 'Phenomenal success of the First Afrikaans Cigarette', which quoted a report from the *Central News* lauding Rembrandt's success and its strategies for achieving it. The second issue in December 1949 went on the offensive with a scathing attack under a banner headline: 'QUOTAS ARE KILLING US! The Afrikaner merely asks for the right to compete.' The article, by an anonymous jurist (presumably James Yeats), argued that protracted rationing with fixed allocations based on past production militated against new enterprises, perpetuated old monopolies, created a black market in quotas and fostered other economic evils. In South Africa, it went on, this was aggravated by the fact that the vested interests that benefited from the system were owned by foreigners, whereas emerging businesses belonged to Afrikaners and their English-speaking compatriots. The state, the article averred, was protecting foreign interests at the expense of nationals by preventing the latter from developing their businesses to the full.[13] The article enraged Eric H Louw, minister of economic development and mines, but the logic was irrefutable – the article emphasised that the Afrikaner 'is not asking for protection or favouritism, merely for the right to compete'.

Rupert went further. He threatened the secretary for trade and industry that he would close the factory in Paarl if he did not get his rightful quota. He also proposed sending girls in Voortrekker dresses to demonstrate at the opening of parliament, carrying posters with the slogan, 'Quotas are killing us!' and to picket there for up to a year. His threats caused quite a hubbub in government circles, supposedly well disposed towards Afrikaner business, and proposals were invited. These led to the introduction of a far more flexible system and the eventual abolition of quotas. Henceforth manufacturers could submit their own assessment of their requirements, which would then be adjusted up- or downwards twice a year, depending on their output in the preceding six months. The battle was won at last, and the increased ability to compete served as a further boost to Rembrandt.

Typical of Rupert who was never one to wait for things to happen but instead made them happen, he registered Rembrandt's trademark in 70 countries. This was something rare at the time – among Afrikaans businesses, only the KWV's trademark had been registered outside of South Africa. Rupert's early grasp of the importance of trademarks, something that would become almost an obsession, was to prove a crucial factor in the global success of his group.

In the early years, Rembrandt's sales representatives did not travel in flashy cars and mostly visited dealers carrying boxes of cigarette cartons on their shoulders. Competitors tended to joke about the activities on the banks of the Berg River. While there was not much money for advertising, Rupert and his associates were inventive, initially on a shoestring budget. Company vehicles, once they could afford them, were painted green and red and acted as mobile billboards, a brand-new technique at the time. Stationary billboards were put up at strategic points. Marketing, and especially advertising, would become a major power source for the Rembrandt Group. Rupert was ahead of his contemporaries in grasping the realities of post-war capitalism. Where they still concentrated mainly on production, he put a new emphasis on marketing. He built up a substantial library on marketing and advertising, requiring his partners and colleagues to read the literature as well, and subscribed to business journals like *Fortune* and newspapers like *The New York Times* and *The Wall Street Journal*. His maxim was a golden rule: 'Advertising can never be simple, sincere and repetitive enough.'

Initially Rembrandt had to compete with the giant United Tobacco (UTC) for prime advertising space in South African media, but within a very few years it had to publish advertisements warning rivals of prosecution for misusing its name. Its aggressive marketing campaigns blazed a trail in the advertising industry. In addition to the emphasis on marketing, Rembrandt's factories were soon more mechanised and its operations more capital intensive than those of competitors, while Rupert kept an eagle eye on productivity.

In 1950 an article in *Inspan*, organ of the FAK and the RDB, hailed Rembrandt as the most successful post-war cigarette company in the western hemisphere. It lauded the company's far-sighted leadership: quality control was superb, probably unique in the country; so was its scientific management, which included sophisticated costing techniques; the latest technology was imported from abroad. The article also referred to Rembrandt's policy of providing employment for white girls in an air-conditioned workplace with comfortable rest rooms, and training white boys in the cigarette industry. The pride expressed at the success of 'the first Afrikaans cigarette factory', situated in Paarl, birthplace of the First Afrikaans Language Movement, was linked to nationalistic feelings among Afrikaners: 'Each nation needs its own – things that are really important – its own language, its own land, its own factories, its own success . . .'[14] An earlier article in *Volkshandel*, official organ of the AHI, also noted approvingly that with its employment policy, Rembrandt had succeeded in 'bringing down labour costs to below the world average'.[15]

In Rembrandt's early years there was a strong emphasis on Afrikaner culture. In 1949 the group sent 63 female employees in Voortrekker dresses, supplied to them by Rupert, to the inauguration of the Voortrekker Monument in Pretoria. A well-known Afrikaans cultural figure, Dr PJ (Piet) Meyer, a later chairman of the AB and chairman of the board of the South African Broadcasting Corporation, served as the group's head of public relations from 1951 to 1959.

Rembrandt's financial statement at the end of the first year showed a loss of £63 000. Rupert has described it as 'the most critical time in my life'. Yet he did not lose his nerve. 'In times of crisis I am always calm.'[16] The following year Rembrandt registered a profit of £104 000. Rupert denied that it was all merit: 99% was sweat, the rest was plain luck – factors beyond their control. But it was a turning-point just the same. After that they never looked back.

Yet Rupert's competitors initially underestimated him. At a gathering of tobacco manufacturers where some referred disparagingly to Rupert as a presumptuous upstart, one man – Bertie Levenstein, an executive at Rand Tobacco and Cavalla – disagreed: 'I think this man is dynamite!' Years later he said: 'I didn't get it quite right; I should rather have said this man is an atom bomb.'[17] When Rembrandt eventually took over Rand Tobacco and Cavalla, Levenstein became a director.

Rupert himself regards 1950 as the year of Rembrandt's great breakthrough. At the group's first annual general meeting in February 1950 the chairman Dr Nic Diederichs announced that its current monthly profit stood at £10 000. By the end of that year, with a turnover of £2 million, it was able to pay its first dividend of three percent on ordinary shares. The South African economy was reviving from wartime austerity, and the industrialisation that had formed part of the war effort was having a ripple effect. It was the type of development that prompted the historian CW de Kiewiet's much-quoted observation: 'South Africa advanced politically by disasters and economically by windfalls.' Rembrandt exploited the favourable climate, expanding its market share in the face of fierce competition – at one stage there were more than 80 brands of cigarettes vying for supremacy. Rembrandt won hands down. It was not just Afrikaner support any more. With Rothmans as its second leg it had a foot in both language camps.

By 1951 its market share was ten percent. More whites were smoking Rembrandt than any other cigarette in the country. A new, longer cigarette, Rembrandt van Rijn, proved particularly popular. The productivity of the female workers in Paarl was rewarded when Rupert announced in 1953 that he was raising the minimum wage for white females and young boys to £1 a day, almost double the wage other tobacco manufacturers had negotiated with a trade union a short time before. This was a prelude to the higher minimum wages for coloureds with which he would cause a stir in South African industry ten years later.

In the starting years Rupert not only sold shares with great enthusiasm, but also bought shares out of his own salary in the Rembrandt Trust, the holding company of the Rembrandt Group. Rembrandt Tabakkorporasie was listed on the Johannesburg Stock Exchange in 1956 and, like TIB and Tegkor, it became an investment of a lifetime. In 1999 Rupert pointed out that shares of R1 000 in the Rembrandt Group bought in 1948 would be worth R17 million, not counting the dividends. In 2002 it was calculated that the first shareholders who bought shares of R1 000 would have earned a spectacular sum of more than R30 million, if the value of Remgro, Venfin and Richemont is included. Rembrandt has made many people millionaires with shares that have increased 3 000 000% in value.

In a welcoming letter signed by Rupert that was sent to each new shareholder in the early years, he asked people 'not to sell your shares lightly. Conserve them for your children.' He heeded his own prophetic advice, and others who did likewise also reaped the benefits.

In 1953 Rupert remarked that the success Rembrandt had achieved up to that point had dispelled the illusion that Afrikaners could not compete with their English and Jewish compatriots in the business world. 'It was essential that someone should break down the illusion.'

Despite Rembrandt's increasing competitive edge and a rise in demand that necessitated extensions to the factory in Paarl, Rupert was aware of the fact that a price war could damage his group. He decided to extend his operations overseas in order to build up profitable new markets, and in the process also came up with innovations that left competitors behind and changed people's smoking patterns internationally.

CHAPTER 8

Innovation leads the way

R upert distinguishes innovative ideas and innovative products as two of the main reasons for the Rembrandt Group's success. His innovative thinking was not just limited to the business sphere.

At the *Tweede Ekonomiese Volkskongres* (Second National Economic Congress) in Bloemfontein in 1950 he advocated partnership as a business philosophy, a partnership that had to be extended to the black population as well. This was an almost revolutionary notion given the spirit of the times, yet he saw it as the only way of turning the benefits of private enterprise into a blessing for all.

Rupert delivered his speech entitled 'The Afrikaner in Industry' two years after the National Party had assumed power. While the political kingdom was now under Afrikaner control, the economic terrain still had to be conquered. The aim of the congress was to take stock of economic progress in the previous decade and draw inspiration from it for the future. In the decade since the First National Economic Congress (according to a 1949 FAK survey) Afrikaners' contribution in respect of turnover in the private sector had almost doubled, but cross-sectorally it still amounted to a mere eleven percent.

Rupert had just turned 34 and was addressing an audience of mostly older and more experienced men. He reminded his listeners that Afrikaners' contribution to industry was still barely six percent – it was too soon to start removing the scaffolding from this small national edifice and start building bridges to others. With regard to those who dominated the economy, he said: 'We are always ready to work *with* you, but not to work *for* you in perpetuity.' And he quoted Kestell's words from long ago: 'We ask no favours. A nation must save itself!'

He provided an overview of South Africa's industrial development in the preceding 25 years, comparing it to an industrial revolution. In this period South African industrial production had rocketed by 700% – faster even than that of Russia and America. This was partly thanks to legislation introduced by Hertzog's NP government after 1924 that led to the establishment of institutions like the iron and steel corporation Iscor, as well as the role played by entrepreneurs such as Hendrik van der Bijl, Hendrik van Eck and Frikkie Meyer in building up the country's biggest basic industries. Yet Afrikaners still controlled less than one percent of the £1 000 million's worth of mining and industrial shares on the stock exchange.

Recalling Ds Kestell's words to students ('I don't dwell on the past or the present but look to the future'), Rupert expressed his own future-oriented thinking with a plea for the upliftment of black people. He based his argument on economic realities. Partly through Afrikaner endeavour, South Africa had been transformed into an industrial country that provided urban employment for thousands of Afrikaners. It was doing the same for hundreds of thousands of black workers. More than 30 000 Africans – both local and from beyond the national borders – were pouring into the major cities annually, leading to a preponderance of blacks in urban demographics. He advocated the 'civilising mission' as a solution to these developments that had brought about 'one of our most vital questions'.

His proposed solution amounted to white mastership in white areas and white trusteeship in black territories, with the proviso that it should be mastership that is earned and based on achievement. He was farsighted enough to envision a day when mining would no longer be able to sustain the economy – South Africa's industries had to developed further to ensure financial strength in the future. The steel and petrol industries had to be developed to make South Africa self-sufficient in the event of international crises. Blacks must know that South African courts would protect their basic human rights. This would make them sceptical of the professed freedom propagated by foreign powers.

He put two specific proposals to his audience. The first was that Afrikaner industrialists should provide a starting capital of £5 000 to launch a non-profit company (he suggested the name 'Bantu Development Corporation') with a view to establishing 'modest local industries in black territories as proof of our bona fides and sincere intentions'. The second proposal was for the establishment of a corporation for European immigration to help meet the need for skilled labour. But he emphasised that the two initiatives should go hand in hand – 'the one must supplement the other'.[1]

Rupert was given a standing ovation by the congress audience, which included his father John Rupert and his former headmaster Dr G von W Eybers. In retrospect his plea for the development of blacks could be regarded as paternalistically couched in the terminology that was current at the time, nonetheless it already expressed the idea of partnership he would proclaim with such conviction in the years ahead. At the congress, his notion of the desirability of economic rapprochement to other population groups was endorsed by both Dr Nic Diederichs and Prof.Wicus du Plessis, who declared that 'we need to start building bridges to the other population groups to strengthen our influence on and our service to the country's economy as a whole'.[2]

Rupert's speech was in many important respects a prelude to the debate about the development of black homelands and the role of urban blacks that would rage in Afrikaner circles in later years. For a long time, however, nothing came of his proposals. As Rupert himself commented laconically, 'There was applause but no action.'

Rupert's innovative thinking on socioeconomic questions was matched by his pursuit of innovation with regard to products. From the outset, the Rembrandt Group concentrated on producing both new and better products in the tobacco industry through research and hard work. Quite early on he introduced the new Golden Throat filter and the All Seal packet, a paper packet lined with aluminium – this innovation came about because Rembrandt had no machines to make cardboard packages. Then, in 1952, fully a year ahead of any other tobacco company in the world, came his biggest innovation yet, which was to change smoking fashions around the globe.

He was never happy about ordinary filter-tipped cigarettes, sensing that smokers subconsciously felt they were being short-changed, since the filter replaced some of the tobacco. So he came up with a brand-new idea: a king-size filter-tipped cigarette. He summoned his chief technician and gave him an ultimatum: within 30 days – not 90! – he had to modify the machines to produce the new format. This was another typical quality of the entrepreneurial Rupert: he demanded much of his employees because of his belief that speed, timing and quality were crucial competitive advantages. With this sense of urgency, he would often remind his associates: 'We are cats on a hot tin roof.'

The chief technician did not hesitate to do what had been asked by 'Mr AE' (as he was called by older employees, to distinguish him from his brothers Mr JP – Jan – and Mr JA – Koos). It was with reason that some of the employees also whispered that 'AE' stood for 'All and Everything'. By the end of 1951 the modified machines were in operation. In 1952, a whole year before their counterparts in the USA and elsewhere, they had succeeded in putting 85mm cigarettes on the market. And not just one brand: alongside Rembrandt van Rijn Filter de Luxe there was a Rothmans King Size Filter as the company's own internal competition, a typical procedure of Rupert's to awaken creative ingenuity and motivate people. 'Because', he observed, 'you don't run the race on your own.'

Other cigarette manufacturers were sceptical about the new, unproved product. Even Sydney Rothman, his technical advisor, refused to market Rothmans King Size or Rothmans King Size Filter (which Rembrandt manufactured under licence in South Africa) in Britain. Not until the eventual takeover of Rothmans of Pall Mall did this Rothmans 'baby', as Rupert called the new cigarette, hit the London market.

Another sceptic was the biggest cigarette manufacturer in Europe, the German Philipp Reemtsma, who had met Jan Rupert in Hamburg in 1950 and was impressed with everything he saw and heard about Rembrandt. When he eventually met Rupert, the two men became firm friends despite initial language difficulties. A World War I pilot himself, Reemtsma had lost three of his sons during World War II. While he suspected that the enterprising young South African would become his main competitor, he asked himself: 'What would you do for your own son?' He decided to take Rupert under his wing and helped him in crucial ways.

In later years the roles changed, with Reemtsma asking advice from Rupert at least once a month. And he insisted on paying Rupert. The depth of their friendship was such that Reemtsma wanted to appoint Rupert as trustee for the interests of his surviving son, Jan Philipp, a child of his second marriage, but Rupert did not see his way open to take on this responsibility as it would have meant moving to Europe.

Reemtsma had grave doubts about the concept of king-size filter-tipped cigarettes. By 1954 this innovation had swept the American market, but America was not Europe. At Reemtsma's home at Bad Gastein in Austria he and Rupert argued throughout one whole night. Round four in the morning they reached a compromise: if filter cigarettes could seize six percent of the market, Reemtsma would concede the point. Never pusillanimous, Rupert predicted it would be 80%.

He was right. By 2000, according to Filtrona International, 93% of all the 5,7 trillion cigarettes smoked in the world were filter tipped. The most widely used filters (69%) were made of cellulose acetate, with Estron as the leading manufacturer. Second came polypropylene filters with 21%, mainly in China.

The episode with Reemtsma reveals much about Rupert's nature. He is a refined and cultivated person, invariably courteous. But he is also someone with firm convictions, who could persevere when others threw in the towel. If he wanted something done, it had to be done. If he was convinced that an innovation was the right thing at the right time, nothing could stand in his way. For this reason some of his close friends have described him as a man of steel.

Rembrandt led the field with other innovations as well. It produced the first mentholated filter-tipped cigarettes in the world; the first 'Multifilter' king-size cigarettes; the first cigarettes with 'Multivent' super-porous paper; the first ultramodern, gold-banded filter; and the world's first luxury-length cigarette.

Five years after its humble start in the old mill in Paarl Rembrandt controlled a substantial part of the South African cigarette market. But this did not satisfy Rupert. He did not underestimate his competitors; he could see the risks of a price war. Besides, he was still fired by the ideal of proving Afrikaner mettle among the top performers in the world. He started looking further afield.

In November 1953 a friend in London informed him that Rothmans, founded in 1890, was selling out to Carreras, an even older British tobacco merchant. This boded ill for Rembrandt, since the licence for manufacturing Rothmans and Consulate in South Africa – two lucrative and carefully nurtured brands – expired at the end of ten years and would have to be renewed. At the last minute the Rothmans-Carreras deal struck a hitch: because of some wartime taxes that did not satisfy the authorities Carreras could face a huge tax bill if it went through. Negotiations were suspended for the time being.

Rupert – already making use of what has since become known as a 'corporate intelligence service' – was kept in the picture. He struck at once. His partner Dirk Hertzog was dispatched to London to make Sydney Rothman a take-it-or-leave-it offer: according to Rupert's calculation Rothmans' break-up value was £750 000, without goodwill. That was what he was willing to pay, not a penny more. Rupert knew Rothman well. He was not a man for snap decisions. If he tried to prevaricate, he told Hertzog, go to the Continent for a while and give Rothman time to think it over.

It turned out exactly like that. On Hertzog's return to London Sydney Rothman accepted the proffered £750 000 (R1,5 million). In one fell swoop Rembrandt acquired a concern that had been in business in England since the previous century, when Louis Rothman had opened his kiosk in Fleet Street. There was just one snag: they were short of some £700 000.

On the evening of Wednesday 18 November 1953 Rupert met AD (Lens) Wassenaar, general manager of the insurance company Sanlam, in the old Carlton Hotel in Johannesburg. He asked Wassenaar if Sanlam could help with a loan: he needed £750 000 to close the transaction, and at once. It had been the managing director of the Sanlam Group, Dr Louw, who had taken receipt of Rembrandt's first cigarette at the Paarl factory five years previously.

Monday 25 November 1953 was the day on which Rembrandt had to pay for the takeover, which left only four days to find the money. Back in Cape Town on the day following his meeting with Rupert, Wassenaar convened a special meeting of Sanlam's board for the Friday. The matter was so urgent that a car was sent to Riebeek West on Friday morning to collect FS Malan, one of Sanlam's directors.[3]

In Cape Town that Friday Rupert put his case, the first time in Sanlam's history that an outsider was permitted to address a board meeting. Using all his powers of persuasion, he managed to secure convertible debentures to the amount of £500 000. Sanlam advanced half of the amount, with its subsidiary African Homes Trust (later Homes Trust, eventually Metlife) and Bonuskor and FVB, both of which were founded by Sanlam, lending the other half. Volkskas bank would provide the remaining quarter of a million.

Monday noon was when the money was due in London. Rupert spent the morning with Jan Hurter, general manager (later managing director) of Volkskas, in the latter's office in Pretoria as they waited for final confirmation that the money had been transferred. Their acquaintance dated back to the days when TIB rented offices in the Volkskas building in Johannesburg. Both were tense, as they knew what was at stake. At quarter past eleven there was still no telex or telegram from Sanlam. At half past eleven Hurter picked up the phone. 'Anton, I'm going to telex London to tell them the money is there,' he said. Rupert would not allow him to do this. He knew that Volkskas, not a big bank at that stage, could be ruined if the transaction should go awry. He reminded Hurter that they had come a long way together, knowing each other since 1941: 'I'm not going to allow you to risk your whole future to help me and to help Rembrandt today.' The minutes ticked by. At ten minutes to twelve the message of confirmation came through at last. At noon the money was in London.

Sanlam could congratulate itself: 'In this way Sanlam helped a South African company take its first step towards becoming a global company.'

Commenting on this closest of close shaves, Rupert observed philosophically, 'If you knew beforehand what's in store for you, you'd never start anything.' When he was asked years later if he ever takes part in Lotto, the officially sanctioned game of chance played by millions of hopeful South Africans every week, he answered with a smile: 'No, I've taken enough big risks in my life!'

In effecting loans with which he financed his expanding business empire, he started following a practice that would yield great dividends in the long run. When money was needed for expansion or whatever, he usually borrowed more than he needed – and then made sure that the debt was redeemed before the due date. That was how Rembrandt established an enviable reputation for creditworthiness over the years.

The Rothmans deal entailed a whirl of overseas activity, including the sale of its 29 tobacco shops. At this point Rupert's youngest brother Koos, a law lecturer at the University of the Orange Free State, joined the group. His first task was to see to the finalisation of contracts. Stationed first in London and later in New York, he became Rembrandt's first overseas representative. Under his guidance 27 of Rothmans' tobacconists were sold – only the shops in Pall Mall and the Burlington Arcade were retained.

Rupert is adamant that his two brothers have been among his most loyal and hardworking supporters. He counts among their virtues that 'they were not ashamed to put a carton of cigarettes on their shoulders to go and sell it'. They also read through all the contracts and financial statements with him before they were printed.

Commitment and loyalty were indeed the kind of distinguishing characteristics that had laid the foundation for the trek abroad, which heralded a new phase for Rembrandt and Rupert. Soon he would spend one day out of every five on aeroplanes, as his son Johann would also do later.

CHAPTER 9

International passport

T he purchase of Rothmans in 1954 launched Rupert internationally. At
the age of 37 he found himself on a playing field where he faced the
toughest opposition in the world.

Unlike many other successful South African business people he did not build
his fortune on the base of the abundance of the country's precious metals, raw
materials and natural resources as he moved overseas. For this reason Bertie
Levenstein, chairman of Rand Tobacco, regards Rupert as the most brilliant entrepreneur to have come out of South Africa. Despite the fact that he could not
lay claim to any built-in advantage, the Rembrandt Group started excelling internationally as the only successful post-war cigarette company in the world. Peter
Drucker, whom Rupert himself considers the best writer on business he has
encountered, refers to this in his book *Innovation and entrepreneurship*.[1] Rupert was
driven by the firm conviction that 'he who doesn't believe in miracles, is not a
realist' – a motto based on the fund-raising appeal of a Jewish aid organisation
he had read about in an American magazine in the 1950s.

At home his overseas ambitions were frowned upon by Sanlam, his biggest
creditor. Sanlam was not keen that Rembrandt should have overseas interests;
the Rothmans brands on the local market were considered sufficient. Apart from
his lack of enthusiasm about overseas industrial involvement, Dr Tienie Louw of
Sanlam was also dubious about the future of the British economy. Sanlam therefore requested Rupert to sell his assets in England and come home.

Rupert found this 'hard to accept' – he knew that unless his group operated
worldwide, international competitors would swallow up his South African interests. But he agreed, and in January 1954 he and Huberte flew to London in
one of the world's first jet-propelled passenger planes, a BOAC Comet 1. On its
next flight a few days later the plane crashed over the Mediterranean, killing all
on board. The accident was caused by metal fatigue. After it happened twice more
to Rupert that a plane in which he had travelled crashed on its next trip, he and
his wife made it their policy never to fly together if they could help it.

In London he sought an interview with Sir Edward Baron, head of Carreras, the
old, established British company that had wanted to buy Rothmans. The founder,
Jose Joaquim Carreras, had opened a tobacconist in London in 1843 and later

manufactured Craven A cigarettes. Rupert offered Baron the opportunity to market the Rothmans brands Rembrandt had bought: 'I know that you wanted them, you negotiated for them and you are going to need them.' Sitting in his splendid office, Baron heard Rupert out. He turned him down flat: 'I don't need you, Mr Rupert. I've got Dunhill.' When Rupert predicted the demise of the brand within a year, the British businessman became so annoyed that 'he more or less threw me out of his office', Rupert relates.

From London he proceeded to Hamburg to try to arrange a similar deal with Wolfgang Ritter, head of the German tobacco group Martin Brinkmann AG. They talked amiably over drinks at Ritter's home on Lake Bremen till three in the morning, but the German, too, declined. Later he was to describe that decision as the biggest mistake of his career. He wrote that Rupert, whose 'incredible instinct for what the consumer wants' he praised highly, laid the foundation for his international success with Rothmans King Size, which became the biggest Virginian filter-tipped cigarette in the world. Ritter also acknowledged that his wrong decision drove Rupert into the arms of Philipp Reemtsma, who would support him.[2] Once again Rupert had reason to thank providence afterwards. As he puts it, 'You shouldn't always be grateful for what you get. Often you have to be grateful for what you didn't get.'

Rupert's control of Rothmans gave him a foothold in the British market, but more importantly, he now had a brand he could market internationally, a launching pad for the group's expansion.

As entrepreneur, Rupert was also constantly moving, building networks, making contacts and keeping a lookout for opportunities. He is an example of what the famous Tom Peters would later say about successful entrepreneurs: You are MBWAs (Managing by Walking Around).

On his return to London from his first meeting with Reemtsma in Austria he was met by an urgent message from his brother Jan, Rembrandt's production chief, who was on honeymoon abroad with his bride Ina (née Wiid). Jan warned him that one of their rivals might be launching a king-size cigarette with the new, improved cellulose acetate filter called Estron, hailed as the miracle filter and achieving success in the USA in cigarettes like Viceroy and Winston. Rupert realised he would have to move fast if he was to secure the rights to the new product. As at other times in his career when the stakes were high, he thought big, and reacted with incredible speed.

He asked Jan to fly to Tennessee at once and arrange a meeting with Eastman Kodak, the American manufacturers. Jan did the groundwork, but it took two days before Rupert and their youngest brother Koos, who was responsible for international marketing, also arrived to join him in America. Together with the group's marketing expert Patrick O'Neill-Dunne they proceeded to the Kingsport factory for their meeting with Eastman Kodak's top executive, William S Vaughan. The only reason why they were able to secure a meeting with Bill Vaughan was that he had been a Rhodes scholar at Oxford. Presumably he was well disposed towards South Africa where Cecil John Rhodes, founder of the Rhodes scholarship fund, had made his fortune. Nonetheless it took some hard bargaining before the deal was finalised on 28 June 1954. It was Eastman Kodak's first contract with a non-American company.

Rupert was shown the machine that produced the miracle filter. It was a somewhat clumsy affair. Its designer, like Rupert himself, had studied chemistry and the two fell into conversation. The prototype had cost $10 000 to produce. Rupert was horrified. 'Is that what you produce for $10 000? You ought to be ashamed of yourself!' The man admitted that the first experimental effort had been too expensive. With that experience behind him, he said, he could produce a much better machine at half the price. Rupert, who realised how badly his group needed the machine, said 'Done!' and offered him $10 000, enough to build two new machines. The man had no option but to accept. 'If I didn't understand the psychology of the chemist,' Rupert said later, 'we wouldn't have been able to obtain the machine, the only prototype.' In addition, the chemist made a few thousand filter bars for another two million cigarettes that were flown back to South Africa.

Rupert had reached his goal to become the first manufacturer outside the USA with the innovation. 'It gave us a huge edge over our competitors and was one of our best investments ever.'

They had the filters and the machine. But they still needed a brand name for the new product. The previous year, when New York was celebrating its tercentenary, Rupert had read in *The New York Times* about the city's founding father Peter Stuyvesant. The Dutch governor, who established the town then known as New Amsterdam in 1653 (hence a contemporary of Jan van Riebeeck), had a wooden leg, which earned him the nickname Peg-Leg Pete. This was a legendary figure on which to build a legend.

Over dinner at O'Neill-Dunne's home he tried out the name on two rivals, Gruber and Cramer, from P Lorillard Company. At the casual mention the one man was so stunned he dropped his fork, and both said there was something in the name. Rupert immediately phoned his trademark department in Stellenbosch and asked that the name Peter Stuyvesant be registered worldwide.

A few days later he had occasion to phone South Africa again, from the Berkshire Hotel in New York. His group was having a sales conference in Durban. 'Have you registered Peter Stuyvesant?' was his first question. No, came the voice over the transatlantic line, the meeting had decided the name was unpronounceable – nobody would remember it. 'We must think of an easier name, like General Lee.' Rupert hit the roof. 'Lee Foo Yong, I suppose! If that brand name is not registered today you're all fired!'

The worldwide registration of Peter Stuyvesant occurred without further delay, but Rembrandt had almost run the risk of not owning the trademark, which might have been snatched up by competitors. The new brand name that combined novelty with tradition would rapidly become the biggest international brand of all cigarettes in Europe.

The launching of Peter Stuyvesant makes a perfect case study of marketing ingenuity. With the choice of the name, the design of the packet, and the advertising and marketing the aim was 'to create a youthful and dynamic image for a new, young international product at home in the whole world'. Rupert tells that a team of bright young salesmen, with the right appearance and dressed appropriately, were selected to sell the dynamic new product. For maximum effect, each new town and city was invaded by a convoy of panel vans emblazoned with the Peter Stuyvesant packet and the slogan that became world-famous: 'International passport to smoking pleasure.'

The new cigarette was so popular that during the launch in the Netherlands, the vans were besieged in the street by customers begging for stock for their local tobacconist. And the marketing was so effective that the group even received letters from customers wanting to procure the 'international passport'!

Timing played an important role in the success. Rupert's view of business people as 'cats on a hot tin roof' created a spirit of urgency that could inspire miracles. Barely a month after the signing of the contract in America the new product was launched successfully on the Rand (the industrial heartland of South Africa) on 11 August 1954, backed by a massive advertising campaign in various media. At the planning meeting held fourteen days before, Rupert's message had been brief and to the point: 'The question is who is going to be first.' Eighteen years later, in 1972, Rupert observed that, for all the money, technology and factories at their disposal today, they could never achieve what they did in those few hectic weeks in 1954 – 'because necessity is the mother of invention. If one decides something can't be done in a week, it can drag on for a year.'

The factory at Paarl was buzzing. It was a race against time. They had to be first on the market with the new miracle filter. Their competitors must get no inkling: the atmosphere was conspiratorial, the excitement palpable. It was teamwork like never before.

When the first Peter Stuyvesant cigarettes came off the conveyor belt in Paarl, two Rembrandt representatives travelled through the night to deliver them to Rupert, bringing to an end his much-needed holiday in the Kruger National Park.

Initially the factory could not keep up with the demand. Rupert himself helped to pack packets into cartons. 'During the day we worked in Stellenbosch and in the evening we went to Paarl to "catch" cigarettes,' he relates. 'The response of the smoking public was astounding.' Smokers were kept informed by the media of when Stuyvesant would be available in their area, and the cigarettes were snapped up. Within three months sales had rocketed from 100% to 1 364%. Six months later it hit 2 066% and, nine months after the launch, 3 730%. Within just one year it was the most sought-after cigarette in South Africa, with sales having increased by a mind-boggling 4 758%.

Rupert had beaten British American Tobacco (BAT) in the South African race. BAT only managed to release its Rex King Size with the Estron filter on the market in October 1954.

Rupert was extremely proud of the new product's design and on occasion referred to Peter Stuyvesant as the 'elusive Pimpernel' because the cigarette 'reminds me of the well-known and charming young nobleman in Baroness d'Orczy's works who saved so many lives during the French Revolution'.

Temperate in his habits, he himself smoked Peter Stuyvesant Extra Mild (or Dunhill Infinite) – mostly ten to twelve and at the utmost twenty cigarettes a day. The 'myrrh and incense' occupied his hands while pondering his next move, he said, and helped him concentrate during tense interviews. He refused to concede, however, that Peter Stuyvesant was his favourite. 'I never discuss the relative merits of the brands we produce, and in fact I try not to tell my friends which brands belong to us. I want each of the brands to fly under its own merits, which is why we maintain a separate sales staff for each one.'[3]

Soon after the arrival of the first Peter Stuyvesants on the market Rupert sent a carton of the distinctive red, white and blue packets to Reemtsma in Germany. Reemtsma, accustomed to quick action, found the packaging amazing and congratulated Rupert in a cablegram: 'Muster Stuyvesant angekommen stop Filter Mischung und Packung volkommen in Ordnung stop Meine Glück wünsche.' This was followed by a letter in which he declared that nothing about the packet could be improved upon. He had had the cigarettes thoroughly tested by his own experts, including his brother Hermann, and the quality was excellent. He commented as follows on the impressive packaging:

'You were wise not to use just the surname Stuyvesant but also the first name; it gives the product a far more personal character. White packets are highly problematic, since they can create an impression of coldness if not accompanied by warm colours. That is exactly what you have done here. The gold on the packet, which sometimes looks heavy, is used very subtly. You neatly circumvented the danger of black by using a paler shade that looks more like olive green. The asymmetrical red stripe running halfway round the packet creates a sense of quality and unique distinctiveness that I have never seen in any other packaging. This asymmetry imparts a dynamic vitality to the packet and a self-assured image, suggesting that this is an established brand and its manufacturer is definitely a company of stature.' [Our translation.][4]

Impressed as he was with Peter Stuyvesant, Reemtsma remained sceptical about the future of filter tips in Germany. On account of increased competition he made various attempts to subdivide existing brands; in Rupert's views attempts that would not succeed, even though they were based on the accepted rules of the old 'Markentechnik' (the German marketing technique). 'The consumer apparently regarded each brand as a separate personality, hence there was a strong need for new brands. The rest of the pre-war brands were practically dead and exhausted.'

The new cigarette was soon introduced successfully in South Africa, the United Kingdom, Belgium, the Netherlands, Australia and elsewhere.

The year 1954 in which they ventured on the purchase of Rothmans was also the year in which the Rembrandt Group took on the world market in earnest. By 1955 Rembrandt South Africa had a capital base of £1 000 000, while that of Rembrandt Beherende Beleggings was £750 000. In the same year Rothmans of Pall Mall was established in Australia. After initial losses Rothmans also started showing good results in Canada, with the first profit declared in 1960. Rothmans Canada operated with a very strong board after Rock City Tobacco Corporation had been sold to Rothmans in the Carreras deal. Rock City's chairman was Louis Saint-Laurent, former prime minister of Canada, who was succeeded in the election of 1957 by John Diefenbaker, the Canadian leader who would agitate against South Africa's continued membership of the Commonwealth a few years later.

When looking for a Canadian chairman for Rothmans Canada, Rupert was advised that no one was better suited for the job than Saint-Laurent. With his help Rupert appointed as directors the kind of distinguished people on whom he felt he could depend. One was Charles Massey, chairman of Lever Brothers, of whose Toronto family it was said that there were only two families in that city: 'The Masseys and the masses.' Another was Robert H (Bob) Winters, president of Rio Tinto Mining Company and a later minister of trade and industry, who subsequently only just lost out to premier Pierre Trudeau for leadership of the Liberal Party of Canada. Also on the board was a confidant of Rupert's who provided important international contacts and advice, the British war hero Sir Francis de Guingand, who would become chairman of the South Africa Foundation.

Rothmans Canada turned into a profitable success story, like the South African operations, while the other overseas companies also started doing well. Rupert's expansion abroad was stimulated by his experience in South Africa, where Rothmans – the 'English' cigarette – had the highest sales in the Afrikaans-speaking Free State, while Rembrandt – the 'Afrikaans' cigarette – sold best in Natal, often described as the 'last outpost of the British Empire'. It convinced Rupert that patriotism counted for nothing when somebody took money from his pocket, and that he could fare as well internationally as at home, while simultaneously countering a possible local price war.

With time, it became evident that Rupert was achieving higher profits overseas than on the home front.

Everywhere Rupert stuck to his policy of working through partnerships. Rembrandt's overseas investments took on a particular pattern. First, the best possible local partners were found and a new company established. In the initial phase and with the launching, advice and assistance were given from South Africa on an ongoing basis. Rembrandt would revitalise the new acquisition. Through cost-cutting and an emphasis on marketing and advertising the business would take off on its own steam. After the local partners had been trained and empowered, however, the Rembrandt Group moved into the background.

The United States was a case in point. Here Rupert obtained a foothold in the market through two small companies: Riggio Tobacco on Long Island in New York and, later, Larus Brothers in Richmond, Virginia, that concentrated on pipe tobacco. In 1954 Riggio was struggling. Rupert summoned Kotie Naudé, who headed his operations in the USA, and Paul Erasmus, then in charge of finance, to his Manhattan hotel. Erasmus, who would later succeed Hoogenhout as the financial head of the whole group and also become a director, relates that this was his first personal encounter with Rupert. When Rupert asked him if they had $22 000 to buy out Frank Riggio's shares, he confessed somewhat sheepishly that their bank balance stood at $3 000. Rupert was flabbergasted: 'How do you run your affairs?' he wanted to know. Naudé had to take the young Erasmus aside and whisper to him that one does not actually say 'No' to Anton Rupert.

From Rupert's bedroom, Erasmus phoned the vice president of finance of Universal Leaf Tobacco, the group's tobacco leaf-supplier in Richmond. He explained that he had to ask a favour: Rupert urgently needed $22 000 to take over Riggio. The financial officer asked Erasmus to hold on while he consulted the tobacco baron Herbert W Jackson Jr, president of Universal. When he returned, he said: 'Mr Erasmus, Mr Jackson is very impressed by your Mr Rupert. That young man is going places.'

The Americans, who by that time had got to know Rupert well, were especially impressed by his knowledge of the American Civil War. 'He knows more about it than we do,' they once told Erasmus. The good impression Universal Leaf's bosses had of Rupert had its origin in an unannounced visit he had paid the company one Friday afternoon in 1954, when he met Jackson Jr and the chief executive officer, Gordon J Crenshaw, for the first time. 'He said he intended to grow his company into a much larger one and to go into many other countries, and he would like to give us all his business,' Crenshaw related. 'Mr Jackson and I looked at each other and thought that it was likely that we were being offered 100% of virtually nothing.'

In retrospect, however, Universal Leaf Tobacco considered Rupert's arrival one of the most important events in the company's history. At first tentatively and then more and more extensively, Universal helped finance Rupert's needs as he expanded internationally and became one of the world's biggest cigarette manufacturers. A book on the American company's history refers to the relationship as follows: 'A man with a keen sense of loyalty to those who aided him along the way, he still gives public recognition to Universal (for whom he remains a key customer) for being willing to listen and then make a commitment to him on that Friday afternoon in 1954.'[5]

When Erasmus rejoined Rupert and Naudé after his successful phone call to Universal, he was congratulated on securing the money. Rupert put his hand on Erasmus's shoulder as they left to go and have a meal: 'You know, Mr Erasmus, the best training school for an accountant is poverty!'[6]

The money was transferred to Chemical Bank in New York on the same day, and Rupert could take over Riggio. They had to close down the factory a year later, however, though Rembrandt continued to market the Lexington brand successfully in South Africa.

Erasmus discovered that Rupert shared his interest in music and the arts and in time they became close friends. What often struck him about Rupert was his unflagging energy, one of his most distinctive characteristics. He could carry on working and concentrating for hours on end and even get up early on Saturdays and walk till late afternoon through the streets of cities like London, Rome and New York, keenly interested in exhibitions and window displays, always on the lookout for innovations and new developments in the industries in which he was involved. And then he could still attend concert performances at night.

Rupert prided himself on not having missed a single day's lessons throughout his school career. Although he was never an athlete or a sportsman, he enjoyed excellent health despite the gruelling pace of his business activities that was not conducive to a balanced lifestyle – he often described aeroplanes as 'flying hospitals'. But, as he himself pointed out in his book *Leiers oor leierskap*, health and physique are not preconditions for achievement. 'A great mind can control a weak body. Roosevelt was a cripple, Julius Caesar an epileptic, and Napoleon had ulcers. Fat or thin is also of no consequence, because Bismarck was obese, Gandhi skin and bone. And yet they all had boundless energy.'

In 1958 Philipp Reemtsma visited South Africa and signed an agreement to market Peter Stuyvesant in Germany. 'Peter Stuyvesant gave us the wings of Mercury and my men sold it across the world,' says Rupert. 'The airline labels on our briefcases not only reflected the spirit of movement, but also became the personification of our theme: "International passport to travelling pleasure".' On his South African visit Reemtsma also had a good look at Rembrandt's advertising and noted the success of the 'international passport' slogan.

Before the launch of the brand in Germany at the beginning of 1959, Rupert made a thorough study of the post-war market. Apart from the preference for new brands, he identified three motives that were inherent in the 'German character': *Heimweh* (nostalgia for home), *Lebenschmerz* (lit. 'existential sorrow', melancholy) and *Fernweh* (longing for faraway places). Whereas the Peter Stuyvesant brand, with its cosmopolitan image, would clearly not appeal to *Heimweh*, it played right into the hands of *Fernweh*. Rupert emphasises that Stuyvesant's theme radiated 'joy of living', something similar to the old motto *Kraft durch Freude* (Power through Joy).[7]

The German campaign linked the notion of pleasure with international travel. It was enthusiastically promoted by Fritz Bühler, a marketing expert from Basle appointed by Reemtsma to design a dynamic German version of the 'international passport' theme. He encapsulated it in the slogan *'Der Duft der grossen weiten Welt'* (The aroma of the great wide world). It was dead right for Germany. Here was a nation hemmed in by other countries on all sides, with only a short coastline in the north. For their holidays they poured across their borders. 'As an escape from unpleasant wartime memories and the unpleasant past, Peter Stuyvesant conveyed to young and old the idea of easily achievable affluence and hope beyond their borders,' relates Rupert. Aeroplanes became a regular feature of Stuyvesant ads at a time when air travel was little more than a dream to impoverished Germans.

Other factors also helped to strengthen the campaign, like the new, distinctive and youthful image of the packet. Modern media like radio, television and the cinema were used for the first time. For the first time since the war march music was used in German advertising: the *Sportsmaster* tune became a hit. Panel vans painted with the logo were used by sales people whose appearance matched the brand.

The new cigarette eventually made history in the field of German brands. A long-time associate of Reemtsma, the marketing expert Hans Domizlaff, architect of Markentechnik, a focus on pre-war brands, had to admit: 'It's beyond my comprehension.' Rupert explains that the older marketing experts were not enthusiastic about Peter Stuyvesant's phenomenal growth rate – it was generally accepted that a fast-growing brand would also fade quickly. In his view, the 'philosophy' of the brand was such that it was planned from the first day to remain youthful and attractive to young and old. He has been told, in Germany and elsewhere, that Peter Stuyvesant confounded the expectations of many marketing experts and that the phrase 'like Peter Stuyvesant' often cropped up in marketing meetings. An important prerequisite for the brand's success had been the fact that it was based on a sound marketing decision – giving the Germans something that appealed to them specifically. 'But in the final analysis – even more important than advertising – success depends on giving value for money through constant quality control. A good product benefits from a brand and advertising; for a poor product, it can mean "sudden death".'

Rupert's passion for brands and marketing techniques has benefited from his keen eye for colour and composition. Ever since his boyhood visit to his uncle Fred Knoetze's newspaper in Somerset East he had been interested in printing and colour. He actually made a careful study of colours, their qualities and effects. According to Hans Knoetze, public relations officer of the Rembrandt Group, Rupert's exceptional feel for colours and textiles is reflected in the great quantity of ties and the metres of material for tailor-made suits he bought to share with people as gifts. Knoetze relates that on birthdays, people would often be called in by Rupert to choose a tie from an amazing collection. 'But you weren't supposed to take too long to choose; with his marketing instinct, he expected you to know instantly what you liked!'[8]

In 1959, a year after Peter Stuyvesant was launched in Germany, Philipp Reemtsma died. Rupert flew to Hamburg to visit him on his deathbed. He considered Reemtsma his 'third father', as Dr Stals had been a 'second father' – besides his own parents, the two older men had had a profound influence on his life and thought. At the hospital he was refused admission to the sickroom. He suspected Reemtsma's wife Gertrud was behind it.

During his lifetime Reemtsma had exacted three promises from his 'adoptive son': Rupert was to take over his business, groom his nephew Hermann Hinrich to run it, and see to it that his own young son Jan Philipp went to a Swiss boarding school. Immediately after her husband's death Gertrud Reemtsma called a directors' meeting from which Rupert, waiting at the door, was excluded. When summoned at last, he was told that the group would continue without him. He offered to market their brands, but that, too, was refused. Leaving, Rupert declared in that case he could do nothing more for them. One man who tried in vain to have the decision reversed was Hans Domizlaff, the marketing expert who had helped Reemtsma to develop some of the most successful German cigarette brands and who had come to know Rupert well.[9]

Rupert was deeply disappointed by the decision, as an interest in Reemtsma would have made his group the second largest tobacco group in the world. He was also prevented from keeping any of his promises to his old friend.

Gertrud Reemtsma continued with the business until Reemtsma's surviving son, Jan Philipp, who was more interested in academia, persuaded her to sell most of the family shares to the coffee company Tchibo. The young Reemtsma, who used his fortune to finance left-wing institutions, was kidnapped in 1996 and released after 33 days for a ransom of 15 million euros.

CHAPTER 10

Women at the helm

With his innovative thinking that often prompted him to break new ground, Rupert was already at an early stage in his career keen that women should be involved in the economy. His notion of female participation, at a time that the male-dominated business world still disapproved of women following professional careers, let alone occupying executive positions, led to a far-reaching innovation in 1955: the establishment of the first South African company owned and set up entirely by women.

The company, *Eerste Nasionale Tee- en Koffiefabrieke Beperk* (First National Tea and Coffee Factories Limited, or Entek), was controlled from the outset by a female board – a quarter of a century after white women in South Africa got the vote in 1930, fifteen years before the women's liberation movement of the 1970s led by activists such as Germaine Greer campaigned for equal rights for women in all spheres of life, and more than 40 years before gender equality became a matter of course in South Africa's transition to a full-fledged democracy in the 1990s.

Women's rights were not high on the agenda in South Africa in the 1950s. Yet a company run by women was not such a foreign idea to a man whose wife could justifiably be regarded as the first company secretary of the Rembrandt Group; also a woman who would have managed his first enterprise Chemiese Reinigers had it not been sold. He had no doubts about women's ability.

With his intense interest in the consumer market, Rupert recognised that women mostly did the household shopping. They bought the family's food, clothing, linen, furniture and crockery. As the most important purchasers and consumers, women also needed to take their rightful place in manufacturing and marketing, he believed.

He approached two friends of his, first Mrs Hobbie le Roux of Oudtshoorn and later Mrs René Morkel of Stellenbosch, and suggested they launch a tea and coffee factory. They would receive the same treatment as all his business partners. He would show them the ropes, give them his support. But it would be *their* baby.

That was how Entek was born. Share capital of £1 million was raised. Each shareholder had to buy at least £100 worth of shares and she had to be a woman: men could only buy shares in their wives' names. The company was floated with 1 362 shareholders, all resident in South Africa and what is now Namibia and all of them female – either individuals or women's organisations. The only exception was Rembrandt Tabakkorporasie, which contributed the £50 000 needed to buy out *Holland-Afrika Koffiemaatskappy* and Ceylon Tea Packers. Entek was registered in Pretoria and on 22 April 1955 it was incorporated into the Rembrandt Group.

Rupert, who had succeeded Dr Diederichs as chairman of Rembrandt in 1955 after the later state president retired on pension from the board, personally sent a circular to all Rembrandt shareholders in which he suggested that there might be 'spouses of shareholders who would also like to have the distinction of being founders of this first Afrikaans Women's Company'. He added that he had already done so for his wife.

The first chairwoman of the board was Mrs Emily Hobhouse (Hobbie) le Roux, who also gained renown as a vivacious but formidable political wife. Rupert had met Hobbie and her husband PMK le Roux (commonly known as PK), who became an MP in the election of 1948 and later chief whip of the National Party, when he arrived at their farm Doornkraal in the Oudtshoorn district to sell shares in the early 1940s. She was named after Emily Hobhouse, the British campaigner for women's rights who became a Boer heroine as a result of her concern for the suffering experienced in concentration camps during the Anglo-Boer War. When Emily Hobhouse's ashes were brought to South Africa after her death and reburied at the Women's Monument in Bloemfontein, Hobbie was one of the bearers of the casket.

She was frank about her limited business experience: 'As a young farmer's wife I ran a shop and a butchery on our farm Doornkraal for about six years. That's all.' At the party to celebrate the floating of Entek the toastmaster presented her with an ashtray inscribed with the words *'Het weer en de vrouwen/zijn niet te vertrouwen'* (Weather and women are not to be trusted).[1] She kept it like a trophy on her dressing table, joking that it was a 'treasure'. Hobbie and the vice chairwoman René Morkel both attended one of Rembrandt's training courses for new appointees. Between them they organised the campaign to canvass shareholders countrywide. They reached the £10 000 mark with £100 shares, then organised a competition that secured a further 13 061 female holders of ordinary shares of £5 and more.

Hobbie le Roux resigned from the board in 1958 when her husband became minister of agriculture. She was succeeded as chairwoman by René Morkel, whose husband PK Morkel, chairman of the board of the Stellenbosse Distriksbank, had also been a Springbok and Western Province rugby player. The other members of the first board, all active members of women's organisations personally asked by Rupert to represent the seven regions of the country, were Mrs Tibbie Visser, daughter of Pres. MT Steyn of the Orange Free State; Mrs Blackie Bosman of Pretoria, wife of JJ (Bossie) Bosman, one of the founders of Volkskas bank in 1935; Mrs Lottie Botha of Durban; Mrs Kitty de Villiers from the Eastern Transvaal, and Mrs Mossie Grobler from the Eastern Cape.

The first board meeting was held in the Rembrandt building in Paarl on 7 December 1955. The public relations officer and company secretary, Margot van der Walt, became more widely known in public life after her marriage to Genl. Magnus Malan, later minister of defence.

Rupert was as good as his word: he helped nurse the new company till it could stand on its own feet. The connection with his business philosophy was evident in its very motto, 'Quality First'. One of the company's first moves, with the help of Rembrandt's international contacts and technical expertise, was to send a chemist to Ceylon (now Sri Lanka), the source of their tea, to ensure that they obtained the cream of the crop. The June 1955 issue of Rembrandt's trade journal *Tegniek* was a special women's edition to publicise the new venture. It carried Hobbie's face on the cover and an article describing the achievements of the two oldest women's organisations in the country, the *Afrikaanse Christelike Vrouevereniging* (Afrikaans Christian Women's Association, ACVV) and the *Suid-Afrikaanse Vrouefederasie* (South African Women's Federation, SAVF), both founded in 1904.[2]

In an editorial, *Tegniek* paid tribute to 'the contribution women had made to the development and prosperity of our country', particularly on the terrain of welfare and culture. 'The establishment of Eerste Nasionale Tee- en Koffiefabrieke is symbolic of women's entry into a new area – the important economic terrain.' The editorial applauded the debut of women – who spent the greater part of the national revenue – in the manufacture and marketing of the products they bought.

Another leaf taken from Rembrandt's book was a massive advertising campaign, both in the press and elsewhere. Mobile cafeterias that sold tea and coffee at agricultural shows helped introduce their products. The women's company's first products were Braganza Tea, Tendertee Tips and Senator Coffee, later followed by Frisco instant coffee. According to René Morkel, the names mainly came from Rupert. He proposed Braganza for the tea, recalling the Portuguese princess Catharina da Braganza who had married Charles II of England in 1662 and popularised tea at the royal court and in the West. The label on the packet depicted her presenting the king with a chest of tea. This was a typical Rupert touch: a product had to have a 'personality and an address', and be linked to a story sales people could tell. It was also Rupert who came up with the name for the ground coffee. 'When you think of coffee, what springs to mind?' he asked Entek's directors. 'I think of a bearded old man in a leather armchair puffing at his pipe and drinking coffee!' Thus the name Senator was born. The name Frisco for their instant coffee also held great appeal for consumers. 'The name itself evokes the impression of something quick, don't you agree?' René Morkel said in an interview with an English magazine that published a highly positive article about the origins of the women's company a quarter of a century later.[3]

In the starting years, a boycott on the part of those people with anti-Afrikaans sentiments who claimed that the company was 'sectionalist' resulted in Entek's products not being available in all shops.

In October 1955 the business journal *Africa X-Ray Report* published a belligerent article by George Clay, a journalist from the *Cape Times*, maintaining that the advent of Senator represented an onslaught on commerce and industry by 'Afrikaner capital'.

'The company ... was to be an "all-women" venture, with Mrs Emily Hobhouse le Roux, "go-getter" socialite wife of the Nationalist Government Chief Whip, as its chairman. Old-established coffee merchants were staggered at the new company's exploitation of aggressive Afrikaner-Nationalist sentiment in the naming of its product.

'But they were more worried by the suspicion that behind this "all-women" enterprise was the keen business brain and administrative genius of Anton Rupert, youthful (39 on 4 October) managing director of the phenomenally successful Rembrandt organisation which in a few years has all but overcome all opposition in the South African cigarette field and has given the long-established liquor marketers a severe fright.'[4]

Clay concluded his article with a dig at Rupert: 'In the first phase the [Afrikaner Nationalist capitalist] movement concentrated on building up its power through purely financial institutions, rather than through big combines. Hence the growth of Sanlam, Santam, Saambou, Federale Volksbeleggings and all the other related insurance, finance and investment companies.

'But in the last five years a new trend has developed. The Afrikaner-Nationalist economic movement is now operating more and more in the industrial and commercial field. And the spearhead of this new drive is the remarkable Rembrandt organisation.'

It was the kind of crude propaganda that left Rupert outraged, especially as he had discovered early in his career that Afrikaans consumers paid little attention to appeals to national sentiment, the National Party had obstructed rather than supported his endeavours, and he had already started expanding internationally.

Tegniek frequently criticised this type of rumour-mongering and boycott appeals. René Morkel took up the cudgels in *Tegniek* on behalf of the chairwoman, whose worst sin appeared to be her connection by marriage to an Afrikaner politician. In an open letter to all boycotters she went on the attack. Since when, she asked, can politicians not be business people, and vice versa? She cited a string of English-speaking parliamentarians who were active in or controlled large companies, among them FC Sturrock, R Stuttaford, JW Mushet, SF (Sydney) Waterson and Harry Oppenheimer. 'Were these firms ever boycotted by Nationalists? And even the family of the chairwoman of the Black Sash controls a big tea and coffee group. Is it not time to stop this nonsensical boycott talk? We have large numbers of shareholders from all groups in South Africa and are in fact true South Africans.' *Tegniek* kept up the pressure. In a later issue, it wrote about the negative and impermissible methods of 'anti-Dutch' competitors who could not hold on to their markets. It pointed out that the enlightened South African public was not fooled: ultimately it bought products according to criteria of quality and price. For this reason boycott movements were doomed to failure.[5]

But the whispering campaign continued. *Tegniek* published details of a political speech by a United party MP, Col. RD Pilkington Jordan, in which he launched a vitriolic attack on Afrikaans businesses. He claimed that all 'purely' Afrikaans companies were under Nationalist control and sectionalist, without any regard for South Africa's true interests. Nationalist Afrikaners were also boycotting non-Afrikaans businesses with 'Hitlerite Germanic thoroughness', he alleged. 'A scheme of this magnitude would have made Captain Boycott's hair stand on end.' Col. Jordan referred sarcastically to the name of an English princess being chosen for Braganza – 'I should have thought that among Nationalists the name of an Afrikaner heroine would have been preferable. I hope, however, that it will sell under its noble title.' [6]

Tegniek responded in an editorial that they had always expressed their opposition to any form of boycott. 'How baseless Col. Jordan's statements are, is also borne out by the fact that a prominent businessman and ex-minister, Mr SF Waterson, declared in an interview with *Tegniek* that he had no knowledge of any boycott by Afrikaners against the enterprises in which he had interests.' The journal also reported that Braganza was now the third best seller among some twenty brands of tea on the South African market despite a boycott movement against Afrikaans businesses, of which they cited several examples. The same issue contained the first of a series of articles on leading English-speaking business people 'to show Afrikaner boys and young men what opportunities existed in South Africa'.

In London, a Bond Street gathering place for homesick South Africans was called Braganza Rendezvous, which belied the allegations of sectionalism. It was started in 1955 by Miems Botha, previously public relations officer of the KWV, whose husband was an attaché at the South African embassy. Nevertheless, the propaganda against Braganza, such as persistent rumours that it was more expensive than other teas, continued for several years. At one stage the company was obliged to run an advertising campaign, also in the English press, to refute diverse allegations that were doing the rounds.

In the early years of Entek, Hertzog was somewhat pessimistic about the new company. He wrote in his memoirs on 23 December 1955 that he was 'ostensibly the "chief adviser" of this women's company', of which his daughter Erna (later Mrs Paul Meaker) was the youngest founding member at three months old. The differences he had with Rupert, 'the real chief adviser', about the prospects of the company were to him also illustrative of their differences in temperament and ways of dealing with staff. 'Anton likes to reprimand, but he seldom fires people. I fire easily but detest scolding or punishing.' Hertzog wanted something to succeed quickly and easily, which made him impatient about waiting for Entek to show results, in contrast to Rupert's long-term approach. 'Anton is a miler and I'm a sprinter. He believes in persistence and "never say die", against my "hope deferred sickeneth the heart".' To Hertzog, 'effectiveness is a maximum result achieved with minimum exertion.' He also hinted that he would have to leave sometime 'without fighting back', as the mental tension inherent in their different temperaments made it inevitable.[7]

Hertzog's evaluation of their different approaches to dealing with staff was correct, just as he described Rupert's long-term approach accurately. Rupert indeed did not like firing people but rather shifted them to other posts. In the few cases where dismissals were unavoidable, he usually left it to others. One of his top executives knows of only one employee who was dismissed by Rupert himself. He also often overlooked mistakes and forgave people. According to his assistant of many years, Jan Groeneveld, he said people were like diamonds; everyone had a shiny facet, it only needed to be polished. It struck Groeneveld that many of the achievers in the group were under-qualified in terms of current norms. They were fully motivated, however, by a man who trusted them unconditionally and believed in their abilities. Groeneveld describes Rupert as someone without any rough aspects. 'Always correct, always courteous, always humble and never familiar. He is a demanding person, never difficult, but don't walk into his office if you haven't prepared your case properly beforehand.'[8]

Yet he could rebuke employees thoroughly. Johann Rupert relates that staff members were often given a dressing-down in an office referred to as the 'thunder room'. In one such case excise duty had been calculated incorrectly, and Rupert severely reprimanded those concerned whom 'he had been teaching how to do it for twenty years'. At the same time he did not like public confrontations, least of all with other Rembrandt people.[9]

The temperamental differences between Hertzog and Rupert never resulted in a break-up. Mutual loyalty predominated in a partnership that stretched over decades. In Stellenbosch they had offices in different buildings for many years – with the joint move to Rembrandt International's building in Alexander Street, the two partners' offices were situated far apart. Hertzog's son Dr Edwin Hertzog commented as follows on these arrangements: 'This is how I had grown up. My father and Dr Rupert were in separate buildings and made appointments to see each other.' [10] Some Rembrandt people hold the view that a part of the group's success could be ascribed to the fact that Rupert and Hertzog 'kept out of each other's way'. Hertzog concentrated mainly on the liquor trade and dealt with the legal aspects of trademarks from his office.

Hertzog, who complained in the early years because Entek, like Distillers, was not growing as quickly as Rembrandt, was also correct in his view that coffee and tea would not show such quick profits as tobacco did. Distillers started progressing after ten years, but was even then 'not yet right', in his words. In the case of Entek, Rupert's long-term view was proved right. Despite boycotts, rumour-mongering and fluctuations in the tea and coffee market during the 1960s, the company became a success. Braganza in particular was popular. In 1960 the company registered its first profit. René Morkel pointed out that this was achieved in the face of fierce competition within a very short period.

Instant coffee and teabags were unknown in the 1950s. Braganza was sold in elegant tins until 1967, when bags were introduced. Five years earlier Entek had launched Frisco coffee powder, a sophisticated product that was an instant hit and saved the company. By the end of 1962 it showed a consolidated net profit of R85 338 and accumulated consolidated profits of R216 916.[11]

In 1983 Entek's brands were sold to Brooke Bond for R3 million. The proceeds were invested profitably in apartment blocks in Stellenbosch and shares in other companies. In 1987 the company became *Entek Beleggings Beperk* (Entec Investments Limited). With the restructuring of the Rembrandt Group in September 2000 it became a subsidiary of Eikenlust (Pty) Ltd, which is in turn a wholly owned subsidiary of Remgro Limited. But in 2002, under the new name and with a totally different field of operation, its three directors as well as the company secretary were still women.

Rupert's pioneering idea predated similar all-women ventures by many years. Wiphold (Women's Investment Portfolio Holdings), an investment consortium controlled by women to create wealth for women, was established in 1994. The Women's Private Equity Fund 1, the first South African fund of its kind catering exclusively for women, was launched in 2003, the brainchild of the entrepreneur

Wendy Luhabe, one of the founders of Wiphold.[12] Luhabe, wife of Gauteng premier Mbhazima Shilowa, had been appointed by Rupert in her first job. A year after she had obtained her BCom degree at the University of Lesotho, he offered her a position in Vanda Cosmetics, a company his group had just taken over. 'To this day I owe a debt of gratitude to Anton Rupert that he noticed my abilities and afforded me the opportunity to work with him,' says Luhabe, in her own right one of the ten wealthiest black South Africans.[13]

Rupert's faith in the economic potential of women never diminished. A solution he has proposed for Africa's food problems is to transform communal land ownership – one of the greatest stumbling-blocks to sustainable economic growth – by allocating land to female farmers on leasehold. His experience at the Small Business Development Corporation taught him that women's creditworthiness far exceeded that of their male counterparts. He also foresaw a major role for women in tourism, a sector that provides employment to thousands. In this regard he likes to refer to one of his initiatives, the Southern African College for Tourism in Graaff-Reinet. The main focus of this college, a Peace Parks Foundation project, is to train black women as managers and proprietors of guesthouses to deal with the envisaged increased tourist numbers in southern African nature reserves. The training is hands-on, conducted in a guesthouse purchased specially by Rupert for this purpose. The college, which was officially opened by South Africa's first lady, Zanele Mbeki, and Huberte Rupert in 2002, addresses client service standards in cooperation with the Southern African Wildlife College at Hoedspruit.

In its first year the SA Tourism College received applications from around 500 prospective students. By 2004 word had spread all over southern Africa, with students from Zambia, Zimbabwe, Swaziland, Mozambique, Malawi, Lesotho and Botswana being trained in Graaff-Reinet.

'Men cannot manage guesthouses. I can't even manage my own home!' Rupert said in 2002 when addressing the culture board of the FAK.[14] 'It is something women do excellently. Women could be the salvation of Africa.'

CHAPTER 11

Across the globe

T he phenomenal success of Peter Stuyvesant helped Rupert to lay the foundations of a business empire that would stretch across the globe. An important development at the end of the 1950s involved the British cigarette company Carreras, which had been outmanoeuvred by Rembrandt when they bought Rothmans.

Carreras, with assets of £26 million, was at that stage effectively in the hands of the Baron family. The Barons controlled 39% of Carreras's shares and all votes at board meetings. Established in 1843, it was the kind of company with a rich tradition in which Rupert was always interested. Russian-born Bernhard Baron had joined Carreras in 1880 and introduced the first cigarette-manufacturing machine in England. Carreras was known for the celebrated Craven mixture, specially made for the Count of Cradock, and produced a popular tobacco with the nostalgic name Arcadia, also the name of their London factory. In 1928 it started operating from a new, air-conditioned factory, the first of its kind in the history of the industry. In 1953 Carreras took over other established tobacco companies with famous brand names.

In 1958 an opportunity arose for Rembrandt to obtain an interest in Carreras.

Rupert first paid a visit to Philipp Reemtsma in Germany to ask advice and enlist his support. Then he went to England to start talks with Sir Edward Baron. He secured the backing of a later faithful ally, the financier Edmund de Rothschild, who knew the Barons well and worked on them to sell their shares and special voting rights to Rembrandt. De Rothschild told the family members with voting rights that Rupert was 'an honourable man who would look after the interests of the employees'. According to him one of the family members was undecided, and 'a certain degree of diplomacy' was necessary to convince him to part with his interests.

Meanwhile Rupert and his companion, Daan Hoogenhout, 'sat chewing our nails' for three weeks in the Westbury Hotel. Talks with Sir Edward were not easy. He was deaf and, according to Rupert, switched off his hearing aid when he did not want to hear well. At last, in November 1958, the deal was clinched. The Barons sold three percent of Carreras B shares and their family votes to the Rembrandt Group for £1 250 000. Then a new obstacle cropped up: the South African government refused Rupert permission to take the money for the deal abroad. The German tobacco brothers Philipp and Hermann Reemtsma saved the day by advancing the sum. Rupert promptly sold Carreras's head office for three times the price of the B shares.

Huberte used the example of the Carreras deal when she told the journalist Rykie van Reenen how Rupert always discussed his major undertakings with her. 'People often ask me if he's not worried about a momentous and risky step he has taken. But he always says: it's not the time to worry once you've made your decision. You must do your worrying beforehand. Once you've taken your decision, you must just push on!'[1]

After signing the contract in De Rothschild's London office, Baron pulled Rupert aside at a window. 'Mr Rupert, tell me, why did you predict Dunhill's demise in 1954?' Rupert's explanation was brief and to the point: they were marketing untipped cigarettes in a filter era; and they underestimated the two leading British brands, Players and Senior Service, which, though in short supply, could push Dunhill off the market. 'You chose the wrong road and you pushed the wrong product. Your timing was out.'

Then Baron wanted to know why it took Rupert and his associates as long as three weeks to come to a final decision. Rupert told him he had been watching the phenomenal success of a new Carreras product, a short and less expensive filter cigarette called Guards, on the streets of London. By the end of the year, he said, Guards sales would have hit 200 million per month. 'What!' the British magnate exclaimed. 'If I'd known that, I'd never have sold my shares!'

The British press was astounded by Rupert's success. *The Times* of London described his company as 'a progressive cigarette-manufacturing organisation with new blood and new ideas and which already has worldwide experience in marketing and manufacturing'. When Rupert was asked by the British press about the reasons for his success, he responded as follows, according to the *Cape and Transvaal Printers' Book*: 'Use the best machinery you can buy. Keep a close watch on every form of waste. Advertise to ensure good sales, which cuts down the costs of distribution and advertising on every packet of cigarettes sold. Spend money on research to give your customers the best value for money. Get there before the other fellow.'[2]

Other British media were less flattering. Dirk Hertzog commented wryly in his memoirs on the reaction of some papers to the takeover of Carreras: 'Now the English Press is complaining of the "cavalier treatment" of "non-voting shareholders who contributed more than £7 million". Scoundrels! When an English family was in control – and the business was going downhill – everything was hunky-dory. Now that we, who have already put Rothmans right, are taking over, there are complaints. British may be masters over Boer, but not a Boer over British – that's the real reason for the hypocritical "misgivings".'[3]

In South Africa, too, Rupert's overseas ventures were viewed with suspicion. By this time he had come to the conclusion that the country's salvation in general and Afrikaners' salvation in particular lay in coexistence, not racial segregation. He was giving practical expression to this conviction through his philosophy of shared advancement and industrial partnership. This was one of the reasons why Rupert was not particularly popular in nationalistic Afrikaner circles. Hans van Rensburg, an Afrikaner hothead and at one stage leader of the extremist Ossewa-Brandwag, once said to Hertzog: 'Why are you people going overseas?' It was a loaded, even accusatory, question, not meant to obtain information. Van Rensburg was speaking on behalf of many Afrikaners who believed that Rupert should concentrate only on South Africa, and specifically on Afrikaners. An Afrikaans company that spread its wings to other countries was considered by many to be unpatriotic.

But Rupert, while as patriotic as any of his opponents, wanted to prove that he could also succeed in foreign countries. An ethnically captive business was not his idea of sound business principles, much less an economy that remained dammed up within an Afrikaner laager. In contrast to many South African companies that were strongly directed inwards, Rupert started reaching out across language, cultural and national boundaries from early on.

He also did not hesitate to speak his mind overseas. Addressing a share-holders' meeting in London early in 1959, the new 42-year-old chairman of Carreras bluntly pointed out the mismanagement of the company before the takeover. 'My first impressions of the business were that many things are not too well done,' he said. Its cost structure compared unfavourably with Rembrandt-Rothmans's. His impressions were confirmed by subsequent visits of his technical advisers. There were 'major defects' in the organisation: lack of sales strength, mainly due to lack of sufficient research, proper planning and packaging; expensive super-structure; outmoded machinery and plant; and a new factory far too large for modern manufacturing conditions. All this would have to be set right. 'It is going to take a considerable time to clear the decks.' The shareholders cheered when he announced plans to sell off various assets and to amalgamate the group's British and Canadian operations.

The previous chairman, Sir Edward Baron, was in New York, but other direc-tors, including Paul and Theodore Baron, listened grimly. When Rupert proposed that the Barons be re-elected as directors, a shareholder asked why these directors who had failed them so badly in the past should be approved. Rupert ruled the objection out of order: shareholders, having no votes, had no say in the appoint-ment of directors, he said.[4] He remained true to his philosophy of partnership.

Carreras's London factory was closed down and Carreras, with Rothmans, moved to ultramodern new premises at Basildon in Essex. The new complex was opened on 4 March 1960 by Prince Philip, who became a close friend of Rupert with whom he shared an interest in wildlife and game conservation.

Through Carreras, Rupert eventually also acquired control of the old, established Dunhill. This well-known company, established in London in 1893 by the remarkable entrepreneur Alfred Dunhill, gave him access to the attractive luxury goods market, which would become one of his group's major assets. Dunhill was the kind of distinguished brand Rupert valued highly: it could be protected and was depression proof. Using all his marketing expertise, Rupert promoted Dunhill enthusiastically, although it had failed in the hands of Canadians and later also under the control of Philip Morris. Carreras under the leadership of Sir Edward Baron could also not turn Dunhill into a success.

Rupert nominated the influential Edmund de Rothschild to represent him on the board, which was chaired by Mary Dunhill. De Rothschild, also a director of Carreras, became a good friend of the family and developed a high regard for Rupert. 'In business circles he is regarded as highly respectable, someone who thinks far ahead and an excellent person with whom complex business deals can be undertaken. Dr Anton is one of those rare people who are tolerant, who shows understanding of those who work for him, and a true builder of the degree of civilisation we have.'[5]

Dunhill proved to be a very good investment. Under the new management it rose to an international quality brand that became the fastest-growing cigarette in the Western world in the 1970s. Rupert ascribed the success to the commitment of his staff, good research and innovative thinking, especially with regard to Dunhill International.

Mary Dunhill was a good friend of Sir Francis de Guingand, Montgomery's chief of staff at El Alamein, who had settled in South Africa after the war and became deeply involved with his adoptive country. Shortly after the takeover of Carreras, Rupert asked Sir Francis (Freddie to his friends) to join the Rembrandt Group. He only had to devote half his time to the group, and was offered remuneration that De Guingand considered generous in view of the fact that he would only work on a half-time basis. As a director of subsidiaries of the international group, he helped to open doors for Rupert in the sanction years that would probably have remained closed to him as a South African, and became one of Rupert's most important mainstays internationally.

In 1958 De Guingand, together with a few friends, founded the South Africa Foundation, a private-sector initiative to promote South Africa's image abroad and foster interracial harmony within the country. The foundation, which exists to this day, was supported financially by most of the big South African companies and over the years invited a great number of well-known business people, industrialists and financiers to visit the country and form their own impressions. He retained his British passport and travelled widely, a roving, unofficial ambassador rubbing shoulders with world leaders and prominent politicians with whom he discussed South Africa's problems.[6]

Integrating Rothmans and Carreras was not plain sailing. Carreras's managing director RWS (Ronald) Plumley wanted to steer his own ship, and hard words fell at a meeting where Rupert reminded him again and again: 'You know the procedure.' In the end he left. Rupert stepped into the breach but knew he was over-committing himself. Over dinner at his Grosvenor House suite he asked De Guingand to help him out. It would mean staying on in London and De Guingand was eager to return to South Africa. But Rupert was persuasive and, reluctantly, he agreed to chair Carreras for a maximum of eighteen months. 'I found myself in the familiar role of healing wounds and taking on a job that was new to me. It was only natural that the late chairman's departure had rocked the ship to some extent and this had resulted in pro and anti ex-chairman factions,' De Guingand wrote.[7] There were many ruffled feathers at Carreras, but with tact and diplomacy he restored morale and equilibrium. In De Guingand's first year profits soared by close on 50%. Modestly he ascribed this partly to plans that were already in place when he took over. 'I can at least say that I helped to keep the ship on an even keel during what could have been a very difficult period.'

This remarkable man remained close to Rupert till his death in 1979. Their regard and esteem were mutual. At a memorial service for De Guingand in Johannesburg, Rupert paid tribute to him for all he had done to promote South Africa's interests. As founder of the South Africa Foundation, 'he did so much to protect the country against double standards.' He had also been a member of the delegation sent to the USA by two remarkable South African pioneers, Bob Hersov and Slip Menell, to acquire the rights to the process of manufacturing oil from coal. Although he had moved among princes, presidents, politicians and bankers worldwide, De Guingand had remained a humble man whose single biggest admirer was probably Joe Butt, his London chauffeur, 'to whom Sir Francis was a faithful and loyal friend, as he was to us all.'

For his part, De Guingand regarded Rupert as 'a great man, a great South African', and he noted: 'He is intensely human and the very opposite to what many people think leaders in the Republic are apt to be.' He ascribed Rupert's success in the business world to his remarkable qualities as a leader, his judgement of people, his aptitude for marketing and advertising, and the strong, small team of able people he had gathered around him. 'But probably the most important factor that helped his success was a new philosophy which he called industrial partnership', De Guingand wrote.[8]

Besides the expansion of his partnership philosophy, Rupert, whose scientific training had taught him the importance of research, was constantly involved in modernisation and technological innovation within the Rembrandt Group. Stringent quality control remained a hallmark. He knew as entrepreneur that for all its long tradition, the tobacco industry had to keep up with the times – half the industrial products that were available in 1967, for instance, had been totally un-known 25 years before. 'We therefore concentrated resolutely on producing new and better products in the tobacco world through research.'

Rupert often stated that in an era of specialisation, he preferred generalists to specialists for leadership positions: versatile people with the ability to see diverse components of an enterprise as a whole, and to distinguish quickly what is im-portant. What is required in business 'is not so much insight into and knowledge of each tiny detail, but rather an overall grasp of how all the components of the organisation fit together and relate to each other.' In this regard, he said, leader-ship could be best illustrated through the example of a conductor of an orchestra: he does not need to be able to play every instrument, but he must indeed know and understand the score. 'Leadership is therefore often more a matter of good judgement than of specialised knowledge. ' From as early as 1965 he repeatedly advocated the importance of versatility and balance in a business leader. 'Spe-cialists cannot easily stand in for others and don't always have appreciation for another's task. Lacking versatility, they find it hard to take part in consensus decision-making.' The solution, as he saw it, was not a reduction in specialisation – instead, it had to be augmented by broad-based, general training. Industrialists needed training in scientific exactitude plus abstract thinking, since business is a mixture of the two. 'Versatility in management requires more than knowledge alone. It involves a broader humanity.'

His business practice reflected this integrated approach. He appointed special-ists for selected needs, and believed they should be remunerated well. But as a firm proponent of the benefits of private initiative he preferred that each employ-ee should also be a salesman. New employees in the group received a broad, gen-eral training for their first three years. If they decided to stay on, they were then shuttled around from one department to another. Thus they might spend a year 'on the road' as sales representatives, then a year in the office learning about group operations and administration; afterwards they would spend time on the factory floor or in quality control. This applied to all levels of the organisation.

In accordance with this modus operandi Rupert's own brother Koos, after a stint abroad as Rembrandt's public relations man, was sent to Port Elizabeth in 1956 to test the market for their new American acquisition, Lexington. The untipped cigarette had too high a moisture content for the damp coastal climate, with the result that it drooped at the end. When the problem had been remedied, the cigarette, now filter tipped, sold like wild fire in its red-and-white flip-top box – especially once Koos had come up with the catchy new slogan, 'After action satisfaction', complete with a catchy advertising jingle for commercial radio. For a while Lexington outstripped even Peter Stuyvesant as the bestseller on the South African market, but then public taste reverted to untoasted Virginia tobacco. Koos, having gained his hands-on experience, returned overseas as the group's London representative in 1958, after his marriage to Rona Davel, who became a well-known writer under the name of Rona Rupert.

Rupert's other brother, Jan, headed many of Rembrandt's and Rothmans' overseas operations. Jan, more jovial and extrovert than his brothers, had been trained in law, but specialised in technical matters and became the group's head of technical planning and acquisitions.

In South Africa the cost of transporting cigarettes from Paarl to Johannesburg led to a dispute in which Rupert became involved, resulting in clashes with the minister of transport, the former trade unionist Ben Schoeman, as well as the assistant general manager of the Railways, JP Hugo. In the late 1950s most goods were still transported by rail. According to a Rembrandt memorandum, the transport costs of a carton of cigarettes exceeded the production costs. They wanted a reduction of high transport costs, a factor that was also seen as contributing to the concentration of industries on the Rand. At a 1959 congress of the AHI in Port Elizabeth Rupert criticised the tariff policy of the Railways, describing it as the country's biggest problem after racial issues: 'Something is wrong when matters are so disproportionate.' The AHI requested a general investigation into the transport system, but Hugo's response was strongly dismissive. The question of tariffs reminded him of a wolf in sheep's clothing, he said. The aim of such an investigation would be to expose the Railways. The AHI should rather come and see him and discuss firm proposals over a cup of coffee. Rupert's comments were frank: 'As a businessman I would hesitate to talk to my shareholders as Mr Hugo has done here. The Institute's members are responsible people. Nevertheless, I admire Mr Hugo's pugnacity and am convinced that, if he were to apply his energy in the right way, South Africa would be the beneficiary.'[9]

Around the same time Schoeman confronted Rupert at a dinner hosted by the American ambassador and said brusquely: 'Rupert, why did you people lie?' – meaning that the memorandum on transport costs was based on inaccuracies.

When Rupert pointed out that the figures had come from the Railways' own documents, Schoeman defended himself by saying: 'Yes, you want to bring down railway tariffs while I want to keep white people employed.' Those were the days when whites, and especially Afrikaners, were given preferential treatment. Schoeman went on to accuse Rupert of employing black people in order to exploit them, whereupon Rupert asked: 'Since when is job creation regarded as exploitation?'

When Rupert apologised to the ambassador, in whose presence the exchange had taken place, the latter responded unexpectedly: 'I'm glad about what has happened. Now people can see that there is not unanimous agreement among Afrikaners'. Schoeman and Rupert also had an altercation at another dinner when Schoeman called out to him: 'Rupert, come here!', and the normally ultra-courteous Rupert retorted: 'Yes, Schoeman, what do you want?', instead of addressing him as minister.

The 1960s were a period of consolidation as well as expansion of Rupert's tobacco and cigarette interests. The takeover of Carreras and Rothmans led to expansion in other parts of the world. Using Rothmans as his flagship, he created a stir with his philosophy of industrial partnership in various countries where he embarked on new initiatives. Partnership companies were established on a bilateral basis in Australia and New Zealand, Malaysia, Singapore, Indonesia, Canada, Jamaica, Northern and Southern Rhodesia (now Zambia and Zimbabwe) and Nyassaland (now Malawi) – eventually even beyond the Iron Curtain in Russia and China.

In Australia, where a new company was started, Rothmans King Size Filter overtook all competitors. The journal *Nation* wondered what that 'dazzling young Afrikaner, Anthony Rupert', was going to do with the interest his acquisition of Carreras had secured him in his Australian rival, British Tobacco Company (Australia) Ltd. According to *Nation*, his solution was to gradually liquidate his 'curious investment' while taking long swipes at the Australian heavyweight. The market was awash with rumours of an impending success story, with Rothmans' £1 shares selling like hot cakes at £3. The journal noted that youthfulness was the stamp of Rothmans. Its Australian general manager was the 36-year-old South African David Engela, who had cut his teeth in London and New York before moving to Australia. Behind him was his chairman Rupert, not yet 43. And behind this youthful vanguard was the solid experience of tobacco experts like Sydney Rothman, which Rupert never ceased to value and draw on in all his operations. His knack for bringing in specialists on an equal footing was also applied in Australia. Sir Kenneth Coles of Coles Stores provided the retail expertise, Clive Ogilvy of 2GB was in charge of publicity, and the intense, ambitious Ronald Irish, whose accountancy skills were supplemented by previous experience in the tobacco industry, served as chairman. Even Bill Gunn's presence on the Australian board had a South African model, namely Jan Henry Moolman, the South African wool farmer who was a 'top panjandrum' of South African wool politics.

The acquisition of Carreras by the London Rothmans was followed by a rights issue on the Australian market that undoubtedly helped to repay loans to London, which had borne Australia's losses in the past, and thus helped finance international expansion. Not that Rupert had difficulty securing loans. 'As the head of two South African investment trusts he gets money on call; but money from shareholders may be cheaper,' *Nation* decided.[10]

In 1961 Rupert moved into the former Federation of Northern and Southern Rhodesia and Nyassaland (Zambia, Zimbabwe and Malawi), where he had to operate via Britain because of South African exchange-control regulations. That same year he formed a partnership company in Malaysia. Two years later be bought Sullana in Switzerland and formed a partnership in Ireland, which became the largest factory in that country. In the Netherlands he obtained a share in Schimmelpenninck cigars.

Rupert is exceedingly proud of what they achieved with Rothmans. 'When we purchased Rothmans, our total sales in England came to 6 million cigarettes per month. We built that business – a great achievement, but we South Africans built it,' he declared in a lecture to commerce students at the University of Pretoria in 1972. 'Today we control more than two thirds of all cigarette imports from the British Isles, and we are the biggest exporters of cigarettes in the world. Young South Africans did the groundwork, the planning, and the product design, and it was done at Stellenbosch.'

From 1954 to 1972, the Rembrandt Group's production had increased dramatically to 12 000 million cigarettes per month. Even Sanlam, initially sceptical of overseas expansion, was satisfied that the European interests had not been sold – the debentures that had been converted into shares, yielded very good earnings. 'In the 1930s and 1940s,' Rupert continued in his Pretoria lecture, 'our aim was to prove that Afrikaners also had a foothold. In the 1950s our aim was to prove that South Africans could compete anywhere in the world.'

Rembrandt under Rupert proved that they could.

CHAPTER 12

Adversaries left and right

I n 1959, the year after the Carreras takeover, Rembrandt's board decided unanimously to establish a partnership company with coloured people in South Africa. Rupert's international success with his partnership philosophy had convinced him that he could follow the same model just as successfully at home.

But in his home country he came up against Prime Minister Dr Hendrik Verwoerd, who was pursuing a rigorist apartheid policy. Government thinking of the time was diametrically opposed to the post-war *Zeitgeist*. By the 1960s, South Africa's racial dispensation was increasingly coming under fire as a result of radical changes in the international arena. Changed attitudes to South Africa were already evident from 1947, when the internationally respected Genl. Jan Smuts, who had drafted the Preamble to the United Nations Charter, returned from a UN session with the sobering message: 'My country is under the harrow.'

At the UN, India initially spearheaded the Afro-Asian criticism of South Africa that intensified over time. India's Mahatma Gandhi had experienced humiliating racial discrimination in South Africa in the early 1900s before he challenged and overcame British colonialism in his home country with his policy of passive resistance. In the USA, segregationist practices were increasingly resisted by the civil rights leader Martin Luther King and the National Association for the Advancement of Colored People. In South Africa, by contrast, the Malan government that came to power in 1948 went ahead with entrenching old, unwritten practices as well as new segregationist measures in law under its policy of apartheid, while the African National Congress (ANC) under the leadership of Oliver Tambo and Nelson Mandela became more and more militant and demanded equal rights.

In defiance of mounting internal and external pressure, however, Verwoerd remained obdurate. The private sector also had to bear the burden, as Rupert discovered when he made a courtesy visit to the prime minister's office to inform him of Rembrandt's envisaged partnership company with coloureds in Paarl.

Plans were already well advanced. According to a memorandum on talks between Rupert, Hoogenhout and Willem Malherbe, various names – Van Riebeeck, Constantia, Ryk Tulbagh, Da Gama, Stellentia Cigarette Company – and some twenty possible brand names had been proposed. A factory site in Dal Josaphat between Wellington and Paarl, complete with buildings, had been purchased. Machinery was installed. All was set for the takeoff.[1]

In the late 1950s there was not yet complete clarity on the policies of the apartheid government. Rembrandt's board therefore requested Rupert to inform Verwoerd of their plans as a matter of courtesy. He was delegated to pay the prime minister a visit in his office – the same man whose offer of a job at *Die Transvaler* he had turned down years ago.

Verwoerd received him cordially but when Rupert explained the reason for his call, he was met with a total rebuff. While not speaking with bitterness about the clash, Rupert's disappointment at being prevented by the political ideology of the time from realising a historic opportunity for the country was still evident after many years. In his submission to the Truth and Reconciliation Commission in 1997, Rupert recalled their conversation. Verwoerd's first objection was that coloured people would not have the money to procure a 50% shareholding. Rupert responded that, in the same way they had established the present Rembrandt, the company would raise capital by selling a few shares at a time to individuals – teachers, civil servants and the like – in the coloured community. Verwoerd did not pursue the point.

His next question was more incisive: who would be the directors? Rupert told him about the policy of his partnership companies in other countries, where local shareholders were appointed to the board. In the present case this would imply a fair number of coloured directors. Verwoerd then pointed out that coloured people lacked the expertise and skills to run a factory, whereupon Rupert said that Rembrandt's technicians would be happy to train them, as they were doing elsewhere in the world in their existing factories. 'Dr Verwoerd then asked if this would mean that white technicians would have to work under a board with non-white directors. I explained that this was exactly what was happening in our overseas partnership companies. To my utter dismay he said that in that case, he would close the factory down. Later he even attacked me in parliament, declaring he would not allow 'a certain Rupert' to exploit blacks.'[2]

A few years later when white civil servants had to work under black ministers in the homelands created in terms of apartheid policy, Rupert wryly recalled this episode.

Verwoerd's negative reaction was one of Rupert's most deeply disappointing experiences. Yet strong public protest or challenging the authorities was not his style. Instead, he concentrated his attention and energies on his overseas interests where he could practise partnership without interference – while at home, where he had to navigate over political minefields, his statements attracted much attention and sometimes landed him in controversy.

Rupert discussed his clash with Verwoerd with Dr Beyers Naudé in 1961 during a day-long car trip when they were returning to Johannesburg from Graaff-Reinet after the funeral of Rupert's father. At Rupert's request, Naudé had conducted the funeral service. The two natives of Graaff-Reinet, whose fathers had been close friends, had both matriculated at the Afrikaans Volkskool, in 1931 and 1933 respectively. By 1961 political events in the preceding two years, including the Sharpeville incident where unarmed black protestors were shot dead by police during anti-pass demonstrations, had had a great impact on the two Afrikaners in their mid-forties.

Rupert told Naudé about his shock at Verwoerd's negative reaction to his partnership proposals, and shared his concern that South Africa could not survive without partnership. Naudé, in turn, had received a great shock at the 1960 Cottesloe conference of the World Council of Churches, where the DR Church's stance towards apartheid as well as the Sharpeville shootings had come under the spotlight. He was at that stage still attempting to achieve change from within the DR Church and had become moderator of the Southern Transvaal Synod in 1961. In later years, Rupert expressed the view that the Cottesloe conference had left Naudé with questions about apartheid. He was convinced that their discussion during the car trip must have raised even more questions in the mind of Naudé, who then started to voice those questions in public. In 1963, Naudé eventually resigned under pressure as moderator and as minister of the DR congregation of Aasvoëlkop in Johannesburg. Afterwards, Rupert blamed himself that their conversation could have contributed to the difficult circumstances that Naudé later experienced when he was banned as a strong anti-apartheid activist. Recalling their conversation, Rupert said pensively: 'Two Afrikaners. Two sons of the Karoo. Two leaders "spoke" when leadership was most sorely needed. Not until three decades later would the political leaders of the Afrikaners "hear" their message.'[3]

Ironically, in the late 1950s Rupert experienced antagonism not only from the government but also from its fiercest opponents. As part of its resistance to white minority rule and apartheid, the ANC launched a boycott campaign that included Rembrandt among its targets. Pamphlets were distributed countrywide encouraging people to boycott the products of Rembrandt and Distillers. As a last resort, Rupert turned to the court. On 8 June 1957 the Pretoria Supreme Court granted a temporary interdict prohibiting the ANC and likeminded organisations – the SA Indian Congress, the SA Congress of Democrats, the SA Coloured People's Organisation and the SA Congress of Trade Unions – from distributing a document propagating a boycott of certain cigarette and tobacco products.

Rupert himself participated actively in various moves to counter the boycott campaign. He went on the offensive when the *Eastern Province Herald* published a report under the headline 'Products of Nat firms boycotted' on 12 June 1957. A letter of protest to the paper with a personal covering letter was delivered to the editor AE Pollock, father of the Springbok cricketers Peter and Graeme, by Koos Rupert himself. In his official letter Rupert pointed out that the report concerned dealt with a court case that was sub judice, as Rembrandt had obtained a temporary interdict against the distribution of pamphlets alleging that the group was controlled by the NP. He demanded an unconditional apology as well as an undertaking that the paper would at no time spread the allegation that Rembrandt was controlled by the NP or any other political organisation. He added that it was not possible to determine the damages that Rembrandt had suffered, but that he was not interested in unnecessary court cases and hoped that the necessary correction would follow speedily.

In the covering letter Rupert held out the olive branch. He wrote that the official letter was aimed at protecting the interests of his shareholders and expressed the hope that the good relations between the two groups could be maintained. The *EP Herald* responded with a full apology and retracted its report unconditionally. 'We have no reason or grounds to believe that the Rembrandt Tobacco Manufacturing Corporation of South Africa Limited is Nationalist controlled, and we have no reason to doubt a statement by Mr AE Rupert . . . that this group is an independent business organisation with many thousands of shareholders, and is not under any political control, whether Nationalist or otherwise.'[4]

Rupert's partner Dirk Hertzog also responded later to allegations of political control when he commented in an internal memorandum on inaccuracies in Dan O'Meara's book *Volkskapitalisme*, in which it was alleged: 'It (Rembrandt) contributed heavily to the HNP (Herenigde Nasionale Party) and ostentatiously sponsored a wide range of cultural groups and projects, all of which were incorporated into its advertising campaigns.' Hertzog declared that no funds had been given to the NP or the HNP, and referred to an occasion when they claimed damages for defamation of the directors where it had been alleged that the company was 'Nationalist controlled'. This had implied that the directors were mismanaging shareholders' money. 'The accusation was then withdrawn and an NP minister even blamed Dr Rupert and me for taking these steps. He was under the erroneous impression that we had maintained it was defamatory to be called a Nationalist!'[5]

Rembrandt suspected its main South African competitor, United Tobacco Companies (South) Limited (UTC), of involvement in the ANC's boycott campaign. In June 1959 they instituted a civil claim against UTC for damages of £5 million, the biggest of its kind in South African legal history up to then. Rupert placed countrywide advertisements declaring that Rembrandt was not under government control and practised no discrimination. A warning was issued, signed by Rupert himself, that anyone stating that the Rembrandt Group was politically controlled would be sued for insinuating that the company was not managed in the interests of its shareholders and was engaging in unsound business practices. A 'public statement' appeared as a full-page advertisement in the Cape daily newspaper *Die Burger*: 'The Rembrandt companies are public companies and shares can be bought freely on the Johannesburg Stock Exchange. You can also buy shares. No political party owns any shares in the Rembrandt Group or receives any income from it. The lists of shareholders are open to inspection by the public.' The statement was accompanied by a list of English and Afrikaans educational, cultural and charitable institutions that had received donations of £100 or more from Rembrandt.[6]

UTC's chairman, LN (Leslie) Bond, responded with a letter to Rupert in which he categorically denied that his company had ever approved any boycott. He promised he would act against any of their staff who had been responsible for a statement that Rembrandt was politically controlled. Rembrandt dropped its claim at once and announced in the press on 28 July 1959 that the dispute had been settled. *New Age*, a paper that was eventually banned by the government, reported the following week that UTC had fired its seven black public relations officers the very day that Rupert announced the withdrawal of the claim. They had been informed in writing that their dismissal was due to 'reorganisation', but according to *New Age* they had been questioned a few weeks earlier by UTC's legal representatives about any possible involvement with the distribution of the ANC's boycott lists, and had been warned not to attend ANC meetings.[7]

As for Rembrandt's case against the ANC's boycott campaign, the temporary interdict was extended once. The day Rupert and his lawyers arrived at the Supreme Court for the final order, Adv. Bram Fischer, who was acting as junior with the equally well-known Adv. Sidney Kentridge for the ANC, approached him on the steps outside and said: 'Anton, why does your company now want to drag us to court?' Rupert, rather surprised, responded: 'But, Bram, why do you people disseminate pamphlets singling out our products for a boycott? You know as well as I do that we're not controlled by politicians and that we don't discriminate, and you know about our policy of coexistence and partnership.'

Fischer, who would later become a leader of the South African Communist Party, then wanted to reach a settlement. After further discussion, Fischer proposed before the start of the court proceedings: 'Would you withdraw your application if we undertook not to do it again? 'But of course,' Rupert said. 'That's exactly what I want.' They shook hands to confirm the agreement. Rembrandt products were never boycotted again by the ANC.

Rupert has described Fischer, grandson of the Free State republican premier Abraham Fischer, as well as another prominent anti-apartheid activist, Patrick Duncan, son of a South African governor-general, as 'among the gentlest people I ever met, but with a hard shell because of their sympathy with the oppressed – reminiscent of oysters which, like tortoises and snails, need a hard shell to protect their tender innards.'

South Africa was going through turbulent times at the start of the 1960s. Race riots in 1960, including the Sharpeville shootings that were condemned world-wide, had a negative effect on the economy. It was also the year in which the British prime minister Harold Macmillan made his watershed speech about the 'wind of change' blowing through Africa. In the same year a referendum was held among white people to determine whether South Africa should become a republic. With a small majority of 52% the old republican ideal of Afrikaner nationalists was re-alised, although many English-speaking South Africans had also voted in favour of a republic. But at the Commonwealth conference in London in 1961 Verwoerd met with fierce opposition to his race policies. He withdrew South Africa's application for continued membership and the country left the Commonwealth. On 31 May 1961, exactly 51 years after the establishment of the Union, the Republic of South Africa came into existence against a background of internal unrest and international censure.

After Sharpeville the property market in South Africa slumped. In the early 1960s Rupert bought the beautiful Fleur du Cap wine estate of 19,87ha at Somerset West for a mere R50 000. This was the one occasion he thought of moving from Thibault Street to the stately mansion, but his wife refused point-blank. When told that entrepreneurs are often characterised as living in the same house for a very long time, she retorted: 'Very sorry, but then Anton is not a good entrepreneur. He bought Fleur du Cap and he wanted to go and live there.' For almost three weeks he hardly spoke to her, but she remained adamant. She regarded the place as a retirement village for veterans of the Indian Army, and she did not drink whisky or play bridge. In Stellenbosch their children cycled to school. At Somerset West she would have to ferry them by car. Their lifestyle was simple, she insist-ed, it would not suit them. Besides, Huberte pointed out to her husband, 'If I die, you won't be able to run it on your own; it's too big. And if you die, I'd have to sell vegetables at the gate to maintain it!'

So the family remained in Stellenbosch and in 1963 the Rembrandt Group bought Fleur du Cap estate as a guesthouse. Over the years the visitors' book of Rupert's guests who were hosted there came to resemble an international who's who: Dutch, British and Basotho royalty; heads of government like Margaret Thatcher and Tony Blair; cabinet ministers like Caspar Weinberger and Henry Kissinger; business people like David Rockefeller and Edmund de Rothschild; politicians like Sen. Edward Kennedy, and ambassadors from countries represented in South Africa. When Rembrandt bought a priceless collection of Dutch East India Company porcelain and antiques from DaimlerChrysler in 2001 it was moved to Fleur du Cap, where it is now on display. Until 1984 the estate also served as a corporate training centre. After that courses – also for trainees from associated companies – were run at the Court House, a Georgian mansion in Sandton, Johannesburg, which accommodates Rembrandt's guests to that city as well.

In Stellenbosch the Ruperts' two sons, Johann and Anthonij, went to school at Paul Roos Gymnasium, named after the first captain of a Springbok rugby team. Hanneli attended Bloemhof girls' school. Huberte took an active interest in her children's schools and Rupert served on a board of patrons of Paul Roos that was constituted in 1966, the school's centenary year. Dirk Hertzog's son Edwin, who was the head boy that year, recalls that Rupert donated a framed poem that hung in the staff room.[8]

'Dr Rupert also donated prizes for the school and Mrs Rupert did a lot for music at Bloemhof,' Edwin Hertzog remembers. He had been impressed in his youth by Huberte's organisational capabilities. A music room had been added to the Ruperts' house, with a piano on which Hanneli could practise. Here Huberte and Marié Opperman organised concerts two or three times a year, when the youngsters performed on the piano, recited poems and generally displayed their talents to an audience of parents. Edwin remembers Huberte as a forthright person who did not hesitate to speak her mind – you always knew where you stood with her, and he thought the other women were rather scared of her. 'She was instrumental in organising the Christmas tree functions for the Rembrandt Group in the early years. I really enjoyed these functions as a child; it was wonderful to have this communal sense of knowing who else's mom and dad also worked at Rembrandt.'

Hanneli, the Ruperts' youngest child, was born with cataracts on both eyes. She recalls that it felt 'as if one was looking through mist', and from the age of five she had to wear spectacles. Her parents were caring and supportive and her brothers were always protective. In 'these very difficult times' during which the family needed spiritual support, Huberte studied books and articles on eye problems so that she could take informed decisions.[9]

On weekends Hanneli often accompanied Rupert on walks in the marshlands of Karindal at Stellenbosch. At the popular beach resort of Hermanus she regularly went swimming with him at Voëlklip beach near their holiday home. Rupert was very fond of the sea, but on their trips to the beach it would sometimes take half an hour just to get down the steps at Voëlklip – people would constantly stop him for a chat. On the beach at Hermanus he said something to his children that they have never forgotten: 'Remember, we are all like grains of sand, no person is better than another. That is why we can dine with kings but also eat with paupers.'

These words illustrate a quality of Rupert that struck many people; in spite of spectacular international success he remained unpretentious and humble. Hans Knoetze, long-time public relations officer at Rembrandt, tells that he and his colleagues also experienced this humility. 'He happily shared the limelight with colleagues. At functions he would personally pour drinks for guests if we weren't quick enough, and set the example. He always saw visitors out to the lift or the parking area. Few left his office without having received a book on art or the conservation of historical buildings as a gift.'[10]

The Ruperts, concerned about the eye problems of their only daughter, believed as a general policy that one should always get the best possible medical advice in the event of sickness or ill health. At an early age Hanneli was taken to Utrecht for treatment. In 1960, when she was five, Dr Hennie Meyer of Pretoria and Sir Benjamin Rycroft both recommended a famous Spanish ophthalmologist, Dr Joaquin Barraquer. They took the little girl to Barcelona and a series of delicate eye operations followed. Notified by Owen McCann, cardinal of Cape Town, a Barcelona priest, Father Arimon, stood by them throughout this trying time. Huberte and Hanneli regularly lit a candle to St Lucia, the patron saint of eye sufferers, at the saint's shrine in the cathedral. Under Barraquer's treatment Hanneli's vision improved markedly – so much so that in later years she no longer needed spectacles at all.

The stay in Barcelona also opened up new fields of interest for Rupert. He was greatly impressed with the architect Antoni Gaudi's modernistic creations, especially the Temple of the Sagrada Familia, a landmark in Barcelona. In course of time the Ruperts met King Juan Carlos of Spain, with whom they established a long friendship. An important influence on Rupert's thinking has been the work of the humanist philosopher José Ortega y Gasset, one of his sources of inspiration in his opposition to state interference and bureaucratisation. Rome declined, said the Spanish philosopher, because the bureaucratised state stifled the creativity, initiative and spontaneity of its citizens. This gave rise to the mass person; the human being stripped of individuality, initiative and dissimilarity. Rupert concurred wholeheartedly. And he added: in a bureaucratised society inventiveness consisted of the circumvention of regulations.

By this time Rupert was an institution in Stellenbosch, the university town that became a cultural brand name thanks to his presence. It would be known as the place where conservation had become a priority, and where the headquarters of the Worldwide Fund for Nature (WWF) South Africa would be established. Stellenbosch also became a brand name for estate wines, a development to which Rupert contributed from the outset. Rembrandt's address became world famous and as the home base of one of South Africa's leading industrial enterprises, Stellenbosch was visited by renowned personalities and international business leaders. Prominent figures from the world of high finance and politics – David Rockefeller, General Motors head Frederic G Donner, Consolidated Goldfields chairman Sir George Harvey-Watt, Sen. Robert Kennedy – visited Rembrandt headquarters. Royal visitors to Stellenbosch included Prince Bernhard of the Netherlands, who would play a leading role with Rupert in the WWF and peace parks, Prince Philip, Duke of Edinburgh, and Prince Burchard of Prussia.

At the age of 75 Lord Montgomery – Monty of El Alamein, who defeated Rommel's forces in North Africa and turned the tide of World War II – smoked his first cigarette ever at a Rembrandt function in the *Burgerhuis* in Stellenbosch in 1962. His chief of staff Sir Francis de Guingand was also present at the function, which reminded the British of the day that Monty, a teetotaller known for his austere lifestyle, told Winston Churchill: 'I don't drink, I don't smoke, I sleep a lot. That's why I'm a hundred percent fit.' To which Churchill responded: 'I drink a lot, I sleep very little and I chain-smoke cigars. That's why I'm two hundred percent fit.'

Rembrandt's reputation for quality was also evident in the way the Ruperts entertained guests. 'Nothing excessive, hearty in the Afrikaner way, but at the same time exquisite and right,' said Huberte.

One function in particular attracted much attention. When the Rembrandt Group held its sixth world conference in May 1962 they hired the passenger liner the *Windsor Castle*, which was specially converted for the purpose, for less than the cost of a similar conference on dry land. The party of 60 delegates representing the countries where Rembrandt had factories went on a five-day cruise from Cape Town to Durban amid a fanfare of media interest. International business people who attended the conference included Dr Paul Rijkens, director of Turman Tobacco and former head of the Unilever Group as well as erstwhile adviser to the wartime Dutch government in exile in England; John Hansard, chairman of Carreras and director of the Samuel Montagu banking group; Sydney Rothman's son and heir; G Ellman-Brown, chairman of Rothmans (Rhodesia) and a cabinet minister of that country; Dato WM McLeod, chairman of Rothmans (Malaysia); Sir Francis de Guingand, world director of Rothmans; Frank Riggio, president of Riggio Tobacco Corporation in New York; and Ron Irish, chairman of Rothmans (Australia). The ship's theatre was equipped as a conference centre, cabins were fitted out as offices. Tobacco experts, researchers and financiers gave lectures and a wide range of topics affecting the industry was discussed.

In Cape Town and Durban, as well as at Port Elizabeth and East London en route, Huberte and Rupert hosted formal receptions to introduce the delegates to local merchants and industrialists. Some of the men were accompanied by their wives. Huberte jokingly referred to them as 'weed widows' and organised sightseeing tours for them at the ports where they called. The receptions were described in glowing press reports. A review of the 'party to end all parties' in the *Natal Daily News* of 17 May 1962 summed up the Durban reception: 'With the Windsor Castle – one of the most luxurious ships afloat today – as a setting, it was all magnificently, even glitteringly, staged. But once again the Ruperts, by their easy charm of manner, managed to invest it with a pleasant informality.'[11]

Huberte always played a leading role in the receptions hosted in South Africa; the smaller, more intimate gatherings held in their home in Thibault Street as well as the bigger receptions that were mostly held in hotels. She took trouble to make foreign visitors feel at home and to introduce them to the country, its people and traditions. Her menus invariably included typically South African fare and lots of fresh vegetables, salads and fruit. Always health conscious, she did not serve rich, indigestible dishes. The best South African wines were offered. At formal dinners she took great pains over seating, trying to avoid 'dead spots' by not putting quiet people together. On occasion guests were provided with cards carrying information about the two people on their right and left, their names, jobs and interests. It gave her great pleasure to see a heterogeneous group of guests with widely divergent tastes and customs '"finding" one another and having a wonderful time together'.[12]

Whenever Rupert returned to Stellenbosch from his many overseas business trips, he followed a strenuous daily routine. According to Huberte, he seldom got home before half past seven or eight and the evening was often spent reading: works on economics, advertising, business trends in every part of the world. 'Especially through journals he would keep in touch with what was happening in the world.'

His personal assistant for 25 years, Jan Groeneveld, described him as 'out and out an evening person'. Before going to work in the morning he would plan his day. By the time he arrived at the office round half past nine he was ready for the fray. Systematically he worked through his planned schedule. Letters were answered promptly – some days he signed as many as 60. According to Groenveld, Rupert lived in 'in compartments from day to day' – what could be done today had to be completed. It made his assistants' task easy to protect him 'against embarrassment and inconvenience'. In the late afternoons he got his second wind. Then he might find time to chat with colleagues. But by the time he left his office the desk would be clear.

This daily routine increasingly had to make way for international involvement. Often he was overseas for weeks on end, up to seven months in one year. At such times Huberte had to shoulder both parental roles, attending parents' evenings at schools and the boys' sports matches, while also being closely involved in the musical education of Hanneli, who became one of South Africa's most talented singers.

Yet she still managed to keep abreast of her husband's business activities. In an interview with the journalist Rykie van Reenen she demonstrated her grasp of the group's extended interests and also advertising and marketing, the field in which Rupert achieved perhaps his greatest success. The public could not be persuaded for long just by advertising, she believed: 'You can perhaps fool people for a while with good advertisements for an inferior product, but don't think you can get away with it for long! The public do not really let themselves be taken for a ride.' Besides, advertising was but one weapon in the industrial campaign. 'It's as if you're conducting a war. You have to be strong on all fronts: not just in your advertising, but also in your manufacturing, your personnel matters, your distribution, your public relations – everything.' This close attention to detail on all fronts, she maintained, was perhaps the main reason for Rembrandt's success. 'Even if there is dust on a salesman's car, it's bad for your company. Everything must be immaculate at all times. Clearly, that's how you create a reputation for quality.'[13]

Although living very privately, the Ruperts built up a close circle of intimate friends in Stellenbosch, as they did in Pretoria and Johannesburg. Their many overseas friends included business people, bankers and art connoisseurs. Besides their life-long friends Prince Bernhard and Prince Philip, others with whom they had forged friendships on overseas visits included Robert Mondavi, who had started a wine revolution in California; Dr Joachim Zahn, head of Daimler-Benz; the shoe manufacturer Tom Bata; Dr Lucas Hoffman of Hoffman Laroche; the conductor Herbert von Karajan; the Swiss banker Bruno Saager of Union Bank; Jurgen Ponto, head of Dresdner Bank; and David Rockefeller, heir to the Rockefeller fortune and president of Chase Manhattan Bank.

Many of his friends were people with whom Rupert liked to engage in what he called 'mental gymnastics' – long conversations with business aquaintances and academics about current affairs, politics, global dilemmas, art and culture. In brief, the diversity of interests and open-mindedness that made Rupert a man for all seasons.

In Stellenbosch he enjoyed intellectual conversations with academics such as Prof. Jannie Swartz from the faculty of education, whose father hailed from Graaff-Reinet; the law professor James Yeats; and Prof. JPJ (Stannie) van Rensburg, professor of Greek, who had translated Homer's *Iliad* into Afrikaans. Other close friends were the poet Dirk Opperman and his wife Marié, the composer Arnold van Wyk and Prof. Jannie de Villiers, professor in gynaecology who was at one stage the rector of the university. Huberte was often present at the discussions on current affairs, speaking her mind and holding views of her own. As her son Johann has remarked, she was very much her husband's intellectual equal.

Edwin Hertzog tells of the 'mental gymnastics' that took place within the Rupert household itself – he occasionally stayed with the Ruperts when his parents went abroad and was quite daunted by the discussions, in which all members of the family freely expressed their views. 'Often they disagreed strongly, with Mrs Rupert leading the way, and Johann inherited this from his mother, I think.' Hanneli Rupert also referred in a magazine interview to the 'spirited discussions' at home, usually as a family during meals. Her father would give his opinions during such discussions, even if some of the others did not agree with him. 'Something that baffles me is how some people can say he's "liberal". Particularly when I think of how openly we talk, where everyone can have his say, I know how untrue this is. He is rather – how shall I put it? – sensibly conservative. It sounds to me as if that's also how he operates in his work.'[14] The term 'liberal', as used by Hanneli in 1971, had a pejorative meaning since it was used in right-wing political parlance in South Africa to label just about anybody who did not rigidly agree with reactionary orthodoxy. To be called 'liberal' at the time was about the same as being called unpatriotic and subversive.

To Hanneli, her father's greatest quality was his honesty. 'If you ask him something, you know you'll get an honest answer. In business life, in conversations, in all of his conduct he's totally honest.'

Besides the stimulating exchanges of ideas Rupert experienced at home, Huberte's love for art, music and culture helped to broaden the horizons and fields of interest of her science-trained husband who had to devote most of his time to the demands of business life. Huberte's interest in art contributed to the habit he developed of spending time in art galleries overseas while waiting for the irregular flights to South Africa. In this way he became acquainted with leading art dealers and connoisseurs – the prelude to the remarkable art collection his family and the Rembrandt Group would acquire over the years.

CHAPTER 13

Shock waves from wages

B usiness confidence in South Africa recovered quite rapidly from the shock waves of the early 1960s. The new republic opened up a range of new opportunities and leaving the Commonwealth did not, in itself and overnight, bring isolation. In this growth period the Rembrandt Group was expanding its interests, acquiring an important South African competitor, Cavalla Limited, in 1961. Eventually the group would dominate the tobacco industry on the subcontinent.

An innovation that attracted international attention was Rembrandt's decision in 1963 to pay a minimum wage of £1 (R2) per day, besides fringe benefits, to every worker, irrespective of race and colour. On 27 October 1963 the *Sunday Express* blazoned a headline across its front page: 'Rupert's dramatic pay rise move.' 'We have confidence in the country and have concluded that we can afford it,' Rupert told the newspaper. He advanced three reasons for this stance. First, he had confidence in the people of South Africa. 'I believe that our power lies in our diversity and in our adaptability to the problems of Africa. I believe that their inherent common sense and goodwill will overcome all problems.' Second, he had confidence in South Africa's growth potential. The United Nations had rated it one of the only three developed countries in the southern hemisphere, along with Australia and New Zealand. Third, the country had well-nigh limitless resources. Apart from its gold reserves, it was one of a few countries that were agriculturally not just self-sufficient but a major exporter.[1]

The news of the pay rise caused a sensation – an American journalist was to describe it as 'one of those economic earthquakes whose shock waves continue and grow'. Over the next few days it hit the headlines in all major newspapers. To those editors who felt resentful about the *Sunday Express*'s scoop Rupert sent an apologetic telex, not for publication, that reflected his concern for good relations with the media. He explained that the announcement of the pay rise had not been an exclusive press release but 'an afterthought', slotted into an interview in response to a telephone call asking him if he had faith in South Africa's future.

On 1 November the *Financial Mail* published a cartoon with the caption 'Breakthrough' on its front page. It showed a photograph of Rupert at the tip of a rocket inscribed 'R2 a day'. The newspaper's editorial praised the announcement: 'With a bold stroke of his pen Anton Rupert has ushered in a new, more enlightened era in South Africa's industrial history. A pound-a-day minimum for all his company's employees fires the imagination, and Dr Rupert's genius for image making has ensured that his name, and Rembrandt's, will long be linked in the public mind with this historic break through the wage barrier, irrespective of whether it has cost the group much or little.'[2]

There was criticism too, some of it quite sharp, notably from Rembrandt's rivals and the agricultural sector. But organisations like the Trade Union Council and the Bantu Wage and Productivity Association hailed it as a trail-blazing event that was bound to inspire other employers to do the same, with favourable widespread repercussions. Certainly there was a big backlog to make up: the University of South Africa's Bureau for Market Research had found that the average monthly income of Sowetan heads of households was R42,05, well below the generally accepted poverty baseline of R46.

Still, the very next issue of the *Sunday Express* reported that at least 50 other South African companies employing hundreds of thousands of black workers had told the Bantu Wage and Productivity Association that they intended following Rembrandt's example.

Allen Drury, the American author of a widely discussed book on South Africa, *A Very Strange Society*, wrote that Rupert had single-handedly brought about an upward revolution in the economic status of black people and that even the most determined of governments would not be able to stop it. In a frank interview with Drury at Stellenbosch in 1966 Rupert spelled out his underlying business philosophy, to which he adhered staunchly throughout his career. 'White and Black, we are each other's shadows', he said, 'particularly here in South Africa where we share the land together: if the African doesn't eat, we don't sleep, and vice versa; even if we are "apart", if he doesn't succeed, we don't succeed, and if we don't succeed, he won't.' Rupert continued: 'The potentials of this continent are beyond belief. What we could all do together in partnership staggers the imagination. We can do it and we will, when they [other African states] have decided it is to the advantage of all to work together, as many of us are trying to do here.'

He derided communism as a foreign ideology based on outmoded economic theories, threatening stability in Africa. 'Politically it is simply another form of imperialism and colonialism, masquerading behind the guise of humanitarianism. Some African states have already learned this for themselves. It offers no answers to the problems of Africa.' He motivated his group's wage increase as follows: 'I suppose I am what you could call a "liberal Cape Afrikaner", yes. I have raised wages in my companies because I think the economic condition of the Bantu must be improved to the benefit of all of us. We must create economic partnership and a better life for all in South Africa, African and European. Economic opportunity is the key to all our problems, I believe. With it will come an amelioration of many things to which the outside world objects. I believe the Bantu's condition will greatly improve in the next few years, the Indian's also; I predict that before long we are going to have a complete integration of the Coloureds in the White community.'

Ensuring stability on the African continent as a whole required stable leadership, which South Africa could provide. He told the American that undermining South Africa was not in the interests of Africa. According to Drury, Rupert concluded thoughtfully: 'Men in the mass are nothing. The individual is everything. I think that is why I love the Karoo. It is stark – it is challenging – there a man is a man, standing or falling by his own efforts . . . Individuals can do everything – but they must cooperate. They must work together for the benefit of all.'[3]

Although Rupert took the lead with higher minimum wages for his group, in later years a few Rembrandt employees complained that their remuneration was low, particularly early on. For a long time there were no share options available: Dirk Hertzog, who like Rupert himself bought shares on the open market at an early stage, opposed the practice. In time, the salary scales improved considerably and were adjusted in line with the market. In the opinion of Gys Steyn, who headed Oude Meester for many years, Rupert paid his employees 'very well'.[4] Thys Visser, CEO of Remgro, is adamant that the Ruperts' proprietary interest contributes largely to the welfare of the group and that of all its employees – if there should be a few isolated cases of pensioners who are dissatisfied, he would not be surprised if they had squandered their retirement funds.[5]

Koos Human of the publishing company Human & Rousseau remembers that Rupert once asked him whether he and his partner Leon Rousseau were paying themselves proper salaries, 'because if you pay yourselves unrealistic salaries it distorts the results.'[6]

Rupert, in his capacity as founder of the Rembrandt Group, also referred to the salary issue in a submission to the Truth and Reconciliation Commission (TRC) instituted after South Africa's first democratic election in 1994 by Pres. Nelson Mandela's government to investigate the period from March 1960 to May 1994. He stated that he had initially been reluctant to respond to the TRC's enquiry as he always assumed that his belief in coexistence through partnership as an alternative to apartheid was common knowledge, especially among business people. It had become clear to him, however, that the philosopher José Ortega y Gasset was correct when he said there is a new generation every fifteen years, and that his group's stance was not well understood in 1997. He therefore pointed out in his submission that Rembrandt introduced a minimum wage of R2 per day as early as 1963, despite strong opposition from other employers, especially in the agricultural sector. More than 30 years later Rembrandt was still paying among the highest minimum wages in the country.

In 1987 all Rembrandt employees with three of more years of service became shareholders in the company, with every employee, from the lowest level to management, receiving the same number of shares. 'Our policy towards employees has always been one of non-discrimination, including equal pay for equal work, fringe benefits which are available to everyone and appropriate training for all employees. We have never forced anyone to converse in any language but their own.'[7]

Johann Rupert, who had succeeded his father as CEO of the Rembrandt Group, stated in his oral testimony at the TRC's hearings on the business sector on 12 November 1997 that the minimum salary package in the Rembrandt Group (for a cleaner in the factory) amounted to R3 600 at that stage, more than a high-school mathematics teacher was earning. When the group experienced problems at one of its factories in Berlin, 30 South African employees, broadly representative of the country's population groups, were sent to deal with the situation – within six weeks they raised the productivity of the German factory by more than ten percent. 'I think this says a lot about our level of training and commitment,' he said.

The initial R1,5 million his predecessors invested abroad in 1955 yielded a net return flow of billions of rands. Johann emphasised that he represents a South African group with South African shareholders. 'This was not achieved by any exports of South African raw materials or finished goods. In other words, we did not build this company abroad off the "black sweat of black workers", unionised workers and hostels. This money went abroad, people went abroad and worked very hard. The value of this investment, held by South African residents, is today in excess of R25 billion. By the way, for many years this exceeded the country's gold and foreign-exchange reserves.'[8]

Anton Rupert's intrepid leap with minimum wages, like his idealism as benefactor to serve the community, was based on his firm conviction that a business enterprise could only do such things if it made a profit. He did not for a moment deny or denigrate the profit motive. Lecturing to commerce students at Pretoria University in 1972, he said: 'If any professor or socialist were to tell you that all profit is of the devil, you must remember that without profit there can be no savings, without savings no investment, and without investment no jobs.' Making a profit is not disgraceful, he maintained – 'in fact, it is a disgrace not to make one'.[9]

He was proud that no company of which he was chairman or managing director had ever gone under, as he pointed out to friends.

Long before it became a popular concept in management theory, Rupert adopted the stakeholder model that emanates from the belief that a business enterprise is not an island in a sea of market relationships, but instead involved with a variety of sectors and people in society. He emphasised three relationships in particular, three stakeholders to whom Rembrandt owed its success: 'Our basic philosophy is that we have three levels of responsibility, namely to our shareholders, to our staff, and to the community in which we operate.' On occasion he added: 'Now my biggest fun in life has been the third one – my biggest pleasure.' This was the other side of Rupert the entrepreneur – his community involvement that was expressed in philanthropy. Not just giving away money because he had plenty of it, but philanthropy based on his all-absorbing outlook on life – personal, business, cultural, civic life – in partnership with others. With the advent of globalisation the notion of strategic alliances has become commonplace. But Rupert was well ahead of his times.

Early in the group's development it was decided to spend part of the profits on what he later described as a partnership between 'Capital and Culture', 'Capital and Art', and 'Capital and Sport'. In 1949, when Rembrandt made its first profit after initial losses, Rupert as chairman and Patrick O'Neill-Dunne, their marketing advisor from Rothmans, each became entitled to 2,5% of Rembrandt's net profit. Rupert told the board that he wanted it to devote his share to good causes. His request was rather impetuous, given the time and Rembrandt's level of development. Many years later, even after the imperative of corporate social investment had become generally accepted, there were still not many companies that set aside such a percentage for this purpose. In 1966 the arrangement was formalised in an employment contract signed in Stellenbosch, but in fact it had come into operation fifteen years earlier, long before the company had risen to national and international eminence. At that time it could well have been seen as a bold, idealistic leap in the dark. Yet in 1972 he told students at the University of Pretoria that it marked a turning point: from that day on he never had a problem securing any donation of whatever kind from any board of directors anywhere on the globe.

The example of his parents had played a particular role in inspiring Rupert to serve the community to an extent matched by few other business leaders in South Africa. 'Cast your bread upon the waters, for after many days you will find it again' – these words of his mother encouraged him as a young man to reconcile social responsibility with his business success. And in 1960, when Rembrandt had started achieving considerable success, his father said to him: 'Boetie, it's very nice that you've accomplished all of this, but what are you doing for your own people?'

John Rupert died the following year at the age of 73. After his retirement he had lived comfortably in Port Elizabeth, looked after financially by his sons. He died intestate – according to the inventory of his estate in the Cape Town Archives his assets, including 100 Rembrandt and 240 Volkskas shares, amounted to R6 205,50 and his liabilities to R197,69, leaving a balance of R6 007,81. His son Jan was appointed executor of the estate.

One of the projects in which Rupert became actively involved in the early 1960s was a major fundraising drive on behalf of the University of Stellenbosch (US) with a view to the establishment of a bursary fund in 1966, its centenary year.[10] Although it was not his alma mater, Rupert was on the council and closely involved with the university's activities. Early expectations of a successful fundraising campaign were dampened by the Sharpeville shootings on 21 March 1960, which reverberated worldwide. Nonetheless the university council decided to go ahead and appointed an executive committee of ten members to guide and advise the Centenary Fund campaign, chaired by Dr Tienie Louw of Sanlam. Rupert, a member of the committee, headed the organisation that had to raise R300 000 from the private sector countrywide. At a gathering in Johannesburg he said the targeted figure was too low – it should be R3 million. When two businessmen friends in the committee, Etienne Rousseau and WB Coetzer, raised the view that Sharpeville had put paid to any fundraising at all, Rupert said there were only two possibilities: 'If our country is about to collapse, you're going to lose your money anyway. If something positive is to happen, we must focus on our universities and officials. We need competent people.' He noticed that the mining magnate Harry Oppenheimer, sitting in the audience, was nodding in agreement.

Oppenheimer was immediately prepared to donate funds for education. The view of the two philanthropists held sway, and the Centenary Fund gained new momentum. This was an unexpected ally, but the relationship between the two men deepened; they joined hands in many philanthropic projects over the years. In a tribute to Oppenheimer when he died in 2000, Rupert declared: 'Someone once asked me if Harry Oppenheimer regarded me as a successful man. I answered 'No'. I would rather like to be man of value, someone who gives more to life than he had received from it. Harry Oppenheimer was such a man.'

Early in 1961 Rupert announced at a dinner for business people in Stellenbosch that Rembrandt, which already employed more than 50 graduates of the university, would contribute R50 000 to the Centenary Fund. 'Our nation's future depends on the universities, on how ready we are to compete, on how we achieve, and not on how we protect ourselves with laws,' he said. 'The question is if we still can afford to give recognition only to those who come first, second or third in long jump, high jump and prancing, but not in brain power. And whether we play too much and work too little here.'[11]

One of the events that made Rupert wary of long speeches occurred in 1961 at a Centenary Fund banquet for top business people in Johannesburg, one of the 80 grand dinners hosted by the US during the campaign. Each speaker was allowed ten minutes. The first, Harry Oppenheimer, kept to the time limit. The chancellor of the US, Dr Eben Dönges, then spoke for twenty minutes. He was followed by the chairman of the executive committee, Dr Hendrik van Eck, who spoke for 30 minutes and quoted long passages about the university's founding years in Dutch. Finally, the rector, Prof. HB Thom, delivered the longest speech of all. By a quarter to twelve the guests were so restive that many left before there had been a proper opportunity to corner them for contributions.

Thom did, however, get credit at a later stage. Huberte requested that the theatre that was established on the US campus, for which she had campaigned for many years, be named the HB Thom Theatre 'because he contributed so much to our culture'. Huberte's massive contribution to the theatre was mentioned in the commendation when she received the university's Pro Bono Merito medal for exceptional service in March 1999, the first South African to be honoured by the university in this way. At the ceremony the rector, Prof. Andreas van Wyk, said that the Rupert family and music were synonymous in Stellenbosch. He noted that Huberte had been involved through the Oude Meester Foundation for the Performing Arts and the Rupert Family Foundation in many gala occasions in the Endler Hall of the university's conservatoire, where numerous overseas artists performed. She also proposed the name of the George van der Spuy accompanist fund in honour of the US professor of singing who had been one of the tutors of her daughter Hanneli, a prominent mezzo-soprano.

The many business dinners and fundraising rallies in aid of the Centenary Fund were highly successful. On 28 February 1966, a few months before the university's centenary in September, the company contributions stood at R2 315 688, with the combined pledged total of 7 515 individual and corporate donations at more than R3 million, namely R3 591 162. Rupert's target of six years earlier had been achieved. When the university wanted to set its sights even higher, however, he refused: enough is enough, he said. That year the US awarded him an honorary doctorate in commerce, his second honorary degree. The first had been a DSc from his own alma mater, the University of Pretoria, in 1960 – after that date he was referred to as Dr Rupert. Subsequently he was similarly honoured by the Universities of Cape Town (1979), Natal (1984) and the Randse Afrikaanse Universiteit (1988).

Not all shareholders shared Rupert's broader vision. In 1962 a newsletter of the *Vereniging van Aandeelhouers van Suid-Afrika* (South African Shareholders' Association) criticised Rembrandt for its liberal support of, inter alia, educational institutions. The amount at issue was R250 000, at a time when the group's gross profits stood at R17 025 004. As a result of the criticism, Rupert started stating his views on corporate social responsibility more strongly in public. He addressed the criticism in his chairman's report to shareholders at Rembrandt's AGM in 1962 under the heading 'Support for universities'. He acknowledged the association's concern that he and his board were being 'too generous with your assets'.[12] Ahead of this time, at least as far as South Africa was concerned, he said bluntly: 'As I see it, the modern company has three responsibilities, namely to its shareholders, to its staff, and to the society from which its success derives and within which it operates.' 'You are the judges,' he told the shareholders, 'but if all of you were as grateful for the contribution we can make to the community as I am, I'd be more than satisfied.'

Rupert emphasised that, since the inception of Rembrandt, public confidence and goodwill had been 'one of the cornerstones on which a sound business must be built'. As for supporting academic institutions, he pointed out that this was a gilt-edged investment in the future of the country. At present, he said, Rembrandt employed over 100 graduates from South African universities. The country's educational institutions were 'the source of present and future strength'.

In typical fashion, Rupert did not simply respond reactively to the association's criticism. He put his words into action and announced at the AGM that the Rembrandt Group was establishing a study fund of R10 000 for deserving children of its own staff. It would be administered as a separate loan fund by the Helpmekaar Study Fund – the educational fund started with the surplus from the Helpmekaar fund for rebels held liable for damages after the Rebellion of 1914. Over the years the Helpmekaar Study Fund provided study loans for thousands of needy young Afrikaners, including eminent figures like economist Prof. CGW Schumann; the heart surgeons Chris Barnard and his brother Marius; the poet Breyten Breytenbach; Dr MH de Kock, former president of the Reserve Bank, and a string of scientists, doctors and business people.[13] More recently it broadened its activities to include loans for young entrepreneurs as well. Rupert was a trustee for many years, until he was succeeded as trustee by his son Johann.

In 1963, a year after the AGM where he had advocated the threefold responsibility of business, Rupert told representatives of the business sector in Pretoria that wealth entailed responsibility. Wealth could lead either to progress or to decadence; if it led to the acceptance of responsibility and 'doing good to others', it was a 'divine asset'. In 1977 corporate responsibility was again the theme of his chairman's address at Rembrandt's 29th AGM. Under the title 'Corporate responsibility' on the cover of his address the group was described as follows: 'The

Rembrandt Group and its partner companies are a unique global organisation of equal partners. The assets of the group exceed R2 400 million and turnover amounts to approximately R4 400 million.' That year Rembrandt's net profit, before tax, was R97,8 million, most of it earned overseas.

On 16 June 1976 Soweto, with the biggest concentration of urban blacks in the country, exploded with student unrest on a scale not experienced in South Africa before. Political unrest spread nationwide and business confidence was at an all-time low. In his 1977 chairman's address Rupert referred to domestic economic problems brought about by 'the recent global recession and political developments in South Africa'. He pleaded with both the authorities and his colleagues in the business sector that the challenge of changes in the country should be faced, not purely reactively, but positively and innovatively: confidence, he said, creates confidence, both at home and abroad. What was needed was positive proof of that confidence, not just in the economy but also in the loyalty and responsibility of all population groups. 'In this regard,' he said, 'I'm thinking particularly of urgent steps to create more opportunities. Redistribution of possessions is a one-off gesture, creating illusions of prosperity – redistribution of opportunities, on the other hand, creates lasting prosperity'. And again he emphasised his theme of a company's threefold responsibility. 'Our Programme of Service to the Community . . . is based on the principle that "he who wants to retain all, will lose all': in other words, that self-interest does not mean selfishness.'

Rupert's philosophy stood in marked contrast to that of the free market guru and Nobel laureate Milton Friedman, whose 1970 article entitled 'The social responsibility of business is to increase its profits' in *The New York Times Magazine* caused a stir. In his book *Capitalism and freedom* he went so far as to call social responsibility in its broadest sense a fundamentally subversive idea. In Friedman's view, since companies were creating wealth, remunerating employees and paying taxes to the state, they had no responsibility to use for social purposes the funds that should accrue to their shareholders.

In Rupert's address of 1977 he referred once again to the shareholders' association's criticism of Rembrandt's investment in social programmes in 1962. He agreed: shareholders were entitled to know how their money was managed. He cited Adam Smith's doctrine that a free market creates the greatest wealth for the greatest number of people, as propounded in *The wealth of nations* in 1776. He quoted Smith's well-known description of business people being led by 'an invisible hand' to do more good for society than they had ever consciously planned. To do so they needed a profit motive, one of the mainsprings of human progress. Without it development got bogged down in excessive centralisation and bureaucracy. Profit was also the yardstick of efficiency. Profit generated the money that paid taxes to fund development projects and services. Technological development, maintaining and expanding production factors, good wages and salaries, the purchase of new equipment, vitally important research with a view to new products – all these depended on profit.

But Rupert went further. Two extremes must be avoided: on one hand for business to concentrate exclusively on profit maximisation, on the other hand the radical trend to blame all social ills on big business and advocate state control. Within the framework of the free-enterprise system, 'the contract between business and society should be expanded so that social responsibility becomes an additional function of the private sector.' The free-enterprise system had always operated in the context of society and thus it had to adapt to changing social circumstances and expectations simply in order to survive. That was why child labour was abolished in Britain and why air and environmental pollution had to be combated.

He endorsed the views expressed a quarter of a century earlier by the founder of the American business journal *Forbes* when the latter wrote that the purpose of the journal in 1917 was to 'promulgate humaneness in business, then woefully lacking', because too many individual and corporate employers were 'merely mercenarily-minded, obsessed only with determination to roll up profits regardless of the suicidal consequences of their short-sighted conduct. They were without consciousness of their civic, social, patriotic responsibilities.' The writer warned that if employers did not change their tactics, politicians would do it for them, and the employers would not like it.

In Rupert's view, 'the best way to do business in the long term is to discharge our responsibilities to the community out of gratitude in order to create a climate within which profitable business can still be done in the future'.[14] This notion, which he expressed in 1977, is today uppermost on the global agenda, with the emphasis on sustainable development.

The state also had to play its part, however, by looking at tax structures that would encourage social responsibility efforts on the part of the private sector. He cautioned against expectations that the state should do everything, which anyway is not in the interest of society. Besides, Adam Smith had warned that if you expect that the state should do something *for* you, you must be prepared that the state could do something *to* you.

'A basis of sound mutual cooperation' was in the interest of both the state and the private sector. He concluded by quoting the Canadian economist WL MacKenzie King, who said in 1919: 'Labour can do nothing without Capital, Capital nothing without Labour and neither Labour nor Capital can do anything without the genius of Management; and Management, however wise its genius may be, can do nothing without the privileges which the community affords.' On these grounds Rupert subscribed to a definition of business as 'honourably serving the public at a profit'.

In his 1977 address Rupert provided a list of services to the community by means of seven institutions in which Rembrandt was actively involved: Historical Homes of South Africa; the SA Nature Foundation, founded in 1968 to promote conservation of the country's natural heritage; the Rembrandt van Rijn Art Foundation; the SA Sport Foundation, serving all population groups since 1964; the Urban Foundation, established in 1976 to address the critical social conditions in urban areas; the Lesotho National Development Corporation; and Edesa, the development corporation established as Rupert's brainchild to advance development in Equatorial and South Africa.

In his approach to corporate social responsibility, as in his companies, Rupert consistently followed a long-term strategy and undertook projects of which the fruits would only be reaped much later. Recognition often also came much later. On 18 April 2002, Remgro (as the group was renamed after unbundling in 2000) was honoured at the annual Birmingham International Festival in Alabama 'in recognition of corporate excellence and social responsibility towards the people of South Africa' over a period of more than 50 years. Remgro's CEO, Thys Visser, travelled to the USA to receive the Silver Crown award, with which the South African companies Pick 'n Pay and Standard Bank had also been honoured.

CHAPTER 14

On political minefields

D uring the 1960s Rupert started playing an increasingly active role in public life. While always wary of being dragged into party politics, he often found himself on political minefields. By this time his long-standing belief in coexistence had not only deepened, but he was also putting it into practice in his personal capacity as well as through the Rembrandt Group.

In 1947, when he had already turned to business, Rupert's political convictions took a direction that was to become more sharply defined in time to come. This was the year before the National Party (NP) of Dr DF Malan, whom Rupert had met in his student years in Pretoria, came to power and put South Africa on the road of statutorily enforceable apartheid. The Nationalist takeover in 1948 was preceded by fierce debates in Afrikaner circles. Furthermore, it occurred in the aftermath of the Second World War. Afrikaners, economically inferior to their English-speaking compatriots, strove for political power not only in pursuit of their ideals of political independence, but also to obtain a secure foothold in the economy. In fact, economic self-reliance for Afrikaners was initially probably a greater incentive for the acceptance of apartheid than ideological and racist convictions.

A debate on South Africa's political future between Judge HA Fagan and physics professor AC Cilliers took place in Stellenbosch in 1947. It was to have a great influence on Rupert, who was in the audience. At the time of the debate Afrikaner nationalism was burgeoning. Fagan, in his younger days an Afrikaans language activist who later became a cabinet minister in the Hertzog-Smuts fusion government in the 1930s, had caused a stir with his commission report on the race issue for the Smuts government in 1946. In it he rejected both total segregation and racial equality as feasible options. Instead he proposed a middle course, acknowledging that black and white would continue to coexist, but economically interdependent. Against Cilliers, whose views reflected popular Afrikaner opinion, Fagan defended the view that racial segregation did not offer a solution to the country's sociopolitical problems. He conceded that there was some segregation in everyday life, but to make it an overriding political ideal would exacerbate conflict, not mitigate it.

That evening, Rupert told himself that Fagan was right. The country's salvation did not lie in racial segregation; instead, South Africans would have to learn to cooperate and coexist. In political terms, Rupert was ahead of his time. In 1948 already he pleaded in vain that South Africa should welcome uprooted post-war West Europeans to provide an injection of skills into the under-skilled South African economy. His plea for development through immigration fell on deaf ears. The NP feared that if such 'aliens' obtained the vote, they would not vote for the nationalist Afrikaner cause.

In the 1948 election the NP had asked whites to vote for apartheid. Given the post-war climate of economic and political disillusionment, also among returning soldiers, they won. Smuts suffered the same fate as the British war hero Winston Churchill. The former Dutch Reformed minister Malan headed the new government. Flying in the face of post-holocaust world opinion, it started to implement its policy of forced racial segregation increasingly wider and more rigidly. Fagan, who would become chief justice in 1957, adopted a philosophical attitude to the outcome of the 1948 election, in which the Nationalists rejected his recommendation about black urbanisation. He did not doubt that whites would remain in the saddle. If territorial segregation worked, well and good. If not, it would nonetheless be a preparatory stage to make the public realise that territorial segregation was impossible, so that they could find the best way of adapting to what was possible.

Fagan's view was closely related to Rupert's notion of coexistence. In any case, Rupert did not regard the dour Malan as a very practical person – he was too much of a 'theoretician'. In his opinion, Malan allowed himself to be influenced by 'typical politicians' like Paul Sauer. Sauer often travelled by car with Malan from Stellenbosch, where they both lived, to Cape Town, and then used the opportunity to plant ideas in Malan's mind.

Rupert made his first public plea for coexistence at the second National Economic Congress in Bloemfontein in 1950 in a speech that signalled his inclusive political thinking (see Chapter 8). His approach was cautious and diplomatic; some of his supporters would later say too cautious and diplomatic. But this was typical of Rupert. He was not keen to get involved in public debates and was even reluctant to respond to public criticism.

Prior to Ghana's independence in 1957, he proposed a 'Malan doctrine' that he regarded as appropriate for the *uhuru* era of decolonisation: a message that South Africa as one of Africa's four independent countries welcomes the new African states as free states. His plea was motivated by a passionate vision of a South Africa organised on the basis of coexistence, both within its borders and externally with fellow African states. The idea did not impress the rulers, and South Africa missed a golden opportunity to extend its influence on the continent.

The 1950s were decisive years for the future politics of South Africa. Afrikaner nationalism went from strength to strength. Coloureds were removed from the common voters' roll and when Dr Hendrik Verwoerd became prime minister in 1958, he started putting his stamp on the political process among Afrikaners and in parliament. Apartheid was interpreted as geographic segregation on racial lines, a form of balkanisation of South Africa. With news of anti-white and anti-Indian ostracism drifting in from elsewhere in Africa, Verwoerd could capitalise on white fears. These were also fed by growing organised protest among South Africa's black population. During a protest march by women in Pretoria pass-books that black people were compelled to carry by law were burned in a huge demonstration of resistance. In June 1955 the ANC, not yet a banned organisation, held a conference at Kliptown where the Freedom Charter was accepted. This document, which declared that South Africa belonged to all who live in it, black and white, and advocated a non-racial, democratic form of government as well as nationalisation of the banks, mines and heavy industries, would become an important source of inspiration for black resistance to apartheid.

In the midst of the gathering storm Rupert steered clear of party politics, but proceeded to proclaim his views on coexistence and partnership wherever the opportunity presented itself.

Following his confrontation with Verwoerd in 1959, he was profoundly dis-illusioned that the head of state was prepared to intervene forcibly in the dynamics of the private sector for the sake of political ideology. The experience also made him highly sceptical of the political leaders of the apartheid years. He had 'no other alternative than to defend our position', and for at least the next seven years he explained his policy in addresses to meetings and business conferences as well as lectures to students. His felt his approach could best be described in the words of the poet NP van Wyk Louw as a form of *'lojale verset'* (loyal resistance). Most of these speeches appear in a collection entitled *Progress through partnership.* Addressing the Afrikaans Chamber of Commerce in Worcester in July 1959,[1] he cited Pres. Paul Kruger's farewell message: 'Take from the past that which is good and use it to build the future.' Kruger might be considered conservative, Rupert pointed out, but he had also been progressive: he had awarded a medal to the first person who brought a motorcar to the Transvaal; he floated above Paris in a balloon; he bought the first submarine patent in the world. 'It would therefore be much better to put the emphasis on "building the future" – or, as I would like to put it: "Use the past as a springboard to the future, not as a sofa."'

Rupert also questioned the laws discriminating against coloureds, whom he regarded in the words of Prof. WJ du P Erlank as 'an underprivileged but integral part of the Afrikaans language community'. Morality could not be imposed by law and Afrikaner legalism would learn its mistake. He went further and criticised two other aspects of government policy: its constraints on immigration and its concept of development of the black homelands, which he considered impracticable and shortsighted. 'We are too scared of industrial development in the black areas. I have already . . . indicated that the developed industrial areas have nothing to fear from the developing areas.'

Verwoerd, adamantly opposed to the deployment of white capital in black homelands (which he regarded as 'neo-colonialism'), reacted that he would not be dictated to by businessmen intent only on filling their own pockets. Angered by this misrepresentation of his motives, Rupert requested an interview a second time.

He was driven to parliament by his personal assistant, Wynand van Graan, in a company car, a blue Chrysler Imperial, which he had been insisting for some time should be replaced. When he emerged from the building an hour later, he was clearly disturbed by the conversation with Verwoerd. He asked Van Graan for the car keys, saying he would drive. When he unlocked the driver's door, the handle came off in his hand. Demonstrating icy control even in the most trying circumstances, he said, 'Mr van Graan, it is really time this car should be replaced.'[2] The episode with Verwoerd was the end of the Chrysler Imperial; it was replaced.

As a result of this clash with Verwoerd Rupert focused his attention on overseas interests, where he could practise his partnership philosophy without restraint. His move overseas was eventually much more profitable than if he had remained only in South Africa – a fact that often caused Rupert to respond with annoyance to allegations that he had benefited from favourable treatment on the part of government. It had rather been the opposite, already early on in the war years when he was not permitted to import cigarette machines, and as also clearly shown by his clashes with, inter alia, Verwoerd and Ben Schoeman.

Rupert's next clash with government opinion was over Harold Macmillan's famous wind-of-change speech a month before the Sharpeville shootings in March 1960. The British premier's message to South Africa's white parliamentarians was: 'The wind of change is blowing through this continent and, whether we like it or not, the growth of national consciousness is a political fact. We must all accept it as a fact, and our national policies must take account of it.' Verwoerd reacted fiercely: there must not only be justice done to blacks in Africa but also to whites. Rupert, by contrast, welcomed Macmillan's frankness. He told the Canadian-South African Businessmen's Association that objecting to the British prime minister's speech was rather like people inviting a preacher from elsewhere to preach to their congregation and then criticising him for speaking about their own sins rather than their neighbours'. He reiterated: white South Africa could not barricade itself or save itself with laws, for laws can never enforce morality. The country was facing both a population explosion and a tide of rising expectations. Europe needed Africa and Africa needed Europe. South Africa, the axis between the two continents, could still show the world the way to coexistence in partnership, but 'the challenge facing us in the great emergency can only be met with the utmost sacrifice'.[3]

In a subsequent press statement[4] to clear up 'certain misunderstandings', Rupert said he had tried to make it clear that 'we are really not as wrong as many people abroad seem to think. With regard to the whole of the West (America included) I advocated economic cooperation with the new emerging states of Africa on a basis of true partnership.' He pointed out that foreign companies in other African states would have to change their attitude radically by opening up investment opportunities to the indigenous populations. 'In this respect South Africa has already gone much further. Any person, regardless of colour and race, is free to buy whatever shares he wants.' He pointed out that Macmillan, with his authority as British prime minister, for the first time honestly and unambiguously focused on a problem that had long been a topic of discussion in South African circles. He concluded: 'I can see no other solution than for the West to embrace much more strongly the direction of economic partnership in Africa. He who wants to keep everything for himself, will lose everything. Moreover, of what avail is it to someone to gain the whole world and lose his soul?'

His next meeting with Verwoerd, even more catastrophic than the one in 1959 when they had clashed about his plans for a factory in Paarl, took place scarcely more than a month later, shortly after the Sharpeville debacle on 21 March 1960.

The reverberations of the tragedy, where the police had shot dead 69 black protestors, spread throughout the country. Albert Luthuli, leader of the ANC, burnt his pass and urged people to stay away from work. On 30 March, 30 000 black people marched from Langa township to Caledon Square in the centre of Cape Town, led by 19-year-old Philip Kgosana. Kgosana who was not a member of the ANC but the Western Cape regional secretary of Robert Sobukwe's Pan-Africanist Congress (PAC), a black nationalist organisation established in 1959 by a group who broke away from the ANC, which was organising a countrywide campaign against the hated pass laws. At that stage the PAC, and not the ANC, was the dominant black resistance movement in Cape Town. The march was peaceful, well organised and disciplined, contrary to white expectations. The leaders were told that if they handed over their protest document and dispersed quietly, there would be no reprisals. The police spokesman, Col. IPS Terblanche, also promised them a meeting with the Minister of Police, Frans Erasmus, a promise that was not kept by government. Instead, the leaders of the march were arrested shortly afterwards and the government introduced legislation to have the ANC, the PAC and the SA Communist Party declared prohibited organisations.

The night after the march, Patrick Duncan and his brother (sons of a former governor-general of the Union, Sir Patrick Duncan) arranged for Rupert to meet Philip Kgosana at a 'neutral' house.[5] Kgosana was wearing shoes without laces, Rupert remembered. He was amazed that such a poor, young person could have led such a huge crowd.

The protest march had been a shock to him, just as Sharpeville, the stayaways and the outflow of money from the country had shocked other whites profoundly. 'I then knew that this was the start of a potentially long-term revolution,' he said in his submission to the TRC in 1997.[6]

Kgosana was out on bail after his arrest, one of 18 000 people arrested in that period. He subsequently fled the country and spent 36 years in exile. In his book *Lest we forget*, Kgosana wrote that Duncan had invited him to meet 'prominent personalities' who were interested in the PAC campaign:

> 'Who did I find in the house but Ngwenya, the ANC Chairman for Cape Town, and Anton Rupert, a hard-core racist member of the Nationalist Party? I was taken aback, but decided to keep cool.
>
> 'For a good 30 minutes, Rupert lectured me about the futility of our action. He told me I was very young and inexperienced, and probably was being misled. He went on to talk about the political evolution of nations, citing examples from European history, and told me that African people could not ride roughshod over history without plunging South Africa into utter destruction. Ngwenya sat there, smiling, as the racist capitalist babbled a lot of nonsense.
>
> 'I told Rupert that the revolution was on, and that nothing could stop the winds of change that were blowing across the continent.'[7]

According to Kgosana, Duncan then said a few words, apparently to narrow the gap between him and Rupert. They were invited to dinner, but Kgosana maintained he was not 'properly dressed' in terms of white standards. Duncan lent him a tie and on his way to the bathroom he reprimanded Duncan's black domestic worker because she had failed to observe their campaign. 'The incident turned the dinner a bit sour, but we went through it exchanging a lot of good-for-nothing talk and comments,' wrote Kgosana, who, according to Rupert, did not have much to say to him that evening.

Kgosana's view of Rupert as 'a hard-core racist member of the Nationalist Party' is indicative of the extent to which perceptions in South Africa diverge. In diametric opposition to this perception, an extreme right-wing paper, *Die Afrikaner*, in 1981 described Rupert's role in the 1960s thus:

'The political climate in the 1960s was extremely unfavourable for Dr Rupert and his ideas. With Dr Verwoerd as prime minister, the tobacco magnate was not a member of the National Afrikaner establishment and, unlike today, he exercised a futile, peripheral influence on politics. Relations between him and Dr Verwoerd were so strained that he was once virtually thrown out of Dr Verwoerd's office.'[8]

Yet another point of view was expressed by ANC leader Albert Luthuli in his evidence in his sensational treason trial in 1956. Asked how he saw the difference in outlook between Afrikaner businessmen and industrialists on one hand and the government and farmers on the other, he said that there were some signs that the former were questioning the policy: some Afrikaner businessmen appeared to favour easing the pressure on blacks. 'I recall Dr Rupert – there are also others, he's not the only one, but I remember him saying: "One must keep the workers in mind, they should be able to ask for better wages."'[9]

The cataclysmic events of 1960 became another turning point in Rupert's life. He put his pride in his pocket, as he put it himself, and asked Verwoerd for another interview. He told the prime minister that he saw these events as the start of a never-ending spiral of insurrection and violence. He was also concerned about the unmistakable swing in international sympathy. One point of conflict, he said, was that black people were not allowed to own property in urban areas. The conflict situation could only be tempered through the creation of stability, for example, by granting freehold rights to workers in areas such as Sharpeville. Blacks should be given the opportunity to own homes, however humble these might be. Verwoerd responded sharply that blacks were temporary residents in white South Africa and would return to their own territories in due course – he set the date at 1978. (This mythical date was to become a target of opposition derision.)

Rupert then proposed 99-year leasehold as an option, citing the example of London, where even the American embassy stood on such property. Verwoerd rejected it out of hand. Not deterred, Rupert proposed a system of 30-year leasehold to stabilise black communities until such time as Verwoerd could realise his dream of segregation and reverse the movement of blacks into urban areas. By now Verwoerd was thoroughly incensed. Rupert, realising that Verwoerd was bluffing and that the black influx into the cities could not be reversed, made a final bid: if he were Verwoerd, he said, he would offer houses at a discount to long-term tenants to ensure stability – in fact, it would be better to give them away rather than allow a revolutionary climate to develop. He based his proposal on the view that home ownership was the basis of savings. A home was also the first form of security a person needed to start anything – black families had to be given security.

Verwoerd liked this even less, and never forgave Rupert for it. The two men never again spoke directly to one another.

Rupert's strong conviction that adequate housing was a prerequisite for a stable, healthy community was not just idle talk. As usual, he put his money where his mouth was and two housing projects were constructed for Rembrandt staff, one at Stellenbosch, the other at Paarl. In Paarlita Park 67 families were housed in attractive cottages with all modern amenities, built in the style of the historical Drostdyhof at Graaff-Reinet. The housing estate, one of the first of its kind in the Western Cape, had a park atmosphere and no motor traffic was allowed. At Stellenbosch Oude Meester provided their coloured workers with equally tastefully designed housing at Stellita Park, with a splendid view of Papegaaiberg and the surrounding wine farms. Huberte and other Rembrandt wives made lined curtains for the cottages so that night-shift workers would be able to sleep by day. Later, in the tempestuous year of 1976, Rupert announced that his group proposed providing housing for their Johannesburg staff as well. The (subsequently banned) newspaper for black readers, *The World*, hailed it as 'a ray of hope in a country otherwise plagued by unrest'. According to the paper nothing was more important to the future of the country than a stable and secure black community. Rupert's announcement was an act of faith and hope. 'What Dr Rupert has done in effect', it said, 'is to waken this country's social conscience. He is saying to his fellow industrialists that nothing is gained by accusing the government of making a mess of things. One must do something about it. Race relations must be improved.'[10]

On 8 April 1960 the ANC and the PAC were declared prohibited organisations. The next day, at the Rand Easter Show, a mentally disturbed white man, David Pratt, shot Verwoerd in the head. While the seriously wounded Verwoerd was recovering in hospital, the senior minister, Paul Sauer, made a dramatic speech at Humansdorp. He said that the old book of South African history had been closed a few weeks earlier at Sharpeville. 'As far as the immediate future is concerned, we would have to reconsider our whole approach to the Native question'. This earned him a rebuke from Verwoerd, who regarded key policy issues as his preserve. At the end of the parliamentary session he nonetheless announced measures very similar to what Sauer had mooted at Humansdorp. These affected passbooks, alcoholic beverages (under grand apartheid blacks were only permitted sorghum beer), urban contact with blacks, better wages and the development of the 'Bantu' territories.

The gulf between Verwoerd and Rupert was so deep that it was never to be bridged. 'I came to the conclusion that we had no other option but to follow a policy of "loyal resistance",' Rupert explained. 'By this I mean that as loyal South Africans we would defend our country abroad, but we would oppose unwise policies at home.'

Sauer, who lived across the street from the Ruperts in Stellenbosch, regretted the way in which Verwoerd cut all ties with Rupert. While they were not close friends, Sauer thought highly of Rupert's business acumen and clear-sighted, progressive thinking. 'Verwoerd never again wanted to hear anything good about Rupert,' said Sauer, who described Verwoerd as 'stubborn'. 'Vorster [his successor as prime minister] was completely different. He rated Rupert's friendship and his value to the country highly.'

But the breach was irreversible and Rupert's advocacy of 50/50 partnership between white entrepreneurs and blacks in the homelands to stimulate development and economic independence merely aggravated matters. According to Sauer, Verwoerd only had faith in people who accepted his views unquestioningly – he resented those who disagreed even slightly with him and never forgot it.[11] Blinded by the ideology of separate development, Verwoerd insisted that state corporations should develop the homelands, not private enterprise.

In March 1961 Verwoerd attended the conference of Commonwealth heads of state in London. It was two months before South Africa became a republic. The country's continued membership of the Commonwealth had become a contentious issue, on one hand because of apartheid and on the other hand as a result of Verwoerd's ideal to declare the then Union of South Africa a republic. Piet Meiring, Head of the South African Information Service, preceded Verwoerd 'to help prepare the way for our request to remain within the Commonwealth'.[12] Rupert happened to be in London at the time. The day before Verwoerd was due to arrive he bumped into Meiring. He suggested that an advertisement be placed in the British press, at his expense, to point out how much Britain would lose if South Africa was kicked out of the Commonwealth. The advertisement duly appeared in all major papers and caused a stir. According to Meiring, Verwoerd was furious when he learned that Rupert had footed the bill. He could not repeat the words Verwoerd had used, said Meiring.[13]

Unintimidated by Verwoerd's inflexible ideological stance, Rupert proposed at Oudtshoorn in 1961 that 'apartheid' be replaced by 'coexistence' – and he was speaking about policy, not just terminology. What he had in mind was an alternative political way of life for all South Africans. South Africa, regarded as a 'heroic nation'at the beginning of the 20th century, was now eschewed as the world's 'polecat', he said. Good deeds would not influence world opinion. What was needed was 'an idea to combat an idea' – an idea that captured the imagination and could be sold worldwide. 'I believe that idea to be "industrial partnership" between developed and underdeveloped communities – between us and the Bantu.' Unlike the proponents of rigorist racial segregation, Rupert did not see the multiracial composition of South African society as a threat. In this respect his thinking differed from that of many South Africans. For him it was rather a challenge to be met with courageous deeds and creative thinking, more so if it concurred with his conviction that a canton system was the most suitable system of government for the country.

Opening the Port Elizabeth agricultural show in February 1961, he made an appeal to his compatriots' reason and common sense. Sharpeville had not shattered his hopes for his country; he believed South Africa's people could promote peace and prosperity on the continent. But it was a gross fallacy to think that the prosperity of white and black South Africa could be divided. It was downright dangerous to think that whites could live in affluence while blacks were struggling to subsist. A laager mentality would get South Africa nowhere, he said. The idea that military power would assure national survival in a hostile world was a pipedream.

The *Eastern Province Herald* welcomed his speech: 'As a nation we remain – let us admit it – self-centred and complacent. It is left to a few far-sighted individuals – people of the calibre of Dr Rupert – to develop a policy of good neighbourliness that would include the whole of Africa.'[14]

A few months later the Institute for Marketing Management named him Marketing Man of the Year. At a dinner to mark the occasion he again warned about apartheid as a policy based on whites' fear of losing their home. The solution lay in industrial partnership with as yet underdeveloped black people. Half the shares in new industries in and around the homelands should be taken up by the Bantu Development Corporation. 'This should be followed by a movement across the colour bar by putting blacks in responsible positions in industry.'[15]

Addressing the African Affairs Society of America in New York in 1962 he said that, however important politics may be, South Africa's racial problems would not be solved by political parties. Sceptical about politicians after his experiences with Verwoerd, he was convinced that the possibility of a solution lay in industrial development. He went further: democracy, he declared, needed a responsible economy more than a responsible polity.

Back home Rupert told students at the University of Pretoria in 1962, the reproach in his voice diplomatically softened by his choice of words: 'It is strange that we could establish a factory on a partnership basis in Malaysia but not in the Transkei. There is no reason for fear. Trust can and must create mutual trust.'

In a no-confidence debate in parliament on 23 January 1962 the opposition leader, Sir De Villiers Graaff, referred to Rupert's views in this regard. He quoted Rupert as saying, 'We must develop at least one of the Bantu homelands on a large scale. An area as big as Pondoland should, for instance, be able to provide for eleven million people if they went to work as productively as the people of the Netherlands.' Rupert, said Graaff, had added as 'gentle criticism' of the government: 'I do not think we can achieve this by methods at present being used without adding to it white industrial partnership.' In his response to Graaff's speech Verwoerd's tortuous economic reasoning was manifest. He explicitly rejected Rupert's partnership policy: unlike Malaysia, Transkei was not an independent country. Here it would be a matter of white guardians permitting a partnership. 'On no account may we get a reputation for imposing any form of economic imperialism. We also must not come with an element of bluff, as is inherent in that proposal.' They would not be able to bluff anyone that such partnerships would not still be white enterprises. These entrepreneurs were sure to exploit cheap labour, which would not be permitted in Bantu territories, for it would destroy their development if they were to become 'second Hong Kongs'. The principle remained that 'there could be no private white ownership or even co-ownership of industries'. Verwoerd's solution was border industries on the peripheries of black territories, and secondly, industrial development 'with the aid of machinery under the trusteeship principle'.[16]

In direct contrast to Verwoerd's views, Rupert knew from experience that industrial partnership worked, and was convinced that such partnership between the developed and developing countries, between the West and the emerging states, could bring about an 'economic rearmament'. In 1963 he wrote that all new enterprises started by outsiders in a country should be based on 'the principle of equal partnership with the local population'. Recalling that he had already advocated at the Second Economic National Congress thirteen years before that whites should assist with the development of black areas on a basis of full industrial partnership, he considered it 'a tragedy' that this policy had not been followed earlier within South Africa as well as in the rest of Africa. 'We would have been able to set the pace for the whole of Africa.'

While some may call this impractical, he believed in it since it had worked in his group. It also seemed to him to be morally the only correct policy. One could not use the labour, communication systems, public services, goodwill and markets of a country without admitting its inhabitants as equal partners. He emphasised that one should put trust and confidence in people in order to gain trust. 'Where there is no trust, life no longer has any purpose or meaning. Albert Schweitzer once said trust is the most important "capital" in any enterprise, since nothing of essential value can be established without it. Trust is risky. But mistrust is an even greater risk, particularly in these times.'

To prove the power of ideas as opposed to force of arms, he cited the examples of Christ and Paul. Christ started with twelve disciples, one of them a traitor; and in Rome Paul stood alone. But both had an idea. Subsequently the Christian church grew into a mighty force throughout the world; the Roman empire crumbled. He again referred to Schweitzer, 'that great benefactor of Africa', who reportedly said: 'Everyone is getting involved in politics – but no one is prepared to work.' 'Let us therefore get to work,' Rupert wrote.[17] He believed firmly that industry was 'the lifeblood' of a country and its people – the only way to pay for public amenities, education, health and other social services.

In an article in *Industry and Trade* in 1963, Rupert emphasised trust and compassion (closely related to the African concept of ubuntu) as prerequisites for the progress and prosperity of South Africa. He advocated such an attitude in the further acceleration of the industrialisation of the country: '. . . compassion among the many races in this multiracial country . . . the compassion to look for points of agreement rather than differences.' He cited the motor-vehicle industry, which in a country like Australia was a major economic activator. He illustrated it with a 'humble example'. One day his two sons of nine and eleven years old showed him a shining automobile belonging to a black man. The car was much better than theirs. He answered: 'You ought to be thankful for that car and should wish that all blacks own such cars – then they won't be jealous of ours.'

Australia's success could be replicated in South Africa if people of all races had the income to buy cars and create a market for the second phase of industrialisation. 'This applied to other branches of industry as well,' wrote Rupert, who had understood at a very early stage that shared prosperity offered part of the solution to South Africa's racial problems.[18] He made no secret of the fact that one of the greatest disappointments of his life was that he had not been able to convince the then rulers of the merits of his partnership policy.

Rupert's repeated pleas that appropriate industries should be established in South Africa's black homelands like the Transkei were rejected by Verwoerd, who was in favour of vertical, rigorist racial segregation with no private enterprise cooperation between white and black in either the homelands or the rest of the country.

Their disagreement on this topic was echoed in an emotional debate in parliament on the economic development of black homelands that took place in 1964. The Deputy Minister of Bantu Administration, MC Botha, challenged the opposition to invest in the homelands. Gray Hughes, United Party MP for an Eastern Cape constituency, pointed out that the challenge was hollow, for when Rupert wanted to do just that, Verwoerd blocked him. This was in keeping with the government white paper on homeland development, based on the Tomlinson report. Daan Nel, Minister of Bantu Administration and a staunch Verwoerdian, said that no white industrialist would be prepared to build up a factory in a Bantu area and hand it over holus-bolus to the black residents. Nor was that what Rupert had in mind, he hinted darkly, and his plans were not acceptable to government either.[19]

Verwoerd's opposition to white investment in black territories was further confirmation of his lack of business sense, a failing that was known in a small circle from early on. This blind spot caused many white traders and businesspeople to vacate the Transkei, further crippling the homeland's precarious economy. Along with communal land ownership, the Achilles heel of many African countries, Verwoerd's poor grasp of economic realities was a recipe for disaster. The upshot was that the Eastern Cape, where the 'independent' states of Transkei and Ciskei were created, became one of the most impoverished and backward regions in the country.

The Verwoerdian homeland policy, more than anything else, resulted in a process of impoverishment in South Africa that became virtually unmanageable. Rupert hammered home the reality: by excluding private enterprise on the part of white entrepreneurs from the homeland areas, central government had to keep pumping in more and more money that the country could ill afford. Homeland policy never stimulated development or generated wealth. Instead, it amounted to giving away wealth. At one stage there were ten homelands, either 'independent' or 'self-governing' states. Each had to have its own government and cabinet, its own parliament, law courts, bureaucracy, in some cases its own army, plus the infrastructure to accommodate these. In the 1980s Rupert told Barend du Plessis, then Minister of Finance, who had explained to him the financial implications of the homelands for central government: 'You are now like a man with ten sons, and each son has signing rights to your bank account'.[20] One result was that the buying power of the rand dropped horrendously, as shown in a graph constructed for Rupert. In 1971 a R100 in 1961 terms was worth R71,50; in 1981 it was R23,90, in 1991 R6,10 and by 2001 a mere R2,70. While the homeland policy cannot be blamed exclusively for this decline, it certainly was a major contributory factor.

One result of Rupert's conflict with Verwoerd was a bit of pure irony. In 1965 the newly established University of Port Elizabeth (UPE) in the Eastern Cape wanted him to be its first chancellor. Verwoerd vetoed it.[21] As a result of his intervention the office went to Rupert's old adversary the Minister of Transport Ben Schoeman, who held it until 1977. By then Verwoerd was dead and the new chancellor was a native of the Eastern Cape and the university's original choice: Anton Rupert. (It was on the occasion of his inauguration that Albert Geyser apologised to him for the attempted tarring-and-feathering incident years before on the UP campus.) Rupert was chancellor of UPE for five years, until 1982. In 1987 he became chancellor of his alma mater, the UP, an office he held until 1997.

At a time that South Africa was increasingly faced with international isolation, also in the field of sport, Rupert embarked on an imaginative initiative, the Sport Foundation of South Africa, in 1964. In 1960 South Africa's racial policies had cost it its membership of the Olympic association, and with that the right to compete in the 1964 Games. The idea for a sport foundation came from Gerhard Roux, Rembrandt's head of public relations, after a visit to South Africa by the New Zealand athlete Peter Snell, who was involved with a similar foundation in his home country. Roux, excited by the idea, spoke to Rupert, who promptly moved into action in his characteristic style, securing the backing of a top South African athlete, Danie Joubert. On 10 November 1964 the Rembrandt Group launched the Sport Foundation, to be administered by Rembrandt staff under the leadership of Gerhard Roux, with a view to raising the standard of amateur sport through expert coaching and training. Rupert pointed out in a speech that the group had already established an art foundation, but a 'sound mind needs a healthy body. We wanted to look after Athens, but also Sparta. That is why we decided to launch the Sport Foundation.'

In those days sport sponsorships were few and far between and there was a desperate need for professional coaching. The Foundation catered for all age groups, for both genders, and, remarkable at that time, for all population groups. Its advisory board included eminent figures in the sporting world, such as Danie Craven (rugby), Ken Viljoen (cricket), Frank Braun (boxing and Olympic Games), Dawid (Sasol) de Villiers and Matt Maré (athletics), JL Barrie (tennis) and Hannes Botha (youth sport). No tobacco advertising was permitted at Foundation sport meetings or on its vehicles: it propagated itself simply as an agency that helped others to help themselves. Top South African sportsmen like Cliff Drysdale, Gert Potgieter and Trevor Goddard were drawn in as part-time coaches. Overseas sportspeople and experts were brought to South Africa, among them the Wimbledon champion Jaroslav Drobny and the Australian test cricket umpire Colin Egar. Two well-known New Zealand athletes gave courses specifically for coloured athletes. Courses for sportspeople and local coaches were offered throughout the country and as far afield as Namibia.

Overseas tours were organised for black athletes, many of them mineworkers, who had been coached with the approval and cooperation of Harry Oppenheimer. As could be seen from later achievements, many of South Africa's best black athletes hailed from the mines, including Josiah Thugwane, winner of the gold medal in the marathon at the 1996 Olympics.

In the case of the Sport Foundation Rupert soon also experienced the kind of state interference he found reprehensible. In 1966 the government established its own Department of Sport. Eventually the universities' sports academies were also overlapping the Foundation's activities, and the advent of television in 1975 brought liberal funding to sport and sport development. In 1989 the Sport Foundation fizzled out, but by then it had provided over 4 000 training courses to some 300 000 sportspeople. The Rembrandt Group explained in a promotional publication what it had regarded as the true role of the Foundation: 'Sport, like music, art, culture and nature conservation, has the wonderful capacity to bring together people from divergent backgrounds, but with a common interest, and to forge ties of goodwill and friendship.'[22]

Rupert looked back ruefully on efforts by the state to do work the private sector could have done much better. He elaborated on this at the junior congress of the AHI in June 1979, where he also criticised the homeland policy. 'When the South Africa Foundation was established in 1959 to promote South Africa's interests abroad, the government did not appreciate it enough and founded the Department of Information. Everybody knows what the consequences were,' he said, obviously referring to the Information Scandal that had rocked the country. 'All I know is that in the field of sport South Africa has now been excluded from almost everything, and that it would perhaps have been better to leave matters like these in the hands of the private sector.'

Another initiative in the sphere of sport followed in 1967, when a number of yachts people decided there should be a South African entry in the tough Trans-atlantic Solo Race. Rupert made a big contribution to the *Voortrekker*, the South African-designed yacht manned by Bruce Dalling, then a lecturer at the University of Natal. Dalling ended second at the final destination in Newport, but was first on handicap. This remarkable achievement led to a resurgence of yachting in South Africa. A direct result was the Cape to Rio (later Cape to Uruguay) yacht race, which attracted many international participants from the outset. The *Voor-trekker* can also be regarded as an early stimulus for the creation of Cape Town's flourishing yacht-building industry.

In the mid-1960s Rupert started focusing strongly on the concept of leadership, particularly on the strength of his exposure to global trends and to leaders in a variety of fields. From a lecture he gave in 1963 at the UP it is clear that as restless thinker and observer of new tendencies he was already concentrating on an issue that would gain prominence in the late 1980s and the 1990s: leadership for the future.

He wrote to numerous leaders of that time to obtain their views on leadership. The list included, inter alia, Gen. Dwight Eisenhower, US President from 1953 to 1960; Clarence B Randall, American business philosopher; David Rockefeller, President of Chase Manhattan Bank; Frederic G Donner, Chairman of General Motors; Gen. Lauris Norstad, President of Owens-Corning Fibreglass Corporation; Field Marshal Sir William Slim, former Governor-General of Australia; Sir Francis de Guingand; Sir Nicholas Cayzer, Chairman of British and Commonwealth Shipping Company; the London commercial banker Edmund de Rothschild; Robert H Winters, former Canadian cabinet minister and Chairman of Rio Tinto Mining Company; Dr Paul Rijkens, former World Chairman of Unilever; Dr Hermann Abs, Managing Director of Deutsche Bank; Prof. Charles Mâlik of Lebanon, former President of the General Assembly of the United Nations; dato Nik A Kamil, leader of the Malaysian delegation at the UN; and South Africans like Dr Frikkie Meyer of Iscor, Rupert's partner Dirk Hertzog, and Clive Menell of Anglovaal.

From the answers he received, Rupert told the students, it was clear to him why the term enthusiasm came from a Greek word meaning 'to be inspired or possessed by a godhead'. To him, 'the heart is the source, the fountain of leadership'. That is why pessimists, cynics and nihilists could not be enthusiasts. Rupert used a powerful metaphor to hammer home his point: 'The fire of enthusiasm creates the driving force to do something, creates willingness to work and to assume responsibility.' He could not stand pessimism and cynicism, remarking to the students that the basic fault of modern capitalism was not inefficiency, but cynicism. He spoke in religious terms of the need for a dream to inspire and to fire one's enthusiasm. It is a 'matter of faith' – there must be a 'leitmotif', coupled with a 'readiness to serve', a 'sense of a calling'. Like the famous management consultant Lyndall Urwick, Rupert also said: 'If a person wants to have a conscious purpose in life, he must know that his life is worth living.' One therefore needs a cause, a purpose, as well as an organisational framework to keep the purpose alive.

Rupert compiled his own list of requirements for leadership from the answers he received. He emphasised that business leadership required a generalist: the leader with the ability 'to see the diverse components of an organisation as a whole, and to grasp quickly what is important'. The greatest need for the future, in his opinion, was 'the development of more and more leaders in all spheres of life – leaders who possess the knowledge, mettle, conviction and human understanding to master the problems of a shrinking world, of freer trade, of the population explosion and the necessity of better living conditions for all people.'[23]

In the 1960s Rupert was not in favour of universal franchise without reservation. On occasion he warned against the phenomenon of 'one person, one vote, once'. Addressing the Economic Club of Detroit in 1966, he quoted Lord Hailey: 'May it never be said that the African asked for bread and was given the vote.' He was not opposed to extending the franchise, but insisted that political development had to rest on a solid foundation of social and economic development. Without that prerequisite democracy could not survive, let alone broaden or deepen. His argument was straightforward: if people shared in the country's wealth and helped to create it, common interests and values were bound to evolve. That was the reasoning underlying his sensational minimum wage increase in 1963 (see Chapter 13).

Apartheid, argued Rupert, was built on the fears of whites. No political policy could succeed if it was built on fear. Policy had to be inspired by common interests and values – and the vision that partnership was in the interest of all.

In July 1966, with Verwoerdian apartheid in full swing in South Africa, Rupert appointed Thom Mtine, a Zambian, chairman of Rembrandt's operations in that country. Again *The World* gave him an accolade: 'There are very few men of his stamp in South Africa. If this country could raise only ten men with the same vision our relationships with the rest of Africa and the world would change overnight.'[24]

Two months later, on 6 September 1966, South Africa was rocked by a tragic and far-reaching event: Verwoerd was stabbed to death in parliament by the assassin Dimitrio Tsafendas. Rupert later came to believe that Verwoerd, who had been born in Amsterdam, was to Afrikaners the same kind of catastrophic outsider that, for example, Hitler had been to the Germans. In his opinion, a similar fate had befallen other countries under leaders who were essentially outsiders. Napoleon was a Corsican, Stalin a Georgian, and Hitler an Austrian. All three had ruled dictatorially and wreaked havoc in their adoptive countries.

'I always realised the man was an academic and a sociologist and not practically minded,' Rupert said about Verwoerd, the former university lecturer who had studied sociology in Berlin in 1933 together with Prof. Geoff Cronjé, another leading apartheid ideologue. He added: 'Apartheid, like communism and fascism, started with a good idea, but was mismanaged by people in practice. When an idea turns into an ideology, it later becomes very hard to turn the car round without capsizing it.' He also recalled that, as editor of *Die Transvaler*, Verwoerd had uttered not a word when the Nazis bombed Rotterdam and occupied the Netherlands in the Second World War, imposing dreadful hardship on that small country and killing many Dutch people, including relatives of Huberte Rupert. That was the nation that had sent a ship, the *Gelderland*, to Delagoa Bay during the Anglo-Boer War to transport the exiled Pres. Paul Kruger to Europe and had granted him asylum. Yet Verwoerd expressed no sign of public sympathy for the land of his birth in its hour of need, and Rupert blamed him and other ungrateful Afrikaners for this.

A sequel to Verwoerd's assassination was a letter Rupert received from the eminent Afrikaans poet NP van Wyk Louw after they had both been awarded honorary doctorates by the University of Stellenbosch. It was dated 12 September 1966, the day before Verwoerd's successor was due to be elected. Louw and friends such as Judge Kowie Marais foresaw disaster if John Vorster, the hardline Minister of Justice, became prime minister – as he duly did. He urged Rupert to reconsider his refusal to enter politics: he was needed at this time. Rupert had long made up his mind on that score. He declined courteously, writing that Louw's letter had moved and humbled him. 'For about 30 years I have felt us to be kindred spirits in loyal resistance. Let me say it frankly: I consider your worth to our nation as far more important than that of any politician. You have an instinctive sense of what lies ahead and there are unfortunately few – too few – of our contemporaries who know.' Rupert went on to say that he had spoken openly to leaders of the University of Pretoria and had elicited an 'extremely favourable reaction'. There was a 'glimmer of the realisation of our task and responsibility as "Afrikaner". But world politics itself keeps buying votes and is increasingly becoming the lowest common denominator.'[25]

In light of the animosity between the two men during Verwoerd's lifetime, it was ironic that the Verwoerd Trust in 1986 awarded Rupert the Hendrik Verwoerd prize comprising a medal and R20 000. Rupert promised the money to the SA Nature Foundation for resuscitating the indigenous flora around Betty's Bay, where the late prime minister had a holiday home. The reaction from far-right Afrikaner movements was damning. Verwoerd's daughter, Mrs Anna Boshoff, wrote to Rupert that her father would have been no less astonished at his receiving the prize than Cecil Rhodes would have been had he known that Verwoerd would one day occupy his house (Groote Schuur, the official prime minister's residence in Cape Town). Ironically, her husband, Prof. Carel Boshoff, was a trustee of the Trust that had made the contested award. In gentlemanly fashion Rupert returned the prize, because she felt it would dishonour the name of her father. He said he would honour the promise to the SA Nature Foundation from his own pocket. Although the Chairman of the Trust board, Willem Cruywagen, tried to persuade him to reconsider accepting the prize, Rupert declined.

Much later, 30 years after the stormy 1960s, a significant revelation was made to Rupert. In 1995, the former MP for Brits Koos Potgieter, chief whip of the NP for 27 years under, inter alia, Verwoerd, invited him for a personal interview to Pretoria. Old and ailing, Potgieter wanted to convey two important matters to Rupert. First, he apologised for an attack on Rembrandt he had made during a speech at Rustenburg in 1957 – it did not reflect his personal view, but was done at Verwoerd's request. Even more startling was his second disclosure: two days before Verwoerd's death he had summoned Potgieter to his office and told him he realised that the policy of apartheid was impracticable and could not be implemented.[26] If that is so, Potgieter asked, then why don't you change it? According to Potgieter, Verwoerd responded that such a step was not politically feasible at that stage: 'You can't turn the car around too sharply, it will capsize.' The quotation convinced Rupert that Verwoerd's thinking had changed radically.

It would always remain an unanswered riddle what Verwoerd, with his drive and intellectual abilities, might have been able to achieve with a fundamental change of direction. As indicated by a letter he had written to the Australian premier Sir Robert Menzies, he had probably already started thinking about integration of coloureds and whites. The economic needs of South Africa, which had achieved a growth rate of six percent under Verwoerd, also required greater utilisation of black workers. The urbanisation process and the flow of black people to centres of economic activity, much more than sanctions and international censure, precipitated the demise of apartheid. Rupert believed Verwoerd had gained new insights at a lunch the two of them had attended shortly before the assassination with Chief Leabua Jonathan of Lesotho, a month before that country became independent. In his opinion, the Basotho leader's pragmatic approach had impressed Verwoerd greatly during a long conversation. He wondered if Verwoerd's successors had not been left to implement a policy in which its own author no longer believed.

Opposition to Rupert's partnership philosophy continued under Verwoerd's successor BJ Vorster, despite the new prime minister's initially more relaxed approach to sport and relations with African states. In 1968 Rupert was criticised in parliament by the government spokesman on black affairs, Adv. GF van L (Sampie) Froneman, who said development of black homeland areas should take place via state-controlled agencies – 'white capital' had to be channelled through these agencies. Rupert's partnership policy, shouted Froneman, would lead to integration. Private initiative on the part of whites in black homelands would merely enrich whites at the expense of blacks. This would be nothing else than exploitation, Froneman maintained.[27]

Rupert's partnership approach not only elicited opposition and derogatory remarks from politicians. Even in his home town, Stellenbosch, he came under fire. He was wryly amused when some of his fiercest critics eventually ended up far to the left of him. A case in point was Sampie Terreblanche, Professor of Economics, at the time a prominent proponent of NP policies and at one time deputy chair of the control board of the South African Broadcasting Corporation (SABC). Terreblanche eventually became more socialist-minded and did such a complete about-turn that in the 1990s he became an equally vociferous critic of the old order, castigating other Afrikaners in particular. Later he became a critic of the new dispensation as well, publishing a work in 2003 in which he blamed the ANC government for doing too little for the poor.

A more vindictive enemy during the 1960s was SED Brown, editor of the *SA Observer*, an extreme right-wing political paper at one time subsidised by the National Party to gain English support. Brown spoke no Afrikaans, yet he spearheaded the acrimonious infighting between *verligtes* (the enlightened) and *verkramptes* (bigots) within the NP, triggered by Vorster's outward-looking policy that elicited far-right resistance. The run-up to this infighting that culminated in a fierce 'broedertwis' (fraternal quarrel) for Afrikaner hearts and minds was an increasing campaign of rumour-mongering directed at prominent Afrikaners. At one stage the *Observer* was printed by the Rembrandt-controlled Pro Ecclesia Press. After repeated personal attacks on Rupert in its columns, he terminated the contract and Brown joined Dr Albert Hertzog, Mr Jaap Marais and his right-wing peers in Pretoria. Brown expressed publicly much of the criticism voiced against Rupert by certain Afrikaners, mostly behind his back. They included those whom Vorster scornfully called the 'super-Afrikaners', who considered themselves the guardians of the nation's culture and religion. A conspiracy theorist par excellence, Brown represented Rupert's association with the Rothschilds and Rockefellers, his friends from 'the left-liberal, integrationist camp', as part of a misguided attempt to 'save Africa from communism' by providing aid for underdeveloped countries, thereby playing straight into the Kremlin's hands. He castigated Rupert for forsaking the Afrikaner cause he had espoused so nobly in his youth and focusing exclusively on money. Other targets of the *Observer's* wrath were Harry Oppenheimer, the SA Foundation and the United States-South African Leadership Exchange Programme. All these bridge builders, along with Rupert, were depicted as mortal enemies of the white Afrikaner nation.

In mid-1966 Ian Robertson, chairman of the anti-apartheid student organisation Nusas, invited John F Kennedy's pro-civil rights brother Robert to visit South Africa. The uproar this caused was symptomatic of NP paranoia at the time. Verwoerd's government went to great lengths to limit the impact of the visit. Robertson was banned for five years and no American journalists were allowed to accompany Kennedy on his four-day tour of the country.[28] Huberte and Rupert, by contrast, hospitably entertained the Kennedys at their home in Stellenbosch. Rupert took Kennedy to a university residence where he talked to students – and asked them what they would do if they found out that God was black! All this was reported in lugubrious detail in the *Observer,* which depicted Kennedy as an 'agent of subversion', envisaging a new world that entailed the destruction of the political and social order in South Africa and its replacement by a totally new system based on 'Unesco's communist-inspired equality doctrine'.

In view of government opposition to the visit and fierce criticism of Rupert for having held talks with Kennedy, Johan Piek, public relations officer of the Rembrandt Group, drew up a memorandum for internal circulation within the group.[29] Kennedy had wanted to see Rupert when he was in New York, having heard about his speeches in America, but he had already left the country. It was common courtesy to receive him when he came to South Africa. Also present at the talks at Rupert's home had been Piet Cillié, editor of *Die Burger*, Dirk Hertzog and Prof. James Yeats. According to Piek's memorandum, the principle that applied in this case was that 'you cannot expect to be received abroad as a guest if you refuse to talk to foreigners in your own country'. In addition to criticism, Rupert also received support from unexpected quarters. Replying to a letter he had received from Rupert to congratulate him on being appointed editor of the *Daily Despatch* newspaper, Donald Woods added a comment: 'Incidentally, may I in turn congratulate you on being one of the leading South Africans to have adopted an adult attitude to the visit of Senator Robert Kennedy. It is a pity there is not more intelligence of the Rupert brand to be found in our Cabinet today.'[30]

The Kennedys, for their part, had been favourably impressed. On his return to America Kennedy wrote: 'Between your hospitality and Stellenbosch's beauty we were like Faust, both moved "to command the fair moment to stay", but to no avail. Not only was our visit with you a most pleasant interlude, but it was for me personally an extremely interesting and helpful one. I think a number of the problems we discussed will yield to solutions if, as you suggested, persons in our country and others work together on them. I hope we will have a chance to continue our discussion both here in the United States and once again soon in South Africa.'[31]

One of the Kennedy entourage was Robert Kennedy's administrative assistant Earl G Graves, who later became one of America's most influential black businessmen and founded the journal *Black Enterprise*. Graves wrote a bestseller, *How to succeed in business without being white*, in which he records how he once paid a business visit to Rupert in Stellenbosch, where he stayed at the Rupert home. Graves was on his way to Germany to meet the head of Daimler-Benz, Dr Joachim Zahn, whose son was at that time working for Rembrandt as group coordinator.[32] Joachim Zahn Jr is convinced that Graves's acquaintance with Rupert was one of the reasons why he could persuade fellow black Americans that a peaceful transition in South Africa was possible. Years after first getting to know Rupert, Graves still played a role with regard to South Africa.[33]

Rupert did not respond personally to the continuous attacks in the *Observer*. When asked by *Tegniek* why he did not defend himself, he said, 'Why should I? It would merely add grist to the mill of a handful of sensation-mongers. Besides, as the old Boers used to say: One doesn't hunt termites with Mausers!'[34] Dirk Hertzog stated a few years later in an internal memorandum that references in Dan O'Meara's book *Volkskapitalisme* to the 'political fervour' of the Rembrandt Group in the initial years 'would have been tempered by an unbiased person with SED Brown's accusations in the *SA Observer* that Rupert was "the biggest liberalist ever to undermine South Africa" and other accusations of a similar nature.'[35]

The sustained smear campaign against leading Afrikaners took on such dimensions that muffled criticism made way for public reprimands. Ds JS (Kosie) Gericke, Vice-Chancellor of the US, and the university's Rector, Prof. HB Thom, both deplored the suspicion-mongering directed at Afrikaners who put the country's case abroad and to those with different opinions. The quarrel came to a head after the Afrikaanse Studentebond (ASB), a student organisation represented on Afrikaans campuses, passed a motion expressing gratitude and appreciation to Brown and the *Observer* at its congress in July 1966. The motion had been proposed by Sam de Beer, a UP student who later became an NP member of parliament and cabinet minister before joining the ANC in the late 1990s. The ASB's motion had repercussions in parliament. Japie Basson, a United Party MP, declared on 2 August 1966 that the list of 'enemies of the nation' was becoming ever longer, and appealed to Verwoerd to look into the extent of witch-hunting and sniffing-out of enemies 'in his own kraal'. Basson, who described Brown as an anti-Semite, a friend of the British fascist Oswald Mosley and in cahoots with white supremacy organisations like the John Birch Society in the Deep South of America, warned: 'The machine is now turning around and starting to devour its own children.'

Dawie, the well-known columnist of *Die Burger*, joined the fray and charged Brown with using the same methods against Afrikaners as those of the notorious American communist hunter Senator Joe McCarthy, namely 'guilt by association'. He described the insinuations about Kennedy's visit to Stellenbosch as scurrilous misrepresentation and expressed surprise that an English-speaking journalist could presume to set himself up as a judge of prominent Afrikaners' credentials. What he found even more surprising was that some Afrikaners attached value to Brown's judgements.[36] Dawie advised Afrikaner students to distance themselves from the paper with its 'poisonous and divisive' suspicion-mongering. Two weeks later at a mass meeting, the Students' Union of Stellenbosch distanced themselves in the strongest terms from Brown and the *Observer*, described as a pernicious influence and an undesirable element in South African politics.

Elsewhere in the political arena the power struggle in Afrikaner ranks continued. In 1969 Vorster at last left Genl. JBM Hertzog's ultra-right-wing son Albert out of his cabinet. The Hertzog supporters could no longer continue their subversive tactics within the NP, and Hertzog formed the *Herstigte Nasionale Party* (HNP, Reconstituted National Party) together with three other MPs. The more enlightened wing of the NP started to set the tone in South African politics. It left progressive thinkers, and also those outside of politics like Rupert, in a stronger position.

The *Observer* still struggled on with dwindling support until Brown's death in 1990. In February 1989 he blamed Rupert for wanting to talk to the ANC leader Nelson Mandela. Rupert said it was time for the true leaders of all sectors of South African society to get together. He would like to sit down with Mandela and discuss the creation of a peaceful environment. 'We must work together, man to man. And no threats.' Brown responded that Rupert had turned his back on a lifetime of conservative principles to adapt to his new friends, the Rockefellers, the Rothschilds, the Harry Oppenheimers and their ilk. He could still be known in South African history as 'the Afrikaner who has done more damage to his own Afrikaner nation and the cause of white national survival in South Africa than even Pieter Willem Botha has already done and is still doing'.

A year later Pres. FW de Klerk unbanned the ANC and released Mandela, and negotiations about a fully democratic South Africa commenced.

Although Rupert was demonised by the right-wing lunatic fringe on account of his belief in coexistence and partnership, his value to South Africa was recognised in other circles for this very reason. In December 1966 the business journal the *Financial Mail*, not noted for its pro-Afrikaner sympathies, proclaimed Rupert Businessman of the Year. His tobacco company was then 25 years old, and the journal declared: 'Business brilliance did it.' The *Financial Mail* commented that when Rupert launched into business many people thought: 'Just another Nat trying to elbow his way into big business.' That image was long dead and buried. 'The king of Rembrandt has tended to stir pride rather than envy in Afrikaner hearts.'

At the age of 50 Rupert had earned his laurels in the business world. He explained his youthful aspirations to the *Financial Mail*: 'I thought, what have Afrikaners and South Africans conspicuously failed to achieve which I might? The Afrikaner had shone in battle – Generals De la Rey and De Wet had respectively invented trench warfare and perfected modern guerrilla tactics. Hertzog had paved the way, in the Statute of Wesminister, for freedom without bloodshed in the birth of new nations. And Smuts, the League of Nations. But Afrikaners had done little in business (many still thought honesty and business incompatible) and South Africans generally little in industry outside their own country. So I decided to correct this . . .'[37]

Rupert was speaking as a patriot, also an Afrikaner, someone rooted in a particular linguistic and cultural community, inspired by fellow Afrikaners. Yet he was also speaking as a citizen of the world, someone whose roots did not restrict him to thinking and acting exclusively, but instead gave him the self-confidence to think and act inclusively. He was speaking as someone who had to balance a variety of interests and passions in his own life: the hardened businessman who had to control extensive business interests, but also (according to the *Financial Mail*) the 'missionary of goodwill', the 'philosopher-ambassador', the philanthropist, the nature lover, the South African legend.

CHAPTER 15

Cross-border partnership

R upert's passion to establish private initiative and free enterprise by means of small business ventures led to his involvement in 1966 in Lesotho, the tiny mountain kingdom entirely surrounded by South Africa. This was at the request of Chief Leabua Jonathan, the first prime minister of the newly independent state known previously as Basotholand, a British protectorate.

Jonathan first approached Rupert in 1963, travelling all the way to Stellenbosch to solicit financial support for his forthcoming election campaign in view of his country's impending independence. Rupert explained that he could not assist in this way, however, as it would be improper to involve himself in the internal politics of a neighbouring country. But when Rupert saw his guests off and observed their dilapidated vehicle, he made a donation towards the costs of their journey home.

Just over a year before Lesotho celebrated its independence on 4 October 1966, Rupert's birthday, he referred to Lesotho as the 'Switzerland' of Southern Africa in a speech at a graduation ceremony in Bloemfontein. On this occasion he emphasised his 'faith in prosperity through open-handedness', and expressed his willingness to offer free advisory services to any of the new governments (Botswana and Swaziland, two other British protectorates adjoining South Africa, were also gaining their independence), if asked to do so, and help them launch industries in genuine partnership. Careful to avoid the slightest suspicion of personal gain, his one condition was that neither he nor the Rembrandt Group should have any financial stake in such ventures.

Shortly before independence Jonathan paid another visit to Stellenbosch, this time in a 1937 Chevrolet. He had tried to obtain Rupert's cooperation through diplomatic channels but had met with strong opposition from the South African government, notably from the ultra-rightist Dr Albert Hertzog, then still a member of Verwoerd's cabinet. So he came in person to invite Rupert to become his country's honorary adviser on industry after independence. Jonathan had already appointed two honorary advisers: Denis Cowen on law, and Prof. Owen Horwood, later South African Minister of Finance, on fiscal policy. Rupert agreed to become the third.

When it became known that Rupert had accepted the invitation, Albert Hertzog, a cousin of Dirk Hertzog, phoned him at his office. Hertzog's objection was extraordinary: 'Anton, if you succeed, the whole world will praise you. But if you fail, we Afrikaners will blame you.' After Rupert had put down the phone he turned to Stuart Pretorius, Rembrandt's group coordinator, who happened to be with him. 'Is the guy crazy?' he asked. 'I'm not even thinking of failure.'[1]

Someone would have to go to Lesotho to do the work. Pretorius told Rupert he thought there was only one man for the job: Wynand van Graan, one of his most senior and experienced colleagues, at that stage the group's representative in Canada. After a moment's reflection, Rupert nodded: 'I think you're right.'

Van Graan's background and business experience made him eminently suitable to head the development task in the neighbouring country. He hailed from Harrismith in the Free State, close to Lesotho. When Van Graan joined Rembrandt in the 1950s, he was appointed in Rupert's office where he gained valuable experience, as Rupert was at that stage personally responsible for advertising and marketing.

At Rupert's suggestion the Lesotho government passed legislation to establish the Lesotho National Development Corporation (LNDC), analogous to the South African Industrial Development Corporation. Van Graan accepted the position of managing director and was duly seconded to the LNDC. Stuart Pretorius, who had studied Sesotho at the University of the Free State, went to Maseru to arrange for Van Graan's arrival. The interview with Jonathan and his deputy prime minister was conducted in Sesotho, and Pretorius's fluency in the language caused the amazed deputy prime minister to exclaim: 'Mr Pretorius, you shock me!'

The family had to have appropriate accommodation – Van Graan had promised his British-born wife that she would be reasonably housed in Africa. However, no suitable house was available in the impoverished mountain kingdom. Jonathan solved the problem by ordering his British-seconded secretary for foreign affairs Jim Hennessy, later the British High Commissioner in Uganda, to vacate the house he was occupying. The old sandstone, two-storey, colonial-style house was made available to the Van Graans.

In 1966 Lesotho was considered the third poorest country in the world. Annual per capita income was R33 – less than the average German spent on flowers every year, according to Rupert – and the national revenue was slightly less than the total revenue of a city the size of Kimberley. There was no railway or water scheme and only two kilometres of tarred road. In the absence of mineral and other resources the economy relied wholly on subsistence agriculture, stock farming and, overwhelmingly, the earnings of hundreds of thousands of economically active young men who worked as migrant labourers on South African mines and farms. 'Our only export,' Jonathan summed up, 'is our muscle power.'

On his acceptance of the appointment as honorary adviser on industry, Rupert revealed much of his philosophy of life. Owing to circumstances beyond its control Lesotho was one of the most impoverished and underdeveloped countries in the world, he said. The development of the newly independent state would take a gargantuan effort, Rupert declared, as it posed the greatest challenge with which any nation had yet been confronted.

'Whether I can be of any help would depend primarily on the Basotho themselves, but also on the support and assistance my own people and my friends, both in South Africa and many other parts of the world, can extend in the practically impossible task.' What Lesotho needed most was people who could act as catalysts to lay the foundation for progress. 'Whether this task would ever be achieved depends on Providence, but I have always believed that "anyone who doesn't believe in miracles is not a realist".' He added: 'The Basotho are a Christian nation, and as a Christian I cannot refuse to help them.'

On a visit to Lesotho's secretary of health in 1966 Rupert was given first-hand information about the country's medical needs. 'The facilities were poor, equipment was outdated and the shortage of doctors acute: one per 40 000 of the population, as opposed to one per 1 800 in South Africa.' Rupert made it a priority and the response was amazing, indicative of the goodwill in South Africa towards the newly independent neighbouring states. Two of Rupert's medical friends, his old university friend Dr Colijn van Bergen and Dr Hennie Meyer, the ophthalmologist who had treated Hanneli initially, took the initiative and were the first to offer their services over weekends in Maseru. The SA Medical Association and the SA Medical and Dental Council endorsed the project enthusiastically: in a letter to Rupert 223 leading surgeons and doctors offered weekend services for free.

In 1968 – the year after the Cape heart surgeon Dr Chris Barnard had gained world fame with the first heart transplant – the Medical Shuttle Service was officially launched, one of the biggest voluntary specialist services of its kind. Rembrandt paid airfares from Johannesburg, Pretoria, Cape Town, East London and Port Elizabeth to Bloemfontein, from where Avis supplied rented cars at discount rates. Stuart Pretorius, shocked by the condition in which the British colonial government had left Lesotho, obtained anaesthetic equipment and surgical instruments from the National Hospital in Bloemfontein. On 3 February 1968 the first group of specialists and theatre sisters joined Rupert in Maseru. Every weekend teams of the 'flying doctors' arrived in the little capital: anaesthetists, ear, nose and throat specialists, dermatologists, gynaecologists, orthopaedic surgeons, ophthalmologists, and plastic and breast surgeons. Women were treated by gynaecologists such as Dr Jannie de Villiers, later rector of the US. Among the surgeons was Van Bergen who dealt with general surgery. Orthopaedic surgeons included Dr Hamilton Bell and Dr Chris Steytler, while Dr Hennie Meyer healed eye diseases and removed cataracts. Another of the pioneers was an old friend of the Rupert family, Dr Von Welfling Eybers of Bloemfontein, who did the first operation. Dr Jannie Louw came from the Groote Schuur Hospital in Cape Town, where Barnard had done his historic heart transplant. The visiting South African doctors, soon known among the Basotho as the 'mercy group', also helped local doctors to improve their services through practical experience.

When Rupert turned his mind to industrial development one of his first steps was to request an interview with the British premier, Harold Wilson. This was complicated as Lesotho considered the British grant-in-aid to the newly independent country skinflint and had broken off diplomatic ties with Britain soon after independence. But Rupert managed to speak to James (Sunny Jim) Callaghan, a top member of Wilson's cabinet and his eventual successor. His argument was simple: if the LNDC succeeded, it would relieve Britain of a great burden. Callaghan expressed willingness to help but pointed out there was little his government could do unless diplomatic relations were restored. He asked Rupert to use his influence with Jonathan to that end. No doubt he was a factor in the equation. At all events, the diplomatic situation was eventually normalised and Britain provided welcome aid to the LNDC.

Rupert also succeeded in persuading the Lesotho authorities to make a very important mind shift: leasehold tenure was granted to industrialists in the mountain state where traditionally only communal land tenure was obtained. The LNDC, a state corporation made up of businessmen who were committed to 'getting it done', put the accent on job creation through small business ventures based on a simple premise: 'It is better to light a small candle than to curse the darkness.' Appropriately, the first industry was a candle factory! It very soon had to triple its output.

Rupert considered it a true example of 'small is beautiful', the title given by the economist EE Schumacher to his much-discussed book *Small is beautiful: A study of economics as if people mattered* (1973). For Rupert, private initiative and free enterprise found their best expression in small business ventures. He advocated this idea with passion at a luncheon he gave for Schumacher at the Lanzerac Hotel in Stellenbosch. The influential German-born economist, who had been the economic adviser to the British Coal Board from 1950 to 1970, based his thinking about the beauty of small things on the Sermon on the Mount and advocated production by the masses as opposed to mass production: 'We need a gentle approach, a nonviolent spirit, and small is beautiful.' He also introduced the concept of 'intermediate technology' for developing countries. Over lunch Rupert explained to Schumacher his small business concept with reference to what they had been doing in Lesotho since 1966. 'It surprised him,' Rupert remarked afterwards. Ten years later he would also start applying the concept of small business successfully in South Africa.

Van Graan was doing essential spadework and turning 'private initiative with an idea' into a reality. After Rupert had convinced the government to introduce leasehold tenure, it acted as a stimulus for industrial development. Maseru's industrial area was situated on terrain that had previously been a sewage dump. A loan was obtained from Britain to install sewers and lay out streets for the new enterprises. Van Graan tackled one project after the other, mostly nothing ostentatious, instead simple and realistic. He worked together with Timothy Thabane, a Mosotho, who would later occupy a prominent position at the World Bank in Washington before he accepted a senior position at the South African Reserve Bank, and eventually became Lesotho's Minister of Finance.

Lesotho also benefited from the goodwill of Free State farmers from South Africa who assisted at an early stage in the development of their independent neighbouring country. In August 1968, when the Basotho's oxen were too emaciated by drought to plough the maize fields, three quarters of the white farmers of Clocolan crossed the border with 232 tractors to help plough more than 1 700 hectares agricultural land in Lesotho. One of the farmers, Nico Hofmeyr, spent three weeks planning the big operation, which was executed with military precision thanks to the use of two-way radios. Five oil companies donated 4 000 gallons of fuel and the Clocolan farmers' cooperative provided maintenance and repair facilities. Later a Ficksburg farmer crossed the border with his tractor and harvester to help reap the crops.[2]

Lesotho is one of Africa's main producers of mohair and the fourth biggest in the world, so it was decided to start a weaving factory. As always, Rupert wanted to obtain the best possible advice. He asked an internationally renowned expert to come to Lesotho to assist with the design of the products. Director of the Stedelijk Museum in Amsterdam, Jonkheer WJHB (Willem) Sandberg, who was vehemently opposed to apartheid, eventually agreed to visit Lesotho in September 1968 to look into the state of affairs. Stuart Pretorius accompanied the Dutchman on a tour of the mountain country, under strict instructions from Rupert to say nothing to influence the visitor.

Somewhere in the mountains they came across a young herdboy, whose face bore scars of what had clearly been a major operation performed by a skilled surgeon. When Sandberg inquired about the operation, he heard the whole story from Pretorius. The boy had been sleeping next to a fire and had rolled into the coals, burning his cheek. A surgeon from the Medical Shuttle Service had performed the operation. To Sandberg it was an eye-opener to hear about everything Rupert and the medical teams had been doing for the local population and his scepticism vanished in an instant, Pretorius remarked.[3] He became a keen supporter of the Lesotho weaving factory, where women sat singing over their looms, weaving traditional patterns in warm, earthy colours. Sandberg was so impressed that he offered to obtain tapestry designs free of charge from internationally recognised artists. Designs were received from renowned artists such as Alexander Calder, Victor Vasarely, Kumi Sugaï, Karel Appel, Christo Coetzee, Joseph Lagasse, Yascov Agam, and others.

On a visit to Switzerland, Van Graan was excited by the carpets and tapestries woven at home industries in that equally mountainous country. On making inquiries he was introduced to Vreni Schmidli, an expert in this traditional Swiss craft. Some time later she phoned him and said she proposed coming to Africa on her own steam. In Maseru she introduced advanced techniques that turned the Royal Lesotho Carpet Weavers into a modern production unit. Its mohair rugs and wall tapestries were soon exported to countries as far afield as Canada and were acclaimed worldwide. In 1970 they won a gold medal at an international handcraft exhibition in Florence.

Pottery was another potential export. Under the guidance of the Finch family from the famous Winchcombe potteries in Gloucestershire, the Kolonyama pottery in Lesotho produced top-quality ceramics, selling its entire output to foreign importers months in advance. Kolonyama pottery won a gold medal at the Rand Easter Show in 1970.

Other LNDC projects included a traditional beer brewery; a wheat-and-maize mill; a tyre-retreading factory; a modern hotel, the Holiday Inn, with a splendid view of Maseru and a casino for tourists (at that stage gambling was prohibited in neighbouring South Africa); a factory producing gutters and down-pipes; a sacking factory; a furniture factory; a fertiliser-packaging firm; a shopping mall; and micro-enterprises manufacturing diverse goods from umbrellas to clothes.

On her first visit to Lesotho, Huberte went for a drive around the capital and its environs. Horrified at seeing no trace of wildlife, not even a bird or a rock rabbit, in the barren hills around the town, she told her husband: 'Anton, you *must* help them!' He did not need pushing. Coexistence between human beings and nature had long been on his agenda. In 1968 he had helped to establish the

Southern African Nature Foundation (SANF) as the local branch of the World Wildlife Fund (WWF). He was at that stage president of SANF and a trustee of South Africa's National Parks Board as well as a member of the executive of the WWF, the organisations from which his much bigger and more comprehensive idea of transnational peace parks would eventually develop. The newly established SANF's first operations were aimed at helping Lesotho and Swaziland to develop nature reserves. Lesotho's first national park, Sehlabathebe, was established in 1971, complete with a research centre.

But not everyone was enthusiastic about Rupert's involvement in Lesotho. In South Africa the NP government continued under the heavy shadow of Hendrik Verwoerd, and the rhetoric was the same: unless Rupert's advice to Lesotho was couched on the lines of South Africa's policy in Transkei, Lesotho would be Africa's prime example of a victim of economic colonialism. As the grandiloquent deputy minister Blaar Coetzee put it, if the Basotho chose to admit 'capitalists and vultures', on their heads be it.[4] Even Rupert's close friend, the law professor James Yeats, asked him what the blazes he thought he was doing. His response was to become a classic 'Rupertism': 'Jamie, in southern Africa we can't get away from it: we are our brother's keeper. And we can't sleep peacefully if our neighbour has no food.'

At one stage there were fears for Rupert's safety. At the insistence of Oupa Kriel, director of Rembrandt Beherende Beleggings, Stuart Pretorius bought a .38 Smith & Wesson revolver to carry with him when he accompanied Rupert to Lesotho. One day, while Pretorius was showing their passports at the border, Rupert saw the revolver in the cubbyhole of the car. 'What do you need that thing for?' he asked Pretorius on his return. 'You want to wage war and I want to develop industries.'

Rupert's lifelong thrift and unpretentious ways amazed his companion. He insisted that they share the same chalet at their hotel in Maseru instead of Pretorius using a separate room: 'There's enough space for both of us; you can sleep here and we'll save money.' When Pretorius saw him cleaning his own shoes and offered to do it for him, he declined: 'Thanks, but I usually do it myself. You won't be able to do it as well as I can.'[5]

Rupert's involvement in Lesotho elicited opposition from the left as well. He and Van Graan had to cope with the anti-South African hostility of the sanction years. In the initial years in Lesotho the leftist opposition leader Ntsu Mokhehle, who eventually became prime minister in 1993, threatened to nationalise all industries if he came to power. Speaking at a press conference, Pretorius posed a rhetorical question to Mokhehle: What industries *were* there to nationalise?

One of the foreigners who conducted a sustained campaign against the South African involvement in Lesotho was the American legal adviser to the United Nations International Development Association (IDA), Charles J (Chuck) Lipton. Wynand van Graan, who maintained excellent relations with the Lesotho government, was informed on several occasions that Lipton was trying to undermine him with an anti-South African whispering campaign. Lipton, who made all sorts of claims in his attempts to influence the leadership of Lesotho, a member of the Commonwealth, inter alia wore a tie of the Commonwealth Parliamentary Society to which he was not entitled, as the USA did not belong to the Commonwealth.[6]

Lipton's campaign against the South Africans did not succeed, and the LNDC continued its operations. Van Graan headed it for two three-year terms, with the last part during the state of emergency that Jonathan proclaimed when he suspended the 1970 elections. Opposition members were detained and the young King Moshoeshoe II could not return from exile in the Netherlands until he had accepted a proclamation that forbade him to take any part in politics. Jonathan's autocracy only ended in 1986 when he was overthrown in a military coup by Major-General Metsing Lekhanye.

In 1972 Jonathan wrote a letter to Rupert in recognition of the role the LNDC had played in Lesotho under Wynand van Graan: 'The LNDC has been built up over a short period from less than nothing into an effective machine which, for the first time, has brought within our grasp the possibility of economic self-sufficiency.' At the end of Van Graan's second three-year term in Lesotho Jonathan requested him to stay on, but Van Graan opted to join Rupert's new project, the Development Bank for Equatorial and Southern Africa (Edesa). This gave the lie to the London journal *XRay*'s report in December 1973 that Chief Jonathan had 'summarily dismissed' Van Graan before he left for Edesa. Its next issue contained a lengthy apology for the 'serious defamation'.[7] But negative criticism of the LNDC appeared in other publications as well. 'I wish the gods would protect developing Africa from the attention of people like these,' Van Graan concluded a letter of protest to the writer of one such publication.[8] Even after his retirement years later at Somerset West, where he died in 2004, people from Lesotho continued to seek his advice.

By the time Van Graan left the country, R25 million had been ploughed into the economy – R25 for every member of the population. At the time, the LNDC acquired R70 of foreign capital for every R1 invested by the corporation. It had used only R210 000 of the initial R500 000 provided by the British government before it became financially independent. To be sure, it had been necessary, as Rupert said, to 'twist arms' to achieve success, particularly to prevent politicians and the Lesotho government from seizing control of the corporation. Rupert was adamant on this score: development should be in the hands of private enterprise. At a closed gathering in front of a student audience in Pretoria in 1972 he threatened that he would speak to the chancellor of the exchequer in London, Tony Barber – 'a friend of mine' – if the Lesotho government dared interfere or expected the LNDC's profit of R800 000 to form part of its budget. That profit, he pointed out, would not have been realised if they had not held out solidly against any political appointments. And if that ever happened, 'we would pull out'. On no account would he compromise on his partnership philosophy.

In February 1978 Rupert was to speak at the tenth anniversary of the Medical Shuttle Service in Maseru. The speech he had prepared contained the following statement: 'If unemployed men could vote for what they really want, they'd vote for more jobs – not merely more politicians. Too much attention is paid to one man, one vote, when what is really needed is one man, one job. Economic independence is hard-earned, but it is the only real independence.' Wynand van Graan, who had been invited from Swaziland to attend the function, saw the speech shortly before the ceremony. He phoned Rupert and warned him that these sentences would not be well received in Lesotho and elsewhere in Africa. Rupert heeded his advice and undertook to leave out the references to one man, one vote.

In the speech he delivered, he praised the South African medical staff for the services that had been rendered over a decade: 3 500 operations by 528 specialists and 524 theatre sisters, and more than 10 000 consultations. 'They all came here as people of goodwill. Of all the helping hands one can extend to one's fellow human beings, nothing equals the hand that heals the sick.' In addition, many doctors and nurses of Lesotho had been assisted and encouraged to improve their own medical knowledge and skills. 'We are all Africans, whatever our colour or creed or persuasion, and our future depends on our mutual loyalty and support,' Rupert stressed. 'We are so interdependent that a lack of trust in one part of our subcontinent affects everybody in the other parts. If we want investments from elsewhere, we have to push each other up the economic ladder. If we pull down those ahead of us, we shall all fall together.'

Unfortunately the unexpurgated speech had already been circulated to the media by the group's public relations department, and the comments on one man, one vote received the widest coverage. In Van Graan's opinion, it sullied relations with the authorities in Maseru for a while.[9]

The Medical Shuttle Service delivered services to the people of Lesotho for a period of 25 years. Safety concerns increased, however, after two cars transporting doctors to Maseru were hijacked. At the same time some of the doctors, who could pride themselves on the fact that not a single patient had died during any of their operations, were worried about dangers increasingly posed by the poor state of equipment in Maseru. The service came to an end in 1993.

After Van Graan's departure, the LNDC, at Chuck Lipton's insistence, was run by United Nations economists. Their lack of insight into local realities nearly cost the corporation its life. At one stage financial problems were so severe that the banks refused to honour its cheques. The situation improved after Jonathan had sent a promising young economist, Sam Montsi, to Swaziland to consult Van Graan on the management of the organisation. He was the first Lesotho citizen to head the LNDC. Montsi, who later became a prominent businessman in South Africa and a director of the petroleum giant Sasol, managed to get the struggling corporation back on track.

Projects such as the weaving factory became the model for long-term success. In 2002 Lesotho's Minister of Natural Resources, Monyane Moleketi, reported that the country was the biggest exporter of textiles in Africa. He was speaking at a certification ceremony at the SA Tourism College in Graaff-Reinet, where Lesotho's first guesthouse managers received their training. In the presence of Rupert and his wife as well as South Africa's First Lady Mrs Zanele Mbeki, he praised Rupert's contribution to his country's progress. He added that Lesotho's exports had benefited greatly from the African Growth and Opportunity Act, the American law that provided incentives for Africa to export goods. (Later, though, the changing global scene, especially cheap Chinese textile wares exported to South Africa, adversely affected the flourishing Lesotho industry.)

In 2001 King Letsie III awarded Rupert his country's highest honour, that of Knight Commander of the Most Loyal Order of Ramats'eatsana, at a ceremony in Maseru. The tribute strengthened Rupert's view that the people of Lesotho would never forget a good deed. He and his wife had remained friends with the king, who often visited them in South Africa, while the queen mother also stayed at Fleur du Cap on a visit to South Africa.

Looking back on his involvement in Lesotho, Rupert said: 'It was an enormous challenge. Something had to be created out of nothing. Knowing that one successful industrialist can inspire a whole community to exchange the begging bowl for the spade, the development corporation strove to create more job opportunities through local industries, thereby making better use of Lesotho's greatest asset – its people.'

He gave an indication of what he saw as some of the essential requirements for development in Africa in a lecture to students at the University of Pretoria in

1972: 'We undertook it [the Lesotho project] despite the fact that we in Southern Africa are so foolish as to still have medieval or nineteenth-century training. We couldn't use a single student from the University of Roma (Lesotho), because once you've become "white collar" you're not prepared to do "blue collar" work, and they study sociology, psychology and political science, and at Fort Hare [South Africa] also anthropology.'[10]

His scepticism about the overproduction of students in such disciplines in developing countries was also expressed in an interview where he said: 'Sociology is the subject where you are taught to give away other people's goods to yet others.'

Rupert's passion for promoting development and job creation never diminished. Many years after the Lesotho project, he remarked: 'I would like to tell Pres. Thabo Mbeki that he should say to the developed countries: "Remember, if we can't export our products to you, we'll be exporting our population (as migrants) to you instead."'[11]

CHAPTER 16
Early moves in the beer market

E ven before he found himself in the minefield of South African politics, Rupert, always on the lookout for alternative possibilities, started eyeing the beer industry soon after he had entered the liquor industry in 1945. In the midst of developing and consolidating his wine and spirit interests and expanding his tobacco empire, he managed to make some exploratory moves in this tantalising field. The challenge lay in the daunting competition any newcomer would face in a highly competitive market dominated by South African Breweries (SAB).

Early in 1946 he asked Daan Hoogenhout's brother Imker to find out more about breweries in South West Africa (present-day Namibia) with a view to establishing good relations and, if possible, cooperation to strengthen his hand in South Africa. On 15 May 1946 Imker wrote Rupert a detailed letter to inform him about two breweries: South West Breweries in Windhoek and the Hansa Bräuerei at Swakopmund. The former was planning to increase its share capital from £60 000 to £80 000 by means of a share issue. Without wasting any time Rupert sent Hoogenhout a telegram on 27 May: he wanted a 'substantial interest' in South West Breweries, was prepared to travel to Windhoek for negotiations, and was interested in acquiring all the shares issued to make up the £20 000 increase of the share capital. At this early stage already it was clear he was prepared to think big.

Hoogenhout had a number of conversations with Van Doorn, secretary and co-manager of South West Breweries. On 3 June 1946 he wrote to Rupert: 'He [Van Doorn] is a refined chap and, in my opinion, someone we can take at his word.'

Hoogenhout was also instructed to keep in touch with Hansa Bräuerei. In 1947 he travelled to Swakopmund for talks with its director and senior co-manager Hans Heusschneider. Hoogenhout invited him to visit Stellenbosch – while Heusschneider could not accept the invitation, he promised his support to Rupert for any brewery he might establish.[1]

Two investigations Rupert requested to be done showed that he seriously considered entering the beer market at this early stage in his career as entrepreneur. The one was to find out where the best brewing equipment could be obtained – typical of Rupert, only the best was good enough. Heusschneider told Hoogenhout during a conversation that the Skoda factories in Pilsen, Czechoslovakia, were the best bet. Establishing a brewery with a capacity to produce 120 000 bottles a month would cost about £100 000, he said.

The other investigation was conducted by one of Rupert's confidants, Dr Jan Steyn. Steyn, the son of Pres. MT Steyn's brother Helgaard, had played provincial rugby and tennis for the Free State before obtaining his doctorate in political economy summa cum laude at the University of Heidelberg in Germany. In Geneva, where he had been in South Africa's foreign service, he was for a while the private secretary of Joseph Avenol, secretary-general of the League of Nations. On his return to South Africa he became the first head of the Security Service, but resigned when Gen. Smuts entered the war. After Gen Hertzog had resigned as prime minister in 1938, Steyn served as his personal assistant without remuneration till Hertzog's death in 1942. In 1948 he was elected MP for Potchefstroom. Steyn, who never married and always wore a distinctive bow tie, was a member of Rembrandt's board for many years and stayed with the Ruperts up to ten times a year when board meetings were held at Stellenbosch.

Rupert thought very highly of Steyn, as he stated publicly during a speech in 1969: 'If there is one man on whom I have depended over many years for great wisdom, it is Jan Steyn. Few of us have the ability to think so philosophically and I now want to confess honestly that there are few other people in my life who have been so close to me, but as far as advice is concerned, no one. Because it has now been many, many years that I could sharpen myself against Jan as a whetstone, and he has the gift not to make me blunt, but rather to inspire me to become sharper. I hope not too dangerously sharp.'[2] Steyn was also the person who once made a cryptic yet profound remark to Rupert: 'What you possess, possesses you.'

Rupert asked him to investigate the possibility of finding a master brewer in war-shattered Germany who was looking for a future abroad. Steyn set about his inquiries methodically. In 1947 he approached a number of contacts in Germany, asking them if they could put him in touch with: a Munich brewery willing to open a branch in South Africa controlled by South African shareholders; a Munich master brewer willing to emigrate to South Africa with his family and undertake the technical management of a brewery; and a master owner-brewer of a small Munich brewery who would come with his family and all the necessary machinery, to start a new factory from scratch. Despite interest from German brewers, nothing came of these tentative moves as there were problems on the South African side with the realisation of plans to establish a brewery. Steyn was requested to keep the German connection alive for some time, although with the warning that, as a brewery would have to be built up in South Africa from scratch, it would take at least two years before beer could be produced. Meanwhile Rupert concentrated on the tobacco industry.

In the early 1950s he again made a serious effort to enter the South African beer market. At that stage there were five breweries in the country: SAB, Ohlsson's Cape Breweries, Chandlers, Stag and Old Dutch. By 1954 he was exploring the chances of obtaining an interest in, if not control of, Stag Brewery Ltd. As Rupert always required, a thorough investigation was conducted. The investigation and the eventual decision were complicated by relationships with friendly organisations and individuals that had to be considered – a seasoned businessman from early on, he did not like disrupting good relations unnecessarily or treading on toes. But when a difficult business decision had to be taken, it was done without prevarication or attempts to be diplomatic. His recommendation on Stag in response to the documents submitted, was scribbled in pencil: 'I consider it [the price] far too high for sound business.' Stag's selling and distribution costs were too high, the turnover was insufficient, and too few outlets committed to selling the brand.[3]

Contrary to what many people thought, Rupert never asked for help from the NP government in his endeavours to enter the beer market. He also never received such assistance; the politicians rather put a spoke in his wheel. Rupert and his associates were aggrieved that SAB was allowed to enter the wine industry a few years later despite the statutory division between the wine and beer markets. In 1960 SAB acquired a controlling interest in Stellenbosch Farmers Winery (SFW), which belonged mainly to Bill Winshaw's family. The takeover was in direct contravention of section 144(c) of the then Liquor Act. The illegality of SAB's acquisition of the shares was confirmed by a Supreme Court judgement in 1962. SFW and Distillers Corporation were parties to this suit, where an application instituted by Johan Piek, public relations officer of Rembrandt, was granted. In 1963, however, SAB's takeover was ratified retrospectively by a legislative amendment introduced by John Vorster, who had recently become Minister of Justice. An important role in this move was played by Vorster's former university residence friend Willem Dempsey, a lecturer in commerce at the University of Stellenbosch, who later became mayor of the town and eventually an ambassador and senator. Dempsey, later a director of SFW, had been asked to convince Vorster of the desirability of the takeover for the wine industry. Vorster was also supported behind the scenes by the shrewd politician Paul Sauer, likewise a director of SFW, who later also helped to get Vorster elected prime minister. Sauer had known Vorster well since 1938, when he had asked the then fifth-year law student at Stellenbosch to accompany him on a political trip to the Eastern Cape where Vorster had to open the gates on the farm roads.[4]

SAB could use its monopoly in the beer market to get hotels and liquor stores, also those not directly under its control, to stock and promote SFW products. Rupert was outraged by the course of events. His public relations officer, Piek, noted in an internal memorandum: 'During the takeover Dr Rupert and others warned strongly that it would be a fatal day for the wine industry. The warnings fell on deaf ears . . .'[5]

The incident is one of the reasons why Rupert responded with indignation to allegations that he and the Rembrandt Group had been favoured by government. It had rather been the opposite – as he had already experienced in the 1940s with the prohibition on the import of cigarette machines as well as the reintroduction of the quota system when the NP assumed power in 1948. 'I've never asked any government department for anything special for my company,' he stated. 'Only once did I speak to a cabinet minister alone, and that was in 1945 when I asked permission to convert a canning factory in Stellenbosch into premises for brandy production. When we objected as a company to the punitive quota system introduced during and immediately after the war, I always went to speak to the minister as part of a delegation from the industry as a whole.' When Rupert was asked on another occasion whether he knew of any Afrikaner companies that had been helped by English organisations, he reflected for a while and then responded succinctly: 'I can't think of any, and I'm grateful for that.'[6]

Rupert's view that success in business depends on sound business principles rather than government support or group loyalties has been corroborated by his son Johann, who was top of the *Financial Mail*'s list of South Africa's twenty most powerful businessmen in December 2003. Johann explained his view in 2002 when asked by the second businessman on the list of twenty, Patrice Motsepe, chairman of the black business chamber Nafcoc, to address members of the organisation on what they could learn from the Afrikaner's economic advance. He also emphasised that black businesspeople should not rely on ethnic sympathies or the state, as the Rembrandt Group had learned.[7]

Early in the 1960s Rupert again became involved in talks about entering the beer market. It became a formidable challenge, because he had to attempt to prove that an Afrikaans entrepreneur could achieve success in this market despite the dominant position of SAB. By this time he had learnt the effectiveness of his partnership strategy and he started courting two overseas companies, Whitbread in England and Heineken in the Netherlands. On 30 May 1961 Colonel Whitbread, chairman of Whitbread & Co., wrote to Rupert: 'Affairs in Africa do not seem to give one much confidence; on the other hand, if you were willing to go on with our project, I think you would find that we would be willing to do so also, being quite aware that we were accepting political and commercial risks.'[8] The correspondence continued and by late 1961 Whitbread was insisting on a personal meeting. This was typical of Rupert's practice of maintaining networks and answering letters promptly. By that time the colonel had resolved on opening a brewery in South Africa and a site just outside Johannesburg had been identified. Whitbread wanted Rupert to be involved in the project, but progress was slow. On 11 January 1962 Rupert sent Whitbread a list of names of shareholders of SAB as well as notes on the company, since they had to take cognisance of SAB in talks about a possible partnership.

In 1962 the South African government lifted the prohibition on black people's consumption of alcoholic beverages. As Africans started switching from illicit home-brewed spirits like skokiaan, mampoer and stuka to malt beer, sales soared.

On a visit to London in June 1962 Rupert informed Whitbread that if it were legally possible, he would be prepared to take up to 50% of the shares in the proposed brewery in South Africa. Whitbread was delighted. In a letter soon afterwards he wrote: 'Again many thanks for coming to see us and hoping this may one day prove a successful joint enterprise.' Still negotiations dragged on. There were legal restrictions on a company like Rembrandt entering the beer market and government would have to amend the act. It was in no hurry to do so.

Meanwhile talks between Whitbread, Heineken and Rembrandt carried on. Rupert proceeded with great caution and at one stage almost got cold feet. In October 1963 Colonel Whitbread wrote: 'I get the impression that our project may be causing you some personal doubts, so let me say that the last thing we should wish is to embarrass you.' Nonetheless he added: 'After careful consideration of your views and those of our friends here and in South Africa, we have decided to go ahead.' In the South African press there was already some speculation about the prospective project. Several journalists tried to obtain Rupert's comments, but he refused to be drawn on the matter.

In December 1963 a Dutch newspaper reported that the London brewers Whitbread & Co. had announced that they, together with the Dutch company Heineken and the South African Rembrandt Group, would be building a new brewery at Isando outside Johannesburg in 1964. In the new company, Whitbread (South Africa) (Pty) Ltd, the report read, Heineken and Whitbread would have a 25% shareholding each; Rembrandt would hold the remaining 50%.[9]

Once again Rupert had acquired an interest in an enterprise with partners that were old, established firms. Again he had chosen his partners carefully, people who also had networks of influential friends and acquaintances. Heineken was an old Dutch brewery with a strong family tradition.[10] Whitbread (London) had been launched in London by Samuel Whitbread I in 1742. Colonel Whitbread, who had close links with the royal family, was chairman of the British company in the 1960s and became vice-chairman of the South African company.[11]

The entry of the 'South African tobacco king' into the beer market was hailed in the local press.[12] According to reports, the new brewery would cost R4 million and have an annual production capacity of 80 000 barrels. At that stage Whitbread (London) had fifteen breweries in the UK, plus 56 bottling and distribution depots. It also had a big market in Belgium, which was then the world's greatest beer-drinking country. Shortly after the official announcement of the partnership, a three-man delegation from Whitbread (London) arrived in Cape Town and at once proceeded to Stellenbosch for a meeting with Rupert.

Rupert had done his homework. The files in the archives show that everything related to the transaction had passed across his desk, and reveal his close attention to detail. At a meeting in August 1963 they had discussed a name for the proposed company, its nature, possible directors, a marketing and sales manager, architects, legal advisors and auditors (Rupert felt strongly about involving Afrikaans firms), shipping lines, and an advertising agency. With regard to the latter, Rupert was opposed to the appointment of Intam and L'Estrange because of their links to one of his competitors in the tobacco and cigarette industry. It was decided to use Lindsay Smithers instead. At a subsequent meeting in November 1963 the Whitbread representatives had said they would accept Rupert's idea of partnership provided there was a 50-50 shareholding between the Dutch and British interests on the one hand and the South African interest on the other. Rupert then made the interesting remark: '. . . under partnership there was no need to strengthen South African representation on the board.' He added that he would like to be on the board himself, and continued: 'We should state our intentions regarding partnership at the time of the announcement but not ask retailers and the public to take up shares until production is about to begin at the brewery. After that, our publicity in South Africa during the building period should be as quiet as possible, other than information about Whitbread in the UK.' He made detailed notes about the history of Whitbread, including a reference that the family was of 'Bedford farmers' stock'.[13] He even inquired about the size of the site for the new brewery and expressed reservations about its location at Isando – in the end it was built on a much larger site at Wadeville, Germiston. His sustained involvement in the project is apparent from a meeting held on 23 April 1964 in Amsterdam, where he recommended that one of their products should be named Culemborg after the birthplace of Jan van Riebeeck, founder of the Dutch East India Company's settlement at the Cape. According to Rupert, the name had a built-in continental as well as South African image.

There were other, more pressing problems in getting the brewery off the ground. Permits for the importation of barley malt were snarled up in red tape. Not only did they involve several government departments, but it was the era of control boards that did all within their power to protect the vested interests of their members. The Wheat Board in particular objected to the importation of barley. According to tests done by Heineken, the barley available in South Africa was not suitable for brewing high-quality beer. While Rupert insisted throughout that he was no more than a 'financial partner' in the venture, he, Dirk Hertzog and others worked hard to persuade government to grant permits. On 27 November 1964 GRAM Johnston of Whitbread (SA) wrote to Hertzog: 'Is there anything that you or Dr Rupert might do to ensure that the minister's support to our request for 3 800 tons of imported malt in 1968 is not successfully opposed by the Wheat Industry Control Board as they will most certainly try to do?'

Samples of the yellow barley malt Whitbread (SA) favoured were submitted to the Wheat Board – and, at Rupert's insistence, to him as well. He was even consulted on the choice of labels and bottle designs. When Colonel Whitbread announced his intention to visit South Africa at the end of 1964, Rupert had a large reception arranged for him. He and Huberte went to great lengths to welcome the colonel and his wife, as was typical of the way in which they received guests. Visitors, like the Whitbreads, not only found flowers and fruit in their hotel rooms but also a book, usually about South Africa's cultural and natural heritage.

The partnership between Rupert, Whitbread (London) and Heineken was finally formalised. Half the shares would be in South African hands, with Rembrandt holding 30%. The other 50% of the shares would be in the hands of the foreign partners, with Whitbread (London) holding 40% and Heineken 10%. Rupert was furious when news of the partners' plans leaked to the *Financial Mail* before an official announcement had been made. He could not reconcile himself to his affairs being discussed in the press before he had issued a statement.

At long last the first beer was brewed. Many people had looked forward to the new products, but a tough battle against the established SAB lay ahead. Rupert knew that Distillers had to enter the beer market in order to be able to survive. To protect his interest in Distillers, and also because SAB made use of 'conditional selling', Rupert started focusing on beer. This was also the reason why he would eventually even cooperate with Louis Luyt.[14]

The year after the establishment of Whitbread the Rembrandt Group consolidated its liquor interests in *Oude Meester Kelders, Distilleerders en Brouerskorporasie* (Oude Meester Cellars, Distillers and Brewers Corporation), which came into being in 1965 through the takeover of fifty companies. Rembrandt held 50% of the shares of the new company. The board, chaired by Dirk Hertzog, met for the first time in April 1965. Other members of the first board were Mr D de W Meyer, Prof. JP Yeats, Mr SL Muller, Mr JAJ Pickard, Mr MD Pieterse (managing director), Adv. AJ van Rooyen and Dr SP du T Viljoen.

A problem soon developed around the directorships of Pickard and Muller. Jan Pickard, a former Springbok rugby player who was married to the daughter of a senior minister, Dr Eben Dönges, and his attorney Louwrens Muller, later a minister in the NP government, acquired shares in *Uniewyn* (Union Wines), a competitor of Oude Meester. Rupert intervened from the group's parent board when the conflict of interest came to his attention, and gave them a choice: either they transfer their interest in Union Wines to Oude Meester at the price they had paid for it, or they resign. He saw it as the only honourable course of action; if not, he himself would resign and put the matter before the shareholders. According to Rupert, Pickard and Muller were enraged but realised they could not serve two masters.[15] They resigned their directorships and were replaced on the board by Prof. WH van der Merwe and Mr JG Grové. Pickard, boss of Picardi, would in time acquire the controlling interest in Union Wines.

Another factor that influenced the history of wrangling between the wine industry and the beer industry was the link-up of Monis with SFW, as a result of which this respected institution in the liquor market ended up in the hands of SAB. Monis, a well-known producer of sherry, sparkling wine, fruit juice and sweet fortified wines, had been founded by the Italian Roberto Moni who came to South Africa in 1906. In the 1960s the board of Monis decided it wanted to join the Rupert stable in preference to SFW. They were of the view that they would be able to cooperate well with people who had a respect for brands. Negotiations were started and progressed smoothly, with Dirk Hertzog acting as chief negotiator on behalf of the Rembrandt Group. A final meeting to settle a few outstanding details was planned for a Wednesday. The deal fell through, however, according to some reports because Hertzog wanted to keep a golf date and send subordinates to deal with the negotiations; according to other reports, on account of technical hitches. Years later Moni's son-in-law Bruno Mori, managing director of Monis, told Rupert and his wife that the Moni group had decided on that same day that they could not work with a chairman who put sport above prearranged business negotiations.

Although the Moni family was divided on the issue of to whom the business should be sold, they had also been negotiating with SFW, who outbid Oude Meester by R4 million. In the end Monis struck a deal with Johannesburg Consolidated Investments (JCI) and, together with JCI and SAB, it took over the Stellenbosch Wine Trust, which meant that Monis effectively took over SFW, and not the other way round. SAB still retained control of both companies.[16] At that time the wine market was much stronger than the beer market – with Monis as well as SFW in its stable, SAB had acquired a crown jewel in the wine industry. In addition, Monis owned the Nederburg wine estate with its graceful Cape Dutch manor house, where the prestigious Nederburg wine auction would be held decades later.

The Monis episode changed the history of the liquor industry. The stakes in the battle to rule the roost at once shot up.

Meanwhile the Whitbread saga continued. The new brewery could not achieve a breakthrough, and by September 1968 the writing was on the wall for the Rupert-Whitbread partnership. On 29 September 1968 Alex Bennett of Whitbread (London) wrote to Sir Francis de Guingand, the chairman of Whitbread (SA): 'When we met at the Brewery the other day, I thought you felt that at our meeting on the 12th September, Anton Rupert might have been unduly depressed about our business in South Africa and complications in Canada.' (Via Rothmans Rupert had obtained an interest in Canadian Breweries.) According to Bennett, Rupert had meant it when he called himself 'an unwilling marketer' with regard to the interests of Whitbread (SA). 'It is plainly not on to try and keep him in on that basis.' In fact, Bennett was convinced Rupert was 'a willing seller of his interests at a discount', which he regarded as 'a great disappointment . . . to me personally'.

The good relations between Rupert and Whitbread (London) were nearly soured by Rupert himself, but especially by Hertzog. Even before Bennett's letter to Sir Francis, Rupert had indicated that he was considering negotiating the sale of his shares in Whitbread to SAB. Whitbread (London) did not like this at all, and insisted that they and Rupert should come to an agreement about his shareholding. Whitbread would then, if necessary, negotiate with SAB themselves. Sir Francis was greatly concerned about the possibility of relations being damaged. On 11 October 1968 he phoned Rupert, telling him in no uncertain terms what he thought should be done, and then followed this with a letter on the same day in which he said Rembrandt should do nothing 'that could be looked upon as slick practice'. In an earlier letter of 7 October he had told Rupert frankly: 'I think you must be very careful not to give the impression that you have a way of getting out on better terms than the other two partners.' Rupert would later, on 23 October, write to Sir Francis: 'Have had very amiable discussions with Bennett and Tidbury this morning . . . They are staying tonight as our guests at Fleur du Cap. All this would not have been possible without your very great help. Thanks a million.'[17]

But Dirk Hertzog's relations with Whitbread (London) were strained. Sir Francis wrote to Rupert about this on 7 October: 'Dirk is alleged to have told Whitbread earlier on in the year that the shares were worthless and that the Group was prepared to write the whole investment off in their accounts.' In an undated note to Rupert he said Bennett had told him Hertzog was said to be accusing Whitbread (London) of wanting 'to get the Brewery cheap by forcing liquidation'. Sir Francis had told Bennett it was nothing but 'vicious gossip'. Concerned about a possible deterioration in the relations with Whitbread, Rupert discussed the issue with Hertzog. On 16 October Hertzog wrote a long letter to De Guingand, which bore evidence of the severe tension that existed between him and the management of Whitbread (SA). He claimed, among other things, that the management had represented him to others as a 'difficult person'. About Whitbread (SA) he wrote: 'Under present control, however, there is no future in it and an increase of capital (preferred in the event of liquidation) simply prolongs the embarrassment and fritters away all hope of salvaging anything.' He concluded his letter: 'I am not quite as black as I may have been painted to you.'

A further complication was that Rothmans' interest in Canadian Breweries had created a conflict of interest for Rupert, since the Canadian firm's Carling Black Label was marketed in South Africa by SAB. But the conflict of interest was not the only reason for the dissolution of his partnership with Whitbread and Heineken; Rupert had no intention to be part of a failure. A final announcement was made on 26 October 1968: Rembrandt would take over the interest of Whitbread (London) in Oude Meester and Oude Meester would give up its minority interest in Whitbread (SA). Whitbread would find a buyer for the shares or, if necessary, buy them itself. This opened the way for Whitbread to start negotiating with SAB.

Once again Rupert found himself outside the South African beer market, a market that continued to elude him.

The next big opportunity for greater entry into the beer market arrived in 1969, the year in which the Rembrandt Tobacco Corporation changed its name to the Rembrandt Group Limited and announced a subdivision of 50-cent shares into 10-cent shares. In the same year the expanding Oude Meester acquired a substantial interest in SA Distilleries and Wines Limited, which included companies such as EK Green & Company, Van Ryn Wine and Spirit Company, Castle Wine and Brandy Company and Henry Collison.

The opportunity to break into the beer market did not present itself in South Africa, however, but in Canada, where Rupert's Canadian subsidiary, Rothmans of Pall Mall, Canada Ltd, had acquired an eleven-percent holding in Canadian

Breweries Ltd (later renamed Carling O'Keefe) in 1968. With further purchases Rothmans secured a majority interest. Then, in May 1969, one of Rupert's cigarette rivals, Philip Morris Inc., came with an aggressive takeover bid headed by its chairman Joseph Cullman III. Philip Morris offered to buy 50% of the issued shares of Canadian Breweries, which included well-known names such as O'Keefe Breweries, Dow Breweries and Carling Breweries. The initial offer of $12 a share was later increased to $15 a share. But Morris did not reckon with Rupert's determination to retain his interest in Canadian Breweries.

He had to move fast to keep Morris out, and in the process he would turn to the network of influential people he had started building up early in his career. First he summoned Rothmans' Canadian head, John H Devlin, and its financial head, Paul Erasmus, to Zürich to discuss a strategy to counter Philip Morris. They thought it would cost at least $100 million. The three left for Grosvenor House in London, where Rupert woke Erasmus one morning at five o'clock with a telephone call to say he had a plan: they could keep Philip Morris out if they obtain a loan of $50 million and buy another $50 million's worth of shares. He requested Erasmus to get Hoogenhout in Stellenbosch to convene an urgent special meeting of Rembrandt's executive. Dirk Hertzog could chair it and he, Hoogenhout and Rupert's brother Jan could take the decision. Hoogenhout called back that same day to say the executive had approved the scheme.[18]

The next day Rupert phoned a Swiss banker at eight o'clock in the morning – the Swiss are at work early – and told him about the Philip Morris dilemma. When the banker asked how much he needed, Rupert said $145 million. The same afternoon at four o'clock Rupert was notified by the bank that the money was available. He had been able to obtain it without a signature.

The Swiss banker later told Rupert his decision had been the result of the favourable impression Rupert had made on him a few years earlier. He had been in the audience when Rupert had addressed international representatives of stock exchanges on 7 February 1961, the day after the opening of the new Johannesburg Stock Exchange and just months after the Sharpeville shootings in March 1960.[19] Rupert, who in turn held the conservative Swiss banker in high esteem, related: 'That day my speech impressed him so much, although we had never met, that it was the reason why he lent me the $145 million.'

The banker also gave him the name of a London broker who could start buying up shares on Rothmans' behalf. Paul Erasmus shuttled between London, Canada and Zürich to complete the necessary documents after he had been granted power of attorney by telex. At last Philip Morris's takeover bid was foiled. On his return to Toronto, Erasmus was greeted by newspaper headlines: 'Rothmans obtains 50% of Canadian Breweries.' Cullmann had been outmanoeuvred within three weeks and had to withdraw his tender. He later bought Miller Brewing Company from WR Grace & Company.[20] Eventually Rothmans bought the controlling share in Canadian Breweries for about $136 million.

Canadian Breweries continued to expand in Canada and by 1970 the company had 32% of the Canadian beer market. In the USA, Canadian Breweries' Carling was the seventh biggest brand, with a market share of four percent. But when Rupert hoped to increase that share by joining forces with an American brewery, he came up against a solid wall of American bureaucracy and anti-South African feeling.

Accompanied by Erasmus, he went to Washington to discuss his expansion plans, which entailed a merger between Carling USA and the established brewery Pabst of Milwaukee, with the Department of Justice. They were received by a female official, sitting with her feet on her desk, who inquired brusquely: 'What can I do for you?' In the icy anti-South African atmosphere Rupert tactfully tried to break down the official's resistance by first telling her how much he had enjoyed his visit to the Kennedy art centre. Her attitude thawed slightly, but she remained adamant that such expansion by a company under South African control would not be permitted in America. When he pointed out that there were no legal restrictions on South African investments, she said maybe not, but she would tie them up in American court cases for seven to eight years.[21] As a direct result of this disappointing experience Rupert remained wary of doing business in America ever afterwards.

In Canada, too, opposition to South Africa was rife and boycotts of South African products were spreading. Canadian Breweries, renamed Carling O'Keefe, was one of the targeted companies. In 1979 Rothmans' American beer interests, in Carling National, were sold for $34,5 million. The previous year Rembrandt had sold its controlling interest in Liggett Myers Inc. (North America), a cigarette company that had also diversified into food and liquor, to the Liggett Group after the latter had sold off its overseas interests to Philip Morris. The deal brought in about $28 million.

The international beer interests never achieved the spectacular success of the cigarette market. This was probably attributable to the different marketing strategies involved even more than the boycotts. Cigarettes were an intimate product that smokers carried on their persons. Beer, by contrast, was drunk mainly in dimly lit bars and beer halls. Besides, in large markets beer was marketed more effectively on television.

Despite everything, Carling did reasonably well in Canada. But Rupert still had no foothold in the South African beer market.

CHAPTER 17

Multinational trailblazer

T he 1960s was a period of expansion and diversification, both at home and abroad.

In 1964 Cavalla, already under Rembrandt's control, bought out Rand Tobacco Company. Bertie Levenstein, later a director of Rembrandt until his retirement, stayed on as chairman of Rand Tobacco. In this year, ten years after acquiring Rothmans, its first overseas venture, Rembrandt was selling more cigarettes in one day than it had sold per month in 1954. This was also the year of its first attempt to break into the South African beer market through the acquisition of a 30% stake in Whitbread SA, which proved to be the prelude to the beer war that was to erupt a decade later.

The following year Rembrandt consolidated its liquor interests in Oude Meester Cellars, Distillers and Brewers Corporation, and the Printpak Company was established through the amalgamation of the interest in the printing company *Kaaplandse Drukkery* (formerly Pro Ecclesia) with the printing branch of Herzberg Mullne Holdings on a 50/50 basis. The latter company had been supplying packaging material to Rembrandt since 1948.

In 1968, following a massive increase in excise duty on cigarettes, Rembrandt had to close down a small factory in Cape Town that it had acquired along with Cavalla. A hundred workers were retrenched with a severance package. The trade-union leader Anna Scheepers, president of the National Union of Cigarette and Tobacco Workers, described the 'golden handshake' of R100 000 as 'the most generous gesture I've seen in my 30 years as trade unionist'.[1] Hardly any of the retrenched workers felt the need to take up the offer of alternative employment elsewhere in the group, which included free transport.

The Rembrandt Tobacco Corporation changed its name to the Rembrandt Group Limited in 1969. A year later it joined forces with Sanlam and acquired control of Master Development Corporation, a property and urban-development company operating in various parts of the country.

Rupert referred to Afrikaner aspirations to acquire a footing in industry when he handed over Pres. Paul Kruger's sash of office to the University of Pretoria at the institution's Spring Day celebrations in 1969. He elaborated on the struggle waged by his generation and the generations before them in respect of three important causes: freedom, language equality and a footing in commerce and industry. 'The struggle for freedom was about an idea; it was not anti-English or anti-British,' he said on that occasion. 'It started in the days of the Dutch East India Company, when as early as 1707 Hendrik Bibault exclaimed in Stellenbosch: "Ik ben een Afrikaner!" [I am an Afrikaner]. It was about the republics of Graaff-Reinet and Swellendam, about Slagtersnek, the Free State Republic, Natalia, Transvaal, Majuba, Spioenkop, Paardekraal and Vereeniging. The struggle for language equality was at first against Lord Charles Somerset for the right to continue using Dutch in the church, court and school. And then later about the new language from Africa, the most modern in the West, Afrikaans. The struggle for a footing in commerce and industry was taken up repeatedly, after the Anglo-Boer War and after the two world wars, each time Afrikaners felt themselves to be politically powerless.'[2]

Rupert's domestic success was accompanied by extensive international expansion. In 1965 Rembrandt obtained a 30% stake in Martin Brinkmann AG, Wolfgang Ritter's tobacco group that dated from 1813. In 1900 the group had been taken over by Ritter's father, the German cigarette manufacturer who was reluctant to buy Rothmans' brands from Rupert in 1954. Along with Brinkmann, the biggest manufacturer of pipe tobacco and third biggest manufacturer of cigarettes in Germany, Rembrandt obtained an interest in House of Edgeworth, the leading exporters of pipe tobacco in the USA. Brinkmann fitted the profile of the kind of company that attracted Rupert: established brands with a rich tradition that could be promoted and expanded through technological innovation. Two years later Rembrandt expanded its interest in Brinkmann, which had just formed a partnership with a Belgian company, Tabacofina SA.

By 1968 Rembrandt had 34 tobacco factories in twenty countries, including Australia, Canada, the Netherlands, Fidji, Cyprus, Malta, Singapore, the Sudan, Brazil, Jamaica, Germany and Belgium. In Stellenbosch, a triumvirate consisting of Willem Malherbe, Thys Roux and Kallie Buys looked after the tobacco interests on the home front. By 1972 Rembrandt was the fourth largest tobacco group in the world and ranked among the top ten in the beer trade. Its issued share capital remained modest – just R5,3 million – but its assets exceeded R1 000 million, it had reserves of more than 35 times the capital, and the annual turnover stood at R2 000 million.

All of this had been essential preparation for the next phase of Rupert's international involvement.

A milestone year for Rupert's philosophy of partnership in business was reached in 1972, when Rembrandt's European interests were combined in Carreras. The new company was named Rothmans International, and he considered it the first truly trans-European partnership company, with interests spanning the continent – from Britain and Ireland to Belgium, the Netherlands, Germany, Spain and Switzerland. Rupert made a distinction between transnational or international companies on one hand, and multinational companies on the other. In his view, transnationals followed the conventional pattern of establishing branches abroad, which then reported back to head office in the mother country. A multinational company based on true industrial partnership – or an industrial commonwealth, a concept he often used – comprised full-fledged partners on an equal footing: a group of companies cooperating internationally, with local shareholding of at least 50% in each country where a new enterprise was established.

Rothmans International was such a multinational industrial commonwealth. It was established shortly after the formation of the European Economic Community (EEC), which later became the European Union. Rupert saw the time was ripe for his partnership philosophy to come to fulfilment ' in a new Europe, because one of the largest economic blocs in human history is on its way – one of the most powerful and most dynamic – the new EEC.' His ideal was that 'we from this remote southern corner would be the first to create a trans-European, pan-European enterprise in which all Europeans could share.'

It was not easy to set up the company. Nonetheless, Rupert remained positive: 'I had great fun in discussions and I had to speak to the most difficult trade union of all – that is the German trade union.' His German was poor – his wife described it as 'Afrikaans with a would-be German accent' – but his message was clear and to the point: 'We were handing Europe back to the Europeans.' With barely concealed pride he summed up later: 'I sold them the idea and they are now the largest tobacco group on the continent. But it was not easy.'[3]

It had taken six months to complete the mammoth unification, he told commerce students at the University of Pretoria on 22 August 1972. Two weeks earlier they had signed the mountain of contracts on which hundreds of lawyers, auditors, tax advisors and bankers had laboured. Their professional services, which cost £1 million, would save millions every year. 'If I were to tell you,' he told the students, 'that we had a hundred qualified auditors working in one weekend, that this company's interests amount to about £200 million, that it employs about 25 000 workers (and remember, we're highly mechanised), that this company enabled us to offer £20 million's worth of convertible debentures in Europe, for which we had £160 million's worth of offers from more than 120 banks, then I also want to tell you why. It is because over the years we have consistently adopted an open-handed policy, have consistently advocated industrial partnership, have never opted for external control, have always dealt with local directors, have never operated the way so many American, British and other companies operate abroad. For we come from a country that knows what it's like not to occupy a position of power. We know what it feels like to have no shares in motor-vehicle companies or banks – that's where we started from, that's how it was in the 1930s . . . And because I knew that, we looked for the necessary friends with whom we could collaborate with full self-respect.'

Rothmans International was the first company of its kind in Europe. Its board of directors read like an international who's who, people in key positions in business in their respective countries who had been personally selected and approached by Rupert. Among the directors were:

> Prince Burchard of Prussia, director of Brinkmann
> Dr DSA Carroll, chairman of Lloyds and Bolsa International Bank
> John M Brown, managing director of Carreras
> Frans van den Berg, president of Tabacofina
> Luis Gomez-Acebo, president of Tobacigar
> Dr F Kristinus, president of Brinkmann
> JC van Marken, chairman of Turmac and the Amsterdam Bourse
> David CS Montagu, chairman of Samuel Montagu & Co.
> Edmund L de Rothschild, chairman of NM Rothschild & Sons
> Bruno M Saager, general manager of Union Bank in Switzerland
> Franz H Ulrich, managing director of Deutsche Bank
> Franz Witt, managing director of Dresdner Bank
> Edmond G Wouters, chairman of Tabacofina
> Robert Wickenden, assistant managing director of Carreras
> Sir Derek Pritchard, chairman of Carreras
> JW Mayo, a British attorney
> Alexander Orlow, president of Turmac.

Rupert, the consummate networker, was proud of the calibre of the people they had drawn together on their board. He told the students they still needed to bring in some Italian and French directors, although that meant getting round the state monopolies in those countries.

His brother Koos has affirmed the view of many of their contemporaries that Rupert's success as an international businessman owed much to his instinctive ability to appoint the right people in the right place and in the right position: square pegs in square holes and round pegs in round holes. Limiting his risks by building networks left him with enough time to focus on the detail of an enterprise, one of his strengths and something he himself considered crucial to risk management. *Press Advertising and Radio Review* wrote in this regard: 'It has been his personal assessment of his personal ability to visualise and his personal attention to detail and insistence on the highest standards which have helped to raise standards throughout the Republic.'[4] This attribute enabled him to check the basics, know his company's figures, monitor progress, ask the right questions and avoid financial risk. 'Successful businessmen pay attention to detail. This also applies to success in other fields of life. What else enabled the geologist Hans Merensky to make his discoveries?' he said in an interview. Reflecting a moment, he remarked: 'Though some businessmen abuse attention to detail in order to cut corners.'[5]

Huberte related that her husband's keen eye for detail made her resort to what she called 'the flower treatment'. Whenever he came home from a business trip he would at once spot if the slightest thing was out of place. Knowing how much he loved flowers and colours, she would make sure the whole house was filled with flowers to welcome him. 'Then Anton didn't notice anything wrong.'[6]

In his assessment of people, Rupert also put a premium on practical experience. In 1973 he told an audience of chartered accountants: '. . . I think a man who has not yet sold something to his fellows at the age of 22 might not be able to achieve success.' This belief in the value of experience was one of the reasons why he felt so strongly that one should not have an inferiority complex on account of not having been to university. When UP students asked him in 1971 what was required for business success, he advised them to flee from the university as quickly as possible after having gained a first degree. 'You can always return later after you've learnt about life.' And he told a meeting of chartered accountants: 'I know of no doctor of law in South Africa who has also been a brilliant advocate, because they sharpen the pencil so excessively that the point snaps off. You study more and more about less and less.'[7]

In August 1972 Rothmans International went public, with assets of $539 million and sales of $2 billion per annum. Not all the reports in the British Press were favourable. Columnist Michael Gillard of the *Daily Express* described Rupert as 'a little-known South African doctor of chemistry [who] yesterday unwrapped his master plan to create the first British based Euro-company born of the Common Market age, and a new £200 million tobacco giant'. Rupert, to whom he referred as 'a friend of South African Prime Minister Mr John Vorster and cash backer of the ruling National Party', now planned to concentrate all his activities outside South Africa and America via Carreras.[8]

Rupert objected strongly to the loaded description, particularly the suggestion that he backed a political party financially. The paper was obliged to print an unconditional apology the next day.[9] He was adamant in his view that no company contributions should be made to any political party, a principle he laid down as company policy.

When Johann Rupert testified before the Truth and Reconciliation Commission (TRC) on behalf of the Rembrandt Group in 1997, he stated that he had studied all the company reports from the earliest days to obtain a better understanding of the group. He could not find a single contribution to the NP. From the age of about five or six he had known that they were not 'with' this party. Besides, any support would have run counter to the widely publicised mutual animosity between his father and Verwoerd. 'There was a fundamental difference in philosophy,' according to Johann.[10]

The establishment of Rothmans International was the crown on the labours of many people. Rupert drew a message from this for the Pretoria commerce students: 'I just want you to know that with a small group of people in this country we are capable of achieving enormous things. You have to ask yourself, what does a man need? Diligence, certainty and imagination? The Swiss bankers say they need knowledge and character – 'aus können wird kann' coupled with character. But above all you need the idea and the ideal and the enthusiasm – and the enthusiasm carries you very far.'

Speaking to the students at the age of 56, he identified as one of South Africa's problems the phenomenon of 'too many of the older people being scared to take risks'. Annoyed at perceptions that most older people in positions of power fell in this category, he told his predominantly younger audience: 'Count me out!' A second problem he identified was that of people scaring themselves with rumours reminiscent of the 1930s. 'If you become scared, we are lost; if you listen to this petty talk . . . you are lost. Close your ears! Life is a ladder and if you pull down the man ahead of you, you will fall down yourself. If you push up the man ahead of you, you get somewhere.'

On this occasion he was acerbic in his evaluation of the South African situation, as if he had become fed up with the pottering in the country to find a new, more productive course economically and especially politically. 'At present South Africa appears to me to be a country with a great number of kings all crowing on their own dunghills . . . You who are young must not let yourselves be influenced by this surfeit of talking – Coloured Parliaments, White Parliaments – these do not produce what we need.' He concluded with an argument that had become almost a refrain: 'Nothing ventured, nothing gained, and enthusiasm brings one a whole mile further.'[11]

At that stage of his life Rupert was spending a great deal of his time on the road, in aeroplanes and abroad as he supervised the execution of the agreements reached with his partners. There were endless consultations with key players, clients and other stakeholders, as well with kings and princes, statesmen and opinion formers.

He maintained a cultured, charming and courteous presence, increasingly attracting the attention of the international media, perhaps more so because of his tendency to keep a low profile. The German journalist Rolf Bigler compared him to Distillers' Richelieu brandy with its 'priceless maturity'. Like his quality wines, Bigler wrote, he was 'temperamental', and like the dark-red cigarette packet of his Dunhill International he was 'solid' and 'promising'. A basically serious person with a shy smile, a twinkle in his eye betrayed his enjoyment. A funny incident could make him laugh, but never boisterously. As Bigler put it, he smiled lost within himself, like a Pierrot without his Columbine.[12] Other observers discerned a shy, quiet, hidden self behind the man of action, a thinker, dreamer and introvert, sensitive and gentle, who nonetheless issued orders, travelled, planned and made sure that things got done.

Rupert did not always consult everybody. Behind the doctor's gracious, introverted manner lay a will of steel, remarked the journal *Fortune*, as well as a certain high-handedness. On one occasion he sold half Rembrandt's share in Rothmans without consulting the executive directors – which incurred a trip to London to placate each director individually and explain his action. His reluctance to reveal too much about himself also led the journal to observe: 'Rupert, touchy and proud, evades topics he does not like and is a master of the reply that evades the question.'[13]

By 1966 he was spending about 69 days a year in aeroplanes between five continents. For seven months of the year he was away from home. As far back as March 1959 he had said: 'I've coined a phrase, "A man in the air is worth three on the ground."' Rupert's frequent and prolonged absences from home did not perturb him. 'I'm amazed by the way in which the Americans rely on their wives. I love my wife and children as much as the next man, but men have to fulfil their vocation. Really, when I think of Magellan and the explorers, it's a bit much to hear young men complain about a temporary separation from their partners.'

In later years he never carried a business card on his travels – for security reasons, since many foreigners were hostile towards South Africans during the sanction years. For the same reason he occasionally signed hotel registers using his first name only. Like most international businessmen, he used only the best hotels: it would be detrimental to a company's reputation if its top executive operated from a second-rate hotel. His primary residence abroad was the suite he hired on an annual basis in Grosvenor House in London, which had a janitor, room service and tight security. In Paris he usually stayed at the Bristol on the Rue Faubourg St Honoré, sometimes at the Hotel George V or the Ritz. In Hamburg he liked the Vier Jahreszeiten, in Zürich the Dolder Grand Hotel or the Eden Au Lac, and in New York he frequented The Plaza on Fifth Avenue, the Hotel Pierre and occasionally Essex House near Central Park.

He kept an inventory of clothing and travel requisites, which enabled him to keep his luggage below the prescribed limit. In the 1970s the introduction of Concorde supersonic passenger jets halved travel time between London and New York. Rupert frequently used these flights, on which he also made the acquaintance of many international personalities. One of these was David Frost, whose television interviews with famous politicians and other newsmakers were broadcast on both sides of the Atlantic. At Rupert's invitation Frost travelled to South Africa on holiday and was offered accommodation during his private visit at Rembrandt's guest house, Fleur du Cap.[14] In London he entertained Rupert at a reception at his home, along with prominent British figures such as Princess Margaret and the playwright Robert Bolt, who wrote *A man for all seasons*.[15]

Early in the 1970s the Rembrandt Group expanded its American tobacco interests. In 1973, Rupert emerged as the biggest single shareholder of the giant Ligget & Myers Group. He had outmanoeuvred HA (Mickey) Newman, chairman of the executive of Western Pacific Industries who had attempted to obtain representation on the L & M board, by buying enough L & M shares to give him effective control of the once mighty American tobacco company that had declined to such an extent that its biggest profit came from Alpo dog food. As a result of this move, *Business Week* described Rupert in an article entitled 'South Africa's mystery man' as one of the world's most powerful and influential multinational industrialists.[16] He told the business journal that his group had entered into a working relationship with L & M and would manufacture their brands under licence agreement in Germany and Australia.

Rupert did not say outright that Raymond J Mulligan, president and chief executive of L & M, had requested him to fend off Newman's bid, but he implied that this had been the case. Mulligan, in turn, said admiringly that the courteous South African had 'stood ready' in the background 'without my knowledge'. As Mulligan did not know much about cigarette manufacturing, he concentrated on L & M's other operations. 'We complement each other,' Rupert said about their relationship. 'I know the cigarette industry, and he follows my advice.' L & M's once proud Chesterfield brand had lost popularity, and at that stage the company was focusing on the king-size filter-tipped cigarettes L & M and Lark.

Rupert felt that L & M's poorly performing cigarette interests could be turned around with aggressive marketing, and launched his St Moritz brand in the

American market through a licence agreement concluded with Turmac Tobacco in the Netherlands. In his view, other subsidiaries of L & M fitted well with his liquor interests in South Africa. These subsidiaries marketed, inter alia, the prestigious American bourbon Wild Turkey, and imported liqueurs such as Metaxa from Greece and Grand Marnier from France, Bombay gin and the aperitif Campari from Italy.

He considered the great number of cigarette brands under his control – including Peter Stuyvesant, Craven A and the expensive Dunhills – to offer something for every taste. He used the variety of brands to appeal to the different ways in which people thought about themselves: Dunhill for cosmopolites, Paul Revere (named after the American silversmith who rode through the night to warn the colonists of Massachusetts that the British troops were on the march) for admirers of America, St Moritz (which derived its name from the Swiss ski resort and playground of the rich) for the continent of Europe, and so on.

Rupert could get very annoyed if anybody smoked competitors' cigarettes in his presence. During interviews he regularly smoked three to four cigarettes, Peter Stuyvesant or Dunhill Light. When a visitor once left a packet of a rival company's cigarettes in his car, he said tersely: 'That's an insult!'

By the end of the 1980s Rembrandt had interests in about 60 factories in 30 countries on all six continents on a partnership basis. In the course of time the group's products would be used in virtually every country in the world.

Rupert offered a fourfold explanation for the group's success:

- *Hard work.* 'We believe that success is achieved by those who produce that extra bit, and that 24 hours in a day are actually not enough.'
- *The concept that 'He who does not believe in miracles is not a realist'.* 'Without this firm belief it would have been impossible to make a breakthrough in a strongly competitive market.'
- *New approach.* 'While we realise that the tobacco industry has a rich tradition, we also know that half of today's industrial products had been totally unknown 25 years ago. We therefore concentrated purposefully on producing innovative and improved products in the world of tobacco through research.'
- *A balanced perspective,* 'based on the understanding that the current fiscal policy in most countries makes if difficult, if not impossible, for the young entrepreneur to make a meaningful contribution to the general welfare.'

The group's strategy was 'to manage that which we know and to invest in that in which we have a say', he said in a lecture at the University of Pretoria (UP) in 1981.[17]

A further component of his partnership policy was the structure of the group: not rigidly hierarchical, but decentralised, with responsibilities where they belong. And, stated Rupert, 'where we deviated from this, it was to our detriment. In a few countries where we took over businesses that did not operate on a partnership basis, we incurred problems. We also believe in consensus decision-making and won't take any decision at board level if a director is strongly opposed to it.' In this regard he was ahead of this time. Today strictly hierarchical management systems are considered unacceptable, and provision is made for a participative management style.

Yet Rupert was never hesitant to state his opinion and to take decisions. He could even explode if a proposed decision was, in his view, poor or did not make business or strategic sense.

In his UP lecture he elaborated on the group's systems, which were aimed at effective communication. 'This is achieved through international group co-ordinators, world conferences, personal contact and the provision of specialised services by a non-profit organisation.' He described the group's style as the delivery of quality, service and open-handedness. 'Unlike the Japanese we simply believe in innovation, not imitation. Through constant research we believe in always remaining ahead. We also don't suffer from what the Japanese call "announcementitis". We are often accused of secrecy, but we believe in first doing and then disclosing.'

In his lecture he summed up the philosophy that he had been putting into practice for 30 years. The aims, the dominant objectives, are partnership, no discrimination, and equal opportunities – to serve all communities honourably, at a profit. Rupert's partnership philosophy was evidently a very clearly defined value system, which he had been implementing long before the role of values in the business world would receive such strong emphasis. In their bestseller *In search of excellence*, TJ Peters and RH Waterman Jr concluded that values feature prominently in excellent companies.[18]

The success that the Rembrandt Group achieved by means of this value system was not only reflected in the healthy state of their financial statements. 'We also experience daily how it builds a bridge of understanding between individuals and nations and serves to create a better rapport and greater mutual goodwill. For longer than three decades I have been pleading globally for true industrial partnership between the developed and the developing countries, because I believe that it holds the answer to the aspirations of the poor populations of the world, and that it can counter domination by the rich countries effectively.'[19]

At the start of the 21st century twenty years later, his plea would still be as relevant as ever.

CHAPTER 18

The stuff of legend

An important diversification process that ensued from Rupert's merger of European interests in Rothmans International in 1972 related to Cartier, one of the brands on the list of the new multinational conglomerate's interests.

The new company's association with Cartier, described as the 'jeweller of kings and the king of jewellers' by the Duke of Windsor, the former Edward VIII of Britain before his abdication in 1936, attracted Rupert's attention as he reviewed their latest acquisitions.

Among affluent clients worldwide the name Cartier was legendary. It was an old, established firm with a rich tradition, the kind of business that appealed strongly to Rupert.

The Paris firm was established in 1847 by Louis-François Cartier. When the Empress Eugénie, consort of Napoleon III, ordered a silver tea service from him he was made. In 1874 his son Alfred succeeded him as head of Cartier. Cartier's premises moved in 1899 to Paris's most fashionable shopping area, the Rue de la Paix, where the shop is still a beacon to tourists. In 1904 Cartier was granted a royal warrant of supplier to the Court of St James by King Edward VII of England. A string of other royal houses followed his example, including those of Spain, Portugal, Russia, Siam, Greece, Belgium and Egypt, as well as the House of Orléans and the principality of Monaco. Celebrities and multimillionaires from all over the world bought their jewellery, watches and valuables from Cartier.[1]

The house of Cartier was also known for the fabulous jewels it sold over the years. Evalyn Walsh McLean, the *Washington Post* heiress, bought both the famous Hope diamond – a blue 67,12-carat stone, said to be under a curse – and the Star of the East, a pear-shaped 94,8-carat brilliant, from Cartier. The Star of South Africa, a globular 47,75-carat gem discovered near Hopetown in 1869 that according to Cartier triggered the country's diamond rush, was reset in a Cartier piece. In 1969 it acquired a pear-shaped 69,42-carat diamond in New York for just over $1 million. Days later actor Richard Burton bought the diamond, at that stage the 56th biggest stone in the world, as a gift for Elizabeth Taylor.

Apart from jewellery, Cartier's wares ranged from luxury leather goods, sunglasses, perfumes and pens to its famous *objets d'art* and 'mystery clocks' (*pendules mystérieuses*) whose hands appeared to float in the air, as well as its stylish Tank wrist watches.[2] Cartier's 'love bracelet', designed by Aldo Cipullo in 1969, was sold only to people who were buying a gift for a beloved. Richard Burton bought one for Elizabeth Taylor. Other famous couples who bought this token of love included Ali McGraw and Steve McQueen, Mai Britt and Sammy Davis Jr, and daughter and father Nancy and Frank Sinatra.

Early in the 20th century Cartier opened branches in London's Bond Street and Fifth Avenue, New York. Alfred Cartier's three sons respectively managed the Paris, London and New York houses, but after they died in the 1950s the business fragmented. That was the situation Rupert found when he started his inquiries about the Cartier brand in which Rothmans had acquired an interest. The brand in question was registered under class 34 of the International Brand Classification, the category that included tobacco, smokers' accessories and matches, and turned out to be a world-famous cigarette lighter. It was the elegant, oval-shaped luxury cigarette lighter that Robert Hocq, the inventor of gas cigarette lighters, had licensed under Cartier's banner. In time this invention revolutionised the luxury goods industry. The new recipe of combining functionality with luxury caused a turnabout in the cosy, exclusive world of the coterie of prominent luxury goods houses.

Soon Rupert met the Parisians Robert Hocq and Joseph Kanoui, the two partners who emerged as key figures in the reunification of Cartier's three branches. In 1972 they started taking control of Cartier Paris. Hocq, the energetic marketing expert, was the chairman while Kanoui was in charge of finance.

In 1973 a confidant of Hocq, the youthful Alain Dominique Perrin, launched a worldwide chain of boutiques called Les Must de Cartier. The name was Perrin's coinage. When asked by Hocq what Cartier meant to him, he replied in English: 'Cartier? It's a must!' The first Les Must boutique opened in Biarritz; the first Parisian one was at no. 7 Place Vendôme, the square at the bottom of the Rue de la Paix. The boutiques catered for a less illustrious clientele, offering items priced more affordably at about $200 to $2 000. These included the popular Cartier cigarette lighters.

The reunification of Cartier's three branches was a complex process that took nearly eight years. Hocq took the lead in taking over the London house in 1974. With Rupert's support he then started regaining Cartier New York, in which several groups had a stake. Perrin, who had joined Cartier in 1969 and could speak English well, sometimes acted as interpreter between Hocq and Rupert during their consultations.

Rupert's diversification into the luxury goods market, which had already started with the acquisition of the stake in Dunhill, was gathering momentum. In 1976 Rupert, who wanted a representative on Cartier's American board, phoned his former head of finance in North America, Paul Erasmus. Erasmus had left Rembrandt in 1972 and acquired Canadian citizenship, but returned to the group in 1977. Along with Robert Hocq's elder daughter Nathalie he served on the board of Cartier New York and also represented Rupert in the negotiations to reunite the various Cartier units. When negotiating with Hocq his interpreter was Mario Soares, the group's representative in Brazil, who could speak French.

It struck Erasmus that Rupert and Robert Hocq had similar philosophies and many shared interests. Rupert's telex to Hocq to introduce Erasmus as the new director read simply: 'Paul Erasmus is a very good friend.' Kanoui, whom Erasmus regarded as a superb diplomat and negotiator as well as a very capable financial expert, also took part in the negotiations, sometimes in Hocq's office at the Place Vendôme. They were entertained lavishly, for Hocq had the Paris agency for Russian caviar.

Nathalie Hocq had joined Cartier Paris in 1974. At one stage in the 1970s it was rumoured in the press that she and Rupert's son Johann, at that time working at Lazard Freres in New York, had a romantic attachment. They went out for a while, and Hocq and his family visited the Ruperts in South Africa. But when questioned by journalists, Huberte denied the rumours: 'Nathalie and Johann are friends. If either of them fell in love, we'd know it right away.'[3] The 26-year-old Nathalie responded that she and Johann (then 28) were 'just good friends'. The relationship did not develop further. During the same period it was also rumoured that Hocq intended to give Cartier to Nathalie and the House of Dior to his other daughter, Sophie. 'I have two daughters, both unmarried. I want to give Cartier to one of them as a dowry and Dior to the other,' he said.[4]

In the meantime the negotiations about the reunification of Cartier were kept very much under cover. Sanctions were in full swing and any leakage about a South African connection would have jeopardised the process.

The finalisation of the American takeover in 1979 saw the creation of Cartier Monde as a reunified, worldwide company. Apart from the original three houses in Paris, London and New York and the Les Must de Cartier boutiques, the firm by this time had shops in Cannes, Monte Carlo, Munich, Palm Beach and Tokyo. Hocq and Rupert amalgamated their interests in an umbrella holding company. So strict was the secrecy surrounding the deal that Rupert's name does not even appear in books written about Cartier at the time. It was merely mentioned that 'another group of investors' acquired Cartier New York in 1976, and that Cartier Monde was established in 1979 as a result of a merger of the groups that owned the houses in Paris, London and New York.[5]

Rupert was also interested in obtaining a licence to market cigarettes under the Cartier brand name. In that case it was agreed that Cartier Paris would furnish Rothmans International with full particulars about the firm and an introduction to its shops and dealers that could assist with promotion. All contact with Cartier would be channelled via Turmac, a Rothmans subsidiary.

The reunification of Cartier ended tragically for Hocq. On the evening of 8 December 1979 he and his wife were walking to their car from an office Christmas party. He was hit by a passing car in thick fog on the Place Vendôme and died under the eyes of Perrin, who was walking just behind the couple. Hocq's death put Rupert in a quandary, since Kanoui was planning to join a banking group. He phoned Kanoui and told him he could not leave him in the lurch at this juncture. He asked him to stay on and, typical of his partnership philosophy, to take over the chairmanship of Cartier. On 6 January 1980 Kanoui became executive chairman of Cartier Monde, with Perrin at the head of Les Must de Cartier. 'It was a wonderful saga to start again and rebuild Cartier,' Kanoui commented. 'And the best aspect of it all is the Cartier spirit – people from the ateliers to the boutiques are proud to be part of the family. The challenge we now face is to continue to beat our opposition, but we have the strength which is inherent in the trademark. We can sell items at hundreds of dollars or millions – none of our rivals have that depth of reserves. We have.'

Nathalie Hocq had such faith in the Ruperts' integrity and business abilities that she offered Rupert the family share in Cartier after her father's death. In this way Rupert effectively acquired the controlling interest in Cartier, the international prestige jewellers, via his tobacco interests.

Internationally as well as at home, where the government was laboriously starting to move away from the rigorist application of apartheid of the Verwoerd era, Rupert was increasingly giving expression to his partnership philosophy. When he spoke of 'private initiative with an idea', he did not see the 'idea' as something vague but instead a way of doing business in practice. More precisely, his philosophy of life, embodied in partnership.

Looking back on the role of this business philosophy in their operations, he said: 'Our achievements overseas were determined by partnerships with equal shareholdings . . . Partnership means trust – a willingness to share responsibility and accountability with others. I would consider it an insult if someone offered me a 49% share in his business.' As far back as 1963 he stated his position unambiguously: 'With our policy of industrial partnership we did away with the concept of financial colonialism by ensuring that in every country where we built factories, at least half the shares in our group of companies belonged to residents of such countries.'

His idea of partnership hinged on wholehearted commitment; a win-win relationship between partners; willingness to enter into a stable, long-term relationship based on common goals; and above all, confidence and trust. Rupert was outspoken on this point: 'Our history in the field of partnership is one of trust. We have never made an unfriendly bid. All our investments outside the traditional areas of tobacco and liquor were made at the invitation of others. Central to our Group's partnership philosophy is a business philosophy that tends to facilitate rather than dictate.' For trust to develop, partners should be open and frank with each other. They should keep each other informed, communicating openly and regularly; unpleasant surprises have a lethal effect on trust.

In 1979 he said in an address to the Afrikaanse Handelsinstituut: 'I do not let friends down. I prefer loyalty and friendship to money.' He constantly emphasised trust and loyalty as core values. This was later illustrated painfully in the saga around Sanlam, Rembrandt, Gencor and his bosom friend Wim de Villiers. In a moment of self-revelation, Rupert added another quality to the idea of trust: self-confidence. He even called it the starting point and first key to success. 'I've learnt that you need to have self-confidence; you have to take calculated risks, take balanced decisions. Your brain always works like a pair of scales: for and against, for and against.'

A good partnership was also embodied in the nature of the representation. Rupert put this into practice by appointing local chairmen of the boards that looked after the interests of the group in the various countries. Local residents served as directors while local staff were recruited and received good training. All chairmen and managing directors of the group were treated as equals.

Joseph Kanoui, for many years the chairman of Cartier, emphasised that this approach was crucial to the successful partnership Cartier developed with the Rupert family from the remote town of Stellenbosch. Like Rupert, he believed that the head of a company should not quarrel with his shareholders; there should be mutual trust, complete transparency and full disclosure of facts. Kanoui maintained his close association with the Ruperts for years and later also became chairman of Vendôme, Richemont's umbrella company for luxury goods. He spent a few holidays with the Ruperts at their Hermanus beach house. Eventually he built his own holiday home at Johann Rupert's golf estate Leopard Creek on the Crocodile River at Malelane in the Lowveld.

Kanoui regarded Rupert as '300% South African', but was often struck by his attunement to places: his ability to capture the spirit of a place, be it a foreign city or country. He saw this as almost a sixth sense, even taking into account that Rupert, 'clearly highly intelligent', naturally relied on thorough research when he entered new markets. He often ended up knowing more about these markets than long-time residents. Kanoui was also impressed by Rupert's talent for selecting capable people and then trusting them completely. But if anyone misled or deceived him, their ways parted.[6]

Critics sometimes questioned the wisdom of running a huge international conglomerate from a head office in distant South Africa. A long-time observer, Dr Joachim Zahn, strategy manager of DaimlerChrysler in South America, pointed out that in the climate that prevailed during the sanction years there was lot to be said for administering the group's affairs 'from the periphery'. Zahn Jr, son of Rupert's old friend Joachim Zahn of Daimler-Benz in Germany, had been Rembrandt's group coordinator in Stellenbosch for a while. According to him Rupert always kept abreast of world affairs. He read and travelled widely, building networks wherever he went. Besides, at Stellenbosch Rembrandt was not exposed to anti-South African pressure groups and organisations. There were no demonstrations, disruption of AGMs or protesters occupying their buildings, which could have been the case if the head office had been situated in London or on the continent of Europe.[7]

Rupert was also criticised, inter alia by the *Financial Mail*, for not divulging sufficient information about his companies and their activities. Rembrandt's annual reports in fact contained precious little about the group's overseas interests. His counter argument was that in the business environment confidentiality was of the essence. If competitors got wind of new moves, it could sabotage the venture. 'Business is based on trust,' he maintained, 'and it is as fragile as a glass menagerie. If everyone in business has to tell exactly what they're going to do for the next decade, that business will be a disaster.'[8]

By 1974 he was using his office at Stellenbosch only about 100 days a year, spending the equivalent of 90 working days a year on aeroplanes to visit overseas offices of the Rembrandt Group, the Rupert-controlled holding company that was at that stage the world's fifth biggest tobacco group, with direct interests in 29 countries. The journal *Business Week* commented on the situation in which Rupert had to do business internationally: 'The South African's pattern of operation is to maintain a low profile, because that is his personal style and because there are obvious disadvantages to identifying consumer brands in the public mind with South African interests.'[9] His regular overseas trips were not only aimed at ensuring that his plans and ideas were being implemented, but also enabled him to maintain personal, face-to-face contact, which he preferred to communication by telephone.

He fully conceded that it might be more efficient to run his business empire from Geneva or some other central location, but felt he had certain responsibilities to South Africa. Responding to a question in this regard, his answer was brief: 'There's too much to do in Africa. I feel more needed here.'[10]

Kanoui relates how he was often struck by the impression Rupert made on people. According to him the former British Prime Minister Margaret Thatcher probably met about 20 000 people in her life, 'of whom perhaps 2 000 are important – but she remembers Anton Rupert'. The Italian industrial patriarch Gianni Agnelli who transformed Fiat – with Lancia, Maserati, Alfa Romeo and Ferrari under his banner as well – into an international motor-vehicle competitor that spearheaded Italy's post-war economic boom, had a platinum plate made for Rupert. And Kanoui recalls a dinner in New York hosted for Rupert by *Time* magazine where the guests included the US secretary of state Henry Kissinger, three American senators and the oil minister of the Shah of Iran. Yet Kanoui's lasting impression is of Rupert's modesty and courteousness.

Rupert's thoughtfulness also deeply impressed Hans Kolles, administrative director of the Cape Town clothing manufacturer Monatic-Alba. In the 1970s Rembrandt took over the company after it had run into trouble. Sidney Back, a director of the parent company IL Back & Co., was at that stage also a director of Rembrandt, whose entry saved hundreds of jobs in the clothing industry. Although Rembrandt sold the clothing factories again after a year or two, Rupert had suits made at Monatic-Alba during that time. According to Kolles his approach differed from that of other directors, particularly the new ones, who ordered suits from the factory – some demanded that their suits be ready within three days, which disrupted the production process. Rupert, however, was always considerate: 'Mr Kolles, there is no hurry. Don't interrupt your production lines; fit these suits in whenever it is convenient for you. It must not affect production. Take your time.'[11]

Perrin came to know Rupert well, and also his son Johann whom he met in New York in the 1970s. Although Rupert as South African had to act discreetly during the sanction years and kept to the background, Perrin remembers his particular charisma, describing it as *rayonnement* – his 'shining presence, the aura of someone who is noticed by everyone when he enters a room'. Rupert sometimes attended board meetings of Cartier and on occasion receptions and launches, but never went to shareholders' meetings. Both Kanoui and Perrin emphasise that he did not interfere in Cartier's affairs, although they kept him fully informed. They met him two or three times a year, and travelled to Stellenbosch to discuss the annual budget and new products.

'He is very astute in marketing, and he would ask a lot of questions. He also listens to people and doesn't forget what one has told him. He truly has a vision: a special way of looking at people, and at the economy, and of gauging long-term outcomes. I've learnt much from him. He's not a person one forgets easily,' according to Perrin.[12]

CHAPTER 19

A bank in the crosswinds

R upert's Lesotho experience and his firm belief in development based on private initiative instead of handouts gave rise to another international development project: the Development Bank for Equatorial and Southern Africa, or Edesa for short. The purpose of Edesa, which was established in 1972, was to provide development aid and capital for private enterprise particularly to countries in southern Africa. Rupert's partner for the venture was his staunch supporter Union Bank of Switzerland, where his friend Bruno Saager played an active role.

The times were not auspicious for such a venture, however, and Edesa had to contend with difficulties from two sides. Initially the South African private sector responded positively, but the government was not enthusiastic about the idea. It expressed its intention of launching its own development bank – a project that would only materialise eleven years later in 1983! The government's attitude did much to dampen the initial interest in business circles.

Overseas the project also elicited political resistance. At the United Nations a smear pamphlet was circulated, accusing Rupert of trying to circumvent his country's economic isolation. Lesotho's ambassador to the UN, Mooki Molapo, spread anti-Rupert propaganda in New York, possibly instigated by Wynand van Graan's old adversary Chuck Lipton. In addition the London monthly *XRay*, which had to apologise for defamatory misrepresentation of the LNDC, reported that Rupert was creating an international institution 'aimed primarily at extending South African capital investment across the whole African continent'.[1]

On one hand, Edesa is the story of a development visionary who not only found his way blocked by international prejudice against his country but also had to experience in his own country that businesspeople did not have the courage of their (private) convictions and chose instead to submit to the prevailing ideology. Yet it is also the story of a leader who demonstrated tenacious perseverance in the face of difficulties.

Rupert threw himself into the project with his usual energy and enthusiasm. In the early months of 1973 more than 120 letters were sent off to top business people, both in South Africa and abroad, requesting that the boards of their companies consider investing £500 000 in Edesa. Overseas contacts included Rockefeller (Chase Manhattan), Ford, De Rothschild, Axel Springer (*Springer Verlag*), Jannott (*Münchener Rück-versicherungs-Gesellschaft*), David Montagu (Samuel Montagu & Co.), Franz Ulrich (*Deutsche Bank*), Philips (the Netherlands) and Lord Stokes (British Leyland Motor Corporation). Within South Africa he approached business leaders like Harry Oppenheimer of Anglo American, Santam's CHJ (Carel) van Aswegen, Punch Barlow of Barlow Rand, Tony Bloom of Premier Milling, FJC (Frans) Cronjé of Nedbank, Marius Jooste of Perskor and Adriaan Louw of Goldfields. Part of Rupert's dream was that his compatriots would set the example.

His letter, dated 18 January 1973, spelled out his dream – and revealed his insight. Referring to the growing divide between the rich North and the impoverished South (more especially Africa), he said so far attempts to narrow it had taken the form of 'massive give-aways'. It had not worked. The solution he proposed was the development of African entrepreneurship, driven by the private sector.

Not long after Rupert started broaching his Edesa vision, the South African government came with a rival scheme: developing the black 'homelands' within the country by way of public and private-sector partnership. The reaction of South African businesspeople demonstrated the extent to which the NP government had succeeded in imposing its ideological will.

Four responses, two from the predominantly English business community and two from the predominantly Afrikaans-speaking business community, tell the story. In a letter dated 8 March 1973, Nedbank's Frans Cronjé congratulated Rupert on a splendid and important idea – then followed the rider: his board felt that South Africa, 'and more particularly the Bantu homelands', should be their priority. Nedbank therefore proposed backing the government's envisaged 'Bantu Development Bank' instead, according to Cronjé. The tenacity with which Rupert pursued his ideal of establishing a 'small-business culture' was evident from a subsequent letter he wrote to Cronjé on 26 March, when it was already clear that he could not elicit the support for which he had hoped. Despite Cronjé's disappointing response, Rupert informed him that '. . . we are therefore proceeding regardless.'

Marius Jooste, managing director of Perskor, the other big actor in the Afrikaans media industry alongside Nasionale Pers, was even less friendly than Cronjé. He wrote on 26 February 1973: '. . . I regret to inform you that we cannot participate in the project. My board is of the opinion that in view of anticipated future competition as well as the fact that the government is starting something similar through Bantu Administration, it is not possible for us to support you in this matter.'

There had been bad blood between the two men in the past when Rupert refused to take shares in Jooste's Dagbreekpers, on the grounds that Rembrandt did not invest in media companies, even though Rupert served for a short while on the board of Dagbreekpers in the 1950s. He did, however, buy the printing company Pro Ecclesia's building in Stellenbosch from Jooste, but Jooste was enraged by his refusal to buy shares.

When Dagbreek Trust gave a banquet in Johannesburg to celebrate its tenth anniversary, Rupert was among the invited guests. He was totally taken aback when the guest speaker, the politician Jan de Klerk (father of the later president FW de Klerk), lashed out at him publicly, implying that his refusal to buy the Dagbreek shares was tantamount to treason. Rupert was convinced that Jooste had written the 'vindictive speech' delivered by De Klerk, brother-in-law of the former prime minister Hans Strijdom. Feeling highly embarrassed, he was surprised to receive a note at his table that had been written to him just after the speech by Strijdom's widow Susan, the sister of Jan de Klerk. Her note read: 'Dear Anton, You should have been the leader.'[2] He related that he felt so flustered, he crumpled up the note – 'I wish I had kept it.'

He soon resigned as alternative director of Dagbreekpers and refused all media directorships thereafter. The Rembrandt Group served all groups in society, he maintained, and he should not show any preferences as far as media groups were concerned.

Like Jooste, Adriaan Louw of Goldfields (29 January 1973) did not respond positively. He bluntly gave Rupert a bit of personal advice: 'The major problem of Black Africa lies in the excessive birth rate of its peoples.' With thinly concealed *schadenfreude* he also pointed out that in 1971 Rupert had refused to buy a minority interest in Goldfields. Many years later Rembrandt did acquire an interest in the mining company.

Responding to Louw's disappointing letter on 2 February 1973, Rupert elaborated on his vision: 'I am giving Edesa my support not because it is of major importance to myself or my group. It is my honest opinion that it is imperative that we should tackle the problem of our Black peoples to safeguard our very existence in this part of the African continent. We are facing the most difficult period in the history of country and it is the responsibility of each and everyone to do something.'

In an interesting letter, Carel van Aswegen of Santam argued that banking law prohibited investment in a bank-controlling company in Luxemburg. He made the following suggestion: 'However, if any of the companies in your group should wish to form part of the proposed company situated in Luxemburg, we would gladly be of assistance by holding those shares in one of our nominee companies in our group so that it will not become known that you are participating in that Luxemburg enterprise.'

The response of eminent overseas businesspeople like Eddie de Rothschild and David Montagu was also disappointing, yet Rupert's resolve was unshaken. If anything, rebuffs and obstacles seemed to strengthen his determination when he believed in an idea. This quality of his would sometimes verge on stubbornness. He continued marketing his Edesa concept, writing letters, addressing boards of directors and organising dinners with influential people. While it provided some inspiration that people like Punch Barlow said: 'You have pointed the way', and that RF Hellings of Pretoria Portland Cement responded: 'The venture under reference is thought-provoking but the investment you seek is formidable'. Nevertheless this was not enough. What he wanted was participation.

He sent his personal assistant Arminius Archer, charged with special responsibility for Edesa, to talk to the mining magnate Harry Oppenheimer. Oppenheimer listened attentively to Archer, later head of the Business School at the University of Stellenbosch, and undertook to submit the matter to his board. Shortly afterwards the Anglo American company notified them by letter that the board had decided against a contribution.

Rupert instructed Archer to arrange another meeting with Oppenheimer, saying to his assistant: 'I'll show you how it's done.' An appointment was arranged, and Archer listened with fascination to the conversation between the two richest people in the country. Throughout the meeting Rupert engaged Oppenheimer in conversation about the race horses of Harry and his wife, Bridget – not a subject that normally interested him much, if at all. As he and Archer were about to leave, Rupert turned back and said: 'By the way, Harry, there's something else I meant to mention – a contribution to Edesa, the development bank I want to set up.' 'Yes,' said Oppenheimer, 'I submitted it to my board.' 'Come on, Harry,' Rupert retorted, 'you and I know how these things work. If you submit something to your board, *you* decide.' Whereupon Oppenheimer yielded: 'Oh, OK then . . .'

That OK was worth R1 million, at that time still equivalent to one million American dollars. Ironically, it also led to one of Rupert's quips, that no good deed goes unpunished! Oppenheimer had asked him to open the Carlton Hotel on 21 November 1972. The recently completed Carlton Centre in the heart of Johannesburg, considered a symbol of Oppenheimer's confidence in South Africa's future, was at that stage the highest building in Africa and the hotel the largest in the southern hemisphere. At the opening ceremony, Rupert remarked that the service in the new hotel was in the best tradition of the old Carlton.

Much better than in another hotel, he joked, where a guest presented the manager with a bunch of flowers: 'These flowers are for the telephonists.' When the manager thanked him for the compliment on their good service, the guest responded: 'Compliment? Not at all – I thought they were all dead!'

With Rembrandt and Union Bank of Switzerland, Anglo American helped to provide the initial capital for Edesa: $1 million each. The 22 shareholders included some of Europe's biggest banks and industrial companies, and even some of the world's biggest motor-vehicle manufacturers. Among them were Amsterdam-Rotterdam Bank NV, Bank of Montreal, Barclays Bank International, Daimler-Benz, *Deutsche Bank Aktiengesellschaft*, Dresdner Bank AG, Ford Motor Company, General Motors, IBM World Trade Corporation, Luxemburg's Credit Bank, Union Castle Mail Steamship Co. Ltd and Universal Leaf Tobacco Company.[3] By the time the board first met in October 1973 Edesa had over $10 million to channel into development.

Rupert and Saager delegated the task of investigating the structure and financing of such a development bank to a Union Bank employee, René Gerber. After doing his homework Gerber recommended establishing a holding company in Luxemburg, a tax haven with no restrictions on money transfers and the number of directors. When the conversation turned to an executive head, Rupert pointed at the 37-year-old Gerber: 'You're the man!' he said.

Gerber became Edesa's managing director, operating from a small administrative office in Zürich. In southern Africa his local counterpart, Wynand van Graan, had his headquarters in Mbabane, Swaziland. Against Van Graan's advice the office was moved to Harare when Zimbabwe became independent in 1980. (In view of the later problems affecting the economy of Zimbabwe under the disastrous leadership of the despotic Robert Mugabe, his presentiments turned out to be well founded.)

Edesa's board was chaired by Prof. Karl Schiller, former West German minister of finance and a prominent economist, who had been approached by Rupert for this task. In discussing the division of responsibility between him and Gerber, Schiller defined it thus: 'I am the star on the Mercedes's bonnet; you are the engine.'[4] On his first visit to Africa Gerber did the rounds of South Africa's black 'homelands' in the company of Archer. Although he spoke five European languages, he also obtained a Tegnidisc language course from Rupert that enabled him to become passably fluent in Afrikaans. Over the years Gerber paid hundreds of visits to the continent.

In the meantime Rupert faced increasing difficulties in South Africa on account of the government's obvious efforts to thwart his plans and solicit the support of local businesspeople for a state-controlled development bank. The South African ministers driving the development bank project were none other than Rembrandt's second chairman Dr Nic Diederichs, now minister of finance, and another well-known figure from Rupert's university days, MC Botha, a cabinet minister not renowned for his vision and enterprise. Rupert did have talks with Botha, but to little purpose. The vast majority of South African businesspeople, not prepared to be characterised as opponents of the government, decided to back Botha's proposal. A scramble to comply with what were considered valid requirements for survival and to oblige the government of the day settled the matter; a similar phenomenon to the footwork of certain businesspeople to 'transform' after the ANC came to power in 1994.

At one stage after he had been officially obstructed Rupert was so discouraged that he even contemplated abandoning the project. He sent his assistant Arminius Archer to Zürich to discuss the matter with Saager. But Union Bank stood firm: too much money had already been invested in the idea. They held the view that if the South African government was reacting so negatively, they should look further north. 'Tell my friend we're going ahead,' Saager told Archer. Archer phoned Rupert at once and could hear his excitement on the line. He made Archer repeat Saager's words three times. That made him decide to persevere, and Edesa got under way.[5]

Rupert never chaired Edesa's board, although as director he attended most board meetings. According to Gerber he participated in the discussions as a 'fatherly guide'. Gerber developed a great respect for Rupert's business insight and ready wit. Once, when Edesa was struggling during a worldwide debt crisis, Gerber recommended a takeover of an ailing Geneva firm. Rupert stopped him in his tracks: 'Mr Gerber, you want to send a chap in a wheelchair to assist another man in a wheelchair!' Another time Gerber asked him if he ever suffered from headaches, Rupert's reply was, 'No, I distribute them!'

The new development bank proceeded to offer expertise and venture capital to sub-Saharan countries, with the exception of South Africa. By the mid-1980s Edesa was involved in 43 projects in 24 countries. The work was being done despite malicious opposition and rumour mongering, not just from the South African regime but from its opponents as well. In 1974 the journal *Africa Confidential* claimed that Edesa was backing the anti-Frelimo movement in Mozambique because of the presence in Swaziland of the Portuguese adventurer Jorge Jardim. When Edesa protested that the allegations were false and defamatory, *Africa Confidential* retracted its statements in a subsequent edition. The allegations were groundless, the correction stated, and Edesa had no association with the movement opposing Frelimo or with Jardim.[6]

Edesa's lifespan can be divided into three phases of roughly a decade each. In the first phase Van Graan, operating from Swaziland, pursued his tried and tested policy of supporting small businesses with loans: potteries, carpet weavers, manufacture of artificial flies for anglers in Malawi. In the second phase it started funding larger undertakings. In its third decade the project started fizzling out as changing circumstances on the continent, including the South African scene, reduced the need for an institution such as Edesa.

Rupert had been advocating something on the lines of the present Southern African Development Community (SADC) since the 1980s, when the Southern African Development Coordination Conference was established with a view to strengthening the hands of its nine member countries – the so-called 'frontline states' – and reducing their economic dependence on apartheid South Africa. Rupert took the idea further. In his chairman's address at Rembrandt's AGM in 1988 he said that southern Africa should follow the example of the European Economic Community and forge a closer union – an economic confederation, possibly on the lines of the Swiss canton system. The customs union between South Africa, Lesotho, Swaziland and Botswana benefited all parties and would have even greater impact if it were joined by Zambia, Zimbabwe and Malawi as well. 'Let us move forward fearlessly towards a future in which discrimination will make way for coexistence, mutual respect, trust and free participation in wealth creation by everybody,' he said in his speech.[7]

Four years later SADC was in fact established at a meeting of heads of state in Windhoek, Namibia, when the transition was made from a conference to an economic community. By 1994, when South Africa joined, it was one of fourteen member states pursuing regional cooperation to promote economic growth and development, alleviate poverty and improve the quality of life of the inhabitants of the region.

After operating throughout sub-Saharan Africa for two decades Edesa was at last able to open an office in Johannesburg in 1991. Wynand van Graan had long left Edesa to head the Development Corporation of the then 'independent' homeland of Bophuthatswana before returning to the Rembrandt Group in 1985. Gerber left Edesa in 1997 after Jürgen Schrempp, chief of Daimler-Benz, had taken over the chairmanship. After 1997 the new managing director, Rudolph Hug, gradually dissolved Edesa. Rupert remained a director until 1995, when he decided to stand down and make way for younger people. By then Edesa had outlived its usefulness and there was some duplication: first SADC, then the

'African Renaissance' advocated by Thabo Mbeki, which was to culminate in Nepad, the new partnership for Africa's development.

Looking back on that period in his life, Rupert said: 'Edesa did not succeed.' And after a few seconds of silence, while staring at the ashtray in front of him: 'I had never been involved, either as managing director or as chairman, in any private enterprise that failed.' A major error, in his view, was that Edesa's biggest investments had been loans to governments or parastatals, which were never honoured. 'That is why many African governments have such large debts which they now want to have written off,' he said with scarcely concealed contempt for governments that want to undertake development work themselves. That task, he consistently maintained, was best performed by private enterprise.

He also expressed the view that Edesa's top management, situated in Europe, did 'banking work' before they had projects on the ground. The idea of Edesa was 'sunk' by government interference in South Africa. Because of government opposition the bank could not be controlled locally from South Africa – 'and then we had to hand it over to foreigners'. In an angry tone he said: 'I don't accept responsibility for something if I'm not the chairman or can't call the management to account. I resigned from the board of Wolnit when they published the company's results before they had been submitted to the board. If I have to break away, I break away. Pik Botha [former minister of foreign affairs] also once told me that he wanted to break away. But he didn't.'

The fact that his Edesa dream could not be realised in the way he had hoped still rankled after many years. With reference to his Edesa experience, he commented with a trace of reproach in his voice: 'One of the reasons why Africa has not progressed is that governments don't keep their word.'

CHAPTER 20

The beer war

I n 1973, more than twenty years after Rupert first contemplated entering the South African beer market, he finally tackled this daunting challenge head-on. At that stage his international beer interests were doing relatively well. In South Africa, however, the market was still dominated by the highly successful SA Breweries (SAB). Louis Luyt, the country's fertiliser king, had started a brewery that was not making headway.

Luyt eventually entered into a partnership with Rupert, an alliance that represented one of the strangest sagas in South African business history. When the joint venture also did not perform satisfactorily, it resulted among other things in a conflict of style and approach. On the one side Anton Rupert, the undisputed gentleman of South African business; on the other, Louis Luyt, a businessman-politician who described himself as a beer-drinking street fighter.

Luyt, whose fertiliser company Triomf was ultimately taken over by Nedbank after disastrous financial problems, also became a central figure in the Information Scandal that rocked South Africa at the end of 1970s, when state funds were funnelled into various dubious projects, among others *The Citizen* newspaper. He was the archetypal self-made man: stepson of an impoverished Britstown family, he carried a chip on his shoulder because he felt some rich people had looked down their noses at them. 'They saw us as outcasts,' he said in an interview. 'This kind of thing had a big impact on me. I wouldn't call it hate. It was more a question of wanting to show these bastards I could make it.' In the business world Luyt was an adherent of the school of the personality cult. 'My philosophy is that a company without a man, a personality, is lost,' he declared.[1] This approach, which could easily degenerate into swagger, would obviously be hard to reconcile with the philosophy of partnership and coexistence.

Yet before Rupert's eventual takeover of Luyt's beer interests in July 1973 there was already cooperation between the two groups after Luyt, who was experiencing problems, had approached Rupert in 1972. It was agreed that Rembrandt, via Oude Meester, would obtain shares in Luyt's brewery – it already held shares in his fertiliser company. In return Luyt became a share-holding director of Oude Meester. The deal was finalised in June.

Initially the partnership worked well. Luyt asked his staff to support and pro-

Left: The Rupert family of Graaff-Reinet: in front are Rupert's parents, John and Hester, with their three sons, Jan, Koos and Anton.

Below: With the 1938 Ossewatrek, a deputation from the University of Pretoria fetched the ox-wagen *Louis Trichardt* from Bulhoek. Anton Rupert, in Voortrekker dress, is furthest left on the steps next to the leader of the Trek, Henning Klopper, who later became Speaker. [Photograph: *Trek*]

Left: Huberte Rupert actively participated in the festivities of the late 1930s. Here she is in a long white dress on a float in 1938, denoting women's contribution.

In 1938 both Rupert and Huberte served on the steering committee of the Afrikaanse Nasionale Studentebond. In the picture, both are in Voortrekker dress: he is at the centre as chairman, with Huberte front left. [Photograph: *Trek*]

The couple with their three children. Anton stands at the back with Hanneli while Huberte is flanked by Johann (left) and Anthonij.

Left: Family picture in Stellenbosch: Hanneli, the Ruperts' only daughter, is between her parents with her brothers, Anthonij and Johann, at the back.

Below: Dr Tienie Louw of Sanlam taking the first 'Afrikaans' cigarette from Rembrandt's machine in their Paarl factory, 4 June 1948. Rupert and Dr Nic Diederichs, second group chairman, are with him.

Above: Mrs Annie Stals, widow of Rembrandt's first chairman, Dr AJ Stals, laying the cornerstone of Rembrandt's Paarl factory, 22 September 1951. The next chairman, Dr Nic Diederichs (left), is at her side, with Anton and Huberte Rupert behind her.

Left: The Ruperts in 1954, arriving in London on the BOAC *Comet* which fell during its next flight.

Left: Anton and Jan Rupert (right) in London discussing brands with their partners Sydney Rothman and Stanley Gray.

Right: Huberte and her daughter leaving for Europe to have Hanneli's eyes operated upon.

Below: A group conference held in Grosvenor House in London, from 6 to 9 January 1959. To the left of Rupert (centre front) is his financial expert, Daan Hoogenhout, with Jan Rupert behind Hoogenhout.

The De Rothschilds of London visiting the Cape. The picture was taken at a dinner held in 1960 in Newlands in honour of the visiting couple. Edmund de Rothschild, at that stage a director of Carreras, and his wife are in the middle.

Field Marshall Lord Montgomery smoking his first cigarette in 1962 in Stellenbosch. Sir Francis de Guingand, Montgomery's war-time head of staff, served as director of the Rembrandt Group for many years.

Three brothers and their wives, photographed in the Ruperts' garden in Stellenbosch: from left to right Huberte and Anton, Ina and Jan, and Rona and Koos.

Left: Ethel Kennedy, wife of US Senator Robert F Kennedy, arriving at the Ruperts' Stellenbosch home in 1966. Between her and Huberte Rupert (left) is Mrs Maria Malan, widow of Dr DF Malan, South African premier from 1948-54.

Below: The Rembrandt board on 30 November 1966. Dirk Hertzog, founder partner, is to the right of Rupert (at the back).

Then State President, Jim Fouché (left), opening an exhibition of Lurçat's tapestries in Stellenbosch. His wife is next to him with Huberte to her left. Rupert stands

between the rector of the University of Stellenbosch, Prof. HB Thom, and Mrs Thom.

Left: Rupert with *Mabalel*, one of Coert Steynberg's best sculptures.

Below: State President CR Swart (with sash) opened the Hester Rupert Art Museum in Graaff-Reinet. Here Swart, Rupert and the mayor of Graaff-Reinett view a bust of Louw Wepener, the Free State soldier born in Graaff-Reinet.

Left: Congratulations! Rupert toasts Sydney Rothman on Rothman's 80th birthday. Rupert especially went to see him on this occasion.

Middle: In October 1985, the National Monuments Council conferred a gold medal on Rupert for the renovation and restoration of Tulbagh, following an earthquake that destroyed much of the town. With him is Mr Justice MH de Kock, Western Cape chairman and son of Rupert's friend Jan de Kock, of whose death Rupert learnt shortly after burying his mother. [Photograph *Die Burger*]

Below: Rupert visiting Pres. Kenneth Kaunda of Zambia on 15 July 1985 in Lusaka. With him are his personal assistant, Frans Stroebel, and René Gerber of Edesa (left).

The couple on Rupert's 70th birthday in 1986. [Photograph: Johan Stander]

Above: Rupert and David Rockefeller of New York at one of the Cape Dutch homes so admired by Rockefeller.

Left: Money matters: Rupert in 1988 as director of the Reserve Bank, next to the Bank's President, Dr Gerhard de Kock (centre front). Rupert's friend Wim de Villiers is to De Kock's right.

Above: In the wild: Rupert and Prince Bernhard (to his left) with a rhino. [Photograph: Ebbe Dommisse]

Bottom left: Rupert, thrilled to be holding a lion cub, in the Kruger National Park.

Bottom right: Prince Philip in October 1995 in Stellenbosch with Rupert at a WWF meeting.

Top: The family at the opening of the distribution centre for Historic Wines of South Africa in 2000 in Montague Gardens, Cape Town. From the left: Hein Koegelenberg and his wife, Hanneli, Gaynor (Johann's wife), Anthonij and his parents and Johann Rupert.

Bottom: Young and old together: Hanneli and her son, Paul, with her father on his 80th birthday, with Johann and Gaynor Rupert and their three children, Caroline, Hanneli and Anton Jr, and far right Huberte and her grandchild Berdine.

Top: Honoured: President Nelson Mandela conferring the President's Decoration of the Order of Outstanding Service on Rupert in 1999 in Pretoria.

Bottom: In the Karoo: Rupert on his son Anthonij's farm Welgevonden outside Graaff-Reinet, with the town visible in the distance.

Frontier: On Rupert's birthday, 4 October 2001, a ranger assists him to the rocky outcrop from where guests viewed the transfer of the first elephants from the Kruger National Park to the Mozambican side of the Greater Limpopo Transfrontier Park. Former President Nelson Mandela is behind him, accompanied by his assistant, Zelda la Grange. [Photograph: Ebbe Dommisse]

Left: Anton and Huberte in conversation with Mrs Zanele Mbeki, wife of the South African President, on 18 October 2002 at the official opening of the South African College of Tourism, which trains guesthouse managers in Graaff-Reinet. [Photograph: UPS]

Below: Summit: Rupert and Pres. Thabo Mbeki on 12 February 2004 at Tuynhuys in Cape Town. [Photograph: Esa Alexander, *Die Burger*]

Opposite left: The big names in nature conservation in the Soestdijk Palace in The Netherlands: Former President Nelson Mandela, Prince Bernhard and Rupert attending a meeting of the Peace Parks Foundation.

With the sculpture of a mother cherishing her twins: Rupert and Nelson Mandela in the foyer of the Peace Parks Foundation with Käthe Kollwitz's *Mutter mit Zwillingen.*

Rupert with Rodin's sculpture *The Cathedral.*

mote the products of the Rembrandt Group. In a memorandum circulated within Rembrandt on 5 February 1973, Rupert and his management noted this with thanks and declared: 'If the cooperation could be mutual, it would be sincerely appreciated.' The memorandum stated further that Rembrandt staff could buy preference shares in the Luyt Group, and stressed 'the importance of cooperation between our Group and Luyt Brewery'. Luyt, who initially showed admiration for Rupert's marketing expertise, also considered Rembrandt's interest in Western Province Cellars with their 180 liquor stores a real asset to the brewery.

In March 1973 Luyt approached the Rembrandt Group with a proposition. He wanted to expand his fertiliser interests to Brazil and thought it would be easier to borrow money against his Triomf shares. He therefore requested Rembrandt to buy out his Oude Meester preference shares for cash; he was also prepared to exchange his Oude Meester stock for Triomf shares.

This was about four months before the cooperation and partnership between Rupert and Luyt came to grief.

The relationship between the two soured for various reasons. One was Luyt's conduct after an explosion at his fertiliser factory at Potchefstroom in which a number of Triomf employees had been killed. Luyt travelled to Brazil during this time and did not remain in South Africa to attend to the problems. Rupert took severe umbrage at such callousness. His brother Koos also warned him that Luyt acted unpredictably. In Rupert's presence he would put his best foot forward, but behind his back he shouted at staff. People close to the conflict situation explained the personality clash between Rupert and Luyt as 'bad chemistry'. In his autobiography Luyt described their relationship as 'not a marriage of convenience, but a disastrous mixture of oil and water in the belief that the large volume might be beneficial to both. It was an alliance between two entirely incompatible, headstrong personalities set to unravel from the very moment it was formed'.[2]

On one occasion in Rupert's office, Luyt opened a packet of light cigars he had brought along. Rupert protested that 'a partner doesn't do this', as the cigars were from a rival manufacturer. He immediately called for a packet of Rembrandt's Anthonij van Dijck cigars, which he handed to Luyt.[3]

Juicy stories about the friction between the two businessmen made the rounds, one of which featured in the book the investigative journalists Mervyn Rees and Chris Day wrote about the Information Scandal. Day was flying with Luyt in his private jet to attend a meeting with Rupert at a time when, according to Day, it was known that Rupert had advised Luyt to keep a lower profile and act in a less flamboyant manner. On the flight back to Johannesburg Rupert's legal representative accompanied them to finalise a contract. The man wanted to go to the toilet, but Luyt would not allow it because, he said, they first had to reach the right altitude. When the legal representative, pale and drawn with discomfort, was finally permitted to go and relieve himself, Luyt said in an aside to Day. 'You've got to show these Cape hot-shots that the action really is in Johannesburg.'[4] Such bombast made a clash with the courteous, sophisticated Rupert inevitable.

Relations worsened with Rupert's decision to buy out Luyt's shares, and at the end of July 1973 the simmering conflict erupted.

Telexes flew to and fro between Rupert and Luyt and public statements were issued, mainly by Luyt. The eruption came within a week after Rupert had bought Luyt's shares, and was triggered by a statement issued by Oude Meester on Monday 30 July 1973. The statement disclosed that Luyt had been paid R1 710 000 cash for his shares; that Louis Luyt Breweries (LLB) had shown a loss of R600 000 for the first four months of the financial year; and that LLB would have to push up its five percent share of the market if it wanted to show a profit. Luyt, who was in London at the time, concluded that the statement had been issued intentionally during his absence, and flew into a rage. He issued a counter statement, repudiating Oude Meester and declaring that its statement 'contains assertions which, if not correctly interpreted, will remove all public confidence in Louis Luyt Breweries' – not that there was much public confidence in the brewery at that stage anyway.

Rupert had already earlier sent Luyt a telex. He said he assumed Luyt had read the various reports in the press about Oude Meester's acquisition of an interest in LLB. He pointed out that some of these reports misrepresented the facts and could be misleading with regard to share values. 'It is clearly our duty to inform the investing public and shareholders and for this reason details of the transaction are being made public,' he continued. Apparently unperturbed, Rupert concluded his telex with 'Kind regards'. Despite Rupert's telex, until Oude Meester's press release there had been no detailed statement spelling out the whole deal and its implications. A head-on confrontation between Rupert and the aggressive Luyt was, however, unavoidable.

Luyt's quarrel with Rupert was not an isolated case, but could be seen as part of a recurring pattern in his stormy career. Luyt's subsequent antagonists in sensational public confrontations included former president Nelson Mandela; his son-in-law Rian Oberholzer, managing director of Rugby South Africa; the Springbok hero Jan Engelbrecht; Francois Pienaar, captain of the Springbok rugby team that won the World Cup; and a rugby public relations officer whom he had dismissed summarily.

Accordingly, in the beer war with Luyt, Rupert's views on trust between partners were sorely tried. The telex an incensed Luyt sent to Rupert on 30 July 1973 was practically a declaration of war. His position at Rembrandt had become untenable, he said. He wanted his Triomf shares back in exchange for the Oude Meester shares, with adjustments for the respective dividends paid; and he wanted to buy the aircraft back at the price Rupert had paid for it minus depreciation. The plane, a Falcon that Luyt had bought from the French aviation company Marcel Dassault, with a licence to carry passengers, had been part of the original transaction. Both Rupert and Luyt had a share in it. It also became a matter of bitter dispute.

Without using the formal form of address that indicates respect in Afrikaans, consistently used by Rupert himself, Luyt sent another telex to Rupert the next day, informing the latter that he was issuing his own press statement as a follow-up to Oude Meester's. His long telex testified to his anger: 'I understand that you have released detailed information to the press, not only about our transaction, but even about the company's affairs. I regard this as an absolute stab in the back . . . especially because you were well aware that I was not in South Africa. I also regard it as very unfavourable for the company's affairs that you have disclosed these figures and it would appear as if it was only done to embarrass me. This mud-slinging can only be to the detriment of the company's future . . .' He reiterated his demands regarding the Triomf shares and the plane. He also announced his resignation with immediate effect as director of Oude Meester as well as director and chairman of LLB. 'I have decided to do this as cooperation with you is absolutely unacceptable to me,' Luyt said.

Rupert, never one to lose his head in a crisis, sent a calm, reasoned telex in reply on the same day, 31 July. He gave a carefully substantiated account of the speculation in LLB shares on the stock exchange, and added: 'Your conclusions are unfair because we have been trying to protect you all along.' He was prepared to consider the exchange of Triomf and Oude Meester shares once the brewery showed a reasonable return on investment. The Falcon jet was a separate issue. Rupert's view was that Luyt could have it back but they would keep the licence. If Luyt wanted that as well, he would have to pay for it. In the telex of 31 July Rupert said: 'We are prepared to return the plane to you at a more reasonable offer. You have told me yourself that the plane is worth more at present.'

In Rupert's first public statement about the row he said that he harboured no grudge against Luyt and was sorry that Luyt had reacted in such a way to Oude Meester's statement. For the first time he revealed instances where there had been differences of opinion in the course of the partnership. He had felt Luyt should not have left for Brazil after the explosion at his fertiliser company;

also that Luyt, as chairman of Luyt Breweries, should have chaired the AGM of the company on Monday morning instead of having departed for London on Sunday evening. According to Rupert, Oude Meester had not interfered in the management of LLB: 'We only gave them advice.' The press statement about the state of the brewery's business had been issued in the public interest, since speculation in LLB shares was rife and they were offered at vastly inflated prices. 'I have never heard of the public losing confidence [in a business] when it learned the truth,' he added.

On 6 August 1973, one of the days on which there was a major row with Luyt, Huberte hosted an evening reception for the acclaimed British novelist Graham Greene at L'Ormarins, the Ruperts' farm near Franschhoek. The publisher Koos Human was one of the guests. He noticed that Rupert, who was at that stage a shareholder in Human & Rousseau publishers, arrived late, his face like a thundercloud. 'But he was the perfect host,' Human recalls. Rupert soon struck up a cordial conversation with Greene. The British writer, a great admirer of the work of Afrikaans novelist Etienne Leroux, was on a three-month trip through South Africa and had spent a few weeks with the Lerouxs on their farm Janee near Koffiefontein in the Free State.[5]

As far as the partnership between Rupert and Luyt was concerned, it was all over. A final meeting was held in Rupert's office in Stellenbosch to finalise the outstanding issues, including the sale of Rembrandt's interest in Triomf Fertiliser and the buyback of Triomf's shares in Oude Meester. Luyt maintained that he had flown to Stellenbosch because their partnership had become a house divided within itself. According to him he told Rupert frankly: 'We are partners, you are not my boss and I want out of this partnership – either I buy you or you buy me out.' Rupert was not at all surprised, according to Luyt; all that mattered to him were the terms on which they would part. Rupert rejected Luyt's offer to buy his shares in LLB, as he was already in the liquor industry, and instead bought out Luyt's interest.

According to Gys Steyn, who attended the meeting on behalf of Oude Meester, the written agreement between the two parties comprised a single page. There were no further legal points to be settled. 'There was no celebration – just a cold handshake and a sense of relief on both sides that this unhappy partnership had come to an end,' Luyt related in his autobiography.[6]

Luyt's big money-spinner Triomf Fertiliser was liquidated in 1986 after he had accumulated debt to the amount of $59 million at Nedbank.[7]

Throughout the saga of the partnership Rupert's strong feelings about shared values in business life had been severely tried by Luyt, whose *modus operandi* went against the grain with him. 'He disappointed me,' Rupert responded briefly afterwards.

Hans Knoetze, public relations officer of the group, observed that Rupert put a very high premium on integrity and honesty. 'If you can buy a person, that person is not worth buying,' he said on occasion to Knoetze, who noted that Rupert adhered to these principles in practice and did not do business with people who did not share his values – as a result of which he probably forfeited potentially profitable deals.[8]

The group's trademark expert, Dr Frederick Mostert, related a typical anecdote about a somewhat similar situation: 'I remember very well how I once suggested to Dr Rupert that we should correct someone's unacceptable business behaviour in such and such a way in order to prevent the same problem in future. He looked me straight in the eye with his characteristic smile and said: 'My friend, you can teach a man many things, but you can't teach him morality.'

Mostert added: 'Something I'll always remember is Dr Rupert's honourable conduct in business. A mere verbal agreement, and even just a handshake, would be honoured in all respects. Such integrity is a rare phenomenon in today's business world where the old Roman law principle of *pacta sunt servanda* (agreements are to be observed) is only honoured after lengthy written agreements have been drafted – and even then sometimes evaded. Dr Rupert's courteousness and respect for his business partners show that he's every inch a gentleman . . . in my view, a "gentleman's gentleman".' His charm and warmth were reflected in the most trivial actions: always insisting that his colleagues or friends go first through a door, being scrupulously punctual for appointments with colleagues despite his busy schedule, and apologising profusely on the rare occasions where he might be a few minutes late.[9]

Luyt did not speak about Rupert in such flattering terms. Early in the 1990s he and Dirk Hertzog's son Edwin, chairman of Medi-Clinic in the Rembrandt Group, ended up next to each other on a plane. When his fellow passenger introduced himself, Luyt remarked laconically to the amused Hertzog: 'So you are also a partner of Rupert's. I used to be one too. His partnership philosophy works this way: *you* are the partner, *he* is the boss!'[10]

In his autobiography, which appeared in 2003, Luyt described his 'ill-advised partnership' with Rupert as one of the worst errors of his career, almost on a par with his association with the Vorster government's *Citizen* project during the Information Scandal. He made a number of other allegations about Rupert, including the false and defamatory statement that Voorbrand had gone bankrupt. Luyt also claimed that the businessmen Jan Pickard and Albert Wessels, both already dead at the time, had warned him against Rupert at the dinner where he was named as Marketing Man of the Year in 1972.

Asked if he had any comment on Luyt's attack, Rupert vouchsafed a single sentence: 'I won't dignify Mr Luyt's statements with a response.'

With Luyt gone from the brewery and the positions he had held, Rupert could now pay attention to his main competitor, SAB. The first priority was to 'clean up' LLB. Luyt had surrounded himself with former rugby players, for whom the Rembrandt Group had no use.

The new brewery was named Intercontinental Breweries (ICB) and kicked off with some internationally known brand names, famous for their observance of the traditional Bavarian brewers' *Reinheitsgebot* (law of purity). Rupert already had an interest in the Bräuerei Drei Kronen, established in 1308 near the medieval German city of Bamberg and in the possession of the Gerner family for centuries. ICB was licensed to brew Drei Kronen in South Africa, as well as the famous Beck's beer from Bremen – at that stage the only brewery outside Germany permitted to do so.

With Rupert's usual perfectionism about detail his promotion drive for Krönenbrau 1308 included authentic German beer wagons loaded with barrels, drawn by six large Shire-horses in imported German harnesses. The accent was squarely on the German origins of his beers – brands like Krönenbrau 1308, followed by Krönenbrau Gold and Colt 45, which were making significant inroads into the beer market. SAB, by contrast, put the emphasis on English names with Lion Lager and Castle Lager the most popular brands. Soon a full-scale price war erupted between the two groups as they competed for market share.

The price war became a hard-fought contest that was not confined to the beer market. In the early 1970s intense competition arose in the wine market as well, especially after Oude Meester launched a sensational new sparkling wine, Paarl Perlé, in January 1970. It made a massive, unprecedented breakthrough among the traditionally beer-drinking black population, who attributed all sorts of health and other benefits to the wine they called 'Pala Pala'. According to a memorandum from Gys Steyn, managing director of Oude Meester, within two years the new wine outstripped all the top sellers, not only on the local market but throughout the world.[11]

SFW, with Monis featuring strongly, fought back by all means and launched several Paarl Perlé-type products, according to Oude Meester with labels that increasingly resembled that of the original Paarl Perlé. Oude Meester applied for court orders and eventually took the matter to the Appeal Court, while the country's top advocates made lengthy submissions and some of the best-known judges, including Chief Justice Rumpff, had to pass judgment on the legality of labels like 'Improved Paarl Perlé', 'Selected Paarl Perlé', 'Grand White Paarl Perlé' and 'The Champagne of Paarl Perlés'.

Ultimately neither side won, least of all the contested Paarl Perlé itself. The sparkling wine's runaway success was eventually undermined by rumours spread among black consumers that 'Pala Pala' caused gastric diseases and male impotence. The rumours became so pervasive that at one stage Rupert requested two directors of SAB to come and see him at his office. He played them a tape about stories being spread against Oude Meester. But even this did not have the desired effect.[12] As a result of the rumour-mongering Paarl Perlé's record sales dropped rapidly, although it continues to be available in the South African market in the 21st century and is still fairly popular.

The rivalry between Oude Meester and SFW was so intense in the 1970s that *Eikestadnuus*, the local Stellenbosch paper which was at that stage controlled by the Rembrandt Group, made almost no mention of SFW. The paper carried no reports about SFW's popular open-air theatre, Oude Libertas, where the world-famous pianist Vladimir Ashkenazy enchanted the audience with Beethoven's Moonlight Sonata at the launching concert in 1977.

The price war, too, was taking its toll. Beer prices were slashed, creating a greater demand that ate into the sales of wine and spirits. As wine surpluses built up the wine industry, especially the farmers, started pressing for a government commission of inquiry. Concern about the situation eventually also manifested in government circles. Willem Dempsey, the intermediary who had managed to get SAB's entry into the wine industry legalised in 1963, asked Rupert to reach an agreement with SAB in the interest of the wine industry. In view of his past experience with Dempsey, Rupert's response was sceptical.

This was followed by an initiative from Senbank, a merchant bank associated with Sanlam. The aim was to achieve consolidation in the beer market as well as the wine market, dominated by two wholesale groups, Oude Meester and SFW. The key person was a director of Senbank, Dr Fred du Plessis, the Transvaal professor of business economics who would be in the centre of the battle that erupted between Sanlam and Rembrandt a few years later. Du Plessis initially approached both Rupert and Dick Goss, chairman of SAB, with his proposal for a possible consolidation, which amounted to SAB and Rembrandt trading their respective beer and wine interests. Rupert was not averse to the idea, but he thought government would not be amenable. As a sensible way out he suggested involving the wine farmers via KWV.

In mid-August 1979 he pointed out to Dr André du Toit, chairman of KWV, that SAB's ownership of SFW was anomalous. He reaffirmed his loyalty to the wine farmers, who had backed him so staunchly in Rembrandt's early years and had been disadvantaged by the beer war. As a possible solution he suggested that KWV form part of the new arrangement so as to gain government approval. Confidential negotiations between KWV and Rembrandt went on for about ten weeks. The participants from KWV were the managing director Ritzema de la Bat and Pietman Hugo, director and Member of Parliament. Rembrandt was represented by Rupert, Daan Hoogenhout and Willem Wilken, auditor from Theron & Van der Poel.

The negotiations with SAB were more difficult. Dirk Hertzog was involved in several of the initial skirmishes. On the final day, a Saturday, Fred du Plessis spent almost the whole day in telephonic contact with the two parties. The deal-maker Murray Louw was with Goss in Johannesburg and De la Bat and Hugo were with Rupert in his office in Stellenbosch. Late that afternoon they finally reached agreement. On the following Monday evening, 5 November 1979, the respective parties signed the Heads of Agreement in Sanlam's boardroom in Bellville. The only drink with which the wine and beer leaders could celebrate was a bottle of whisky found in the drinks cabinet in the boardroom.

A week later cabinet approved the arrangement, which heralded a new era for the two industries. SAB bought out ICB, thus securing 99% of the beer market. Both Rembrandt and SAB sold their wine and spirit interests to a new company, Kaapwyn (CWD), in which Rembrandt, KWV (via a new company, KWV Investments) and SAB each held 30% of the shares and the public the remaining ten percent. Rembrandt secured managerial control of CWD.[13]

As could be expected, not everyone was happy about the settlement. Dirk Hertzog felt that an alternative option, with Rembrandt obtaining a 30% interest in SAB, would have been preferable. His son Edwin said he knew there had been differences of opinion. 'My father once told me specifically that this was the one decision with which he definitely disagreed, but he accepted it and discussed it with Dr Rupert. Then he said that a ship could only have one captain and if this was what Dr Rupert wanted, he had to resign himself to it.' Dirk Hertzog also mentioned to his son that he was fully entitled to differ from Rupert, but that he would never do so in a way that could embarrass Rupert.[14]

Jan Pickard, chairman of Picbel and Union Wines with their extensive wine interests, complained that he had asked to put his case but was not afforded the opportunity to do so. He had been told to trust the 'heavyweights'. 'I had been hanged without a trial,' he said, and added that the two newly created monopolies were not in the national interest.[15]

The managing director of ICB, Gerhard Steinmetz, had not been aware of the confidential negotiations. He was only informed at the last minute, when the contract was about to be signed, and was furious. People close to Rupert felt that in the case of such a delicate transaction that could possibly fail he was not keen to inform the sales staff – it could discourage them while their attention should remain focused on sales. Steinmetz, who had been sent by Rupert to ICB earlier to sort out the problems, said that in his view ICB, with fourteen percent of the beer market, was about to take off and Rupert should have held out. 'Dr Rupert told me later that selling ICB had been his greatest mistake.'[16]

Rupert's son Johann confirmed that his father considered it the most stupid business decision he had ever taken, but he was obliged to do it for the sake of the wine farmers. Dick Goss of SAB also told Johann Rupert afterwards that with the restructuring they had been surprised by the strong position of ICB. In his opinion ICB would have made a breakthrough in the beer market within a year.[17]

Johan Piek, public relations officer of the group, summed up Rupert's dilemma in a memorandum: 'Should the beer war have been continued until SAB was forced to its knees, with the wine farmers possibly going under in the process, or should the wine farmers have been assisted in their hour of anxiety, about which they had been warned in the past? For a man like Dr Anton Rupert, who has always known and lived by loyalty, it was not personally a hard decision. He would choose the side of the wine farmers who had demonstrated their trust in him in the early years of the group – the pioneers of Rembrandt. Once again loyalty tipped the scales!'[18]

The settlement did not mean that the problems were over. From early 1980 the question whether CWD constituted a new form of monopoly formed part of an investigation by the Competition Board into restrictive practices in the supply and distribution of alcoholic beverages in the country. A majority report concluded that CWD indeed constituted a monopoly and had to close down. A minority report submitted by AJ Marais, however, accused the board of double standards: if a wine monopoly was undesirable, the same applied to beer. He argued that a counterweight to SAB would do the market good, whereas the closure of CWD would greatly harm the Western Cape economy. The government then came under pressure from both the wine industry and the Afrikaanse Handelsinstituut to intervene. The wine farmers were traditionally a powerful lobby in parliament, and the government was sensitive to their demands. At the same time rival liquor groups that wanted to see CWD dissolved – notably Union Wines of Jan Pickard, son-in-law of Dr Eben Dönges and one of the National Party's most generous donors – were exerting strong pressure on the government. They were concerned that KWV, the sole supplier of brandy, would not be able to remain neutral, and of course they were also worried about the stronger competition.

It was a total impasse. The buck was passed to Dr Dawie de Villiers, Minister of Trade, Industry and Tourism. Over a period of about a year De la Bat made eighteen appointments with him to discuss the situation. De Villiers, a popular former Springbok rugby captain, eventually convened a meeting of the NP's industry study group at short notice, apparently to approve the Competition Board's recommendation for submission to the cabinet. Pietman Hugo, director of the KWV who was a member of the study group in his capacity as Member of Parliament, got wind of this shortly before the meeting and immediately informed Koot van Staden, an NP whip and right-hand man of the prime minister, PW Botha.

When Botha found out what was happening, he instructed that the cabinet's full economic committee be convened. Rupert was invited to the summit meeting together with De la Bat, Hugo and André du Toit. Botha himself chaired the meeting. According to De la Bat, Rupert remained silent throughout the meeting. 'He realised that it was a dispute between the farmers and the politicians, and that the farmers' lobby had to do their work. This is something else one can say about Rupert – he knows when to keep quiet,' related De la Bat. The upshot was that Botha turned down the Competition Board's recommendation. As an afterthought he proposed reducing the 316 outlets previously allocated by the cabinet to CWD to 100. But when De la Bat protested that there was no way he could justify such a decision to the stakeholders, Botha conceded the point and left it at 300 outlets. As the delegation left the room, Rupert just smiled.[19]

On 25 March 1983 Dawie de Villiers issued a press statement that announced that the minority recommendation of the Competition Board had been accepted: the stringent separation between beer interests and the wine and spirit industry would be enforced.

Rupert said in his chairman's report of that year: 'You will recall that I have often in the past pleaded from this platform that liquor sales should remain in the hands of the small man and that control of beer and the products of the vine should be separated. Mindful of the support your group had received from the Boland wine farmers in its formative years, it was surely the right decision whereby not only the interests and the future of the wine industry could be secured, but also the objectives could be achieved of separating, on the one hand, the wine and beer interests and on the other, the retail and wholesale interests. Via CWD the wine farmer is now for the first time a partner in the marketing of his own product.'[20]

Under the new arrangement in the wine industry, Rupert also chaired an annual marketing conference of SFW, as he had done for Distillers over the years. As a rule it was attended by some 30 executives of the companies involved. De la Bat of the KWV sometimes attended as director of the two companies, together with Gys Steyn, managing director of CWD, and other top executives of Distillers and SFW like Michiel le Roux and Ronnie Melck. They had to submit comprehensive reports on all their products, complete with marketing strategies, advertising budget and the positioning of each product for the next financial year. Everyone who was responsible for a product had to do a presentation to the conference. Rupert constantly asked questions and commented on 'a thousand and one points of detail,' according to De la Bat. 'It was an impressive one-man show which unmistakeably revealed his marketing insight and experience. From half past eight till four in the afternoon and sometimes later he had them all sweating.' It struck him that Rupert had 'a bee in his bonnet' about labels. 'Sudden changes to the labels of established, successful brands made his hair stand on end. He had a very long-term vision of brands.'[21]

In 1988 CWD was restructured into two separate companies, Distillers Corporation and SFW, which were both listed on the Johannesburg Stock Exchange (JSE). In 2001 the two merged to form Distell, which was also listed on the JSE.

Looking back, one might say that Anton Rupert lost the beer war. But the real victory was his: SAB was out of the wine industry. In addition, it had enabled him to expand more easily in another market, luxury goods, where he would eventually be typified as the King of Luxury.

CHAPTER 21

Small business is big business

T he pioneering work done by Rupert in the field of social responsibility, such as the increased minimum wage and his industrial initiatives in Lesotho, was for a long time in the second half of the 20th century not followed up with a similar sense of urgency in South African politics. Inspired by 'loyal resistance', he often spoke out against the slow pace of change and short-sighted government actions.

In a speech delivered in Bloemfontein in 1971 Rupert stressed the importance of private initiative and the threat posed to it by excessive legislation, regulation and bureaucratisation. At that time South Africa was taking the first steps towards entering the television era, after much agonising and debate amongst government leaders – television would only be introduced in 1975, years later than in most other countries. Addressing the Bloemfontein audience, he said with unconcealed irritation: 'But what do things look like here, where public expenditure continues to increase as a result of our constant demand for services, and where we have just been kindly informed by the chairman of the Broadcasting Corporation that the ideal form of television would be that of non-profit utility company. I ask you, who will pay the taxes for the ever-growing public expenditure if everybody were to operate without profit?'

One of the reasons for this irritation came to the fore in a conversation Rupert had had the year before with Sir Alec Douglas-Home of Britain. Sir Alec had complained that more than half the population of the UK was state employed. This security (for people with salaries) came at a high price: Britain's economic growth rate had declined to the lowest in the West, despite the country having more technological expertise at its disposal than the entire southern hemisphere put together.

Rupert's resistance against a legalistic approach, excessive regulation and the bureaucratisation of all and sundry stemmed not only from his conviction about private enterprise. Also, his emphasis on small business, private initiative and deregulation was not motivated by a narrow and self-centred desire to make money. To him, private initiative was embedded in the basic rights of freedom that characterised a democratic culture, the kind of culture in which creativity, innovation and individuality could best be realised. A free market and a democratic culture went hand in hand. His conviction in this regard had been strengthened by the ideas of the philosopher José Ortega y Gasset (1883-1955).

When opposing the notion of television as a state-controlled utility company in his 1971 speech, Rupert also spoke about freedom of the press. He pointed out that the paper with which John Fairbairn and Thomas Pringle had achieved the hard-won freedom of the press at the Cape in 1828 had been called *The South African Commercial Advertiser*. A free press ensured its freedom by relying on advertising for revenue; only then could people's views be heard and freedom of speech be guaranteed. Otherwise, what remained would 'look like *Pravda*'. (In later years the Rembrandt offshoot Venfin put Rupert's words into action by investing in the South African commercial television service e.tv.)

Rupert was adamant: control and regulation aimed at limiting initiative, freedom and fundamental human rights brought neither more order nor prosperity. He made it clear that he was not opposed to control as such, but the kind of control that restricted or even suspended rights of freedom. This was what he had experienced at the hands of Hendrik Verwoerd when he had been prevented from forming a partnership with coloured entrepreneurs in Paarl.

When Verwoerd's successor John Vorster took over the premiership in 1966 he raised some hopes with his outward-looking policy and relaxation of racial restrictions on sport, but resistance to his government grew as reforms were not implemented fast enough. On 16 June 1976, with mounting pressure on government to expedite reform, South Africa's biggest black township Soweto erupted into violence, and this time the youth were at the heart of it. The immediate trigger had been the imposition of Afrikaans as a compulsory teaching medium in black schools. But the protest action went much wider, fired by the slogan 'No education before liberation'. Revolting against the acquiescence of their fathers and mothers, the youth lost their fear for the laws and the guns of the apartheid government. As far as the government was concerned, most black townships countrywide became ungovernable. Anxiety prevailed about social, economic and political stability in South Africa. The revolt, which astounded supporters and opponents of the government alike, became a turning point in the country's history, epitomised by the statue erected in Soweto of the schoolboy Hector Petersen who had been the first casualty in the insurrection. The date of his death, 16 June, was commemorated annually long before it became a public holiday – Youth Day – in 1994.

The events of 1976 had a profound effect on Rupert. The fear he expressed in 1960 after the march led by Philip Kgosana in Cape Town had become a reality: a revolutionary climate prevailed throughout the country, with children participating in the revolt.

Rupert and Harry Oppenheimer met in London and decided to convene a meeting of business leaders to give urgent attention to the crisis. The conference held at the Carlton Hotel in Johannesburg on 29 November 1976 had as its theme 'Quality of life of urban communities'. In addition to prominent whites, it was attended by the Committee of Ten, a group of influential black leaders led by Dr Nthatho Motlana from Soweto.

Rupert, deputy chairman of the conference, had had a very good relationship with Oppenheimer, although they were never close friends. 'We had great respect for one another,' Rupert said in later years. 'Harry was a bit of a loner.'[1]

What the events of 1976 also illustrated to Rupert was the strong socioeconomic component of South Africa's racial problems. People were not only protesting against the denial of political rights but against social misery and appalling forms of poverty in black areas. Much more starkly than the tragic events at Sharpeville in 1960, the 1976 uprising in Soweto and other urban areas made many whites realise that the established political order could not guarantee peace and stability in the future, and that reforms were urgently needed. Business leaders like Rupert and Oppenheimer campaigned within the Urban Foundation, which was to result from the conference, for socioeconomic development and basic rights such as home ownership and access to the economy for urban blacks. This initiative was an ambitious attempt on the part of the private sector to address a situation in which the government had failed in its responsibility towards the black population of the country.

Rupert was one of the main speakers at the conference. As in many of his speeches, he started by situating South Africa in the context of global developments. After all, his partnership idea included the principle of the interdependence of countries. He pointed out that the West was being seduced by wealth, which in turn made it tempting to take the easy option of disregarding others and one's own safety. 'This is how Knossos, the rich and civilised capital of ancient Crete, fell in a night to the invading Myceneans. This is how Rome fell to the Barbarians.' Affluent (predominantly white) South Africans, he stated flatly, were dominated by fear – 'the fear of survival as a separate entity, the fear of being overrun by numbers, the fear of possible tyranny by an unenlightened majority resulting in one man, one vote once'.

'We cannot survive unless we have a free market economy, a stable Black middle class with the necessary security of tenure, personal security and a feeling of hope for betterment in the heart of all our peoples. And the urgency of the challenge is underlined by the fact that nearly half of the population of the Republic was born since Sharpeville.'

Getting down to practical solutions, he outlined seven aspects that would improve the quality of life of urban blacks: job creation, job-oriented training, payment of a living wage, creation of commercial opportunities, extended home ownership, improvement of existing housing, and provision of sporting and other amenities to improve social life in the modern concrete jungle. To this end he proposed the appointment of a task force with the following brief:

'To establish an Urban Development Foundation to accommodate and co-ordinate, on an ongoing basis, the private sector's endeavours at improving the quality of life in the urban black townships. The essential motivation for the Foundation's existence would be that it would seek to encourage and assist as a catalyst the transformation of South Africa's urban black communities into stable, essentially middle-class societies subscribing to the values of a free enterprise society and having a vested interest in their own survival. The Foundation would be the vehicle for development aid and counselling provided by the private sector in close consultation and collaboration with black leadership, to whose management it would transfer all programmes at the earliest possible stage. It follows that the Foundation should include amongst its trustees recognised urban black leaders.'[2]

The upshot of the business leaders' conference was the establishment of the Urban Foundation. The immediate aims were to improve housing in the townships and promote home ownership, encourage private initiative, provide amenities, build schools and improve black education. In the process human resources in black communities had to be mobilised so as to get beyond a paternalistic culture.

The new foundation was headed by Judge Jan Steyn (not to be confused with Rupert's friend Dr Jan Steyn, a director of Rembrandt), a jurist with a social conscience who was admitted to the bench in Cape Town in 1964 and afterwards had been involved in Nicro, an organisation for the rehabilitation of criminals. His father had been a minister of religion and his mother, Dr Zerilda (Droskie) Steyn, was known for her pioneering work in urban housing and care of the aged.

Rupert and Oppenheimer approached Steyn personally to undertake the task, and after careful consideration he decided he would be able to make a greater contribution at the Urban Foundation. On an eye-opening visit to Soweto he discovered that the huge black city (its official population was 600 000 at the time, in fact it was closer to 1 500 000) had just one cinema and one sports field. It convinced him of the need and he took on the challenge. He also realised at the conference in 1976 the extent to which black people experienced the national policy as humiliating and oppressive.[3]

Steyn considered the participation of Rupert, who maintained his usual low profile in this initiative, to have been of decisive importance to the Urban Foundation. He not only gave Steyn his full support throughout, but helped ensure that optimal use was made of the foundation's financial resources. He even offered some of Rembrandt's staff to assist the foundation. In Steyn's opinion, the involvement of prominent Afrikaners like Rupert, Andreas Wassenaar from Sanlam, Wim de Villiers from Gencor, David de Villiers from Nasionale Pers and later Jan van der Horst from Old Mutual contributed to a reluctance on the part of the Nationalist government to disparage the Urban Foundation when it undertook initiatives that were not in line with rigid apartheid policies.

At the same time, the black community's response was ambivalent. Some recognised leaders supported the foundation, but with reservations: would it help change the political system of the country? Would it not be just another patch job? Black radicals regarded the Urban Foundation's social upliftment initiatives as mere delaying tactics aimed at putting off the inevitable revolution. They also mistrusted the foundation's opposition to international sanctions against South Africa, which were advocated by the ANC as well as Archbishop Tutu. Jan Steyn considered sanctions a campaign that contributed little to vital reform. On the contrary, they rather had a negative effect and delayed the imperative political change in South Africa, he wrote in 1990.[4]

When Steyn stepped down as chairman of the Urban Foundation in 1990 on his appointment as chairman of the Independent Development Trust, he could look back on fourteen years in which the foundation had made a real contribution to improving the lives of disadvantaged urban communities. It had erected thousands of houses in black townships, promoted the abolition of influx control, and played a significant role in education and skills development in black communities. The leasehold Rupert had implored Verwoerd to consider finally became a reality under the leadership of the Urban Foundation – 99-year leasehold was introduced in 1979.

In 1995 the Urban Foundation, along with the Consultative Business Movement, was absorbed into President Nelson Mandela's newly established National Business Initiative (NBI). It represented the private sector's collective response to the new government's Reconstruction and Development Programme (RDP), operating mainly in the same socioeconomic fields where the foundation had been active over the years.

Although the Urban Foundation did valuable work in improving black people's living conditions, prospective black entrepreneurs were initially not sufficiently exposed to business life. Three years after the establishment of the foundation, Rupert, still seriously concerned about inequalities and poverty in South Africa, embarked on a new initiative. Prodded by his son Johann, a fervent proponent of small business development, he established the Small Business Development Corporation (SBDC) with the help of the Rembrandt Group on 3 March 1979. The aim of the SBDC was to provide limited funding to selected small businesses as well as expert advice and training, in order to stimulate entrepreneurial talent among all population groups. This was in line with Rupert's conviction that democracy had to be underpinned by social development and economic progress. Besides, it was his way of overcoming his frustration with the politics of the day.

The corporation was launched with initial capital of R1 million, the principle of 'partnership with the people' and the credo that 'small business is big business'. Without much publicity, the announcement read: 'The Rembrandt Group and the Rupert family hereby announce the establishment of the Small Business Development Corporation with nominal capital of R1 million.' The SBDC conformed fully to Rupert's partnership model. He himself chaired the multiracial board of directors, including Habakuk Shikwane, a black industrialist; FM (Fred) Harris, a coloured building contractor; JN Reddy, an Indian banker; and MJ (Tienie) Oosthuizen, a white director of Rembrandt.

Rupert was particularly interested in the establishment of small manufacturing units. The corporation sponsored numerous projects in what were known as beehive developments: small businesses set up with basic equipment in abandoned factories. As in the case of his other initiatives, and in accordance with his partnership policy, he invited other established businesses to participate. The SBDC would be a 'catalyst' in job creation in South Africa, he said, using one of his favourite terms that recalled his training as a chemist.

He did not attach much value to theories that could not be put into practice. On the establishment of the SBDC he cited the example of the United States of America, where nine million jobs were created within eight years, up to 1977. Three million of these had been created by individual states and local governments, and almost none by the central federal government. About 500 000 jobs had been created by the biggest thousand companies; the rest, 5,5 million jobs, by smaller businesses. While fully aware that a business like his own had to be 'big or dead' in a shrinking and increasingly competitive world, he refused to accept that wealth creation could only be left in the hands of big business. His background as the son of a lawyer in a rural town had made him a proponent of small business, he often said. In this regard he liked to refer to his hometown of Graaff-Reinet, especially the intersection of Somerset and Bourke Streets. 'At the one corner was the church, with the printing works right across the street. On the other corner was the smithy, where the blacksmith also lived. On another corner was a shop.'[5]

This memory of the town of his youth made him react strongly against the notion of 'Western planners' that factories and industries had to be banished from cities. In a lecture entitled 'Small business is big business' at the University of Pretoria in 1979 he set out his views in detail.[6] He firmly believed that the free enterprise system could best be expressed in small business, referring to small business as 'the roots of a system with an unrivalled record of wealth creation'. He was told by Tom Bata, the world's biggest shoe manufacturer, that Italy, which manufactured the finest shoes in the world, did so by way of home industries – it had three million of them, flourishing in the heart of cities like Rome and Florence. This obviated the counterproductive system of establishing factories far from residential areas, compelling workers to get up at five in the morning, travel at great cost to their workplaces and return home weary round nine at night. 'I want to hope that when we do development in black homelands,' he said, 'we would allow the black people to run businesses in their backyards and garages.'

Rupert cited the example of one of the SBDC's earliest investments. An American softdrink company had paid for a man to do a welding course. The SBDC then helped him to set up his own business. With a dig at the government, Rupert said: '… I should rather not identify him and where he works, otherwise he'll probably get a visit from a factory inspector!'[7]

Habakuk Shikwane, one of the corporation's own directors, had started off manufacturing cane furniture in his backyard in Soweto round the same time that Rupert was making his own modest start in tobacco in Johannesburg. Eventually Shikwane moved to a black 'homeland' and became the biggest manufacturer of cane furniture in the southern hemisphere. His shrewd advice helped shape SBDC policy in many respects. When an applicant wanted R10 000, he counselled, dole it out in instalments as the need arose, otherwise he might be tempted to use the money to buy a car instead of developing his business.

One of the SBDC's prime targets was Soweto, where government had hitherto prohibited all industry, even in people's own backyards. In Soweto the SBDC rapidly 'discovered', according to Rupert, a hundred people who benefited the country 'illegally' by creating value in their backyards. The corporation also assisted the first black lawyer in a black township to get his practice going. A coloured township butcher was helped to acquire a vehicle for deliveries, his two children accompanying him on his rounds. These projects thrilled Huberte no less than Rupert: 'In the first beehive project outside Johannesburg all races worked together. The Indian T-shirt manufacturer answers his black neighbour's phone when he's out selling his wares. A white university lecturer hired a unit for a while to build himself a fibreglass boat and taught his neighbours how it's done. Everybody helps everybody else. It's beautiful,' she said.

Rupert emphasised that the unsophisticated component of the population should not be subjected to sophisticated regulation. 'Don't start imposing trade unions and factory law immediately. Let the man start small and provide jobs.' If South Africa's reservoir of creative energy were not channelled, he predicted, like water it would stagnate and rot. 'It should be generated, motivated and activated to blow like a fresh breeze through our economy. South Africa has too many mouths to feed for us to be able to afford to sit back. We must go forward – with confidence – without fear.'[8]

Small business was also the theme of his speech at Rembrandt's AGM in 1979. With its rapidly growing population and government still dragging its feet about the much-vaunted homeland development – which, in twenty years, had made no progress – South Africa was, as Rupert put it, 'sitting on a powder keg of unemployed people': 'A man without a job is a desperate man. We can see this in the ever-growing stream of unemployed from the rural areas to our cities. Even the influx-control measures do not deter these people.'[9] On this occasion he also pleaded for programmes that could accelerate the training of skilled workers. He pointed out that current job-creation policies rested on the assumption that mechanisation and automation would lead to sustainable growth and increased production capacity. This had happened to a certain extent – but at a high price. For the emphasis was on the scarce commodity, capital, instead of the abundant one: labour. The result was growing unemployment.

For Rupert, free enterprise was not merely about wealth creation for its own sake. It made the development of full human potential possible. Besides wealth, the free enterprise system ensured a number of other rights: the right to own property, the right to choose a vocation according to one's own preference and ability, the right to choose one's own lifestyle, the right to freedom of association and the right to freedom of movement.

Rupert liked to think in terms of contrasting extremes and then striking a balance between them. In his opinion, people who could not list both the advantages and disadvantages of a policy, viewpoint or strategy had not yet learnt to think creatively. In fact, at Rembrandt they kept a 'black book' in which employees had to record the pros and cons of proposals. According to Rupert the book was 'famous' to some employees, 'notorious' to others. 'You quickly fall victim to tunnel vision if your brain can't think pro and con,' he said. 'If someone asks me a question, my brain works in terms of pros and cons, advantages and disadvantages. Only then can you take decisions.'[10]

An example of how he used antithetical positions to make his own point occurred at the group's AGM in 1977. He first set out the one extreme: Those who use Adam Smith, the father of the theory of capitalism, to defend the view that the only function of business is to maximise profits 'without taking into consideration any factors outside the field of business.' At the other extreme was the radical viewpoint: Everything wrong in society was the fault of capitalists. The private sector could not be trusted to let justice be done – capitalists were only interested in money.

Rupert opposed both views. In fact, his opposition found expression in his partnership philosophy. That is why he even talked of a 'contract' between business and the community within which it operates. This contract, he said in 1977, must be 'expanded' so that the social responsibility of the business sector could come into its own. And this was especially possible within the free enterprise system. Rupert did not argue against the idea that the profit motive was a driving force of progress and a measure of efficiency. What he emphasised, however, was that this was not all it involved. Community service and development was part of the free enterprise system, which found its best expression in small businesses.

An example he liked to use was what he called the most important biochemical discovery of the 20th century, the structure of the DNA molecule. It was not made in a modern laboratory in America, but in a bicycle shed in Cambridge! He found it interesting that so many small enterprises had been started in people's garages, even in farmhouses and vestries of churches. A garage he regarded as an eminently suitable environment for the start of small businesses: overheads are low and the rudimentary facilities stimulate innovative thinking and the development of a strategy. It offers the kind of environment that inspires people to achieve success, a sense that things can only get better.

In his lecture at the University of Pretoria, he stated that it was necessary to send a 'young man ... with a Polaroid camera' to places like Singapore, Hong Kong, Taiwan, Florence and Barcelona to photograph and report on what people in small businesses were doing. Not long afterwards he put this idea into action. One day in 1979 Hans Knoetze, a former journalist who had been employed as a liaison officer at Rembrandt since 1974, was summoned to Rupert's office. Without any preliminaries, Rupert asked if there might be any circumstances at home preventing him from going on a trip. 'I nearly fell off my chair,' Knoetze recalled. 'The reason for the strange question was that he had an assignment for me.' Knoetze regarded the assignment as typical of Rupert. 'The fact that it would be my first trip abroad, that I would travel alone and among others had to visit a country like South Korea that was virtually inaccessible to South Africans at that stage, did not bother him. Dr Rupert never thought twice about giving people responsibilities and you would do everything not to disappoint the trust he showed in you. He liked to say that he does not give assignments to a committee because a committee does not lie awake at night thinking about a problem, but an individual does.'

Knoetze first attended a congress on small business in Berlin, where he built up valuable contacts from Taiwan, Hong Kong and South Korea. After visiting each of these countries as well as Singapore and Tokyo in Japan, he returned with a wealth of information about the flourishing small businesses of the Far East. Ten years later he was sent to China on a similar mission, which made him realise that, given the enormous resources of Chinese history, it was only a matter of time before the present generation burst into creative economic activity. With their rich history the Chinese were 'standing on the shoulders of giants', Knoetze thought, which he compared to the image he had of Rupert: 'As colleagues of Dr Rupert, young and old, we were also standing on the shoulders of a giant, and that was the reason why we could perhaps see further than those who had not been exposed to his exceptional leadership . . . He had the ability to broaden people's horizons, not only in respect of the things in which he involved one, but also because of the knowledge and experience he shared so readily. Working for him was not a job, it was an experience.'[11]

Shortly after Rupert had established the SBDC, the South African government came with an initiative of its own. Growing political unrest among black South Africans, unemployment and increasing international isolation led to a summit at the Carlton Centre in Johannesburg on 22 November 1979. Chaired by Prime Minister PW Botha, it was attended by some 300 business leaders, including Harry Oppenheimer, Anton Rupert and black businessmen like SM (Sam) Motsuenyane and JN Reddy. Botha, who was starting to feel the pressure of isolation and sanctions, spelled out his concerns. Portugal's withdrawal from Angola and Mozambique meant that South African liberation movements now had bases much nearer home. 'As a result of the collapse of law and order within their borders and the concomitant inability to address socioeconomic and security problems, some southern African states have become susceptible to overtures from Soviet Russia,' he said.[12] In view of these developments of Marxist-oriented states on its doorstep, South Africa had to reconsider its priorities. Botha proposed the creation of a constellation of southern African states where ' law and order' as well as 'free enterprise' would prevail. He requested the business sector to contribute to 'a southern African strategy', 'stability through regional development' and the development of 'national states' (the black homelands) as first priority'.

In Rupert's speech at the summit he highlighted what he saw as 'two crucial problems': improving the living conditions of urban blacks, and creating jobs through small business. He pointed out that about five million small enterprises in Japan employed 80% of workers in the private sector. With reference to these statistics, he said: 'To create jobs one must think small.' He proposed the creation of a small business development corporation with a 'multiracial' board of directors and starting capital of R100 million, half of it provided by the state. 'I shall personally propose to my Group that we contribute one tenth, that is R5 million, of the private sector's R50 million to such a corporation.'[13] Money alone would not solve the problem – small business also had to be promoted through investments in training and aftercare of new entrepreneurs. He proposed that the state provide a further R2,5 million for initiatives of this nature.

Rupert's proposal was accepted, but to his immense frustration the new SBDC took more than a year to materialise. Government's obsession with control, established parastatal interests and differing opinions about the shape the new SBDC should take led to endless delays that irritated the business sector in general and Rupert in particular. The proposals government eventually put on the table also did not accord with his notions of an equal partnership between government and the private sector. At the end of his tether, he wrote to Botha in August 1980 to inform the prime minister that he was withdrawing his offer made at the Carlton talks. In his two-and-a half-page letter he did not mince his words in criticising what had happened since the summit. He found it particularly disturbing that he had to hear on the radio that the Industrial Development Corporation (IDC), a parastatal organisation, was to extend its loan facilities to small businesses, especially in Soweto. In Rupert's view this was supposed to be the function of the SBDC. A tax-paying SBDC could not compete with the state-funded IDC, he informed Botha. This latest episode reminded him strongly of 'other instances where the state, rather than support positive initiatives by the private sector, preferred to duplicate them, with unfortunate results'. He cited three examples, including his experience with Edesa, where unfulfilled government intentions effectively put paid to investments in the development bank. In view of government's manifest resistance to private sector initiative, he was withdrawing his offer made at the Carlton talks.

Botha could not afford to have the project founder by losing the support of business leaders. Rupert was attending the opening of the restored Reinethuis in Graaff-Reinet when he received a phone call from Pik Botha, Minister of Foreign Affairs. 'The boss wants to talk to you,' he said. 'Who's the boss?' Rupert asked. The boss, it turned out, was PW Botha, now in a more conciliatory mood and requesting Rupert not to withdraw his offer. In a subsequent letter Botha informed him that he had instructed the central banker Dr Gerhard de Kock, leader of the special constellation committee, to expedite the establishment of the new SBDC. He expressed understanding for Rupert's 'dismay' about the delay and assured him that 'a misunderstanding had occurred somewhere' and that he was looking into the matter. He expressed his appreciation of Rupert's original offer: 'Like you, we are really serious about offering optimal opportunity for developing private enterprise among all South Africa's people.'

Botha's reference to 'all South Africa's people' indicated how economic realities had caused cracks in the wall of apartheid. Where apartheid had unleashed centrifugal forces, Rupert's partnership philosophy – in conjunction with economic realities – generated centripetal energies. Recognising this, Botha acknowledged the importance of obtaining the support of business leaders. At that stage he showed awareness of Rupert's contribution to a better future, something he would forget in the 1980s when he had to deal with the threat of financial sanctions. Still, Botha deserved credit for his speedy resolution of the problem that had arisen around the SBDC. He assured Rupert in his letter that '... I share wholeheartedly your aversion to the tendency to transform all good ideas into state institutions'.

The new SBDC was duly floated in November 1980 with an authorised shareholding of R150 million, split equally between government and the private sector. Rupert, who chaired the launching committee, prevailed on Rembrandt to contribute the first R5 million and in a matter of four weeks he could announce that R63 million had been raised from the private sector – well in excess of the targeted amount. In February 1981 the new and expanded corporation was registered as a public, fully taxable company. Rupert chaired the board of 27 private sector directors and seven state appointees. A government-business partnership to promote private initiative by way of small enterprises, a concept Rupert had been advocating for three decades, had finally come into existence in South Africa. It also removed development from an ethnic context: prospective entrepreneurs would be assisted irrespective of race or gender. Rupert saw this as proof of 'positive thinking and action'.

The first managing director was Prof. WB (Ben) Vosloo, a Stellenbosch professor of political science and a director of Rand Merchant Bank, which had been taken over by Johann Rupert (a former student of Vosloo) on his return from America in 1979. Vosloo, who had obtained his doctorate at Cornell University in the USA, put his considerable energies and ability into promoting small business among all population groups.

He insisted, in the face of many claims from individuals and institutions that theirs had been the leading role in the establishment of the SBDC, that 'the person who had set the ball rolling in concrete terms was Dr Rupert, with strong encouragement from his son Johann.'[14] Vosloo regarded Rupert in all respects as the 'impresario' in the formation and functioning of the SBDC. 'He did the spadework before and during its establishment and had remained consistently involved as chairman of the board till 6 October 1995.' For his part Rupert acknowledged on more than one occasion to Vosloo that Johann, not yet 30 years old at the time, had played a major role in convincing him of the crucial importance of an institution for small business development. During Vosloo's term as director of Rand Merchant Bank, from 1979 to 1981, conversations with Johann as well as what happened at board meetings had made him aware of Johann's strong views on the necessity of promoting small business in South Africa, which included addressing the need for medium- and long-term capital provision.

Vosloo recalled being struck by an aspect of Rupert's philosophy that emerged during a conversation they had in his car one evening while returning to Stellenbosch from the airport. 'We were talking about the general lack of integrity among some business people when he remarked that "a person who is himself dishonest cannot trust others", and also that "if you want to succeed in business, you must be willing not only to trust in people, but also to trust them in turn".' According to Vosloo, Rupert had illustrated what he meant by this by referring to the biggest deal of his life that had been concluded with a handshake, when Sydney Rothman had offered Rupert his interest in Rothmans at a particular price. 'The accountants and legal people later worked out the precise details of the deal.'

Rupert himself regarded trust as the most important thing life had taught him – how to gain it, how to create it, how to retain it. 'This applies to trust between husband and wife, husband and children, children and their parents, colleagues, partners, acquaintances. It is built over time, it's a long-term investment in quality. This includes self-confidence, trust in yourself, which is so important to the survival of our young people today – a humble self-confidence.' Trust was something one had to sustain at all cost, he believed. 'No major international businessman would be successful in the long term if he betrayed people's trust. It takes long to build trust, but one slip-up and it's gone,' he stated.[15]

In 1981 the SBDC changed its name to Small Entrepreneurs Limited – Rupert's suggestion again. By now he was devoting himself to problems that, in his opinion, were obstructing or even blocking the initiative of small entrepreneurs. Top of the list was the stifling web of First World standards imposed by a massive bureaucracy, which effectively enmeshed small businesses in endless red tape – a situation that still prevails in South Africa at the beginning of the 21st century. Rupert's solution was unequivocal: deregulate. The second major obstacle was the commonly held view in some circles that big was more important than small in the business field, and therefore merited preferential treatment. Here Rupert's answer was an 'alliance' between big and small business, which would result in job creation, improved quality of life and social stability.

His thinking was not only limited to South Africa. On 18 January 1985 he helped establish Neu-Europa Hitec & Biotec in West Berlin, a development corporation analogous to the SBDC, with the emphasis on advanced technology. This happened after a visit to South Africa by the West Berlin Minister of Trade and Transport, Elmar Pieroth. He invited Rupert to Berlin on behalf of the mayor, Richard von Weizsäcker, who later became the president of the Federal Republic of Germany. They wanted his help and advice to deal with unemployment in their divided city. Rupert proposed that a renewal company be established. In one night he wrote a foundation charter that he submitted to Pieroth the following morning. In the document he motivated his proposal by referring to the ingenuity for which Europe had always been known and the many technological innovations that had originated in Berlin, among others the train, the motorcar, television, radar, the rocket and the computer. 'And yet today Europe's future is uncertain owing to the practical application of originally European inventions by American and Japanese production and marketing know-how. Europe must make better use of its creative abilities by providing opportunities to its talented young inventors.' Quoting Lenin who had said that whoever owned Berlin, owned Europe, Rupert emphasised that Berlin had more young scientists studying at university than any other centre in Europe. 'Thus the need for a new European Hitec & Biotec corporation, with its headquarters in Berlin. It is an investment in the future – your future.'[16]

Rupert set the example by taking up some of the first shares himself, and helped recruit other shareholders, which included Deutsche Bank, Dresdner Bank, Commerzbank, Allianz Versicherung, the Hoechst chemical company and Daimler Benz. The first chairman of the broad was Heinz Nixdorf of Nixdorf Corporation, with Jürgen Sarrasin of Dresdner Bank and Hans-Otto Wieschermann of Henkel as alternative chairmen. His most difficult task proved to be breaking down what he called the 'European sclerosis' – a mistrust of youthful daring and enterprise. In the course of his peregrinations he visited East Berlin – his was the first private plane to land there after the fall of the Berlin Wall in 1989. On a visit to factories in the former East Germany, show window of communism, he was struck by the antiquated buildings and machinery, and the fact that they needed twelve to fourteen workers to do a job that one Rembrandt employee could handle with ease.

Eventually Neu-Europa did not progress satisfactorily owing to a lack of sufficient and enthusiastic support, and it became a disappointment to Rupert. This was reflected in a letter he received from Pieroth: 'The world has really changed since you first landed with your private plane in East Berlin, I hope for the better. What is missing, is more of your self-help assistance. This must be applied far more widely.'[17]

In the meantime, with the advent of democracy in South Africa in the early 1990s, serious differences in opinion arose between the SBDC under Rupert and the new entrants to the political scene. It centred on the role of the state in small business development. Even before the 1994 elections various development bodies became targets for all sorts of opportunists who were vying for control over key positions and funds. A campaign against the SBDC was headed by Trevor Manuel, who was to be Minister of Trade and Industry in the post-election ANC government, and his eventual director-general, Alistair Ruiters. Manuel and Ruiters were at that stage still strongly in favour of centralised control and, like the NP before them, believed that the government was better able to run such affairs than the private sector. The main reason why they wanted to change the situation lay in the restrictions on state interference and control entrenched in the SBDC's articles of association.

During the manoeuvres to bring about a restructuring Johann Rupert, who would succeed his father as chairman of the SBDC, was appointed a director of the organisation on 31 August 1993. He soon took the lead with his father in negotiations with the new ANC government representatives, at a time when other business leaders, in Ben Vosloo's opinion, were mainly protecting their own interests and were currying favour with the new political leaders. According to Vosloo, the atmosphere during the talks was strained. He responded frankly to allegations from certain politicians and black business people that the SBDC had not done enough to promote the interests of black entrepreneurs and was biased in favour of white business people: 'The SBDC has created more employment for black people than any other institution in the country. In the thirteen years of our existence we have created 370 000 jobs, of which 80% have been for black people.' Vosloo was also of the opinion that at that stage there were very few successful black business people who had not been assisted at some time or another by the SBDC, which he considered the biggest developer of business infrastructure in black areas. 'We believe that we are one of the most successful organisations of our kind in the world. There is nothing on the African continent that can be compared to us.'[18]

The two Ruperts, alert to the kind of state interference that generated inefficiency and corruption in the development corporations of the erstwhile black homelands, strongly advocated scaling down the state's role in the SBDC. In fact, Rupert's right-hand man in Lesotho, Wynand van Graan, had encountered so much corruption when he headed Bophuthatswana's Development Corporation that he resigned and became head of Bonuskor in Johannesburg. After lengthy negotiations, in the course of which Johann Rupert played a key role by jointly compiling a memorandum of understanding with Ruiters, they agreed that the state's shareholding should be brought into line with its representation. But this required a 'ransom'. In exchange for the restructuring, the state was initially supposed to receive an amount of R499,8 million, according to an agreement approved by the shareholders on 6 October 1995. This was also the board meeting at which Rupert retired as chairman and was succeeded by Johann. Ben Vosloo, who later moved to Australia, retired at the end of 1995, although he still assisted the corporation as a consultant for a while. Jo Schwenke succeeded him as managing director.

Before the SBDC's offer was finally approved, however, the Department of Finance insisted on an increased amount of R599,8 million, which was approved by the board at The Court House on 18 April 1996. Assets to the value of R599,8 million were transferred to the state in the form of cash, share transfers, set-off and fixed property.[19]

During the negotiations Manuel, who later also created a stir with his criticism of the market as an 'amorphous entity' when he became Minister of Finance, eventually arrived at the insight that the private sector was better able to address small business development than the state. This contributed to his satisfactory management of the country's macroeconomic policy, so that he is commonly considered one of South Africa most successful ministers of finance.

The state gradually reduced its shareholding in the SBDC from 50 to 20%. Listed companies own 70% of the shares and a share trust of SBDC employees the remaining ten percent. Remgro is the second biggest shareholder, with sixteen percent. In October 1998 the organisation changed its name to Business Partners Limited. In terms of the restructuring agreement it withdrew from the informal sector and confined its activities to small and medium enterprises in the formal sector.

In a survey of twenty years in the field, Business Partners reported that its financing of 188 projects to the amount of R11,2 million in 1981/1982 had increased to 766 projects to the amount of R578,5 million in the 2001 financial year. In these two decades it had approved investments of over R4 billion and increased its shareholders' value by more than R1 billion.[20]

Schwenke is proud of the fact that since its inception the organisation has shown a profit ever year, and that the initial investors have been amply rewarded for their investment. In his opinion, the success of Business Partners, which essentially invests in people, could to a large extent be attributed to Rupert's interest in people and the people-oriented approach that characterised his entire career. Integrity and honesty had also been watchwords at Business Partners from the start, and sound corporate governance was pursued long before the King Report on the topic. A strict division was maintained between the offices of the non-executive chairman and the managing director, under Rupert as well as Johann. In line with the Ruperts' dislike of ostentation and showiness, Business Partners' headquarters are neat and serviceable because the results are what count, says Schwenke.[21]

The company as facilitator had helped to create and sustain an estimated 500 000 jobs. Despite this massive effort on the part of the private sector, by 2003 South Africa had lost more than a million jobs since the ANC came to power in 1994, and the official unemployment rate stood at a very high 40% of the economically active population. This can be attributed partly to the country's rigid, prescriptive labour laws, the kind of laws Rupert would like to deregulate.

Rupert in 1976 (Urban Foundation – together with Oppenheimer) and Rupert in 1980 (Carlton summit and his letter to Botha) must get the credit for an important chisel that cracked the walls of apartheid.

For Rupert, the individual was the key person in the development of small business. He was convinced that creativity started with the individual – that the entrepreneur with the right idea at the right time and in the right place was the heartbeat of private initiative. As far back as 1959, addressing the Worcester Business Chamber, he said frankly that one should start with the small to correct big problems. What was required, however, was an individual with drive and vision who could take the lead – private initiative and creative innovation did not come from a committee. In 1996 he said: 'A brilliant idea only comes to life when it is carried by the driving force of a man who believes in it so passionately that he accepts all risks and surmounts all obstacles. Courage is to be aware of everything that stands in the way and yet still carry on unceasingly.'[22]

He also liked to support his views on small business with references to the Industrial Revolution in Britain and the USA. According to him it started small – with owner-managed enterprises that became big enterprises within the lifetime of the owners. Well-known names like the Wedgwoods, Cadburys, Fords and Carnegies fitted this pattern. Rupert had an unshakeable belief in the innovative and creative abilities of the free individual. After all, small and independent enterprises were not the products of boards, committees, fund managers or governments but of an entrepreneur's initiative, ambition, creative thinking and perseverance.

Free enterprise was to him the successful antipode to collectivism and socialism: 'There's enough of a Scotsman in every human being to make us work harder when our own welfare is at stake. Who would get out of bed in the middle of the night to repair his neighbour's windmill or doctor his sick cow? When everything belongs to everybody, nothing belongs to anybody and nobody cares.'

Because South Africa was a land of 'glaring contrasts', with a 'sophisticated economy' and a 'totally unsophisticated economy' existing side by side, Rupert saw the country's future as lying not in mass production, but in production by the masses – as had happened in South Korea and was also the case in Italy. In addition to job creation, he attributed other major advantages to the small business enterprise: it was flexible and readily adaptable to changing circumstances; it was conducive to innovation, in that personal initiative was not stifled by management; entrepreneurs were free to take risks in their own interest, which made the small business enterprise a bulwark against socialism; and it contributed to the stability and social welfare of communities – in remote rural areas it often constituted the only source of employment, hence it counteracted the fragmentation of communities.

Some commentators have regarded Rupert's partnership idea as the precursor of the entry of black entrepreneurs into the South African economy in the 1990s. 'Actually, what is now happening on a large scale is what Anton Rupert advocated years ago with his term "partnership",' wrote the business magazine *Finansies & Tegniek* in 1997. 'Rupert proved the success of his approach in his own company by expanding his group globally. In a certain sense he could be called the father of black empowerment.'[23]

Rupert, firmly convinced that trade unions and governments did not create jobs on a meaningful scale, remained concerned about job creation in South Africa. To his son Johann, who has stated plainly that trade unions rather destroy jobs, he said with reference to protests and strikes: 'The more they dance, the more they toyi toyi, the more jobs are going to Hanoi.'[24]

He saw free enterprise, private initiative and innovative leadership as inextricably linked. According to Rupert, it was innovative individuals like Bartholomew Dias who sailed round the Cape of Storms and Martin Luther who initiated the Reformation, Alexander Graham Bell who developed the telephone and Henry Ford who implemented mass-production techniques.

Rupert's fervour to change the world for the better and his determination to accept risks and overcome obstacles were nowhere more strongly evident than in his passion to entrench a small business culture in South Africa and its neighbouring countries. He had championed that idea several years before someone like the scenario planner Clem Sunter from Anglo American, who in the mid-1990s expressed the wish that the political transition would be followed by a 'passion for business'. Sunter is also strongly in favour of small business and argues for 'a new, energetic and enthusiastic entrepreneurial class with world-class aspirations'.[25]

Sunter is following in Rupert's footsteps. If Dias had been an intrepid visionary who sailed into the unknown because he was driven by an unshakeable conviction, Rupert, who had implemented the idea of small business in practice years ago, could be seen as the South African Dias of the endeavour to establish small business as the energy source of development and progress.

CHAPTER 22

The feud between Rembrandt and Sanlam

T he beer war with Louis Luyt and SAB was followed shortly afterwards by another tempestuous chapter in Rupert's career: the feud between Rembrandt and the insurance giant Sanlam, a saga in which many high-profile Afrikaans business leaders became embroiled.

On 30 March 1982 Rupert wrote a trenchantly-worded letter to 'The Chairman and Directors' of Sanlam that spoke volumes about an intense conflict that had broken out between Rembrandt and the insurance company. With reference to a measure Andreas Wassenaar and Fred du Plessis from Sanlam wanted to push through at the mining house General Mining to strengthen Sanlam's control, he wrote: 'We cannot allow that you make us a prisoner of the megalomania of a few individuals. We do not go along with this and will contest it publicly, in our own as well as in the national interest.'[1]

A subtext in the feud between two of the leading Afrikaans companies was the ill feeling that existed between Wassenaar and Du Plessis, chairman and managing director of Sanlam respectively, on the one side, and Wim de Villiers, executive chairman of General Mining, on the other. De Villiers, a mining-industry veteran with a doctorate in mechanical engineering, had joined Anglo American in 1950. After a stint as managing director of LTA Engineering he served briefly as Sanlam's adviser on industry, and in 1970 joined General Mining (later Gencor), where he was executive head and later executive chairman until 1982. Rupert developed a high regard for the dynamic, though sometimes recalcitrant, De Villiers who built up General Mining into the second biggest mining house in South Africa, surpassed only by the Oppenheimers' Anglo American. They became personal friends and also served together on the board of the Reserve Bank.

Wassenaar, whose wife was the daughter of a former Lord Mayor of London, Sir Frederick Wells, had qualified as an actuary in Scotland before his meteoric rise from the mid-1930s onwards at Sanlam, where he was considered one of South Africa's most influential businessmen. Of the four major role players in the Rembrandt-Sanlam feud, Du Plessis, a former professor in finance and banking at the universities of Potchefstroom and Pretoria respectively, had the least practical business experience. The former academic, renowned for his capacity for hard work, entered the business world when he had to attempt to save the ailing Trust Bank. In 1978 Du Plessis was appointed managing director of Sanlam and four years later it was announced that he would succeed Wassenaar as chairman on 1 October 1982.

The discord between these four men represented one of the most bitter periods in the course of the Afrikaner's rise in the economy. For Rupert, what mattered above all in the dispute was his notion of partnership and representation. But more was at stake: his loyalty, too, to his friend Wim de Villiers.

How had it come about that Rembrandt and Sanlam, formerly the two friendly heavyweights in Afrikaans business, had virtually declared war on each other? Why did matters take such a turn that, according to his wife, the events had a 'very depressing effect' on Rupert? After all, prior to the dispute the relationship between the two companies had been characterised by good cooperation for more than a quarter of a century. When Rupert was in a tight spot in the 1950s during his efforts to finance his daring offer to take control of Rothmans, he had turned to Sanlam, where Wassenaar helped him in the nick of time. Many years later, in the saga that unfolded during 1974-75 around General Mining's take-over of the mining house Union Corporation – with Sanlam in control of General Mining – it was Sanlam's turn to approach Rupert for help. Wassenaar wrote about this in a personal document: 'Because Rembrandt was considered a friendly company, I phoned Dr Rupert in London (at his hotel suite). My question to him was whether Rembrandt had much cash overseas. His answer was "Yes".' Rupert himself said in later years: 'I always believed that Volkskas and Sanlam deserved my support, because they had helped me with what I needed.'[2]

On 15 July 1974 it became known the South African industrial conglomerate Barlows had entered into a merger agreement with the independent mining house Union Corporation (Unicorp). The new company, to be called Unicorp Barlows, would be a major player in the South African economy. Renowned business personalities Mike Rosholt and Ted Pavitt would be joint managing directors. Also featuring prominently in this plan were high-profile South African business leaders such as CS (Punch) Barlow, who would be chairman of the new company, Frans Cronjé, Len Abrahamse, GS (Gerry) Muller, Dick Goss and Mandy Moross.

The announcement was expected, and caused an uproar. One newspaper headline read: 'Merger creates a new SA colossus.'[3] The terms and conditions of the agreement were unacceptable to the market, however, and gave rise to fierce controversy. The new situation was obviously of great significance to General Mining, which had been taken over by *Federale Mynbou* (Federal Mining) in 1963 in a transaction universally seen as a breakthrough for Afrikaner interests in mining. For long it was believed that this development had been made possible by a wise and magnanimous Harry Oppenheimer of Anglo American who favoured the entry of Afrikaners into the top echelons of South African mining houses, and consequently sold his shares in General Mining to Federale Mynbou. In due course, however, a different view was advanced, one which held that the move had instead been motivated by a desire to protect Oppenheimer's interests in the founder of the diamond industry, De Beers, which held sway as a virtual monopoly in the global diamond market through its control of marketing through the Central Selling Organisation. Thirty years later a similar situation arose: when Anglo American ordered the unbundling of JCI (Johannesburg Consolidated Investments) in 1994 to ensure increased black participation, the diamond sector was specifically excluded so as to leave Anglo/De Beers in control. And at the turn of the century Oppenheimer's son, Nicky, relinquished substantial interests in Anglo in favour of control of De Beers, which was delisted.

In the early 1970s General Mining was in a fairly solid position in the mining industry. But in August 1974 its local competitor, Goldfields, announced its intention to make a counter offer for the Unicorp shares. The fat was now truly in the fire. Newspapers started speculating that General Mining was interested in Union Corporation. In fact, a three-man delegation of General Mining stakeholders was dispatched to London to talk to Hambros merchant bank, which had a six percent interest in Union Corporation and a 45-year affiliation with the South African mining house. They requested a London merchant banker to accompany them, which was how the merchant bank Morgan Grenfell became involved. At a meeting on 19 August 1974 where they made an offer for the Unicorp shares, they were told flatly by Wheatley, an executive director: 'I am not interested. The board will not be interested. The meeting is over.' That left General Mining with just one option: to buy up shares of Union Corporation in the open market.

On 5 September 1974 Barlows and Unicorp announced that they had abandoned their proposed merger. This set the stage for one of the most intense and audacious corporate battles in South Africa's history. Only two contenders remained in the arena, General Mining and Goldfields – the latter, ironically, a company that would be taken over by Rembrandt many years later. In the contest for the control of Union Corporation, however, Rupert found himself on the side of General Mining. In fact, his involvement gave General Mining its competitive advantage.

Anglo American had an agreement with General Mining, dating back to the Federale Mynbou takeover in 1963, which set out the procedure to be followed in the event of either party seeking control of another mining house. Should the parties consider a joint takeover, the party that initiated the move and acquired a dominant position would offer the other an interest of not less than 40% at cost or at the current market price. WB (William) Coetzer, a heavyweight in General Mining and Federale Mynbou who had also been a member of the first board of Rupert's Voorbrand, immediately approached Harry Oppenheimer about possible cooperation in a Union Corporation takeover. The talks were of critical importance. After all, the takeover of Union Corporation would decide whether General Mining or Goldfields would be South Africa's top mining house, after Anglo American. On a later occasion Wassenaar of Sanlam also participated in the talks with Oppenheimer, which were not very successful. Anglo American was more interested in Union Corporation's paper (Sappi) and platinum (Impala) holdings than its mining concerns.

In the meantime Goldfields, under the leadership of Adriaan Louw, proceeded with its plans to gain control of Union Corporation. On 26 September 1974 the company announced officially that it would make an offer for Unicorp. General Mining had been driven into a corner. Four days later they made a counter offer, but owing to a lack of financing General Mining announced it would be for just 50% of Unicorp shares. The tug of war was on, causing a stir in London financial circles. One newspaper headline proclaimed: 'London looks at Afrikaner interest in Unicorp.'[4] The contest between General Mining and Goldfields was soon regarded as a battle between Afrikaner and English-speaking interests. On 8 October 1974 Unicorp rejected Goldfields' offer; at the same time it was said that no formal offer had been received from General Mining. In any case, London financiers turned up their noses at backing an offer for a mere 50%, and General Mining had to retract.

A second, improved offer by Goldfields was also rejected by Unicorp, especially after the price of Goldfields shares had started to drop. Media speculation increased and on 16 November 1974 Goldfields extended the closing date of its second offer till early 1975, putting General Mining in a spot: if the Goldfields offer was accepted, it would be left with a minority interest in Unicorp, placing it in a very weak position. It embarked on the extremely risky game of buying up Unicorp shares on the open market. According to a Johannesburg newspaper, General Mining had at that stage about a twenty percent shareholding in Unicorp.[5] A few days later another newspaper claimed that General Mining had increased its holding to 22%.[6]

The position of Anglo American was a crucial issue. Through its London subsidiary Charter Holdings, Anglo had a ten percent interest in Unicorp which, according to some sources, Oppenheimer was said to have promised to General Mining on the basis of their 1963 agreement and subsequent talks. Mindful of the understanding that existed between them and Anglo American, the people at General Mining pinned their hopes on being able to add Charter's shares to their own when the takeover battle intensified. The Charter holding would give General Mining access to over 30% of Unicorp shares, and that percentage was still increasing through open-market acquisitions. On 24 November 1974, however, Goldfields again improved its offer. It seemed as if General Mining would have to throw in the towel. Yet it continued buying Unicorp shares. On 1 December 1974 a Sunday paper reported that General Mining already owned about 30% of Unicorp shares, taking this as proof that it had won the battle against Goldfields.[7]

Goldfields responded by upping its offer yet again, and Unicorp's board recommended that this time it should be accepted. General Mining, its back to the wall, seemed doomed to a minority shareholding. Then another disaster struck. On 5 December 1974 there was speculation, which was confirmed on 10 January 1975, that Charter Holdings had accepted the Goldfields offer. Oppenheimer's right-hand man, Julian Ogilvie Thompson, at least had the decency to inform De Villiers before the formal announcement. He visited De Villiers at his holiday home in Hermanus and hinted that all was not necessarily lost, provided Unicorp's Sappi and Impala interests were transferred to Anglo. Incensed, De Villiers rejected this and told Thompson: 'You expect us to carve up the corpse while it's still alive.'[8]

The 'understanding' with Anglo American on which General Mining had banked had not been strong enough. The Sunday paper *Rapport* commented: 'It seems that in the rivalry over Union Corporation Genmin has now finally been edged out as a suitor, and by none other than its partner Anglo American.'[9] This was a blow to cooperation and commitments between Afrikaans- and English-oriented business interests.

General Mining was in a corner. It could either submit to Goldfields' offer and get rid of its minority shareholding, or it could try to buy still more shares on the market to block Goldfields' offer. The latter option was obviously extremely risky, and exercising such an option depended on two assumptions. The first was the availability of sufficient capital. Sanlam, with Pepler Scholtz as managing director, was able to provide some help. Wassenaar committed Sanlam to a further R50 million – a dangerously high figure, as the insurance company had about R200 million cash available at the time. According to Wassenaar, this gave rise to a dispute between him and General Mining's De Villiers. Wassenaar later wrote in a personal document that De Villiers had been 'terribly indignant' and had 'kicked up a fuss about the fact that Sanlam had so much less available than what had been estimated initially'.[10]

The second assumption regarding the option to be exercised was even more challenging than Sanlam's shortage of funds. As there were few Unicorp shares to be bought in Johannesburg, the shares had to be acquired abroad. And because Sanlam could not do it, someone else had to be found. It was at this stage that Wassenaar phoned Rupert in London. Wassenaar maintained in his personal document: 'I assured him that Sanlam would see to it that he would not suffer any damage.' Many years later Rupert still remembered the call. He was leaving for the airport to board a plane to the Canary Islands when he was summoned back to take the call. When Wassenaar explained that money was urgently needed to buy up Unicorp shares abroad, Rupert, mindful of Sanlam's assistance when he himself had been in a tight spot, promised he would give serious consideration to helping General Mining (and Sanlam).[11]

Meanwhile there was panic in the General Mining camp, particularly after the decision of Charter Holdings. According to Wassenaar, Etienne Rousseau, a respected Afrikaans businessman and someone who would also feature in the saga around De Villiers and Rupert, was 'panic-stricken'. Others shared his doubts about the wisdom of proceeding with the option.

Rupert, however, did not waver. Through his Swiss banking contacts with whom he had built up a relationship of trust over the years he organised a credit line for the purchase of Unicorp shares. Such was the trust between the parties that the agreement with the bank was only signed a month later, after some of the money had already been used to buy shares. Credit to the amount of DM100 was made available.

A number of 'ghost buyers' purchased the shares. In addition to the credit line Rupert had obtained, Drexel Burnham of New York was involved in buying shares for General Mining, including two blocks of shares that had been in French hands. The broking firm Greenwells was used in London, with Peter Davidson one of those involved. Large purchases of Unicorp shares took place in London and Europe amid widespread speculation about the identity of the buyers, with headlines such as 'Mystery buyer of Unicorp comes back'. The newspaper in question wrote: 'GPSA [Goldfields] and its merchant bankers, Hill Samuel, are as bemused by the identity and objective of the London buyer as General Mining.'[12]

At the same time a rumour was circulating that Goldfields intended making a new offer, which they denied on 9 January 1975. The mistrust between General Mining/Sanlam and Anglo American also deepened, as it was suspected that Anglo had entered into an agreement with Goldfields about Sappi and Impala, the holdings on which Anglo had set its sights.

An important ruling of the London Stock Exchange suddenly became relevant to the contest. As soon as any company acquired a twenty percent share in a particular business, it had to disclose any additional purchases on a daily basis. When it reached 30%, it had to make an offer for the balance at the highest price paid to secure the first 30%. On the basis of this rule the London panel supervising stock exchange transactions started investigating the 'ghost buyers', a step that aroused suspicion in South Africa – why did a London institution have to determine the rules for a local corporate contest? General Mining (by then holding 29,9% of Unicorp shares) and Volkskas, which admitted purchasing shares on behalf of a client, appeared before the panel to answer questions, but they were acquitted of collusion. The identity of the 'ghost buyers' remained a mystery. But on 19 January 1975 a South African newspaper was already reporting on 'Genmin's great victory' after 'one of the toughest takeover battles in the country's history'.[13]

During this crucial period in the intense and risk-laden battle, in which Scholtz as managing director of Sanlam had to act like a cat on a hot tin roof, Wassenaar was on a cruise to the Antarctic. Based in a hotel in Cape Town, Jan van den Berg of General Mining did yeoman work organising buyers of Unicorp shares to eliminate the threat posed by Charter. An Italian, Eric Tenderini of Johannesburg, lent a hand by acquiring more than five percent of Unicorp shares via his London family trust and the Johannesburg investment group Unisec, of which he was managing director. Wassenaar acknowledged his 'excellent role in this battle'. After the 'battle' Van den Berg's colleagues at General Mining presented him with a small replica of Union Corporation's coat of arms. According to Wassenaar, De Villiers was 'outraged' by this gesture as he allegedly refused to recognise the key role Van den Berg had played.[14]

The overseas 'raid' was so successful that by 25 January 1975 Goldfields conceded victory – a narrow one to be sure, for it needed just 51% to gain control and the General Mining camp held a bare 49,87%, but victory nonetheless. With the help of Rupert, who via his agent had bought about 8,65% of Unicorp's shares, General Mining had gambled and won. With reference to these events, Rupert wrote much later, on 30 March 1982, to 'The Chairman and Directors' of Sanlam: 'During 1975, in response to an urgent request by Dr Wassenaar, we risked more than DM100 million to rescue your company from a situation in which, with a very big investment, it would have been the prisoner of another mining house. In the process we ran the risk that had our rescue attempt failed, we would have found ourselves in a similar fix. We tested our overseas credit to the hilt in order to assist you.'

On 25 January 1975 it was generally accepted that General Mining, with the assistance of Rupert, had won the contest. When Wassenaar returned to Cape

Town from his South Pole holiday in February it was all over – bar the footing of the bills. Sanlam's account at Volkskas was overdrawn, and there was the DM100 million debt for the credit Rupert had arranged. At this point De Villiers proposed to Wassenaar that Sanlam offer Rupert a 25% holding in Federale Mynbou, General Mining's parent company. That would give Rembrandt two directors on the board of Federale Mynbou and considerable leverage. A 'material condition' of the agreement between Sanlam and Rembrandt was that the debt to Rembrandt (R36,5 million) would be paid in Deutschmark, free of charge, at Deutsche Bank in Frankfurt or whatever bank Federale Mynbou appointed. The agreement also stipulated that Sanlam would support the appointment of two Rembrandt representatives to the board in future, 'provided Rembrandt's shareholding does not drop below twenty percent of the issued capital of Mynbou'. Sanlam wanted an undertaking that Rembrandt would 'respect the controlling position of the Sanlam Group' in Federale Mynbou, but this controversial clause was eventually scrapped from the agreement. Rupert related later that he had told De Villiers: 'I'm not signing that'.[15]

The proposed clause highlighted an issue that would emerge later in the feud between Rembrandt and Sanlam: Sanlam's leaders wanted a strong controlling position. In fact, Sanlam also wanted to secure the first right of refusal on any shares of Federale Mynbou that any member of the Rembrandt Group or its nominee might wish to sell – but without Rembrandt being granted the same right in return. On account of the substantial amount of DM100 million Rembrandt had to invest, this clause was not acceptable to Rupert, and he asked for it to be deleted. As an annexure to the contract, the following concluding paragraph was issued as a press statement: 'The companies welcome the opportunity for mutual cooperation that will be created by this new and powerful partnership.' In 1981-82, these words would be at the heart of the dispute between Rupert/De Villiers and Wassenaar/Du Plessis.

Initially there was a good understanding between Rembrandt and Sanlam, although it took Rembrandt a while to accept the offer made to them during February/March 1975. The contract was eventually signed at Fleur du Cap on 11 November 1975.

In December 1979 the merger between General Mining and Unicorp was formalised and General Mining Union Corporation Ltd – Gencor – was floated in 1980, with Wim de Villiers as executive chair and Unicorp's Ted Pavitt remaining as vice chairman. The controlling interest in Gencor was held by Federale Mynbou, in which Sanlam and Rembrandt between them held a 71% stake. As a result, Sanlam became one of the largest conglomerates in the country after Anglo American and Old Mutual.

As far as Rupert was concerned, Rembrandt's relationship with Sanlam was a partnership based on his long-standing principles on which he was not prepared to compromise: mutual trust, a win-win situation, long-term commitment, and in particular the kind of representation befitting a partnership and conducive to consensus decision making.[16] It was precisely these factors that caused the eventual blow-up between Rembrandt and Sanlam as well as the personal animosities. Essentially four prominent Afrikaners – Rupert, Wassenaar, Du Plessis and De Villiers – were responsible for unprecedented drama, with Etienne Rousseau as a fifth important role player.

Du Plessis was emerging as a powerful force in Sanlam. Wassenaar, who had had serious reservations about Du Plessis at one stage, finally gave him his full support. According to Wassenaar there had been complaints against Du Plessis in 1979 that had necessitated an investigation on his part, but in his personal document he did not specify their nature – in any event, auditors found the complaints to be groundless.[17]

Sanlam under Du Plessis evidently wanted to put distance between the insurance giant and Rembrandt. It was a long and complex tale that left Wassenaar embittered and caused him to refer Rupert and De Villiers with a certain degree of venom in his later document about the events. Wassenaar was clearly profoundly affected by the saga. Rupert, too, spoke about the events with a lump in his throat.

In 1979 there was still close contact between Rembrandt and Du Plessis, who was involved in the negotiations between Rembrandt and SAB during the beer crisis and its eventual resolution that led to a new dispensation in the wine industry.

However, there was already some discomfort in Sanlam about relations with Rembrandt. Sanlam had a major financial stake in Rembrandt and, not unreasonably, wanted to be represented on its board. According to Wassenaar, Rupert agreed to this on condition that the director was Wim de Villiers. This condition was rejected by Sanlam as Wassenaar wanted his investment head, Willem Pretorius, on the board. Further friction arose when Sanlam wanted to market a non-smokers' policy at preferential rates. Du Plessis sought an appointment with Rupert to discuss the matter, but according to Wassenaar Rupert was not prepared to talk to Du Plessis, to the latter's intense annoyance. A week before Du Plessis requested the appointment, on 19 March 1980, Rupert had delivered an address at Sanlam's AGM, but from this point relations rapidly went downhill. On 27 March Rupert wrote Du Plessis a letter in which he expressed his surprise and distress at the proposed policy: 'The essence of the free enterprise system lies in the freedom of the individual to exercise his personal choice. It seems to me that Sanlam wants to restrict this choice.' He mentioned other contentious points: Sanlam had sold off some of its Rembrandt shares 'at ridiculously low prices' (mostly taken up by Old Mutual); it had 'frozen' his contributions to *Tegniek* (the business journal initiated by Rupert); and it had cancelled its own contributions to the SA Nature Foundation, one of Rupert's projects. He expressed his conviction that these actions on the part of Sanlam 'were connected with your fears and the steps against smokers now contemplated by Sanlam'. All of this led him to the following conclusion: 'The long-standing good relationship between our organisations has become impaired to such an extent that a parting of the ways is indicated.'

Du Plessis wrote back the same day. He found it 'a great pity' that Rupert was reacting so 'sharply' to him and Sanlam. He explained the circumstances pertaining to Rupert's objections and asked for a personal interview to discuss the whole matter. Responding in a letter of 31 March, Rupert wrote: 'You have already hurt my feelings in the past. Broadly speaking, our philosophies of life and business appear to be so divergent that it would be better to part ways without attracting publicity.' At the time of the beer negotiations Du Plessis had issued a press statement, reported in *The Citizen*, which Rupert had found hurtful. Although Du Plessis had objected to the paper about its interpretation of his statement, it still rankled.

According to Wassenaar, he visited Rupert on 28 April 1980 to discuss the strained relations between Sanlam and Rembrandt, at the recommendation of the Sanlam board. It is doubtful whether Wassenaar, who could be irascible at times, was the right person for the job – at that stage he was already in the Du Plessis camp. As could be expected, he did not do much to defuse the situation. Rupert reportedly said to him during the conversation: 'He (Du Plessis) is going to break Sanlam.' Rupert himself said he had told Wassenaar: 'Be wary of Du Plessis.' According to Rupert he had warned Wassenaar because the ailing Trust Bank continued to struggle despite attempts under Du Plessis's leadership to salvage the situation. He added: 'I did not trust him with financial management.'[18]

Rupert related an interesting tale to illustrate the good relationship that had developed between Rembrandt and Sanlam over the years. When Trust Bank ran into difficulties, Wassenaar wanted Volkskas, in which Sanlam had a substantial shareholding, to take over the bank. Rupert discussed this with his friend Jan Hurter of Volkskas, with whom he had shared anxious moments years before as they sat waiting for confirmation of Sanlam's financial assistance during Rupert's bid to take over Rothmans. Hurter did not want Trust Bank, however, which upset Wassenaar. In order to salvage the situation, Rembrandt, which had acquired a twenty percent stake in Volkskas in 1977, bought out Sanlam's shareholding in Volkskas.

Despite this history of cooperation, Wassenaar reported to his board on 28 April after his conversation with Rupert: 'Dr Rupert is looking for arguments against Sanlam and we would be making a mistake if we continue considering him a friend of Sanlam, or Rembrandt a well-disposed organisation.'

De Villiers had also been making his own moves. Even before 1980 he had persuaded Wassenaar to help him secure the executive chairmanship of General Mining by getting the then chairman William Coetzer to step down. According to Wassenaar, De Villiers and Etienne Rousseau wanted Coetzer replaced as chairman of Federale Mynbou as well, on the grounds that Coetzer was too 'old' for the job. In his personal document, Wassenaar wrote in this regard: 'If I should have been asked to give my own view, it would have been that Dr Rousseau was even less suitable than Dr Coetzer.'

These manoeuvres were important to the unfolding of whole story of conflicts of interest and personal vendettas, which up to 1982 was still taking place mostly behind the scenes. Wassenaar and Du Plessis, with their own agenda, were convinced that Rupert and De Villiers were in cahoots to obtain control of Gencor in favour of Rembrandt. The mistrust between the protagonists in Gencor was evident from the way in which Wassenaar became distraught after a 'Johannesburg businessman' had warned him in 1981 that Rupert was intent on gaining control of Gencor.[19] By this time the battle lines had been drawn, and Andreas Wassenaar and Fred Du Plessis were pitted against Wim de Villiers of Gencor and his friend Anton Rupert.

On 3 August 1980 Wassenaar and De Villiers had an acrimonious interview. It is clear from Wassenaar's notes that he mistrusted De Villiers. He talked, inter alia, about a 'gossip campaign that had to stop', and accused De Villiers of discussing Coetzer with Rupert. He also alleged that De Villers had discussed the highly controversial question of Unicom, the computer company in which Wassenaar had a personal interest, with Rupert. Unicom would become one of the major points at issue in the dispute. The main theme of the conversation, however, was whether De Villiers had promised Rupert that decisions on Gencor and Federale Mynbou would be taken on a consensus basis. According to Wassenaar, De Villiers responded that such a question put him 'in a quandary'. In response to a direct question in this regard from Wassenaar, however, De Villiers admitted to telling Rousseau that he would resign if Du Plessis were appointed to the board of Gencor, according to Wassenaar.

The juggling for positions continued. Early in 1981 Rousseau felt convinced that De Villiers, then vice chairman of Sanlam, would not be ready to succeed Wassenaar as chairman. This gave rise to new intrigues, including a plan that PJ (Piet) Riekert should take over the chairmanship. Eventually Rousseau, on the recommendation of Wassenaar, became vice chairman of Sanlam in 1981. During this time De Villiers suffered a heart attack. According to Wassenaar, Rousseau remarked to him that 'an ill man cannot manage such a group'. Then followed an attempt to oust De Villiers.[20] But when Wassenaar as chairman of Sanlam addressed the board of Federale Mynbou with a view to securing the recommended retirement of De Villiers, he received no support – a defeat he resented.

At this stage another situation presented itself that added to the ill feeling between Wassenaar and De Villiers: acute problems around Unicom, the computer company in which Wassenaar and his son had a personal interest. In 1977 Wassenaar and Fred Street had formed Unicom, a Johannesburg company that focused on the rapidly growing market in mini computers. The managing director was Dirk Wassenaar, son of the chairman of Sanlam who was also the most influential director of General Mining. General Mining held one third of the shares, the Wassenaar family 25%, and Street close on 42%. When the company failed to make the grade, relations between the founding partners soured to such an extent that Wassenaar wrote Street a painful letter on 12 September 1979: '. . . it was your idea to get Genmin in . . . I swallowed the bait and persuaded Dr De Villiers to take up a minority shareholding . . . I am ashamed that I have dragged Genmin into a business association with you . . . on Monday, September 10, I experienced one of the most humiliating moments of my life when I apologised to the board for this. I had to do this in order to make it possible for me to live with my conscience . . . I hate to be deceived by a man I called a friend, as much as anybody hates to be bitten by his own dog. I hope we shall never see one another again . . .'[21]

Street left the country and because Wassenaar could not afford to buy out his shares, General Mining came to the rescue and ended up with a 75% shareholding. But Unicom continued to struggle despite Wassenaar involving closely himself in the affairs of the company, even to the extent of becoming embroiled in disputes with an official of General Mining he suspected of intentionally sabotaging potential contracts for Unicom. As Unicom continued to go downhill, several top people at General Mining remained supportive of Wassenaar, particularly out of gratitude for the strong support he had given them in the 1975 takeover and also out of sympathy for the fact that he faced personal bankruptcy. The amounts at issue were not substantial from the perspective of a large corporation, but General Mining was concerned about pumping shareholders' money into another company as well as the principle that these matters had not been thrashed out at board level. Relations with De Villiers, initially friendly, worsened after Wassenaar had reproached De Villiers harshly, according to witnesses: 'I rescued you, I made you, made you the boss of Gencor. What have you done for me?' This occurred at the onset of the detailed talks about the final merger with Union Corporation, at the same time as concerns were growing about the implications of Unicom.

By 1981 Gencor decided it could no longer support Unicom financially and proposed liquidating it. The news infuriated Wassenaar, who threatened to 'break' De Villiers. He went to see Rupert. His son was in trouble, he said, and De Villiers no longer wanted to help. According to Rupert, Wassenaar was 'enraged' about this. He tried to make Wassenaar see reason. De Villiers could not be expected to continue committing Gencor financially and he would not attempt to influence him to do so. But if Wassenaar gave him a fortnight, he would see what he could do to help. By then it was too late to salvage either Unicom or the relationship between Wassenaar and De Villiers. Against this background, Huberte Rupert commented: 'Wassenaar had a blind spot.'[22] Willem Pretorius referred to Wassenaar's 'irrational side' as far as the Unicom issue was concerned.[23]

Ultimately, Wassenaar was obliged to accept Gencor's intention to withdraw from Unicom. He wanted R750 000, but settled for R400 000 after mediation by Coetzer – according to De Villiers this settlement was not acceptable to Gencor management, but it had been ordered by the board. 'Gencor suffered a loss of R1 925 000 after Dr Wassenaar took over Gencor's interests for R1 . . .', De Villiers reported.[24]

On 4 March 1982 De Villiers submitted a comprehensive proposal for a restructuring of Gencor to the board of Federale Mynbou, including the appointment of six full-time managers of Gencor to the board. Wassenaar and Du Plessis interpreted this as another move to give Rupert control of Gencor, whereas they wanted to entrench Sanlam's position. Accordingly Du Plessis, seconded by Wassenaar, proposed at the start of the meeting that one of their men, Marinus Daling, be appointed director of Federale Mynbou. The proposal caused an uproar. In the course of the discussions Du Plessis stated that Sanlam could not agree to the appointment of so many manager-directors unless Gencor's articles of association were amended to make it just as easy for Sanlam to get rid of directors as it would be to appoint them if De Villiers's proposal were accepted. In the end it was decided, as a compromise, to leave both proposals for Federale Mynbou's April board meeting.

Meanwhile Dirk Hertzog, Rembrandt's representative on the Federale Mynbou board, wrote a letter to Federale Mynbou's secretary on 9 March 1982, asking that the 'augmentation' of Gencor's board 'should go ahead without delay'. Wassenaar interpreted this as proof of Rembrandt's intention to acquire control via a management-friendly board. Hertzog sent a copy of his letter to Du Plessis, expressing the hope that he 'could expedite the matter' – to Du Plessis and Wassenaar this letter was like a red rag to a bull.

On 22 March 1982 Hertzog wrote directly to Du Plessis after he had received certain documents from De Villiers. According to these, Wassenaar and Du Plessis were prepared to support the expanded board with the proviso of amendments to the articles: manager-directors could be fired if they failed to comply with the will and wishes of the controlling shareholder. Hertzog wrote: 'They would become puppets of the chief executive of the controlling company.'

The subsequent correspondence showed that the profound mistrust between Rembrandt and Sanlam had turned into a feud. According to Wassenaar, he and Du Plessis came to the conclusion that they could not rely on Rousseau's loyalty to Sanlam. 'We must therefore either get rid of him at the boards of Federale Mynbou and Gencor, or Federale Mynbou's board should be expanded to fifteen so that we can appoint other directors on whose loyalty and sincerity Sanlam will be able to rely.' Sanlam's board rubber-stamped their plans in March 1982. It was resolved to nominate MH (Marinus) Daling for appointment to the boards of Federale Mynbou and Gencor; to expand Federale Mynbou's board from twelve to fifteen by means of an ordinary resolution; and to appoint Riekert, PL (Flip) la Grange and P (Pierre) Steyn to the three new positions thus created. Whether Wassenaar and Du Plessis actually believed that Rupert was seeking control of Gencor or not is a moot point. What is clear is that they were resolved to entrench Sanlam's dominance and to get rid of De Villiers.

On 30 March 1982 Rupert wrote in his letter addressed to 'The Chairman and Directors' of Sanlam that the Sanlam board should give him and Hertzog the opportunity to address them so that he could explain his position. The issue of partnership was to him an integral part of the original agreement with Sanlam. He stated his position unambiguously in the letter: 'We had . . . entered into a partnership agreement with your company and Federale Mynbou Beperk.' He requested 'politely, yet urgently' that the board should receive them as soon as possible 'in order to clear the air between us'. But he also warned: 'If you are not prepared to do this, you will have to suffer the serious consequences of public disclosure of our concerns and knowledge.'

Not surprisingly, the tone of the letter and the threat upset the recipients. Under the influence of Wassenaar and Du Plessis, the Sanlam board refused Rupert a hearing – unlike years before when he had been the first outsider ever to address Sanlam's board at the time of his first overseas operation. The board was in any case not strong and independent enough to oppose Wassenaar and Du Plessis. In his personal document Wassenaar recorded that he considered Rupert's letter 'presumptuous' and illustrative of his 'arrogance' in expecting to be permitted to address Sanlam's board.

At Federale Mynbou's board meeting in Johannesburg on 1 April 1982 Sanlam made it quite clear that it would not tolerate any expansion of Gencor's board that jeopardised its control. At its AGM on 6 May 1982 the whole matter finally erupted in public when Sanlam's earlier resolution to appoint three additional directors was passed, in the face of strong opposition from Rembrandt and Volkskas. They had argued that it should be dealt with as a special resolution requiring a 75% majority, in which case Sanlam would lose as the shareholding of Rembrandt and Volkskas amounted to 35%. However, the chairman, WB Coetzer, ruled that it was an ordinary resolution requiring only 50%. Subsequently, Du Plessis said at a press conference that Sanlam's eagerness to acquire three additional directors stemmed from its desire to ensure that Gencor would not be taken over by minorities. There was a difference between Rembrandt's and Sanlam's views of 'control philosophy', he explained: 'In the case of conflict about control philosophy the majority shareholder has to dictate the situation, and this is what the clash is about.'

When Rembrandt took the matter to the Supreme Court, it lost the case.

The gloves were off now between Rembrandt and Sanlam. The public attacks astounded financial journalists like Jim Jones, later editor of *Business Day*, who had not expected Rupert – 'normally discreet, aloof, mysterious, and not at all prone to lashing out publicly in print' – to speak out so forcefully in public. It also puzzled him that the two groups should engage in a public wrangle about a technical point that could surely have been settled in the boardroom.[25]

On 17 June 1982 Sanlam placed an advertisement in the press in which Du Plessis attempted to justify Sanlam's position and also alleged that a point of dispute with De Villiers had already been settled in 1980-81. In the end Sanlam could not get its amendment of the articles of association passed by Federale Mynbou. Rembrandt, backed by Volkskas, managed to block it at an extraordinary shareholders' meeting. But Du Plessis did not give up. Following another route, he took the proposal to Gencor, where Rembrandt with a smaller shareholding would not be in a position to block the resolution in favour of amending the articles. It was also seen as a method to drive De Villiers into a corner; after all, he was the one who had to convene the extraordinary shareholders' meeting and see to it that the proceedings were legitimate. Warning lights were therefore flashing for De Villiers, who evidently shared Rupert's philosophy of a partnership.

According to Wassenaar's personal document he went to see Oppenheimer to secure the support of Anglo American, whose five percent holding, added to Federale Mynbou's 50% stake in Gencor, would be enough to pass the resolution. Thus Sanlam had to make use of Anglo American to outmanoeuvre Rembrandt – something to which Oppenheimer consented. Other shareholders were also lobbied by Sanlam.

Wassenaar recorded in his document that, in order to put pressure on De Villiers, who had to chair the special meeting and vote on behalf of the open proxies, he put very specific questions to De Villiers at Sanlam's board meeting of July 1982. In retrospect, it was a clever ploy, forcing De Villiers to either compromise himself or to resign. According to Wassenaar, De Villiers's response was straightforward: he would act on his convictions and vote against the proposals on the agenda. Years later Wassenaar wrote in his personal document: 'After I had drawn the board's attention to the fact that Dr De Villiers held the position of executive chairman because we, Sanlam, had appointed him to it, I pointed out that we could not continue having him in this position if he wished to frustrate our decisions. I then proposed formally that we request Dr De Villiers to resign from all the positions he held in our group.'

When De Villiers saw which way the wind was blowing, he agreed to chair the meeting and exercise the open proxies in such a way that Sanlam's proposals would be passed. Within a matter of days, however, he wrote to Wassenaar from Johannesburg to say he was reverting to his initial position. The Rubicon had now been crossed. A week before Gencor's extraordinary meeting Rembrandt sought an urgent court interdict to stop the meeting, claiming that the notice was inaccurate and misleading. Wassenaar suspected that De Villiers knew about the intended interdict but did not inform Sanlam. The mistrust was massive. When it turned out that some notices had been dispatched a day late, the meeting was called off. The press statement, compiled by Sanlam but edited and issued by De Villiers, put Sanlam in a bad light and gave Rembrandt the moral high ground – to Wassenaar's chagrin. At the same time there was speculation in the press that Sanlam's eagerness to enlarge Federale Mynbou's board was prompted by the sensational 'discovery' that three of its appointees to the board would be prepared to side with Rembrandt in a bid to take control of Gencor. In an internal memorandum Gencor's financial director, Tom de Beer, identified the three alleged 'disloyal directors' as De Villiers, Pavitt and Rousseau. Their votes could place Sanlam in a minority position of 5 : 6. De Beer was of the opinion that Sanlam's fears could only be justified in light of 'Sanlam's absolute distrust of Gencor's top management'.[26] Although De Beer eventually became chairman of the Broederbond, any Broederbond involvement is unlikely. On Sanlam's side

Wassenaar was a member of the secret organisation but Du Plessis was not; on the other side De Villiers was a member and Rupert was not.

In Stellenbosch Rembrandt was increasingly disgruntled about the lack of deference shown to their chairman after the way he had tipped the scales in favour of General Mining, and therefore Sanlam, at the time of the Unicorp take-over. On 1 August 1982 Rupert acted in a totally uncharacteristic way, declaring in public that 'Sanlam constituted a threat countrywide' and condemning its 'dictatorial management'. The envisaged summary dismissal of directors was comparable to an appointment with a noose round one's neck, he said. Du Plessis retaliated immediately, saying this was not Sanlam's style and that '. . . Dr Rupert was possibly experiencing this closer to home.'

On 3 August Sanlam convened a meeting to discuss the crisis. A week later De Villiers summoned Gencor's top management to an urgent meeting where he handed the chair to Pavitt and unburdened himself, describing the tribulations of the past two years. Most of the 86 people present backed their chairman and were opposed to Sanlam, especially Du Plessis and Coetzer, who also attended the meeting. Basil Landau reportedly described the mortification to which De Villiers had been subjected as 'the most despicable thing I've ever heard of.'

De Villiers repudiated press reports about the disloyal directors 'with absolute contempt'. He asked Du Plessis directly whether he believed this, to which Du Plessis replied, 'No.' When he asked Coetzer if it was true that he (De Villiers) had been asked to resign on the day Du Plessis had expressed his confidence in him in public, Coetzer looked away and said nothing.

At Sanlam's board meeting on 18 August Wassenaar, who was now on the war path, proposed after a brief motivation that De Villiers be asked to resign from all positions he held in the Sanlam stable. With a few amendments, the motion was carried. De Villiers was not present and was given no opportunity to defend himself. Pavitt succeeded him as chairman of Gencor.

The day after De Villiers's formal resignation Rembrandt held its AGM. In his chairman's address in this highly public forum, Rupert did not hold back. Addressing the matter of Federale Mynbou, he said: 'Yesterday we learnt with deep regret of Dr Wim de Villiers's decision to resign as executive chairman of the Gencor group which he had built up over the past two years into one of the biggest mining groups in the world, and with a 45,8% increase in annual revenue. With this, the business world is losing one of the noblest and greatest among us. We had hoped and prayed it would not come to this, and we had also done our best to prevent it, but it had not been possible.'

Rupert disclosed that Wassenaar had already told him on 11 February 1981 in his office that he 'would eliminate (De Villiers) and that he would get "Dupie", (Dr Du Plessis) to do it.' He continued: 'The result was inevitable. However, a scapegoat had to be found. Rembrandt had been attacked repeatedly, even by means of full-page advertisements that cost thousands of rands of policy-holders' money . . .' He gave a synopsis of Rembrandt's assistance at the time of the Unicorp takeover, the contract from which they had required clauses to be excised 'because we wanted to be investors with a say and not just minions', and the joint press statement at the end welcoming the 'new and powerful part-nership'. Du Plessis had not even been present at the signing of the contract about which he was now making untrue statements, Rupert said. 'In terms of the contract we always considered ourselves the junior partner and were consulted about everything until about 15 March 1982, when Sanlam adopted a totally new, dictatorial management philosophy at the insistence of Dr Du Plessis. From that point on everything was different and the vendetta against Dr De Villiers intensified. Among other things, the board of Sanlam refused to grant Mr Hert-zog and me a hearing.'

He vehemently repudiated 'the nefarious lie' that was still being circulated about Rembrandt supposedly conspiring to gain control of Gencor. 'It is also se-riously defamatory to claim that Rembrandt ever wanted to hijack Sanlam's con-trol of Gencor.' According to Rupert, the disagreements arose from the drastic amendments to the articles of association that would have entitled Du Plessis to fire directors at will. Rembrandt, in contrast, considered it important for boards of controlled companies to be able to maintain a strong loyalty of their own.

He concluded the references to Federal Mynbou in his address with a dig at Sanlam, quoting from the commission report of Prof. DG Franzsen who had in-vestigated the country's fiscal and monetary policy in 1970: 'Insurers as such do not necessarily have the expertise to act as entrepreneurs in other spheres and investment decisions are not necessarily taken objectively once they become in-volved in the control of enterprises. This increases the possibility of errors of judgment when making investments and may mean that they do not necessarily earn the highest return on investments. For these reasons the commission sees merit in overseas practices restricting insurers' interest in individual business enterprises.'[27]

On 30 October 1982 De Villiers wrote to a good friend in the Sanlam stable: 'When I now see those two hands [the Sanlam symbol] squeezing someone in such a way, I accept it as the most unpleasant and disgusting experience in my life . . . As far as Sanlam is concerned, the matter is a great victory for every value I cannot accept.'[28]

A few days later, on 2 November, Rupert wrote to Du Plessis: 'We had hoped that with the victory you gained with Dr De Villiers's early retirement there would now at last be peace.' He then referred to an article about the harmful effects of smoking in Sanlam's staff journal *Die Fakkel*, which 'unfortunately indicates the opposite'. Rupert continued that the Rembrandt Group had loyally supported Sanlam for years without requesting competitive quotations for policies for the management of pension funds. With the establishment of Kaapwyn quotations had been mandatory, therefore 'we were obliged to place certain smaller policies at two other companies because their tenders had been R373 000 less *annually* than Sanlam's'. He then posed the question: 'Is the publishing of the attack in your official journal a result of this?'

Du Plessis responded on 8 November that the letter in *Die Fakkel* about which Rupert complained had appeared under a pseudonym and 'could in no way be connected with any decisions on your part about the placement of your pension business'. He invited Rupert to discuss the matter of De Villiers in detail with him 'in order to eliminate the misunderstandings that exist.'

Further unpleasantness followed when Rembrandt wanted to increase its shareholding in *Tegniek*, the business journal that had been started originally by TIB. According to Rupert the aim was to bring Rembrandt's shareholding to the same level as that of Sanlam and its subsidiaries, but Sanlam objected to the proposal. Rupert wrote in a letter dated 3 February 1983 that he found 'it hard to understand your objections unless they emanate from the fact that Rembrandt would not accept unquestioningly at Mynbou and Gencor your new policy of absolute control over companies in which you hold more than 50% of the shares.'

On 16 February Du Plessis refuted Rupert's interpretation in a letter. In his view, he wrote, their disagreements about Federale Mynbou and Gencor had no bearing whatsoever on the shareholding in *Tegniek*. And he added: 'May I ask, on the other hand, if the interview the editor of *Tegniek* requested with me and about which he was so enthusiastic that he spent a lot of time here, and which would have been published in *Tegniek* for the past four months but has not yet appeared, had anything to do with the Mynbou/Gencor matter, and if you had personally instructed that the interview should not be published?' He again requested a personal interview 'to determine whether any agreement could be arrived at'.

The upshot of the squabbling was that a new owner of *Tegniek* emerged. On 1 August 1984 the business journal was taken over by Nasionale Pers (Naspers), which changed the format from a monthly journal to a weekly financial magazine. The name later changed to *Finansies en Tegniek*.

Eventually an attempt at reconciliation between Sanlam and Rembrandt took place at Groot Paardevlei, the stately Cape Dutch mansion at Somerset West which was at that stage the home of Sanlam's chief executive. Present at the 'peace talks' were Rupert and Wassenaar, Gerhard Steinmetz, Dirk Hertzog, Louis Rive (an influential civil servant who headed the postal services), as well as Du Plessis, Tjaart van der Walt and Flip la Grange from the Sanlam camp. The meeting did not yield any results.

Rupert, who emphasised that he wished to live with an eye to the future and not remain stuck in the past, remarked about the meeting: 'As we walked out that evening, Wassenaar punched me on the arm and said: "Go on, damn you. You were the only one willing to help me." '

Yet when Rupert, deeply moved, phoned Wassenaar later that evening to talk about the incident and to tell him that he harboured no ill feelings, Wassenaar hung up on him. Reflecting on the events many years later, Rupert gazed pensively into space and continued to defend Wassenaar: 'Perhaps he had felt humiliated at having to ask me for help. Lens (Wassenaar) was a totally honest person. Circumstances played a role in it all. It was an absolute tragedy that he and De Villiers parted ways.'[29]

When Rupert looked back on the sorry episode in 2001, several of the main actors in the long-running drama had already died. Fred du Plessis (57) was killed in a car accident outside Somerset West in 1989. Andreas Wassenaar, aged 83, succumbed to a heart attack at his Claremont home in 1991, only three months after Wim de Villiers, by then a cabinet minister, had collapsed at a luncheon and died in hospital at the age of 69. In an eulogy, Pres. FW de Klerk referred to him as 'one of South Africa's greatest sons'. According to friends of De Villiers he had made his peace with William Coetzer at the latter's deathbed, but he never forgave Wassenaar.

It would eventually take more than a decade before the rift between Sanlam and Rembrandt was healed. The reconciliation was brought about mainly by the man whose appointment had initially been a point of dispute, although he himself had not been involved in the power struggle: Marinus Daling, who restored relations with Rupert. An intermediary who played a key role in the reconciliation efforts was the share broker George Huysamer, at that stage president of the Afrikaanse Handelsinstituut.

It was also under Daling's leadership that Sanlam was listed on the Johannesburg Stock Exchange, but by that time the Sanlam empire built by his predecessors such as Andreas Wassenaar and Tienie Louw had shrunk considerably. Gencor had unbundled, Sancorp (holder of Sanlam's strategic investments in Johannesburg) was dismantled, and shares were sold holus-bolus at the best prices they could fetch in a rush to have Sanlám listed on the stock exchange ahead of its main rival, Old Mutual. The sale of Sanlam's shareholding in big players like Billiton and Sappi contributed, inter alia, to the more modest position Sanlam occupies in the South African economy compared to its heyday. And when Sanlam rid itself of its shareholding in these two companies, Remgro reluctantly followed suit, partly because its minority interest had also become diluted and as a result had become strategically less important.

CHAPTER 23

Heroes and lepers

D espite his misgivings about the political direction of his country's leaders, Rupert continued expanding and diversifying the Rembrandt empire both at home and abroad. In effect, the Rembrandt Group was operating on two different tracks, one in South Africa, one overseas. This brought great advantages to shareholders. Millions of rands were also repatriated to South Africa from overseas countries, amounting to more than R2 billion by the turn of the century, according to Rupert. Confidence in South Africa, as expressed by Rupert shortly after Sharpeville, has always been and still is a characteristic of the group.

An important development in the 1970s was that Rupert intervened as peacemaker in a serious dispute between Sanlam and Volkskas, with Rembrandt eventually buying Sanlam's interest in Volkskas.[1] Other opportunities locally were also exploited, and the diversification of the group within South Africa started intensifying from the 1970s. In 1979 Rembrandt acquired a stake of 49% in W&A Gilbey and twenty percent in Legal and General Volkskas Insurance. The following year they expanded their interests to other sectors of the economy: Henkel (50%), the oil company Total (twenty percent), and the diamond mining company Trans Hex (54,1%). Substantial mining interests were acquired: Rembrandt's interest in Federale Mynbou was increased to 30,25% in 1981, and in 1987 the group acquired a ten percent stake in Goldfields of SA. Also in 1981 interests were acquired in Stewarts & Lloyds of SA (ten percent), Momentum Life Insurers (30%), Boland Bank (ten percent), and Metkor (twenty percent). The latter shareholding was increased to 50% in 1984, the year in which Rembrandt's interest in Volkskas was pushed up to 30%. In 1985 the group acquired holdings in Huntcor (87%), Bonuskor (25%), and Fralex (34,6%). A further fourteen percent in Total and 25% in Bonuskor followed in 1987, as well as an interest in Standard Bank Investment Corporation (ten percent). In 1988 the Bonuskor interests were combined with those of Hunt Leuchars & Hepburn.

The consolidation of all these interests put the Rembrandt Group effectively in control of Volkskas and Bonuskor. Furthermore, Rupert and Donny Gordon of Liberty were partners in control of the mining group Goldfields, which led to their becoming partners in Standard Bank as well as Trans Atlantic, a British subsidiary of Liberty. As a result of a disagreement Richemont, the international arm in which Rembrandt's foreign interests had been combined, sold its interest in Trans Atlantic, while Rembrandt got rid of its stake in Standard Bank but remained a partner in Absa (into which Volkskas had been merged) and Sage.

Partnerships also spread to other core sectors of the South African economy, including chicken farming. The Rembrandt Group acquired a stake in Rainbow Chickens, which was turned around slowly after a difficult period and started improving.

In addition to expanding the group in South Africa, Rupert was putting much effort into promoting Rembrandt's overseas interests. During the sanction years of the apartheid struggle, however, he had to operate discreetly and cautiously abroad. For security reasons, he tried to avoid publicity and took precautions against attacks on his trips. His work overseas spanning decades would finally bear fruit with the establishment of Richemont in 1988, a development in which his son Johann played a decisive role. The whole array of international brands with which Rupert had achieved such success had now been brought together under one umbrella.

In the 1970s, however, the international expansion and consolidation of his business empire still lay in the future. At home the political problems were dragging on. Portugal's withdrawal from Angola and Mozambique had removed the buffer between apartheid South Africa and independent Africa, and the Carter administration in America contributed to increased overseas pressure on the country. Moreover, the Vorster government became embroiled in the Information Scandal, when sensational rumours of misappropriation of taxpayers' money circulated in the mid-1970s. Rupert became aware of some of these irregularities and exposed them.

Public funds were pumped into an initiative for the ostensible purpose of improving South Africa's image abroad. Eventually it came to light that millions of rands had been channelled from the defence budget to the then Department of Information for secret projects, the most controversial of which was the purchase of publications to put the government's case.

The main actors behind a conspiracy to establish, inter alia, a new English daily newspaper, *The Citizen*, under the secret code name Project Annemarie were the Minister of Information, Dr Connie Mulder, his departmental head Dr Eschel Rhoodie, and the head of the Bureau for State Security, Gen. Hendrik van den Bergh, the shadowy confidant of Premier John Vorster from their days in the internment camp at Koffiefontein.

As front for the new daily they chose none other than the swaggering fertiliser magnate Louis Luyt, who had clashed so fiercely with Rupert in the beer war. Luyt was told that Vorster had personally expressed the wish that he should be the front for the project. Rhoodie, a slippery customer, subsequently said that when Vorster gave the green light for the establishment of *The Citizen*, he had cautioned them: 'Be careful that you don't get your coattails caught in the door.'

Rhoodie advanced R12 million of treasury funds to Luyt, who promptly invested it in Triomf Fertiliser and proceeded to organise the new publication. But they did not cover their tracks well enough and their plans started to leak out. Luyt looked tired and worried when he at last informed Rhoodie's departmental right-hand man, Les de Villiers, that an anti-government newspaper, *The Rand Daily Mail*, appeared to be aware of the abuse of public funds.[2] De Villiers at once flew to Switzerland to arrange with a 'friendly Swiss banker' to throw the *Rand Daily Mail* off the scent. De Villiers returned with a letter declaring that Luyt had borrowed 12 million Swiss francs from a reputable Swiss bank. That was to be his alibi.

The first issue of *The Citizen* appeared on 7 September 1976. From the outset the newspaper lost money hand over fist, up to R400 000 per month. Then came an even more critical development. Rhoodie summoned De Villiers to his office and informed him 'with a rueful smile' that he had just received an alarming call from Vorster. Bruno Saager, the Swiss banker who had provided Luyt with the letter about the 'loan', had told Rupert that the government was involved in *The Citizen*.[3]

Rupert, who always maintained that the end does not justify the means, was deeply perturbed on learning that the South African government had acquired an interest in a newspaper in the private sector by using taxpayers' money. On his return from Switzerland he stopped off in Johannesburg and drove straight from the airport to Pretoria to see his old university friend, Dr Hilgard Muller, the suave, level-headed Minister of Foreign Affairs. Rupert insisted on a confidential interview.

Muller was undoubtedly aware of the 'unconventional diplomacy' that Rhoodie and Van den Bergh were conducting on the territory of his own department, the domain of professional diplomats whom Rhoodie scornfully dubbed 'the pinstripe brigade'. When Rupert informed him that his Swiss banker-friend had divulged that government was ploughing big money into a South African newspaper, Muller flushed scarlet. He sprang to his feet and, disregarding his promise of a confidential interview, said: 'Wait here. You have to speak to the boss.' Once Vorster had been put in the picture, Rupert found himself having a second 'confidential interview'. Vorster heard Rupert out, his face expressionless, and denied any knowledge of the whole affair. But he undertook to take immediate steps to set matters right and promised he would respect the confidentiality of their discussion.

Rupert proceeded to Stellenbosch. That same evening Saager phoned him in a state of great agitation: Rhoodie and De Villiers were on their way to Europe to see him. Rupert immediately phoned Vorster, protesting against the breach of confidentiality. Vorster was evasive but said he would stop them. A while later he phoned back and said he was sorry, they were already aboard the flight.

The two had a hard time getting hold of Saager. De Villiers later wrote that on 18 September 1976 they finally tracked him down at a spa in an Italian village. Although he was on holiday, the 70-year-old banker, who had just emerged from a sauna, was dressed in the typical sober light-grey suit that was the mark of seniority at Swiss banks. As he listened to Rhoodie's explanation of their problem, Saager – whose name De Villiers did not mention in his book; it only emerged later in the investigation of Judge Rudolph Erasmus[4] – was increasingly wiping perspiration from his forehead.

Whatever they told him, it appeared to satisfy him and he promised to do his best. According to De Villiers, that was apparently good enough to persuade Rupert that it had 'all been a great misunderstanding': there was no real government involvement in *The Citizen*. Rupert did not discover how he had been hoodwinked till late October 1978, when Judge Anton Mostert, who had started investigating foreign-exchange contraventions, put him in the picture.

Six months after their Swiss mission, however, De Villiers was regretting that their appeal to Saager had not failed – as would have happened if Rupert's warning had been heeded. *The Citizen* was in deep trouble, its debts soaring and Luyt having to foot the bills from his own pocket, for which he had to obtain a personal loan from Volkskas. Furthermore, Standard Bank refused to renew his credit facilities for a Swiss loan of $3 million unless he submitted his balance sheets. He had to terminate the facility and redeem the loan. Within a few months his personal exposure exceeded R3 million.

Meanwhile Luyt was caught up in running battles with the equally self-important Rhoodie about who was the real boss of *The Citizen*. In his autobiography he records telling Rhoodie: 'You are a James Bond. You don't talk to me like that. I hire guys like you. I don't work for them. I don't work for Dr Mulder either, I am doing these things for nothing.' He considered Rhoodie probably the most dishonest person he had ever met. Soon they were not even on speaking terms: 'We were riding a tiger, sitting at opposite ends. Only, I found myself at the front end, having to feed it. I decided that the time had come to stop the madness.'[5]

By now the Information Scandal was sending shock waves through the country. The one-man commission of inquiry of Judge Mostert uncovered damning evidence of misuse of public money. A new judicial commission headed by Judge Rudolph Erasmus of the Free State Supreme Court eventually described the Department of Information as a mare's nest of clandestine operations, with secrecy as a 'Judas cloak' for anyone who wanted to steal, cheat or engage in any kind of chicanery. Vorster had already disbanded the department, but it was too late.

In the midst of the growing crisis Rupert's old friend and business associate, State President Nic Diederichs, died in office. Rupert paid a moving tribute to him at the memorial service in Bloemfontein on 26 August 1978. Starting his address in English before the international audience that included several diplomats, he said: 'Moral man is sometimes privileged to leave imprints – footprints, hand-prints, voice prints and man-prints. Our beloved President Nicolaas Diederichs, likewise, leaves an imprint – a "man-print". A man-print of great culture and great humility.' He elaborated on Diederichs's extensive cultural interests as well as his respect for the customs of Africans and their respect for older people. In his high office Diederichs had remained the beloved, humble servant of all his people – a friend to all, an enemy to none.

At the funeral John Vorster looked haggard. Three days later he was admitted to hospital for observation. He resigned as prime minister, and on 28 September 1978 was succeeded as NP leader by PW Botha. Botha, who promised 'clean administration' and had warned South Africans at Upington to 'Adapt or die', took office as the country's seventh prime minister. Vorster was subsequently inaugurated as state president. Connie Mulder, Minister of Information, who had lied to parliament about state funding of *The Citizen*, resigned from the cabinet on 7 November ahead of the first report of Judge Erasmus (who had been appointed by Botha), which was issued on 6 December.

The chairman of *The Citizen*, Hubert Jussen, testified before the Erasmus commission that he had been informed on 8 November, the day after Mulder's resignation, that the newspaper would no longer receive any government funding. Desperate for R400 000 to keep it in print for one more month, Jussen approached various business leaders, Rupert among them. 'I wouldn't touch it with a bargepole,' Rupert told him. When Jussen spoke to his wife about his problems, she responded angrily: 'Now you're sitting here like a blasted Dutchman and you're trying to rescue the country. Name one Afrikaner who will give the money and say go and rescue it – not one!' She then personally lent him the R400 000.[6]

Vorster, who had boasted of taking three steps forward and two steps back in order to at least gain one, resigned a few months afterwards. Judge Erasmus's second report did not absolve Vorster from blame as his first had done, and the former premier and state president disappeared from the political scene, the Information Scandal having tarnished his reputation. In the increasingly difficult times he could not provide decisive leadership, and he was probably the one leader of South Africa who had to be kept afloat by motions of confidence in the NP caucus and cabinet.

Luyt repaid the 'loan' government had provided for the establishment of *The Citizen* with a cheque for R10 118 000. Rhoodie, who had fled the country, was extradited from France, convicted on five charges of fraud and theft, and received an effective jail sentence of six years. He successfully appealed against his conviction and sentence, however, and lived a free man in Atlanta, Georgia, in the USA till his death.[7]

The entire episode did not serve to increase Rupert's confidence in politicians. He referred to his experiences with politicians when addressing the junior congress of the Afrikaanse Handelsinstituut in 1979:

'When I wanted to enter into a partnership for economic development with the coloureds, the then prime minister (Verwoerd) threatened that he would subvert our plans. Then the state established the Bantu Development Corporation on condition that no white person participated. After ten years of frustration it was decided in 1959 that whites could get involved on an agency basis. In 1974 it was realised that this plan also did not work well enough, and a kind of triangular partnership was allowed. Now it is being accepted for the first time that full partnership is the only way to ensure growth.'

This speech followed on two important developments since 1976, when the revolt of black youth had shaken the country and raised serious concern in the business sector. Rupert became a major driving force behind both the Urban Foundation and the Small Business Development Corporation, which aimed to improve the living conditions of urban blacks on the one hand, and create jobs through the establishment of small businesses on the other. The business sector and the government exchanged ideas at two large joint conferences, the Carlton conference and the Good Hope conference, and Rupert participated actively in both (see chapter 21).

In 1981 Rupert's opposition to excessive regulation came strongly to the fore at a conference of business people and political leaders: 'We have too much bureaucracy, too many administrative laws and regulations. For every new act put on the statute book, parliament should scrap at least seven.' In the same year he again advocated the abolition of black communal land ownership so that black farmers could be allowed to own and farm their individual piece of land. If there were no private land ownership in the homelands and 99-year leasehold was granted in Soweto and other urban areas, 'every enterprising black youth would head for the cities', he told a Rembrandt AGM. On the same occasion he pointed out that influx control could be blamed as much on British colonialism as on Afrikaner nationalism. The first legislation dealing with influx control had been instituted by Sir George Grey's administration in 1857. The Afrikaners also could not carry the sole blame for apartheid, he continued. He referred to Dr David Welsh's book *The roots of segregation,* which showed that the precursor to apart-heid had been the system implemented by Theophilus Shepstone in Natal.[8]

In the meantime South Africa had become increasingly isolated international-ly on account of apartheid. The domestic political situation deteriorated and the writing was on the wall for the old dispensation. At the same time resistance to reform and renewal was growing in extreme right-wing circles, directed in par-ticular against PW Botha's notions of 'healthy power sharing'. In 1982 the NP split, with a grouping to the right that wanted to preserve Verwoerdianism un-der Andries Treurnicht, the former Dutch Reformed minister who aspired to fol-lowing a path similar to that of DF Malan, from the pulpit to a newspaper editor and then prime minister.

Against the background of these turbulent events Rupert delivered one of the strongest speeches in which he spelled out his beliefs about the political direc-tion South Africa should take. His address to the Johannesburg Afrikaans Cham-ber of Commerce on 21 October 1981 was in many respects a personal manifesto of peaceful progress, again inspired by his philosophy of partnership.

He analysed Afrikaner history in terms of three treks, all three in search of freedom. The first was to escape from the Dutch East India's monopolistic politi-cal and economic control of the settlement at the Cape in the 17th century. More than a century later came the second: the Great Trek to the interior, when people of Dutch origin wanted to get away from British imperial rule. This put them into contact with black peoples further north, leading to both treaties and armed conflict. British imperialism eventually clashed with the Boer Republics that had been established, and two wars of liberation were fought against the British em-pire. Thus the Afrikaners were the first freedom fighters of the twentieth century in southern Africa. They lost their struggle for freedom and South Africa became a union.

The trek to the interior of South Africa was completed within the union with the migration of Afrikaners to the cities, especially during the Depression of the 1930s. 'In the cities,' Rupert said in 1981, 'the character of the Afrikaner was shaped further. Here Afrikaners consolidated and increased their economic power, and later also their political power.'

The second trek culminated in the Afrikaners' mobilisation of political power, embodied in the NP's takeover of the reins of government in 1948. Within apartheid, a laager was then created behind laws and regulations to protect white people in general and Afrikaner political hegemony in particular. Pressure on the system of apartheid, from inside as well as outside the country, triggered the third trek. Unlike the first two, said Rupert, it was not a physical migration: 'It is a mental trek – away from discrimination – towards participation in freedom by all population groups.'

Rupert's appeal was one among many voiced by concerned South Africans in the 1980s. Such appeals did not have the desired effect, however, despite Botha's initiatives to amend the Constitution, whereby a tricameral (white, coloured and Indian) parliament was created and he himself became the executive state president. On 16 March 1984 Botha and Mozambique's Pres. Samora Machel signed the Nkomati Accord, a treaty that was expected to lead to greater détente between South Africa and its neighbouring states.

By September 1984, however, a renewed black nationalist and revolutionary onslaught erupted in South Africa. With the help of ANC underground cells, black townships were made ungovernable. Images of soldiers imposing order as well as gruesome 'necklace' murders and violent resistance were shown for months on end on TV screens worldwide. South Africa found itself in an economic and political vice. Trade sanctions had been taking a toll all along. Now there were attempts to impose financial sanctions.

In January 1985 Rupert hosted a dinner at Fleur du Cap for Sen. Edward Kennedy, youngest brother of Pres. John F Kennedy of the US. In a letter to Kennedy he warned him against the consequences of disinvestment in South Africa. He had interrupted his holiday to meet Kennedy because, he said, he vividly remembered his brother Bobby's visit to his home and their intimate conversation twenty years before. To his dismay, Kennedy had followed the same route on his visit as that of Meg Greenfield of *The Washington Post*. Instead of a trip to the exciting new city of Mitchells Plain (outside Cape Town), Kennedy saw only Crossroads (a squatter camp). 'Some of my compatriots take pleasure in only revealing our horrors and none of our achievements.'

In his letter to Kennedy he admitted that there were some inhumane slums, but few countries in the world could claim that they had no slum areas. 'We are doing our best. The proof is that many millions vote with their feet for our troubled society by crossing our borders in search of jobs and food.' He pointed out that for three decades he had been advocating a new approach to the problems of the developing world in the form of fully-fledged business partnerships with local populations rather than one-off donations. 'If you want to do a good deed for the world,' he wrote, 'positive advice to your countrymen to invest actively in partnership with the blacks in Africa and to transfer skills will be of far greater benefit to everyone than all the negative advice to disinvest. That simply leads to a vacuum that will be filled by others.'

Rupert concluded with an outline of what the Small Business Development Corporation was doing to assist mainly black entrepreneurs. 'We shall continue doing so, for our future lies here in Africa!'[9]

Against the background of violence and threats of sanctions, rumours abounded that the Botha government was contemplating radical reforms. Great expectations built up around the so-called Rubicon speech Botha was due to deliver on 15 August 1985 at the Natal NP congress in Durban, fuelled, inter alia, by the Minister of Foreign Affairs Pik Botha, who went to Europe to inform governments about it. Newspapers reported that 'real negotiations' were in the offing and that full power sharing, with full citizenship for all, would follow.

In the event, this much-vaunted speech turned out to be a damp squib. Botha came across as being very aggressive, but he did repudiate a fundamental concept of apartheid by promising that black homelands that did not want independence would be permitted to remain part of South Africa. Afterwards, it was widely speculated that Botha's original speech had been amended by certain conservative members of cabinet because they considered it 'too daring'. Rupert, who along with Louis Rive and Wim de Villiers in the private sector had been consulted ahead of the occasion, confirmed this. His intelligence network informed him that one of the main objectors had been FW de Klerk, at that time the conservative leader of the Transvaal NP, who threatened that his caucus would rebel if Botha did not amend the proposed speech.

By this time Rupert's appeals to his compatriots were becoming even more urgent. In a speech to the Institute of Marketing and Management on 29 September 1985 he declared: 'Do not embalm the corpse of apartheid, bury it. If you need to jump from cliff to cliff over an abyss, you can't do it step by step.' In a press interview he quoted the Swiss warrior-theologian Huldrych Zwingli: 'For God's sake, do something brave!'[10]

Despite his strong views he turned down an invitation to accompany other businesspeople on a trip to meet leaders of the then banned ANC. In 1985, a small delegation headed by Gavin Relly of Anglo American held talks in Lusaka, Zambia, with an ANC group led by Oliver Tambo. Rupert said subsequently that he had no objections to the meeting, but warned that it could be counterproductive 'if it is not realised that differences do exist'. He also objected to 'the dogma of violence', probably with reference to the ANC's guerrilla campaign.[11]

The Rubicon speech triggered worldwide reaction. The rand dropped to unprecedented levels – eventually as low as 36 American cents. Money fled the country and foreign banks, with Chase Manhattan at the forefront, started withdrawing credit facilities. The government was obliged to negotiate a debt moratorium. In an attempt to avert the danger of financial sanctions, Rupert was asked to identify a foreign mediator and introduce him to the government. He contacted the Swiss banker Fritz Leutwiler, who, with the assent of 28 creditor banks as well as the South African government, took on the task of mediation.

At a meeting in Zürich on 20 November 1985 a deeply concerned Leutwiler told Rupert that unless South Africa embarked on major reforms he would have to pull out: he did not want to be known as an apologist for apartheid. He also pointed out the very real risk that foreign banks could confiscate South African state and parastatal assets abroad. The very next day Rupert personally conveyed Leutwiler's message to Botha. At a second meeting with Botha the following day he and a group of businessmen informed the president about their conference with American business leaders in London ten days before.

Early in 1986 Leutwiler visited South Africa. On 10 January, the day before Leutwiler was due to see Botha at his holiday home at the Wilderness in the southern Cape, Rupert had a meeting with him in Pretoria. He gave the Swiss mediator press cuttings of Botha's speeches during 1985 and Harry Oppenheimer's commendations of Botha's reforms.

Fourteen days later Rupert sent a six-page private letter to 'Highly esteemed President Botha'.[12] He wrote in response to the two meetings with Botha in Pretoria, and repeatedly raised the issues about which Leutwiler was deeply concerned. It was probably the most important and meaningful letter Rupert ever wrote to a politician. Abandoning his customary diplomatic approach, he stated bluntly that the November meetings with Botha had left him with the following conclusion: firstly, that Botha's attitude was one of 'rather to be poor than to yield', and secondly, 'that you were not prepared to say that you would renounce apartheid.' He devoted four pages to refuting these two premises: 'If I understood you correctly, I am deeply concerned about this attitude.'

Rupert's frustration with Botha's obduracy and political stubbornness radiated from the letter. His patience with the leaders of the then government had evidently run out.

He emphasised unemployment as 'the biggest cause for concern – fertile ground for intimidation and subversion', and pointed out that the Economic Advisory Board's estimated 5,5% growth rate to provide employment for a growing population had not been maintained for some years. The national debt had escalated from R2,7 billion in 1970 (when gold was trading at one tenth of the current price) to R60 billion in 1985. And inflation, which he had already described as Public Enemy Number One in a lecture twelve years earlier, was more rampant than ever – the highest since 1920, when it had triggered rebellion among white workers on the Reef in 1921. The value of the rand had dropped through the floor, dampening any hopes of foreign investment. The state was unable to pay its debts. Inflation was eroding the savings of the solid middle class. The country was drifting towards revolution. Poverty rather than capitulation? With confidence in the country's currency at a nadir, it was heading for a future that would be both 'poor' and 'black'. (In later conversations Rupert often referred to a remark made to him by a Swiss banker that had always stuck in his mind: 'A government that does not protect the value of its currency turns all its citizens into crooks.')

As for apartheid, he pointed out to Botha that as far back as 1947 the heated debate between Judge HA Fagan and Prof. AC Cilliers had convinced him that 'the truth is not enclosed in apartheid, but lies elsewhere'. Since then he and his group had proved the practical feasibility of industrial partnership on several continents. Yet when they tried to do so in a venture with coloureds at Paarl in 1959, 'Prime Minister Verwoerd threatened to close the factory,' despite a unanimous resolution of the Rembrandt board supporting the idea. 'The result was ostracism, and everything that was done by the business sector was immediately neutralised by the state.' Rupert gave some examples: the establishment of the SA Foundation in 1959 was immediately countered by the creation of a Department of Information, with its flawed ethics of 'the end justifying the means'. The Sports Foundation evoked the birth of a Department of Sport and Recreation, Edesa an announcement of a State Development Bank.

Returning to apartheid, 'that word for which we have been crucified,' he posed the question: 'Is it the cornerstone of our survival? Certainly not. I believe that the belief that apartheid guarantees the interests of the white man's survival is a myth. As a matter of fact, it jeopardises his survival. Apartheid is seen by too many as a transgression against humanity – the neo-Nazism of a *Herrenvolk.*' He launched into an impassioned personal appeal to Botha: 'Reaffirm your rejection of apartheid. It is crucifying us; it is destroying our language; it is degrading a once heroic nation to be the lepers of the world. Remove the burden of the curse of a transgression against mankind from the backs of our children and their children.' He continued: 'I realise that you have to withstand the onslaught from fiery "political priests" both from the far right and the far left. I believe that you are upholding the golden mean: a sensible middle-of-the-road policy, based on balanced thought, which stands for coexistence without discrimination. I know that you believe that we have been brought together here by the Almighty in his supreme wisdom and that our power lies in our diversity to accomplish all our tasks. It lies within your power and it is your duty to free our people from rancour and bitterness, and to imbue them with hope and love for their fellowman.'

He followed this with a sombre warning: 'Should you fail in this God-given task, then one day we shall surely end up with a Nuremberg.'

Needless to say, Botha did not heed his words. Rupert's *cri de coeur*, an appeal from the heart in which he had summarised his entire philosophy of life, fell on deaf ears.

The letter formed part of the written submission Rupert sent in October 1997 to the Truth and Reconciliation Commission (TRC) Pres. Nelson Mandela had instituted under chairmanship of former Archbishop of Cape Town, Desmond Tutu. The deputy chairman of the TRC, Dr Alex Boraine, said on 12 November 1997 to Johann Rupert, who delivered verbal testimony on behalf of the Rembrandt Group, that his father's letter had been a surprise to him. Boraine expressed the hope that everyone in the country would read the letter one day, because big business was regarded as being skilful in the field of public relations. A private letter, however, could not be regarded in the same light. It is a remarkable declaration, Boraine continued, 'the tragedy being that, like so many other pleas, it was not heard as effectively as it should have been.'[13]

One of the commissioners, Wynand Malan, was not present when Rupert's submission came up before members of the TRC, but he recalled from informal conversations that it had had an impact on some of the members who had harboured certain prejudices. Rupert's submission showed that an individual and his group 'at least wanted to do something positive', unlike politicians, according to Malan.[14]

In his written submission to the TRC Rupert explained his philosophy as follows: 'I take responsibility for all those who share my belief that coexistence through partnership is the best solution to our problems. I believe that this cause has been worthwhile and in all humility believe that we have no need to apologise for what has been achieved.' He added: 'We have never done any business with any government, have not received any favours from government, nor has any prime minister or president asked my advice in the period under review.' And further: 'We have suffered greatly in certain overseas markets because of the stigma of apartheid. But, nevertheless, we survived thanks to our belief in coexistence through partnership.'[15]

In his testimony Johann Rupert elaborated on his father's and his own opposition to apartheid. 'We considered the system an immoral, oppressive attempt at social engineering'. Afrikaners had only two options open to them, however: either emigrate, or try to fight the system from within. On the maternal side the Rupert family's South African ancestry dated back to 1662, and they decided to stay and resist the system from within, in the spirit of what the Afrikaans poet NP Van Wyk Louw described as 'loyal resistance'. But the NP had seen itself as a permanent government and the critical distinction between government and state disappeared – 'not very different, I'm afraid, from certain signs visible today'. He pointed out that under apartheid all opponents of racial discrimination were promptly branded unpatriotic liberals and, of all things, communists, whereas abroad the Ruperts were accused of racist fascism. 'During these attacks, and despite these attacks, we have remained what is now called a profile of patriotic bourgeoisie, which practises 'loyal opposition'. We endeavoured to build progress through partnership.'

He recalled an occasion in Johannesburg when an eminent member of the previous government had told him in front of one of South Africa's foremost and most powerful business leaders: 'Rembrandt is not big, we will break you', and had added menacingly: 'Politics is a cut-throat business, and I mean that literally.'[16] What he did not mention before the commission was that the cabinet minister in question was Magnus Malan, then Minister of Defence, whose wife Margot had been the first company secretary of Eerste Nasionale Tee en Koffie, the all-female company in the Rembrandt Group.

PW Botha answered Rupert's letter on 29 January 1986. In his reply (which Rupert did not include in his submission to the TRC) Botha maintained he had had a 'pleasant conversation' with Leutwiler and had found him wiser, stronger and more sympathetic 'than some businesspeople in my own country who are more interested in temporary profits than in the government's struggle for stability, also on their behalf.' Venomous as he could be at times, Botha added: 'I have many good friends who advise me. I gladly listen to advice from good friends. But I tend to ignore advice that does not sound genuine to me. Dr Kissinger also warned about this in his writings.'[17]

Another chance had been lost to start moving with dignity out of South Africa's crisis situation. Stubbornness, instead of greatness of mind and wisdom, set the tone.

Despite his clashes with NP leaders such as Verwoerd and Botha, Rupert consistently maintained that he would defend his country abroad, but was entitled at home to criticise when he saw fit. 'I remain wary of governments and am always engaged in loyal resistance,' he joked. 'Abroad I shall defend my country to the death, but here I consider it my duty as responsible citizen to take a critical stance towards the actions of leaders.'

Rupert was also ready to assist foreign friends when their association with South Africa caused problems during the sanctions years. At one stage Paul Fentener van Vlissingen, the Dutch owner of Makro, a wholesale company operating in South Africa, was under pressure from anti-apartheid organisations and decided to withdraw the company from the country. Rupert, who had got to know Van Vlissingen in nature conservation circles, offered to buy the business from him for one rand and run it for an indefinite period. Then, once the situation had been normalised (significantly, he did not doubt that it would be), he would sell it back to him at the same price. In the event, Van Vlissingen said he could unfortunately not accept this generous offer, inter alia on account of the danger that Rupert's interests in Europe could become a target for terrorist activities.[18]

Towards the end of 1986 Rupert expressed his disappointment at the slow pace of progress in South Africa in an interview with the magazine *Leadership*, which put his photograph on the cover: 'I am only sad that it took so long to convince people that apartheid or separate development, regardless of the good intentions with which it might originally have been imposed, can never be a practical solution for South Africa. It is a myth that apartheid is a safeguard for the Afrikaner's survival. On the contrary, it endangers the existence and future of all.' What he regretted, he said, was 'my inability to have persuaded more of my fellow countrymen that peaceful coexistence in South Africa could best have been achieved through partnership and sharing. And that we shall not be able to sleep in peace if our needy neighbours do not eat.'

He remained convinced that a canton system was the most appropriate system of government for South Africa. 'Personally, I believe that the Swiss canton system with its maximum local autonomy is the most successful example of its kind for a country with a multicultural population,' he said.[19] He considered three cantons as probably the most practical dispensation for South Africa – rather than the nine provinces, some struggling to keep going, into which the country had been divided in 1994. But what had become increasingly clearer to him was that such a canton system should in essence be a dispensation organised on the basis of coexistence and common interests – especially economic interests.

Throughout his career Rupert avoided public confrontation whenever possible. One exception took place in 1987 at a dinner of the South African-German Chamber of Commerce and Industry at the Carlton Hotel in Johannesburg, where he was due to deliver the keynote address to some 600 guests. Putting his prepared notes aside, he responded fiercely to a provocative speech by Fritz Ziefer, the German *chargé d'affaires*, who warned the German and South African business leaders to act as 'political sentinels' and meet their obligation to reform the country's economically, politically and morally 'indefensible system'. Ziefer's speech was received with undisguised hostility and some guests, including leading

German businesspeople in South Africa, hissed, laughed, groaned, and even booed him as he spoke.[20]

Rupert, visibly upset, shot from the hip. He mentioned his assistance with small business development in West Berlin some years earlier. The German government should not bring 'false tidings' to South Africa, as Kaiser Wilhelm had brought Paul Kruger in the late 19th century, a message that had been partly responsible for Kruger embarking on a war that cost the lives of 28 000 women and children in concentration camps. Then he turned on Ziefer: 'Don't bring us bad tidings. Bring us good news.' He continued by saying that he accepted the obligation and was speaking from the heart when he said: 'We have a long history of friendship with Europe and your country in particular – but messages are dangerous.'

Rupert was given a five-minute standing ovation. Afterwards he walked over to Ziefer's table to shake hands, but an altercation broke out, in the course of which Rupert told him that Germany was one of the last countries in the world that could preach morality, citing, inter alia, the German genocide among the Herero in erstwhile German South-West Africa (Namibia) as an example. In a subsequent newspaper interview Rupert refused to comment further, 'except that Mr Ziefer assured me the criticism in his message had been directed at the German business leaders in South Africa and did not relate to us.'[21]

Shortly after this incident Rupert had another disagreement with Pres. PW Botha. Around this time the Sharpeville Six were making international headlines. Eight people had been charged with murder under the controversial 'common cause' clause for complicity in a mob-stoning following a rent increase. It ended with the death of the deputy mayor of Sharpeville on 1 September 1984 after being set alight. Although they could not be directly connected with the murder, five men and a woman were sentenced to death. (One of them, Duma Kumalo, subsequently staged a play, *He left quietly,* based on the experience.) With the black townships seething hotbeds of insurrection, South Africa had among the highest execution rates in the world. The number of hangings had increased from about 40 per year in the 1970s to 164 in 1987, a year when the USA with its huge population recorded only 25 executions. Rupert received requests from eminent people overseas to see if he could obtain clemency for the six. On 17 March 1988 he wrote a short letter to Botha:

'Highly esteemed State President
'Please forgive me if this letter should make things even more difficult for you. That is not my intention.

'I want to ask you humbly if you could not please commute the death sentence of the "Sharpeville Six" in the interests of our children and grandchildren. We should at all costs avoid creating another six Jopie Fouries.[22]

'Any reprieve should be accompanied by the clear warning – *this is the last* – any similar murders after today will have only *one* consequence – the worst.

'Our future is in your merciful hands.

'With sincere greetings

'In friendship

Anton Rupert.'

Botha replied four days later. He took exception to the analogy between the Sharpeville Six (not all of whom, he pointed out, were from Sharpeville) and Jopie Fourie. He referred Rupert to the trial judge's report and the court report of the five appeal judges, as well as the convention governing clemency by the head of state, which had been observed since 1910. 'I must say that I was deeply disappointed after I had read your letter, but it proves to me once again how the best among us are falling victim to orchestrated propaganda against our country and a Government which is trying to uphold civilised values in South Africa.'

The matter did not end there. Under growing international pressure a re-trial was instituted and on 23 November 1988, after nearly 1 000 days on death row, the six were at last reprieved by Botha. They were released in 1991 once Pres. FW de Klerk had started negotiations with the ANC.

In the late 1980s the irascible Botha became increasingly isolated in his presidential office in Tuynhuys (Garden House), jokingly nicknamed '*Kruithuis*' (Gunpowder House) by detractors. Although Botha had revoked a whole series of the most oppressive apartheid measures during his term of office – influx control, the pass laws, Section 16 of the Immorality Act (which prohibited sex across the colour line) and the Mixed Marriages Act – he also attempted to ward off the onslaught against his regime by proclaiming a state of emergency. Draconian media restrictions were introduced and the security forces were given emergency powers, including the right of summary arrest.

Botha did start with preparations for releasing the most important imprisoned black leader, Nelson Mandela, whom he received and had talks with at Tuynhuys. But Botha disappeared from the political scene in 1989 after suffering a stroke. His resignation came into effect on 15 August 1989, four years to the day after he had delivered his controversial Rubicon speech. Botha's successor, FW de Klerk, the erstwhile hardliner, forged ahead with preliminaries to negotiations that had been started tentatively by Botha. The fall of the Berlin Wall in 1989 and the collapse of the communist bloc afforded De Klerk the opportunity to embark on new initiatives. On 2 February 1990 he announced the unbanning of all prohibited organisations, including the ANC, the South African Communist Party and the Pan Africanist Congress, in an epoch-making speech to parliament that envisaged a totally new South Africa. Nine days later Mandela walked out of prison, a free man for the first time in 27 years. Mandela and De Klerk eventually shared the Nobel Peace Prize.

For the first time, Rupert could feel that his philosophy of coexistence through partnership was also finding expression in political developments. Yet he found it necessary to warn against nationalisation, a policy that was still being advocated by Mandela in his first speech after his release on the Parade in Cape Town. At a public dinner in Johannesburg on November 1990 where he presented the state president's prizes for export achievements to the winners, Rupert cautioned that any drive to promote exports would fail if private initiative were jettisoned. Without it, no meaningful reform and renewal would be possible. Attempts to redistribute wealth through government intervention in the economy would have the same disastrous consequences as it had under socialism in Eastern Europe and would also trigger a brain drain, he warned. 'Where do we find economic progress and the highest living standards today? In countries where private initiative is the fuel of the economy: Japan, Germany, Taiwan, South Korea, Hong Kong and Singapore. And where do we find the greatest misery? In countries that embraced the ideology of communism and socialism. Africa and East or Central Europe offer numerous examples.'

Rupert repeated on this occasion that he was not an advocate of capitalism, but that he knew of no better system than free enterprise. As in the former communist countries, communal land ownership was what kept Africa trapped in poverty. The Achilles heel of communism, which had conquered continents since 1917, was its impractical, unrealisable economic theories. In his Johannesburg speech he warned further that increased state control and taxation would be the surest way to strangle any attempt at wealth creation in South Africa. Foreign investors would steer clear of a country where company tax was among the highest in the world. (Since 1994 the ANC government has steadily lowered both personal and company taxes, to the amazement of those who had shared Rupert's convictions.) Finally he pointed out that, notwithstanding the worldwide failure of nationalisation, successful private-initiative companies, including the Rembrandt Group, were still being targeted by critics. In his view the secret lay in the right mix of big and small business. Strong companies with their ready access to capital and technology did not necessarily pose a threat to the economy. They were an asset, according to Rupert.

The Rembrandt Group's track record was proof of this. By 1990 its initial foreign investment of R1,5 million in 1953 had increased to such an extent that the group had been able to return over R1 000 million to South Africa, Rupert stated at the AGM of Rembrandt Controlling Investments on 25 July 1990. Although many people thought the group was primarily successful within South Africa, its greatest successes had in fact been in overseas companies such as Richemont, in which Rembrandt shareholders initially held the controlling stake. In addition, the success achieved locally with the SA Nature Foundation, Historical Homes of South Africa and the Small Business Development Corporation (SBDC) could be attributed mainly to private initiative.

In the Rembrandt's Group annual report for 1990 Rupert elaborated on this theme: 'Our experience has been that if you create opportunities for others to look after their own interests, they also look after yours. Progress is contagious and if wealth is shared, it leads to greater wealth. Sustainable development is only possible if people are given a say and are thereby also placed in a position to take co-responsibility for their own future. Development is not stimulated by the right to political participation, but by free economic participation.' One of the greatest problems facing South Africa was how to reconcile the striving for political independence with the ability and experience to sustain it economically. In Rupert's view, 'partnership – between private initiative and the state; between the formal and informal sectors, between developed and developing people – is the most effective way to bring about a redistribution of opportunities and skills, which, coupled with a dynamic free-market economy, would result in the desired redistribution of wealth everybody is talking about'. But with the difference being that 'it would be newly created wealth'.

Even in the heyday of apartheid, he declared, the Rembrandt Group had consistently believed industrial partnership and coexistence, and not enforced segregation, to be the most appropriate economic model for South Africa. In many quarters such a business philosophy had been suspect: it would lead to either integration or exploitation, it was said. The reverse was true. 'In a country where everyone is economically interdependent, partnership is the key to peaceful coexistence because it is based on trust, which is an unrivalled source of power in human relations. Without trust there can be no development, mutual goodwill, progress or sustainable peace.' Homeland development had failed because it had not allowed for the realities of the integrated South African economy. 'If the South African economy had organised itself years ago on a basis of free participation by way of partnership, nationalisation as a method of wealth redistribution would probably not even have been an issue today.'

Rupert's economic views remained closely connected to his political views, which he shared with Mandela in 1990. Mandela, destined to become a South African icon commanding respect worldwide, had contacted Rupert to discuss what could be done to achieve a peaceful transition. The appointment was scheduled for 8pm at The Court House, the mansion where the Rembrandt Group entertained guests in Johannesburg.

Mandela arrived early and they talked till eleven. In response to a question by Mandela, Rupert advised him on three issues which could be summed up cryptically as 'contain the far right; contain the far left; stop the brain drain'. A few years later Mandela confessed to Rupert that he had failed to resolve the third of these.[22]

In 1991, the year after his meeting with Mandela, Rupert stated in the group's annual report that much had been said and written in the past year about the concentration of power in the economy, with frequent references to Rembrandt. He highlighted a few aspects in this regard:

- In virtually no company does Rembrandt have a stake in excess of 50%, apart from the original interests.
- Rembrandt has never acquired shares where not invited to do so by other groups. The main reasons why Rembrandt is approached are either to prevent hostile takeovers or to enable the management of a particular company to do longer-term planning.
- Rembrandt usually appoints at most two or three directors in other boards on invitation.
- Rembrandt only gives advice when it is appropriate and welcome.
- Rembrandt has 20 000 direct shareholders, with insurance companies and pension funds holding a large portion of such shares. This means that the company in effect belongs to millions of policyholders and pensioners.

The early 1990s saw astonishing progress to a fully-fledged democracy in South Africa, hailed internationally as a 'miracle of reconciliation'. The talks at Kempton Park culminated in a new Constitution and the first democratic elections held on 27 April 1994. A week before, on 20 April, Rupert wrote a letter to FW de Klerk, who was then still state president:

'Dear Friend, I pay tribute to you! When I woke at 3.30 this morning, it was with a vivid sensation that I should get up and send you this message of appreciation.

'It takes courage to wage war, but greater and nobler courage to make peace . . . God be praised that you could step back from the verge of a civil war. I praise your perseverance, your wisdom and your courage . . . Leadership often means loneliness. Faith-inspired thinking comes from long spells of reflection in the desert. May it turn out so that in our barren, arid country we find solutions to some of humanity's problems in living harmoniously in true partnership through coexistence. It may call for superhuman, divine humility.'[23]

As a result of the ANC's overwhelming election victory, Mandela was inaugurated as the first president of a democratic South Africa, with Thabo Mbeki and FW de Klerk as deputy presidents.

Rupert developed a great respect for Mandela. 'Mandela has a humanity about him,' he said with scarcely concealed esteem for the man who in turn regarded Rupert as his 'older brother' and with whom he worked closely to realise the dream of the Peace Parks project. 'His years in prison have made him wiser and have left him without rancour.' It has struck him that Mandela had a higher regard for Botha than for De Klerk. What he appreciated about Mandela, Rupert noted, was that he trusted Afrikaners. Rupert himself expressed the conviction that 'Afrikaners and black people *can* get along. We are Africans.'

After the 1994 elections Rupert heard about another revelation that could have changed the course of South African history, similar to the earlier one about Verwoerd's apparent change of mind shortly before his death. On 15 August 1995 he hosted a luncheon for the later German chancellor Gerhard Schröder, then Premier of Lower Saxony, at his son Anthonij's farm L'Ormarins at Franschhoek. Schröder was accompanied by German public officials and businesspeople. Claas E Daun, a German businessman with interests in South Africa, made a surprising revelation in an open discussion session after the meal. According to Daun, Chris Hani, then leader of the SA Communist Party, had sat next to him on a flight from Europe to South Africa shortly before he was assassinated in April 1993. Hani, who was returning from a visit to a number of countries in Eastern Europe, told him that communism was 'dead', Daun said.[24]

To Rupert this was news of exceptional importance, as he was as sceptical about communism as about apartheid. This stemmed from his deep faith in the value of private ownership and property rights. Peoples who did not recognise private ownership could not survive in the modern world, he insisted. The San whose rock art he admired so much, the indigenous Americans, the Inuit, the Australian aborigines – they found it the most difficult to adapt to the modern world and their survival was most threatened because they did not know private ownership. For this reason, he also praised Pres. Vladimir Putin for starting to introduce leasehold in the previously communist Russia. Rupert frequently proclaimed that when the Bolsheviks took over in Russia, all that happened was that 'czars and serfs' became 'commissars and comrades'.

In Rupert's view, Hani, who had exerted a strong influence in the ANC-SACP alliance and could have contributed to a more rapid abandonment of socialist fallacies, had died prematurely, as had been the case with Verwoerd. He had often wondered what profound influence the changed views of these two leaders, Verwoerd and Hani, might have had on the country and the course of its history had their lives been spared.

In the changed circumstances of the new dispensation in South Africa Rupert was more convinced than ever about the future role of the Afrikaners as a catalyst, a role he has described as early as 1971 as one of 'devoting our energies to the upliftment of our compatriots and our neighbouring states'. In 1996 he described this role as follows: 'I believe that no other small people in history had ever voluntarily transferred as many assets as we did in our attempts to create ten republics in our country.' This was in the heyday of communism, after apartheid had become an ideology – an experiment he had always insisted would lead to failure. 'Now we have a new situation, with nine provinces instead of ten. We again have a new capital in Nelspruit, in Kimberley, a shifting of the capital of Lebowa to Pietersburg (later renamed Polokwane), new buildings, and still that is by no means where it ends . . .'

Asked whether the Afrikaner had a future, Rupert responded that survival was rather a question of grace on the part of Providence. 'But about the Afrikaners: we are among the best people from the civilisations to whom we owe our origins. We here in Africa are the most important Westerners in the world. We are the catalysts in this country. This is a message I get from several African countries. They say please, you must not be ploughed under here. You are the instruments to bring about renewal and innovation.' He also added a warning: 'It worries me, however, that governments have a tendency to become radical. Here, in history, in many places. If blacks should fail in government, they might be likely to blame the whites . . . But I think we are all too far advanced on the free-market road for that to happen easily. The fact is that the world has grown so small that nobody can do as they please any longer. All are connected economically. And money is like mercury, it runs through one's fingers.'[25]

He repeated that the new South African government should not rely on donor aid, but that leaders of developing countries should learn that there were a few simple yet essential requirements without which progress would be impossible:

1. Law and order had to be instituted and maintained.
2. A sound and adequate monetary system had to be maintained.
3. An impartial and honest public service had to created.
4. Adequate transport and communication systems had to be created and utility services delivered.

On several occasions Mandela consulted Rupert about major decisions. In July 1998 he asked Rupert and Marinus Daling, chairman of Sanlam, for their views on the proposed appointment of Tito Mboweni, then Minister of Labour, as head of the Reserve Bank ahead of other candidates such as James Crossley and Timothy Thabane, both deputy presidents of the Reserve Bank, and Maria Ramos, then director-general of finance. Rupert reacted negatively, responding that the rand would drop by 30% – not, as Mandela might think, because Mboweni was black, but because he was a politician. Financial markets were wary of political appointments to top positions that should be independent of government intervention.

The ANC government, intent on black empowerment and transformation, went ahead with the appointment (or 'redeployment', a term that features often in ANC terminology) of Mboweni. Immediately after the announcement of his appointment, the rand, which was trading at about R3,60 to the dollar in 1994, duly dropped to new lows of R6,70 against the US dollar and R11,10 against the British pound.

Mboweni was subsequently taken on a tour of introduction to conservative central bankers abroad by his predecessor Chris Stals. According to observers Mboweni derived much benefit from the visits.

Rupert was equally dubious about Finance Minister Trevor Manuel's introduction of a capital gains tax, which, while offering a minimal return to the treasury and was a difficult tax system to administer according to experts, put another damper on foreign investment.

In a country such as South Africa with a currency declining in value, he observed, a foreign investor investing here with a strong currency would have to deal with being taxed on shrinking returns in terms of his initial investment. 'Beggars can't be choosers,' he warned.

By and large, however, the new South Africa was vindicating some of Rupert's most cherished principles, one of which was his long-standing belief that strength lies in diversity. The subcontinent's diversity of flora and fauna, cultures, human talents and skills was its greatest resource, with the strength to be found in diversity also finding expression in Rembrandt's business philosophy. 'Rembrandt strives as catalyst to exploit this source of power in partnership with the communities of southern Africa to our mutual benefit.' In 1981 Rupert pointed out in his book *Prioriteite vir medebestaan* (Priorities for partnership) that the motto on South Africa's then shield of arms, *Ex Unitate Vires*, was translated as 'Unity is strength', or sometimes 'Unity creates strength'. He continued: 'and that is so, but strength does not lie in similarity. I believe that our true strength lies in diversity. Laminated wood is much stronger than single-ply wood and that is why South African society can be built better and stronger, because we are like laminated wood. Perhaps our motto should be: "Our strength lies in diversity".'[26]

The new South African shield of arms, which officially came into use on 27 April 2002, indeed bears the motto: Unity in Diversity. This is the translation of *!ke e: /xarra //ke*, the motto as it appears on the shield of arms in an extinct Khoisan language. Rupert's wish was realised in striking fashion two decades after he had first voiced it.

CHAPTER 24

The oracle of trademarks

T he value Rupert attached to trademarks from the outset was the key to the business success he was to achieve internationally, when he gained control of some of the world's best-known firms with time-honoured trademarks. The vision that led to crown jewels like Cartier, Alfred Dunhill, Vacheron Constantin, Van Cleef & Arpels, Montblanc, Baume & Mercier, Piaget and Chloé being added to the Rembrandt empire had been inspired above all by his aim to expand and fortify his group with world-famous trademarks.

His intimate knowledge of marketing and almost uncanny marketing instinct contributed to his success in this regard. For decades, Rupert personally approved virtually all labels, packaging, advertisements and publicity material of the Rembrandt Group. Nothing appeared on the market if it had not first been scrutinised by him.

In 1988 Rembrandt's overseas interests were amalgamated in Richemont, a Swiss company listed on the stock exchanges of Johannesburg and Zürich that owed its establishment primarily to the initiative and drive of Rupert's son Johann. The new company comprised some of the mainstay tobacco interests as well as illustrious luxury goods. By that time Rupert's group had, via Rothmans International, direct investments in Cartier, Piaget and Baume & Mercier as well as indirect investments in Dunhill, Montblanc and Chloé. Rothmans had gradually been expanding the luxury goods interests they initially ran under the Dunhill trade name.

A golden thread of tradition ran through most of the luxury brands that found a new home under the Richemont umbrella.[1] Some of these prestigious trade names had been in decline before the Ruperts took them over and revived their internationally known products.

The heavyweight among these legendary names is still Cartier, the renowned firm of jewellers in which Rupert became involved in the early 1970s. The Les Must de Cartier boutiques and Cartier were merged in 1981; the new chairman of Cartier International was Alain Dominique Perrin, who was later also appointed chief executive officer of Richemont. In 1982 Joseph Kanoui's wife Micheline took charge of Cartier's jewellery design, a position held for 40 years by the legendary Jeanne Touissaint famed for her sixth sense of taste, 'goût Touissaint'.[2] In 1993

Cartier's Joseph Kanoui became head of Richemont's luxury branch, Vendôme. By the turn of the century Cartier was responsible for more than half of Richemont's business and employing about a third of its 15 000-strong work force.

Among the trademarks under Richemont the one with the longest history is Vacheron Constantin, the oldest Swiss watchmaker still in operation, which was founded in 1755. Vacheron Constantin's oldest trademark registration, for watches and watch holders, dates from 20 December 1880, barely two months after the first Swiss trademark registration had been filed by Theodore Ermatinger. (England, however, had stolen a march on the Swiss as far as trademarks were concerned: the first English trademark to be registered was for Bass & Co.'s Pale Ale in 1876.[3])

Another early watchmaker in the Richemont stable is Piaget, a Swiss family business that had started manufacturing precision watches in La Côte aux Fées near Geneva in 1874 – later models included the Protocol, Polo, Dancer and Tanagra. Piaget's motto is a saying of one of the family's ancestors: Always do better than what is necessary. The tradition passed on for generations among the Piagets symbolises the high esteem in which Swiss watchmakers are held to this day. The Piaget watch factory at La Côte aux Fées in the Swiss Jura Mountains is shared by another venerable watchmaker firm, Baume & Mercier, founded in 1830 but with roots stretching back to the beginnings of the Baume family's watchmaking business in 1542. B & M had been taken over by Piaget in 1965.

Richemont also invested in women's fashion with the takeover of Chloé, established in 1952 and situated in Paris's Rue du Faubourg St Honoré in the centre of French haute couture. The great innovation of the founders has been *prêt-à-porter de luxe* – affordable, off-the-rail quality clothing made from the best materials.

One of Richemont's best-known companies, Alfred Dunhill, was established in London in 1893. Its entrepreneurial founder was one of the most ingenious inventors of his day, with 600 patents registered in his name. Alfred Dunhill had a motto that inspired everything he did: It had to be useful. It had to operate reliably. It had to last. It had to be the best of its kind. He started off with leather goods; then came clothing. With the advent of the automobile he turned to motoring accessories. Dunhill himself made history of a different kind when he became the first Briton ever to get a speeding fine – for driving down London's Portsmouth Road at 22,5 mph in 1903! His first range of watches was launched in the same year. By 1907 he was manufacturing pipes and pipe tobacco, and later a range of luxury items. A famous photograph taken at the conference of Yalta at the end of World War II shows Churchill and Stalin sharing a sofa, the former smoking a Dunhill cigar, the latter a Dunhill pipe – with Roosevelt looking on disapprovingly. Yet Dunhill had an uphill battle in many countries, and folded completely in Canada. Indeed, Rembrandt's first cigarette machines were bought from that bankrupt factory in 1947. But it was not till the Carreras deal that the parent company came under the Rembrandt Group's control. By 1969 Dunhill was the fastest-growing brand among Virginian cigarettes with Dunhill International. The distinctive dark red and gold packet of Dunhill International, Rupert said in that year, was the simplest of packets and had taken only five minutes to design: '. . . that cigarette with its new idea is perhaps our greatest and most valuable asset for the future'.[4]

Montblanc, manufacturer of prestige writing materials, claims that its Meisterstück fountain pen is the best in the world. The Maastricht Treaty was signed with a Meisterstück, as was the treaty for the reunification of Germany. After his sensational *'Ich bin ein Berliner'* speech, Pres. John F Kennedy signed the Golden Book with a Montblanc. Montblanc, founded in Hamburg in 1908, is characterised by the symbol of a snow-covered Swiss mountain. The number 4810 on the tip of each fountain pen refers to the height of the famous peak in metres.

Trade names such as those of the luxury goods that had found a new home under Richemont's roof by 1988 were an important addition to equally illustrious names in the international tobacco industry like Rothmans and Peter Stuyvesant. The amalgamation of these names represented the crowning achievement of the encyclopaedic knowledge Rupert had amassed about trademarks, mainly from practical experience in business as his formal studies in law and commercial subjects in the late 1930s and early 1940s had not prepared him for this. From early on, however, he had sensed the vital importance of trademarks to his companies, and read as much as he could about the subject.

As far back as 1950, when he was only 34, Rupert had pointed out that South Africa 'lagged behind enormously' with regard to trademarks, a field to which his group was to pay close attention in future. 'As far as I know,' he said at that stage, 'among Afrikaans enterprises only two trademarks have been registered internationally, namely the key mark of the KWV and the Rembrandt trademark.'[5] His early practical experience in South Africa had proved to Rupert that 'patriotic' trademarks like Patriot, Landdros, Drosdy and Oom Bart did not necessarily succeed in the consumer market. Besides, he had become convinced that he had to expand internationally to ward off a price war with powerful competitors, quite possibly backed by foreign capital. In the 1940s the name Rembrandt, his own inspired choice, already gave an international dimension to his group. Keenly aware even then of the importance of trademarks in an international environment, he made sure that the name Rembrandt was registered in 70 countries. Within South Africa the group's oldest trademarks are in the liquor trade. The earliest, Collison, first registered in 1895, was still being renewed a century later. Overseas the veteran is The Empire Scotch Whisky, first registered in 1884 and subsequently continuously renewed.

In 1961 Rupert created a new department within the Rembrandt Group, today known as Intellectual Property Services, to render specialist services in the field of intellectual property protection as subsidiaries of Remgro/Richemont. These services include attending to the registration, protection and policing of trademarks and patents, copyright issues, licensing, litigation, combating of imitations and advisory services. In South Africa the Trade Marks Act protects the trademarks of 34 classes of goods and eleven classes of services against specific forms of infringement through adulteration and abuse by third parties.

Rupert gave such intensive, painstaking attention to trademarks that a world authority in this field, Dr Frederick Mostert, considers him 'the oracle of trademarks'. Mostert, honorary chair of the International Trademark Association and chief adviser on intellectual property to the Richemont, Remgro and Venfin Groups, explained as background that when trademark companies launch a new product, a limited protection programme is usually initiated in just 20 or 30 countries. 'It is rare in today's world and requires exceptional courage and confidence on the part of marketers to embark on a comprehensive programme from the outset. Imagine my astonishment, therefore, at my first meeting with Dr Rupert in his office in Stellenbosch where we were discussing the launching programme of a new product and I asked him in how many countries the trademark in question had to be protected. His reply was instant: "Globally, of course, my friend!" As if any other possibility did not even merit consideration.'

To Mostert this was a moment he would never forget, symbolising the level of excellence at which the group operates when trademarks and immaterial property are developed and considered. 'To be part of a group with such a sweeping approach to immaterial property is a trademark specialist's dream.' Rupert had explained his reasoning about the value of trademarks to Mostert in the following way: If he had to face a choice of having all the group's factories burn down and retaining only its trademarks, or a scenario where the factories remained intact but the trademarks were declared invalid, he would obviously choose the survival of the trademarks. Factories can be built up again, but it takes decades to establish the reputation of trademarks, which cannot recover easily from a sudden disaster.

Mostert pointed out that the importance of intellectual assets in Richemont/Remgro/Venfin is reflected by the infrastructure the groups have built up around these interests. By the turn of the century the groups employed more than 40 in-house specialists stationed in London, Geneva and Stellenbosch, who liaise on a daily basis with lawyers in over 200 countries (in every country where trademarks can be registered). The legal experts who look after the security of the groups' immaterial property are involved from the very start of a product's development to the eventual prosecution of imitators anywhere in the world. In the process these specialists handle more than 60 000 applications for and registrations of trademarks and other intellectual assets and some 5 000 conflicts, besides controlling thousands of Internet domain names.[6]

Mostert was also struck by Rupert's direct involvement in the naming of new products. Many of the most successful products of the Rembrandt Group owe their names to his flashes of inspiration: Rembrandt itself, Oude Meester, Stellenryck. Another example is Amarula, the name he proposed for the famous South African liqueur registered globally as a trademark – the one Rupert considered the most valuable of the Distell group's trademarks. This cream liqueur, blended with the berries of the indigenous marula tree, was developed by Distillers at Stellenbosch under the guidance of Jack Thirion. The distinctive label depicting an elephant and marula trees was registered in South Africa on 5 May 1983. Amarula has since then become a top seller around the world, especially in South America.[7]

Rupert's attention to marketing extended beyond product names. He went into the background, the legacy, the design, and even the colour scheme of every product. Various people in the group remarked on his penetrating interpretation of each brand. He could explain extensively how consumers would respond to every detail of a product's label and packaging. Particularly illuminating was his interpretation of the psychology of colours and how colours had a different impact on consumers in different parts of the world. For instance, to him red was a revolutionary colour in the cold northern hemisphere; green was the parallel in arid parts of Africa and the Middle East.

In brief, said Mostert, 'as far as I am concerned Dr Rupert is the oracle in the field of trademarks. His insight is of immeasurable value in a world that is increasingly geared towards trademarks and intellectual assets.'[8]

Pans Taljaard, who became head of Rembrandt's art department during the 44 years he spent with the group, considered Rupert an exceptionally creative person and had profound respect for his abilities in the field of design. Although he had worked abroad, including more than three years in London with Rothmans International, Taljaard said he had never encountered anyone who could match Rupert's intuition and insight when it came to packaging. They had worked together in the early years before the advent of computer graphics, when all designs and drawings were done by hand. 'Dr Rupert had an intimate knowledge of typefaces and type sizes, of shades of colour, but also of the quality of paper or cardboard as well as of the printing presses and machinery used for printing designs,' he recalled. 'I've never encountered anyone who came close to him; he outclassed everybody when it came to feel and instinct, and to this was added his knowledge of human nature and the market.'

Their close cooperation enabled him to 'read' Rupert and to know how his mind worked when it came to products, Taljaard maintained. Rupert once summoned Taljaard to London from Stellenbosch to assist with a label for an American beer, Carling Black Label. When Taljaard arrived the following day, the American marketer was waiting with Rupert at his suite in Grosvenor House with some twenty proposed designs, for which he had paid $1 000 each. None of these satisfied Rupert. With his insight into Rupert's thinking, Taljaard was able to produce a rough sketch within half an hour. Rupert, who had often told Taljaard that a word to the wise was enough, approved the design on the spot and the American obtained an appropriate label at a much lower cost.[9]

Rupert's perfectionism about the quality and appearance of products kept staff on their toes. According to Gerhard Steinmetz, a senior official of the Rembrandt Group, Rupert always 'concerned himself' with packaging. Once when he had picked up Rupert at Johannesburg airport, they walked past display cases containing some of the company's products. Offended by the quality of the display, Rupert said: 'It's wrong.' When Steinmetz replied that it was not something that involved him, Rupert retorted: 'You're involved with everything to do with the company. You see that that display is fixed. Speak to the parties responsible for it.'[10] Other employees came in for similar admonishments at times. Rupert was intent on instilling the notion that everybody shared the responsibility for the company's affairs and that an all-inclusive team effort was required.

Once he and Steinmetz were discussing new packaging. When Rupert mentioned an idea that had come to him, Steinmetz asked: 'Where's the money going to come from to market it?' Rupert, who himself remarked jokingly at times that he 'has a short fuse', flew into 'a devil of a temper' and snapped: 'If we always just have to think of money, how would we get anywhere?' According to a senior official Rupert did not like opposition when it came to his ideas on marketing and packaging. In Taljaard's experience, Rupert 'could get pretty grumpy' if plans and proposals seemed foolish to him. Officials recalled a simple point he always made: 'If I'm not prepared to buy an article myself, how can I expect anyone else to?'

Even his bitter adversary Louis Luyt conceded that Rupert had an extraordinary flair for marketing. In his autobiography Luyt referred to a report in the

Financial Mail where he was quoted as saying about Rupert: 'He's a fantastic label man as well as the biggest market innovator I've ever met' – and he meant every word of it. In the days of their partnership Luyt once showed Rupert the labels of some products he proposed marketing. Rupert put one of the beer cans on a shelf, stepped back and surveyed it. Then he put on his spectacles and went right up to it. 'Do you have a packet of thirty Stuyvesant in your office?' he asked over his shoulder. Luyt did not, but undertook to have one fetched right away. 'I want an unopened one, with the cellophane still wrapped around it,' Rupert cautioned. When Luyt's secretary returned with the cigarettes, Rupert tore the gold strip from the cellophane, went to the shelf and wound it round the beer can. 'Now, does that not look better?' he asked rhetorically. Luyt wrote that he had to agree: 'Anton Rupert's genius when it came to creating product images and appealing to markets could hardly be disputed. Unfortunately, as it turned out later, my new-found partner was of the firm belief that only he knew about marketing and whatever he said was law. This, of course, was unacceptable to me and slowly the cracks began to show.'[11]

Rupert's eye for detail was a byword. His former personal assistant Mike Botha related that when Rupert opened a copy of the book *Kuns as avontuur* (Art as adventure), he unerringly spotted the one spelling error in the prestige Rembrandt publication that was issued in four languages, to the dismay of officials who had brought him the copies hot off the press.[12] In another case a minimal change to a brand name led to improved performance, according to Jan Groeneveld, who had been Rupert's personal assistant for 25 years. At a point when Klipdrift brandy was selling poorly, Rupert asked why the final 't' of the name had been dropped on the label. When the letter was reintroduced, sales recovered: apparently brandy drinkers, at least subliminally, preferred the older, High Dutch ring of Klipdrift to the Afrikaans version of the name.[13]

Dr Edwin Hertzog, chairman of the Medi-Clinic Corporation and son of Dirk Hertzog, had served on Rembrandt's executive committee before the restructuring of the group. Rupert's attention to detail also left a deep impression on him. 'You would never get anything written by him that wasn't perfect to the last letter, and with any product he created it was always the case that the dot had to be here and the colour should be such, and so on.' Yet, said Hertzog, recalling his experience of meetings of the executive committee, Rupert was not really keen on things always being ordered and arranged with 100% precision. An official with 'a typically German approach as businessman' wanted the Rembrandt Group to operate in precisely demarcated sections: this is the organisational structure; this is the plan for the following year; this is the budget. 'Dr Rupert never worked in such terms during my time; his approach was much more flexible: 'Let's see what will happen, we shall decide when it is necessary to do so . . . He did not operate in little blocks and circles,' according to Hertzog.[14]

Rupert often emphasised to his marketers that reliable quality was the primary requirement for a brand, even more crucial than price. Yet a competitive price was important in ensuring long-term viability of a brand. An official of Distillers told Koos Human of Human & Rousseau Publishers in which Rupert was at one time a shareholder that he had often advised them 'not to be afraid of high prices'. And when Human once asked the then Rembrandt PRO Johan Piek why the group did not produce matches, the explanation was: 'They're too cheap.'[15]

A brand had to have a distinctive 'personality', according to Rupert. That personality was made up of diverse components – name, price, packaging, flavour, texture, aroma, feel, the lot. The impression the personality of a brand left in the memory of a buyer should be positive, lasting and trustworthy. At the same time the depiction of the brand name on the packaging had to be optically striking, appropriate to the product and easy to grasp. If a product had an exceptional image, like a CocaCola bottle, it should be protected and nurtured.

Rupert referred to the success examples of Cartier, Dunhill, Piaget, Baume & Mercier, Rothmans and Peter Stuyvesant as brands that were in essence the product of a personality and were sustained strongly by a personality.[16] While he insisted on continuous analysis of existing brands and improvements where necessary, he did not believe in tampering with successful brands. Wolfgang Ritter, head of the German tobacco group Martin Brinkmann, pointed out that Rupert's scrupulous product improvement was based on an important principle: how to prolong the life of a brand. Ritter observed that Rupert emphasised that the benefits of a product had to be communicated simply and intelligibly in advertisements – he abhorred sensational advertising. In this way he could create a distinctive image for each of his brands. He would never sell a product if he did not value it himself. And he warned against trying to develop brands that would cater for all tastes. A product had a specific target group, and everything should be focused on that group.

According to Ritter, Rupert declared that it takes ten years to become a good financial expert, twenty years to become a good engineer, but an entire lifetime to become a brand expert – and when such experts finally understand branding techniques at the end of their working lives, they retire and their expertise is lost to the company.[17]

When asked if he was someone who believed in advertising, Rupert replied: 'Yes, but if you were to ask me what is most important in a business, it is firstly the quality of a product, secondly the quality of the staff and thirdly capital.' He did not like the word advertising, he said – advertising is communication and one communicates one's product. 'You have to *live* in marketing. The client is king. You have to satisfy the expectations of your clients and that is where you build trust.'

The success Rupert achieved with marketing even caused one of the most re-nowned advertising gurus of his time, David Ogilvy of the global advertising agency Ogilvy & Mather, to eat his words. At an early stage in his career, Rupert had approached Ogilvy at his Madison Avenue office about marketing Rothmans in the USA. Ogilvy was riding the crest of the wave at the time – 'at 60 miles an hour the loudest noise in this new Rolls-Royce comes from the electric clock' was his brainchild – and his agency handled major accounts such as Shell, American Express, Sears Roebuck, IBM, Rolls-Royce, Hathaway shirts, Schweppes and Guinness. He admitted later that success had gone to his head. In any event, he turned down Rupert's brief so arrogantly that his guest's parting shot was: 'Mr Ogilvy, I hope to meet you again – when you are on your way *down*.'[18] Some years later, by which time Rothmans and Rembrandt had proved their mettle, Ogilvy arrived for dinner at a restaurant in Geneva. Scanning the tables, he spotted Rupert at one of them. He crossed the room and, kneeling on the floor beside him, said, 'Sir, I am on my knees and going down.' Amid roars of laughter Rupert reached out his hand to Ogilvy, who admitted on his knees that he had let a golden opportunity pass him by.[19] After that the two were friends for many years, also serving together on the executive committee of the Worldwide Fund for Nature (WWF). Ogilvy, who had described Rupert as 'a man in a million', died in 1999 in his fourteenth-century château, Touffou, in France.

Another person who regarded Rupert as probably the greatest marketing brain of his time was Georg Domizlaff, son of the marketing expert Hans Domizlaff who had helped to build up Philipp Reemtsa's products in Germany and who was considered the grand master of trademarks in the 1920s with his *Markentechnik*. The younger Domizlaff had held executive positions in Rothmans and later British American Tobacco and often had dealings with Rupert, who held the view that Hans Domizlaff, rather than the Americans, should be seen as the architect of branding techniques. In Georg Domizlaff's view, Rupert's exceptional marketing instinct was counterbalanced by a stubborn refusal to budge from an idea. Domizlaff related that at one stage he thought the cigarette Lord Ultra, the packet of which had been designed by Rupert, was not performing satisfactorily in Germany. Domizlaff himself then designed a totally new packet aimed at a younger market. When the new design was submitted to the Rothmans management in London, Rupert took one look and said: 'I don't like it.' Domizlaff pressed on regardless and in a short while sales of the brand trebled. Domizlaff, contrite at a possible affront to someone whose expertise and accomplishments he greatly admired, wrote a letter of apology. Rupert's brief reply read: 'Dear Georg, Doing the wrong thing is better than doing nothing at all. Congratulations on Lord Ultra's success.'[20]

Rupert's consistent focus on trademarks was confirmed by an article on 'The King on Luxury' in the prestigious American wine magazine *Wine Spectator*: 'Rupert has never strayed from his desire to build trademarks. He's done it in the tobacco industry and in luxury goods. And he's produced some high-profile wine and spirit brands.' The article quoted the views of Anthony Greener, former managing director of Alfred Dunhill and later chairman of Diageo, the world's biggest wine and spirits group, on Rupert: 'One of his great skills is awareness of the trends of fashion and what consumers are interested in. He has a great feel for brands and how they talk to different customers, and how people from different affluence levels and nationalities will use the products. He understands human nature.' According to Greener, on his trips to London Rupert was often seen walking up and down Bond Street and Jermyn Street, where the best retail shops in the city are located. ' He'd come back and tell us he'd seen this or that. He was excited. It was his way of keeping in touch.'[21]

A trustee of the Rupert family foundation, Frans Stroebel, gave a striking example of Rupert's feel for what customers preferred.[22] The paper manufacturer Sappi, in which the Rembrandt Group had an interest at one time, published a book of scenic landscapes in aid of the SA Nature Foundation. The cover carried a picture of a lion. When Rupert was shown the book by Stroebel he remarked that the publication was a good idea, but that people would not necessarily buy it as the cover was not eye-catching enough. Perturbed at the comment, the advertising agency responsible for marketing the book had eleven other covers designed and tested the twelve versions on customers at CNA's bookstores. Stroebel then showed Rupert the same twelve books, with the request that he should select the best ones. After glancing once at them, he laid nine aside, then selected one of the remaining three as the best cover.

It so happened that his first choice concurred with that of the customers at CNA. The other two he had selected were their second and third choices. Bottom of the list at the CNA was the original cover that Rupert had turned down. Within a year the whole edition of 10 000 had sold out.

CHAPTER 25

A sip of wine as a way of life

Anton Rupert did pioneering work in establishing the reputation of South African wines and brandies on world markets. Moreover, his international connections formed the basis on which a partnership was created between two of the most famous families in France and South Africa: Rupert & Rothschild Vignerons.

The respect Rupert commanded in the industry was acknowledged in 1996 when he was appointed president of the International Wine and Spirit Competition (IWSC), an independent British-based organisation established in 1969 to 'promote the quality and excellence of the world's finest wines, spirits and liqueurs'. Previous presidents included doyens of the wine industry such as Robert Mondavi of California, the Marquis Piero Antinori of Italy, Robert Drouhin of France and the Marquis Leonardo de Frescobaldi of Italy. Rupert was approached by the IWSC shortly after the abolition of apartheid in South Africa. He was the logical choice for the position, according to the executive director Peter Duff: 'Anton Rupert is the founding father of the distilling and wine industry in South Africa,' Duff explained, 'but our body refused to have a South African during apartheid. When the climate changed in that country, Robert Mondavi, who knows Anton Rupert well, proposed his name (as president). Anton represented South Africa as the country moved from a police state to a more open society.'[1] He was later succeeded as president of the IWSC by, inter alia, Sir Anthony Greener of Britain and Baroness Philippine de Rothschild, owner of Château Mouton in Bordeaux.

As far back as 1979 Rupert was honoured for his contribution to the South African wine industry when he received the KWV's highest award. The then minister of agriculture, Hendrik Schoeman, presented him with a set of silver wine goblets at the historic Groot Constantia estate, where the Dutch Governor Simon van der Stel had produced the finest Cape wines of the late 17th century. In his laudatory address the minister pointed out that Rupert had recognised the significance of wines of origin and estates 25 years before the introduction of the wine-of-origin system in South Africa. The interest he had acquired in the famous old wine farm Alto in 1947 and his marketing agreement with the Jordaan family of Theuniskraal in the same year were merely a prelude to what he would achieve with other wine estates in the 1970s.

No other firm had done more to change the image of brandy in South Africa than the Oude Meester Group, the minister said. The stigma that used to cling to brandy as a drink for hardened boozers in rowdy pubs had been replaced by the Oude Meester image, the Rupert image: truly the refined, matured product of the heart of wine. In his person and in his acts of leadership Rupert symbolised dedication, balance and the maintenance of the highest standards for the wine industry. 'These are precisely the qualities that the wine industry would like to identify with the civilising message of wine,' Schoeman declared.[2]

An initiative in the wine industry with which Rupert was closely associated was the establishment of the *Bergkelder* (Mountain Cellar) in Stellenbosch, a project that started after Rembrandt had transferred all its liquor interests to the Oude Meester Cellars, Distillers and Breweries Corporation in April 1965. Ambitious plans were made to construct a vast underground wine cellar, similar to the famous cave cellars in France and Germany, that would be the first of its kind in the southern hemisphere. The Bergkelder was constructed on a piece of land on the southern slope of *Papegaaiberg* (Parrot Mountain) on the outskirts of Stellenbosch. The granite of Papegaaiberg proved too soft for deep tunnelling to create the proposed cave cellar, however, and they had to settle for a temperature-controlled production cellar and a smaller maturation cellar excavated into the mountainside. But even that project was to be modified. When the plans were submitted to Rupert, he considered the envisaged buildings too costly: 'We don't want a white elephant. The reception rooms are too lavish. We don't want visitors on the premises; how we make wine has nothing to do with outsiders.' So the size of the cellar was cut by one third, and the reception area was reduced to a tasting room for internal use. Rupert also disapproved of the modernistic style of the proposed laboratory. At his request, it was redesigned to blend in with the historical architecture of old Stellenbosch.[3] The laboratory was relocated on the mountain slope with a view on the Bergkelder and included a wine-tasting room, linked to the underground maturation cellar.

The Bergkelder was opened by the minister of economic affairs, Jan Haak, in 1968. At the ceremony Niel Joubert of the Spier estate, one of the architects of the wine-route project together with Frans Malan of Simonsig and Spatz Sperling of Delheim, advocated the idea that Rupert's partnership concept should also be emulated in the wine industry between the producers, the wholesalers and the retail sector.[4] The Bergkelder's wines were matured in the cool, dark and moist underground tunnels, some in hand-carved wooden vats. Brands like Fleur du Cap, Stellenryck, Drostdyhof and Grünberger gained international renown. In addition, wines from several estates were entrusted to the Bergkelder for aging and marketing in its Vinotèque.[5]

As usual, Rupert made sure that top-class experts were appointed at the Berg-kelder, winemakers like Dr Piet Venter and Dr Julius Laszlo. The Hungarian immigrant Laszlo, appointed by Rupert in the mid-1970s, was to play a major role in modernising viticulture and wine making in South Africa. One of his innovations was to mature wine in oak casks instead of the earlier large wooden vats, thereby improving the quality of chardonnays and cabernet sauvignons.[6]

Rupert's devotion to heritage and tradition could be glimpsed in the family's involvement in three historic wine farms, managed by his children: La Motte, L'Ormarins and Fredericksburg, all in the Franschhoek valley where French Huguenots had started farming operations after their arrival at the Cape in 1688. This is where the interests of the Rupert and Rothschild families have been combined in the Rupert & Rothschild Vignerons partnership.

In 1984 Rupert and Huberte's younger son Anthonij, already the owner of the L'Ormarins estate, bought the historic 90-hectare wine farm Fredericksburg that had been established by the Nortier brothers to the north of Simonsberg, between Plaisir de Merle and Backsberg, in 1690. At that stage the farm was in a dilapidated state and the vineyards had been neglected. Replanting of noble varieties started in 1986. The cellar was modernised to comprise a fermentation cellar with some 50 stainless-steel tanks, a bottling room and an underground maturation cellar with about 3 000 wooden vats.

The oldest dwelling on the farm was a two-roomed, whitewashed cottage dating back to 1705, which had been the home of Daniel Nortier's widow Marie Vitu, an enterprising Huguenot refugee from the French persecution of Protestants. The manor house had been altered several times since that period, and Anthonij embarked on the restoration of the buildings in 1991 after their history had been carefully researched. As an expert on Cape Dutch architecture and period Cape furniture who also served as a director of Historical Homes, he could pursue his particular interests at Fredericksburg as well as L'Ormarins.

Besides the shared interest of a love of wine, the French connection became a factor in the partnership created between the Ruperts and the Rothschilds in the 1990s. At that stage Rupert was already on friendly terms with Baron Edmond de Rothschild of the French branch of the family, while he had become acquainted long before with the British banker Edmund de Rothschild, who had been involved in the Carreras takeover and became a director of Rothmans International. These were the kind of connections that led the magazine *Wine Spectator* to observe about Rupert: 'He has prospered by staying behind the scenes. With characteristic discretion, he has quietly weaved a web of business and personal connections throughout the world by using his fabled charisma and justified reputation for fairness, business acuity and plain good sense.'[7]

Edmond de Rothschild and his son Benjamin had known the Ruperts for about fifteen years by the time they decided to enter into a partnership, according to Bertrand Otto, managing director of Rothschild's private interests. Shortly after the signing of the cooperation agreement in 1997, Otto said: 'Edmond de Rothschild has been wanting for some time to do business, on a friendly basis, with Anton Rupert.' The Rothschilds, doyens of international banking and high finance, had a South African connection dating back more than a century, when they had financed the formation of the De Beers diamond company. The founder of the family dynasty of Europe's most renowned bankers was Mayer Amschel Rothschild – the Rothschild name was derived from the sign of the red shield under which he had done business in Frankfurt. From there he had dispatched his five sons to the main centres of Europe like the five arrows on the family crest.

Baron Edmond de Rothschild, a fifth-generation Rothschild and an only son, was considered the wealthiest of all the Rothschilds. Benjamin is also his only son. The family's extensive wine interests in France include a one-sixth share in the famous First Growth (*Premier Cru*) Château Lafite-Rothschild in Pauillac and ownership of Château Clarke, a *cru bourgeois* in Listrac, as well as two nearby wine estates, Peyre-Labaide and Malmaison. Among the family's numerous assets is a bank in Geneva, the Swiss city where Edmond lived all his life in the magnificent Château de Peregny overlooking Lac Leman (Lake Geneva). Switzerland was his country of residence, he explained jokingly, because 'the Swiss don't nationalise you and they let you invest where you will'. (This was with reference to the actions of France's socialist Pres. Francois Mitterand, who had nationalised his cousin Guy's Rothschild bank in 1980. Whereupon Guy de Rothschild emigrated to America and declared indignantly: 'A Jew under Pétain, a pariah under Mitterand, I've had enough.')

The partnership that was created consisted of two father-and-son combinations: Edmond and Benjamin de Rothschild, and Anton and Anthonij Rupert. The aim was to produce world-class wines at Fredericksburg, an estate with its roots in both the French Huguenot and Cape Dutch traditions, and market them internationally. The news was announced in 1997 at Château Clarke, one of the Rothschild estates in France. Eighty-one-year-old Rupert took the opportunity to attend Vinexpo, the world's biggest wine fair, in Bordeaux, where he personally manned the Fredericksburg stall, greeting visitors and answering questions about the new venture. 'I'll die if I do nothing,' he said on that occasion. 'We have a joke in our company. One day there was no work on my desk, so I started another company, and my assistants said, 'God save us! Give him something to do or he will start something else!'

A 1996 Fredericksburg chardonnay was served at a reception held at the

Rothschilds' Bordeaux estate, and greatly impressed the many wine connoisseurs who were present. According to a spokesperson from the Rupert business empire, the South African exhibiters at Vinexpo were heartened by this vote of confidence on the part of the Rothschilds.

Baron Edmond de Rothschild died in 1997 at the age of 71, before he could taste the first red wine from Fredericksburg. 'He was a loyal friend,' declared Rupert, 'and that's the best one can say about any man. He was a very generous man who helped people. It was a great pleasure and an honour to have known him. This is a very sad day for me and for his many friends.' One of the new partnership's red wines, a merlot-cabernet sauvignon blend, was named Baron Edmond after him. The other Fredericksburg red wine, Classique, is a blend of merlot, cabernet sauvignon and cabernet franc. The third wine made by Rupert & Rothschild on the estate is a chardonnay named after Benjamin's mother, Baroness Nadine. She had been an actress and model, Nadine L'hopitalier, when she bowled the baron over, leading to one of the great romances of the 20th century – among other gifts, he presented her with a fabulous black diamond necklace. She was also a novelist and wrote books on entertaining and etiquette.

In John Platter's guide *South African Wines 2003* both Baron Edmond and Baroness Nadine are adjudged top-class wines. Fredericksburg is visited four times a year by the world-famous oenologist Michel Rolland, who acts as consultant to Rupert & Rothschild and advises cellar master Schalk-Willem Joubert. Rolland has gained renown for perfecting a number of wine techniques that have served to transform wine making. But viticulture is not the sole preoccupation of the owners of Fredericksburg. Much attention is also paid to conservation and the environment. Rupert & Rothschild Vignerons became the first South African winery to be awarded the internationally recognised ISO 14001 environmental certificate, which emphasises aspects such as nature and water conservation, recycling of waste products, cost control, efficiency and a safe working environment. The process is audited by one of the world's leading certification bodies, National Quality Assurance, with its head office in London and representation in 42 countries.

The two other wine estates in which the Rupert family are involved, the old Huguenot farms L'Ormarins and La Motte, were bought by Rupert in 1969 and 1970 respectively. As at Fredericksburg, the old homesteads on these farms have been renovated extensively.

Anthonij Rupert had studied economics at Stellenbosch University, but soon realised that, unlike his brother Johann, he had no real taste for the world of big business. In 1975 he proceeded to Geisenheim in Germany, where he studied viticulture for two years. On his return to South Africa he chose to farm at L'Ormarins. The farm had been allocated in 1694 to Jean Roi, who hailed from the town of Lourmarin in Provence and was one of the first Huguenots to arrive at the Cape. As far back as 1833 L'Ormarins was producing South Africa's first champion white wine and brandy. But by 1977, when Anthonij Rupert took over, it had fallen into some decay. He took on the challenge of improving and modernising the vineyards, and restoring the old homestead to its former glory.

The lower slopes of the mountain had been turned into peach orchards. These were chopped down to make room for vineyards. Above these new terraces were constructed, where the noble cultivars are grown. At the top end of the farm a waterfall cascades from the mountain, feeding the farm reservoirs to ensure an optimal water supply to the vineyards. The flow is electronically controlled. The diversity of soils and micro-climates permit a diversity of grape cultivars yielding distinctive wines. L'Ormarins' grapes are harvested at night by workers wearing mine helmets fitted with lamps.

Anthonij lived on the estate along the slopes of the Franschhoek mountains, in the stately Cape Dutch mansion with its neo-classical gable. The original wine cellar, its massive walls restored, was turned into a wine-tasting venue and wood-aging cellar. Wooden vats, imported from France, were emblazoned with the coats of arms of the original Huguenot settlers of the Franschhoek valley. Great attention was paid to good labour relations at L'Ormarins and neat labourers' cottages and a community centre were built in the Cape Dutch style to blend in with the scenic beauty of the surroundings.

The Rupert family's third farm, La Motte, was allocated just 42 years after the arrival of Jan van Riebeeck at the Cape in 1652. In 1799 the Huguenot owner Pierre Joubert named it after his Provençal hometown of La Motte D'Aigues. It changed hands many times over the years, eventually becoming one of Cecil John Rhodes's many fruit farms. After Anton Rupert had bought La Motte in 1970, the house, water mill and wine cellar were restored and a new maturation cellar was built. When his daughter Hanneli – by then married to Hein Koegelenberg, former winemaker-manager of the Windmeul Cellar in Paarl – took it over in 1984, she organised regular concerts in the historical cellar.

Hanneli's husband Hein Koegelenberg took over the overall management of the three estates after Anthonij's tragic death in a motor accident during a storm one Saturday night in October 2001. Koegelenberg is also the managing director of Historic Wines of South Africa, which markets the wines of the three estates from a technologically sophisticated maturation and distribution centre in Montague Gardens, Cape Town. The wines of the three estates, as well as those of some other estates, are labelled there before being distributed.

Although he is associated so closely with the Cape wine industry, to Rupert the liquor industry and wine estates in particular represent a way of life rather than a highly profitable investment. This is borne out by the economic facts. The profit of the Distell Group as a whole only amounts to about 3 percent of Remgro's South African profits. If the overseas interests are taken into account, the profit contributed by the liquor interests amounts to less than 1 percent. Wine is much more of a lifestyle – gracious, cultured, traditional – than a money-spinner. As such it was part of the Ruperts' family life.

Good wine is a customary accompaniment to meals in the Rupert home. 'I like wine,' Rupert said. 'I like both white and red quality wines with meals.' When Rupert did not go home for lunch in Stellenbosch, he tended to frequent either the *Volkskombuis* (People's Kitchen) with its traditional Cape cuisine or his favourite Italian restaurant in town where a table, known as 'Rupert's corner', was reserved for him. At lunchtime he usually prefers a light white wine, in South Africa often the latest vintage La Motte Sauvignon Blanc from his daughter's farm in Franschhoek. With dinner he prefers a Bordeaux-style red, or perhaps a cabernet sauvignon or merlot.

Rupert personally does not have a wine cellar and has never collected wines. 'I don't have a wine cellar, I have a fridge,' he said. 'It's not important to me. I've never had the time to keep a wine cellar and I don't think the difference between a great wine and a good wine is big enough to warrant spending that kind of money. I don't like squandering. I was brought up that way and I attach more importance to giving than to receiving. It's as simple as that.'

CHAPTER 26

The old order changeth

T he 1980s saw both an era drawing to a close and the dawn of a new one. While Rupert increasingly focused on conservation initiatives, his business interests were characterised by several new developments. This was partly due to the loss of a number of the pioneers who had helped build the Rembrandt empire.

The first was Daan Hoogenhout, who had been Rupert's financial right-hand man for decades. Hoogenhout became seriously ill and died of cancer at the age of 62 on 24 April 1981. Hanneli Rupert conveyed the news of his death by telephone to her father who was in Port Elizabeth to award honorary doctorates at the local university, of which he was the chancellor. It was a poignant moment. Dr Stals had been dead thirty years; Dr Nic Diederichs died in 1976. But they had been older men. Daan was the first of the younger members of the small band that believed in miracles to follow them.

In a moving address at Hoogenhout's funeral, Rupert paid tribute to 'the full, rich life of our friend' who had meant so much to them over the years, and who had been afforded the opportunity by God to serve his country and all its people as a pioneer. He referred to the challenges they had to face in the founding years of the group: 'What was it that sustained us? A belief in miracles, a policy of partnership, and openhandedness in practice. Daan helped our people to pull themselves up from the mud by their bootstraps. Daan, a child of the Depression, ended his race as an international businessman of stature, and as a director of some of our country's biggest mines, banks and industries.' Rupert also used the opportunity to thank Hoogenhout's wife Anna, his 'faithful and beloved partner through all the years, as well as their children and grandchildren, for their great compassion and affection.'[1]

On 17 August 1984 Rupert's brother Jan, the technical expert who had headed the Rembrandt and Rothmans overseas operations and held various positions in the group, died unexpectedly at the age of 61, leaving his wife Ina and three children. During that year the youngest Rupert brother, Koos, who had been a director for some years, became managing director of the Rembrandt Group.

Then, on 1 December 1991, on his 77th birthday, Rupert's pioneer partner Dirk Hertzog died. He had remained involved with the group almost to the day of his death. Hertzog was survived by his wife Lorraine, who had been a para-plegic since a motor accident in 1968. She died a few years later, also on her 77th birthday. Hertzog's estate amounted to more than R9,6 million, with bequests to family members and godchildren. The remainder of the estate was divided equally among his children. He left his holiday house in Hermanus and his car to a long-standing friend of the family, Bea Nagel, divorced wife of the auditor Ryk Nagel, who had acted as his companion after his wife became an invalid.

Hoogenhout's illness triggered a significant renewal in the group: the arriv-al of the next generation. The Rupert brothers, Hertzog and Hoogenhout had a long-standing agreement that their sons would not join Rembrandt. Rupert himself once said that, although he admired family businesses, he did not trust them. He regarded the involvement of his brothers Jan and Koos in the group as exceptions to his rule that nepotism was not to be tolerated. 'They have been with the business since the beginning, and when you start with nothing, there's a difference,' he declared.[2] The situation changed, however, once his old com-panions started falling away. Gerhard Steinmetz recalled that when Hoogenhout became seriously ill, he went to Rupert and said: 'Mr Hoogenhout is not going to make it. Why don't you get his son involved?' Rupert agreed pensively, but added: 'Not at Rembrandt. Only at Trans Hex.' Thus Niel Hoogenhout was the first of the new generation to join the old guard. He eventually left for Canada.

The arrival of the younger Hoogenhout opened the way for Rupert's son Johann, Hertzog's son Edwin, and Jan Rupert's son Jannie to join Rembrandt.

Johann Rupert had started off studying commerce and law at Stellenbosch University. A keen cricketer who played a few times for the Western Province B team, he had to give up the game because of a knee injury. At that stage the idea of working for his father did not appeal to him. He needed just two subjects to complete his degree and had been admitted to write both examinations, but the university (which was to award him an honorary degree in 2004) insisted that he repeat both courses. One of the people who advised him at the time was Ben Vosloo, professor of political science, later head of the Small Business Develop-ment Corporation. He reminded the younger Rupert of an old Zulu proverb: 'Nothing grows beneath a big tree.' Vosloo's suggestion that Johann should work out his own salvation contributed to his decision to equip himself further for a business career by gaining experience overseas.

At this point he got an opportunity to spread his wings: His father's business associate David Rockefeller offered him an opening at Chase Manhattan Bank in New York. After two years with Chase Manhattan he joined the investment bank Lazard Frères, where he worked for three years. There he learned, in his own words, to work very hard, a fourteen-hour day six days a week – 'and to my surprise, I found I enjoyed it'. In 1979 he returned to South Africa and started Rand Merchant Bank in Johannesburg, having taken over its licence after Rand Bank had gone under. While on holiday in Hermanus he met his future wife, Gaynor Downie, and they were married in 1982.

In 1980, just after Johann's return from New York, Rupert first suggested to his son that he join Rembrandt. Johann told him he would do so only if the entire company was privatised. In New York he had 'learnt about all these wonderful things like management buy-outs and leverage buy-outs,' he related. 'I told my father that Rembrandt was totally undervalued and that I could show him how we could restructure and privatise the company. Then he looked at me and said: "Johann, but how can any transaction that benefits us as a family also benefit the other shareholders? Because we know more than the other shareholders. You see, at any price we could buy it would be unfair to the outside shareholders." And it was the first time anyone ever said that, said it pertinently, and it was a hundred percent correct; it was altogether the ethically correct decision. Then I decided, in that case, I would never take that hand. Anyway, there was such strong resistance against me among the senior officials at Rembrandt. On more than one occasion it was said openly that if I should ever join the company, they would leave by the other door.'[3]

This was not the end of the story. A few years later the younger Rupert's reluctance to join his father's company would be overturned by changed circumstances.

In August 1982 Rupert invited Edwin Hertzog and Jannie Rupert to join the fold. Jannie, a mechanical engineer, went into the production side and eventually became a director of Richemont SA. Edwin Hertzog, 33 years of age, a qualified anaesthetist, was at a loose end. He agreed to try Rembrandt for three years. The younger Hertzog recalled that Rupert had told him the views of his wife should also be taken into account when considering a move to Rembrandt. His closeness to the Rupert family over the years made it clear to him how important Huberte Rupert's role had been in some of her husband's decisions: 'He used her as a sounding-board. I think her role was important.'

To Edwin Hertzog, Rupert had been 'an absolute hero' since his childhood days. 'He is a giant figure in terms of what he has achieved and the value he has created for our Hertzog family is astounding – of course, my father also contributed and I have done a little bit myself recently. One can only have reason to be immensely grateful to him.' In addition to Rupert's powerful intellect and unflagging physical and mental energy, what impressed Hertzog was the quality General Electric CEO Jack Welch referred to as the ability 'to energise other people'. In Hertzog's view, Rupert 'hasn't only got lots of energy; he is also an impressive energiser of other people'. Another aspect that struck Hertzog was Rupert's long-term thinking. 'He has always been attuned to the future and not just the present.' He confirmed that Rupert preferred generalists to specialists. The reason why he liked to surround himself with people like Louis Rive (former postmaster-general) and Jannie de Villiers (former rector of Stellenbosch University), according to Hertzog, was that they were spiritually rich people with perspectives that stretched further than just the specific fields in which they had gained recognition.

'My father always said he believed a company should have only one captain steering the ship and about this there was no doubt: Dr Rupert was the captain and he had a track record without equal; my father had tremendous respect for him. He also used to refer to this capacity for work, this typical energy of Dr Rupert's – which my father himself didn't have. My father did not believe that you should work till midnight, but Dr Rupert could work and sit through nights and weekends in England and other places. '[4]

At Rupert's suggestion Edwin Hertzog and Johann Rupert were appointed to Rembrandt's executive committee a few months after the latter's arrival in Stellenbosch, where they served in the old hierarchy from 1986 to about 1991. According to Hertzog the board met once every two months, but the Rembrandt exco 'called the shots'. Serving on the committee with people who were all twenty to forty years older than him, he had the opportunity to observe Rupert's modus operandi and his working relationships with fellow directors. As chairman Rupert was by that time in his seventies, an age at which most people had retired. 'But he had this enormous intellect, although of course he was no longer so physically active, and you know older people tend to be more cautious and conservative. As my father always said: "The older people have to step on the brake and the young people have to step on the accelerator. That's how the car, the company, moves forward.' Rupert exercised absolute control, according to Hertzog: There would be a discussion about a possible investment or about donations, but nothing would happen or be decided before he had given his view. 'Then all the other views would be shaped around his or be adjusted or polished accordingly . . .'

While Edwin Hertzog had been struck by Rupert's control on the one hand, he also noted that there was a 'period of inertia' with regard to the core business on the other hand, although Rupert was actively involved in the various foundations of the group and his family. 'There were so many things where I sometimes felt Rembrandt could have played a more active role, there were business opportunities . . . But of course there was much uncertainty about the country as well, from about 1986 to 1991. People were wondering: Would things work out in South Arica? Who was going to govern the country and what would become of us? Dr Rupert could sometimes be awfully alarmist. At times he could become really outspoken and worried, or be critical of things where I sometimes wondered whether it was necessary to get so upset about it.'[5]

Jan Engelbrecht, secretary of the group for many years, corroborated Hertzog's observations about Rupert's position of authority. Before the start of board meetings in Rembrandt's boardroom, directors and officials would usually stand around chatting, but as soon as Rupert entered everyone stopped talking. Officials were expected to pay scrupulous attention to every fact, comma and full stop in reports they submitted to the board. Rupert once adjourned a board meeting after a few minutes because a departmental head had failed to correct five spelling mistakes in his report. According to Engelbrecht, Rupert made it clear that the sloppy preparation indicated negligence, and the board could not take decisions on the basis of such a report.[6]

Hans Knoetze, Rembrandt PRO and later a trustee of the Rupert Family Foundation's family trusts, also commented on Rupert's precision. 'As speechwriter, I could never mislead him with partially correct facts. He is particularly attuned to language and the finer nuances of phraseology. He is almost over-sensitive about giving offence. He would always change a text to remove a possible sting or to give a positive slant to something that may appear negative.' Rupert was even more mindful of this when he had to speak overseas. 'He always said that you don't criticise your own people abroad; you do it at home in the vestry. Winston Churchill also said that, but added that sometimes he couldn't get home fast enough!' Knoetze related that Rupert tolerated mistakes when it was clear one had really tried, but dereliction of duty and half-hearted efforts were like red rags to a bull. The watchword was 'when in doubt, find out' – and preferably in advance, 'because he has the incredible ability to notice a typing or a factual error, even if it is the only one in a document,' according to Knoetze.[7]

Engelbrecht also noticed Rupert's solicitude as far as all aspects of the company were concerned. When Rupert arrived at work one morning, a hosepipe lay across the road at the entrance to the group's headquarters. He got out of his car and rolled up the hosepipe before driving through the gate. It was a standing instruction that all company vehicles had to be clean and polished at all times. A young salesman parking a dirty car next to the bay where Rupert had just parked was ordered to have his car washed immediately.

Knoetze was struck by Rupert's attentiveness to people and their distress, and his constant interest in colleagues' weal and woe. And appreciative: 'Expressing appreciation, a hand on your shoulder when saying thank you for something that was actually just part of your duties. That is how we knew him. Always a word of thanks after a function, a speech or some occasion or other where we had been privileged to make things run smoothly for him. I still treasure the cover of that speech on which he wrote, "Excellent. This is obviously not my own work." It was this warm, human style of his that brought out the very best in us.'

In his position as group coordinator, Stuart Pretorius observed that Rupert sometimes had to sign up to three files of letters every day. He welcomed every new shareholder by letter. Pretorius recalled that Rupert once remarked to him after a rather heated telephonic exchange of words with another businessman: 'You know, Mr Pretorius, a truly great person and a small person have one thing in common: They don't know it.'[8]

Rupert always came to work dressed formally, usually in a dark tailor-made suit from the best Saville Row material, with brand names like Dormeuil or Holland & Sherry. He loved designer ties, particularly red ones, and preferred Italian shoes. For appointments he would wear a suit or at the very least a jacket and tie, 'out of respect for the other person'. Professional conduct and informal clothing did not go together, he maintained: 'I believe the average investor does not want to entrust his money to people who seem too casual. My sense is that one doesn't attend a shareholders' meeting in beachwear.'

With his medical background, Edwin Hertzog was of the view that private hospitals could be a feasible industry. Rupert, who had originally also wanted to study medicine, responded positively to his plans and requested him to do market research on the prospects of private hospitals in South Africa's major cities. On the strength of Hertzog's findings, Rembrandt's executive committee approved funds in 1983 to build one hospital with about 100 beds in Cape Town's northern suburbs. Prof. Jannie de Villiers, a gynaecologist, former rector of Stellenbosch University and a long-standing director on the board, was appointed executive chairman. Edwin Hertzog, as managing director, was authorised to do what he deemed necessary. ' I was scared stiff, and went to the medical library at Tygerberg Hospital to look for books on how to build hospitals. When I realised that most hospitals in the country had been built by the provinces, I went to the provincial health department. I was completely unimpressed by what I found there, but I did make contact with their architects, ' Hertzog related.

The financial expert he approached to help him on a part-time basis was Thys Visser, financial manager of WP Cellars' head office who later became deputy chairman and chief executive of Remgro. They got on excellently and in 1984 the Medi-Clinic Corporation was founded. When Hertzog had completed the first hospital, the Panorama Medi-Clinic in Tygerberg, Cape Town, the 100 beds had increased to 325. 'But I was never told you may not spend more than this,'

Hertzog explained. 'As the corporation grew, I just kept on motivating and it was actually a great risk – obviously I realised that if the first project should fail, I would also go down. Fortunately, everything worked out well. Today Medi-Clinic Corporation has 35 hospitals with 5 000 beds,' he said in 2001.[9]

Johann Rupert's move to Rembrandt was prompted by a change in circumstances. A situation that upset the Ruperts terribly arose in 1984 while Johann was on a week-long business visit to London, accompanied by his wife Gaynor and Coleen Carinus, wife of his childhood friend Johan Carinus, a prominent Stellenbosch farmer. When they called on his father at his suite in Grosvenor House, Rupert was in an agitated state. 'He was as white as a sheet,' Johann recalled. It turned out that Rupert, by now 68 years old, had just been informed by Rothmans' chairman, Sir Robert Crichton-Brown, that in future he would only be welcome at Rothmans as a shareholder, not as part of management. The reason given was that anti-South African sentiments had reached such a pitch that the Rembrandt connection was becoming a millstone round their necks. After all, they operated in countries like Malaysia where South Africans were not admitted at all. Rupert was very aware of this. Indeed, Rembrandt had sold half its shares in Rothmans to Philip Morris for that very reason, a transaction in which Johann Rupert had been involved. As a result, Rembrandt and Philip Morris each owned 34% of Rothmans' shares.

Johann was incensed at such treatment of his father. 'The man tells my father (and my father had appointed him), "You're no longer welcome here as part of the management . . ." I thought my father was going to suffer a heart attack.'

The younger Rupert decided there and then that the time had come to join Rembrandt. He discussed it with Gaynor. His father had always wanted them to settle in the Cape. Had he not bought him two wine farms to entice them? Johann had given one to his sister, and he did not want to compete with his brother Anthonij, the family's wine farmer. But now they would have to go to the Cape. As he told his wife, 'I can't allow Sir Robert Crichton-Brown (an Australian formerly known as Bobby Cohen) to do this to my father.'

Johann Rupert's main dilemma was the future of his colleagues, many of whom were still at Rand Merchant Bank. He did not want to sell them out to a large bank or leave them at the mercy of their competitors. The only people he felt he could trust completely, although they were major competitors, were his friends GT Ferreira, Paul Harris and Laurie Dippenaar at Rand Consolidated Investments (RCI). They had helped him before by warning him in 1982 against risky loans to Martin Summerley, who operated a scam in the Magnum Group. That experience was also a life-long lesson to him, which made him decide that as a businessman he never wanted to be at the mercy of someone else, whether a bank or any other person.

At Johann's suggestion Rand Merchant Bank merged with RCI in their mutual interest. RCI could at last obtain the banking licence they had been unable to secure in their own right, and the merger was also the prelude to the success story of the Rand Merchant Bank/First Rand financial services group. The benefit to Johann was that it left him free to move to Stellenbosch.

Johann set two conditions on which he would join Rembrandt. One was that his father would permit him to transfer all Rembrandt's international interests to a separately listed company abroad, which made sense in view of the growing threat of sanctions. The second was that he be given the use of the company plane, because 'I wanted to see my wife and children and there was no chance that I would constantly be flying all over the world if I could not use that plane'. No salary was discussed, just the two conditions. Both requests were granted and Johann duly moved to Stellenbosch. He was initially appointed as an executive director of Rembrandt, with nobody reporting to him. Fortunately, he said, Edwin Hertzog was already there.

Johann's reservations about Rembrandt's overseas structure were two-fold: The foreign companies had made mistakes in his view, and sanctions against South Africa were gathering momentum. In 1986 a debt moratorium was declared by the South African government. A Safmarine vessel had been confiscated in an American port and the credit facilities of South African banks were withdrawn. What if they started confiscating Rembrandt's assets, he asked his father.

That was the beginning of the restructuring of Rembrandt's international interests under the umbrella of Richemont, a development in which Johann played a crucial role. He realised they could not continue as before, 'and I also decided these guys needed a bit of law and order.' He kept his father, as chairman, fully informed of the potentially far-reaching activities in which he was engaged.

Just after his arrival in Stellenbosch, a controversial Cartier board meeting took place overseas that was to give rise to an intense battle at board level. At that stage Cartier was controlled by Rembrandt and Rothmans, each with 47,5%; a company in Belgium, Sofina, held the remaining five percent. Sketching the background, Johann related that it was December; his parents were already at their holiday home in Hermanus. 'I was in New York on business when I got a call from our former colleague Joe Kanoui. In tears he told me they had just come out of a board meeting of Cartier where Sir Robert Crichton-Brown, the chairman of Rothmans, had told them that henceforth they would be reporting to Rothmans; they had nothing to do with Rembrandt or the Ruperts – because of sanctions, et cetera – and no communication with Stellenbosch was allowed.'

Yet the only reason why Rembrandt had sold half its shares to Rothmans in the first place was to protect Cartier in the event of sanctions. He had been involved with Cartier from 1975, Johann said. 'Among other things, I went out with our partner's daughter (Nathalie Hocq) for years, so I know the family, I know Joe Kanoui . . . We are all friends, but again as a result of sanctions, et cetera we endeavoured to have third parties as shareholders in order to protect Cartier.'

The South African dealmaker Murray Louw, who had been present at the meeting, also called Johann and informed him that Sir Robert had further said that all jewellers were thieves – he would be watching them, for he had learnt in Australia that people in the jewellery industry stole. 'This he said to the most sophisticated French board members, and he claimed to be saying it "with Dr Rupert's knowledge and consent". I then phoned my father in Hermanus and told him: "You now have two options: You either lose the cooperation and the support of the entire Cartier team, or you pull Sir Robert Crichton-Brown up short." '

Eventually Johann came up with another plan: an ingenious move to ensure control of Rothmans. He and Kanoui flew to Belgium and, together with Sofina, launched a new company in Luxemburg, Luxco, which became the holding company for Rembrandt's and Sofina's joint 52,5 percent interest in Cartier. 'We then gave Sofina ten percent of Luxco and we had ninety percent of Luxco, and we informed Rothmans, "By the way, this is the new structure."'

The news hit the Rothmans board like a bombshell. Johann kept his cool: Unless Sir Robert vacated the chair, he would listen to no further communication. When he finally did see Sir Robert, ' he kept on calling me "my boy" and treated me like a child'. He proposed that Rembrandt should trust Rothmans and sell their shares to Rothmans Australia. Johann scornfully rejected the idea. When he probed more deeply into Sir Robert's background, he found that the man had pulled off a similar deal in an Australian firm of insurance brokers, and that he had also accomplished such a reverse takeover when he arrived in England.

Johann duly informed Rothmans' board in England that he wanted to convene an extraordinary shareholders' meeting to ask for Sir Robert's resignation. Johann, then in his mid-thirties, was unfazed when a senior director, John Mayo, told him he could not do it because 'you are South Africans'. He retorted: 'Mr Mayo, where in the Companies Act does it say that South Africans are not allowed to vote?' According to Johann, that was when the board saw 'we were serious, very serious, and Sir Robert Crichton-Brown was replaced by Sir David Montagu.'[10]

Johann went ahead with Richemont. He sold all his shares in Rand Merchant Bank, because he wanted the bank to assist him in his new venture and he would be guilty of self-enrichment if he awarded the huge contract to a firm in which he had an interest. At his father's insistence he informed his colleagues at Rembrandt of the project – Rupert had cautioned his son that 'I do not want to get a reputation for acting unpatriotically. You have to convince all your colleagues.' One of the Rembrandt old guard, Gerhard Steinmetz, refused to back Johann's plans and tried to persuade Dirk Hertzog and his son Edwin to withhold their support. 'Not only did Mr Hertzog very politely show him the door, he also phoned my father,' Johann related. 'These guys didn't want to do it because they saw they would be relinquishing their power. The argument was: Why should we give away our assets? Of course, these were not management's assets in the first place, they belonged to the shareholders.'

Problems also arose when Johann approached Philip Morris, to whom Rembrandt had sold half its share in Rothmans, to obtain their consent to the transaction. But once Philip Morris realised that Rembrandt would not sell its remaining Rothmans shares, they decided to pull out themselves. Rothmans, not charmed by the prospect of Rembrandt buying out Philip Morris's shares, decided to throw a spanner in the works. At the next board meeting Johann was duly put through his paces.

In the first place he received the documents less than 24 hours before the meeting. Only then did he learn that Rothmans London was planning to buy out the Rothmans houses in Singapore and Australia. Johann at once smelled a rat and asked Sir David Montagu not to submit the proposals, since he needed time to study them. He suspected that some information had been leaked, as the share price had already gone 'through the roof'. His request was refused.

When he walked into the boardroom, the thirteen other directors were already seated around the table. He was shown to the remaining chair directly opposite Sir David, who was soliciting approval for the purchase. He knew the underlying aim was to push through the deal, however unlucrative financially, simply to make it impossible for Rembrandt to buy out the Philip Morris shares. Montagu started with the director on Johann's right, which meant Johann would be the last to be consulted. One by one the others agreed to the proposal. When it was finally his turn, his was the lone vote against. But Johann held his ground. Questioning the financial sense of the purchase of Rothmans Australia, he exposed spurious arguments based on a discrepancy between higher Australian interest rates as well as the strength of the Deutschmark (with which the Australian assets would be bought) as opposed to the Australian dollar. Questioning the directors' retort that they thought the Australian dollar would appreciate, he asked whether they thought the Australian interest rates would fall while the currency would simultaneously strengthen. 'I started to get the board's attention. Then I said: "Apples and pears are being compared here." Thank God I had spent those years at Lazard Frères and had had my own bank,' Johann explained. 'Because these chaps were told to put the transaction there, not because it was a sound financial deal, but to make it impossible for Rembrandt to buy the Philip Morris shares. That was the sole reason.'

Soon he had an ally against the chair – none other than Henry Keswick, head of Jardine Matheson Holdings and a close friend of Montagu's. Keswick asked: 'Mr Chairman, is it correct that you did not ask your proprietor and you are going against his wishes?' When Johann demurred that they did not own all the shares, Keswick said firmly: 'Young man, you *are* the proprietor.'

Johann went further. They would also, he pointed out, be using a German pension fund, in other words German workers' money, to buy assets in Australia. Another close friend of the chairman's, Cob Stenham, financial director of Uni-Lever and chairman of Bankers Trust, responded to this by urging caution. The upshot was that the proposal was turned down.[11]

In 1989 Rembrandt finally bought out Philip Morris's shares in Rothmans after negotiations lasting for months.

In the early 1990s Johann Rupert and a team of senior Rembrandt staff, including Dillie Malherbe, son of the Rembrandt veteran Willem Malherbe, and colleagues such as Jan du Plessis and Jan Dreyer, spent three years in London creating an operational structure for the new company. With their ownership of Richemont now a matter of public knowledge they no longer had to keep a low profile, which Johann saw as beneficial to corporate discipline.

Johann himself came up with the name Richemont for the new overseas luxury-goods conglomerate. After a late-night business conference in Geneva he caught a few hours' sleep at the Hotel Le Richemond, which marketed itself as 'one of the real palace hotels of Switzerland and Europe as a whole'. When he asked for his bill early the next morning – he had to catch a six am flight from Geneva – he was shocked at the amount of 1 400 Swiss francs for a stay of a few hours. The cashier retorted that Le Richemond was a luxury hotel. Sitting in the plane Johann mulled over the incident. He was looking for a name for a conglomerate manufacturing and selling luxury goods. He decided on Richemont – but not spelled with a *d*; Richemont with a *t*, that was it. Besides, it started with an *R*, like so many names with which the Ruperts had been involved: Rembrandt, Rothmans, Rupert International, even his own Rand Merchant Bank, and Reemtsma. Once the copyright section had established that the name was not registered anywhere in the world, Richemont became another strong R-name in the Rupert stable.[12] A later addition that followed this pattern is R&R, the acronym for the trade name under which the Ruperts and Rothschilds market the wines of the Fredericksburg wine estate.

The Rembrandt Group's overseas interests – not just luxury goods but also its strategic interests in the tobacco industry – had already been transferred to Compagnie Financière Richemont AG in 1988. All Rembrandt Group shareholders obtained one share in Richemont for every Rembrandt share they owned. Listed as a Swiss company, Richemont's original head office was in Zug. As in other Rupert businesses, valuable artworks were displayed in the building – more especially in the Huberte Goote gallery on the ground floor, named after Johann's mother.

Via a holding company, Compagnie Financière Rupert, the Ruperts controlled 50,45% of votes in Richemont. In 2004 they bought out the minority shareholders in Compagnie Financière Rupert (23%, half of which belonged to the Hertzog family), giving them full control over Richemont. The first chairman of Richmont was Dr Nikolaus Senn, honorary chair of the erstwhile Swiss Union Bank and an old friend of Anton and Huberte Rupert. In 1988 Rupert invited Senn and his wife Charlotte to the Salzburg Festival. According to Senn, who regarded Rupert as 'a very intelligent, well-balanced, deliberate and very clever entrepreneur,' Rupert asked him during a long walk to serve as chairman of the new company Richemont.[13] Senn agreed and was chairman for fourteen years until Johann Rupert, hitherto the chief executive officer, succeeded him as executive chairman in 2002.

In 1990 Johann was confronted about Richemont by Cyril Ramaphosa, secretary-general of the South African trade union federation Cosatu and subsequently the ANC's chief negotiator at the Kempton Park negotiations on the country's transition to democracy. At a dinner at a Cape Town restaurant where the two men met for the first time, Ramaphosa, at one stage mentioned as a prominent contender for the role of possible successor to Nelson Mandela, wanted to know why the new company had been established overseas. At the time, the ANC had strong communist leanings and nationalisation was in the air. Johann gave a straight answer: 'Cyril, it's actually very simple, and you can tell that to your stakeholders. I have to protect the assets of my stakeholders, the shareholders, against your stakeholders – so that if they want to steal stuff, they won't be able to do so. No capital has left the country; no capital *will* ever leave the country; and all the revenue still returns to South Africa. I've given my word to Dr Gerhard de Kock (former president of the Reserve Bank), and over the years we have not taken out a single penny.'

Ramaphosa then 'nearly split his sides' and said: 'Oh, you Afrikaners!' When Johann asked what he meant by this, Ramaphosa said he had just put the same question to Julian Ogilvy-Thompson, chairman of Anglo American, and that Ogilvy-Thompson had told him all kinds of stories about marketing agreements with Russia, et cetera . . . Johann said such talk was just nonsense, and he and Ramaphosa subsequently became good friends.[14] Ramaphosa even served as a director of the Peace Parks Foundation for a while, but found he could not devote sufficient attention to this on account of other obligations.

Johann Rupert was also involved in the negotiations about the last remaining sticking points of South Africa's final new constitution, which was finalised in 1996. He was invited to a conference of negotiators aimed at reaching agreement about the last two controversial issues: the right of trade union members to prevent lock outs, and property rights. The younger Rupert, a proponent of small business, was strongly opposed to the envisaged lock-out clause, which would prohibit employers from locking trade union members out of the workplace in the event of strikes. He had been warned against this by the former British prime minister Lady Margaret Thatcher, who had told him that the scrapping of this clause constituted her greatest victory over the militant British trade unions. The clause could favour trade unions to such an extent that they could occupy factories and workplaces and break down everything on the premises if they did not get their own way.

The meeting, chaired by Pres. Nelson Mandela, was attended by about 60 people, including cabinet ministers, politicians from opposition parties, prominent businesspeople and trade union representatives such as the secretary-general of Cosatu, Mbhazima (Sam) Shilowa, a member of the central committee of the South African Communist Party who would become premier of the Gauteng province in 1999. Mandela started the proceedings by addressing the younger Rupert directly: 'Johann, I know that you have reservations about the lock-out clause. But you have to trust the government in this matter.' Whereupon Johann replied: 'Mr Mandela, you know I have great respect for you and that I love you like a father. But it's not you that I have to trust. Because I don't trust Sam (Shilowa).' He continued by mentioning that four workers of his group had been murdered by trade union members during a strike at Heidelberg. The veracity of his statement was confirmed by the ANC's chief negotiator, Cyril Ramaphosa. Rupert then said that if the lock-out clause were to be enforced, he would close down all his factories and mines in South Africa the next day. This would obviously have a devastating effect on the stock exchanges and the South African economy as a whole.

After Johann had spoken, there was an uneasy silence and the meeting was adjourned after five minutes. Outside, Ogilvy-Thompson came up to him and muttered: 'A bit aggressive, a bit aggressive . . .'. When the meeting finally resumed, Ramaphosa said that they had struck a 'deal' with the National Party (NP) with regard to property rights. Marinus Daling of Sanlam subsequently walked over to Roelf Meyer, the NP's chief negotiator, and said he heard they had entered into a 'deal' with the ANC. Meyer replied: 'No, not a deal, an understanding.' To which Daling responded: 'Roelf, I'm not a politician, but could you explain to me what the difference is between a deal and an understanding?' Meyer failed to provide an answer.[15]

Ultimately, the lock-out clause was not included in the final constitution, while property rights enjoy protection.

In 1996 Richemont's luxury-goods subsidiary, Vendôme, took over Vacheron Constantin, the oldest Swiss watchmaker still in business. The following year the Italian watchmaker Officine Panerai was added to the group. Another three famous watchmakers, the German firm A Lange & Söhne and two Swiss firms, Jaeger-LeCoultre of Le Sentier and IWC of Schaffhausen, were acquired in 2000. The acquisition of these three firms was financed by the sale of the group's preference shares in British American Tobacco, as well as the proceeds of the sale of the group's interest in Vivendi, which brought to an end a short-lived entry into pay television, initially in Nethold and then in Canal Plus.

The French leatherware manufacturer Lancel was taken over in 1997. In 1999 the group acquired a 60% stake in the Parisian jewellers Van Cleef & Arpels, which was increased to 80% in 2000. Other luxury subsidiaries of Richemont include Montegrappa, an Italian manufacturer of luxury writing materials; Seeger, a leading German leather-goods manufacturer; and Shangai Tang of Hong Kong. In Britain, there are the clothing and accessories groups Hackett and Old England. Another venerable British institution is James Purdey & Sons, the firm of gunsmiths whose exclusive, hand-engraved shotguns and sporting rifles have a tradition dating to 1814. A register of every client since that date is still maintained. Prospective buyers must have their measurements taken before the gun is made, a prerequisite often entailing a special trip to London in order to secure a firearm of the highest quality.

In various cases there is competition within the group between subsidiaries operating in the same field, but pooling of shared knowledge also takes place.

In 1999 Richemont bought out the minority shareholders in Vendôme at 26% more than the market price, gaining full control of Vendôme's luxury-goods interests, at that stage worth $5,7 billion. Johann Rupert explained at the time that in the luxury trade, privatisation offered protection against the sudden fluctuations in share prices to which public companies, in the full glare of the media spotlight, are exposed. It was regarded as a classic Rupert move: the combination of privacy and success that Johann's father had mastered so many years before.

At the start of the 21st century it was decided to move Richemont's head office from Zug to Geneva, which strengthened Geneva's claim to the title of the world's watch capital. The subsidiaries of Richemont jointly constitute the second biggest manufacturer of luxury goods in the world, with only LVMH (Louis Vuitton Moët Hennessy) a bigger competitor.

At home in South Africa Anton Rupert retired as chairman of the Rembrandt Group in 1992 and was succeeded by his son Johann as non-executive chairman. Rupert remained chairman of the holding companies TIB, Tegkor and Rembrandt Beherende Beleggings for a few years. He also retired as chairman of Rembrandt's advisory board, which was dissolved in 2003 after long-standing associates such as Prof. Jannie de Villiers, Dr Oscar Dhlomo, Habakuk Shikwane and Bertie Levenstein had served on it.

At the start of the new century the group owned four corporate jets. They were at Rupert's disposal at a fee, also for overseas flights, following a board decision that he should not use commercial airlines. The aircraft subsidiary, Falconair, falls under M&I, a service company that rents out aeroplanes to the group and associated firms, besides handling the group's staff funds and other services.

Rupert's passionate interest in nature conservation and game parks started moving increasingly in the direction of transfrontier peace parks, a message that was boosted by South Africa's peaceful transition to a fully-fledged democracy in the 1990s. It gathered such momentum that by his 80th birthday in 1996, the Peace Parks Foundation was established.

On the tobacco front, too, times were changing. Governments were clamping down on tobacco sales. And Rothmans International was facing increasingly tough competition from the big international conglomerate, Philip Morris, which had an annual cash flow equal to Rothmans' market capitalisation.[16]

Owing to his medical background, Edwin Hertzog had been conscious of the health problems associated with tobacco at a much earlier stage. From a young age, he had observed the growing resistance to smoking and tobacco. He concluded that Anton Rupert, with his scientific training and background, had decided tobacco was fighting a losing battle.[17]

Stricter anti-smoking legislation was being enforced more and more widely in South Africa and elsewhere. In 1993, before the ANC came to power in the 1994 elections, the South African parliament adopted a law controlling tobacco products whereby health warnings were introduced on cigarette packets and smoking on public transport was prohibited.[18]

In view of these developments Rembrandt and Richemont first merged their respective tobacco interests in Rothmans International in 1996, then merged with British American Tobacco (BAT) in 1999 to form the second biggest international tobacco company. The interest in BAT is held by a joint Rembrandt-Richemont company, R&R Holdings (Luxemburg). This left them in a strong enough position to take on Philip Morris should the occasion arise.

Rupert never hesitated to give his son Johann full credit for the establishment of Richemont. One occasion on which he did so publicly was in his speech at the annual dinner of the Cape Town Chamber of Commerce in 2000, where *Die Burger's* Business Leader of the Year was announced for the tenth time. At the gala function where he was pronounced the newspaper's Business Pioneer, Rupert said frankly that Johann's commitment and attention to detail had been decisive factors in the formation of Richemont.[19]

Edwin Hertzog remarked that people who worked for Rembrandt's cigarette companies were 'sad and unhappy' about the deal with BAT, as a result of which management control was relinquished but a dividend yield was ensured. According to Hertzog, the reason for the unhappiness was that 'in South Africa there used to be a certain credibility and acceptance that if you worked for Dr Rupert, you were doing something better than just selling cigarettes'. He added: 'This is where the hard decisions of the business world come into play. I have no doubt that this deal was the right decision for the company and the shareholders . . . But cigarette people no longer have that glamour of working for the Rupert empire.'[20]

Even more stringent legislation against tobacco and smoking followed in 1998 in South Africa under the ANC government. All tobacco advertisements and sponsorships were prohibited, smoking was banned in all public places including workplaces, and cigarette sales to children younger than sixteen were prohibited. Excise tax was increased to 52% of the retail price of cigarettes. According to research on the tobacco industry, the combination of strict legislation and more expensive cigarettes has led to a considerable decline in consumption among all age groups. A perhaps unintended consequence, however, was the 'freezing' of the tobacco industry, which meant that well-known brands became more solidly entrenched – with advertising prohibited, no new competitors could risk entering the industry.

A further international measure against smoking followed in 2003, when the

World Health Organisation unanimously accepted the Framework Convention on Tobacco Control (FCTC) on 21 May. This convention, the first global health treaty in several decades, requires of member countries to impose restrictions on tobacco advertising, sponsorships and promotions, to introduce new regulations on packaging and indoor air-conditioning, and to control illicit trade in tobacco and secondary smoking.[21]

For the old Rembrandt Group, which had already started moving away from direct manufacturing of tobacco products, further diversification into other fields of business seemed obvious. In 2000 the Rembrandt Group in South Africa underwent sweeping restructuring. The original pyramidal structure ended when the group unbundled, without prejudice to existing shareholders. On Rupert's recommendation the group's underlying investments were split between two listed companies: Remgro and VenFin.

Rembrandt's established interests in tobacco, wine, spirits, financial services, mining and industry generally went to Remgro. The erstwhile manufacturing industry, with its thousands of employees, has shrunk to what is essentially an investment company with huge, diversified interests but only a small staff complement. Rembrandt's technological investments in the IT industry were pooled in the much smaller VenFin. Rupert had reservations about the mushrooming of IT companies – he felt that, like radio in the early days, the industry was vastly inflated, and he was proven right when the IT bubble burst. Yet the need for instant communication between worldwide interests has led to heavy investment in computers and the Internet. In 2003 the combined South African staff establishment of Remgro, VenFin and M&I Management Services numbered just over 200 employees. The vast majority of the international group's employees are employed by Richemont's overseas subsidiaries in the manufacture of luxury goods.

The share capital of Remgro and VenFin, both listed on the JSE Securities Exchange, was restructured in a new class of shares known as B shares in each of the two companies, most of which were issued to the Rembrandt Trust (Pty) Limited, the holding company of the Rembrandt Group. These unlisted B shares have a higher par value than the ordinary shares of the two companies, ensuring that the Rembrandt Trust retains control of the entire group.

As in the case of Richemont, Remgro is effectively controlled by the Ruperts via the Rembrandt Trust, in which Anton Rupert has for years had by far the biggest interest. The Rembrandt Trust owns all the unlisted B shares of Remgro and is entitled to 42,2% of the total voting rights. At the start of the 21st century only Anton Rupert and his children owned shares in the Rembrandt Trust, after the smaller holdings of the Hertzog family (5,6%) and the Hoogenhouts as well as the outside shareholder Sanlam had been bought out.

BAT took over the Rembrandt Group's old head office in Alexander Street, Stellenbosch. Remgro and VenFin have moved to premises at Technopark just outside Stellenbosch, while Johann Rupert has offices at Groot Paardevlei at Somerset West. His father has moved his office to Millennia Park, the old Gilbeys building near the Adam Tas Bridge in Stellenbosch.

Although Rupert was no longer directly involved in the activities of the group in the 1990s, he continued to give advice from time to time. One occasion was a transaction in which Edwin Hertzog became involved in 1999: the merger of a number of prestigious wine farms. The old Rupert stalwarts Alto, Le Bonheur and Uitkyk were to be merged with the interests of Hans-Joachim Schreiber, immigrant-owner of the farm Neethlingshof. The idea was a joint venture between Distillers (later Distell) and the interests of Schreiber's Hygrace company in Neethlingshof, Olives, Hill & Dale and Stellenzicht.

Edwin Hertzog, chairman of Medi-Clinic, was at that stage a director of Distillers as well as joint deputy chairman of Remgro, together with Thys Visser. Schreiber, a German with interests in Singapore, had handled gold sales for a German bank and then fell out with his employer. Rupert, who was aware of this, called in Hertzog and warned him, the son of his founder-partner, that one should rather not do business with the likes of Schreiber.[22]

Hertzog was in a quandary. According to him the decision to enter into the transaction had been taken on business grounds, and he alone could no longer halt it. In the view of senior Rembrandt people he had committed an error of judgement, however, by not recusing himself from the board discussions where the transaction was approved. At that meeting it was decided to establish a new umbrella organisation, Lusan, its name being derived from the wine farms Le Bonheur, Uitkyk, Stellenzicht, Alto and Neethlingshof. Moreover, Schreiber became the chairman of Lusan, whose products are marketed by Distell.

The Hertzog family is still a major shareholder elsewhere in the group. According to Remgro's annual report for 2002, Edwin Hertzog owns 1 732 614 shares in Remgro (with a market value of around R70 per share at that time), as against Johann Rupert's 687 070 shares. Johann is, however, also a director and beneficiary of the Rembrandt Trust.

When Anton Rupert and family entered *Forbes'* list of billionnaires in 1996, they came in at number 241, with estimated assets of $1,6 billion. According to *Forbes*, at that stage the Ruperts, besides their interest of $816 million in Richemont, controlled 86% of the tobacco market in South Africa and had significant shareholdings in gold-mining companies, banks and the wine industry. The empire had been built, according to *Forbes*, by Anton Rupert, then 79, and his 'brash and energetic' son Johann, then 46.[23] The only other family from Africa to be listed by *Forbes* in 1996 was the Oppenheimers, whose assets were estimated at $2,5 billion at that stage.

In 1996 the monthly journal *Bilanz* rated the Ruperts fifth on a list of the richest people in Switzerland, with estimated assets of close on R23 billion. In 2002 the combined market capitalisation of the Richemont, Remgro and VenFin groups was some R140 billion (at that stage about $14 billion). Two-thirds of the income was earned abroad.

PART IV

BENEFACTOR

CHAPTER 27

Patron of the arts

R upert's interest in the arts, initially stimulated by his wife's studies under Prof. Matthys Bokhorst during their student years, deepened during his overseas visits. On business trips abroad, especially while waiting for the irregular flights to South Africa, he spent many leisure hours browsing around art galleries in European capitals, broadening his comprehensive knowledge of and appreciation for the works of major artists.

The very first artwork he bought for Huberte still stands in their home: a teak carving of a female bust by Elza Dziomba, a birthday present purchased in the early 1940s. Ruperts admits to a predilection for sculpture: 'In that respect I'm an African.'

Rupert the African also has a soft spot for San rock art, in its own right a distinctive phenomenon in the peace parks about which he could wax lyrical at times. Hundreds of rock paintings, many of them centuries old, are to be found in some peace parks. To him, these are the world's oldest artworks as well as the oldest open-air museums. He sponsored a project of the painter Townley Johnson to copy examples of rock art in southern Africa. Johnson sold more than 600 such drawings to Rupert.

Appropriately, one of the Rembrandt Group's first major art purchases was a collection of nineteen original Rembrandt etchings, first exhibited in Port Elizabeth's Feather Market Hall in 1956. It was the prelude to the establishment of the Rembrandt van Rijn Art Foundation eight years later, the oldest of the foundations established on Rupert's initiative to carry out the group's programme of service to the community. Besides this, the Rupert Family Foundation eventually comprised five family trusts that promote the arts, music, historical homes, nature conservation and education. These foundations are funded from family income and have no connection with the group.

In 1957 the Rembrandt Group commissioned the first of about 50 films on the paintings and sculptures of prominent artists, mostly South Africans: Pierneef, Irma Stern, Maggie Laubser, Jean Welz, Anton van Wouw, Maud Sumner, Walter Battiss, Lippy Lipshitz. Thus art was 'brought to the masses' in public cinemas.

In 1959 Rembrandt sponsored a countrywide bursary competition for young South African artists as part of the 50th anniversary of the Union of South Africa in 1960. Entitled 'Joy of Living' – Rupert's idea – it aimed to promote interest in art among the youth and invited entries from talented young people of all population groups. The judges, too, came from all communities. More than 2 500 entries were received from some 600 school pupils. One prizewinner, a young girl from arid Namaqualand, painted a group of children joyfully looking up after a shower of rain. Another prizewinner was Amichand Rajbansi, who later turned to politics and gained notoriety as the 'Bengal tiger' that 'handed out carrots'.

When the Eastern Cape prizewinners were fêted in East London on 19 September 1960, it made headlines in local papers as the first public multiracial reception in the city's history. In a front-page report in the *EP Herald* entitled 'All races attend cocktail party', Councillor CK Rowland, chairman of the East London Fine Arts Society, was quoted as saying: 'It is greatly to the credit of the organisers that they had seen fit to invite to the official opening members of the dark-skinned races. It has assisted racial well-being and is one of the most far-sighted things that has been done in business circles throughout the Union.'[1]

But not everybody congratulated the two Rembrandt representatives who had organised the reception, Rupert's personal assistant Wynand van Graan and the well-known radio personality Gerhard Roux. 'Mixed' parties were taboo in the heyday of Verwoerdian apartheid. Van Graan explained that the teachers of some of the coloured prizewinners had inquired whether they could attend the function. The teachers' spokesman was Dennis Brutus, who would later be the driving force behind the South African Non-racial Olympic Committee (SANROC) that opposed apartheid in sport. Roux had met Brutus earlier at sports events, and he and Van Graan had approached him beforehand to avoid a possible boycott of the prizegiving ceremony. They had readily agreed that the occasion would be open to all, as Joy of Living was intended above all to showcase the diversity of the country, to give wider exposure to the work of young artists, and to allow different populations groups to reach out to each other.[2]

The storm abated fairly quickly, and the young artists' works were displayed in seven centres across the country. It was the first time that almost all people in South Africa were afforded the opportunity to witness the creative art of the youth. A selection of works from the exhibition was also taken to Japan and the United States of America. The youth project was the final run-up to the group's comprehensive programme of promotion of the arts that became strongly established in the 1960s, a period during which Anton and Huberte Rupert also acquired an impressive core collection of South African art.

In 1964 the Rembrandt van Rijn Art Foundation was founded. Over the years it has exhibited some 50 art collections, including works by major international artists, at nearly 300 exhibitions in South Africa and neighbouring countries, attracting more than four million visitors. One of the Foundation's first projects was to open an art centre at the Rand Easter Show in Johannesburg, South Africa's leading annual industrial show. In an editorial in *Die Burger*, the poet WEG Louw lauded the 'art patronage' of 'a well-known Afrikaans company'. Thousands of visitors viewed the exhibitions of the work of famous artists every year until the Rand Easter Show moved from Milner Park to a new venue in the 1980s, whereupon Rembrandt transferred the art centre to the University of the Witwatersrand, situated next to the old show grounds.

A key person in this period was Danie van Niekerk, later a publisher, who had joined Rembrandt's public relations department in 1964. When Rupert learned of his interest in art and sculpture, he was charged with establishing the various collections: Rembrandt's in South Africa, the Stuyvesant Art Foundation abroad (later transferred to the Richemont Art Foundation). Van Niekerk had to report to Rupert on an almost daily basis about art auctions, art books and travel programmes; he had to keep abreast of prices and organise exhibitions around the world. He had to consult Rupert on all purchases of art works, which turned into excellent investments.

A painter with whom the Ruperts were on friendly terms in the early years was the financially successful, though often controversial, Russian immigrant Vladimir Tretchikoff, who had followed his wife and daughter to Cape Town from Indonesia after World War II. Flamboyant and not noted for modesty, his work included ultra-realistic, popular pieces like *The dying swan* that were dismissed as kitsch by art critics. (His response was, 'I cry all the way to the bank!') In his autobiography, Tretchikoff related how he had made the acquaintance of the Ruperts thanks to a letter of introduction from Patrick O'Neill-Dunne of Rothmans. An amusing incident took place after the almost penniless Tretchikoff had held his first successful exhibition. He and his wife, Natalie, visited a furrier where she tried on an expensive mink coat with a far-away look in her eyes. He promptly bought it for her, but their friends thought they were crazy – particularly Rupert and his wife (whom Tretchikoff called Huba). 'People with sense would first buy a little house, then a little car,' Rupert admonished him sternly. 'Bottom of their list would be a fur coat for the wife. And what the heck did you do?' But Tretchikoff held his own: 'Anton, we really do mean to buy a house. In fact it's always been one of the three things on our list – a house, a car and a fur for Natalie. It's not my fault they come in the wrong order.'[3] Rupert initially bought a few of Tretchikoff's paintings but his interest soon waned. One Tretchikoff was destroyed in a fire, the rest were sold.

As patron of the arts Rupert developed a refined personal taste, thanks to his exposure to local as well as international artists. Van Niekerk related how he and other Rembrandt employees would often find Rupert in his office pensively study-ing the design of a new cigarette packet. 'Then he would turn it around slowly, scrutinise it from all sides, take it to the window to examine it in better light. The precise design, lettering, the exact shades of colours were of the utmost im-portance to this master of marketing.' Apropos of this, Van Niekerk wondered whether this 'precise, concentrated experiencing of colour, form and design was not perhaps part of and the source of his interest in art? Is art not also a form of packaging?'[4]

In European art, Rupert preferred the German expressionists to the French impressionists, and the sculptures and graphics of the German artists Käthe Koll-witz and Ernst Barlach were close to his heart. Among South African artists he considered Irma Stern and Jean Welz the greatest painters the country had pro-duced. The Rembrandt Group published glossy publications on the work of both these artists. Van Niekerk regards the publication on Stern, *Fees van kleur* (Festi-val of colour) by Marion Arnold, as perhaps the finest book ever published on a South African artist.

In 1967 Van Niekerk was appointed chief executive of the *Suid-Afrikaanse Akademie vir Wetenskap en Kuns* (South African Academy for Science and Art). The Akademie had already come under fire from the far right of the political spectrum when it awarded its top literary honour, the Hertzog prize, to the novelist Etienne Leroux for *Sewe dae by die Silbersteins* (English version: *Seven days at the Silbersteins*). At an extraordinary meeting of the Akademie, objections were raised to Van Niekerk's appointment – it was alleged that he was an employee of the 'liberalist' Rembrandt organisation, 'planted' in the Akademie at the behest of Anton Rupert. The allegations of possible involvement by Rupert were refuted by the chairman, Dr S Meiring Naudé. Naudé added that Van Niekerk (who later became head of Tafelberg Publishers) was the best candidate.[5]

A week later the columnist Rykie van Reenen said in a column in the Sunday paper *Rapport* that the allegation of Van Niekerk being 'planted' at the Akademie was ironic, as Rupert himself had mentioned to her shortly before that he was going to have great difficulty replacing Van Niekerk, especially at a time when seven large exhibitions were doing the rounds of illustrious European galleries such as the Louvre and the Tate. But he accepted the loss of Van Niekerk philo-sophically, telling Van Reenen: 'It is a policy at our company never to appoint a man who is not also sought after by others. And also not to stand in a man's way. Particularly not if he wants to render broader service to the nation. In fact, we consider it a privilege to help train people for that purpose.'[6]

Jean Welz had been approached to paint an oil portrait of Rupert in 1964. Ini-tially he was not enthusiastic – he did not think the 20th century was an era for portraiture – but a conversation with the poet WEG Louw, at that stage the arts editor of *Die Burger,* made him change his mind. Welz related in an interview that he had started off by doing four charcoal sketches of Rupert in his Stellenbosch office.[7] During the first sitting he asked Rupert what colours he liked best. Red and olive green, he was told. In his studio in Worcester Welz brooded for a long time about the motives for painting a portrait. He found some in a book about Picasso. A portrait, any work of art for that matter, he read, should be a study not of nature but of the human soul, its fear in the face of death and the unknown. At the same time a portrait does not merely depict its subject or the artist's conception of the model: It documents an epoch. Finally, there is the glory of the subject as a creature made in the image of God. For two and a half years Welz pondered on the problem of painting the Rupert portrait. Then the answer dawned on him. In the South African political climate people were judged not so much by their usefulness to society as by their allegiance or antipathy to prevailing political ideas. 'In difficult times such as the present, where the purely political aspect is often overemphasised when one evaluates the worth and character of a fellow human being, it seemed to me of crucial importance to salvage the idea of the honest person as such.'

Consequently, Welz decided 'without hesitation . . . to adopt a monumental approach: a monument to the honest man, in this case, the honest Afrikaner'. He painted Rupert in profile, which he considered more striking than a frontal view.

The portrait was nearly complete before Rupert finally came to Worcester. Welz had battled with the profile – the features, soft yet pronounced, reminded him oddly of President Paul Kruger. He asked Rupert directly: 'Where does your likeness to Paul Kruger come from?' Rupert replied without hesitation: 'From the Karoo. The Karoo leaves its mark on the people who live there.' Welz did not show his excitement at this answer, but that evening he tackled the painting 'in a final storm'. He had found the setting for his monument: 'I knew where to place the honest Afrikaner, I knew it had to be the Karoo. I am also overwhelmed by the majesty of the Karoo.' He filled in the background, a vertical Karoo landscape without any sky. All the Karoo colours appeared around Rupert's figure, and 'the red and olive green came in handy'.

One of the Rembrandt Group's best known collections, bought at Rupert's behest, is that of Rodin and his contemporaries. It comprises mainly small bronzes, hunted down piece by piece in Europe, some at the Rodin Museum in Paris. There are 39 Rodins, including a cast of his famous standing figure of Balzac, and works by some of Rodin's contemporaries, including his brilliant young friend Antoine Bourdelle as well as Rosso, Maillol, Renoir, Degas and

Picasso. Rodin's 'Cathedral', depicting two hands clasped in prayer, was mounted on a pedestal in Rupert's office. It was bought for R1 780. Today it is valued at some R6 million.

The September 11 attack on the World Trade Center in New York in 2001 indirectly affected the Rembrandt Group's collection of Rodins. The firm that suffered the greatest loss of life in the tragedy, Cantor Fitzgerald, also suffered the most serious art loss: a collection of Rodin sculptures that had been exhibited on the 105th floor of one of the towers. Estimations of the number of Rodins that were actually in the WTC vary from dozens to a few hundred.[8] As a result, the cultural importance of the Rodins owned by Rupert's foundations has increased, while their value has probably also risen considerably.

Another collection that aroused great interest during countrywide exhibitions in South Africa was Art of the Space Age, a collection of modern optic and kinetic artworks by artists such as Victor Vasarely, Yaacov Agam, Jesu-Raphael Soto and Attilio Pierelli, among others.

In the late 1960s Rupert bought a collection of modern 'Scultura Italiana' from the art dealers Galleria Obelisco near the Spanish Steps in Rome. His eye had been caught initially by a statuette in the show window, Augusto Perez's *Re et regina* (King and queen), and inside he discovered many other sculptures he liked. In a bookshop nearby he found an artbook in which many of the valuable sculptures in the Italian gallery were discussed, including those of the modern masters Marino Marini and Giacomo Manzù.[9]

The manager of the gallery, Cesare Bellici, years later told Van Niekerk the whole story. One day during their exhibition of modern Italian sculpture and graphics, including about 36 sculptures, said Bellici, they noticed a well-dressed man in a dark suit, closely scrutinising the works and making notes in his catalogue. 'We wondered whether he was an art critic from some or other journal. Then, after about an hour, he came to us and asked: "What does the whole collection cost?" We were flabbergasted – something like this had never happened to us. Then he introduced himself: He was a Mr Rupert from South Africa.'[10] Rupert, shrewd businessman as well as art connoisseur, calculated the total of the prices listed in the catalogue and made the gallery a cash offer. He managed to acquire the entire collection at a substantial discount.

Rupert and Huberte together developed a particular interest in tapestries, an art form that had nearly died out until it was resuscitated in its modern form by Jean Lurçat, a former surrealist painter who turned to this medium in the 1940s. Rupert regards Lurçat's monumental *Le chant du monde* (The song of the world) tapestry cycle as the greatest artwork of the twentieth century he has seen. This series of panels, the biggest contemporary tapestry cycle in the world – 80 metres long and 4,5 metres high – hangs in an ancient hospital, the Hôpital Saint-Jean, in the French tapestry city of Angers. The cycle was inspired by another famous tapestry, *Apocalypse d'Angers*, which depicts the Biblical apocalypse. This medieval tapestry, the biggest in the world, was completed in 1380 and is housed in the nearby castle of Angers.

Lurçat's modern counterpart depicts the destruction of nuclear warfare on the first four panels, then one of human beings in harmony with nature. The last five celebrate human creative powers, including Lurçat's counterpoint to the science that has created the atom bomb – the science of space exploration. The work contains many of the themes that have had a great influence in Rupert's own life: the bombing of Hiroshima, the destructive as well as the creative power of science, joy of life, coexistence, and humankind in harmony with nature.

The Rembrandt Group owns 61 Lurçat tapestries, the largest private collection in the world. Two travelling exhibitions of his work were presented by the group in South Africa, in 1979-80 and again in 1994-95. Lurçat's widow Simone (he died in 1966) travelled from Paris to Stellenbosch for the opening of the second exhibition in the university's Sasol Museum. Rembrandt also owns three other modern French tapestry collections. As early as 1969 a selection of 37 of these tapestries was displayed at the opening of the university's art gallery in the old Lutheran church in Stellenbosch, a building that was a personal gift from Anton and Huberte Rupert to the university. The background music for the occasion, *Musique pour Triéze*, had been specially composed by the South African composer Arnold van Wyk.

Rupert's admiration for the German expressionists Kollwitz and Barlach led to an exhibition of a collection of their graphics and sculptures in Stellenbosch in 1969, which was the first time works of these two artists were shown jointly outside of Germany.

In the Nazi era Kollwitz had been warned not to exhibit her works and was fired from her position as director of the *Meister Atelier für Graphik*. An avowed pacifist, her works are an impassioned protest against suffering and injustice. Before her death near Dresden towards the end of World War II, she expressed the hope that a new, better world would arrive: 'But one day a new ideal will rise, and there will be no more war. I die with this firm belief. One will have to work hard for it, but it will be attained . . . It is a new vision, the vision of the brotherhood of Man.'[11]

On a visit in the 1960s to his good friend Richard von Weizsäcker, then mayor of West Berlin and later president of the Federal Republic of Germany, Rupert learned that there were still plaster casts of Kollwitz's works in her studio, which had been bombed during the war. He negotiated with her surviving son Hans to have them cast in bronze. (Her younger son, Peter, had died in Flanders at the beginning of World War I.) Six bronze casts were made of one of her biggest and most impressive sculptures, *Mutter mit Zwillingen* (Mother with twins), of which Rupert acquired two. This moving sculpture, which was also exhibited on a travelling South African exhibition of her work in 1997-98, depicts a mother lovingly embracing her two children, as if they form part of her. It stands in the entrance hall of Rupert's office building in Millennia Park in Stellenbosch.

The many other exhibitions organised by the group also included a joint exhibition in 1980-81 of the work of two South African art pioneers, JH Pierneef and Anton van Wouw, who had been good friends. Forty of Pierneef's paintings and twenty of Van Wouw's bronze sculptures were shown together.

The Rembrandt van Rijn Art Foundation also acts as curator of the art works that belong to the Rupert Family Foundation for the Arts. In 1981, in collaboration with South Africa's national art galleries, it launched the most imaginative exhibition of contemporary South African art yet held in the country. The project was known as the Cape Town Triennial, a three-yearly exhibition showcasing a selection of the best visual art of leading local artists. The exhibitions were also taken to other cities. Four Triennials were held between 1982 and 1991. Winners received the Rembrandt gold medal and a substantial cash prize – the most recent prize to be awarded, R25 000, went to William Kentridge, an artist who has gained international renown. Kentridge is the son of Adv. Sidney Kentridge, who had been Bram Fischer's senior advocate when Fischer had agreed with Rupert years before that the ANC would stop its boycott of Rembrandt products.

The Triennial artworks stirred lively interest, as well as some controversy. Over a decade more than 452 000 people visited the 33 exhibitions. In 1992 the Foundation terminated its sponsorship, which had amounted to hundreds of thousands over the years. In a press statement it declared that 'changing circumstances' necessitated reconsideration of the Group's funding priorities in view of social needs. The money hitherto channelled into the Cape Town Triennial would henceforth be used to combat unemployment in South Africa.

Underlying the decision, it was speculated in media reports at the time, was 'an element of tension' between the Rembrandt van Rijn Art Foundation and Ms Marilyn Martin, new director of the South African National Gallery in Cape Town, who would be closely involved with the Cape Town Triennials. She evoked criticism with controversial pronouncements against 'Eurocentric art'. Informed cultural commentators were of the opinion that she had offended Rupert with statements such as: 'What is inferior, though, is our diet of third- and fourth-rate productions of opera, of plays that are no longer relevant anywhere, of so-called international exhibitions that mean nothing.' As well as: 'We are told that our culture is threatened. What culture? South Africa has no reputation as a culture-conscious country, quite the opposite. The country has never had a culture policy and the promotion and education of the individual and the nation by means of culture have never been on the agenda. Money has never been spent on culture.'[12]

At a later stage Rupert indicated in a newspaper interview that he had an aversion to critics who condemned 'Eurocentricity' in art. 'I do want to say that I can't stand the stories about Eurocentricity,' he declared. 'The Japanese have the highest appreciation for Western music. The Chinese play Western music. What nonsense is it to say it's Eurocentric? The best museums I have ever seen are in Taipei, Taiwan, with treasures of Chinese civilisation from 4 000 years ago. Does it now make me Sinocentric to say that those things are valuable, moving, the traces of people through the ages? That is why the conservation of all forms of heritage is so important to me. Buildings, places, art and particularly the ecology. We must keep what we have and know where we come from if we are to know where we're going,' he said.[13]

The sponsorship of the Cape Town Triennial was not replaced after Rembrandt had withdrawn its support.

Rembrandt's overseas partners also built up collections of their own. One is a remarkable Canadian collection of Inuit art made of soapstone and whalebone; another is the second biggest collection of modern British artworks after that of the Tate Gallery in London. In 1991 extensive damage was caused by fire in a London warehouse where some of the art treasures of the Stuyvesant Art Foundation were stored. The damage to the Rembrandt Group's assets, which had previously been exhibited in various countries, was estimated to be at least R23 million at the time.

One of the group's finest galleries, the Rembrandt van Rijn Art Museum, is a historical house in Dorp Street, Stellenbosch, which had been built by Lambertus Fick in 1780. The house in the Cape Dutch style was bought by the Krige family in the 19th century, and saw the marriage between Isie Krige and the later South African prime minister Jan Christiaan Smuts in 1897.

Many of the group's artworks have been used to beautify the workplaces of its employees, as in the South African head office in Stellenbosch and before that in factories in Paarl, Heidelberg and the Netherlands. The art collections require the full-time attention of Van Niekerk's successors in Stellenbosch, among others Leo Kruger and later Deon Herselmann.

According to Dr Frederick Mostert, the group's trademark specialist, the artworks displayed by the Art Foundation in the group's offices is a source of pleasure to its employees. 'There is no doubt that these artworks have a positive influence on the workplace. They promote productivity – definitely in my case and I'm sure my colleagues will agree.'[14]

Huberte Rupert, who was honoured by the Akademie in 2004 for her contribution to art and culture, took the initiative with a new art museum constructed close to her husband's head office in Stellenbosch. After a fire at the Rupert home she felt that their personal collection of artworks and their library should be kept on safer premises, where they would also be accessible to more people. Some of the best works that used to adorn company buildings are displayed in the new Rupert Museum that Huberte established in cooperation with her daughter Hanneli, along with selected pieces from the Rembrandt van Rijn Art Foundation. The museum complex, designed by the architect Hannes Meiring in the style known as Cape Dutch farm architecture, is characterised by its simplicity: a large shed with five pointed gables, oval windows and Cape Malay plastering, giving it a lime-washed effect. Indigenous trees and shrubs dot the surrounding land without any formal landscaping – it looks like a farmyard and park. Inside, however, the latest technology has been installed to protect the priceless contents against all hazards, including burglary, fire and damp.

Rupert shares Huberte's love of music, especially classical German and Russian composers, and music is one of the fields that benefit from the Ruperts' interest as benefactors. Huberte chairs the Rupert Music Foundation, which sponsors orchestras and concerts in particular. Of course, they take a keen interest in their daughter's singing career. As a mezzo soprano, Hanneli studied under Prof. George van der Spuy at Stellenbosch and obtained her B.Mus and B.Mus Hons degrees with distinction. She then proceeded to Europe, where she studied under Pierre Bernac, Paul Schilhawsky, Erik Werba, Ingalill Linden and Ernst Haefliger. She made her professional debut in 1979 and was acclaimed as a talented *Lieder* and oratorio singer. She has often performed with orchestras in France, Germany, Denmark, Austria, Switzerland and South Africa, as well as in broadcasts on Austrian, Turkish and South African television. She is especially known for her interpretation of the music of Mahler, Bach and Brahms. In 1992 she performed with the National Symphony Orchestra in Washington's Kennedy Center. Under the baton of Mstislav Rostropovich, she was the alto soloist in four performances of Mahler's *Das Lied von der Erde*, and each time received standing ovations from packed auditoriums. Several CDs have been made of her renderings of composers ranging from Brahms to Wagner and Mahler.

In 1976 the Oude Meester Group established a foundation aimed at promoting music and theatre in South Africa. The Oude Meester Foundation for the Performing Arts has made a massive contribution to musical life in the country, inter alia by supporting concerts by artists of international stature, the National

Choir Festival and prizes for promising young musicians. The Foundation also provides support for master classes by musicians and theatre specialists, aimed at improving the quality of local artists. Excellence in the field of professional theatre in the Western Cape is recognised annually by the Foundation's Fleur du Cap awards, considered to be among the most sought after in the country.

On their overseas travels the Ruperts were regular concertgoers. Over a period of sixteen years they regularly attended the annual Whitsun Festival in Salzburg, Austria, where they made the acquaintance of the German conductor Herbert von Karajan, who became a good friend. In 1977 they attended the Salzburg Festival in the company of the German banker Jurgen Ponto, the Spanish ophthalmologist Joaquin Barraquer (who had treated Hanneli), the Canadian shoe manufacturer Tom Bata, and their wives. Shortly afterwards Ponto, chairman of the Dresdner Bank, was murdered in Germany by members of the infamous Baader-Meinhoff gang following a failed kidnap attempt. Three weeks after Ponto and his concert pianist wife had been his guests in Salzburg, Rupert flew to Germany to attend the banker's funeral.[15]

In his opening speech at the Cape Art Festival in 1968, Rupert summed up his response to aesthetic experience and his views on 'the human value of the arts'. He gave a résumé of highlights in his own encounters with the arts over the years, including musical events such as 'Orpheus and Eurydice' directed by the great Fürtwaengler in his first post-war concert at La Scala in Milan; Dietrich Fischer-Dieskau in the *Lieder* cycle *Die Schöne Mullerin* accompanied by Gerald Moore; 'Aida' at the ruins of the Caracalla baths in Rome; visual experiences like the world exhibition of Rembrandts in Amsterdam on the tercentennial anniversary of the artist's birth, an exhibition of all Picasso's sculptures at the Tate in London . . . He elaborated on the feeling 'when one suddenly discovers the most beautiful French impressionists in the Art Institute in the concrete jungle of Chicago. And when one encounters for the first time in the Art Gallery in Bremen the works of Paula Modersohn-Becker, mother of the German expressionists, and of whom our own Irma Stern and Maggie Laubser are also offspring.' At such times, Rupert declared, 'fatigue and lethargy disappear. Then one's cup overflows with joy.' As someone coming from the world of science and technology, he concluded, 'I realise the value of the arts in humanising cities and normalising the enormous powers at the disposal of modern human beings.'[16]

An incident in the musical world in which the Ruperts were involved and that reached the media, happened in October 1993. Rupert and Huberte had bought two tickets for a recital of Mozart's Requiem, in which Hanneli was performing at the Cape Town city hall. But when they arrived with their tickets, their seats were already occupied – by the later Minister of National Education, Kader Asmal, and his Irish wife. When the Ruperts indicated that they were occupying seats that had been paid for, the Asmals refused to vacate them. The septuagenarian couple then seated themselves on the steps of the gallery to listen to the concert.

With reference to the incident, a reader from Bellville, Bets Botes, wrote in a letter to *Die Burger*: 'What a wonderful example this true gentleman is to us all. He does not kick up a fuss. He does not scold anybody. True to the inner nobility that has become so characteristic of his style over the years, he and Mrs Rupert quietly sit down on the steps to enjoy the evening. Our world today is in terrible need of people of the calibre and stature of an Anton Rupert. Bravo and hats off to this humble great man.'[17]

CHAPTER 28

Lure of the wild

I ncreasingly convinced of the need for coexistence between humans and nature, Rupert became closely involved with nature and game conservation from the 1960s.

The Worldwide Fund for Nature (WWF), with its famous panda logo, was founded in 1961. By the end of the 20th century, it was the largest international conservation body in the world. Operating in 90 countries, it is engaged in numerous areas, from wildlife and nature conservation to global warming, the hole in the ozone layer and saving the rain forests.[1] When the founder-president Prince Bernhard of the Netherlands wanted to start a branch in South Africa in 1966, he approached Anton Rupert, already a trustee of the National Parks Board. In particular he was perturbed by the South African government's schemes for the Etosha pan in northern Namibia, then still South West Africa and governed by the Republic under a League of Nations mandate. The government intended to create ethnic homelands in the mandate territory that would lead to a balkanisation of the Etosha game park. Prime Minister Verwoerd took exception to Prince Bernhard's criticism and did not support the establishment of a WWF branch in the country.

Two years after Verwoerd's death in 1966 Prince Bernhard repeated his request and Rupert tried again. This time the obstacle was the Wildlife Society, which declined to become a branch of the WWF. That was why the Southern African Nature Foundation (SANF) was created. But it was not the only reason. According to WWF policy, branches confine their activities to their own countries. In line with his philosophy of partnership, Rupert was keen to involve the whole subcontinent of southern Africa. Besides, with anti-South African feeling rampant at the time he foresaw that a purely South African venture would have limited impact.

The SANF was established on 14 June 1968. Its head office was in South Africa, but it was to operate from Malawi southwards. To prevent any competition with the Wildlife Society, only corporate membership was allowed. Rupert was the first president, with an executive committee that included Dr Rocco Knobel of the National Parks Board, Dr Jan van der Horst of Old Mutual, LCV Walker and James Verwey, the first executive director. Rupert made it his business to canvass members from the South African business community. By the end of its first year 72 companies had joined and the SANF had an income of R131 000. Soon it was one of the few non-profit organisations in the country that could pay its own way. All donations went strictly to conservation.

The first projects were beyond South Africa's borders. Thanks to efforts such as these by the SANF, environmental conservation, which had undergone a transformation worldwide after initially being seen as the concern of a small group of campaigners, was also starting to influence people's everyday lives in southern Africa. The first two southern African countries to benefit from the SANF's activities were Swaziland and Lesotho. In Swaziland an amount of R47 224 went on expanding the Mlilwane nature reserve, which was handed to the government of the new country during its independence celebrations on 7 September 1968. For the first time in a hundred years lion and elephant – the country's national symbols – returned to Swazi soil. In 1970 the SANF assisted with the establishment of Lesotho's Sehlabathebe nature reserve while Rupert was doing pioneering work in that country as honorary economic adviser.

The first project in South Africa was a donation of R120 000 to construct a weir in the Letaba River, the first permanent dam in the Kruger National Park. It was named after the donor, the American millionaire Charles Engelhard.

In 1971 a special chair in environmental management, the first of its kind in the southern hemisphere, was instituted at Rupert's alma mater, the University of Pretoria. It was sponsored by the SANF. The university, which had awarded him an honorary D.Sc degree in 1960, the first of his five honorary doctorates, wanted it to be called the Anton Rupert Chair of Nature Management. In his speech on the occasion Rupert asked, however, that it should rather be named after the versatile Afrikaans journalist, lawyer, poet and naturalist Eugène Marais, to commemorate the centenary of his birth. Marais's study of the collective mind of a termite colony, *The soul of the white ant,* was allegedly plagiarised by the Nobel prizewinning Flemish writer and naturalist Maurice Maeterlinck, who was able to read Afrikaans. Expressing his admiration for Marais's genius, Rupert quoted Robert Ardrey: 'As no gallery of modern art can fail to be haunted by the burning eyes of Vincent van Gogh, so the pages of no future science can fail to be haunted by the brooding, solitary, less definable presence of Eugène Marais.'[2]

He had reserved his request until the last minute, Rupert said, for fear that a discussion in the university council might be sidetracked into a controversy about Marais's morphine addiction. The university granted his request, and the Eugène Marais Chair of Nature Management was later followed by chairs at other universities in environmental law, conservation biology, environmental education, and environmental policy and management.

As in the case of other projects he tackled in the field of social responsibility, Rupert looked for partners. The WWF, in whose international executive he served, had been struggling to collect sufficient funds. In the first decade of its existence it raised barely $1 million. Rupert then came up with a plan – 'Conservation without money is conversation', he quipped. In 1971 he persuaded Prince Bernhard to launch Club 1001 as a fundraising agency, to which Rupert seconded one of his personal assistants, Charles de Haes. A thousand people in over 50 countries were approached for contributions of $10 000 each to cover the WWF's operational and scientific costs. South Africa, with 71 contributors, was fourth on the list of donor countries. In just fifteen months De Haes managed to recruit 400 members, leaving the WWF with a solid bank balance of $4 million. In 1972 Rupert predicted that this 'crazy idea' would raise $10 million. Over the years he was proved correct.

According to Prince Bernhard, Rupert was acutely conscious of the stigma of his South African citizenship during the apartheid era. He did not mind operating behind the scenes and he had learned from experience how to maintain a low profile in international circles. As treasurer of the WWF board, he personally helped finance the establishment of new branches all over the world, Prince Bernhard said. Then, out of the blue, at an AGM in Switzerland in the early 1970s, he announced his resignation. 'Hell, you can't resign,' Prince Bernard exclaimed. 'We'll talk about it later.' After the meeting they had a private discussion, when Rupert explained that he could not jeopardise the WWF's reputation through the involvement of a South African, as South Africa had a bad name because of the country's policy of apartheid. 'But you can count on me as long as I live, but not on the front page.'[3]

The board of trustees of the SANF (renamed WWF SA in 1995) consisted of leading South African business and community leaders. An advisory committee identified conservation priorities and obtained the best independent scientific advice to guide the Foundation's activities. In its first five years the SANF contributed over R500 000 to 35 conservation projects in southern African countries, including projects in Malawi, Botswana, Angola, Swaziland, Lesotho, Zimbabwe and Mozambique.

In Malawi a major research project was instituted to protect the fish in Lake Malawi, which fed more than a million people. The Foundation embarked on the project after Dr Tony Ribbink of the Smith Institute in Grahamstown had expressed concern that fishermen trawling with long nets would decimate the lake's fish population. When the relevant cabinet minister in Malawi refused to receive the report, Rupert asked for a personal interview with President Banda, who took the necessary steps to protect the fish. The SANF also funded a project to train nature conservationists from Malawi to run the Lake Malawi National Park. This park, since declared a World Heritage site, has more endemic vertebrates (mainly fish) than any other park in the world.

In Mozambique, white rhino were resettled in two nature reserves. In Angola, a survey was done of the country's flora and fauna. And in Zimbabwe, the Foundation funded a massive operation to capture 30 black rhino which were under threat from poachers and move them to the Gonarezhou Park in that country. Another SANF project was an urgent investigation into the problematic elephant and buffalo populations in north-eastern Botswana. In 1975 a wildlife survey was undertaken in Damaraland and the Kaokoveld in present-day Namibia, before launching a comprehensive conservation programme that was considered an international priority.

In 1974 a countrywide drive was launched by the SANF to raise funds for the establishment of nature reserves in the Karoo. Thousands of school children helped to sell special stamps for this fund. For the first time in South Africa's history two important nature reserves, the Karoo National Park at Beaufort West and the Karoo Nature Reserve at Rupert's home town, Graaff-Reinet, were established by the public. In Lausanne, Switzerland, Rupert presented Prince Bernhard with 2 000 of the stamps as a symbolic title deed to the hundred acres of Karoo land that he had bought on a previous visit to South Africa. 'There is no other area like the Karoo,' Bernhard said. 'It is recognised internationally as a unique natural treasure and your plan to establish new parks deserves the highest praise and support from us all.' The prince had fallen in love with this primordial landscape, and his daughter, Princess Irene, bought a farm at Nieu Bethesda near Graaff-Reinet.

The first springbok and black wildebeest were released at the Karoo National Park at Beaufort West in 1977 and the area was declared South Africa's eleventh national park. The plans for a unique nature reserve encircling Graaff-Reinet did not come to fruition until 1992, when the town's golf course was purchased to consolidate the conservation zone. This has made Graaff-Reinet the only South African town to be entirely surrounded by a nature reserve.

August 1983 saw the advent of Flora '83, the biggest exhibition of wild flowers ever held in South Africa. It marked the start of an SANF campaign to conserve South Africa's indigenous flora, which became the biggest conservation project of its kind in southern Africa. New reserves were created in areas noted for their biodiversity. In conjunction with Cape Nature Conservation and the petrol company Total, the SANF puchased Oorlogskloof near Nieuwoudtville, a veritable

treasure trove of indigenous flora. Steenkampsberg, known as the 'flower paradise of the Highveld' and breeding ground of three species of wild crane, was
proclaimed. And Beacon Hill farm near Port Edward was purchased to conserve
South Africa's largest concentration of rare and threatened tree species.

In the Pilanesberg area, where Huberte had grown up, the SANF was involved
in the massive Operation Genesis in 1979. Within six months some 4 000 animals
were captured in Botswana, Namibia, Natal and the Cape and resettled in the
newly established Pilanesberg National Park. The park is home to the Big Five
(lion, elephant, leopard, buffalo and rhino) and has the third largest rhino population in the world. The nearby Sun City, built by casino king Sol Kerzner, is the
playground of the rich and the park soon became a major tourist attraction. By
the turn of the century it was drawing 500 000 visitors annually, about half as
many as the much larger Kruger National Park.

Besides its field projects the SANF has also published some valuable books.
The capture and care of wild animals, a pioneering study, has become an indispensable reference work internationally. *Mammals of Moçambique,* a manual on 180
land and marine mammals, appeared in 1975, and *Trees of Southern Africa* three
years later.

In 1985 Rupert achieved a crucial breakthrough for conservation in South Africa
with his groundwork for the establishment of the National Parks Trust Fund, to
be used for the expansion and improvement of the country's national parks. The
fund kicked off with a special contribution from two Arab sheiks, the brothers
Naghi, who donated $1 million each. Their donation was given to Rupert, a good
friend, out of gratitude for what he had meant to them. He had broken his rule
not to give any advice on shares and investments in the case of the Naghi brothers, who were Rothmans' Middle Eastern representatives. When the gold price
soared to a giddy $800 a fine ounce they asked him what they should do with their
gold shares. Rupert said that if they were his, he would sell them at that level.
They were so grateful about this advice that they decided to give him a donation. When Rupert received a cheque from the Saudi British Bank for $2 million
(at that stage equivalent to R4,4 million), made out to him personally, he signed
it over to the account of the SANF.

The South African government was persuaded to make a matching donation,
and a trust fund was started with initial capital of R9 million. The annual interest is spent on national parks and the acquisition of new conservation areas. The
SANF's contribution to South Africa's network of parks and protected areas has
been one of its greatest achievements, particularly thanks to the National Parks
Trust Fund. By 2003 some R45 million had been spent for these purposes. More

than 69 000 hectares of land had been bought by the trust fund, of which Rupert became chairman in 1986.

On Rupert's initiative the WWF's 25th Jubilee Club was established the following year. Twenty-five benefactors donated $1 million to commemorate the WWF's 25th birthday in 1986.

In his broad concern for large ecosystems Rupert did not overlook the contribution of outstanding individuals to nature conservation in Africa. On 27 August 1990 he awarded the SANF gold medal and a prize of R10 000 to Petros Ngomane, Swaziland's chief game ranger, who had become his country's first game ranger in 1959. In 1965, while he was trying to arrest a poacher, the man stabbed him in the neck, smashed his rifle over the ranger's head, then stabbed him eight times in the chest. After a few months in hospital, to which he had been admitted in a critical state, Ngomane returned to his post. Twice he infiltrated gangs of poachers and rhino horn traders, leading to the arrest of these criminals. 'It is people like you who give me faith in the future,' Rupert said when he presented the medal to Nogamane.[4]

An old friend of the Ruperts, Hans Hoheisen, owned not only the well-known Delheim wine estate at Stellenbosch but also a 15 000 hectare farm adjoining the Kruger National Park. Worth some R17 million in the early 1990s, Timbavati was one of the few farms where elephant could still roam freely in the wild. In 1992 Hoheisen donated this paradise to the SANF, the biggest donation of its kind ever made in the world. It was the first expansion of the Kruger Park since it was launched under that name in 1926 and at that time the only private nature reserve to be administered as part of the Park. 'In his quiet, modest way, without publicity, he has made an impact in the field of conservation that will continue to amaze our children in decades to come,' Rupert wrote in a tribute after Hoheisen's death in July 2003 at the age of 98.[5]

Hoheisen's generosity triggered further donations, which enabled the SANF to purchase the luxury Ngala camp on a neighbouring farm. Ngala yields an annual income of between R2 million and R3 million, which has been used to expand the West Coast National Park (at Saldanha north of Cape Town, only the second South African national park to preserve a stretch of the coastline), the Mountain Zebra Park near Cradock and the Karoo National Park at Beaufort West.

In 1993, the SANF's 25th anniversary year, the German government decided to erect a R20 million SA Wildlife College on Hoheisen's former farm in honour of this German descendant's magnanimity. With the aid of people from nearby villages, who also provided some building materials, the college was constructed within eighteen months. Rupert has pointed out that since offering its first course in 1995, it has trained over a thousand nature conservationists, game rangers, field guides and other experts. He envisaged that around 10 000 people from all over southern Africa would be trained there in the next five years.

Another spin-off in 2003 was the establishment of an institute to research wildlife diseases, which holds benefits for other areas in Africa as well. Hoheisen's donation was lauded by Prince Bernhard: 'It is the kind of vision from which the whole world can benefit.' Just before his death in 2003 Hoheisen received a letter from Nelson Mandela, emeritus patron of the Peace Parks Foundation, who wrote: 'You have given the nation a magnificent gift of lasting and immeasurable value. The wisdom and generosity of your gift will ensure the protection and survival of seriously threatened wildlife, not just in South Africa, but also in many other countries.'[6]

The SANF also received other munificent donations. In 1992 a major ecosystem reserve was started in the Great Fish River valley when Sam Knott, a prominent Eastern Cape farmer and businessman, bequeathed sixteen farms to the SANF. Elizabeth Harding left R6 million in her will for the conservation of bird life in the Western Cape. The Cape Peninsula, South Africa's biggest tourist attraction, has a remarkable biodiversity comprising 2 285 plant species, 105 of them endemic. The Cape floral kingdom and *fynbos* are world renowned. In 1993 Sir Edmund Hillary of Everest fame visited South Africa to promote the Table Mountain Fund. It was created at the request of various concerned conservation organisations and management bodies to rehabilitate the Peninsula's mountain range from Signal Hill to Cape Point. The entire area, including Table Mountain, has since been proclaimed a national park.

Besides assistance with the establishment or expansion of six national parks, including the Addo Elephant National Park outside Port Elizabeth, the SANF has helped to create or expand a great number of nature reserves, like the Karoo Nature Reserve near Graaff-Reinet and the Baviaanskloof wilderness area in the Eastern Cape.

The SA Natural Heritage programme, one of the most important conservation campaigns of its kind in South Africa, was launched in 1984 to involve private landowners in nature conservation. The upshot has been a whole network of small conservation areas on privately owned land to augment the country's network of formal parks and reserves. Over the years the SANF has spent millions on the rehabilitation of rural areas generally through schemes aimed at benefiting impoverished communities, inter alia via the Green Trust, which is run in conjunction with Nedbank. The Green Trust is aimed at reconciling human needs and environmental conservation.

The Foundation has undertaken and assisted innumerable other projects to conserve South Africa's biodiversity, which the World Conservation Monitoring Centre at Cambridge rates third in the world, after Brazil and Indonesia. South Africa only constitutes 0,8% of the Earth's surface, but houses more than 8% of the world's higher plant species, 8% of birds and 5,8% of the mammal species. To promote the conservation of, inter alia, the Cape *fynbos* floral kingdom with its 8 500 species, the SANF plays a leading role in the Flora wildflower show, the biggest show of indigenous flowers in the world.

In 1984 a countrywide programme was launched to mark and then release line fish. By 1993 over 3 000 anglers had marked some 70 000 fish and important data had been collected by the country's ichthyologists. The country's population of southern right whales has increased by about 7% annually since Dr Peter Best started his programme in 1969, the longest running scientific monitoring programme of a whale population in the world. Other rare and threatened species to have benefited by SANF involvement are black rhino, roan antelope, wattled crane, the riverine rabbit and the African penguin.

'There is little doubt that the picture of conservation in South Africa would have been very different had it not been for the SANF's work behind the scenes over the past 25 years,' said Dr Allan Heydorn, former head of the Foundation, in 1993.

CHAPTER 29

Title deeds to the country

C oncern about the increasing neglect of South Africa's historical buildings, particularly homes built in the characteristic Cape Dutch style,
gave rise to the establishment of Historical Homes of South Africa.
Over the years, the organisation has saved or helped save hundreds of examples
of South Africa's architectural heritage from demolition. As a result of these initiatives Anton Rupert's name has become inextricably linked to imposing towns
such as Stellenbosch, Tulbagh and Graaff-Reinet, whose historical buildings
have become major tourist attractions.

As far back as the 1950s friends of Rupert's, notably Frans Smuts, professor of
classics at the University of Stellenbosch, had voiced their concern about the dete-
riorating situation regarding the preservation of old buildings. Despite the idealistic efforts of institutions like the erstwhile Historical Monuments Commission
and the Simon van der Stel Foundation, only a few hundred of the thousands of
Cape Dutch homesteads and other old buildings from the 18th and early 19th
centuries remained. During the 1950s, in particular, many buildings of historical
importance were razed by bulldozers in the name of 'progress' and 'development'.

Yet South Africa had a long history of conservation. In 1657, only five years
after the Dutch East India Company (VOC) had started its victualling station at
the Cape of Good Hope, Commander Jan van Riebeeck issued a proclamation to
protect the indigenous forest at Hout Bay. Thirty years later, Governor Simon van
der Stel issued an edict to protect indigenous antelope species. One of the best-
known examples of a successful preservation action towards the end of the 19th
century was the sustained effort by Marie Koopmans-de Wet to save the Castle
in Cape Town. This formidable lady, who had been born in the Koopmans-De
Wet house in Strand Street, Cape Town, campaigned on several occasions for the
survival of the Castle, the oldest extant VOC fortress in the world. When the Cape
government wanted to build a road through one of the Castle's bastions so that
Darling Street could run directly into Sir Lowry Road, Prime Minister Cecil John
Rhodes sent his private secretary to Mrs Koopmans-de Wet to sound out her
feelings: would she mind if just a 'tiny little tip' of the Castle was cut off to make
way for the new road? 'Tell Mr Rhodes,' she said, 'that his nose is just a tiny little
tip of his face. Let him cut it off, then look in the mirror.'[1] The Castle, one of the
country's most famous cultural landmarks, was preserved.

Typically, Rupert took the initiative regarding the remaining historical buildings after his friends, especially Smuts, had urged him to become involved. Later he recorded his belief in the importance of preserving cultural heritage: 'Civilised people cannot live on bread alone. A nation that neglects its cultural treasures undermines its own civilisation and sows the seeds of its own decline.'[2]

In 1959 Rupert was approached about a preservation project when the Stellenbosch town council decided to restore the historic *Burgerhuis* in the centre of the town and preserve it for posterity. It was situated just half a block away from his later head office in Alexander Street. The badly dilapidated Cape Dutch homestead, with a gable the artist JH Pierneef had described as one of the Cape's most beautiful, had been built in 1797 by Antonie Fick, grandson of a German immigrant. Rembrandt offered to rent it so as to cover the restoration costs. Already Rupert was applying the principle that guided all his later projects: there is no point rescuing an old building unless it could be put to sustainable use. That meant it would pay for itself – and yield a profit. Appropriately, the building eventually became the headquarters of Historical Homes of South Africa Limited, with a fine collection of antique Cape furniture, VOC glassware, Arita porcelain and copperware on display.[3]

The groundwork for the establishment of the company Historical Homes commenced in 1965 when Rupert made a public appeal for the preservation of the remaining Cape Dutch homesteads. 'Sixty years ago there were about 3 000 of our graceful Cape Dutch houses – today there are fewer than 500 left. Of these, only 275 have retained their original character and, according to a recent survey, only a scant 100 could be considered sure to survive.'[4]

The response was encouraging, especially after Rupert had consulted his network of influential people. On 31 March 1966 Historical Homes, a subsidiary of the Rembrandt Group, was registered under the Companies Act. Its 136 founder members included 36 public companies, all the financial mining houses, newspaper groups and banking institutions. Thus an extremely heterogeneous membership was coordinated in a property-investment company focusing on buildings of historical or aesthetic value.[5] The members represented the most diverse interests ever brought together in a single organisation in South Africa.

Once again the new enterprise was based on Rupert's partnership philosophy. 'That is why,' he declared, 'I advocate a policy of partnership between capital and culture: to help preserve our legacy, but also to provide a climate that is conducive to the creation of cultural goods for the generations to come. History proves that material progress does not necessarily have to be in conflict with the flourishing of culture.'[6]

Rupert became the first chairman of Historical Homes, a position he would retain for decades and one of the few he did not give up when he started scaling down his commitments in the 1990s. Imker Hoogenhout was the first managing director and the first board consisted of Prof. Frans Smuts, Dr WEG Louw and Messrs AJ van der Riet, WHR Hill and W van Heerden. Smuts's company Koloniesland, which had done pioneering work in Stellenbosch in saving a number of historical buildings from demolition, merged with Historical Homes in 1967.

The starting capital was R550 000, R50 000 of it contributed by Rembrandt. All refurbished or restored buildings 'that form a link with our past on account of historical or aesthetic considerations' were rented out. From the outset, the preservation of valuable and irreplaceable cultural heritage was dealt with on business principles. To run the restoration work on a profit basis, Historical Homes assembled an experienced team of builders that undertook numerous projects. The foreman, Herold Alexander, who had been in charge of the restoration work since the formation of the company, was especially thanked by Rupert for his faithful service when the 25th anniversary of Historical Homes was celebrated on 4 October 1991. The occasion coincided with Rupert's 75th birthday; as a gift, he was presented with the chisel Alexander had used when restoring the company's first house in 1966.

The company's policy of making conservation pay through functional, dignified use of restored buildings proved to be sound. Initially the houses were put mainly to residential use, but over the years they were increasingly rented out as office space, apartments, restaurants, clothing stores, art galleries, museums and antique shops. Office premises, it was found, suffered the least wear and tear. The first year the net profit was just over R13 000. The next year they doubled the figure. Historical Homes continued making a profit every year and by 2002 it had reserves of over R10 million.

The activities of Historical Homes are concentrated mainly in three towns that are visited by hundreds of tourists – Stellenbosch, Tulbagh and Graaff-Reinet – but the company provides assistance in various other places where historical houses are restored and put to productive use.

Rupert's home town of Graaff-Reinet, where Historical Homes provided assistance with the restoration of façades and other construction work in respect of some 250 buildings, eventually became the South African town with the largest number of proclaimed historical monuments, some 300 in all. It is also the only town in the country encircled by a nature reserve.

Many buildings, especially the attractive façades, have been preserved in their original state after representatives of Historical Homes spoke to residents, providing cooperation and guidance. Much of this was due to Rupert's stalwart representative at Graaff-Reinet, Gerhard Froneman of Historical Homes. At his funeral at Somerset West in 2002 it was said that Froneman had driven more than 400 times to Graaff-Reinet, a distance of 650 km. Froneman acquired extensive knowledge of restoration projects, among other things by visiting Williamsburg in Virginia, USA, which the Rockefellers had restored to an exact replica of the original 17th-century settlement. Froneman believed that the restoration project in Graaff-Reinet was in many respects more extensive than that of Williamsburg, one of America's most popular tourist destinations. The main difference between the two was that Graaff-Reinet consisted of buildings that had survived and been restored to their former glory, while the 20th century had not been excised from the town.

In 1962 Rupert said in an address to the African Affairs Society of America in New York that when David Rockefeller had visited him in Stellenbosch, he had been amazed at the rich cultural legacy left by the Dutch colonists in South Africa. Rockefeller and his older sister and brothers, including Nelson Rockefeller, former governor of New York, had grown up in their parental home with the Dutch name Kykuit. On his visit to South Africa David Rockefeller, who became a good friend of the Ruperts, said to Rupert: 'Anton, these buildings are the title deeds to the country you love.'

One of the oldest buildings in Graaff-Reinet that had been under threat of demolition, the Dutch Reformed Mission church, was saved through Rupert's personal intervention shortly before the founding of Historical Homes. It is the fifth-oldest church building in South Africa, and had been built and consecrated in 1821. With its four lovely gables it is one of only three cruciform churches in the country to have survived. Once, when the original thatched roof needed to be replaced, the then minister's wife toured the country to raise money. President Paul Kruger of the Transvaal Republic was one of the donors. Under the Group Areas Act the coloured congregation had to vacate the premises and the historical church was sold to the Total oil company, which proposed building a filling station on the site.

The demolition date was set for 20 April 1965. Rupert got wind of it and on 17 April, a day before he was due to fly overseas, he stayed over in Johannesburg and had a meeting with Total chief Alphonse Hough to make Total an offer to rescue the church. However, Hough was not amenable to giving up his plans for the strategic site on the town's main street. In the end, Rupert hinted that it would be a shame if Rembrandt's and Distillers' hundreds of sales representatives who spent every day on the road were to be so outraged by the demolition of a historical church that they decided to shun Total filling stations altogether. Hough then realised that it would be better if the church were saved for posterity.

Rupert not only wanted to preserve the building for posterity, but also to use it productively as 'a living cultural asset' and a source of joy and enrichment for the town's residents as well as its growing numbers of tourists and visitors. Historical Homes restored the little church and it was turned into an art museum, which was officially opened on 26 July 1966. The collection of artworks consists of a selection of paintings, graphics and sculptures by leading South African artists who had been asked by Rupert personally to donate one of their finest works to the museum. The 126 works of 103 artists are considered one of the best South African art collections, particularly art of the 1960s. The oldest work on display is Moses Kottler's first bronze, *Oom Fanie*. Paintings include works by Walter Battiss, Gregoire Boonzaier, Maggie Laubser, Maud Sumner, Alexis Preller, Irma Stern, David Botha and Adolf Jentsch.

The museum is named after Rupert's mother, Hester Rupert. Her photograph, together with a charcoal sketch of Rupert by Jean Welz, hangs in the entrance hall. Both the building and the artworks were donated in trust to the town council. On Rupert's 52nd birthday in 1968 the Hester Rupert Museum, which has become one of the greatest attractions of Graaff-Reinet, was proclaimed a national monument.

The old *Drostdy* (magistrate's residence) of Graaff-Reinet was built in 1804 according to a design by the renowned architect Louis Michel Thibault. The imposing gabled building in the town's main street was restored by Historical Homes and turned into a hotel complex for the Rembrandt Group. Expert advice was obtained from Dave Rawdon, owner of the Lanzerac Hotel in Stellenbosch and the historic Lord Milner Hotel at Matjiesfontein, for the restoration and furnishing of the Drostdy Hotel.

The Georgian buildings flanking the hotel on either side were converted into an auditorium and a restaurant, the Camdeboo. The slave quarters in the colourful old Stretch's Court at the back became hotel rooms. The adjoining Ferreirahuis, birthplace of prominent South African banker-businessman GT Ferreira of First Rand, now comprises luxury suites with a private garden and fountain. Kromms Inn nearby is an informal pub that serves light meals. The Victorian buildings in Bourke Street have been turned into staff quarters with a private swimming pool. Stretch's Court was renamed Drostdyhof in 1970, when it was incorporated as part of the Drostdy Hotel. Drostdyhof was officially inaugurated by Prime Minister John Vorster, who praised Historical Homes in his opening address: 'I am glad to have the opportunity today to thank Historical Homes of South Africa on behalf of all population groups for the very important task you have taken upon yourselves with the preservation of so much of our most precious human-made cultural legacy . . . There is now fortunately a company which can act swiftly and effectively, which can buy, restore or repair, and all of this on a self-sustaining economic basis.'[7]

The John Rupert Little Theatre, a restored building of the London Missionary Society named after Rupert's father, was officially opened in 1980. At the opening ceremony Gene Louw, the then administrator of the Cape Province, also lauded Rupert's preservation initiatives: '. . . my admiration for the many talents, the mettle and the perseverance of the great South African Dr Anthony Edward Rupert, a leader of leaders and a man who still believes in miracles. What he has achieved with regard to the preservation and restoration of our cultural treasures stands as a monument to the finest qualities that can be combined in any individual.'

Rupert and Rembrandt established the *Red Reinet* (Save Reinet) Foundation in 1981 with a view to the town's bicentennial celebrations in 1986. The main aim was the restoration and preservation of the façades of more than 250 buildings in the historical town centre. The Foundation endeavoured to assist the owners of typical Karoo-style houses on a partnership basis. The owners, all founder members of Red Reinet, g ave permission for their properties to be proclaimed historical monuments. Rupert encouraged the residents of Graaff-Reinet to paint their houses white and green: white walls and green doors and window-frames. White ensured coolness in the hot Karoo summers and green complemented the Karoo plains perfectly, he maintained. Face brick he regarded as unsuitable there; it should rather be used on the Highveld, in places like Pretoria and Johannesburg.

Besides the art museum named after his mother and the theatre named after his father, Rupert had another mission church in Graaff-Reinet restored and named it after his brother Jan. The Jan Rupert museum contains the 32 panels of landscape paintings by the artist JH Pierneef that had once adorned the main concourse at Johannesburg's Park Station. They were taken down in 1971 and restored at the Pretoria Art Gallery, but not rehung in the station building. In 2002 Rupert negotiated with the railway company, Spoornet, and the paintings came to Graaff-Reinet on loan to be exhibited there. 'We don't realise how fortunate we are to have these artworks in our town,' said Theuns Eksteen, chairman of the Reinet Trust.

Historical Homes also owns buildings in a few other Eastern Cape towns that have been restored to their original state and are used productively. In Port Elizabeth two British settler homes from the 1820s are occupied by private tenants, as are five adjacent settlers' homes from the mid-19th century in Grahamstown. At King William's Town the Kaffrarian Museum, a little stone church built by the Baptists in 1853, is rented out as a mission museum.

Apart from the Burgerhuis in the historic town centre, which serves as Historical Homes' headquarters, the most important monuments to Historical Homes in Stellenbosch are to be found in the oak-lined Dorp Street. There are several architectural showpieces among the 34 buildings in Stellenbosch owned by the company. They include the old *Diaconieshuis* (Parish House) (1799), which is rented out as an antique shop, the Old Parsonage (1760), which accommodates a gold- and coppersmith, the Oude Meester Wine Museum (no longer in use), the Old Smithy and the Old Bakery (1850), which serve as offices and a shop for a watchmaker and gunsmith. The Vredelust homestead and cottage are let to a firm of consulting engineers. Restored Victorian and other old buildings in Dorp Street are semi-detached and detached homes, such as Saxenhof (1704) and Gymnasia (1866), building of the erstwhile Stellenbosch Gymnasium, precursor of the present university. The Rembrandt van Rijn Art Foundation has been housed until recently in one of the most impressive building complexes in Dorp Street, Libertas Parva, which belongs to Distell. The complex is adjoined by cottages designed by Sir Herbert Baker, where the Volkskombuis restaurant is situated.

Rupert's one failure with a building project with historical theme at Stellenbosch was his attempt to restore the town's old *drosdy* (magistrate's residence/court house). The first drosdy was built in 1687, eight years after the establishment of the town, on a site now occupied by the *Kweekskool*, the Dutch Reformed Seminary that has since become the university's Faculty of Theology. After a fire the drosdy was rebuilt in 1763 as an elegant H-shaped Cape Dutch homestead with one of the earliest rococo gables at the Cape. It was considered the acme of Cape Dutch architecture, emulated in many subsequent designs. In 1858 the Seminary took over the building. Initially the only modification was the words *Sole Deo Gloria* inscribed on one of the gables, but when the building became too small a second storey was added, changing the façade beyond recognition. Further ornate baroque additions followed.

In 1979 Rupert announced that the Oude Meester Group would construct an exact replica of the old drosdy on a vacant site at the lower end of Dorp Street in honour of the town's tercentenary. Like the other old buildings, it would be put to use as the country's first *vinothèque* and wine exchange (*bourse du vin*), with ample cellars below where red wines could age under perfect conditions. Anticipating objections to a facsimile, he cited replicas of splendid old buildings put up in Leipzig and Danzig after they had been destroyed in World War II. The drosdy would also form a unified whole with the nearby Rembrandt van Rijn Art Gallery, the Stellenrijk Wine Museum, the Brandy Museum and the cottages designed by Baker.

The project unleashed a storm of protest, from, amongst others, architects. The Stellenbosch architect Paul le Roux, calling it 'a step backwards', asked in a letter to *Die Burger*: 'What is the difference between a fake Rembrandt painting or literary plagiarism and a replica of a drosdy on a new site? There is no difference. All three are fake, despite the fine-sounding motivations.'[8] Another architect who objected to a rebuilt drosdy was Boets Smuts, son of Prof. Frans Smuts who had initially planted the idea of the value and preservation of historical houses in Rupert's mind.[9] Others supported the scheme, citing examples of similar replicas at Franschhoek and Swellendam. The debate raged on in the letters column of *Die Burger*. Upset by the objections, Rupert decided to abandon the project.

Years later, Le Roux contacted Rupert, for whom he had a high regard, to explain that his letter to the press had been a last resort since he would have preferred to discuss the issue with Rupert in person. Rembrandt officials had prevented him from reaching Rupert, however, and he expressed regret at the course he was forced to adopt. He informed Rupert that there had been broad-based opposition from influential residents of Stellenbosch to his plan, but they had not been prepared to confront him openly. Their objections were based on the notion that authentic historical and contemporary buildings were the essence of Stellenbosch, and that replicas were unwelcome. After all the years, the two men buried their differences and there was no ill feeling on either side.[10]

Rupert always remained concerned about preserving the distinctive character of Stellenbosch. As recently as 2003, when plans were mooted to build a brand-new conference complex in the middle of Stellenbosch, he wrote to the mayor objecting to the travesty of erecting such a huge centre with the inevitable appendages – hotels and further traffic congestion – in that locality. The project had 'the potential of sounding the death-knell for the town's historical centre,' he warned. The university had ample conference space and if more were needed, premises could be erected on the outskirts where they would not destroy the traditional small-town atmosphere which other university towns the world over appeared to treasure. Rupert received strong support from a number of council members of the university, although at that stage it seemed as if the town authorities had not yet given enough thought to solutions that would preserve the historical town centre, such as creating an inner zone where only pedestrians are allowed and providing a ring road with parking areas around the town.

A major restoration project in the Western Cape in which Historical Homes was involved, was undertaken in the town of Tulbagh. In 1969 Tulbagh was hit by a severe earthquake that caused extensive damage to buildings. Imker Hoogenhout and Gerhard Froneman, who succeeded the former as CEO of the company, took the lead in producing a fully restored Church Street with 28 Cape Dutch houses. Both were awarded gold medals by the National Monuments Commission. Historical Homes still administers the Tulbagh Trust, the collaborative body formed at the time of the disaster.

Historical Homes owns and restores properties elsewhere as well. At Swellendam, the old Boys' School, originally a wagon-making shop built in 1825, is leased to the Olyfkrans College and two residences dating back to the 1830s are rented by private families. Assistance has also been provided with many other restoration projects, ranging from the water mills at Mamre, Elim and Genadendal to the fishermen's cottages at Waenhuiskrans (Arniston). The Bo-Kaap Museum in Cape Town's Malay Quarter was opened by Rupert's Indonesian friend Julius Tahija after the group had helped fund it. Sponsorship was provided for the publication of Prof. JJ Oberholster's book *Historiese monumente van Suid-Afrika*.

At Heidelberg in Gauteng, where Rembrandt had its northern tobacco factory, the group took over the old station building, inaugurated by Pres. Paul Kruger in 1895 when he opened the south-eastern railway line to Natal, and turned it into a transport museum. This is where Rupert's father's 1920s Chevrolet ended up. Bicycles dating back to the early 19th century and early 20th-century vintage cars are displayed here, as well as authentic South African cars like the GSM Dart-Flamingo and the Protea. Here the home that once belonged to the Afrikaans poet AG Visser was purchased by the Rembrandt Group, as was Totius's old house in Potchefstroom. In Pretoria the group bought the house of the sculptor Anton van Wouw, which Rupert handed over to the University of Pretoria on 21 May 1974 on behalf of the group, saying that he had got to know Van Wouw 35 years before in the same house, and 'that today it is to me more than just an ordinary honour to be able to hand over this house to my old alma mater.' Many of Van Wouw's best-known sculptures are displayed in the house. Among the sculptures of Van Wouw that Rupert admires, he considers the bronze of two kneeling Boer combatants entitled 'Bad news' his most heartrending work.

With properties valued at R85 million in 2003, Historical Homes has proved that the preservation and utilisation of old buildings is extremely lucrative. In 1990 it paid a special dividend of 100c, that is 100%, equivalent to the company's issued capital. That year Stellenbosch had 140 proclaimed properties, as opposed to a mere seven in 1966. This point was made forcefully by Martiens van Bart, property editor of *Die Burger*, who referred to Historical Homes' excellent financial results to underscore the short-sighted folly of financial institutions who prefer to demolish the nation's architectural heritage for the sake of 'development' rather than restore it and put it to functional, profitable use.[11]

Rupert has succeeded in his initial aim of proving that preservation is economically feasible and can be a profitable investment. In the process Historical Homes has not only silenced many sceptics, but its example has spread country wide as a catalyst. More and more South Africans have realised that it is worthwhile to keep cultural treasures and heritage alive and productive. This was summed up by Rupert in the annual report of Historical Homes of 1973: 'The norm of its success should be seen in equal measure in the image it conveys to the outside world, the influence it radiates and the contagious power of the example it sets.'

In a lecture entitled 'Is the preservation of our heritage economically justifiable?' that he delivered in his capacity as honorary professor at the University of Stellenbosch on 25 August 1975, Rupert explained what in South Africa was worth preserving. It was the one and only time he had been asked by the university of the town in which he lived to give a lecture, although he was a member of the university council. The following day he delivered the same lecture at the University of Pretoria, where he lectured frequently and where his collected lectures were published in the glossy publication *Pro Munere Grates*.

In this lecture he referred to the diversity of buildings to be found in South Africa: temporary homes of the early stock farmers and migrants (wattle-and-daub and beehive stone cottages); gracious Cape Dutch homesteads with their distinctive gables; symmetrical, flat-roofed houses typical of Karoo architecture; British and German settler architecture in the Eastern Cape; Georgian and Victorian architecture all over the country, as well as 'ostrich palaces' from the same era in and around Oudtshoorn; and interesting examples of black African architecture, including traditional Ndebele huts decorated with polychrome geometrical designs.

He then formulated a number of reasons for preserving old buildings and cultural heritage:

- We must preserve because a nation without a history is like a person without memory. Historical buildings represent the milestones of history in material form.
- We must preserve because buildings from the past are tangible proof of the fact that we have been here for a long time and that we belong here. The historical buildings are the title deeds to the country we love.
- We must preserve because we may not just blithely obliterate the footprints of our ancestors.
- We must preserve because by retaining what was good from the past, we prevent boring uniformity.

- We must preserve because a city that grows organically is much more the product of humans than something that is planned for them. Oscar Niemeyer, planner of Brazil's new capital Brasilia, could not stand living in Brasilia and instead fled back to Rio de Janeiro. In Brasilia everything had been planned, nothing was unexpected. In Rio, on the other hand, every street had its surprises.
- We must preserve because our old villages and towns had been planned before cars started dominating our lives. That is why I prefer Graaff-Reinet and Stellenbosch with their feeling of 'togetherness' rather than the whizzing lanes of 'travellers to nowhere'.
- We must preserve because today it is in most cases sociologically better and economically cheaper to repair than to simply demolish.

He concluded the lecture: 'Every civilised country is proud of the tracks it had made on its developmental road – and the visible tracks of our cultural heritage are our historical buildings. Let us then preserve them carefully and keep them in trust for posterity, for they are truly "the title deeds to the country we love". May the generations to come never have to accuse us of having obliterated our footprints ourselves.'[12]

Historical Homes has played an important role in helping to curb the 'demolition frenzy' that caused such immeasurable damage in many historical places in South Africa. The Cape Town preservation architect Dirk Visser confirms that Historical Homes' policy of using historical buildings for practical purposes is the correct approach, since preservation and restoration for their own sake have become virtually impossible in the modern era. 'Restored buildings must be utilised productively to combat rising costs. From a marketing perspective there is no problem, as restored buildings are highly sought after. There are waiting lists of people who want to rent such buildings. On the other hand, the company enjoys the benefit that its buildings constantly appreciate in value.'

CHAPTER 30

Mother tongue and fatherland

D espite his travels that took him all over the globe, Rupert remained a South African patriot. Central to this is his connection with the Afrikaans language, interwoven with his view of different aspects of his identity that coexist harmoniously. He formulated the various loyalties and identifications that make up his notion of himself as an Afrikaner in the following way: 'I am a human being with a Christian conscience, a child of the Christian civilisation. Secondly, I am a speaker of Afrikaans. Thirdly, I am a South African. Fourthly, I am a Westerner, and fifthly, a citizen of the world.'[1]

His language consciousness is an ongoing association that started early in his life. He went to school at the first Afrikaans-medium high school in the Cape, and as a student he closely identified himself with the adoption of Afrikaans as medium of instruction at the University of Pretoria. His training in his home language to the highest tertiary level of the physical sciences as well as his sub-sequent international success as businessman provides an impressive testimonial for the importance of mother-tongue education.

To Rupert, the Afrikaans language is part of a national culture that developed over three centuries and could be compared 'with pride' to that in other countries. Two original and important contributions to world culture by Afrikaans-speaking South Africans (a grouping in which Rupert generally includes coloured Afri-kaans speakers) he considers to be 'our unique Cape Dutch architecture and the vigorous, flexible Afrikaans language, the youngest and most modern language of the Western world'. In a lecture at the University of Pretoria in 1975 he elaborated on his view of the distinctive culture of Afrikaans speakers as being of Africa and inextricably linked to the continent. 'As a whole, our civilisation and our culture is as little European or Western as our language is pure Dutch.' While Afrikaans speakers might have had European origins, they are essentially African. Their cultural identity 'that has been shaped over more than three hun-dred years, also carry the stamp of Africa and of living together with the cultures of this continent . . . The cultural and spiritual assets of our ancestors are a legacy that may not just be bequeathed; it has to be acquired anew by every generation.'[2]

His involvement with the language question, which still remains a burning issue in South Africa, has continued after the country's transition to a fully-fledged democracy. The period after 1994 saw the start of an alarming exodus of skills, with increasing numbers of Afrikaans speakers among those to leave. This has been exacerbated by a number of attempts on the part of government to scale down the role and functions of Afrikaans. In this situation, Rupert observes that if there is one factor that can ensure Afrikaans speakers' commitment to their country and will keep them here, it is the Afrikaans language; it is as important to them as the love for the country that virtually all South Africans share.

In his book *Prioriteite vir medebestaan* (Priorities for coexistence) (1981) he high-lighted the unique characteristics of the Afrikaans language: 'Afrikaans-speaking South Africans of today are the descendants of the only migrating European communities who established a new language in their new fatherland. Linguists today regard Afrikaans as a fully-fledged and independent branch of the Indo-Germanic languages. Moreover, it is the only language in Africa that carries in its name also the name of the continent on which it was born.'[3]

The rise of the Afrikaans language is indeed remarkable, given that in the 20th century only four languages became fully standardised and were used in all fields of public life, including science, technology and tertiary education: Malay-Indonesian, Hindi, Hebrew and Afrikaans.

Rupert emphasised his view of Afrikaans as an inclusive and common mother tongue of all who speak it – not belonging to academia or bureaucrats, but to all who cherish it – when he agreed to sponsor the writer Antjie Krog's Afrikaans translation of Nelson Mandela's book *Long walk to freedom*. He even perceived symbolism in the translated title, saying it would help Afrikaans along on its 'long walk to freedom' to find 'its rightful place in southern Africa as a young, exuberant language of Africa'.

At the launch of the book in 2001, Rupert declared: 'I don't believe one should obliterate one's footprints. The footprints of culture and civilisation are particularly visible in our buildings and in our writings – in the language we speak. This has been important to us as a group of companies. We believe that if you know where you come from, you also have a clearer vision of where you are headed.' He highlighted the role of language, above all, in helping to foster mutual understanding and respect for each other's circumstances and ideals among people, and referred to contributions made by the Rembrandt Group in this regard.

In 1959, for instance, the group sponsored the Afrikaans translation of Homer's epic *Iliad* from the original Greek, a task to which Prof. JPJ van Rensburg had devoted seven years. The Ruperts had been visiting the Van Rensburgs at home when the muted atmosphere caused Huberte to ask their friends what was wrong. She was told Van Rensburg could not find a publisher for his translation of the Homeric poem, the first transcription of which dated from 600 BC, as it was too expensive. As they drove home, Huberte said: 'Anton, this looks like a challenge for you.' Rupert felt the loss to Afrikaans would be too great if this classic work by Homer, considered the founder of Western literature, remained unpublished. He recommended to his board that Rembrandt should publish the pioneering work, and came up with a characteristic innovation: a large number of copies were printed and shareholders were made a special offer to obtain the book at a fair price. A few years later Van Rensburg's translation of Homer's *Odyssey* was published by Human & Rousseau without financial support from Rembrandt, but with the address list of all who had ordered the *Iliad*.

In the 1960s the group launched what Rupert has described as 'probably our most important contribution in the field of mutual understanding and communication': the Technidiscs, a series of language courses on gramophone records produced in cooperation with Sanlam. The series provided for the acquisition of indigenous languages, including isiXhosa and isiZulu, as well as various languages of immigrants to South Africa such as German, French, Italian, Greek and Portuguese. More than 30 000 courses had been sold before a publisher purchased the series in 1978.

A response to the launch of the Technidiscs that Rupert remembered in particular was that of Lord Fraser, well-known blind member of the British House of Lords, who ordered an Afrikaans language course. Rupert later met Fraser, who had extensive interests in Lesotho, through the Rembrandt employee Wynand van Graan whom he had seconded to the Lesotho Development Corporation. Fraser of Lonsdale was one of the influential people Van Graan had met during his stay in Lesotho. The trading house of Frasers was a household name in the kingdom where two brothers, Donald and Douglas Fraser, had owned more than 50 trading posts in the 19th century. After the war of 1880-81 they moved their base to Wepener in South Africa. Their nephew Ian Fraser, who had been blinded as a fighter pilot during World War I, was the heir to Frasers Ltd. In addition to his business interests, Lord Fraser had also been the governor of the British Broadcasting Corporation during World War II. He visited South Africa each year in the European winter and stayed in his imposing mansion in Wepener. Years later a farming couple from the district, a Mr and Mrs Swanepoel, transformed it into a guesthouse known as Lord Fraser House.[4]

After the military coup in Lesotho, Britain instituted sanctions against Chief Jonathan's government. As a British citizen Fraser could not travel to Lesotho, and Van Graan responded to a telephonic request to come to Wepener to inform him about the situation. Some time later Van Graan introduced Fraser to Rupert, on whom the blind British aristocrat made a deep impression. Rupert arranged for the Stellenbosch University choir to perform on the occasion of Fraser's 70th birthday, a gesture typical of him according to Van Graan, and one that was much appreciated by Fraser.

Rupert also helped to introduce the dynamic Afrikaans literature to a wider audience. An anthology of Afrikaans poems, *Afrikaanse Lyrik*, sponsored by Rembrandt, was translated by Helmut Erbe into German in 1959 to give German-speaking citizens a taste of the best Afrikaans poetry. This was followed in 1962 by *Afrikaans poems in English translation*, a collection compiled by AP Grové and CJD Harvey, with translations done by, among others, Harvey, Guy Butler and Anthony Delius.

In the 1940s Rupert and Huberte became good friends with the Afrikaans poet Dirk Opperman and his wife Marié. They had met in Johannesburg and the friendship was renewed when Opperman became a lecturer at the University at Cape Town. When he later moved to Stellenbosch as professor, the Oppermans' home Kiepersol at 3 Thibault Street was a stone's throw from the Ruperts' residence.

According to Opperman's biographer, John Kannemeyer, Rupert had a high regard for Opperman as a poet and the combination of artistry and logical-analytical thinking in his mental make-up. He asked Opperman for advice at times and was so impressed by his abilities that he wanted to employ the poet as copywriter – 'an offer Opperman declined smilingly yet emphatically'.

In 1956 the Ruperts organised a reception at the Stellenbosch farm Nooitgedacht for Mimi Coertse, who was starting to acquire world fame as an opera singer in Vienna. Huberte related years later that when she was once searching for sheet music for Mimi at a music shop in Salzburg, the owner had expressed the view that Mimi's rendition of the 'Queen of the Night' in Mozart's *Magic Flute* was the best any singer had yet sung this aria in Vienna. At Rupert's request Opperman wrote a quatrain, 'Mimi Coertse', for the Stellenbosch function.

At that stage Rupert held the view that he, Opperman and Piet Cillié, perspicacious editor of *Die Burger*, should form a triumvirate to provide political and intellectual leadership in Afrikaans circles. According to Kannemeyer, all three men were probably too independent and stubborn to have implemented such a plan successfully.

Rupert was impressed by the Cape production of Opperman's drama *Periandros van Korinthe* (Periander of Corinth) and said he could not get the protagonist out of his mind. When he heard that Opperman had never been to Greece, he arranged an overseas study bursary for him, in accordance with Rembrandt's policy of returning a portion of its profits as donations to the nation. Opperman, who eagerly embraced the opportunity to undertake an extensive study trip on his first overseas visit, referred to this in a poem in his last volume of poetry

Komas uit 'n bamboesstok (Comas from a bamboo reed). The 'Prince of Commerce' had enabled him to 'mount Pegasus' and given wings to his 'hobby'.

After his trip Opperman wrote Rupert a report on his experiences. His volume of poetry *Dolosse* (knuckle bones used for soothsaying) (1963) was in part the fruit of his travels, and at least twelve of the poems related directly to what he had experienced in Europe. Opperman also dedicated his drama *Vergelegen* to Rupert. At the launch of the publication in Cape Town on 21 September 1956 he handed Rupert a copy with an appropriate quatrain as inscription. The poet described Rupert as representing a great vision to Afrikaners through the way in which he reconciled within his activities 'the farmer, commerce and the arts', reminiscent of the Golden Age of their ancestors in the Netherlands.[5]

In 1967 Opperman wrote a foreword to a collection of Rupert's speeches (*Wie in wondere glo)* (Those who believe in miracles); speeches which, according to Opperman, had mostly made headlines because they always contained something new and surprising that captured the imagination. These addresses were examples of morally committed literature, the words of a man who wants to inspire the community with his ideas and wants to combat misconceptions and dangers, the poet wrote. Rembrandt's annual reports proved how the ideals formulated in the speeches 'have not only been dreams and illusions, but are realised in practice in higher figures, new business, new countries, new boards'. Opperman regarded Rupert as an exception to the process of alienation that increasing specialisation had brought humanity. As a 'prince of commerce' he was able to appreciate the business world as well as science and art, and virtually all his speeches contained as a subtheme a plea for the versatile human being. 'He holds up to us the image of a Michelangelo, a Leonardo da Vinci, of Athens as well as Sparta. What we actually have in these speeches is the vision of a neo-renaissancist.'[6]

Rupert also admired the other great Afrikaans poet-writer NP Van Wyk Louw, and felt that a monument should be erected to the brothers NP Van Wyk Louw and WEG Louw. One of the people he discussed this idea with was Piet Cillié. He had De Waal Park in Cape Town in mind as a possible site for such a monument. Family members of the Louw brothers were presumably not enthusiastic about the plan, however, and it was not taken further.[7]

Rupert was at one stage the biggest shareholder in Human & Rousseau publishers that had been started by Koos Human, former head of publications at Nasionale Boekhandel, and Leon Rousseau, the biographer of Eugène Marais (with his highly acclaimed *Die groot verlange* [The great longing]). Human recalls that Rupert once told him: 'Remember, you are in show business.' According to Human, in the years 1960-61 they had published 'with great bravado' a series of translated non-English detective stories, marketed as *'Billikboeke'* (inexpensive books) and sold at the low price of 95c for hardcover editions. 'Rupert said it was a mistake. We should rather sell them at R1.75 and market them as the world's best detective stories.'[8]

At Rupert's instigation art books in Afrikaans such as *Kuns as avontuur* (Art as adventure) were published by Rembrandt and made available to shareholders, while the country's architecture was described in *Historiese monumente van Suid-Afrika* (Historical monuments of South Africa). In commemoration of the group's 25th birthday the Rembrandt van Rijn Art Foundation compiled *Suid-Afrikaanse kuns van die twintigstge eeu* (South African art of the twentieth century), an art collection in book form that the group's PRO Johan Piek described in a circular of 22 September 1966 as 'the finest book of its kind ever published in South Africa'. Staff and shareholders could obtain it at half price. Such contributions were extended in the 1990s with glossy publications in honour of Irma Stern and Jean Welz, two of the country's most prominent artists.

Rupert was instrumental in the establishment of a research centre for Afrikaans at the then University of Bophuthatswana, donating R100 000 to that institution. At his request the centre was named after the language activist CP Hoogenhout in honour of the latter's grandson Daan Hoogenhout, Rupert's deceased colleague, who had grown up in what was at the time known as the black homeland of Bophuthatswana. The centre's activities included literacy projects and beginner's courses in Afrikaans. At the opening ceremony Rupert said that Afrikaans, the friendly language, belonged to everyone in South Africa – he described the language as a *'kanniedood'* (a type of drought-resistant aloe) that had the ability to hold out and keep on.

A year later he conducted the opening of the *Boekehuis* (House of books) at Calvinia, the brainchild of his sister-in-law Rona Rupert, wife of his brother Koos, who had produced 33 stories for children and young people by the time of her death in 1995. The Boekehuis is situated in a typical Karoo-style house of 1860 that was restored by Erwin and Alta Coetzee, and contains an exceptional collection of books on the Karoo. Among those who attended the official opening in 1993 was the photographer Cloete Breytenbach, who observed how Rupert handed the Coetzees a generous cheque that ensured the survival of the project as a cultural centre and refuge for writers. 'Anton Rupert is a *mensch*,' Breytenbach remarked in 2002 – a spontaneous and significant compliment on the part of a photojournalist who had found enough reason in the course of his newspaper career to become cynical about public figures and politicians whose feet of clay had struck him all too often.[9]

Rupert had expressed his view of Afrikaans in a striking fashion a few years earlier, on 20 February 1987, when he was awarded a medal of honour for service to the nation by the *Federasie van Afrikaanse Kultuurvereninge* (FAK, Federation of Afrikaans Cultural Societies). He considered the speech he delivered on that occasion under the title *'Moedertaal en vaderland'* (Mother tongue and fatherland) so important that he requested it should only be published in its entirety to prevent possible misunderstandings – the only time he ever directed such a request to the media.

The speech was not published anywhere in full at the time. This only happened on 18 August 2001, the day after Rupert had addressed the Cape Town Chamber of Commerce at a dinner where *Die Burger's* Business Leader of the Year was announced. He had received a standing ovation after his speech on the role of peace parks in Africa's young democracies. The year before, when he had been named as the newspaper's Business Pioneer, the main speaker, the academic Dr Jakes Gerwel, who served as director-general of Nelson Mandela's presidential staff, had praised him 'an exemplar of Afrikaansness that can be captured by the word "urbane".'

Rupert's speech of 1987 sounds as fresh and relevant in the new century as it did almost two decades ago. The FAK that he was addressing was one of the influential institutions representing the elite among white Afrikaans speakers that drew criticism from members of other groups in South Africa as well as dissenting Afrikaner intellectuals as appropriating the Afrikaans language in a narrow, exclusionary spirit.

Announcing at the start of his speech that he had a deeply felt need to bring the FAK an 'unconventional message' out of gratitude for the honour they had bestowed on him, he told his audience he was acting as an 'advocate for our common mother tongue, Afrikaans, and our common fatherland, South Africa.' In an unusual approach, he spoke in the first part of his speech 'symbolically and in the first person' on behalf of the Afrikaans language, reminding its speakers of the many strands of its origins that had contributed to this joint creation of a new language in Africa: the contributions of Dutch Protestants, Malay slaves, the French Huguenots. Afrikaans had been a 'humble' language, looked down upon as not welcome in fancy churches and schools, a language that had to struggle for public acceptance even among the elite of its own speakers.

'I was the language of those who had been "wronged", of those who were to call themselves Afrikaners – the carriers of Afrikaans - but also of the coloured people who nurtured me in the kitchens and of christianised black people who are not recognised as Afrikaners. And them someone came, perhaps with good intentions, yet thoughtlessly, and created the word "apartheid" in me, a word that was to become "apart hate" to the whole world – the only word in me that people know worldwide. And thereby I have come to be regarded as the language of the oppressor. Non-white people who use me as their home language have never been prohibited from worshipping in churches of other languages. But there are churches that use me as their language of worship that show the door to fellow Afrikaans speakers, even those who share the same faith.'

Referring to people who love Afrikaans, Rupert said that a monument had even been erected on Paarl Mountain out of this love for the language and in its honour. 'But there is another landmark for those who loved me and perhaps now hate me. It is a landmark of desolation – a part that was ripped out of the heart of old Cape Town. District Six – a landmark of the removal of many who had loved me. Today only minarets remain as evidence of the earlier presence of those who had used me as language in their worship.'

It had been forgotten, Rupert said, that the language had not only grown out of love but also through the actions of those who wanted to restrict it, such as Lord Charles Somerset who had unwittingly ensured the future of Afrikaans by eliciting resistance to his policy of forced Anglicisation and his banning of the use of Afrikaans in schools, churches and courts at the Cape. 'And those who ostensibly love and cherish me forgot the lesson and impeded my growth by attempting to impose me on others, as in the schools in Soweto in 1976.'

Addressing the FAK directly in the name of Afrikaans, Rupert said: 'You use my name Afrikaans in the middle letter of your name. May I, "your language" ask you: Do you allow everyone who honours me as mother tongue to join your ranks? . . . Are you going to let me, your own mother tongue, be restricted on account of prejudice? My future depends on your decisions. You were and are and remain my advocate! You are the FAK.'

Broadening his theme, Rupert said to FAK members: 'But your responsibility stretches further than just your mother tongue. You also have a related responsibility towards your "fatherland".' After referring briefly to the historical background that had led to the creation of numerous independent states in southern Africa as well as the many separate entities into which South Africa itself had been divided as a result of the 'homeland' policy, he said: 'But to be able to survive, this southern African community would need to come together again in future. It is imperative.' He outlined the irrevocable economic interdependencies and connections that existed between the peoples of southern Africa and the infrastructural as well as cultural systems (languages, faith, a free-enterprise orientation, legal system, etc.) they shared. 'As a group of companies we have been working for years in partnership with this whole area. We know most of the black leaders and can testify that we have experienced nothing but goodwill and friendliness. Why then the fears?'

Southern Africa was a wonderful region, he said, blessed with a diversity of flora, fauna and people as well as abundant natural resources. The economic performance of South Africa in the previous year despite trade boycotts showed what an African country could achieve. Yet there were thousands who were leaving this part of the world out of fear, and others trying to prevent change out of despair.

'But it is now time for everyone who calls himself an Afrikaner, and thereby professes that he is from Africa, to accept the calling to serve the "fatherland" together with other compatriots.

'We cannot and may not selfishly claim our mother tongue Afrikaans only for ourselves. The language belongs to all who make it their mother tongue. Likewise, we cannot and may not claim the fatherland for ourselves alone. South Africa belongs to all who make it their fatherland.

'Your future and mine does not lie in fear-ridden division, but in fearless co-existence.'

CHAPTER 31

Peace parks as African elephant

'In a world of war and turmoil we sell peace and tranquillity'
ANTON RUPERT

I n the 1990s, Rupert's long-standing belief in harmonious coexistence between humans as well as between humans and nature took on a new dimension. He came up with the visionary idea of establishing peace parks in southern Africa. At the age of eighty, a stage when most people had long since retired, he launched himself into what he himself called the grandest, most ambitious scheme of his life.

The concept of peace parks, particularly in areas that had seen major conflict, was not completely new, but Rupert linked it to transfrontier conservation and utilisation of game and wildlife. One of the most famous peace parks marks the epicentre of the nuclear explosion at Hiroshima in 1945 – an enduring reminder of the destructive power of the nuclear bomb, though one which Rupert never had the opportunity to visit on his extensive international trips. There is another at Nagasaki. The first transnational peace park was created by Canada and the USA as far back as 1932, when the Waterton Lakes National Park in Alberta was linked with the Glacier National Park in Montana to promote good bilateral relations and transnational conservation. It is one of the few transfrontier conservation areas that can be considered a peace park in its true sense, with a joint management system and unrestricted access for visitors.[1] Rupert regards Switzerland, the seven-century-old central European mountain state with its numerous autonomous cantons, as the oldest peace park on earth. He also believes a peace park to be the only solution to the centuries-old problem of Jerusalem.

In 1990, with South Africa poised on the threshold of a new era of reconciliation, Rupert launched a campaign to promote peace parks on the subcontinent. At the time he was president of WWF South Africa, then called the SANF, and in that capacity he sought an interview with Mozambican president Joaquim Chissano to discuss the possibility of permanent links between the protected regions in southern Mozambique and their counterparts across the borders of South Africa, Swaziland and Zimbabwe. Chissano agreed that the idea should be investigated and WWF SA undertook a feasibility study, which was submitted to the Mozambican government in September 1991. There were further studies, but the ongoing civil war between Renamo and Frelimo delayed the process. The project gained new momentum, however, after the successful transition to a fully-fledged democracy in South Africa, where a new, fully representative government came to power following the elections of 27 April 1994.

During Pres. Nelson Mandela's first two years in office the country experienced a surge of eco-tourism, but the benefits did not spill over to neighbouring Mozambique. Rupert then requested another meeting with Chissano, which was to be held on 27 May 1996, six years to the day after their first interview. The appointment was set for ten o'clock that morning, but Rupert was left to cool his heels for five hours. By the time the president at last received him he was thoroughly disgruntled, and said so. But, he added, he considered the cause he was advocating greater than any discourtesy the Mozambican head of state saw fit to show him. And he was not looking for any favours – on the contrary, he wanted to do one. Then he outlined the significant economic advantages that might follow for Mozambique if Chissano supported the peace park proposals.[2]

Rupert's blunt honesty had the desired effect. He and Chissano formed a firm relationship that grew over the years. Three weeks later a conference in the Kruger National Park was jointly chaired by the South African and Mozambican ministers of transport, Mac Maharaj and Paulo Muxanga. It was agreed that their two countries should collaborate, together with Zimbabwe and Swaziland, to exploit the economic potential of peace parks. In June 1996 the World Bank made its own recommendations in a report entitled 'Moçambique: transfrontier conservation areas pilot and institutional strengthening project'. The report introduced a significant new angle on the traditional concept of protected national parks by emphasising the manifold use of resources by local communities through the creation of transnational conservation areas across hitherto jealously guarded borders of sovereign states.[3] In such transfrontier parks homogeneous ecosystems can be consolidated and ancient game migration routes restored. Another important facet of the new approach is that rural populations are involved in the nature reserves so that they, too, can benefit from the anticipated tourist boom.[4]

Peace parks could also have a significant political consequence: leaders of warring states could find the joint management of a peace park a face-saving strategy for resolving border disputes.

By the end of 1996 South Africa's tourist industry was burgeoning and interest in peace parks was growing across the subcontinent. It was increasingly realised that tourism has the potential to become the economic engine to create much-needed employment in southern Africa. By this time the SANF had become WWF South Africa, whose activities were limited to that country in keeping with the international WWF's policy. Rupert saw great possibilities in Africa's open spaces, where peace parks could be established, employment created and training provided to develop tourism. He was also concerned about global population growth and the increasing pressure on the world's natural resources. 'The past thirty years saw the loss of one third of all fresh water in the world, 30% of all fish and 30% of all natural forests,' he observed in 2002.[5] Accordingly, he addressed the WWF's international body and requested that WWF SA be permitted to operate outside of South Africa's borders and raise donations internationally for the purposes of the subcontinental peace parks process, but his request was refused. Not wanting to disappoint his friends in southern Africa, Rupert came up with a plan of his own: in February 1997 the Peace Parks Foundation (PPF) was established with a R1,2 million donation from the Rupert Nature Foundation.

At his insistence, WWF SA was given three directorships on the board of the new Foundation to confirm that the two bodies were not in competition. Joint monthly meetings are held to share information about their respective activities, and the organisations cooperate closely on projects such as the Southern African Wildlife College at Hoedspruit. The PPF therefore performs the task that was started by the SANF in 1968: to assist South Africa and its neighbours in the field of conservation. Its role is described as that of facilitating the creation of transfrontier conservation areas in support of sustainable economic development, the protection of biodiversity, and the promotion of regional peace and stability across the subcontinent.[6]

The PPF is registered as a non-profit organisation. Rupert was the first chairman and former President Nelson Mandela is emeritus patron. Seven Southern African leaders served as honorary patrons: Pres. Festus Mogae (Botswana), King Letsie III (Lesotho), Pres. Bakili Muluzi (Malawi), Pres. Joaquim Chissano (Mozambique), Pres. Sam Nujoma (Namibia), King Mswati (Swaziland) and Pres. Robert Mugabe (Zimbabwe). South African president Thabo Mbeki became the eighth honorary patron in 2002. The Foundation has an advisory committee comprising representatives of the wildlife authorities of member countries of the Southern African Development Community (SADC).[7]

Throughout his life Rupert was absorbed in all sorts of projects, usually several simultaneously. That was his nature. His family knew that better than anyone else. But when he started at his advanced age with the idea of peace parks in the unstable environment of a number of African countries, they were hesitant – all except his younger son Anthonij (Tonie to the family), who shared his enthusiasm and backed him to the hilt. Gradually, while the peace parks concept gained momentum and wider acceptance, the family felt more at ease. Rupert himself could see nothing against it, and advanced at least one strong argument in its favour: he often said it was essential to do something useful with your retirement otherwise you die. He once mentioned to Prof. John Rowett, British professor of history, that all his academic friends in Stellenbosch had died fairly soon after their retirement. In his view, they had missed the stimulation of exchanges of ideas with students and could not find some new interest to keep them occupied. Rowett later told him he had found out a that most of his own predecessors had also died within five years after retiring.[8]

In his speeches on peace parks, Rupert has emphasised that successful realisation of the idea rests on four pillars. The first is the development of peace parks once the necessary international agreements and protocols have been signed, securing the protected space required to establish meaningful eco-tourism opportunities. The vast African continent, with its relatively sparse population mainly concentrated along rivers and the seaboard, has ample space. Unemployment and poverty, which he considers the world's major pollution hazards, can be counteracted by economic utilisation of the peace parks, enabling people to help themselves and promoting sustainable economic growth. In the process Africa's unique animal kingdom and natural scenery will be preserved. In the six peace parks in which South Africa is involved, this phase is already well advanced.

The second pillar is efficient management to ensure that the conservation areas realise their economic potential. To this end, wildlife managers and game rangers are trained at the SA Wildlife College. Thirdly, tourists will only flock to the conservation areas if proper accommodation facilities and services are provided. That is why Rupert established the Southern African College of Tourism at Graaff-Reinet, where mainly women are trained to run their own guesthouses – women are better at this than men, in his view. Fourthly, tourists, and international tourists in particular, should have adequate access to the peace parks for eco-tourism to become a flourishing industry. The government-controlled SA Airways keeps a tight hold on air travel, and Rupert has frequently appealed to the South African authorities to make more charter flights possible. Tourism is the world's biggest industry, he has pointed out, but Africa's share is only 1,9% of the global tourist trade, compared with tiny Switzerland's 20% and even bigger percentages in France and Spain.[9]

The PPF has made considerable headway in its role as facilitator in the six transfrontier parks in which South Africa is a partner: Ai/Ais-Richtersveld (with Namibia), Greater Limpopo (with Mozambique and Zimbabwe), Maloti-Drakensberg (with Lesotho), Limpopo-Shashe (with Botswana and Zimbabwe), Kgalagadi (with Botswana) and Lubombo (with Mozambique and Swaziland).

Beyond South Africa's border the Foundation also assists projects in the Okavango/Upper Zambezi (Botswana, Angola, Zambia and Zimbabwe) and Lake Malawi/Nyasa/Niassa (Malawi, Mozambique and Tanzania).

The first peace park in southern Africa, Kgalagadi (which means 'land of thirst'), was officially opened on 12 May 2000 by Pres. Mbeki of South Africa and Pres. Mogae of Botswana, who unveiled a life-size bronze statue of two gemsbok in headlong flight. In his speech Pres. Mbeki referred to 'that wise old man, Anton Rupert', although Rupert himself did not attend the ceremony; he wanted to avoid the limelight and believed the honour should go to others.[10] The park unites the adjacent gemsbok parks of South Africa and Botswana, previously separated by a border in the form of a dry riverbed. According to Dirk Parris, parks director of South Africa's National Parks, the Kgalagadi is of exceptional value to conservation. Large-scale nomadic and seasonal migrations of game, the prey of large predators, require vast open spaces, which the Kalahari Desert still provides.[11]

The enormous Greater Limpopo Transfrontier Park will unite South Africa's Kruger National Park (itself larger than the whole of Switzerland), Coutada 16 (a former hunting concession area in Mozambique), Zimbabwe's Gonarezhou National Park and a few smaller areas. Here progress is delayed by major problems, such as the troubled situation in Zimbabwe (although Pres. Mugabe continues to support the project) and the need to consider the interests of the populations of these remote areas, who have to be involved in all the plans. Apart from land-hungry peasants, hazards such as drought, veld fires, poachers and floods put constant pressure on all game reserves. Transfrontier posts have to be set up and visa problems ironed out. Livestock must be safeguarded against infection by wildlife diseases. Tourism needs to be planned, rest camps and guesthouses have to be built and new fences erected. People have to be trained to manage the transfrontier areas and the private sector must be involved in providing infrastructure and tourist facilities.

Despite these mammoth hurdles the first 25 elephants (out of 1 000 to be translocated from the Kruger National Park to Mozambique) were released at a ceremony on the Mozambican side of the three-metre-high electrified fence on 4 October 2001, Rupert's 85th birthday. The guests of honour watched from a hastily erected wooden pavilion on a small hill. A small herd of elephants were already in a boma directly below the hill, when a second group comprising bulls, cows and calves were driven to the entrance in a huge trailer. The trailer gates were thrown open and one by one the newcomers stepped into the blazing African sun, their hides glistening black from hosing to keep them cool on their journey. The dusty grey herd in the boma eyed the new arrivals curiously. Slowly the giant patriarchs and matriarchs of Africa's animal kingdom approached each other, trunks waving, their young following on wobbly legs. Then the two herds met in a magical moment of salute.

The guests of honour included the South African and Mozambican ministers of environmental affairs, Valli Moosa and Fernando Sumbana, and emeritus-patron of the PPF, Nelson Mandela. In his speech at the opening ceremony the former president hailed the new park as one of Africa's success stories. 'The world can learn from us how to use our natural heritage to the benefit of all,' Mandela said. He also referred to the prospects of increased international conflict: 'The peace park, however, is an example of how relations between nations can be improved.' He concluded with an anecdote about the residents of his home village Qunu in the Transkei, who wanted to know when he was going to pay lobola (bride-price) for his Mozambican wife Graça Machel, widow of former Mozambican president Samora Machel, who had died in a plane crash. To the amusement of the assembled guests, he pointed to the herd of elephants newly released on Mozambican soil: 'Today I have paid my lobola!'[12]

Not only had the elephants returned to an area where they roamed in the past, but the event, made possible by a first contribution of R10 million from the PPF, also symbolised the union of two countries that would be stronger collectively if they joined forces.

Rupert told the press how between 1887 and 1902 Afrikaner farmers, along with foreign hunters, had virtually wiped out elephants in the Lowveld (where the Kruger National Park is situated). Fifteen years after the last elephant in the area had been shot, a herd of between fifteen and 30 elephants crossed over to the Kruger National Park from Mozambique, so by 1942 they were again to be seen at Skukuza. 'Those who now gossip that South Africa is giving away its elephants should remember that story, as well as that the thousand elephants to be moved to Mozambique would have had to be culled anyway because there are too many elephants in the Kruger Park (between 9 000 and 10 000),' he said.[13]

In Mozambique, by contrast, the protracted civil war caused large-scale extermination of all game. Besides the current translocation of 1 000 elephants, 6 500 animals of other small and big game species would go to Mozambique. In due course 49 fish species (including the rare lungfish), 116 reptiles, over 500 varieties of birds, 147 varieties of mammals and more than 2 000 plant species would repopulate the Mozambican side of the peace park. There would be facilities for wildlife watchers, four-wheel drive tours, lake cruises, tiger-fishing excursions; and birdwatchers would be able to feast their eyes on the feathered diversity of tropical marshlands.

He envisaged that the big new, united peace park would create employment and markets for southern Africa. 'Tourism, which provides employment for one out of every ten people in the world, is the key to the successful protection of wildlife in the peace parks and to its sustainable survival.' The Hoedspruit airport is just an hour's drive from the peace park. Charter flights could bring tourists from as far as Munich to Hoedspruit within ten hours. There would have to be guesthouses to accommodate far more than the 4 000 overnight visitors catered for by the Kruger Park. He based his calculations on Orlando, Florida, where a marshland had been transformed into one of the world's greatest tourist attractions, Disney World. The Germans said they liked South Africa because it was spacious (*weit und breit*), he added. 'There is space here. Here you find the greatest variety of people, plants and animals. Come to South Africa and you will never be bored.' And he directed his favourite reminder to his own compatriots: South Africa should offer visitors safety, security and service with a smile.[14]

The translocation of the first herd of elephants to Mozambique also led to a special birthday message Rupert received from Dr Maurice F Strong, chairman of the first Earth Summit in Rio de Janeiro in 1992, where the conservation of the planet was discussed in depth by participants from all over the world. 'I cannot think of a more appropriate celebration than the start of the great migration of elephants across the South African-Mozambican border, which could not have happened without your strong, enlightened and unwavering leadership,' Strong wrote. 'This is but the latest example of the impressive range of contributions you have made throughout your remarkable career to your country, your industry and the world community.'[15]

On 11 December 2002, the first stretch of the 353-km border fence between the two countries was cut by ministers Moosa and Sumbana on behalf of their governments: three smallish gaps in the fence that will allow game to roam freely between the two countries.

Rupert is also delighted with the development of the Maloti-Drakensberg peace park, the transfrontier conservation area that links the high, mountainous areas of KwaZulu-Natal in South Africa and Lesotho. The project was officially opened on 22 Augustus 2003 after support had been provided by the World Bank. It is particularly dear to Rupert's heart, partly because of his involvement with Lesotho since 1966, and also because of the over 50 000 San paintings on cliffs and rock-faces in what he regards as the oldest open-air museum in the world. 'Because of the dry rock surfaces some of them could be as old as 25 000 or 30 000 years,' he wrote. 'We admire the pyramids, the Imperial Museum in Taipei, Chinese art from 4 000 years ago because they are old, but our rock artists had left their mark long before anyone else. We must harness all these things to become tourist attractions, it is the way forward . . .'[16]

Like the rock art, he also regards his home town, Graaff-Reinet, as an excellent example of how tourism can be harnessed. Most visitors only drive through, but just outside the town the world's biggest fossil field is to be found on the Rubidge farm. There are more than a hundred examples of dinosaur fossils and other remains. 'We have Jurassic Park there. And we have the world's greatest collection of San rock art in our mountains.'

Funding the peace parks project is an important priority for Rupert, who believes that good managers are essential to run such parks professionally and successfully. Such managers can only be appointed if the necessary funds are available. To this end Rupert and the two other founder members of the PPF, Prince Bernhard and Nelson Mandela, launched Club 21 in Geneva to lay the foundation for the funding of the PPF's activities. Club 21, aimed at promoting peace through conservation in the 21st century, was established to canvass 21 founder members who would donate $1 million each. Prince Bernhard hosted the first meeting at the Soestdijk palace in the Netherlands on 9 June 2002.[17] Good progress was made with international donors from countries where tax relief is granted for such donations.

For a long time Rupert experienced severe problems with South African donations, however, as the South African government offered no tax relief to donors. At one stage he seriously considered leaving South Africa and moving the Peace Parks Foundation abroad.

Rupert tackled finance minister Trevor Manuel head on. At the beginning of 2002, a few weeks before the announcement of the new budget, he wrote a lengthy letter to Manuel, stating that he was 'deeply frustrated' at the inability to resolve the issues regarding tax-deductible donations. He detailed the difficulties the PPF and the SA College for Tourism in Graaff-Reinet (to which his family had donated more than R12 million for capital and training costs) experienced with their tax status and finding local donors under the present dispensation. A submission was made in 2001, he reminded Manuel, but the matter was deferred to the 2002 budget. As part of its international fundraising strategy, Rupert continued, the PPF had established subsidiaries in the USA, Britain, Switzerland, the Netherlands and Germany where individuals and companies can make tax-deductible donations. Great success had been achieved with these efforts, especially with facilitating the establishment of six transfrontier peace parks between South Africa and its neighbouring countries. This facilitation role had been recognised in a tripartite agreement between the department of environmental affairs and tourism, the South African National Parks Board and the PPF. In the past few years the PPF had already raised and allocated more than

R218 million for the establishment of these parks. As a result, other funds amounting to more than R250 million had been made available for the projects, with a potential R660 million for a project on Mozambique's side of the Greater Limpopo Transfrontier Park.

Another example he brought to Manuel's attention was the $15 million the World Bank had made available for the Maloti-Drakensberg Transfrontier Park. The granting of the donation had reached a stalemate, which was only ended once the PPF became involved at the request of four ministers and five directors-general of Lesotho who visited Stellenbosch and were accommodated at Fleur du Cap. All of this was done while the PPF enjoyed no tax benefit in its homeland, South Africa.

The PPF had launched the Club of 21 to help fund its activities, with membership fees set at $1 million. Fifteen of the envisaged 21 members had already joined, including DaimlerChrysler, Philips, Vodafone, Deutsche Bank, Prince Bernhard, Dr Lucas Hoffman, Paul Fentener van Vlissingen and the Schlettwein Family Trust. All these members enjoyed tax relief in their countries of origin. 'These members and the prospective ones we are approaching are now posing the question as to how many South African entities have become members. We are embarrassed to have to explain to them that should a South African company donate R11,5 million, it would receive no tax benefit. Why government refuses to create a tax-friendly environment for South African donors to make such amounts available to causes that will benefit all South Africans, remains a mystery to them.'

Rupert mentioned that he could also not explain to such donors why the R30 million the Rembrandt Group had donated to the Business Trust, with the specific request that R20 million be appropriated for the SA Wildlife College at Hoedspruit and R10 million for the SA Tourism College at Graaff-Reinet, never reached its destination. Support for these two deserving institutions had been ignored, while the Business Trust wasted money on sponsoring a negative advertisement alerting tourists to the risk of a malaria mosquito instead of promoting tourism. Minister of Environmental Affairs and Tourism Valli Moosa promptly stopped the advertisement once Rupert had brought it to his attention.

He pointed out to Manuel that the PPF-sponsored translocation of elephants to Mozambique, on the other hand, generated favourable worldwide publicity to the tune of more than R100 million, according to a calculation by the government departments concerned. 'As a result of our success and because of our local tax problems, there is now increasing pressure from our international board members and associates in Club 21 to proceed with the establishment of peace parks on a worldwide basis. They see the reason for not getting tax benefits as a lack of understanding and appreciation of our role by government. We have had offers of office accommodation, inter alia, in Geneva and the Netherlands. As a result of the non-acknowledgement by our government by not granting us the same tax status as the other countries mentioned, an urgent decision therefore needs to be taken whether we must still maintain our base here. Should the problem not be resolved, we shall have to seriously consider moving our offices abroad . . .' He added: 'This is a situation only you can rectify'.[18]

The letter to the Minister of Finance had the desired effect. Manuel did include a tax-deductible concession for South African donors in the 2002 budget. Besides the Rupert Family Foundation, South African members of the Club of 21, chaired by Johann Rupert, include Remgro, Richemont, VenFin, Absa, De Beers, the Donald Gordon Foundation and Kumba Resources. Apart from the $1-million donations there are many smaller donations from members of the Peace Park Club, the public, private foundations and international development agencies.

At that stage the South African president, Thabo Mbeki, was the only leader in southern Africa who was not an honorary patron of the PPF. Rupert requested an appointment and when Mbeki received him on 30 May 2002 at his official residence in Cape Town, he agreed to become the PPF's eighth honorary patron. Rupert was delighted at Mbeki's decision, particularly on account of his leadership role in Nepad, the new partnership for Africa's development. On this occasion Rupert emphasised that South Africa, while already a popular tourist destination, was still not getting enough tourists. The following day he proposed by letter to Pres. Mbeki that South Africa should persuade the world's eight major industrial countries to subsidise passenger flights to the country. According to his calculations, a subsidy of a thousand flights for 400 000 visitors would cost $120 million; the visitors would spend $1 600 million in South Africa and would create 50 000 jobs. Once tourists have visited the country, the good news would spread by word of mouth.[19]

A study conducted for the SAFRI, the Southern African Initiative of German Businesses, found that the ripple effect of tourism on regional economies was far broader than was previously thought, extending to industries as diverse as advertising, printing, electronics, banking, construction, security services, textiles, furniture manufacture and interior decoration, and vehicle, shipping and aircraft manufacture.[20]

In conversations with numerous influential world leaders as well as in speeches to important institutions Rupert has repeatedly emphasised Africa's potential. He does not believe it to be the 'dark' or 'lost' continent; Africa is merely undiscovered by the rest of the world.[21]

He points out that while Africa constitutes 21% of the Earth's surface, it only has eleven percent (750 million) of the world's population. It is also often forgotten that democracy in Africa is still fairly young. More than a century ago, when the scramble for Africa was at its height, the colonial powers carved up the continent between them with the Treaty of Berlin (1885), and by 1950 there were only four independent countries: South Africa, Egypt, Ethiopia and Liberia. The collapse of the Berlin Wall a century later put an end to American and Russian interference and no Marxist regimes have remained on the continent. In fact, African countries are truly independent at last. By 2000 there were 42 multiparty democracies, with the rest in transition away from authoritarianism. Despite some tendencies here and there towards an autocratic form of government, this was not the direction in which most of Africa was moving, Rupert declared.

Pliny is known for his saying, 'There is always something new out of Africa.' Carthage (now Tunisia) was once the trade centre of the world, the first Hong Kong or Singapore. When Hannibal from the affluent city-state of Carthage tried to invade Rome with elephants, Africa held the key to globalisation. Alexandria in Egypt was also a Greek city on the African continent. 'It had happened in North Africa. Perhaps southern Africa with its peace parks can once again play the role of a world leader,' Rupert said. Sustainable conservation can attract millions of tourists to peace parks in Africa and by involving rural populations in these initiatives, the continent's greatest problem, unemployment, can be beaten. 'People talk about Asian tigers. Is it possible to speak about African elephants in future? The peace parks may just be the catalyst to attract the tourists that could accelerate our economy.'

All the development work of the PPF is performed with a small staff of fifteen, headed by landscape architect Prof. Willem van Riet, from the Foundation's headquarters at Millennia Park, Stellenbosch. From there they can monitor game parks throughout Africa on video and also do the necessary planning with the aid of modern computer technology. Three-dimensional virtual images are compiled of landscapes where new peace parks are envisaged, while eleven coordinators within the existing parks liaise with headquarters.

Internationally, the peace parks concept is gaining support. Rupert has pointed out that at the global conference of the World Conservation Union (IUCN) in Amman, Jordan, the international conservation community declared through the chairperson, Dr Maria Koch-Weser, that the influence of the peace parks stretched much further than the conservation of biodiversity, and that they were playing a major role in promoting cooperation between countries and regions and building trust.[22]

The South African journalist Tony Weaver, who has been following the activities of the PPF for years, maintains that peace parks offer a wilderness experience that reconnects human beings with their innermost yearnings, and Africa offers that experience par excellence. He cites the psychologist Carl Jung, who visited East Africa in 1925 and felt safe there from Europe, the 'mother of all demons', his liberated psychic energies blissfully reverting to the primeval wilds. In many ways, says Weaver, the peace park concept is a Jungian vision, enabling Africans to live in harmony with nature in their restored, ancient game reserves – with the added benefit of earning a livelihood from global tourism.[23]

The message that conservation is ultimately about people has been described by *National Geographic* as almost the mantra of conservation in Africa. 'If you don't have sustainable development around these parks, then people will have no interest in them, and the parks will not survive,' said Eugene Moll, former director of the SA Wildlife College.[24]

Rupert's commitment to the peace parks is a quality that has struck someone who worked closely with him over the years, the trademark expert Dr Frederick Mostert. Referring to Rupert's contagious and inexhaustible enthusiasm to keep on moving forward and broadening his vision, Mostert said: 'The expression for which he would probably be mostly remembered is: "I have always been grateful for the doors that have closed for me otherwise I would not have come to where I am today." This is clearly still as relevant to him today, where he wants to open new doors with the same fire.' To Mostert, Rupert's passionate involvement in protecting the wildlife of southern Africa is an example of his youthfulness of spirit – 'there is not the least thought that he no longer has the stamina or is too old to tackle such an enormous challenge. But like Monet on his deathbed, he would probably also say when that day should arrive: "What a pity, I was just getting it!" To Dr Rupert, the journey is almost always more interesting than the ultimate destination. The hallmark of a great mind.'[25]

There are promising signs of support for the concept of peace parks in various quarters, some of them unexpected. Nepad has indicated that the PPF could help to create 22 transfrontier parks in Africa, which might be the organisation's most internationally prestigious project to date. 'I know of no political movement, no philosophy, no ideology, which does not agree with the peace parks concept as we see it going into fruition today,' Mandela declared. 'It is a concept that can be embraced by all. In a world beset by conflict and division, peace is one of the cornerstones of the future. Peace parks are building blocks in this process, not only in our region, but potentially in the entire world.'[26] In 2003 SADC's fourteen members intimated that they wanted to cooperate. That same year the American Congress resolved to support the PPF by calling on NGOs and foundations to back its projects, which opened the doors to donors in the USA.[27]

The PPF has also been involved in imaginative plans elsewhere in the world. On 13 March 2001 former President Mandela personally met the South Korean president to promote the idea of turning the demilitarised zone (DMZ) between North and South Korea into a peace park.[28] This is the home of various endangered species, including the Siberian tiger. The dispute about North Korea's nuclear capacity has delayed progress so far. According to Rupert, 'such a project can do much to heal the division that keeps the two nations separated.' In Europe the concept of transfrontier parks is taking off: in the Mont Blanc range between Switzerland, France and Italy; the Prespa park in the Balkans between Macedonia, Albania and Greece; and the disputed islands north of Hokkaido, which are claimed by both Russia and Japan. In South America there is the *Si-a-Paz* (Yes-to-Peace) park straddling the San Juan River, the border between Costa Rica and Nicaragua, and another between Brazil, Chile and Ecuador. In India the southern African success story provides a guideline for attempts to establish a peace park between India and Pakistan to settle their protracted wrangling about Kashmir; and Aamir Ali, retired member of the International Labour Organisation and a lifelong mountaineer, wants Siachen in the Himalayas to be declared a peace park to end the unofficial war in that region. 'The idea has truly taken root in southern Africa, a troubled area in the past decades.'[29]

The WWF's sister organisation, the World Conservation Union (IUCN), which has been promoting the idea of transfrontier conservation for years, estimates that there are 169 potential transnational conservation areas globally, which could involve 113 countries, and at the start of the new millennium the strongest impetus is coming from Africa. This view was confirmed by an editorial in *National Geographic* in 2001: '. . . in southern Africa an intriguing idea is taking hold: Perhaps conservation of wildlife and habitat can transcend political differences and political boundaries to become a stepping-stone to lasting peace . . . More regions of the world might look into this model . . . Amid such tantalizing possibilities one thing is certain: Courageous leaders who bequeath a legacy of peace will long be remembered for their vision.'[30]

A decade after Rupert has embarked on the idea of peace parks in southern Africa, he says that his wildest expectations have been exceeded. In his view, the energy that has been unleashed has gained such momentum that the concept now enjoys international support as a vehicle of sustainable development. 'Our objectives with peace parks are very clear: biodiversity, conservation, economic development, job creation, and peace and understanding between the countries concerned. Our biggest challenge in the next decade is to develop capacity. We want to assist governments of the SADC countries to train more than 10 000 game rangers, field guides, veterinarians and guesthouse managers over the next ten years. Fortunately, all heads of state of SADC are patrons of the Peace

Parks Foundation, which confirms their political will and support. Pres. Thabo Mbeki supports the concept specifically because it supports the Nepad principles (using Africa's own initiatives and entrepreneurship to attract foreign capital).'

Rupert has remained involved with the international WWF, where he served as vice-president first under Prince Bernhard and later under Prince Philip. In 2003 the WWF awarded him their 'Oscar for conservation', the conservation medal of the Duke of Edinburgh. Rupert, the first South African to receive the engraved gold medal since its institution 23 years before, could not attend the ceremony at Buckingham Palace on 26 November 2003 as he was indisposed. His wife Huberte, accompanied by their son Johann, received it on his behalf. In 1995 the medal was awarded jointly to the South African National Parks Board, the Richtersveld community and the Natal Parks Board. The only other winner from Africa was Emmanuel OS Asibey from Ghana, who was awarded the medal posthumously in 2002.

In a letter to Rupert, Prince Philip expressed his delight at the award. 'I can think of no one who has done so much for conservation – and the WWF – for so long. The WWF might not have been able to survive the early years without your active support and advice,' Philip wrote.[31] And the director-general of WWF International, Dr Claude Martin, added his own praise: 'Successful businessmen who contribute their initiative, energy and experience to conservation with such resounding success are a very rare species. (Rupert) remains an inspiration for the way in which he shares the reward for his talents to the benefit of society. His influence extends to all facets of life, but his love and passion for earthly habitat is probably his greatest legacy.'[32]

The day after the award ceremony the links between the WWF and the Peace Parks Foundation were strengthened further. A memorandum of understanding between the WWF and the PPF was signed at Soestdijk palace in the Netherlands in the presence of Prince Bernhard, founder member of both organisations.

By this time Rupert was scaling down his official duties in the conservation bodies. On 11 October 2003 he retired as president of WWF SA at the organisation's meeting at Graaff-Reinet, but he retained his position as patron.

Two months later, on 11 December 2003, the first female game rangers graduated at the SA Wildlife College at Hoedspruit, where students from all over southern Africa are trained. The 34 trailblazing women who received certificates as game rangers and nature conservators were from Botswana, Lesotho, Malawi, Namibia, Swaziland, Zambia and Zimbabwe. The ripple effect of Rupert's dream was extending more and more widely.

PART V

HALLMARK

CHAPTER 32

A man for all seasons

Rupert's decision to scale down his responsibilities by the end of 2003 came after he had undergone two major operations that kept him inactive for a while. He returned to his office as soon as it was feasible to attend to the peace parks and related matters.

An earlier setback on 28 October 2001 was the death in a road accident of his younger son, Anthonij, shortly after his fiftieth birthday. His death was a bitter blow to the parents: to Huberte, who had always been lovingly protective towards her middle child, but also to Rupert, who had received from this son, an intense nature lover, the strongest support of all in the family for his vision of peace parks. At the memorial service for Anthonij in the Dutch Reformed Church at Simondium, close to Fredericksburg, his brother Johann who delivered the dedication speech remarked that his brother was probably the only Karoo farmer who never shot game on his farms.

A letter from former President Nelson Mandela was read out at the memorial service. Few experiences in life are as painful as the death of a child, wrote the patriarchal statesman, expressing the sincere hope on behalf of many South Africans that the Ruperts would themselves find the peace that they had so long striven to bring about in the lives of others.[1]

President Thabo Mbeki sent a letter of condolence to the family, noting Anthonij's bonds with the house of Rothschild in France. Anthonij's personal qualities, as well as his professional devotion to wine and culture – firmly in the Rupert tradition – had helped to make foreigners aware of the heights of achievement that were to be found in South Africa, Mbeki wrote. He concluded as follows:

'It is, I hope, an appropriate moment for me to note the sturdy commitment to our democratic country by the Rupert family which, as we all seek to move away from the past, is deeply appreciated and valued.'[2]

A few days after the memorial service Huberte, accompanied by her daughter Hanneli, left for Geneva to undergo a neck operation on 4 November 2001. Concerned family members and friends wondered whether the operation should not be postponed, but the woman with the indomitable personality decided to go ahead. The outcome was successful.

After Anthonij's cremation a bronze plaque in his memory was installed in the wine-tasting centre of his beloved farm L'Ormarins. It reads:

ANTHONIJ EDUARD RUPERT
2 October 1952 – 28 October 2001
Geseënd is hy wat liewer gee as neem.
To be truly blessed is to give rather than to receive.

These words also reflect Rupert's strong conviction that a person of value puts more into life than he gets from it. He has consistently maintained this view of life and it is fundamental to the various tasks and projects he undertook in the name of coexistence and for the benefit of his fellow human beings. It was supported by the success that he achieved as entrepreneur and businessman, spurred on by the intellect and drive that was noticeable well into his senior years.

If there was one thing that he could wish for, it would be: 'I wish that I can say I added value to this life. I don't care for the successful people, I like someone who adds value. It can be done by a teacher. I regard teachers as probably the very people who are able to build our nation . . . Successful, no, I would wish to be someone who added something to a life, left it better than how I found it . . . It doesn't apply only to me, I wish it for everybody,' he stated in an interview.[3]

In 2004 the magazine *Forbes* placed Johann Rupert and family at number 342 on their annual list of the wealthiest 500 people in the world, with estimated assets of $1,7 billion – by itself an indication of how the assets have passed from father to son. The only other family in Africa on the 2004 *Forbes* list was still the heir of the Oppenheimers' gold and diamond empire, Nicky Oppenheimer and family, at number 103 with estimated assets of $4,4 billion. At the very top of the *Forbes* list was once again the world's wealthiest man, the IT guru Bill Gates of Microsoft, with assets of $46,6 billion. He was followed by Warren E Buffet, with estimated assets of $42,9 billion.[4]

As benefactors who want to be of value to others, the Ruperts have received innumerable requests for financial aid through the years. Both husband and wife are careful with money. 'What my husband and I have today, we saved. And we are still just as thrifty,' Huberte confided in a magazine interview. 'If we give, we rather give to the arts, to nature foundations, to education or for the preservation of our heritage.'[5] In deserving cases assistance is given, but with a firm proviso: You find the first half and we will pay the second. In this way people 'do something themselves and they are appreciative of you, but then you are not in a position of superiority', Rupert believes. He is strongly opposed to the foolishness of giving too easily. 'I am deeply aware of the great danger of doing something for others without their total participation.' He sticks to the firm belief that people must be helped to help themselves, although he states with a smile: 'No good deed ever goes unpunished.' The problem is that if you help one, you must help the others. 'Take, for example, our five family foundations. Most of the time we do not publicise what they do because we make more enemies of those we do not help than of those we help.'[6]

Many affluent people have contributed to charity over the ages, but the American steel magnate Andrew Carnegie was probably the first person who stated openly that wealthy people have a moral duty to give away their fortune. This has perhaps a special significance for the Ruperts since the American philanthropist also had a connection with their hometown, Stellenbosch. In 1912 he donated £6 000 to the university library for the extension and maintenance of the book collection, afterwards named the Carnegie library, one of many such libraries established worldwide. (Later the university library was renamed the JS Gericke Library.) In addition, the Carnegie Corporation financed the investigation into poverty amongst the poor whites of South Africa in the 1930s. In America Carnegie created a tradition of industrialists who gave away their fortunes once they had made them.[7]

Rupert's lifelong involvement with good deeds and works mirrors the ideals of Carnegie, whose verdict was: 'The day is not far distant when the man who dies leaving behind him millions of available wealth, which was free to him to administer during his life, will pass away "unwept, unhonored, and unsung", no matter to what uses he leaves the dross which he cannot take with him. Of such as these the public verdict will then be, "The man who dies thus rich dies disgraced."'[8] Carnegie's gospel of wealth led another great benefactor, the oil magnate John D Rockefeller, grandfather of Rupert's friend David Rockefeller, to write to Carnegie in 1889: 'I would that more men of wealth were doing as you are doing with your money but, be assured, your example will bear fruits, and the time will come when men of wealth will more generally be willing to use it for the good of others.'[9]

A pertinent question about Rupert's career is what would have happened if he had entered the political arena, taking into consideration that success in one area does not necessarily ensure success in another. Had he followed a political career and had he been able to apply his partnership model successfully, the traditionally black areas would have been more developed, instead of the mainly poverty-stricken rural areas that remained. In the whole of South Africa the hurtful and dehumanising facets of segregation, from which apartheid with its rigorous rules of separation and forced removals developed, would most probably have followed a less harsh and more humane course.

Rupert's idea of a canton system for South Africa, with at least three cantons, would probably also have featured more strongly. Had such foundations of federalism and devolution of power been built on much earlier, South Africa might have achieved a stronger federal system rather than the simplistic Westminster model of winner-takes-all and a centralised bureaucracy that came into being in 1994, when FW de Klerk had to negotiate from a substantially weaker position. If someone with the stature of Anton Rupert had entered politics, it would probably also have served as a role model for more competent people from the private sector, rather than professional politicians, a phenomenon that the historian Paul Johnson regards as the scourge of the twentieth century.[10] Professional politicians are increasingly dominating the political stage. In the new dispensation in South Africa, their role is strengthened by the system of simple proportional representation that gives exclusionary powers to party bosses and the party machine while the all-important dividing line between state and party is blurred.

Rupert, however, has consistently remained outside party politics. He confirmed his position in a letter he wrote at the end of 2002 in response to a cry of distress from the frustrated leader of the Inkatha Freedom Party, Mangosuthu Buthelezi, who complained amongst other things that he was largely ignored by the government in spite of being the Minister of Home Affairs.[11] Rupert responded that he understood 'the heartache in your political voice' when Buthelezi described the lost opportunities in the country's growing democracy. Buthelezi would, however, be the best judge of his own role, Rupert replied. He should be led by his conscience. Rupert himself had decided at an early stage that business and party politics could both benefit by allowing a healthy distance and sufficient space between the disciplines.

Concerning the national agenda, Rupert asserted his resolve to stand by what he believes and not to become a victim of doubt and fear. He expressed concern about the grip of poverty and believed that leasehold for individual farmers and the deliberate inclusion of women in this form of empowerment in a region such as KwaZulu-Natal would alleviate the problem. It was an extension of the small business concept that had been implemented so successfully since the 1980s, he wrote.[12]

Rupert, all along 'skittish about governments and always in loyal opposition', remains a prime example of the kind of voice from the ranks of civil society that pricks the conscience of governments, thereby ensuring the advancement and success of democracy. He also involves himself persistently in the search for practical and viable solutions to problems experienced by all sectors of the country's population.

In October 2003 he addressed a letter to Pres. Mbeki in which he made proposals about unemployment, 'which right through history triggered more upheavals and revolutions than most other causes'.[13]

He remembered clearly that Adolf Hitler took over in Germany in 1930 when the unemployment rate was 30%. (In South Africa the official unemployment figure, expanded definition, was around 40% at that stage, whilst about a half million new job seekers enter the labour market each year.)

In his letter, Rupert elaborated on coexistence and partnership, small business as big business, tourism, housing and property rights. As early as 1960 he had pleaded with Dr Verwoerd for black home-ownership. Now he pleaded for a new inexpensive and durable concept of dome buildings to solve the housing crisis in South Africa.

The new building method reminded Rupert of the domed building that remained standing in Hiroshima following the nuclear explosion of 1945. A dome is one of the strongest man-made constructions ever designed. These dome-shaped houses were already being built in South Africa and could possibly be used not only in the new peace parks, but also more widely. People are able to build such homes themselves in two days with the aid of a balloon that is inflated on top of the foundation. The building is constructed over the balloon, windows, doors and all, and afterwards the balloon is deflated. Rupert discussed the idea of domed houses – inexpensive, fire-proof and durable buildings of various sizes, cool in summer and warm in winter – shortly afterwards with Pres. Mbeki in Tuynhuys in Cape Town on 12 February 2004. He contended that these domed buildings, reminiscent of the African traditional hut construction, could solve the problem of shack fires that caused so many deaths in the country's squatter camps. Mbeki showed great interest in the idea.

Rupert's idea of peace parks, the most extensive project he has undertaken in his career, and also one of the most daring, has gained greater momentum by the 21st century, arousing interest far beyond Africa. Peace parks and their great tourism potential offer hope to many states on a continent that *The Economist* described at the beginning of the 21st century as 'hopeless Africa'. (The business magazine did, however, change its tune to 'Africa smiles' in a special supplement on the continent in 2004.)[14] This is why the concept of peace parks arouses such interest in the SADC and Nepad.

Rupert's concept of transfrontier peace parks is remarkably attuned to the spirit of the times as far as intensified environmental awareness, ecological threats to the planet and the realities of the era of globalisation are concerned. Reaching out across borders, which is a prerequisite for peace parks, goes hand in hand with the discernible process of the gradual fading away of the nation state. As is already the case in multinational entities like the European Union, there is also an increasing awareness in Africa that international cooperation is a necessity for peace and prosperity to flourish. Rupert's commitment and perseverance with regard to this dream calls to mind the meaning of the Greek word 'enthusiasm' that he observed in his study of leadership: to be inspired or possessed by a godhead.

His peace parks initiative links the ecological and economic components. 'This is of critical importance,' he states. 'The biggest problem in Africa is unemployment. The desperately poor cannot be convinced of the necessity of conserving natural resources. But if they grasp the economic perspective, they soon become enthusiastic conservationists. The development of transfrontier parks will create employment for millions of people.' He points out that visitors to the Kruger National Park see only one percent of the total area, highlighting the potential for tourism in South Africa and its neighbouring states. In his view, peace parks represent the last chance to attain rapid and sustainable development in the marginalised rural areas of Africa.[15]

On 12 November 2004 Rupert was honoured for his exceptional role in conservation with the prestigious Four Freedoms Award of the Franklin and Eleanor Roosevelt Institute. The ceremony took place at the Castle in Cape Town. Previous winners of the award, people who give 'special meaning' to the four freedoms described by President Roosevelt in 1941 in a speech to the American Congress, were, amongst others, the Dalai Lama, the Czech president Václav Havel, UN High Commissioner for human rights Mary Robinson, Médecins Sans Frontières, and King Juan Carlos of Spain. At the ceremony, Rupert dedicated his award to his wife.

Shortly afterwards, on 1 December, Rupert's lifelong friend, Prince Bernhard of the Netherlands, his co-founder of the WWF and the Peace Parks Foundation, died at the age of 93 years. At the memorial service in the Endler Hall in Stellenbosch a grieving Rupert said: 'This is the most trying day I have ever experienced. To lose the most loyal friend you ever had, breaks your heart.' He and other dignitaries, including former President Nelson Mandela, who sent a message, honoured Bernhard as 'the greatest protector of nature in the twentieth century'.

It is not only on account of his vision as benefactor and conservationist that Rupert is held in such high esteem in South Africa and Africa. As entrepreneur and business leader Rupert has no equal in South Africa. He towers above all as an extraordinarily gifted and multifaceted entrepreneur who started with practically nothing, without the help of any of South Africa's abundant natural resources, and built an international business empire in which some of the world's best-known trademarks sparkle like stars. And this happened to a large extent during the sanction years, when South Africa was an international pariah and South African business people were regarded with hostility.

What are his most special qualities?

The *SA Financial Gazette* summarises them as follows:

- Intellect – and a remarkable ability to concentrate. In addition, the ability to think creatively.
- The ability to work hard. He not only spent twelve hours a day at the office but also took home what he called 'creative work'.
- Courage – 'industrial courage', or the willingness to take calculated risks. He could not have chosen a more difficult and more competitive industry than the tobacco industry. Large groups with vested interests controlled this sector. Rupert challenged them. And won.
- The ability to inspire loyalty in his colleagues. His company was the living example of an industrial partnership.[16]

In the business world his partnership philosophy brought him international fame. In most cases it brought reciprocal success, often magnificently so.

As any successful business leader he sometimes had to take hard decisions that were not universally popular. As a result, his partnership approach in business could not always be equally successful. When reciprocal trust was absent, as in the case of Louis Luyt and Jan Pickard, a parting of the ways was inevitable.

However, he spread his philosophy of partnership, far wider than the business world. It found expression in initiatives that will keep his name alive for years to come: a partnership between 'Capital and Art', 'Capital and Sport', 'Capital and Culture', 'Capital and Nature . . .'

He could expand his business empire with characteristic purposefulness and perseverance, qualities supported by the spirit of urgency and the infinitesimal attention to detail that he regards as essential for a successful business leader.

In addition, blessed with a scientific brain, he could stay abreast of technological developments well into his advanced years – an asset that contemporaries with a more conventional business training could but envy. This contributed to the innovative thinking and innovative products that were such essential features in the growth of the Rembrandt Group as a multinational success story.

In spite of Rupert's success, internationally as well as back home in South Africa, it is remarkable that this child of the Depression, a capitalist but not a materialist, remained a humble person, known for his motto: 'We can dine with kings but also eat with paupers.'

His politeness and refinement are legendary; as is the old Afrikaans tradition of taking an interest in people's family and parentage. ('Oh yes, his grandfather was such and such, and he was the one who always did this or that . . .') His interest in the individuals with whom he conducted dealings contributes to the high esteem in which people hold him across the globe.

As business leader he set high standards. It is significant that he regarded General Charles de Gaulle of France as a remarkable contemporary example of trust, a leader whom he quoted as follows: 'Whatever commands the leader gives, they must be clothed in shining nobility. He must aim high, demonstrate his vision, act on a large scale and establish his authority . . .'[17]

Rupert's contemporaries acknowledge his stature. Donald Gordon of Liberty Life, himself a heavyweight amongst South Africa's leading businessmen, remarked to the financial journalist David Meades at a special occasion: 'Anton Rupert is the greatest businessman that South Africa ever produced.'[18]

The Stellenbosch futurologist Prof. Philip Spies summarised Rupert's approach to life by quoting Ortega: '. . . to work for the sake of an idea, seeking by magnificent exertions to arrive at the incredible.' In a letter, Spies thanked him for being a role model for his generation by virtue of his constructive action and panoramic vision at a stage when the Afrikaner establishment had descended into the worst kind of mental rut and group-think bog. 'When we ordinary people were frightened, you not only "spoke out" but also "thought out", "acted out" and created, with the courage of a true leader . . . My greatest hope for the country is that a couple of "Anton Ruperts" from all population groups will appear who will become role models for the youth and serve as activators for the future . . .'[19]

Former President Nelson Mandela, who came to know Rupert well, regards him as a 'super heavyweight industrialist', combining a remarkable vision with a profound social conscience. 'As long as there are people of Dr Rupert's calibre and commitment, South Africa will never be a land without hope.'[20]

The commendatio at the awarding of honorary membership of the *Suid-Afrikaanse Akademie vir Wetenskap en Kuns* (South African Academy of Science and Arts) to Rupert in 2002 summarises his virtues succinctly, finding combined in him the erudition of Jan Smuts, the sensitivity to higher values of NP van Wyk Louw, the business acumen of Tienie Louw and the courage to act of Christiaan de Wet. 'For the Afrikaners he is a man of hope, an inspiration.'[21]

The historian Hermann Giliomee, author of the highly acclaimed book *The Afrikaners: Biography of a People*, holds that Rupert belongs in the pantheon of leading Afrikaner figures as one of the five greatest: together with President MT Steyn of the Orange Free State ('the first modern Afrikaner'), Andries Stockenström, pioneer statesman of the Eastern Cape, Judge HA Fagan, multifaceted jurist with a long-term vision, and the writer ME Rothmann (MER), pioneer amongst Afrikaans women journalists. 'They create a paradigm of the kind of Afrikaner that one would like to see; people who emerge from history with honour and integrity.'[22]

Perhaps the most important of Rupert's characteristics is his positive outlook on life: the ever-present attribute of focusing on the positive rather than on the negative; of accepting setbacks as challenges.

Rupert often emphasised that he lives in the future. For young people in South Africa who have doubts about the future, he proffered simple but valuable advice: become adaptable and be irreplaceable. 'All knowledge doubles every ten years. Knowledge creates new opportunities. I saw that as far back as the 1960s. There are numerous opportunities today for people with initiative. Their initiative could in turn help others and create employment,' he said in an interview. 'If you do not keep up and innovate, you are left behind. Our biggest problem (in South Africa) is our loss of knowledge. There are Afrikaners who could play a leading role and today they are sitting in Australia, Canada . . .'[23]

Rupert, the irrepressible optimist, remains positive about the potential of South Africa and indeed Africa for young people who wish to grasp the opportunities.

The economist-historian David Landes concludes his magisterial work *The wealth and poverty of nations* with a passage that could be applicable to the career and positive philosophy of life of Anton Rupert: "The people who live to work are a small and fortunate elite. But it is an elite open to newcomers, self-selected, the kind of people who accentuate the positive. In this world, the optimists have it, not because they are always right, but because they are positive. Even when wrong, they are positive, and that is the way of achievement, correction, improvement, and success. Educated, eyes-open optimism pays; pessimism can only offer the empty consolation of being right.'[24]

Rupert not only created wealth for his country. He has also played a role, often unrecognised, in promoting civilised values in South Africa. This is the reason why he will not only be remembered for what he has done and what he has achieved. He will be respected above all for who and what he is: A man of value for all seasons.

South Africa will remain a land of hope and the world will be a better place if the values by which he lived, particularly coexistence and partnership, continue to survive and prosper in the future.

Rembrandt structure

before 2000 restructuring

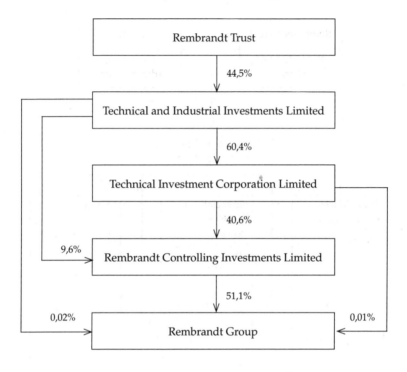

Rembrandt structure

after 2000 restructuring

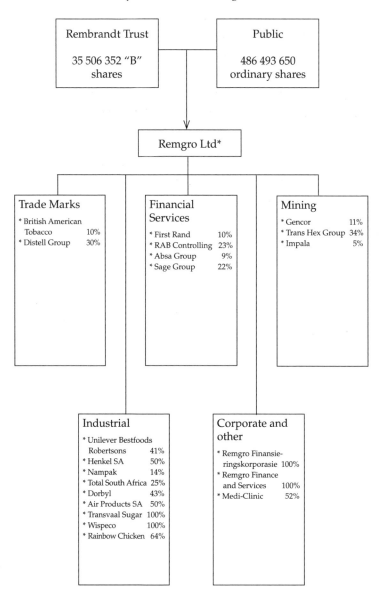

Rembrandt Trust	Public
35 506 352 "B" shares	486 493 650 ordinary shares

Remgro Ltd*

Trade Marks
* British American
  Tobacco   10%
* Distell Group   30%

Financial Services
* First Rand   10%
* RAB Controlling   23%
* Absa Group   9%
* Sage Group   22%

Mining
* Gencor   11%
* Trans Hex Group   34%
* Impala   5%

Industrial
* Unilever Bestfoods
  Robertsons   41%
* Henkel SA   50%
* Nampak   14%
* Total South Africa 25%
* Dorbyl   43%
* Air Products SA   50%
* Transvaal Sugar 100%
* Wispeco   100%
* Rainbow Chicken   64%

Corporate and other
* Remgro Finansie-
  ringskorporasie 100%
* Remgro Finance
  and Services   100%
* Medi-Clinic   52%

* Remgro structure as on 31 March 2004

Rembrandt-structure
after 2000 restructuring

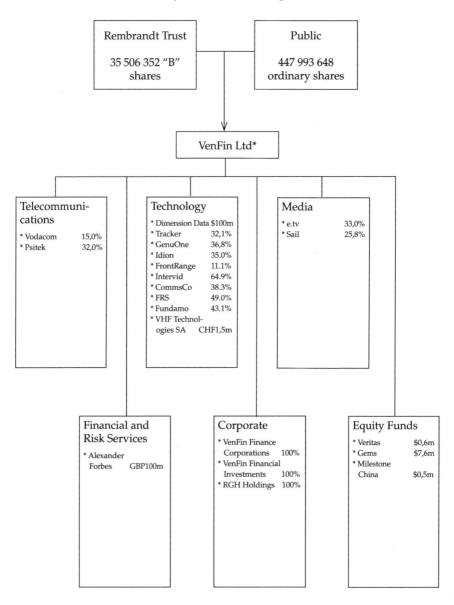

Rembrandt Trust	Public
35 506 352 "B" shares	447 993 648 ordinary shares

VenFin Ltd*

Telecommuni-cations
* Vodacom   15,0%
* Psitek   32,0%

Technology
* Dimension Data $100m
* Tracker   32,1%
* GenuOne   36,8%
* Idion   35.0%
* FrontRange   11.1%
* Intervid   64.9%
* CommsCo   38.3%
* FRS   49.0%
* Fundamo   43.1%
* VHF Technol-ogies SA   CHF1,5m

Media
* e.tv   33,0%
* Sail   25,8%

Financial and Risk Services
* Alexander Forbes   GBP100m

Corporate
* VenFin Finance Corporations   100%
* VenFin Financial Investments   100%
* RGH Holdings   100%

Equity Funds
* Veritas $0,6m
* Gems $7,6m
* Milestone China $0,5m

* VenFin structure as on 30 June 2004

The Pioneers

On the occasion of the Rembrandt Group's 20th anniversary, which coincided with the establishment of Cape Wines in 1979, the group's industrial journal *Tegniek* published a list of its first shareholders in recognition of those who had stood by the company through thick and thin, and on whose support the new company could rely in the future.

The names of these pioneer shareholder are listed below.

JJ Ackermann, Malansdam, Malmesbury

D le R Basson, Dekkersvlei, Klein-Drakenstein

PJ Bestbier, Goede Hoop, Kuils River

DC Bosman, Bleakhouse, Faure

HLB Bosman, Somerset West

PJ Bosman, Welmoed, Lynedoch

A du T Botha, De Eike, Rawsonville

HJF Botha, P O Box 45, Rawsonville

DJ Botma, P O Box 30, Ceres

AW Bredell, Mooiwater, Gordon's Bay

HG Bredell, Firgrove

JJ Bredell, Uitspan, Klapmuts

P vd S Bredell, Vredehof, Firgrove

SW Bredell, Onderustenburg, Firgrove Station

JH Brink, Altena, Barrydale

PF Brodie, Sandhills, Worcester

EJ Bruwer, Mont Blois, Robertson

J Bruwer, De Hoop, Riebeek-Kasteel

JP Bruwer, Mont Blois, Robertson

WJS Bruwer, Goedemoed, Klaasvoogds

BN Burger, De Nuy, Nuystasie, Worcester

JJ Burger, PK Koo, Montagu

JS Burger, Vendome, Huguenot

PW van H Burger, PK Koo, Montagu

WJ Calitz, St Helena, Calitzdorp

JG Carinus, Dwars-in-die-Weg, Stellenbosch

JBZ Conradie, Koelfontein, Prins Alfred Hamlet

HL Deetlefs, Grooteiland, Rawsonville

J de W Deetlefs, Lebensraum, Rawsonville

N de Kock, Die Eiland, Somerset West

SC de Kock, Monkeyland, Orchard

GD de Villiers, Vleisplaas, Barrydale

WD de Waal, Schoone Oord, Kersfontein, Paarl

AP de Wet, Le Chasseur, Robertson

DVH de Wet, Edendale, Bonnievale

HC de Wet, Rawsonville

JCH de Wet, Lorraine, Rawsonville

JK de Wet, Retreat, Robertson

JP de Wet (jr), Kograh, Caledon

PD de Wet, Boontjieskraal, Caledon

GG du Plessis, Lanquedoc, Klein-Drakenstein

CPJ du Toit, Malanstasie, Wellington

DS du Toit, Knolfontein, Riebeek West

JP du Toit, De Gift, Riebeek West

PJ du Toit, Louwshoek, Rawsonville

SF du Toit (G/Sn), Weltevrede, Breërivier

JG Esterhuyse, Robey, Orchard

WJ Esterhuyse, La Fontain, Orchard

CWP Everson, Klipheuwel, Rawsonville

GJ Euvrard, Waterbron, Riebeek-Kasteel

HD Faure, Moddera, Barrydale

HM Faure, Kohlenberg, Faure

JA Faure, Vergenoegd, Faure

JA Fernhout, Vreeland, Ceres

CLN Fick, Ysbrandskop, Krigestasie, Caledon

W Fullard, Lifford, Barrydale

JP Gildenhuys, Firgrove

H Groenewald, Matjieskloof, Rietpoel, Caledon

HSN Groenewald, Alexanderskloof, Rivier-sonderend

CH Heatlie, Orange Grove, De Wet, Worcester

CK Hopkins, Vergenoegd, Lynedoch

CW Hougaard, Verdun, Firgrove

JS Hugo, Robertsonvallei, Franschhoek

APW Immelman, Altenburg, Suider-Paarl

JC Jonker, Weltevrede, P O Box 6, Bonnievale

AW Jordaan, Theuniskraal, Tulbagh
DG Jordaan, Prosper Fair, De Doorns
HJ Jordaan, The Grange, De Doorns
JS Jordaan (jr), Mountain Lodge, De Doorns
LP Jordaan, Môreson, De Doorns
Joubert Broers, La Provence, Vlottenburg
DD Joubert (C/Sn), Goedgeloof, Vlottenburg
DD Joubert (H/Sn), Soverby, Lynedoch
RJ Joubert, By-den-Weg, Vlottenburg
SW Joubert, Lentelus, Barrydale
JJ Kellerman, Klipheuwel, Sandhills
RJ Kellerman, Klipheuwel, Sandhills
JF Kirsten, Vredenhof, Noorder-Paarl
CP Kotze, P O Box 23, Ceres
DJ Kotze, Kotzeshof, Moorreesburg
DJA Kotze, Leeukuil, Moorreesburg
JN Kotze, Koransrug, Moorreesburg
CF Kriel, Uitkyk, Hex River
FJ Kriel, Excelsior, Hex River
JR Kriel, P O Box 1, Riviersonderend
NJ Krige, Bonterivier, Lynedoch, Stellenbosch
CW le Roux (S/Sn), Goudmyn, Rawsonville
JD le Roux, Mooi Kelder, Noorder-Paarl
JG le Roux, Vendome, Hugenot
JS le Roux, Langhoogte, Bot River
MM le Roux, Franschhoek
RE le Roux, Highstead, Wellington
JA Loubser, Sonneskyn, Noorder-Paarl
PJ Loubser, Doornkuil, Malmesbury
PG Lourens, Kliprivier, Swellendam
H Louw, Roulou, Firgrove
L de J Louw en AJ Schoeman, Diepkloof,
    Malmesbury
MS Louw, Ebenhaezer, Riebeek-Kasteel
DF Malan, De Hoop, Wellington
JN Malan, Goedehoop, Wellington
PC Malan, Cordies Rus, Wellington
B vd M Malherbe, La Rochelle, Simondium
DJ Malherbe, Bloekomhof, Franschhoek
JH Malherbe, Rhebokskraal, McGregor
JS Malherbe, Dekkersvlei, Klein-Drakenstein
SG Malherbe, Goudmyn, Klaasvoogds
WD Malherbe (S/Sn), Die Hoek, McGregor
RP Marais, Onverwacht, Wellington
UH Maske, Excelsior, Franschhoek
JW Muller, Elandsfontein, Ceres
RH Myburgh, Klein Welmoed, Firgrove

PB Naude, De Hoop, Hex River
PS Naude, Bluegum, Hex River
SF Naude, De Hoop, Hex River
A de W Neethling, Halfaampieskraal, Klipdale
JH Neethling, Kastanjeberg, Stellenbosch
TJ Neethling Vredenburg, Vlottenburg
EH Nellmapius, De Oude Drostdy, Tulbagh
JHLC Oats, Annandale, Lynedoch
JCD Olivier, Welgeluk, Oudtshoorn
PM Olivier, Onverwacht, Oudtshoorn
HSH Page, Goede Rust, Franschhoek
CJ Palm, Goede Hoop, De Doorns
CJ Palm (R/Sn), Goede Hoop, De Doorns
RJ Palm, Goede Hoop, De Doorns
D de V Rabie, Brakvlei, Nuy, Worcester
JC Rabie, Rust Roest, Nuy, Worcester
NAR Rabie, Oudeschuur, Nuy, Worcester
W de V Rabie, Nonna, De Wet, Worcester
D du P Redelinghuys, Middelplaats, Oudtshoorn
EJF Retief, La Rochelle, De Doorns
GH Retief, P O Box 28, De Doorns
J du T Retief, Hexberg, Wellington
JH Retief, The Pines, Hex River
TJ Roos, Rus-en-Vrede, Firgrove Station
DF Rossouw, Christina, Orchard
DS Rossouw, Alfalfa, P O Box 3, Bonnievale
AD Roux, La Dauphine, Franschhoek
DR Roux, La Provence, Franschhoek
JW Roux, Goedvertrou, Vlottenburg, Stellenbosch
JW Roux, Uitkyk, Firgrove
PJ Roux (CP/Sn), Scholtzenhof, Firgrove
JJ Schoeman, Vadersgawe, Oudtshoorn
HD Schwartz, De Doorns
GMA Smit, Leeurivier, Wellington
WS Smit (jr), Koopmanskloof, Koelenhof
MM Smuts, Grasrug, Malmesbury
P vd B Smuts, Malkopvlei, Riebeek West
EL Steyn, Elsana, P O Box 64, Malmesbury
FP Theron, Rooiland, Tulbagh
JF Theron, Brandwag, Tulbagh
PF Theron (J/Sn), Die Vlakte, Tulbagh
DG Truter, Onverwags, Wellington
HJ Uys, P O Box 3, Barrydale
EG van der Merwe, Grootvlakte, Rawsonville
HN van der Merwe, Le Chasseur, Robertson
JE van der Merwe, Swartdam, Riebeek West
WJ van der Merwe, Monte Rosa, Rawsonville

G van der Westuysen, Maastricht, Durbanville
JJU van der Westhuyzen, Rosenburg,
Malmesbury
A van Niekerk, Non Pareil, De Doorns
PB van Niekerk, Koelenhof
WJM van Niekerk, Mosselbank, Durbanville
DC van Velden, Overgaauw, Vlottenburg,
Stellenbosch
JA Vermeulen, Rhebokskraal, De Wet
FF Versfeld, Klaasenbosch, Constantia
WF Versfeld, Klaasenbosch, Constantia
GP Viljoen, De Vlei, De Doorns
JJ Viljoen, Middelplaas, P O Box 55, Caledon
JL Viljoen, Buffelskraal, De Doorns
DJ Visser, Hex River, Citrusdal
AHG Voigt, Nantesstraat 6, Paarl
FN Wilson, Dagbreek, De Doorns
JS Willemse, Quarrie, Klipdale
TJ Willemse, Quarrie, Klipdale
E Wium, Eikenhof, Vlottenburgstation
FO Zierau, P O Box 19, Paarl
JB Zulch, Kweperfontein, Ceres
PM Burger, Tot-u-Diens, Montagu
JMC Cloete, Mondesir, Hexrivier
C le R de Wet, Schoongezicht, P O Box 7,
Robertson
AJ Jonker, P O Box 13, Bonnievale
H Louw, Klein Amoskraal, Malmesbury
JH Momberg, P O Box 25, Vlottenburg
NJ Myburgh, Klein Welmoed, Stellenbosch
FJJ Rabie, Leipzig, Nuy
WJ du P Roux, Die Fonteine, Firgrove
JHJ Schoeman, Non-Pareille, Dal Josafat, Paarl
PR Schoeman, Vadersgawe, P O Box 142,
Oudtshoorn
HJ Uys, Normandy, Firgrove
H Viljoen, Buffelskraal, De Doorns
WJ van der Merwe, Monte Vista, Rawsonville
E Wium (jr), Eikenhof, Vlottenburg

Voorbrand Tabakmaatskappy Beperk
JJ Schoeman, PK Elim, Vlakteplaas, Oudtshoorn
SET Maree, De Hoop, PK De Rust, Oudtshoorn
JS Basson, Rheboksfontein, Darling
JG Terblanche, Voorbedacht, PK Matjiesrivier,
Oudtshoorn

JC de Waal, Uiterwyk, PK Vlottenburg,
Stellenbosch
JS le Riche, Little Wenlock, Sarentaweg, Kuils
River
JK de Wet, Retreat, Robertson
FCJ Bester, Klipbank, Hopefield
JP Basson, Rheboksfontein, Darling
CJA Basson, Swartwater, Darling
D de Waal, Uiterwyk, Vlottenburg

Tegniese en Industriële Beleggings Beperk
JJ Ackermann, Malansdam, Malmesbury
GJH Albertyn, Nachtwacht, Bredasdorp
DJ Basson, Elandsfontein, Ceres
JS Basson, Rheboksfontein, Darling
WB Basson, Noordwal, Stellenbosch
JP Bekker, Kruisrivier-Wes, Calitzdorp
MJ Bekker, Kruisrivier-Wes, Calitzdorp
PJ Bosman, Welmoed, Lynedoch
AJ Burger, Talana, Montagu
JG Carinus, Bluegum Grove, Lynedoch
SJ Cillie, Vrugbaar, Wellington
JA Conradie, Werda, Nuy, Worcester
PJ Conradie, Kanetvlei, Sandhills, Worcester
AJ de Villiers, Vredenburg, Simondium
J de Vos, Uitkamp, Durbanville
D de Waal, Uiterwyk, Vlottenburg
JC de Waal, Uiterwyk, Vlottenburg
WD de Waal, Schoone Oord, Kersfontein, Paarl
JC de Wet, Lorraine, Rawsonville
JCH de Wet, Lorraine, Rawsonville
E du Preez, The Pines, Suider-Paarl
AJ du Toit, Paarl-Vallei, Noorder-Paarl
AJF du Toit, Nieuwe Plantasie, Paarl
JP du Toit, P O Box 15, Riebeek West
JP du Toit, De Gift, Riebeek West
TJ Eksteen, Labori, Suider-Paarl
H Forrer, Schoongezicht, Firgrove
JAM Fourie, Wynandsrivier, Oudtshoorn
DJ Gerryts, Dennegeur, Koelenhof, Stellenbosch
HC Gerryts, Stenefeld, Koelenhof
VEK Green, Waterval, Dal Josafat, Paarl
SP du T Hauptfleisch, Langrug, Windmeul, Paarl
AJ Jonker, Mooiuitsig, P O Box 15, Bonnievale
HC Jonker, P O Box 12, Bonnievale
JC Jonker, P O Box 6, Bonnievale

AW Jordaan, Theuniskraal, Tulbagh

DC Joubert, Groenberg, PK Bovlei, Wellington

JP Jourdan (sr,), Roodezand, Sandhills, Worcester

JP Jourdan (jr), Roodezand, Sandhills, Worcester

FJJ Kirsten, Eureka, Noorder-Paarl

JM Kirsten, Irene, Noorder-Paarl

DM le Roux, Vredenburg, Hoofstraat, Paarl

DP le Roux, Angora, Bonnievale

FJ le Roux, Helderzicht, Firgrove

FPS le Roux, Tuiste, Paarl

JF le Roux, Driefontein, Malanstasie

PMK le Roux, Doornkraal, De Rust

PE Loubser, Prospect Hill, Klipheuwel

AW Louw, P O Box 1, Tweekuil, Malmesbury

D van V Louw, Babylonstoren, Simondium

NM Louw, Neethlingshof, Vlottenburg

TJW Louw, Bergpad, Suider-Paarl

JF Malan, Oakdene, Wellington

J le R Marais, La Motte, Simondium

NP Momberg, Middelvlei, Stellenbosch

PL Moolman, 2 Moolmanstreet, Paarl

DJ Morkel, Al-te-Na, Strand

PK Morkel, Bellevue, Koelenhof

JG Muller, Wavou, Tulbagh

JW Muller, Elandsfontein, Ceres

JC Potgieter, Kraaldoorns, Calitzdorp

JCD Potgieter, Kraaldoorns, Calitzdorp

JJ Potgieter, Welbedagt, P.K. Welbedagt

JJA Potgieter, Welbedagt, P.K. Welbedagt, Oudtshoorn

FJJ Rabie, Leipzig, Worcester

JH Retief, The Pines, Hex River

AJ Reyneke, 33 Main Road, Paarl

TJ Roos, Rus-en-Vrede, Firgrove

F Rosseau, Sonnekus, St James

DR Roux, La Provence, Franschhoek

J Roux, Hartebeestkraal, Suider-Paarl

P Roux (jr), De Hoop, Suider-Paarl

P Roux (sr), De Rialto, Suider-Paarl

PJ Roux, L'Arc D'Orleans, Wemmershoek, La Motte

JJ Schoeman, Vadersgawe, Oudtshoorn

JJ Schoeman (JH/Sn), Elim, Vlakteplaas, Oudtshoorn

PP Schoeman, De Rust, Oudtshoorn

MJJ Slabber, Middelpos, Malmesbury

WS Smit (jr), Koopmanskloof, Koelenhof

AP Steyn, Waterkloof, Firgrove

D de W Theron, Montpellier, Tulbagh

EO Theron, Sandhills, Worcester

EO Theron, Rhodesand, Sandhills, Worcester

JF Theron, Brandwag, Drostdy, Tulbagh

HPJ Thormahlen, Remhoogte, Stellenbosch

PJ van der Merwe, Merwida, Rawsonville

JN van der Westhuizen, Bonfoi, Vlottenburg

JNJ van der Westhuizen, Bon Foi, Vlottenburg

SW van Niekerk, Uitspan, Klapmuts

BGD van Wyk, Baumgarten, Barkly West

WKFE Wagner, Simondium

I Zuidmeer, Bordeaux, Kersfontein, Paarl

Honours and awards

Honorary degrees

D.Sc.   University of Pretoria, 1960
D.Com.   University of Stellenbosch, 1966
LL.D.   University of Cape Town, 1979
D.Lit.   University of Natal, 1984
D.Com.   Randse Afrikaanse Universiteit, 1988

Distinctions

1961   Marketing Man of the Year (SA Institute for Marketing Management)
1965   Frans du Toit medal for Business Leadership (SA Akademie vir Wetenskap en Kuns)
       Protea award (Society of Marketers)
1966   Businessman of the Year (*Financial Mail*)
1968   Silver medal for Outstanding Service (Historical Monument Commission)
1971   Golden Honorary Medal (Afrikaanse Handelsinstituut)
       Honorary Citizenship of his hometown, Graaff-Reinet
1974   Commander of the Order of the Golden Ark (awarded by Prince Bernhard of the Netherlands)
       Award for Communication and Leadership (Toastmasters Council)
       Award of Cape Provincial Institute of Architects
1977   Award of Cape Three Centuries Foundation
1978   DF Malan medal for Service to the Nation (SA Akademie vir Wetenskap en Kuns)
1979   Wildlife Society Medal
1980   President's Decoration for Outstanding Service
1981   MS Louw prize (Afrikaanse Handelsinstituut)
1982   Gold medal of the Institute of Architects
1983   Business Statesman of the Year (Harvard Business School Club of South Africa)
1984   Honorary citizen of Stellenbosch
1985   President's Award (SA Institute for Marketing Management)
       Gold medal (National Monuments Council)
1989   Member of Honour Award (WWF)
1990   Gold medal (SA Nursery Association)
1991   Endangered Wildlife Trust Statesmanship and Conservation Award
1992   Special honorary medal (SA Akademie vir Wetenskap en Kuns)
       Golden honorary medal (Afrikaanse Handelsinstituut)
       Management Excellency (Business School of the University of Witwatersrand)
       Businessman of the Year (*Cape Times*)
1999   President's Decoration of the Order of Outstanding Service
       Business Pioneer of the 20th Century (*Die Burger)*
2000   Jewish Achiever Award – Humanitarian nomination
       Molteno medal

Award of the Afrikaanse Handelsinstituut
Gold medal and Gift to the Earth Award (WWF-SA)
First Lifetime Achievement Award (*Sunday Times Business Times*)
TUCs Alumnus of the Century
2001 Knight Commander of the Most Loyal Order of Ramats'eatsana (KCHMOR, awarded by King Letsie II of Lesotho)
Legion d'Honneur (France)
Lifetime Achiever Award (Fedhasa)

Honorary membership

1964 Afrikaanse Sakekamer, Stellenbosch
1971 Centre for International Politics, University of Potchefstroom
South African Cruising Association
1974 The Chief Executives Forum Inc.
SA College of Medicine
Cape Town Symphony Orchestra Club
1976 Lesotho Medical Association
South African Orthopaedic Society
1977 South African Amateur Athletics Society
1978 South African National Art Museum
1987 Life member, Institute of Administration and Commerce of Southern Africa
1988 Life member, Institute of Directors of Southern Africa
1990 Southern African Institute of Management Scientists
1991 Nederlands-Suid-Afrikaanse Kamer van Koophandel
2002 Honorary member, SA Akademie vir Wetenskap en Kuns

Rupert's business philosophy

Business philosophy

* *He who wishes to retain all, will lose all.* Man can only survive through a willingness to share. This vision was realised in the company's early years as soon it could afford to put aside profits for community causes.

* *Help others to help themselves.* This philosophy led, for example, to the involvement of the group in medical assistance and aid to neighbouring states and to the upliftment of urban communities.

* *Nobody can do business with the poor.* This served as motivation for the founding of a development bank (Edesa) to encourage entrepreneurship in Equatorial and southern Africa.

* *Goodwill or wealth is not created by giving gifts.* Economic independence is more difficult to achieve than political freedom, but it is more permanent. From this vision an initiative such as the Small Business Development Corporation flowed.

* *Progress is contagious, and if prosperity is shared, it leads to greater prosperity.* If you create opportunities for others to look after their own interests, they will also look after your interests. The group experienced this for itself overseas where it never experienced problems with boycotts due to its policy of co-partnership.

* *Always put yourself in the shoes of the other party.* Show understanding for his point of view; put yourself in his shoes before you assume that you understand how he thinks and feels.

* *Trust creates trust.* It may well be risky to trust, but a lack of trust and suspicion create even greater risks that may easily lead to disaster. This is the heartbeat of co-partnership – without trust no agreement can survive.

Maxims

General

* He who does not believe in miracles, is not a realist. To see your dreams come true, you need to be a practical dreamer; a realistic optimist.

* I often thanked Providence for not receiving what I wanted at the time.

* Where there is a will, there is a way; the will becomes the way.

* Emotion brings about action, but reason determines the outcome.

* For each crisis, for each fear and for every problem there is a hidden opportunity to discover.

* We can only make ourselves indispensable through service and achievement.

* Worry is like a wheelchair; it keeps you occupied, but it leads you nowhere.

* A guaranteed route to feeling miserable is to spend time worrying about how to be happy.

* No good deed remains unpunished.

* Let us use the past as a springboard to the future and not as an easy chair.

* Versatility comprises more than mere knowledge; it supposes a broader humanity.

* Survival is not an automatic right. It must be earned.

Regarding business

* A company has a threefold responsibility: to its shareholders (to keep their investments safe and profitable); to its staff (to ensure that their work remains a meaningful and satisfactory experience); and to society (to be a good citizen reciprocating the trust and goodwill granted by the public).

* Partnership is not exploitation, but the shared creation of prosperity and its fair distribution.

* The best definition of a business that I know of is that it is a body that serves the community honourably at a profit (quoted in Remgro's annual report for 2002).

* You never appoint a super optimist as the executive head of a company; you make him the public relations officer. Neither do you appoint a super pessimist as the executive head; you make him the accountant. And neither a super diplomat as the head, because eventually he comes to believe his own lies.

* Never throw away old shoes before you have bought a new pair – don't rid yourself of your old markets (or clients) before new ones are established.

* Organisation is the enemy of innovation.

* Each point of control is a potential point of corruption.

* We believe in the mobilisation of ideas and the ideal is not to be a conglomerate, but a club of entrepreneurs.

* I believe that the advantages of democracy and free enterprise can only be maintained and developed through true partnership between the industrialised countries and developing countries.

Regarding the community

* Self-development is the only lasting development. Without it the beggar's staff is never exchanged for the spade.

* Never try to do more for people than they can do for themselves.

* Economic independence is difficult to earn but it is the only lasting independence.

* In the nuclear century where nations have the capacity to annihilate all of mankind, we live like scorpions in a bottle.

* In southern Africa you cannot escape being your brother's keeper; we cannot sleep if our starving neighbours cannot eat.

* We are a microcosm of the world's problem with living together harmoniously. I pray that we who live in this wide and arid country may find some of the answers for meaningful cohabitation in true partnership.

* It is better to light a small candle than to curse the darkness.

* Of all the assistance that one person can extend to another, there is nothing that surpasses a healing hand.

* Our true power does not lie in our similarities but in the rich diversity of our plants and animals, arts and cultures and human skills. We are like plywood, which is much stronger that a single beam.

On conservation

* If we chop down the tree to reach the fruit, we condemn our children's children to a lifestyle based on survival rather than quality.

* Conservation has long ceased to be merely an effort of one generation to conserve the heritage of a previous generation for the enrichment of posterity. It has attained a new dimension, namely the safeguarding of our future.

* The best time to begin is always now. If you wish to leave something behind tomorrow, you must begin today.

* Prevention is better than cure; extinction is forever.

* Historic buildings are the visible footsteps of our cultural heritage, the title deeds of the country we love. If these footsteps are erased, a nation's memory vanishes and they become travellers from somewhere on the road to nowhere. (On this subject, David Rockefeller, when he saw some of the historic houses, said to Rupert: 'Anton, these buildings are the title deeds of your country's history.')

Afrikaans business tradition

Ethical guidelines for conducting business were spelt out by Rupert and provided to all employees of the Rembrandt Group. In a speech in 1957 he identified the following six foundation stones for an 'Afrikaner business tradition'.

Some employees had it framed for display in their place of work. The guidelines, under the heading 'Afrikaans Business Tradition', read as follows:

HONESTY
because honesty always lasts the longest

PROPRIETY
because it creates trust in friend and foe

COURTESY
which means dignity without pride and friendliness without fawning

SERVICE
in respect of your client, your nearest, your nation

MUTUAL SUPPORT
so that you can elevate others while you yourself are moving up, because when you dislodge others, you will plunge down together

BELIEF
that all things come to pass for the greater good if one and all do their duty

Transfrontier Conservation Areas (TFCAs) of the SADC
Over 120 million hectares envisaged

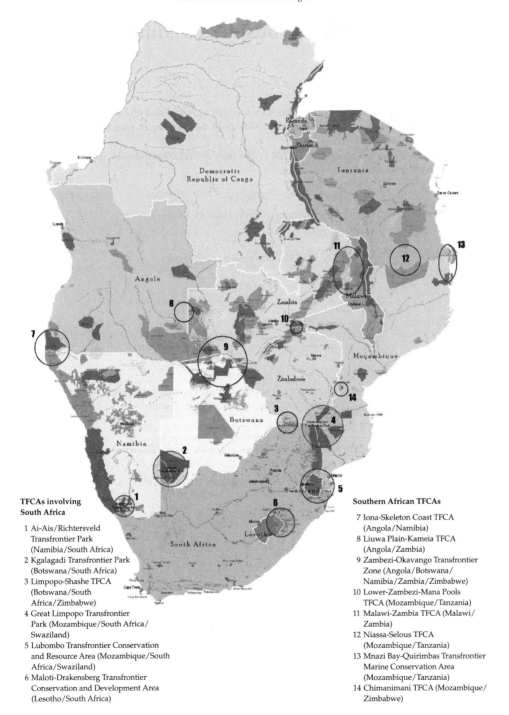

TFCAs involving South Africa

1 Ai-Ais/Richtersveld Transfrontier Park (Namibia/South Africa)
2 Kgalagadi Transfrontier Park (Botswana/South Africa)
3 Limpopo-Shashe TFCA (Botswana/South Africa/Zimbabwe)
4 Great Limpopo Transfrontier Park (Mozambique/South Africa/Swaziland)
5 Lubombo Transfrontier Conservation and Resource Area (Mozambique/South Africa/Swaziland)
6 Maloti-Drakensberg Transfrontier Conservation and Development Area (Lesotho/South Africa)

Southern African TFCAs

7 Iona-Skeleton Coast TFCA (Angola/Namibia)
8 Liuwa Plain-Kameia TFCA (Angola/Zambia)
9 Zambezi-Okavango Transfrontier Zone (Angola/Botswana/Namibia/Zambia/Zimbabwe)
10 Lower-Zambezi-Mana Pools TFCA (Mozambique/Tanzania)
11 Malawi-Zambia TFCA (Malawi/Zambia)
12 Niassa-Selous TFCA (Mozambique/Tanzania)
13 Mnazi Bay-Quirimbas Transfrontier Marine Conservation Area (Mozambique/Tanzania)
14 Chimanimani TFCA (Mozambique/Zimbabwe)

End Notes

CHAPTER 1

1 Interview with Rupert, 27 March 2002.

2 The nuclear explosions in the two Japanese port cities and the subsequent events have been described in various books on the Second World War.

3 In the Hertzog Annals of the *Suid-Afrikaanse Akademie vir Wetenskap en Kuns* (South African Academy for Science and the Arts), 1963.

4 The Rupert family has appeared annually on the *Forbes* list of billionaires since it was first published in 1996.

5 Dirk Opperman referred to the 'prince of commerce' in poems as well as in his preface to Rupert's book *Progress through partnership*.

6 Information about the peace parks appears, inter alia, in annual reports of the Peace Parks Foundation and publications such as those by Martin Pabst, Anthony Hall-Martin and Sedia Modise (see p. 439-441).

7 John Maynard Keynes, *General theory of employment, interest, and money*, p. 570. The extended quotation reads: '. . . the ideas of economists and political philosophers, both when they are right and when they are wrong, are more powerful than is commonly understood. Indeed, the world is ruled by little else. Practical men, who believe themselves to be quite exempt from any intellectual influences, are usually the slaves of some defunct economist. Madmen in authority, who hear voices in the air, are distilling their frenzy from some academic scribbler of a few years back. I am sure that the power of vested interests is vastly exaggerated compared with the gradual encroachment of ideas. Not, indeed, immediately, but after a certain interval; for in the field of economic and political philosophy there are not many who are influenced by new theories after they are twenty-five or thirty years of age, so that the ideas which civil servants and politicians and even agitators apply to current events are not likely to be the newest. But, soon or late, it is ideas, not vested interests, which are dangerous for good or evil.'

CHAPTER 2

1 JA Heese, *Die herkoms van die Afrikaners 1657-1867*.

2 Most of the Xhosa chieftains believed the sixteen-year-old Nonqwase and her uncle Mhlakaza. In the mass hysteria that followed her millenarian vision – not something unique to Africa – the livestock was slaughtered and grain destroyed at the command of the 'new people' that Nonqwase described. She predicted that cattle herds would rise up out of the earth with the spirits of the ancestors and that the grain pits would be filled on a day when the sun would rise blood red in the west. The sea would dry up and the British rulers, who had been driving the Xhosa back more and more and occupying their grazing, would be driven off. On the given day, 18 February 1857, when most of the livestock had already been slaughtered and the grain stocks were exhausted, the sun rose as usual over the land of the Xhosa. The 'day of two suns' never dawned. Famine claimed tens of thousands of lives, while vultures circled over the rolling hills. The colonial governor, Sir George Grey, had to send emergency supplies. The emaciated Xhosa population of British Kaffraria, the area between the Keiskamma and the Kei River that stretched inland to north of the

Amatola Mountains, declined in one year from an estimated 105 000 to 37 500, as a result of deaths and jobseekers moving away from the area.

3   The original district of Graaff-Reinet encompassed the later districts of Albania, Alexandria, Bathurst, Uitenhage, Prince Albert, Willowmore, Jansenville, Somerset East, Cradock, Graaff-Reinet, Aberdeen, Beaufort West, Murraysburg, Richmond, Hanover, Colesberg, Middelburg, Steynsburg and parts of Tarka and Burgersdorp.

4   'Trekbokke', as migrating herds of springbuck were called in those days, moved in an unending stream through the town for three days and three nights in 1849, according to a parson's son of Beaufort West, the later Sir John Fraser. Samuel Cronwright-Schreiner, husband of the author Olive Schreiner, described a large herd of migrating springbuck in 1895 that was 15 miles wide and 138 miles long (24 km by 226 km). He estimated that half a million buck grazed on one plain. According to a resident of the district, Walter Murray, the last big herd of 'trekbokke' close to Graaff-Reinet reached the farm Roodebloem just outside the town in 1902, coming from the north.

5   The builder Rupert wrote, for example: 'Later had ik vele werklieden die onder my werken, waarvan waren metselaars, schreinwerkers, schildereers, papier plakkers enz. Ik bouwde zoo op eenen grooten schaal, en vele bouwen werden door my opgerichten alhier.' [Later on I had many workmen who worked under me, such as masons, joiners, painters, paper-hangers, etc. Thus I built on a large scale, and erected many buildings here.] According to his document, well-known residents of the town and the district were among his clients, including the Murrays of Roodebloem and the brothers Conradie of Onverwacht. He supplied a long list of people from Graaff-Reinet, the Camdeboo and the surrounding area for whom he had built. He concluded as follows: 'Ik wensen al de boven gemelden te danken voor de ondersteuning aan my gegeven gedurende die voorbygaande jaren in die amp die ik aan gevoerd heb, en steeds zyn allen nog myn vrienden vandaag. Allen hunnen bezoeken my, en doen allen in hunnen vermogenheid voor my gedurende myn ziekte. De Heere zegen allen en blyf by hen.' [I wish to thank all the abovementioned persons for the support given to me during the many years of my career, and all of them are still my friends to this day. They all visited me and did all in their power for me during my illness. May the Lord bless and keep them all.].

CHAPTER 3

1   Afrikaans had been introduced as medium of instruction at the Hoër Volkskool in Graaff-Reinet before it was acknowledged as official language countrywide; thus before former Graaff-Reinet resident Dr DF Malan introduced the new language law in parliament in 1925 as Minister of the Interior. This meant that Afrikaans replaced Dutch as official language alongside English, the language with which the arch-imperialist Lord Alfred Milner, British High Commissioner, had tried to anglicise Afrikaners after the Anglo-Boer War with his Anglicisation policy.

2   Quotation from the *Jansenville Chronicle*, 14 June 1914.

3   Quoted in Taffy and David Shearing's book *Commandant Gideon Scheepers and the search for his grave*, one of the most recent works on Scheepers.

4   Guy Butler, in *Afrikaans poems with English translations*, p. 267.

5   Speech when he opened the Port Elizabeth agriculture and industry exposition on 24 February 1967.

6   Radio interview with Pieter Naudé, broadcast on 31 May 1961.

7   Report in *Die Burger*, 13 August 1999: 'Anton Rupert, 'n man van waarde'.

8   EP du Plessis, *'n Volk staan op: Die Ekonomiese Volkskongres en daarna*, p. 27.

1   It had grown from the old Transvaal University College and the original acronym remains current as a nickname to this day.

2   A Boer laager of 40 burghers under the command of Comdt PJ Riekert, Justice of the Peace and also head of the ZAR (Transvaal Republic) border police, lay in ambush to surprise a British occupation force on their way from Bulawayo to Mafeking in the Sequanoi mountain pass, close to Derdepoort, when the laager and the settlement were attacked simultaneously. The attack was carried out by a British column of 300 soldiers under the command of Lt-Col. GS Holdsworth, with the support of about 6 000 members of the baKgatla marching from Bechuanaland across the border. The attack against the laager was fended off, after which the baKgatla marched to the settlement of Derdepoort, where they plundered and burnt down five houses, two shops, the office of the commandant, the police office and the school. Eleven civilians were murdered and sixteen women and children were assaulted and chased over the border on foot to Sekwani in Bechuanaland.

Besides it being the first time in the war that the British had used black people for military purposes, it was the first incident in the war where Boer women and children became war victims. In some ways, it was therefore the prelude to the horrors of the concentration camps which were condemned by the later British premier Sir Henry Campbell-Bannerman as 'methods of barbarism'. Two women of the Riekert family, one Huberte's grandmother, survived the attack. They were first warned by a black servant about the impending danger, and after the walk to Sekwani, a British soldier brought them back, along with other women, to the Boer laager. The soldier, TSM James Bateson, who was on horseback, helped the women and children across a river and approached the Boer laager with a white flag made from a piece of one of the women's petticoats. He received a letter from the Boers to guarantee his safety until he was reunited with his unit. A document in which Mrs HHA (Stroh) Riekert, a daughter-in-law of Huberte's great-grandmother, recorded their hardship at Derdepoort, is still in Huberte's possession. The account was included in the book *Vir vryheid en vir reg* by Marthinus van Bart and Leopold Scholtz, which was published in 2003 by Tafelberg, thanks to a generous sponsorship from Huberte.

3   In Burgersdorp in the Eastern Cape, home of the first Afrikaans language monument, the editor of the *Albert Times* wrote that English should be the language of parliament and government, 'and let the taal be the language of the working class, so that progress will be synonymous with every thing English'. Then the Boer will 'be in his proper place viz. a rough and ready servant, well adapted to the country and fit for hard manual labour and exposure, and adverse to using his brains'. The 'Boer of the future' would be representative of 'the great unwashed of all the races' – abuse reminiscent of the notorious 'lesser breeds without the law'. The editor concluded his wartime diatribe: 'A ruling nation must be a nation with high traditions and ideals, and so let us always sing Rule Britannia.'

4   The Voortrekker ox-wagon ('kakebeenwa') stood on the campus for a number of years and was used at student events before being returned to the ATKV. The Louis Trichardt wagon was also used as hearse for the big funeral in Johannesburg of the renowned champion wrestler Johannes van der Walt, who rebelled during the Second World War and was fatally wounded by a policeman. The wagon, named after the Voortrekker leader who had died of fever in Lourenço Marques, was eventually moved to the ATKV museum at Hartenbos.

5   In HP Lamont's book, a character claimed, for example, that the Voortrekkers practised slavery, that DRC ministers had 'no mercy, no kindness or no human kindness in their miserable hearts', and that the 'back-veld Boer' only took a bath with his baptism, marriage and burial. This raised heated emotions and four young men kidnapped Lamont, tarred and feathered him, and released him on Church Square. The four men – Dr M Steyn Vorster, JW van N Trichardt, and two brothers

FCK and SPE Jacobsz, great-grandchildren of Pres. Paul Kruger – were defended in court by Dr Hjalmar Reitz, MP, and the poet Adv. Eugène Marais.

6   At that stage the president of the ANS was Dr Hans van Rensburg, who had been appointed by Gen. Jan Smuts as administrator of the Free State. He resigned in 1941 and became commandant-general of the right-wing totalitarian *Ossewa-Brandwag* (OB). With the split between Van Rensburg's OB and Malan's National Party, which preferred the democratic way, the ANS also started to decline, and after the war the movement was replaced by the countrywide *Afrikaanse Studentebond* (ASB).

7   Dirk Hertzog had political connections on both sides of his family. Gen. JBM Hertzog, his father's brother, was prime minister for fifteen years, from 1924 to 1939, and Dirk remembered how his Uncle Barry carried him around at night as a 'screaming baby' in 19 Goddard Street in Pretoria. His mother's brother, the novelist and politician Adv. JHH de Waal, was the second in command of the National Party after Dr DF Malan went into opposition in the 1930s. His grandfather on his mother's side, David de Waal, mayor of Cape Town and member of the Cape parliament for Piketberg, was the brother-in-law of 'Onze Jan' Hofmeyr, founder of the Afrikanerbond, and before the Jameson raid he was also good friends with Cecil John Rhodes, with whom he had undertaken an expedition to Mashonaland in the then Rhodesia.

8   Dirk Hertzog in conversation with staff of the Rembrandt Tobacco Corporation, 13 February 1985.

9   Gen. Jan Smuts and Eugène Marais were both exceptionally talented and exceptionally versatile. Smuts, lawyer and soldier, a hero of the Anglo-Boer War and field marshal in the Second World War, was, among other things, also the author of a book on the philosophical concept of 'holism' as well as the respected statesman who in 1945 formulated the goals in the preamble to the Charter of the newly established United Nations ('We the Peoples of the United Nations, determined to save succeeding generations from the scourge of war, which twice in our lifetime has brought untold sorrow to mankind . . .'). Marais, also a lawyer and a newspaper editor at the age of nineteen, was far ahead of his contemporaries as an expert on animals in their natural state, and wrote some of the very first timeless poems in Afrikaans.

10 Gen. Jan Smuts, who strongly criticised the use of blacks in the war by the British, wrote that 'if people in the outside world should know a hundredth part of what was being done inside the Republics, the whole of Christianity would tear their clothes and call out to heaven against such indescribable barbarism'. It was Smuts's task to visit the camps in which women were kept by the British forces, and he wrote in his letter to Pres. Steyn that '. . . I never thought I would see such sights of misery in all my life. Almost all the women and children suffered from malaria and other diseases, resulting from privation and bad nutrition, without a doctor, without medicine, without any comfort in this world; almost without clothing and, after all the plundering by the enemy, without food. And these women did not only come from the poor and backward classes, but some were from the most renowned families in the country. But no hardship could break the spirit of these noble martyrs, and with one voice they all urged me and the burghers to persist to the end.'

He referred in his letter to Mrs Riekert, 'a lady that our nation can be proud of, [who] furnished a hospital in Rustenburg at her own expense where she, amongst other things, nursed 15 of the ill and wounded that Chief Comdt CR de Wet had left there on his great march to Bethlehem.' Smuts further narrated how Mrs Riekert, with her daughters and daughters-in-law, had been banished by the British to the farm Paardekraal outside Rustenburg, in close proximity to hostile blacks, where they suffered from a lack of food and endured terrible fear.

CHAPTER 5

1   Giliomee, p. 348.

2   EP du Plessis, *'n Volk staan op: Die Ekonomiese Volkskongres en daarna*, p. 231. Du Plessis's book is one of the best sources on the rise of the Afrikaner in business life in the first half of the twentieth century.

3   Prominent names at the time were the retail chains *Uniewinkels* and *Voortrekkerwinkels*. *Boere Saamwerk Beperk* ('die wolboer se reddingsdaad') [the wool farmer's act of rescue] and *Wol Groeiers Afslaers* were active in the wool industry. Volkskas was involved in banking, as well as Sasbank, to whom many Railway workers entrusted their money, especially members of *Spoorbond*, the union founded in 1933 as antipode to the National Union of Railway and Harbour Servants. Other well-known names in those years were *Kopersbond* ('die Afrikaner se groothandelsmaatskappy') [the Afrikaner's wholesale company], *Sonop Mode-spesialiste* ('die eerste reddingstap in die Oranje-Vrystaat') [the first rescue step in the Orange Free State], the *SA Diensburo* ('die enigste suiwere Afrikaanse Vendu-afslaers in Johannesburg') [the only purely Afrikaans auctioneers in Johannesburg] and the *Volks-Korrespondensiekollege* ('Ons reddingsdaad is om jong Afrikaners op te lei om hulself te red') [Our act of rescue is to train young Afrikaners to rescue themselves]. *Utolo Beperk* and *Vobi*, or rather *Volksbioskope (Edms) Bpk*, entered the arena of the film industry but had to make way for Schlesinger's African Mirror. The Free State attorney-businessman JG (Kaalkop) van der Merwe of Heilbron, president of the AHI for several years, was involved in several such-like enterprises that did not succeed.

4   *Voorbrand* literally means 'firebreak'. As a metaphor, 'to make *voorbrand*' means, appropriately, to prepare the ground, to blaze a trail.

5   *Oosterlig*, 31 March 1977.

6   C.P. Hoogenhout (1843-1922), head of the Groenland school at Wellington, was a founding member of the *Genootskap van Regte Afrikaners*.(GRA, Association of True Afrikaners). The GRA, founded on August 14, 1875, was the driving force behind the Afrikaans Language Movement that elevated Afrikaans, already the spoken language of thousands by then, to the language of school, Bible and pulpit.

7   Blacking and Zureena were found guilty in a controversial court case and both were given a suspended sentence of four months in jail. Blacking, an internationally acclaimed anthropologist who had, among other things, conducted ground-breaking research on the music of the Venda, at that stage decided to leave the country. He married Zureena and the couple moved to England, where they became prominent academics.

8   The other members of the executive were Dr AJ Stals, Dr N Diederichs, W Bührmann, LL Tomlinson, DP de Villiers, A van W Cloete, CJ Schlebusch and two co-opted members, Profs CGW Schumann and WFJ Steenkamp. The AHI naturally strove to promote the interests of Afrikaans business people, but it was stated at the outset that the organisation did not aim to oppose other existing organisations and associations, but rather to cooperate with them as far as possible and to improve business life by means of 'a constructive and positive policy'. Still, the government was unwilling at first to register the AHI as non-profit enterprise in terms of the Companies Act, as there was doubt whether the Institute would not only serve sectional interests but also the national interest. However, the then Minister of Justice, Dr Colin Steyn, agreed that the registration could take place provided the AHI could agree with the Association of Chambers of Commerce. This prerequisite was met and an agreement was reached that the AHI would limit its membership to Afrikaans speakers and that it would not insist on Afrikaans-speaking members terminating their membership of the Chambers. In addition, a liaison committee was established between the two entities to facilitate consultation and concerted action in cases of mutual interest.

9   Rupert's report on the tobacco industry in the Rembrandt archives.

CHAPTER 6

1 Interview with *Huisgenoot* in 1991.
2 *Wine Spectator*, 28 February 1999.
3 Piet Meiring, *Bane en baanbrekers*, pp. 143-144.
4 Hertzog's memorandum dated 25 January 1983 in the Rembrandt archives.
5 Hertzog's memorandum dated 16 November 1962.
6 Alfred Baumgartner describes the incident in *The first 35 years of Distillers Corporation (SA) Limited*.
7 Interview with Huberte Rupert, 23 April 2001.
8 Article by David Meades, *Beeld*, 28 September 1996.
9 The value of loyalty in the corporate environment was confirmed in a survey International Survey Research (IRS) conducted among 40 big global clients between 1999 and 2001 (*Sunday Times*, 13 October 2002). IRS, which covers more than 2 700 organisations in 100 countries, found that there is a direct link between employees' commitment and loyalty and the profitability of a company. On the basis of surveys among 362 950 employees, Roger Maitland, deputy chairman of IRS, stated that employees' evaluation of leadership was the key component of their commitment. According to Maitland, 'what this shows, is that popular ideas that commitment is built from the bottom up and is influenced most strongly by direct superiors, are wrong. It is the leaders of a company that carry that responsibility.'
10 Alfred Baumgartner, *The first 35 years of Distillers Corporation (SA) Limited*, p. 137.
11 Alfred Baumgartner describes various brands and prices in *The first 35 years of Distillers Corporation (SA) Limited*.

CHAPTER 7

1 *Financial Mail*, 12 September 1980.
2 Interview with *Wine Spectator*, 28 February 1999.
3 Rupert tells how he met Stals in the dark war days of 1941, after Stals had bid farewell to his concerns at the Council of Trade and Industry and the Shipping Council for the sake of his convictions. Stals performed a service of love at the small office of the Reddingsdaadbond as economical adviser 'to serve his people in the important area where we lagged so far behind'. He had known Stals for years as chairman of Voorbrand, the mother of the later Rembrandt. His belief and perseverance contributed to the establishment of Saambou and the expansion of Volkskas.

'All these things he did – not to enrich or exalt himself, because he is a humble man. He did these things because he realised the importance of the self-sufficiency of a people, and knew that every people needs its own for its existence – its own language, its own land, its own factories, its own success.

'But what he asks for himself, he also wishes unto others . . . their own place in the sun. His power comes not from envy and jealousy – in fact, I have never heard him gossip – but from the aspiration to do things himself, to live and let live. And because his point of view is so reasonable and his aspiration so positive, his strength is so powerful.'

Rupert continues to say that Stals, who grew up in the days of the Anglo-Boer War and the Afrikanerbond, knew what it was like to be powerless and without rights. He knew what strength it had cost to save a people. 'Because he knows what suffering is, he is great in spirit and acknowledges his fellow man's right to existence. Because he himself has excelled in building a nation, he knows the strength of standing on your own feet.'

Stals's 'do unto others as you would like them to do unto you' is strange to some, to others even amazing. All great men one meets, leave their image in one's mind. 'With Dr Stals, it is the image of refinement of spirit,' Rupert concludes.

4   ELP Stals, 'Geskiedenis van die Afrikaner-Broederbond 1918-'94', p.216.

5   Stals, pp. 578-581.

6   Particulars of Rupert's short-lived membership also appear in JHP Serfontein's book *Brotherhood of power: An exposé of the Afrikaner Broederbond.*

7   Hertzog's memorandum dated 25 January 1983 in the Rembrandt archives.

8   13 February 1985 in conversation with staff of the Rembrandt Tabakkorporasie at The Court House.

9   History of the tobacco industry in, among others, Iain Gately's book *Tobacco: A cultural history of how an exotic plant seduced civilization.*

10 Mrs HJ Muller's notes in the Rembrandt archives.

11 Rupert on 3 October 1971 in an interview with the Sunday paper *Rapport.*

12 Interview with Jan Prins in *Dagbreek en Sondagnuus*, 15 November 1964.

13 The article in *Tegniek* highlights the example of newsprint: 'Afrikaans speakers are almost twice as many as English speakers, but owing to historical factors the paper consumption of Afrikaans newspapers is only about a seventh of that of English newspapers. The reason for this is simply that English newspapers existed here while Afrikaans was still fighting for its existence against Dutch. If the Afrikaans newspapers are to be restricted to their current paper consumption, the Afrikaners would have to continue to read English newspapers, simply because the papers in their own language may not be expanded! If there had been such a policy in the area of banking or insurance, how could we ever have built a Volkskas or a Sanlam?'

14 Article in *Inspan*, October 1950.

15 Article in *Volkshandel*, March 1950.

16 Interview with *Huisgenoot*, 9 October 1959.

17 Interview on 2 April 2001.

CHAPTER 8

1   Rupert's speech to the *Tweede Ekonomiese Volkskongres* in, inter alia, the Rembrandt archives.

2   EP du Plessis, *'n Volk staan op: Die Ekonomiese Volkskongres en daarna*, p. 234.

3   The story is told in JP Scannell's book *Uit die volk gebore: Sanlam se eerste vyftig jaar.*

CHAPTER 9

1   Drucker writes in *Innovation and entrepreneurship*, published in 1985: 'Industry and market structures sometimes last for many, many years and seem completely stable. The world aluminium industry, for instance, after one century is led by the Pittsburgh-based Aluminium Company of America which held the original patents, and by its Canadian offspring, Alcan of Montreal. There has been only one major newcomer in the world's cigarette industry since the 1920s, the South African Rembrandt Group. And in an entire century only two newcomers have emerged as leading electrical apparatus manufacturers in the world: Philips in Holland and Hitachi in Japan.'

2   Wolfgang Ritter wrote about this in his book *Die bessere Idee.*

3   *Business Week*, 28 September 1974.

4   Reemtsma's letter in Rembrandt's archives.

5   Duke, Maurice and Jordan, Daniel P. *Tobacco merchant: The story of Universal Leaf Tobacco Company*, p. 96.

6   Interview with Paul Erasmus, 29 July 2003.

7   Rupert summed up the conclusions of the investigation into the cigarette in Germany as follows:
    * It is new and somewhat foreign (Philipp Reemtsma tempered this foreign aspect by replacing the words on the packet 'The man who founded New York in 1653' with 'The man from Friesland who founded the city now known as New York in 1653').

* It is immediately evident that the cigarette is filter-tipped and longer.
* The packaging, which gives the immediate impression of a tobacco product, is dynamic and energetic.
* It is not a speciality product, but can cover the whole cigarette market.
* The packaging reflects the careful attention that has gone into it and has a masculine as well as a feminine appearance.
* The packaging suggests cleanliness and mildness of taste as well as pleasurableness.
* There is a balance between restraint and conspicuousness.

8   Interview with Hans Knoetze, 12 November 2001.
9   Interview with Georg Domizlaff, son of Hans Domizlaff, 23 February 2004.

CHAPTER 10

1   *Die Burger*, 7 May 1955.
2   These organisations, the first organised cooperation between women in the country, date back to the days of the Anglo-Boer War, when women's committees were established in several places to help relieve the distress of prisoners of war, women and children. With the establishment of nursery schools, old-age homes, maternity homes, community centres and boarding houses for the low-salaried, the women's organisations for years had been doing the welfare work that was only taken over in part by the state in 1937, when a department of social welfare was instituted.
3   Article by Rosemary Northcott in *Women's Value*, August 1981.
4   The journalist George Clay elaborates on an 'Afrikaner business empire' and continues: 'The coffee men knew that behind Rupert again would be the full might of the tightly-knit Afrikaner-Nationalist business empire that has risen spectacularly in ten years to great strength and influence, an empire controlled by leading Nationalist politicians including Dr Nico Diederichs, MP, Dr Albert Hertzog, MP, Professor AI Malan, MP, Mr JH Greybe, MP, and such 'backroom boys' as Mr CR Louw (chairman of SANLAM – assets over £33 million, and the Federale group of investment and finance companies, vice-chairman of the Nasionale Pers, and director of many other companies), Dr MS Louw (chairman and managing director of Bonuscor, big-time investment corporation promoted by SANLAM), Professor CGW Schumann (Dean of the Faculty of Commerce at Stellenbosch University, one of the top Nationalist intellectuals and director of major Nationalist undertakings) and Dr JFJ van Rensburg (former commandant of the extremist Ossewabrandwag).' The author claims that Eerste Nasionale continued in every respect the pattern laid down by other members of the "Afrikaner Nationalist capitalist empire" – at a time when the National Party was accused rather of being somewhat socialistic, if not simply Naziist. Apart from the advertising campaign, in which much is made of cultural and historical references, the author alleges that a whispering campaign was being conducted by the politically faithful, similar to the one that put Rembrandt cigarettes on the map. 'Nationalists are being urged to buy Nationalist – to support the Nasionale firm and drink Senator coffee.'
5   *Tegniek*, September 1956.
6   *Tegniek*, January 1957.
7   Quoted from Hertzog's hand-written memoires.
8   Interview with Jan Groeneveld, 23 October 2002.
9   Interview with Johann Rupert, 3 September 2001.
10 Interview with Edwin Hertzog, 1 November 2001.
11 Report in *Tegniek*, November 1962.
12 *Die Burger*, 14 February 2003.
13 *Insig*, March 2005.
14 *Die Burger*, 29 November 2002.

CHAPTER 11

1 'Byvoegsel' to *Die Burger*, 9 May 1959.
2 *The Times* and *Cape and Transvaal Printers' Book*.
3 Hertzog's memoirs, dated 5 November 1958.
4 *Daily News*, Durban, 25 February 1959.
5 Personal communication from Edmund de Rothschild.
6 Genl.-Maj. Sir Francis de Guingand, *From brass hat to bowler hat*.
7 De Guingand, p. 106.
8 De Guingand, pp. 104-105.
9 *Die Transvaler*, 24 September 1959.
10 *Nation*, 1 August 1959

CHAPTER 12

1 Memorandum on Paarl project, dated 17 June 1959, in Rembrandt's archives.
2 Rupert's submission to the Truth and Reconciliation Commission, dated 20 October 1997.
3 Notes by FH Stroebel made during conversations with Rupert in 2004.
4 *Eastern Province Herald*, 17 June 1957.
5 Hertzog's memorandum, dated 25 January 1983.
6 *Die Burger*, 23 Julie 1959.
7 *New Age*, 6 August 1959.
8 Interview with Edwin Hertzog, 1 November 2001.
9 Interview with Hanneli Rupert, 5 December 2001.
10 Interview with Hans Knoetze, 12 November 2001.
11 The Wayfarer in his column 'The talk of the day', 17 May 1962. The column continued: 'If he gives a party – and last night he gave one of the biggest and most lavish this city has seen for many a long year – it is always in impeccable taste and without the slightest ostentation. This is part of the genius of this man who can think easier in millions than most men can in thousands; whose boundaries encompass a world while most men think of the borders of a particular country. His make-up is a natural, if almost reserved, quietness. He travels more about the world in one year than any six tycoons you can name put together. And he manages to do it without a single fanfare.'
12 *Sarie Marais*, 28 March 1962.
13 'Byvoegsel' to *Die Burger,* 9 May 1959.
14 Interview with *Sarie*, 15 December 1971.

CHAPTER 13

1 *Sunday Express*, 27 October 1963.
2 'Pound a day', editorial in the *Financial Mail*, 1 November 1963.
3 Allen Drury, *A very strange society: A journey to the heart of South Africa*.
4 Interview with Gys Steyn, 19 February 2003.
5 Interview with Thys Visser, 24 April 2003.
6 Communication from Koos Human, June 2003.
7 Rupert's submission to the TRC, dated 20 October 1997.
8 Johann Rupert's testimony to the TRC, 12 November 1997.
9 Rupert's lecture at the University of Pretoria, 22 August 1972.
10 The fundraising campaign is described in more detail in HB Thom (convenor), *Stellenbosch 1866-1966: Honderd jaar hoër onderwys*.

11 Rupert's speech on 22 April 1961 in Rembrandt's archives.

12 *Jaar van vordering* (Year of progress), Rembrandt Tobacco Corporation, 1962, p. 13.

13 Information about the Helpmekaar in JD Kestell, Voorwoord, *Helpmekaar gedenkboek*.

14 Rupert's chairman's address at Rembrandt's AGM, 1 September 1977.

CHAPTER 14

1 Rupert's speech on 31 July 1959 at Worcester, included in *Progress through partnership*.

2 Interview with Wynand van Graan, 2 December 2002.

3 *Rand Daily Mail*, 12 February 1960.

4 *Die Burger*, 15 February 1960.

5 Patrick Duncan jr, a well-known figure in liberal Cape circles who had links with the PAC and also liaised with Rupert, later died abroad. While he was genuinely concerned about the suffering of black people, he was somewhat eccentric. An aristocratic relative of the Duncans, Lord Brand, once asked Rupert to keep an eye on Duncan jr: 'Would you mind taking care of that young man? He is a bit around the bend.' Like Sir Patrick, Lord Brand (as Robert Henry Brand) had been a member of Milner's 'Kindergarten', the group of young Oxford graduates brought by British high commissioner Alfred Milner to South Africa after the Anglo-Boer War to take over the public service, supervise reconstruction and promote imperialistic ideals, inter alia by making English the only official language as well as the medium of instruction in schools. Lord Brand later became a leading British businessman who also played a prominent role in international affairs.

6 Rupert's submission to the TRC, dated 20 October 1997.

7 Philip Atta Kgosana, *Lest we forget*.

8 The quotation about Rupert and Verwoerd appeared in *The Afrikaner* in 1981.

9 Excerpt from the evidence of Albert John Luthuli in the supreme court case of *Rex vs Adams and Others*, according to an affidavit by Archibald Sholto Douglas, notary public, on 5 May 1960 in Pretoria.

10 Editorial in *The World*, 24 August 1976.

11 Sauer's views appear in Dirk and Johanna de Villiers's book *Paul Sauer*.

12 *Hoofstad*, 21 September 1981.

13 Piet Meiring wrote about this in his book *Bane en baanbrekers*.

14 Editorial in the *Eastern Province Herald*, 27 February 1961.

15 Report 'Apartheid is based on fear' in the *Rand Daily Mail*, 29 September 1961.

16 Debates in parliament, *Hansard*, 23 January 1962.

17 'Hertzog-annale' of the Suid-Afrikaanse Akademie vir Wetenskap en Kuns, December 1963.

18 Article in *Industry and Trade*, May 1963.

19 *Hansard*, 15 May 1964.

20 Communicated by Jan Groeneveld, November 2003.

21 Report in the *Evening Post*, 22 January 1966: 'Dr V rejected Rupert: Millionaire was first man to be chosen as Chancellor of UPE'. The report quoted from the book *Notes on the formation of South African foreign policy* by the American commentator Prof. Edwin Munger that had just been published. Munger referred to Rupert as an example of a prominent Afrikaner whose views were ignored by the government as far as foreign policy was concerned. For example, the prime minister had apparently blocked Rupert's appointment as chancellor of UPE, wrote Munger.

22 *Deelgenootskap in die praktyk* [Partnership in practice], compiled by the public relations division of the Rembrandt Group, p. 73.

23 Rupert's lecture on leadership for the future, delivered on 3 September 1965, appears in *Dr Anton Rupert: Pro Munere Grates*.

24 *The World*, 4 July 1966.

25 Exchange of letters recorded in Jaap Steyn's biography *Van Wyk Louw: 'n Lewensverhaal*, pp. 1058-1059.

26 A document on Rupert's conversation with Potgieter on 31 May 1995 obtained from Mike Botha, who was Rupert's personal assistant.

27 *Eastern Province Herald*, 12 March 1968.

28 Report in *Time*, 17 June 1966.

29 Piek's memorandum was dated 14 June 1966.

30 Letter from Donald Woods in Rembrandt's archives.

31 Letter from Sen. Robert Kennedy in Rembrandt's archives.

32 Dr Joachim Zahn jr also became a close friend of the Ruperts and sometimes looked after their house when they were abroad. One night he had to sleep on the sofa because their dog, Faustus, a Weimaraner, slept on his bed and refused to budge. During this time he completed his doctorate after Rupert had asked him how much time he still needed. Without thinking, he said six weeks – Rupert then gave him six weeks' leave to complete his thesis, on condition that he reported back to the group conference in Europe afterwards.

33 On 4 December 1991, a meeting between Nelson Mandela and American businesspeople and political leaders was held in Graves's corporate head office on Fifth Avenue in New York. Mandela consulted the Americans about black empowerment: 'If we don't have a very strong business class, it would be hard to make real progress.' Three years later, after Mandela had become president, Graves was also instrumental in bringing about a 100$ million investment by Pepsi-Cola in South Africa.

34 Interview in *Tegniek*, April 1965.

35 Hertzog's memorandum, dated 25 January 1983.

36 Dawie's column with the caption 'Rusie oor 'n skadelike blad' (Quarrel about a harmful paper) appeared in *Die Burger* on 6 August 1966.

37 *Financial Mail*, 30 December 1966.

CHAPTER 15

1 Communicated by Stuart Pretorius, 23 October 2003.

2 GME Leistner, *South Africa's development aid to African states*, pp. 12-13.

3 Communicated by Stuart Pretorius, 23 October 2003.

4 *Hansard* of 12 October 1966.

5 Communicated by Stuart Pretorius, 23 October 2003.

6 Lipton also maintained on occasion that he was a close friend of the Kennedy family of the USA. Van Graan was present when, after the assassination of Sen. Robert Kennedy, brother of the assassinated Pres. John F Kennedy, Lipton remarked to bystanders: 'The person I really sympathise with is his wife Rose.' Van Graan angered Lipton even further by pointing out that Rose was the mother of the Kennedy brothers, something any close friend of the family would be expected to know. Sen. Robert Kennedy's wife was Ethel Kennedy.

7 'Nothing could be further from the truth,' stated *XRay* in its apology. Van Graan had terminated his services of his own accord, with the thanks and good wishes of Chief Jonathan and the board of the LNDC. The journal apologised to Van Graan 'for this serious defamation'.

8 In a letter dated 14 August 1978, Van Graan objected strongly to several allegations in Gabriele Winai Ström's book *Development and dependence in Lesotho: The enclave of South Africa*, published by the Scandinavian Institute of African Studies in Uppsala, Sweden. For example, that eight laws had been passed to serve the interests of the South African government. He rejected the allega-

tion that Rupert, who had been appointed Lesotho's honorary adviser on industry in his personal capacity, had anything to do with the country's politics. Also false was Ström's allegation that representatives of the British government's Overseas Development Agency (ODA) had criticised Lesotho's invitation to South African businessmen. Rupert was the only South African business-man advising Lesotho – and he had personally persuaded the British government to finance the LNDC through the ODA. Van Graan also castigated Ström for 'insultingly insinuating' that mining companies such as Rio Tinto, Lonrho and Newmont Mining were stealing diamonds in Lesotho, while full reports on their operations were available from the Department of Mining.

9 Interview with Wynand van Graan, 2 December 2002.

10 Lecture at the University of Pretoria, 22 August 1972.

11 Interview with Rupert on 17 May 2002.

CHAPTER 16

1 Corrspondence in Rembrandt's archives.

2 Rupert in a speech at the celebration of Rembrandt's 21st birthday on 14 June 1969 in Paarl.

3 Documents in Rembrandt's archives.

4 Dirk and Johanna de Villiers, *Paul Sauer*, p. 148.

5 Internal memorandum by Johan Piek in Rembrandt's archives.

6 Conversation with Hermann Giliomee, quoted in his study 'Afrikaner entrepreneurship and the Afrikaner economic advance, 1900-1990: A tale with a puzzle and some twists', undertaken for the Centre for Development and Enterprise. Giliomee's conclusion (in private correspondence) is that English businesses did Afrikaners a tremendous favour by *not* assisting them with forms of affirmative action and empowerment schemes.

7 Johann Rupert complied with the request of an old friend, Motsepe, chairman of African Rainbow Minerals Gold, who in 2003, with the unification of business organisations, became the first chair-man of the combined body of South African businesspeople. His speech attracted much attention, especially because the impression had taken hold among a group of black businesspeople and intellectuals that Afrikaners owed their business success to the support of the National Party. He said to a group of 1 800 black businesspeople at the Nafcoc conference at Sun City that they could not rely on government or other blacks to make their businesses succeed; his father had also learnt not to rely on Afrikaner sentiment. It is only the quality of the product and the price that count. The Rembrandt Group had in fact done much better abroad than in South Africa. Afrikaners also bought Rothmans cigarettes because they thought the imported product was better. When he (Jo-hann) had experienced problems at Rand Merchant Bank, although his loans were covered well enough, Volkskas called in his loans and he received no support from Afrikaners. The people who had helped him to fend off an attack against the bank were Jews and Derek Keys, the later Minister of Finance. 'Don't think that you will achieve success by relying on either the government or fel-low Africans,' the younger Rupert said to the black businesspeople. He warned that there would be great failures, but an unintended result of the apartheid years was that it had taught blacks to think laterally. At Business Partners he saw how black entrepreneurs, especially women, suc-ceeded with small businesses. He encouraged black businesspeople to start with small enterprises and then expand organically. Their perception of the Afrikaner's route to wealth was incorrect. He remarked that the audience might cry 'Viva!' when union leaders made militant noises, but this would not help to counter unemployment and poverty; it could only be ensured by economic growth. This was greeted with 'Vivas!' from the audience. (He complained afterwards to the editor of the *Sunday Times* about the heading of the Sunday paper's article on his speech, 'Afrikaner path to wealth stinks, Rupert warns Nafcoc'.)

8   Correpondence in Rembrandt's archives.

9   Report in *Algemeen Handelsblad* in the Netherlands, 7 December 1963.

10   The founder, Gerard Adriaan Heineken, had bought De Hooyberg in 1863 at the age of 22, the larg-
     est brewery in Amsterdam that dated from 1592. He used a new German method of bottom fer-
     mentation. When a move was made to a new site with its own laboratory at the Stadhouderskade
     outside Amsterdam, Dr Ellion, a student of Louis Pasteur, developed a yeast that forms the base of
     the unique Heineken taste to this day. Heineken expanded much over the years, especially in the
     United States, where the first shipment of Heineken arrived in the harbour of Hoboken three days
     after the ending of Prohibition in 1933. In the 1940s Alfred Henry Heineken, grandson of Gerard
     Adriaan, helped with new marketing techniques to establish Heineken as the largest imported
     brand in America. The flamboyant Freddy Heineken, who had studied advertising techniques in
     the USA, had a strong belief in brands and marketing – a characteristic he shared with Rupert. He
     believed that 'beer can travel' and 'the brand will travel', and this created the foundation for the
     success of Heineken, which had become the largest beer exporter in the world by the 1960s.

11   Samuel Whitbread I, founder of the brewery, was also a devoted philanthropist. The London to
     which his mother sent him as a child was the London of George II and George III, of Pope and
     Dr Johnson, and of the great religious revival under the leadership of the Wesleys and George
     Whitefield. He was inspired by this. Samuel Whitbread I was not only a successful businessman,
     but also a member of parliament for Bedford for 22 years. He played an active role in the struggle
     against slavery, and therefore Rupert's partnership was also one with a family with a rich tradition
     of philanthropy. In addition, the Whitbreads were especially known for their support to the
     theatre. After Sheridan's Drury Lane Theatre had burnt down in 1809, Samuel Whitbread II was the
     chairman of the committee that raised funds for the repair of the theatre in 1811. Col. Whitbread,
     deputy chairman of the South African enterprise, was also a director of the Old Vic Trust.

     The Whitbreads also enjoyed good relations with the British royal family. As early as 1787
     King George III, Queen Charlotte and the three princesses visited the Whitbread brewery. And
     in November 1962, shortly before the partnership with Rupert, Queen Elizabeth II and the Queen
     Mother made a private visit to the brewery

12   *Die Burger*, 7 December 1963.

13   Documents in Rembrandt's archives.

14   Interview with Gerhard Steinmetz, 1 November 2001.

15   Communicated by Rupert, 2002.

16   More details about Monis in Romi van der Merwe, *A magic blend: SFW 1925-2000*.

17   Correspondence in Rembrandt's archives.

18   Interview with Paul Erasmus, July 2003.

19   Rupert delivered his Johannesburg speech, titled 'Prosper from our good fortune', in front of stock
     exchange representatives from England, Scotland, America, Canada, the then Rhodesia (Zimbab-
     we), France, Germany, the Netherlands, Belgium en Switzerland. He argued for a new partnership
     with the rising states of Africa, through which their trade and industry could be expanded on
     the basis of partnership with Western countries. He also wanted to 'try to help the [audience] to
     recover a correct perspective of South Africa's problems – so that "we can live with our problems",
     as Gen. De Gaulle had put it so aptly'. He emphasised South Africa's important strategic position
     as the 'axis' between Africa and Europe, and pointed out that the country had switched from an
     agriculture- and mining-based economy to rapid industrial development, with an average annual
     real growth rate in income of 4,4% in the 40 years from 1918 to 1958. And he pleaded for confidence
     in the future, because confidence created confidence. In this regard he quoted Albert Schweitzer,
     the philosopher-benefactor for whom he had a great admiration, who had said in his speech on

accepting the Nobel Peace Prize in 1954: 'For any enterprise, confidence is the capital without which no effective work can be carried on.'

20 *Business Week*, 28 September 1974, pp. 80-85.

21 Interview with Paul Erasmus, July 2003.

CHAPTER 17

1 *Rand Daily Mail*, 7 May 1968.

2 Rupert's speech at the University of Pretoria.

3 Rupert told the story of the formation of Rothmans International as honorary professor at the University of Pretoria on 22 August 1972. His lecture, 'The first European Community company', initially remained confidential.

4 *Press Advertising and Radio Review*, 1965.

5 Interview with Rupert, March 2001.

6 Interviews with Huberte Rupert, February-August 2001.

7 Rupert's speech to chartered accountants, July 1973.

8 *Daily Express*, 2 August 1972.

9 The apology read: '*The Daily Express* regrets that its City page report yesterday on the new Carreras merger contained inaccuracies. Our report stated that Dr Anthony Rupert was a cash backer of the National Party (in South Africa). We unreservedly accept that neither Dr Rupert, nor any of the companies with which he is associated, make financial contributions to any political party. *The Daily Express* apologises to Dr Rupert for the embarrassment our report has caused.' A later internal memorandum of Rothmans International mentions that the author of the offending column, Michael Gillard, had to leave the newspaper on account of that story and several others and later went to work elsewhere in the media.

10 Johann Rupert's oral testimony before the TRC, 12 November 1997.

11 Lecture at the University of Pretoria on 22 August 1972.

12 *Wirtschaftswoche*, 27 June 1973.

13 *Fortune*, 10 August 1981.

14 Communicated by Rupert, 2002.

15 Margaret bemoaned her fate as fundraiser for a charity organisation; according to her, the British cared more for animals than for people. One of the guests, the playwright Robert Bolt, author of *A man for all seasons*, the dramatised account of Sir Thomas More's clash with King Henry VIII, said to the princess: 'But, m'am, don't you know? The British are a violent people.'

16 *Business Week*, 28 September 1974.

17 'Bestuur – wetenskap of kultuur' in S Marx (editor), *Dr Anton Rupert: Pro Munere Grates*.

18 TJ Peters and RH Waterman, *In search of excellence*.

19 'Bestuur – wetenskap of kultuur' in S Marx (editor), *Dr Anton Rupert: Pro Munere Grates*.

CHAPTER 18

1 Among its clients were the Aga Khan, Indian maharajahs, the Rockefellers, the Vanderbilts, the Fords, the banker JP Morgan; film stars like Ingrid Bergman, Frank Sinatra, Marcello Mastroianni and many others; businesspeople, bankers and the aristocracy of Europe.

2 The Tank, invented in 1917, was inspired by the armoured tank that helped the Allied forces win the First World War. It appeared on the market in 1919, and became a status symbol to a host of famous people. Jackie Kennedy, Brigitte Bardot, Jeanne Moreau, Bob Hope, Warren Beatty, Margot Fonteyn, Andy Warhol, the fashion designers Hubert de Givenchy and Yves Saint Laurent, the supermodels Claudia Schiffer and Naomi Campbell – these and many other celebrities joined the

Tank cult. The writer Truman Capote owned eight of these watches. Rudolph Valentino insisted on wearing his Tank in every scene of his last film, 'The son of the sheikh'.

3   *Beeld*, 5 July 1978, p. 1.
4   *Beeld*, 5 July 1978, p. 1.
5   Books about Cartier from this period include Hans Nadelhoffer's *Cartier: Jewelers extraordinary*, Anne-Marie Clais' *Les Must de Cartier* and Gilberte Gautier's *La saga des Cartier 1847-1988*.
6   Interview with Joseph Kanoui, Paris, 16 June 2003.
7   Personal communication from Joachim Zahn Jr, Paris, 15 June 2003.
8   *Fortune*, 10 August 1981.
9   *Business Week*, 28 September 1974.
10 *Fortune*, 10 August 1981.
11 Interview with Hans Kolles, 23 June 2003.
12 Personal communication from Perrin, Paris, 16 June 2003.

CHAPTER 19
1   *XRay*, December 1973, p. 1.
2   Communicated by Rupert himself.
3   Letter from René Gerber to Ström, 20 February 1979.
4   Communicated by Gerber, Zürich, 2003.
5   Interview with Arminius Archer, 20 August 2003.
6   *Africa Confidential*, 6 September 1974 and 8 November 1974.
7   Chairman's address at Rembrandt's AGM, 15 September 1988.

CHAPTER 20
1   Louis Luyt, *Walking proud*, p. 76.
2   Louis Luyt, *Walking proud*, p. 76.
3   Communicated by Arminius Archer, 20 August 2003.
4   Mervyn Rees and Chris Day, *Muldergate: The story of the Info Scandal*, p. 89.
5   Leroux and Greene became acquainted through correspondence after Green, the author of novels such as *The Third Man, The Quiet American, Our Man in Havana* and *The Power and the Glory*, had read a translated version of Leroux's best-selling novel *Seven Days at the Silbersteins*. Leroux and his wife Elizabeth frequently visited Greene in his apartment at Antibes in the south of France where he lived for forty years with his lover 'Yvonne'. His acquaintance with Afrikaners led him to some interesting conclusions. 'Apartheid was an abomination to Greene and he frequently said in those early years that he believed Afrikaners would cut the Gordian knot in abolishing apartheid,' Mrs Leroux recalled.
6   Louis Luyt, *Walking proud*, p. 76.
7   Louis Luyt, *Walking proud*, pp. 123-136.
8   Interview with Hans Knoetze, 12 November 2001.
9   Communication from Dr Frederick Mostert, August 2002. He added: 'I'm particularly struck by Dr Rupert's acknowledgement of his wife, Mrs Huberte Rupert. I've almost never heard him make a speech at a function in which he did not express his gratitude and appreciation towards Mrs Rupert. Dr Rupert would also, where humanly possible, attend farewell functions for colleagues going on retirement. I'll never, ever forget how he flew all the way from Cape Town to attend my own father's funeral in Johannesburg. His humanity stretches wide and deep.' (His father was Judge Anton Mostert, who initially exposed the Information Scandal.)
10 Interview with Dr Edwin Hertzog, 1 November 2001.

11 Memorandum from Gys Steyn in Rembrandt's archives.

12 Interview with Rupert, 2003.

13 Particulars about the deal appear in DJ van Zyl's book *KWV 1918-'93*.

14 Interview with Edwin Hertzog, 1 November 2001.

15 'Ek is sonder verhoor opgehang', report in *Die Burger*, 15 November 1979.

16 Interview with Gerhard Steinmetz, November 2000.

17 Interview with Johann Rupert, 3 September 2001.

18 Memorandum from Johan Piek in Rembrandt's archives, dated 29 December 1979, i.e.at the time of Rembrandt's 21st birthday.

19 Communication about the negotiations from Ritzema de la Bat, August 2001.

20 Rupert's chairman's report, 1983.

21 Interview with Ritzema de la Bat, August 2001.

CHAPTER 21

1   Interview with Rupert, 2002.

2   Quotations from Rupert's speech 'Challenges facing the private sector'.

3   Interview with Steyn, 3 September 2003.

4   Report in *Die Burger*, 23 August 1990.

5   'Kleinsake is groot sake' in *Dr Anton Rupert: Pro Munere Grates*, p. 200.

6   'Kleinsake is groot sake' in *Dr Anton Rupert: Pro Munere Grates*, pp. 187-201.

7   'Kleinsake is groot sake'.

8   'Kleinsake is groot sake' in *Dr Anton Rupert: Pro Munere Grates*, p. 201.

9   *Cape Times*, 31 August 1979.

10   Interview with Rupert, 2002.

11   Interview with Hans Knoetze, November 2001.

12   *Op weg na 'n konstellasie van state in Suider-Afrika*. Summit between the prime minister and business leaders, November 1979. Publications department, Department of Foreign Affairs and Information, Pretoria 1980, p. 10.

13   *Op weg na 'n konstellasie . . .*, p. 25.

14   Communicated by Ben Vosloo, May 2001.

15   Interview with Rupert, 2002.

16   *Die Burger*, 3 February 1985.

17   Letter from Pieroth from St Petersburg in Russia to Rupert, dated 2 June 2002.

18   Article in *Taalgenoot*, May 1994.

19   Record of the negotiations in the corporation's annual reports of 1996 and 1997.

20   Annual Report of Business Partners, 2001.

21   Telephonic interview with Schwenke, 23 January 2004.

22   Article in *Huisgenoot*, 1996.

23   *Finansies & Tegniek*, 4 April 1997.

24   *Sunday Times*, 30 August 1998.

25   See Clem Sunter, *The high road: Where are we now?*

CHAPTER 22

1   Correspondence in the archives of Rembrandt and Sanlam.

2   Interview with Rupert, 20 April 2001.

3   *Rand Daily Mail*, 16 July 1974.

4   *Rand Daily Mail*, 4 October 1974.

5   *The Star*, 22 November 1974.

6   *Die Transvaler*, 26 November 1974.

7   *Sunday Times*, 1 December 1974.

8   JDF Jones, *Through fortress and rock: The story of Gencor*, p. 158.

9   *Rapport*, 12 January 1975.

10 Wassenaar's personal document about the events was kept confidential for a long time.

11 Interview with Rupert, 20 April, 2001.

12 *Rand Daily Mail*, 11 January 1975.

13 *Rapport*, 19 January 1975.

14 Wassenaar's personal document. Van den Berg later left General Mining.

15 Interview with Rupert, 20 April 2001.

16 Interview with Rupert, 20 April 2001.

17 According to Willem Pretorius (in an interview on 22 April 2001), the investigation related to alleged contentious foreign exchange transactions by Du Plessis in his personal capacity. Eduan Pretorius, managing director of Senbank, had become concerned about rumours in this regard. He shared his concerns with Pretorius, who advised him to speak to Wassenaar. The complaints were then referred to the two senior partners of Bankorp's auditors, who found that the complaints were devoid of substance.

18 Interview with Rupert, 20 April 2001.

19 According to Willem Pretorius, Wassenaar later told him that the businessman in question had been Graham Beck, the horse breeder who also owned the farm Madeba in the Robertson district. Beck and Wassenaar, both keen on horse racing, bumped into each other at a race where Beck then made this remark, probably in passing. At that stage Wassenaar was so mistrustful of De Villiers and Rupert, however, that he took it seriously.

20 Wassenaar's memorandum, which was not submitted to Sanlam, said, inter alia, that it was 'doubtful' whether Federale Mynbou could function under someone 'who could not exert his full powers in the management affairs of the group when required to do so by circumstances'. He recommended: 'It is therefore deemed necessary that Dr De Villiers step down as executive officer from 1 January 1982.'

21 JDF Jones, *Through fortress and rock: The story of Gencor*, pp. 166-167.

22 Interview with Huberte Rupert, 23 April 2001.

23 Interview with Willem Pretorius, 22 April 2001.

24 JDF Jones, *Through fortress and rock ...*, p. 168.

25 JDF Jones, *Through fortress and rock ...*

26 Tom de Beer's memorandum.

27 Rupert's chairman's address, 26 August 1982.

28 Letter by Wim de Villiers.

29 Interview with Rupert, 20 April 2001.

CHAPTER 23

1   See also chapter 2, The feud between Rembrandt and Sanlam.

2   Louis Luyt wrote about this in his autobiography, *Walking proud*.

3   Len de Villiers expands on this in his book *Secret information*.

4   'How the Info men deceived Anton Rupert', *Sunday Times*, 17 February 1980.

5   Louis Luyt described the situation in detail in his autobiography.

6   'Rupert almost sank Citizen twice!', *Sunday Times*, 25 May 1980.

7   Mervyn Rees and Chris Day wrote comprehensively about Rhoodie's involvement in their book *Muldergate: The Story of the Info Scandal*.

8   *Cape Times*, 28 August 1981.
9   Rupert's letter to Kennedy in Rembrandt's archives.
10 *Sunday Star,* 29 September 1985.
11 Quoted in an unpublished study by David Welsh about South Africa's transition.
12 Rupert's letter, dated 24 January 1986, was later also submitted to the TRC.
13 Dr Boraine's comments during Johann Rupert's verbal testimony were included in the TRC's report.
14 Telephonic interview with Wynand Malan, 17 March 2003.
15 Rupert's submission to the TRC, pp. 7 and 8.
16 Johann Rupert's testimony in the TRC's report.
17 PW Botha's letter in Rembrandt's archives.
18 Faxed message from Fentener van Vlissingen, dated 3 September 2001.
19 *Leadership*, November 1986.
20 *Beeld*, 2 November 1987.
21 *Rapport*, 4 November 1987.
22 Interview with Rupert, 27 March 2002.
23 Rupert's letter in Rembrandt's archives.
    Document about this obtained from Mike Botha, who was Rupert's personal assistant.
24. Interview with *Rapport*, 1996
25 Anton Rupert, 'Krag in verskeidenheid,' in *Prioriteite vir medebestaan*, p. 13.

CHAPTER 24
1   Particulars about Richemont appear in a luxury publication issued by the company itself.
2   The history of Cartier appears, inter alia, in Hans Nadelhoffer, *Cartier: Jewelers extraordinary.*
3   Information about Rembrandt's and Richemont's trademarks and companies in the groups was obtained from Frederick Mostert and David Broodryk of Intellectual Property Services.
4   Rupert's speech at Rembrandt's 21st-anniversary celebrations in 1969, in Rembrandt's archives.
5   Rupert's speech at the Tweede Ekonomiese Volkskongres in Bloemfontein in 1950.
6   Communication from Frederick Mostert, August 2002.
7   Information obtained from Distell in the course of 2003.
8   Communication from Frederick Mostert, August 2002.
9   Interview with Pans Taljaard, 14 October 2002.
10 Interview with Gerhard Steinmetz, 1 November 2001.
11 Louis Luyt, *Walking proud*, pp. 76-77.
12 Interview with Mike Botha, 22 May 2002.
13 Interview with Pans Taljaard, 14 October 2002.
14 Interview with Edwin Hertzog, 1 November 2001.
15 Communication from Koos Human, June 2003.
16 Internal publications of the Rembrandt Group.
17 Wolfgang Ritter related this in his book *Die bessere Idee.*
18 Ogilvy told part of the story in his book *Ogilvy on advertising.*
19 Communicated by Georg Domizlaff.
20 Interview with Georg Domizlaff, 20 February 2004.
21 *Wine Spectator*, 28 February 1999.
22 Communicated by Frans Stroebel, 2003.

CHAPTER 25

1   *Wine Spectator*, 28 February 1999.
2   *Die Burger*, 5 February 1979.
3   Alfred Baumgartner, *The first 35 years of Distillers Corporation (SA) Limited*.
4   *Die Burger*, 8 September 1968.
5   Interview with Jacques van de Walle, 15 October 2003.
6   More details are to be found in the *Complete book of South African wine* by John Kench, Phyllis Hands and David Hughes.
7   *Wine Spectator*, 28 February 1999.

CHAPTER 26

1   Rupert's address at Daan Hoogenhout's funeral at Stellenbosch, 27 April 1981.
2   Article in *Business Week*, 28 September 1974.
3   Interview with Johann Rupert, 3 September 2001.
4   Interview with Edwin Hertzog, 1 November 2001.
5   Interview with Edwin Hertzog, 1 November 1961.
6   Interview with Jan Engelbrecht, 7 February 2002.
7   Communications from Hans Knoetze, 12 November 2001.
8   Telephonic interview with Stuart Pretorius, 15 August 2003.
9   Interview with Edwin Hertzog, 1 November 2001
10 Interview with Johann Rupert, 3 September 2001.
11 Interview with Johann Rupert, 3 September 2001.
12 Interview with Johann Rupert, 23 October 2002.
13 Communication from Nikolaus Senn, May 2003.
14 Interview with Johann Rupert, 3 September 2001.
15 Interview with Johann Rupert, 26 August, 2003.
16 Interview with Johann Rupert, 26 August 2003.
17 Interview with Edwin Hertzog, 1 November 2001.
18 This was the last law placed on the statute-book by the NP government.
19 Rupert's speech, August 2000.
20 Interview with Edwin Hertzog, 1 November 2001.
21 South Africa was one of the first forty countries to sign and ratify the convention, which has since been accepted by 192 member countries, on 16 June 2003 in Geneva.
22 Interview with Edwin Hertzog, 1 November 2001.
23 *Forbes*, 1996.

CHAPTER 27

1   *Eastern Province Herald*, 20 September 1960.
2   Interviews with Wynand van Graan, 2 December 2002, and Gerhard Roux, 14 November 2003.
3   Vladimir Tretchikoff, *Pigeon's Luck*.
4   Danie van Nierkerk, 'Rupert word tagtig', *Insig*, October 1996.
5   *Rapport*, 15 October 1967, p. 7.
6   'Op die randakker', *Rapport*, 22 October 1967.
7   Article on 27 October 1966 in the journal of the Pretoria Art Museum.
8   According to *The Economist*, 13 October 2001.
9   The artbook is Roberto Salvini's *Scultura italiana moderna*.
10 Danie van Niekerk, 'Rupert word tagtig', *Insig*, October 1996.

11 Quoted in the preface to a brochure written by Hannelore Fischer, director of the Käthe Kollwitz Museum in Cologne, when Kollwitz's works were exhibited on a travelling exhibition in South Africa in 1997-1998.

12 Article by Marilyn Martin in *Die Burger*, 10 May 1992.

13 'Gesprek met 'n ware heer,' interview with Izak de Villiers, *Rapport*, 1996.

14 Communication from Frederick Mostert, August 2002.

15 Ponto, who had to take a different route to work each day for security reasons, opened his front door on the day of his death to a goddaughter, Suzanne Albrecht, who had arrived with a bunch of flowers and 'two friends', with fatal results. Ponto's murder was one of the most sensational horror incidents during a year in which terrorism held sway in West Germany, with several attacks on leading West German businessmen and industrialists. The gang members who were given jail sentences were followers of Andreas Baader and Ulrike Meinhof, leaders of the Rote Armee Fraktion, the terrorist movement aimed at ending capitalism in German society and removing American troops from German territory by means of bombs, murders and kidnappings.

16 Rupert delivered his speech on 15 August 1968 in the South African National Gallery in Cape Town.

17 Letter to *Die Burger*, 3 November 1993.

CHAPTER 28

1 The WWF, with its headquarters at the town of Gland near Geneva in Switzerland, was established after the naturalist Sir Julian Huxley had written a series of articles about threatened natural life for the London *Observer*. Among the many people who responded was a London businessman, Victor Stolan. Nature can only be saved, he wrote in a letter, if drastic and immediate steps are taken to collect the large sums of money required. The WWF was founded less than a year afterwards.

2 Rupert delivered his speech on 30 August 1971 in Pretoria.

3 Prince Bernhard quoted in *Wine Spectator*, 28 February 1999.

4 *Die Burger*, 28 August 1990, p. 15.

5 Column in *Die Burger*, July 2003.

6 *Die Burger*, 12 July 2003.

CHAPTER 29

1 FS Malan, *Marie Koopmans-de Wet*.

2 *Prioriteite vir medebestaan*, p. 14.

3 Marise van Wyk, 'Bewaring en die rol van Historiese Huise van Suid-Afrika Beperk', p. 28.

4 Annual report of Historical Homes, 1970, p. 5.

5 Marise van Wyk, 'Bewaring en die rol van Historiese Huise van Suid-Afrika Beperk', p. 31.

6 *Prioriteite vir medebestaan*, p. 15.

7 Annual report of Historical Homes, 1970, p. 5.

8 *Die Burger*, 11 June 1979.

9 Interview with Boets Smuts, 2003.

10 Interview with Paul le Roux, 2003.

11 Marthinus van Bart in *Die Burger*, 8 September 1990.

12 *Dr Anton Rupert: Pro Munere Grates*, p. 142.

CHAPTER 30

1 Anton Rupert, *Wie in wondere glo*, pp. 12-13.

2 *Dr Anton Rupert: Pro Munere Grates*, p. 127.

3 Anton Rupert, *Prioriteite vir medebestaan*, p. 12.

4 Christopher Danziger, *A trader's century – the fortunes of Frasers*.

5 JC Kannemeyer, *DJ Opperman: 'n Biografie*.

6 Opperman's foreword to *Wie in wondere glo*.

7 Communicated by Danie van Niekerk, March 2003.

8 Communicated by Koos Human, June 2003.

9 Communicated by Cloete Breytenbach, September 2002.

CHAPTER 31

1 Martin Pabst, *Transfrontier peace parks in Southern Africa*, p. 50.

2 Interview with Rupert, 2002.

3 World Bank report, June 1996.

4 See also Martin Pabst, *Transfrontier peace parks in Southern Africa*, p. 37 et seq.

5 Rupert referred to this, inter alia, at DaimlerChrysler's conference in Cape Town in 2002.

6 Annual report of the Peace Parks Foundation, 2001.

7 Interview with Rupert, 2003.

8 Annual report of the Peace Parks Foundation, 2002.

9 Rupert has explained the theme of the four pillars in various speeches as well as in discussions with government leaders and influential businesspeople.

10 Interview with Rupert, 2002.

11 *Pretoria News*, 15 May 2000.

12 Mandela's speech on 4 October 2001, obtained from the Nelson Mandela Foundation.

13 *Rapport*, 28 October 2001.

14 *Rapport*, 28 October 2001.

15 Letter by Dr Maurice F Strong from Toronto, dated 4 October 2001.

16 *The parks for peace* (DaimlerChrysler 2001), p. 15.

17 Annual report of the Peace Parks Foundation, 2002.

18 Rupert's letter to Manuel, dated 30 January 2002.

19 Rupert's letter to Mbeki, dated 31 May 2002.

20 Martin Pabst, *Transfrontier peace parks in Southern Africa*, p. 42.

21 One such speech Rupert delivered at DaimlerChrysler's conference in Cape Town in 2002.

22 Rupert referred to this at DaimlerChrysler's conference in Cape Town in 2002.

23 *Cape Times*, 2 October 2001.

24 *National Geographic*, September 2001.

25 Communication from Frederick Mostert, August 2002.

26 Annual report of the Peace Parks Foundation, 2001.

27 The resolution in the American Congress, which coincided with the visit of Pres. George W Bush to southern Africa, was tabled – with the consent of the senate – in the house of representatives by Sherwood Boehlert, a Republican from New York, on 16 July 2003. He had visited South Africa two years before as member of an American delegation headed by the speaker of the house who attended a presentation about the PPF at L'Ormarins, Anthonij Rupert's farm.

28 *The parks for peace* (DaimlerChrysler 2001), p. 8.

29 Report in *The Times of India*, 23 June 2001.

30 In September 2001 *National Geographic* published a feature article on peace parks entitled 'Without borders'.

31 Letter from Prince Philip, dated 31 October 2003 from Sandringham. The medal was named after the British royal after he retired as president of the WWF in 1996.

32 Newsletter of the Peace Parks Foundation, 1 December 2003.

CHAPTER 32

1 Message of condolence from Nelson Mandela, read out at the memorial service for Anthonij Rupert on 30 October 2001.

2 Letter from Pres. Thabo Mbeki, dated 27 November 2001.

3 Interview with Izak de Villiers, *Rapport*, 29 September 1996.

4 'The world's richest people', *Forbes*, 26 February 2004.

5 Huberte Rupert in an interview with *Sarie*, 15 December 1971.

6 Rupert in an interview with *Rapport*, 29 September 1996.

7 The collections of paintings and sculptures that Henry Frick, Andrew Mellon and other pioneer financial magnates acquired with their riches formed the foundation for the American national art galleries in New York and Washington. Leon Levy, an American financier who died on 6 April 2003 at the age of 77, also gave away $140 million, of which $20 million went to the Metropolitan Museum of Art in New York, according to *The Economist*, 26 April, 2003, p. 76.

8 Andrew Carnegie wrote, amongst other things, in *The gospel of wealth*: 'This, then, is held to be the duty of the Man of Wealth: First, to set an example of modest, unostentatious living, shunning display or extravagance; to provide moderately for the legitimate wants of those dependent upon him; and after doing so to consider all surplus revenues which come to him simply as trust funds, which he is called upon to administer, and strictly bound as a matter of duty to administer in the manner which, in his judgement, is best calculated to produce the most beneficial result for the community – the man of wealth thus becoming the sole agent and trustee for his poorer brethren, bringing to their service his superior wisdom, experience, and ability to administer – doing for them better than they would or could do for themselves.' He continued: 'He is the only true reformer who is as careful and as anxious not to aid the unworthy as he is to aid the worthy, and, perhaps, even more so, for in almsgiving more injury is probably done by rewarding vice than by relieving virtue.'

9 John D Rockefeller, quoted in *The Rockefeller Foundation: A history*.

10 Paul Johnson, *The history of the modern world*.

11 The direct cause of Buthelezi's memorandum for a conversation with Rupert, dated 25 November 2002, was the floor-crossing legislation that the ANC was in the process of carrying through. He also referred to several other issues, amongst which his refusal to accept the position of deputy president after the election of 1999, because Pres. Mbeki had put as condition that the ANC (and not the IFP) must then receive the premiership of KwaZulu-Natal. He also complained that his role in the government, where his contributions were mostly ignored, was characterised by increasing difficulties and problems. To realise Rupert's and his dream of making the country the Switzerland of Africa thus put him before an extremely difficult choice. But no matter what he would decide, he would serve the long-term goals of their beloved country, he wrote.

12 Rupert wrote a letter in response to Buthelezi's memorandum on 2 December 2002.

13 Rupert also requested in his letter to Mbeki, dated 23 October 2003, that leasehold, modelled after the pattern followed in China in recent years, should be granted to all the people in South African areas in communal possession controlled by tribal leaders. In China 30-year leasehold was granted to 98 million rural families, and the result was that productivity rose sky high. In the letter he also mentioned three other possibilities of job creation: fighting land erosion, removing alien plants (so that water could be saved) and the improvement of subsidiary roads (only 15 percent of the country's roads are tarred).

14 *The Economist* published a much-discussed front-page article 'Hopeless Africa' on 11 May 2000. Four years later, on 15 January 2004, the magazine published a special supplement entitled 'Making Africa smile'.

15 Interview with Martin Pabst in *Transfrontier peace parks in Southern Africa*, p. 12.

16 *Financial Gazette*, 17 December 1965.

17 Gen. Charles de Gaulle is quoted in Rupert's lecture 'Leierskap vir die toekoms' [Leadership for the future] in *Dr Anton Rupert: Pro Munere Grates*. The quotation comes from De Gaulle's *Le Fil l'Epée* (translated in English as *The edge of the sword*), that he wrote after the Pyrrhic victory of 1918 and in which he gave his soldier's advice to France.

18 The event was the opening of the new Liberty Life head-office on 8 September 1982 in Braamfontein, Johannesburg. Gordon asked Rupert to conduct the opening – just as Harry Oppenheimer of Anglo American had asked him to conduct the opening of the new complex of the Carlton Hotel in Johannesburg. Rupert, in his position as chairman of the Small Business Development Corporation, typically sang the praises of Donny Gordon at the Liberty opening ceremony. Rupert said he knew of no better example of a small businessman who in a short span of time had achieved such a measure of success. He considered it proof that miracles could still happen. Within a quarter of a century, Liberty, which had virtually brought about a revolution in the life-insurance industry in the country, had become something of a legend. When the first policy was issued on 1 October 1958, the capital amounted to only R100 000. But, thanks to innovation and aggressive marketing, a wide range of new products was launched, and Liberty became the first life-insurance company listed on the South African stock exchange. 'South Africa, with its multi-racial society, today offers the best school for anyone who wants to learn how to do successful business in any place in the free world. The Liberty Life Centre symbolises the wonderful opportunities that South Africa offers to enterprising businessmen,' Rupert declared.

19 Letter from Dr Philip H Spies, dated 2 July 2001.

20 Message from Mandela on the occasion of the *Sunday Times* Business Times Lifetime Award for his contribution to business and community development in South Africa on 7 November 2000 in Johannesburg.

21 The commendatio for honorary membership of the Academy, awarded to Rupert at Stellenbosch on 21 June 2002, was compiled by the historian Prof. Dr Pieter Kapp.

22 Communication from Prof. Hermann Giliomee, 12 February 2004.

23 Interview with Izak de Villiers, *Rapport*, 29 September 1996.

24 David Landes, *The wealth and poverty of nations*, p. 524.

Sources

INTERVIEWS

We thank the many people who provided valuable information, either by way of interviews or in written communications. First and foremost there is Anton Rupert himself and members of his family: his wife Huberte, his son Johann, his daughter and son-in-law, Hanneli and Hein Koegelenberg, and his brother Koos. Others, listed alphabetically, are:

Dr Arminius Archer
Tom Bata
Elsie Bosman
Dr André Breedt
Cloete Breytenbach
Hanna Botha
Miems Botha
Mike Botha
Dr Theo Botha
David Broodryk
Revd Geoff Davies
Ritzema de la Bat
Georg Domizlaff
Dr Hermien Dommisse
Theuns Eksteen
Jan Engelbrecht
Paul Erasmus
Gerhard Froneman
Rene Gerber
Jan Groeneveld
Dr Hermann Giliomee
Kriek Grundling
Deon Herselmann
Dirk Hertzog
Edwin Hertzog
George Hofmeyr
Eben Human
Koos Human
Joseph Kanoui
Dr Pieter Kapp
André Kilian
Hans Knoetze
Hans Kolles
Leo Kruger
Bertie Levenstein

Paul le Roux
Andrew Marais
David Meades
Erna Meaker
Hannes Meiring
Dr Frederick Mostert
Alain Dominique Perrin
Jennifer Preller
Stuart Pretorius
Jan Prins
Flip Rademeyer
Edmund de Rothschild
Gerhard Roux
Prof. Jan Sadie
Jo Schwenke
Nikolaus Senn
Bertha Slotegraaf
Boets Smuts
Gerhard Steinmetz
Gys Steyn
Judge Jan Steyn
Carolyn Stone
Frans Stroebel
Pans Taljaard
Dr Colijn van Bergen
Jacques van de Walle
Elizabeth van der Merwe
Dr Boy van Eeden
Wynand van Graan
Danie van Niekerk
Thys Visser
Paul Fentener van Vlissingen
Dr Ben Vosloo
Terry Whitlock
Dr Joachim Zahn

BOOKS

Baumgartner, Alfred. 1979. *The first 35 years of Distillers Corporation (SA) Limited.* Private edition.

Beyers, CJ & Krüger, DW (eds) 1977. *Suid-Afrikaanse biografiese woordeboek.* 1st edition. Cape Town: Tafelberg.

Booysen, Beyera Fourina. 1986. ''n Geskiedenis van Jansenville, dorp en distrik, 1855-1955.' MA dissertation, University of Port Elizabeth.

Botha, Hendrik Jacobus. 1965. 'Die moord op Derdepoort, 25 November 1899.' MA dissertation. University of Pretoria.

Botha, Theo A. 1991. 'Graaff-Reinet tydens die Anglo-Boere-oorlog, 1899-1902.' MA dissertation, University of Port Elizabeth.

1994. 'Graaff-Reinet tydens die Eerste Wêreldoorlog, 1914-'19: 'n Sosio-ekonomiese ondersoek.' PhD thesis, University of Port Elizabeth.

Bull, Esmé. 1991. *Aided immigration from Britain to South Africa.* Human Sciences Research Council.

Carnegie, Andrew. 1933. *The gospel of wealth and other timely essays.* Garden City, NY: Doubleday, Doran & Co.

Clais, Anne-Marie. 2002. *Les Must de Cartier.* New York: Assouline Publishing.

Coetzee, J Albert (ed.) 1941. 'Ons reddingsdaad.' Brochure. Johannesburg: Head Office of the *Reddingsdaadbond.*

Danziger, Christopher. 1979. *A trader's century – the fortunes of Frasers.* Cape Town: Purnell.

Davenport, TRH. 1977. *South Africa: a modern history.* Johannesburg: Macmillan.

De Guingand, Francis. 1979. *From brass hat to bowler hat.* London: Hamish Hamilton.

De Kiewiet, CW. 1964. *A history of South Africa, social and economic.* Oxford: Oxford University Press.

De Villiers, Dirk & Johanna. 1977. *Paul Sauer.* Cape Town: Tafelberg.

De Villiers, Les. 1980. *Secret information.* Cape Town: Tafelberg.

De Waal, Pieter. 1918. *De Waal geslag.* Cape Town: Nasionale Pers.

Drucker, Peter. 1985. *Innovation and entrepreneurship.* Johannesburg: Heinemann.

Drury, Allen. 1967. *A very strange society. A journey to the heart of South Africa.* New York: Trident Press.

Duke, Maurice & Jordan, Daniel P. 1995. *Tobacco merchant: the story of Universal Leaf Tobacco Company.* Lexington: University Press of Kentucky.

Du Plessis, EP. 1964. *'n Volk staan op: die Ekonomiese Volkskongres en daarna.* Cape Town: Human & Rousseau.

Esterhuyse, WP. 1986. *Anton Rupert: Pleitbesorger vir hoop.* Cape Town: Tafelberg.

Gately, Iain. 2001. *Tobacco: A cultural history of how an exotic plant seduced civilization.* New York: Grove Press.

Gautier, Gilberte. 1988. *La saga des Cartier 1847-1988.* Paris: Michel Lafon.

Giliomee, Hermann. 2003. *The Afrikaners: biography of a people.* Cape Town: Tafelberg.

Giliomee, Hermann & Adam, Heribert. 1981. *Afrikanermag: opkoms en toekoms.* Stellenbosch: University Publishers.

Giliomee, Hermann. 2003. 'Afrikaner entrepreneurship and the Afrikaner economic advance, 1900-1990: a tale with a puzzle and some twists.' Unpublished study conducted for the Centre for Development and Enterprise.

Graves, Earl G. 1997. *How to succeed in business without being white.* New York: HarperBusiness.

Hall-Martin, Anthony & Modise, Sedia. 2002. *Existing and potential transfrontier conservation areas in the SADC region.* PPF, Stellenbosch.

Heese, JA. 1971. *Die herkoms van die Afrikaner 1657-1867.* Cape Town: AA Balkema.

Jay, Peter. 2000. *Road to riches.* London: Weidenfeld & Nicholson.

Johnson, Paul. 1983. *The history of the modern world.* London: Weidenfeld & Nicholson.

Jones, JDF. 1995. *Through fortress and rock: the story of Gencor, 1895-1995.* Johannesburg: Jonathan Ball.

Joubert, Dian. 1972. *Toe witmense arm was.* Cape Town: Tafelberg.

Kannemeyer, JC. 1986. *D.J. Opperman: 'n biografie.* Cape Town and Pretoria: Human & Rousseau.

Kench, John, Hands, Phyllis & Hughes, David. 1983. *The complete book of South African wine.* Cape Town: Struik.

Kestell, JD. (foreword) 1918. *Helpmekaar gedenkboek.* Cape Town: Nationale Pers Beperkt.

Keynes, John Maynard. 1936. *General theory of employment, interest, and money.* Macmillan, Cambridge University Press.

Kgosana, Philip Atta. 1988. *Lest we forget.* Johannesburg: Skotaville Publishers.

Landes, David. 1988. *The wealth and poverty of nations.* New York: WW Norton & Co.

Leistner, GME 1970. *South Africa's development aid to African states.* Pretoria: Africa Institute.

Luyt, Louis. 2003. *Walking proud.* Cape Town: Don Nelson.

Malan, F.S. ±1924. *Marie Koopmans-de Wet.* Cape Town: Juta.

Marx, S. (ed.) 1986. *Dr Anton Rupert: Pro Munere Grates.* Lectures as honorary professor of business economics, University of Pretoria. Pretoria: Book Productions.

Meiring, Piet. 1988. *Bane en baanbrekers.* Silverton: Promedia Publications.

Mohn, Reinhard. 1996. *Success through partnership.* New York: Doubleday.

Mostert, Noël. 1992. *Frontiers.* London: Jonathan Cape.

Muller, CFJ. 1968. *Vyfhonderd jaar Suid-Afrikaanse geskiedenis.* Pretoria: Human & Rousseau-Academica.

Nadelhoffer, Hans. 1984. *Cartier: Jewelers extraordinary.* London: Thames & Hudson.

Ogilvy, David. 1985. *Ogilvy on advertising.* New York: Vintage.

O'Meara, Dan. 1983. *Volkskapitalisme: class, capital and ideology in the development of Afrikaner nationalism, 1934-1948.* New York: Cambridge University Press.

Opperman, DJ. 1983. *Groot Afrikaanse verseboek.* Cape Town: Tafelberg.

Pabst, Martin. 2002. *Transfrontier peace parks in Southern Africa.* München: Chairman's Office, Southern Africa Institute of German Business.

Pama, C. 1983. *Die groot Afrikaanse familienaamboek.* Cape Town: Human & Rousseau.

Pelzer, AN. 1979. *Die Afrikaner-Broederbond: eerste 50 jaar.* Cape Town: Tafelberg.

Peters, TJ & Waterson, RH jr. 1982. *In search of excellence: lessons from America's best run companies.* New York: Harper & Row.

Rautenbach, CH (ed.). 1960. *Ad Destinatum: Gedenkboek van die Universiteit van Pretoria.* Johannesburg: Voortrekkerpers.

Rees, Mervyn & Day, Chris. 1980. *Muldergate: The story of the Info Scandal.* Braamfontein: Macmillan.

Rembrandt Group Limited, Department of Public Relations. 1988. *Deelgenootskap in die praktyk.* Goodwood: Nasionale Boekdrukkery.

Richemont, Department of Public Relations. 1990. *Richemont.* London: Lowe Bell.

Ries, Alf & Dommisse, Ebbe. 1982. *Broedertwis.* Cape Town: Tafelberg.

1990. *Leierstryd.* Cape Town: Tafelberg.

Ritter, Wolfgang. 1970. *Die bessere Idee.* Stuttgart: Verlag Günther Neske Pfullingen.

Rosenthal, Eric. 1963. *Manne en maatskappye.* Cape Town: Human & Rousseau.

Rupert, Anton. 1967. *Leiers oor leierskap.* Private publication. Cape Town

1967. *Wie in wondere glo.* Cape Town: Nasionale Boekhandel.

1974. *Inflasie – hoe tem ons openbare vyand nommer een?* Private publication. Cape Town.

1981. *Prioriteite vir medebestaan.* Cape Town: Tafelberg.

Sadie, JL. 2002/1. 'The fall and rise of the Afrikaner in the South African economy.' *Annals of the University of Stellenbosch.*

Salvini, Roberto. 1961. *Scultura italiana moderna*. Milaan: Silvana editoriale d'arte.

Schnell, ELG. 1954. *For men must work*. Cape Town: Maskew Miller.

Scannell, JP. 1968. *Uit die volk gebore: Sanlam se eerste vyftig jaar*. Cape Town: Nasionale Boekhandel.

Schwär, F & Pape, BE. 1958. *Duitsers in Kaffraria, 1858-1958*. King William's Town: King Printing Company.

Serfontein, JHP. 1979. *Brotherhood of power: an exposé of the Afrikaner Broederbond*. London: Collings.

Shearing, Taffy & David. 1999. *Commandant Gideon Scheepers and the search for his grave*. Private edition. Sedgefield.

Southey, Nicholas & Mouton, FA. 2001. 'J.A.I. Agar-Hamilton: forgotten historian.' Seminar paper, Department of History, University of South Africa.

Stals, ELP. 1998. 'Geskiedenis van die Afrikaner-Broederbond 1918-'94.' Unpublished.

Steyn, JC. 1987. *Troue Afrikaners*. Cape Town: Tafelberg.

2001. *Van Wyk Louw: 'n Lewensverhaal*. Cape Town: Tafelberg.

Sunter, Clem. 1996. *The high road: Where are we now?* Cape Town: Tafelberg and Human & Rousseau.

Thom, HB. (convenor). 1966. *Stellenbosch 1866-1966: Honderd jaar hoër onderwys*. Cape Town: Nasionale Boekhandel.

Tretchikoff, Vladimir. 1973. *Pigeon's luck*. London: Collins.

Van der Merwe, Romi. 2002. *A magic blend: SFW 1925-2000*. Stellenbosch: Stellenbosse Boerewynmakery.

Van Wyk, Marise. 1991. 'Bewaring en die rol van Historiese Huise van Suid-Afrika Beperk.' Honours dissertation, Afrikaans Cultural History, University of Stellenbosch.

Van Zyl, DJ. 1993. *KWV 1918-'93*. Cape Town: Human & Rousseau.

PERIODICALS AND NEWSPAPERS

Africa Confidential

Albert Times

Beeld

Business Week

Cape Times

Daily Dispatch

Daily Express (London)

Daily News (Durban)

De Oude Emigrant, 13-16 December 1938

Die Afrikaner

Die Beeld/Rapport

Die Burger

Die Transvaler

Eastern Province Herald

Evening Post

Financial Gazette

Financial Mail

Forbes

Fortune

Graaff-Reinet Advertiser

Hoofstad

Huisgenoot

Inspan

Jansenville Chronicle

Lantern

Leadership

Nation

National Geographic

New Age

Onze Courant /Ons Koerant

Oosterlig

Pretoria News

Rand Daily Mail

SA Observer

Sarie Marais

Skakelblad (University of Pretoria)

Sunday Express

Sunday Times

Taalgenoot

Tegniek/Finansies & Tegniek

The Argus

The Economist

The Star

The Times (London)

The Times of India

The World

Time

Tobacco Reporter

Trek

Volkshandel

Wapenskou

Wine Spectator

Wirtschaftswoche

Woman's Value

Xray

Index of Life and Work of Anthony Edward (Anton) Rupert

Index of names

McLeod, Dato WM 136
Macmillan, Harold 133, 154, 155
McQueen, Steve 209
Maeterlinck, Maurice 350
Maharaj, Mac 378
Maillol, Aristide 341
Malan, DF 21, 25, 28, 42, 57, 87, 128, 151, 152, 281, 416n1
Malan, Frans 309
Malan, FS 97
Malan, Magnus 113, 287
Malan, Manie 72
Malan, Margot 113, 287
Malan, Tini 24
Malan, Wynand 286
Malherbe, DF 45
Malherbe, Dillie 325
Malherbe, F du T 82
Malherbe, FEJ (Fransie) 82
Malherbe, Joubero 67
Malherbe, Willem 128, 199, 325
Mâlik, Charles 166
Mandela, Nelson 14, 128, 142, 173, 226, 240, 286, 290, 291, 293, 294, 296, 326, 327, 355, 369, 374, 378, 379, 382, 384, 388, 389, 393, 398, 400, 425n33
Manuel, Trevor 250, 251, 296, 384, 385, 386
Manzù, Giacomo 342
Marais, AJ 233
Marais, Eugène 49, 350, 372, 417–418n5, 418n9
Marais, Jaap 170
Marais, Kowie 168
Maré, Matt 164
Marini, Marino 342
Maritz, Gerrit 21
Maritz, Manie 26, 27
Martin, Claude 390
Martin, James 87
Martin, Marilyn 344–345
Marx, Karl 33
Massey, Charles 105
Mayo, JW (John) 201, 323
Mbeki, Thabo 185, 223, 294, 379, 381, 386, 390, 393, 396

Mbeki, Zanele 118, 184
Mboweni, Tito 296
Meades, David 74, 400
Meaker, Erna 116
Meiring, Hannes 346
Meiring, Piet 43, 70–71, 159
Melck, Ronnie 235
Menell, Clive 166
Menell, Slip 123
Menzies, Sir Robert 169
Merensky, Hans 202
M.E.R. (ME Rothman) 55
Meyer, Dawid de Waal 53, 86, 193
Meyer, Frikkie 58, 93, 166
Meyer, Hennie 135, 177, 178
Meyer, PJ (Piet) 91
Meyer, Roelf 328
Milner, Alfred 41, 416n1, 424n5
Mitterand, Francois 311
Modersohn-Becker, Paula 347
Moerdyk, Gerard 48
Moerdyk, Sylva 48–49
Mogae, Festus 379, 381
Mokhehle, Ntsu 181
Molapo, Mooki 216
Moleketi, Monyane 184
Moll, Eugene 388
Mondavi, Robert 138, 308
Moni, Roberto 193
Montagu, Sir David CS 201, 217, 219, 323, 324, 325
Montgomery, Bernhard, Viscount of Alamein 136
Montsi, Sam 184
Moolman, Jan Henry 127
Moore, Gerald 347
Moosa, Valli 382, 383, 385
Mori, Bruno 193
Morkel, PK 112
Morkel, René 111, 112, 113, 114, 114–115, 117
Moross, Mandy 255
Morris, Philip 122, 196
Moshoeshoe II, King 182
Mosley, Oswald 173
Mostert, Anton 278, 279

Mostert, Frederick 229, 301, 302, 345, 388
Motlana, Nthatho 238
Motsepe, Patrice 189
Motsuenyane, SM (Sam) 245
Mswati, King of Swaziland 379
Mtine, Thom 167
Mugabe, Robert 220, 379, 381
Mulder, Connie 276, 278, 279
Muller, GS (Gerry) 255
Muller, Hilgard 277
Muller, HJ 87
Muller, Louwrens 193
Muller, SL 193
Muller, Willie 59
Mulligan, Raymond J 205
Muluzi, Bakili 379
Murray, Amy see Asher, Amy
Murray, Andrew 20
Mushet, JW 115
Muxanga, Paulo 378

Nagel, Bea 316
Nagel, Ryk 316
Naghi brothers 353
Napoleon III 108, 167, 208
Naudé, Ada 26
Naudé, CFB (Beyers) 26, 27, 85, 130
Naudé, Jozua Francois 26, 27, 85
Naudé, Kotie 106, 107
Naudé, S Meiring 340
Neethling-Pohl, Anna 40, 42, 63
Nel, Daan 163
Nel, Hans 43
Newman, HA (Mickey) 205
Ngomane, Petros 354
Niemeyer, Oscar 367
Nixdorf, Heinz 249
Nongqause 19
Norstad, Lauris 166
Northcliffe, Lord 79
Nortier brothers 310
Nortier, Daniel 310
Nujoma, Sam 379

Oberholster, JJ 365
Oberholzer, Rian 226

General index

458

Simon van der Stel Commission 357
small business development 56, 57, 236–253, 280, 282–283
Small Business Development Corporation (SBDC) 118, 241–242, 246–247, 248, 249–251, 280, 283, 292, 316
Small Entrepreneurs Limited (previously SBDC) 248
Small is beautiful: a study of economics as if people mattered 178
Smith Institute 351
Sofina 322, 323
South Africa Foundation 105, 122–123, 171, 285
South African Academy for Science and Art *see* Suid-Afrikaanse Akademie vir Wetenskap en Kuns
South African Breweries (SAB) 186, 188–189, 190, 192, 193–194, 195, 224, 230, 231, 232, 233, 235, 262
South African Broadcasting Corporation (SABC) 170, 236
South African Coloured People's Organisation 130
The South African Commercial Advertiser 237
South African Communist Party 132, 156, 291, 295, 327
South African Congress of Democrats 130
South African Congress of Trade Unions 130
South African Distilleries and Wines Limited 195
South African Farm Products Protective Association Limited 71
South African Indian Congress 130
South African Industrial Development Corporation 176
South African Information Service 43, 159
South African Medical Association 177
South African Medical and Dental Council 177
South African National Gallery 344
South African National Parks Board 181, 349, 381, 384, 390
South African Natural Heritage programme 355
South African Non-racial Olympic Committee (SANROC) 338
The South African Observer 170, 171, 172, 173
South African Party (SAP) 25, 42, 71, 87
South African Reserve Bank 147, 179, 254
South African Shareholders Association *see* Vereniging van Aandeelhouers van Suid Afrika
South African Wines 2003 312

South African Women's Federation *see* Suid-Afrikaanse Vrouefederasie
Southern African College for Tourism 118, 184, 380, 384, 385
Southern African Development Community (SADC) 222, 379, 389–390, 397, 414
Southern African Development Coordination Conference 222
Southern African Initiative of German Businesses 386
Southern African Nature Foundation (SANF, later WWF SA)) 150, 168, 169, 181, 263, 292, 307, 349–350, 351–356, 377, 378, 379
Southern African Sports Foundation 150, 164, 285
Southern African Wildlife College 118, 354–355, 379, 380, 385, 388, 390
South West Breweries 186
Soweto uprising (1976) 148, 237, 238, 375
Spoorbondkas 69, 419n3
Sports Foundation of South Africa *see* Southern African Sports Foundation
Springer Verlag 217
Stag Brewery Ltd 188
Standard Bank 150, 278
Standard Bank Investment Corporation 275, 276
State Development Bank 285
Stellenbosch 81–82, 133, 134–136, 158, 309, 345, 358, 363–364, 395–396
Stellenbosch Farmers Winery (SFW) 188, 193–194, 230–231, 234–235
Stellenbosch Wine Trust 193
Stellenbosse Distriksbank 112
Stellenrijk Wine Museum 363
Stellenryck 302, 309
Stellenzicht 332
Stewarts & Lloyds of SA 275
Stuyvesant Art Foundation 339, 345
Suid-Afrikaanse Akademie vir Wetenskap en Kuns 340, 415n3
Suid-Afrikaanse kuns van die twintigste eeu 373
Suid-Afrikaanse Vrouefederasie (SAVF) 113
Sullana 127
Sun City 353
Sunday Express 140, 141
Swaziland 350, 351, 354, 378
Swellendam 365
Swiss Union Bank 326